ACCOUNTING
DESK BOOK

EIGHTH EDITION

The Accountant's Everyday
Instant Answer Book

Revised by
Douglas L. Blensly, CPA and Tom M. Plank, MBA

Institute for Business Planning

Eighth Edition
© 1985 *by*

Institute for Business Planning, Inc.
Englewood Cliffs, N.J. 07632

10 9 8 7 6 5 4 3

Library of Congress Cataloging in Publication Data

Casey, William J.
  Accounting desk book.

  Adapted from the first four editions by
William J. Casey and IBP Research and Editorial Staff.
  Includes index.
  1. Accounting.   I. Plank, Tom M., 1919–
II. Blensly, Douglas L.   III. Institute for Business
Planning, Inc.   IV. Title.
HF5635.C33   1984   657'.02'02   84-25161
ISBN 0-87624-011-2

A WORD ABOUT THE VALUE
OF THIS DESK BOOK

This ready-reference instant-answer manual has been used for over twenty years as a source for reliable accounting and tax information. It covers the topics that most frequently cross the desks of business and professional accounting and finance people.

In order to keep pace with the many changes in the accounting and tax treatment of business transactions in the past couple of years, another cover-to-cover overhaul was necessary. The result is the all-new Eighth Edition which continues to be one of the most concise yet wide-ranging guides to today's real accounting world found anywhere in print.

The new "lion" of a tax law is just one area where you will find answers on how to handle many tough questions. Scarcely any area of interest has escaped the author's notice: Individual tax and financial topics . . . bankruptcy . . . imputed interest rules . . . S corporations .. . restrictions on premature accrual of expenses . . . finance leases . . . new LIFO reserve requirements . . . how small businesses can raise capital more easily . . . a 35-page analysis of the latest tax law . . . the new public accounting standards manual . . . and much more.

In short, there has never been a more valuable and timely edition of this ready-to-use, time-tested classic.

INSTITUTE FOR BUSINESS PLANNING, INC.
Publisher

ABOUT THE AUTHORS

Douglas L. Blensly is a Certified Public Accountant (California). He graduated "cum laude" from California State University, Los Angeles, with a B.S. degree in Business Administration. He is currently the accounting and auditing partner for the public accounting firm of Martin, Werbelow, Pyle and Schlinger in Pasadena, California.

Mr. Blensly is on the California Society of CPAs committee on Accounting Principles and Auditing Standards and the Los Angeles Chapter Committee on Relations with Faculty and Students. He is also a member of the Auditing Section of the American Accounting Association.

Mr. Blensly is the author of *The New Look in Financial Statements,* a booklet on review and compilation services, monographs on various accounting and business topics, and currently has three accounting books on press. He speaks regularly on accounting and auditing matters before various professional groups in California. He is a member of the accounting faculty, California State Polytechnic University (Pomona), and formerly was on the accounting faculty of Pasadena City College.

Mr. Blensly is an editorial advisor to the "Practitioners Forum" column of the *Journal of Accountancy.*

Tom M. Plank, President, Pasadena Business Institute, Inc., is a specialist in SEC Accounting Rules and new security issues and annual report filings with the SEC. He gives in-house seminars on accounting and auditing topics to accounting personnel of companies in commerce and industry and in public accounting firms.

Mr. Plank has served on the accounting and finance faculties of various major universities in Chicago and Los Angeles. His business experience includes that of an officer for a commercial bank, a securities analyst for an investment banking firm, and a consultant for various corporations.

Mr. Plank has published over 25 articles in various journals, and is the author of three business books, *SEC Accounting Rules and Regulations, The Age of Automation,* and *The Science of Leadership,* and currently has three accounting books on press. He is an accounting editor for a major publishing house.

Foreword

Most accounting books and articles, in quoting or referencing the AICPA standards, mention as a source the original number of the APB, ARB, SAS, FASB, etc. Reference to those individual pronouncements often involves the further trace to a prior announcement, which amended a prior one, which amended . . . and so on. Also, every opinion, by itself, is dated and pinpointed in time and cannot in itself indicate *subsequent* changes thereafter. Unless one makes manual changes and references to the opinions as they are amended by later pronouncements, he may be working with a provision which is outdated or voided by a later one.

There is only one adequate timely publication which constantly updates the standards—paragraph by paragraph—as changes occur. This two-volume *Current Text* is published by the Financial Accounting Standards Board. Volumes 3 and 4 *Current Text* replaces the AICPA's four-volume *Professional Standards*.

Material Disclosed in the *Current Text**

The FASB *Current Text* is an integration of currently effective accounting and reporting standards. Material in the *Current Text* is drawn from AICPA Accounting Research Bulletins, APB Opinions, FASB Statements of Financial Accounting Standards, and FASB Interpretations. Those pronouncements are covered by Rule 203 of the Rules of Conduct of the AICPA Code of Professional Ethics, which states:

> *Rule 203—Accounting principles.* A member shall not express an opinion that financial statements are presented in conformity with generally accepted accounting principles if such statements contain any departure from an accounting principle promulgated by the body designated by Council . . . to establish such principles which has a material effect on the statement taken as a whole, unless the member can demonstate that due to unusual circumstances the financial statements would otherwise have been misleading. In such cases, his report must describe the departure, the approximate effects

---

*See Appendix G for the itemized content of the two volumes of *Current Text*.

thereof, if practicable, and the reasons why compliance with the principle would result in a misleading statement.

Interpretation No. 2 of Rule 203 states:

> *Status of FASB interpretations.* Council is authorized under Rule 203 to designate a body to establish accounting principles and has designated the Financial Accounting Standards Board as such body. Council also has resolved that FASB Statements of Financial Accounting Standards, together with those Accounting Research Bulletins and APB Opinions which are not superseded by action of the FASB, constitute accounting principles as contemplated in Rule 203.
> In determining the existence of a departure from an accounting principle established by a Statement of Financial Accounting Standards, Accounting Research Bulletin or APB Opinion encompassed by Rule 203, the division of professional ethics will construe such Statement, Bulletin or Opinion in the light of any interpretations thereof issued by the FASB.

The *Current Text* also incorporates the supplemental guidance provided by FASB Technical Bulletins and AICPA Accounting Interpretations.

The *Current Text* does not in any way supersede, change, or otherwise affect the pronouncements from which it is drawn. Although edited by the FASB staff, the abridged text has not been subjected to the FASB's due process procedures used for issuing FASB Statements. The authority of the *Current Text* is derived from the underlying pronouncements, which remain in force.

Material Excluded from the *Current Text*

The *Current Text* does not include FASB Statements of Financial Accounting Concepts, APB Statements, or AICPA Terminology Bulletins. Those documents may be found in *Original Pronouncements through June 1973* and *Original Pronouncements July 1973–June 1st, 1983,* the companion publications to the *Current Text* that contain the complete text of all pronouncements arranged in chronological sequence.

The *Current Text* also does not include AICPA Industry Accounting or Audit Guides or Statements of Position, except as specialized principles in them have been extracted and issued in FASB Statements. Nor are Statements of International Accounting Standards included. All of those documents, however, are available from the American Institute of Certified Public Accountants, 1211 Avenue of the Americas, New York, NY 10036.

The *Current Text* is a condensed version of original pronouncements. Descriptive material, such as information about Exposure Drafts, respondents' comments, background information, and reasons for conclusions and dissents, is generally excluded. However, certain material contained in other than the standards section of an original pronouncement is included to help the reader understand or implement the *Current Text*. Readers wishing to better understand the rationale behind a pronouncement or seeking background information should refer to the original pronouncement from which the related *Current Text* material is drawn. This is easy to do because each paragraph in the *Current Text* contains a source reference to the original pronouncement.

Organization of *Current Text*

The *Current Text* integrates financial accounting and reporting standards according to the major subject areas to which they apply. The subjects are arranged alphabetically in sections that are grouped into two volumes. The first volume (General Standards) contains those standards that are generally applicable to all enterprises; the second volume (Industry Standards) contains specialized standards that are applicable to enterprises operating in specific industries. Each volume presents flowcharts to assist in identifying the disclosure requirements for the sections contained in that volume. A comprehensive Topical Index appears at the end of each volume. The *Current Text* includes disclosure checklists in flowchart form.

Each **section** is identified by an alpha-numeric code. (The numeric part has been arbitrarily selected to allow space for future additions.) The alpha-numeric code in the General Standards volume follows an alpha-numeric-numeric pattern (for example, A99), and the code in the Industry Standards volume follows an alpha-alpha-numeric pattern (for example, Aa9). Each volume has a key cross-reference guide which contains a list of topics arranged alphabetically that might logically be sought under each letter and the section code where each topic can be found.

Paragraphs within each section are numbered consecutively, according to the following numeric format:

Paragraphs .101–.399: Standards
Paragraphs .401–.499: Glossary
Paragraphs .501–.999: Supplemental guidance (not covered by Rule 203)

All **section-paragraph references** are made in the following form: B05.127 or In6.102. For example, B05.127 refers to Section B05, "Balance Sheet Classification: Current Assets and Current Liabilities," paragraph .127, and In6.102 refers to Section In6, "Insurance Industry," paragraph .102.

Terms defined in the **Glossary** for a section are in boldface type the first time they appear in that section.

Source references are provided that indicate the original pronouncements from which material in each paragraph and footnote is derived. They appear in brackets and use the following abbreviations:

FAS	FASB Statement of Financial Accounting Standards
FIN	FASB Interpretation
FTB	FASB Technical Bulletin
CON	FASB Statement of Concepts
APB	AICPA Accounting Principles Board Opinion

ARB	AICPA Accounting Research Bulletin
AIN	AICPA Accounting Interpretation
ch	chapter
fn	footnote

For example, the source reference [FIN21, ¶15, fn3] indicates paragraph 15, footnote 3 of FASB Interpretation No. 21, *Accounting for Leases in a Business Combination*. Similarly, the source reference [AIN-APB11, #8] indicates the eighth AICPA Accounting Interpretation of APB Opinion No. 11, *Accounting for Income Taxes*.

Transitional language and editorial changes that *add* wording to an original pronouncement to maintain a consistent editorial style within the volumes appear in brackets. If an original pronouncement *deletes* wording from a previous pronouncement and it does not provide substitute wording, the amending pronouncement is not included in the source reference described in the preceding paragraph. Only the source reference for the earlier pronouncement is noted. However, Appendix B identifies the sources for all such deletions. Certain editorial deletions have been made to original pronouncements either to maintain a consistent editorial style or for clarity. Those deletions also are not noted. However, in such cases the deletions have not affected the substance of the text. Other changes have been made to conform format (for example, ''iii'' my have been changed to ''c'') or terminology, as follows:

Term in *Original Pronouncement*	Term in *Current Text*
should (meaning *must*)	shall
see (in making a reference)	refer to
which (in a restrictive clause)	that
where (not location)	if
when (not specific timing)	if
entity (if used broadly)	enterprise
company	enterprise
corporation	enterprise
earned surplus	retained earnings
capital surplus	additional paid-in capital
additional paid-in surplus	additional paid-in capital

Effective Dates and Transition Provisions of Underlying Pronouncements

The effective dates of FASB Statements of Financial Accounting Standards, FASB Interpretations, APB Opinions, and Accounting Research Bulletins, and the issue dates of AICPA Accounting Interpretations and FASB Technical Bulletins are summarized in Appendix C. That appendix also presents the transition paragraphs of more recent pronouncements whose effective dates and transition provisions are such that they might be initially applied in annual financial statements issued on or after June 1, 1983.

Users may need to refer to Appendix C to determine if the requirements of recently issued pronouncements are effective in their particular circumstances. Users concerned with accounting and reporting standards for financial statements of prior years also may need to refer to the original pronouncements that were effective for those years. Appendix B lists changes to original pronouncements as the result of subsequent pronouncements.

CONTENTS

SECTION ONE—ACCOUNTING

What Accounting Is All About • Seven-Step Cycle • The
Accountant

American Institute of Certified Public Accountants
• Auditing Standards • Financial Accounting
Standards • Prelude to GAAP Outline • The Pervasive
Measurement Principles • Broad Operating Principles • The
Principles of Selection and Measurement • The Principles of
Financial Statement Presentation

Business Structure Considerations

Introduction • Deferred Compensation Plans • Pension
(And Profit Sharing) Plans • Profit Sharing Plans • Actuarial
Gains and Losses • Defined Contribution Plans • Insured
Plans • Companies With More Than One Plan • Social

Security Benefits and Pension Plans • ERISA Requirements
• Other Deferred Compensation Contracts • Key-Person
Life Insurance • Miscellaneous Considerations • 401 (k)
Plans

Acquisitions • The Purchase Method—Business
Combinations • The Pooling-Of-Interests Method—Business
Combinations • Foreign Subsidiaries • Inter-Company
Transactions • The Indefinite Reversal Criteria and
Undistributed Earnings of Subsidiaries • Goodwill in
Business Combinations • Negative Goodwill

Disclosures • Disclosures Itemized • Restatements
• Timing and Permanent Differences—Income Taxes
• Permanent Differences • Timing Differences
• Reporting for Business Segments

Guidelines for Interim Reporting • Price-Level Financial
Reporting

SECTION TWO—TAXES

The Tax Reform Act of 1984 • The Accountant's
Problem • Accountants' Responsibility • Accounting for
Income Taxes • Choosing a Taxable Year • Change of
Accounting Method

Cash • Accumulated Earnings Tax • Accounts Receivable
• Inventories • LIFO • Securities and Other
Intangibles • Property, Plant and Equipment • Investment
Credit (ITC) • Leasehold Improvements • The Cost of
Acquiring a Lease

Types of Liabilities

SECTION THREE—MANAGEMENT

SECTION ONE

ACCOUNTING

1

The Accountant and Accounting

[¶101] WHAT ACCOUNTING IS ALL ABOUT

In 1941, the Committee on Terminology of the American Institute of Accountants defined and explained the term ''accounting'':

> Accounting is the art of recording, classifying and summarizing in a significant manner and in terms of money, transactions and events which are, in part at least, of a financial character, and interpreting the results thereof . . . . careful attention to the significant words, 'the art of recording, classifying and summarizing' will rule out any interpretation that no more is indicated than bookkeeping. The recording and classifying of data in account books constitute an accounting function, but so also and on a higher level do the summarizing and interpreting of such data in a significant manner, whether in reports to management, to stockholders, or to credit grantors, or in income tax returns, or in reports for renegotiation or other regulatory purposes.'' (Accounting Terminology Bulletin No. 1, August 1953)

In the AICPA Professional Standards for Accounting (''The Environment of Financial Accounting'') that definition was superseded as follows (October 1970):

> Accounting is a service activity. Its function is to provide quantitative information, primarily financial in nature, about economic entities that is intended to be useful in making economic decisions, in making reasoned choices among alternative courses of action. Accounting includes several branches, for example,

> Financial Accounting
> Managerial Accounting
> Governmental Accounting

3

[¶101.1] Accounting Information

Accounting information can be classified into two categories—financial accounting and managerial accounting. Financial accounting is information for the users of financial statements, i.e., creditors, stockholders, financial analysts, governmental regulatory agencies, trade associations, customers. (This is not to say, however, that the same information is not of interest to management.) Financial accounting, then, concerns the financial position, earnings, liquidity, and operating performance generally of the enterprise.

Managerial accounting is primarily for internal control purposes: cost-volume-profit analysis, efficiency, productivity, planning and control, pricing decisions, operating and capital budgets, and a variety of specialized reports which management needs for the decision-making process.

[¶ 101.2] Accounting Principles

Accounting can be thought of as a system—a system of assumptions, doctrines, tenets, and conventions, all included in the concept "Generally Accepted Accounting Principles" commonly referenced by the acronym GAAP. These principles developed by a process of evolution over a long period of years much in the same way that the common law developed, by way of an analogy. Very few accounting rules are embodied in statutory law, as government has for the most part deferred the promulgation of accounting standards to the private sector of the economy. Let's examine a few of the fundamental notions (concepts) that underlie accounting principles and practices as they exist today.

[¶ 101.3] Accounting Concepts

The *matching principle* requires that the revenues of the accounting period be precisely matched with the expenses of that same period that were incurred to generate the revenues.

The *accrual principle* considers revenues and expenses to be an inflow and outflow of *all* assets, not just the flow of cash in and out of the enterprise.

The *historical cost principle* requires that economic resources be entered into the system at cost, when the transaction occurs. The price paid is, on the face of it, considered to be the value of the asset.

The *realization* notion means economic events are accounted for only when the enterprise has been a party to one side of a *bona fide* transaction. For example, if a parcel of land has appreciated in value, the gain cannot be recognized until the land has been sold.

Associated with the realization concept is the idea of *substance-over-form* standard. All transactions must have "economic substance" as opposed to "sham" transactions entered into for some "creative accounting" purpose.

The *entity* concept concerns any person or group of persons having a name, common purpose, and *transactions with outsiders*. A relationship between the entity and external parties must be clearly established. The form of organization of the enterprise is not relevant with respect to the entity being an *accounting unit*.

The *going-concern* assumption considers the entity as one that will operate indefinitely.

The *consistency* standard requires the accounting procedures applied during a given accounting period be the same procedures that were applied in previous periods. The purpose of the consistency principle is to ensure that the statements of the enterprise for the current and prior periods are comparable.

The *conservative doctrine* directs that when the enterprise is exposed to uncertainty and risk that are material, accounting measurement and disclosure should be approached with a high degree of caution and in a prudent manner, until evidence develops that there is a significant reduction or elimination of the uncertainty.

Finally, is the all-important *disclosure* principle. The financial statements must present for the users all the relevant information that is necessary in order *not* to be misleading. This includes not only errors of commission, but also errors of omission of material information.

[¶ 102]   **SEVEN-STEP CYCLE**

1. Recording a transaction is the starting point for a double-entry bookkeeping system. First, the financial structure of the organization should be analyzed as consisting of many interrelated aspects, each one of which is called an account. Documents provide the input into the system.

2. The amounts that have been entered in various journals (the books of original entry) are transferred to a general ledger, a procedure called posting. The general ledger has a page for each account in the organization's financial structure. In addition to the general ledger, a subsidiary ledger is used to provide detailed information about the accounts in the general ledger.

3. The posting procedure is followed by listing the balances in all of the accounts, to determine if the sum of all of the debit balances exactly equals the sum of all of the credit balances. This procedure is called taking a trial balance, and is done at the end of the accounting period.

4. The accountant must next make certain adjustments to implement the accrual method of accounting. This method requires the recognition of revenue when it is earned (the revenue realization principle) and recognition of expenses when they are incurred (the matching principle). Adjusting entries are made at the end of the accounting period, initially recorded in the general journal, then posted to the associated general ledger accounts. If an entry requires an account

that is not in the general ledger, the accountant simply opens a new account with the appropriate account label.

5. Prepare an adjusted trial balance. The adjusted trial balance combines the balances in the original trial balance with the effects of the adjustments. The adjusted trial balance can be thought of as an update of the trial balance.

6. The financial statements can now be prepared. The balances in the accounts are the data used to develop the financial statements.

7. The last step is to close (zero out) the nominal accounts—i.e., the revenue and expense accounts—because the balances in these accounts do not cumulate. This procedure involves the appropriate debits and credits necessary to transfer the profit (loss) into the owners' equity accounts.

[¶ 103]   **THE ACCOUNTANT**

What is an accountant? Simply and best-described, an accountant is one who has *been trained* in accounting. This training may have been obtained in educational institutions or in practical experience, or in both.

There are practicing accountants; non-practicing accountants.

There are private accountants; public accountants.

There are experienced field accountants; non-experienced ones.

There are accountants who are teachers, writers, advisors, etc.

There are accountants who, having met state requirements for education, experience and examination, are granted certificates authorizing them to practice public accounting within that state, "certifying" them as qualified under that state's law.

One of the qualifications to be met for certification, which has been universally accepted by all the states, is earning passing grades on all the following examinations. The examinations are prepared for each semi-annual sitting (usually in May and November) by the AICPA.

1. Accounting Practice (in two parts)

2. Auditing

3. Accounting Theory

4. Business Law

The time for the exams is set by the AICPA uniformly for all states (and territories, etc.). The questions on each exam are changed from sitting to sitting, seldom, if ever, being repeated verbatim. The exams contain both objective questions (multiple-choice) and questions requiring essay-type answers or mathematical solutions in accounting formats. Most states have imposed time-frames within which all the exams must be passed in order for them to remain valid toward certification.

Once qualified as a certified public accountant under state law, the new CPA is immediately offered the opportunity of becoming a member of:

1. The American Institute of Certified Public Accountants (the AICPA).
2. The respective state society of Certified Public Accountants (locally in a county chapter of the same).

For CPAs who are members of the AICPA, the "standards" are mandatory (with the possible penalty of reprimand or expulsion for non-conformance). The standards have also been adopted (sometimes enlarged) by most of the state societies. What is important is the *existence of these standards*. The *fact* of their existence coupled with the widespread *recognition* given them (by owners and the investing public, lending institutions, stock markets, governmental regulatory bodies and other users) makes the *knowledge* of them imperative for those who do not wish to be held legally or professionally liable for *divergencies* from what are called, "Generally Accepted Accounting Standards and Principles." Moreover, proof of rigid adherence to professional accounting standards may be a valid legal defense in a court of law for a non-member, as well as for a member, or for a non-certified public or private accountant as well as for a certified one. Alternatively, deviations from these standards may, in court, preclude an accountant from leaning on the profession as a defense. *How* these standards are set is discussed briefly later.

The term "auditing" has not yet been used in this book. *Management* is responsible for the function of financial accounting (and reporting). The *auditor* is an independent person who examines management's financial accounting (and reporting) and *attests* to its conformance with, or deviations from, "generally accepted accounting principles." In an "opinion" which accompanies the management-prepared financial statements (impliedly and in actuality adjusted to conform with the auditor's detailed error-findings during extensive testing of the system and records), the auditor puts his professional stamp of *relative* approval to the statements presented, as well as to the methods used in arriving at the figures presented. In addition, the auditor attests to certain information (financial notes) which is now mandatory or advisable for certain disclosures.

The wording of attestations ("opinions"), as well as the auditing process itself, has been fairly well-defined and prescribed by the AICPA in "auditing standards" which are separate from, but based upon "financial accounting" standards.

This text is *not* concerned with the auditor's function or the attestation he must make after the examination of management's records and report.

This text *is* concerned with pointing out the *techniques* and *standards* to be followed which, hopefully, would result in an unqualified or "clean" opinion from that independent auditor. The *knowledge* of these factors is important to *both* management and auditor—management (internal or private accountants), to assure proper preparatory and running procedures per the standards; the auditor, to examine management's conformance to those standards. The closer both are to the knowledge of the guidelines, the less likely will be significant and possibly non-conforming divergence from those guidelines.

[¶ 103.1]   Rules of Conduct for the Profession

There is one aspect of the accounting profession which is perhaps more important than skill in the eyes of the outside observer—*Integrity*. The integrity of the individual and the profession of which he is a member—and his uprightness, honesty, sincerity, soundness—are of crucial importance.

For CPAs who are in public accounting, the AICPA has developed specific rules of conduct which constitute the standards of ethics for the membership.

The affirmative ethical principles toward which CPAs should strive are embodied in these five broad concepts of conduct:

1. Independence, integrity and objectivity.
2. Adherence to general and technical standards.
3. Responsibilities to clients.
4. Responsibilities to colleagues.
5. Acceptance of all responsibilities and practices for conduct to enhance the stature of the profession and its service to the public.

CPA members of the AICPA who are *not* engaged in *public* accounting must observe only the following specific rules:

1. The rule of integrity and objectivity.
2. The acts discreditable rule.

Other public accounting organizations also specify rules of conduct geared to the same goal of the highest possible ethical standard.

[¶ 103.2]   Legal Liability

Despite the high standards of conduct and performance demanded within the profession, despite precautions taken for near-perfect performance, even the most dedicated accounting professional, public or private, individual or firm, is always faced with the risk of a lawsuit over some engagement or work in which he participated or supervised.

Some of the charges against which an accountant may have to defend himself against clients or third parties are:

Negligence (especially failure to detect fraud)

Breach of confidentiality

Misleading, misrepresented, insufficient or incorrect reports issued under the accountant's attestation

Charges brought by the Securities and Exchange Commission (or other regulatory agencies) for improprieties, negligence or fraud, or lack of proper disclosure (errors of omission) in connection with registration statements or periodic reports filed.

The accountant may face monetary damage suits (civil suits) or criminal fraud charges (criminal suits), or both.

Professional liability insurance, to some extent, mitigates the risk of monetary loss.

The decision may ultimately rest with judges or juries and be predicated upon the adequacy of the defense offered by the accountant. The strongest defense would undoubtedly be proof of rigid adherence to the professional standards, documented by thorough proofs of work and reasonable effort.

To support the "reasonable effort" concept, many accountants are not using statistical sampling for certain phases of proof-testing. Because the use of sampling techniques has gained such wide acceptance in many other fields, judges and juries may more readily accept conclusions based on what some consider "scientific" principles, which are more generally known than are accounting techniques which may or may not impress the layman.

The AICPA Rules of Conduct and most states now permit members to practice as "professional corporations or associations" (primarily for tax benefits), with the stockholders jointly and severally liable for acts of the organization or its employees. Incorporation is thus prohibited for the avoidance of personal liability.

2

Who Determines the Standards?

[¶201] **AMERICAN INSTITUTE OF CERTIFIED
PUBLIC ACCOUNTANTS**

In society at large, citizens are not praised for *upholding* laws; they are condemned or punished for *breaking* laws or *failure* to conform to the laws. On a smaller scale, the professional accountant is not applauded for adhering to standards; he is, or may be, criticized, reprimanded, ostracized or faced with monetary or criminal penalties for noncompliance with the standards or for *failure* to conform with accounting standards.

Most professional accountants will agree that, despite criticism for certain actions or nonactions, the AICPA is the one dominant organization of accountants. The Institute speaks with recognized authority for the *entire* profession of accounting (for members and nonmembers alike). When the AICPA speaks "officially," on-the-record, adherence is compulsory for members. When the AICPA speaks "unofficially," off-the-record, adherence is *not* compulsory. BUT—(and to emphasize it)—*but*—a member who violates an *unofficial* pronouncement had best have a good defense for his alternate position if it conflicts even with this *unofficial* AICPA position.

The AICPA is the national organization of certified public accountants in the United States. Its membership is made up of thousands of certified public accountants engaged in one or more of every conceivable phase of the accountant's function in society.

There are two requirements for membership:

1. Possession of a valid certified public accountant certificate issued by a state, territory or territorial possession of the United States or the District of Columbia, and

10

2. Passing an examination in accounting and other related subjects, satisfactory to the Board of Directors of the AICPA.

Members are governed by *four* sets of standards:

1. The Bylaws of the AICPA; (not discussed)
2. The Code of Professional Ethics; (discussed briefly)
3. Auditing Standards; (discussed briefly)
4. Financial Accounting Standards (discussed and enlarged in this entire section of the book).

[¶ 202] AUDITING STANDARDS

Auditing Standards (which are *not* the subject of this book) are divided into three parts:

1. Generally Accepted Auditing Standards (AU 150)
2. Statements on Auditing Standards
3. Auditing Interpretations.

The first category of Generally Accepted Auditing Standards consists of: General standards, standards of field work and standards of reporting.

The *Generally Accepted Auditing Standards* (GAAS) are *compulsory*. They were approved and adopted by the membership of the AICPA.

The *Statements on Auditing Standards* are determined by the Auditing Standards Board, the senior technical committee of the Institute. Rule 202 of the Institute's Code of Professional Ethics recognizes these statements as interpretations of GAAS and considers them pronouncements requiring members to be prepared to justify departures. (Preface to AU 100)

Auditing Interpretations are prepared by the *staff* of the auditing standards division and reviewed by members of the executive committee. An interpretation is *not* as authoritative as a "statement." But here too, members should be prepared to justify departures if the quality of their work is questioned. (Preface to AU 9000)

The major foundation upon which generally accepted *auditing* standards are built is found in the first standard of reporting of those auditing standards:

> The report shall state whether the financial statements are presented in accordance with generally accepted accounting principles. (AU 410.01)

It is these "generally accepted accounting principles" (GAAP) which underlie the Financial Accounting Standards.

[¶ 203] FINANCIAL ACCOUNTING STANDARDS

Financial accounting standards, since May 7, 1973, have been determined by the Financial Accounting Standards Board (the FASB), which, by action of the Council of the AICPA, was designed to replace the old Accounting Principles Board (the APB).

> *Status of FASB interpretations.* Council is authorized under Rule 203 to designate a body to establish accounting principles and has designated the Financial Accounting Standards Board as such body. Council also has resolved that FASB Statements of Financial Accounting Standards, together with those Accounting Research Bulletins and APB Opinions which are not superseded by actions of the FASB constitute accounting principles as contemplated in Rule 203.
>
> In determining the existence of a departure from an accounting principle established by a Statement of Financial Accounting Standards, Accounting Research Bulletin or APB Opinion encompassed by Rule 203, the division of professional ethics will construe such Statement, Bulletin or Opinion in the light of any interpretations thereof issued by the FASB.

The FASB is *not* a division of the AICPA or a committee thereof. It is an autonomous organization in which the AICPA has representation. It is one of a three-part rule-making process, with each part performing important and distinct functions in the process of setting accounting standards:

The Financial Accounting Foundation is governed by a nine-member board of trustees comprised of five CPAs, two financial executives, one financial analyst, and one accounting educator. The president of the AICPA is a trustee. The trustee's primary duties are to appoint members of the Standards Board and the Advisory Council, to arrange financing, to approve budgets and periodically to review the structure of the organization.

The Financial Accounting Standards Board (FASB) is an independent body with seven full-time, salaried members, at least four of whom are CPAs drawn from public practice; the other members are persons well versed in financial reporting. The FASB's primary duty is to issue statements on financial accounting standards, including interpretations of those standards.

The Financial Accounting Standards Advisory Council comprises not less than 20 members who are experts in the field. The Council works closely with the FASB in an advisory capacity, consulting with the Board to identify problems, set agenda priorities, establish task forces, and react to proposed financial accounting standards.

The net result of the recognition of the new FASB was to make the following designated pronouncements the *official,* binding standards to be observed:

> Those *prior* pronouncements of the *old* Accounting Principles Board (the APB) which were *not* changed by the new FASB:

1. APB Opinions

2. APB Statements

3. Accounting Research Bulletins:

   Plus the new pronouncements (rules) of the FASB:

4. FASB Statements

5. FASB Interpretations

[¶ 203.1]   An Important Distinction

The (old) "Accounting Interpretations" (that is the terminology used) were prepared by the AICPA staff and were *not,* when issued, considered to be official. They were answers to practitioners' questions. These "Accounting Interpretations" are *still* in effect, still unofficial, but recommended for use, with the burden of departures on the individual accountant. There will no longer be any new "Accounting Interpretations,"—at least not under that title.

The new terminology for these unofficial answers to practitioners' questions (since June 1973) is *"Technical Practice Aids."* These have been added to the body of *unofficial* interpretations of standards.

Note that the "interpretations" issued by the FASB, however, carry the title, "FASB Interpretations" and, under Rule 203 cited previously, *are official* pronouncements.

[¶ 203.2]   Unofficial Pronouncements

The following are the unofficial pronouncements issued by the AICPA as guidance for members (who might have to explain departures therefrom):

The Accounting Interpretations (up to June 1973)

The Technical Practice Aids (from June 1973 on)

Terminology Bulletins

Guides on Management Advisory Services

Statements on Responsibility in Tax Practice

Statements of Position of the Accounting Standards Division

Accounting Research Studies (these are different from "Accounting Research Bulletins" which *are* official)

Industry Audit Guides

Most other publications of the AICPA, unless clearly specifying their official nature. (Reference here is to *accounting* publications.)

Reiterating the concept of the first paragraph of this chapter, the responsibility to know the standards and to follow them rests with the individual accountant.

The whole body of compulsory rules and interpretations (though some are unofficial) is surprisingly small in terms of printed material.

There are other areas of accounting specialization, such as: income taxes, cost accounting, SEC filings, statistical sampling, computers, mathematical "decision-making," etc., which require unique education and research. Though peripheral and adjunct, they are guided by the main body of standards, but not explicitly spelled out by them.

The FASB is developing a series of Statements of Financial Accounting Concepts. Four statements have been issued through December, 1981:

1. Objectives of Financial Reporting by Business Enterprises
2. Qualitative Characteristics of Accounting Information
3. Elements of Financial Statements of Business Enterprises
4. Objectives of Financial Reporting by Nonbusiness Organizations

[¶ 204]   PRELUDE TO GAAP OUTLINE

[¶ 204.1]   Standards and Regulations

Until 1973, accounting principles had been established by the American Institute of Certified Public Accountants. In 1973, the Financial Accounting Standards Board was organized as an independent standard-setting body, with the AICPA continuing to set the standards for auditors. Corporations whose securities are publicly held must conform to rules set by the Securities and Exchange Commission, a federal government agency. The Internal Revenue Service administers the tax statutes and regulations at the federal level. There is no standard setting authority for managerial accounting, but there is a program available for accountants to qualify for a certificate in management accounting (CMA). The Institute of Internal Auditors administers an examination for an accountant to be designated a certified internal auditor (CIA).

A well-defined body of knowledge and precise, for the most part, methodology has been developed for accounting procedures over a long period of time. Existing techniques and new approaches continue to be studied by the authorities in an effort to keep accounting standards consistent with changes and innovations in business practices, legislative changes, and socioeconomic changes in our society.

The following is an outline of Generally Acceptable Accounting Principles (GAAP):

   I. OBJECTIVES OF FINANCIAL ACCOUNTING
  II. BASIC FEATURES AND BASIC ELEMENTS OF FINANCIAL ACCOUNTING
     A. Basic Features—The Environment
     B. Basic Elements—The Individual Company
       1. Economic resources, obligations and residual interests
       2. Changes in those resources—events that cause them to increase or decrease

   *3. GAAP—for recording and reporting them:
   *A) The Pervasive Principles
   *B) The Broad Operating Principles
      *1) Selection and measurement
      *2) Financial statement presentation
   C) Detailed Operating Principles.

*3 (A) and 3 (B) (1) & (2) are covered in the outline below. They pertain to the practical application of the principles, which are described in more theoretical and historical-development terms in the prior sections of the outline.

GAAP

(Generally Accepted Accounting Principles).

[¶ 205] THE PERVASIVE MEASUREMENT PRINCIPLES

Six principles establish the basis for implementing *accrual* accounting:

1. *Initial Recording:* of assets and liabilities, income determination, revenue and realization.

2. *Realization:*
   Revenue —when earning process is complete.
            —when an exchange has taken place.
   Expenses—gross decreases in assets.
            —gross increases in liabilities.
   Classes of expenses:
   Costs of assets used to produce revenue—cost of goods sold, selling—administrative expense, interest expense.
   Expenses from non-reciprocal transfers—taxes, thefts, floods.
   Costs of assets other than product disposed of—plant, equipment.
   Costs of unsuccessful efforts.
   Declines in market prices of inventories.
   Does *not* include repayments of borrowings, expenditures to acquire assets, distributions to owners (including treasury stock) or adjusting prior period expenses.

3. *Associating Cause and Effect.*

4. *Systematic and Rational Allocation.*

5. *Immediate Recognition*:
         Costs of the current period which provide no future benefits (those which have been incurred *now* or *prior*) or when allocating serves no useful purpose.

         Measurement is based on its own exchanges: contracts not recorded until *one* party fulfills commitment; not all changes are recorded, not internal increases and not price changes in productive resources.

Assets usually are recorded at cost, or unexpired portion
of it. When sold, difference increases the firm's net assets. The cost principle: use acquisition price (historical
cost). Cost also refers to how asset was originally recorded, regardless of how determined.

6. *The Unit of Measure*—U.S. Dollar—no change is recognized for
change in general purchasing power of the dollar.

[¶ 205.1]   The Pervasive Principles—Modifying Conventions

Modifying conventions are applied because too rigid adherence to the measurement principles might produce undesirable results, exclude other important
events, or even at times be impractical.

The modifying conventions are:

1. *Conservatism*

2. *Emphasis on the importance of income* (LIFO is an example)

3. *Judgment of the accounting profession as a whole* with regard to:
The usual revenue recognition rule—recognition of contracts in progress.

Segregation of extraordinary items.

Avoiding undue effect on net income in one single period
(installment sales).

[¶ 206]   BROAD OPERATING PRINCIPLES

Two broad principles are:

1. The Principles of Selection and Measurement.

2. The Principles of Financial Statement Presentation.

[¶ 207]   THE PRINCIPLES OF SELECTION AND MEASUREMENT

These principles guide the selection of the *events* to be accounted for; they
determine *how* the selected *events* affect items; and they guide the *assignment of
dollars* to the effects of the *events*.

The types of *events,* classified, are:

1. External Events

A. *Transfers* to or from *other* entities

(1) Exchanges (reciprocal transfers)

      (2) Non-reciprocal transfers

        (A) With owners

        (B) With outsiders

    (B) *Other-than-transfers*

  2. Internal Events

    A. Production of goods or services

    B. Casualties

The outline presented next breaks down each of the types of events above and briefly highlights, where appropirate:

When to record the transaction

How it is *measured*—what value to use

Some *discussion* and/or *examples*

In that order: when to record, how to value, discussion, examples. In addition to the events themselves (above), there are:

    3. *Additional* principles which relate to the *changes* in events, which determine their effects.

    4. Principles governing assets and liabilities that are not resources or obligations (such as deferred taxes).

[¶ 207.1]   1A—External Events—Transfers To or From Other Entities

(1) Exchanges (reciprocal transfers)

Assets—Acquisitions: Record as acquired (some not carried forward are expenses); cost, face amount, sometimes discounted value; sometimes fair value in non-cash exchanges (allocate fair values for individual assets in group)—excess is goodwill. Cash, accounts receivable, short-term receivables at discounted amount when no or low interest stated.

Assets—Dispositions: When disposed of, at cost adjusted for amortization and other changes; in partial dispositions value is based on detailed principles (FIFO, LIFO, average).

Liabilities—Increases: When obligation to transfer assets or provide services is incurred in exchanges; value is established in the exchange, sometimes discounted (long-term)—pension obligations, loans under capitalized long-term leases, bonds, notes bearing little or no interest (the difference is amortized over period to maturity).

Liabilities—Decreases: When discharged through payments or otherwise; use recorded amounts. If partial, may have to apportion to recorded amount.

Commitments—*Not* recorded when unfulfilled on both sides, unless: one party
fulfills its part; some leases are recorded: *losses* on firm commitments are recorded. Long-term leases are recorded as assets by
the lessee, with the corresponding liability.

Revenue from Exchanges—When product is sold, service performed, resource
used by others, and when asset is sold producing gain (or loss);
recorded at price in the exchange, sometimes reduced for discounts or allowances. Exceptions: long-term construction contracts, revenue not recognized on purchases, certain products with
an *assured* selling price—sometimes recorded over long periods
without reasonable assurance of collection (installment method;
cost recovery method). (Under the installment method, proceeds
collected measure the revenue, but expense is measured by multiplying cost by ratio of collection to sales price. In cost recovery
method, use all proceeds collected until all costs are recovered.)

Expenses—Directly associated with revenue from exchanges—use costs of assets sold or services provided, recorded when related revenue is
recognized. If other than a product, the remaining *undepreciated*
cost is subtracted from the revenue obtained.

(2) Non-reciprocal transfers:
    (A) *With owners:* Investments and withdrawals recorded as they occur:

Increases—by amount of cash received; the discounted value of money
claims received or liabilities canceled; fair value of non-cash assets received (often, the fair value of *stock issued*).

Decreases—cash paid; recorded amount of non-cash assets transferred;
discounted present value of liabilities incurred.

In "pooling," assets and liabilities are combined as on books (no
change); "purchase" method entails use of fair value.

Investments of non-cash assets recorded when made; sometimes measured at cost to founder (rather than fair value).

    (B) *With outsiders:* assets, when acquired, when disposed of, when discov-
ered; for non-cash assets given, usually use fair value; liabilities, at face
value, sometimes discounted.

[¶ 207.2]   1B—External Events—Other Than Transfers

Examples are: Changes in prices of assets, changes in interest rates,
technological changes, damage caused by outside influences.

Favorable events—Generally not recorded, except at time of later exchange. Retained on books at recorded amounts until exchanged (assets) or
until satisfied (liabilities). Exceptions are: When using the equity
method; foreign currency translations; marketable securities under

new rules, written down to market, up to cost, as fluctuates; obligations under warranties.

Unfavorable events—Decreasing market price or utility of asset, adjusted to lower market price or recoverable cost, usually governed by specific rules such as cost or market for inventories. A loss is recognized when utility is no longer as great as its cost, obsolescence; adjust write-offs or write-off entirely currently if it is completely worthless, or down to recoverable cost. Damage caused by others, record when occurs or discovered—to recoverable cost. Increases in amounts currently payable because of higher interest rates only generally not recorded until liquidated. Increases in non-U.S. Dollar liabilities are recorded in terms of U.S. Dollar because of currency translation.

[¶ 207.3]   2A—Internal Events—Production of Goods or Services

Production is the input of goods and services combined to produce an output of product which may be goods or services. It includes: Manufacturing, merchandising, transporting and holding goods.

Recorded at historical or acquisition costs (previously recorded) as used in the production process during the period; deducted from revenue to which related in the period sold. Costs are usually shifted or allocated from initially recorded asset accounts to other accounts in a *systematic* and *rational* manner.

Costs of manufacturing or providing services—Costs of assets completely used plus allocated portions of assets partially used; allocations are assumed, based on relationship between assets and activities; note that "costs" refers to amounts charged initially to assets—they become "expenses" when allocated to expense as follows:
If benefit only one period—expense then.
If benefit several periods—expense over periods involved (depreciation, depletion, amortization).

Expenses—Some items are recognized as expenses immediately and charged directly thereto. Enterprises never "acquire" expenses, as they acquire assets. Costs may be charged as expenses immediately under the principle of immediate recognition when they pertain to the period involved and cannot be associated with any other period, such as officer salaries and advertising.

Revenue—Under certain conditions and special standards, revenue may be recognized at completion of production or as production progresses (precious metals industry; long-term construction contracts). Ratio of performance to date must be capable of being reasonably estimated and collection *reasonably* assured. Take losses *immedi-*

ately. Revenue is measured by an allocated portion of a predetermined selling price, less product or service costs as they progress.

[¶ 207.4]   2B—Internal Events—Casualties

Sudden, substantial, unanticipated reductions in assets *not* caused by other
entities, such as:
> Fires, floods, abnormal spoilage.

Recorded when they occur or when they are discovered.
Measured by writing them down to recoverable costs and a *loss* is recorded.

[¶ 207.5]   3—Additional Principles Which Related to The Changes in Events, Determine Their Effects

Dual effect—Every recorded event affects at least *two* items in the records.
The double-entry system is based on this principle.

Increases in assets arise from:
- A. Exchanges in which assets are acquired
- B. Investments of assets by owners
- C. Non-reciprocal transfers of assets by outsiders
- D. Shifts of costs during production
- E. External events (equity method)
- F. Increases ascribed to produced assets
    - with *opposite effect* of:
- 1. Decrease in other assets
- 2. Increase in liability
- 3. Revenue recognition
- 4. Sometimes, neutral effect—production costs shifted.

Decreases in assets arise from:
- A. Exchanges in which assets are disposed of
- B. Withdrawals of assets by owners
- C. Non-reciprocal transfers to outsiders
- D. External events which reduce market price
- E. Shifts and allocations
- F. Casualties
    - with *opposite effect* of:
- 1. Increase in other assets
- 2. Decrease in liabilities
- 3. Increases in expenses:
    - Immediately, if used up;
    - Or if future benefit cannot be determined.

Increases in liabilities arise from:
- A. Exchanges in which liabilities are incurred
- B. Transfers with owner (dividend declaration)
- C. Non-reciprocal transfers with outsiders
    - with *opposite effect* of:
- 1. Decrease in other liabilities

   2. Increase in assets
   3. An expense.

Decreases in liabilities arise from:
  A. Exchanges in which liabilities are reduced
  B. Transfers with owners
  C. Non-reciprocal transfers with outsiders
     (forgiveness of indebtedness)
     with *opposite effect* of:
   1. Increases in other liabilities
   2. Decreases in assets
   3. Revenue

Increases in owners' equity arise from:
  A. Investments in enterprise
  B. *Net* result of all revenue and expenses in a period
  C. Non-reciprocal transfers with outsiders (gifts)
  D. Prior period adjustments.

Decreases in owners' equity arise from:
  A. Transfers to owners (dividends)
  B. Net losses for a period
  C. Prior period adjustments.

Revenue arises:
  A. Primarily from exchanges
  B. Occasionally from production
  C. Rarely from transfers or external events with *opposite effect* of:
   1. Usually an asset increase
   2. Decrease in liability (called "unearned revenue").

Expenses arise from:
  A. Exchanges—costs directly associated with revenue are recognized when assets are sold or services provided.
  B. Non-reciprocal transfers with outsiders
  C. External events other than transfers
  D. Production:
    1) Costs of manufacturing products and providing services *not* included in product costs (example—overhead)
    2) Expenses from systematic and rational allocation, excluding those assigned to product costs of manufacturing
    3) Expenses recognized immediately on the acquisition of goods or services
    4) Costs of products for which revenue is recognized at *completion* of production or as *production* progresses (precious metals, percent-of-completion contracts).

[¶ 207.6]   4—Principles Governing Assets and Liabilities That are Not Resources or Obligations

Certain items are shown as assets that are not in reality resources, such as deferred charges for income taxes; and certain items are shown as liabilities that are not in reality liabilites, such as deferred credits for income taxes.

Accounting for them is governed by detailed principles, such as accounting for deferred federal income taxes.

The effect of recording these items is an increase or a decrease in assets or liabilities, with a corresponding decrease or increase in expenses on the income statement.

[¶ 208]   THE PRINCIPLES OF FINANCIAL STATEMENT PRESENTATION

The general objective is to provide reliable information on resources, obligations and progress. The information should be useful for comparability, completeness and understandability. The basic features involved in financial accounting are: the individual accounting entity, the use of approximation and the preparation of fundamentally related financial statements.

[¶ 208.1]   "Fair Presentation In Conformity with GAAP"

1. GAAP applicable in the circumstances have been applied in accumulating and processing the accounting information; and

2. Changes from period to period in GAAP have been properly disclosed; and

3. The information in the *underlying* records is properly *reflected* and *described* in the financial statements in conformity with GAAP; and

4. A proper balance has been achieved between:
   A. The conflicting needs to disclose the important aspects of financial position and results of operation in conformance with conventional concepts, and to
   B. Summarize the voluminous underlying data with a limited number of financial statement captions and supporting notes.

[¶ 208.2]   There are 12 Principles of Financial Statement Presentation

1. Basic Financial Statements—minimum requirements:
   A. Balance Sheet
   B. Statement of Income
   C. Statement of Changes in Retained Earnings
   D. Statement of Changes in Financial Position
   E. Disclosure of Accounting Policies
   F. Disclosure of Related Notes
      Usually presented for two or more periods.
      Other information may be presented, and in some cases required as supplemental information: Price-level statements; information about operations in different industries; foreign operations and export sales; major customers (segment reporting).

2. A Complete Balance Sheet (or "Statement of Financial Position")
   A. All Assets
   B. All Liabilities
   C. All classes of owners' Equity.

3. A Complete Income Statement
   A. All Revenues
   B. All Expenses.

4. A Complete Statement of Changes in Financial Position
   > Includes and describes all important aspects of the company's financing and investing activities.

5. Accounting Period
   > Basic time period is one year
   > An interim statement is for less than one year.

6. Consolidated Financial Statements
   > They are presumed to be more meaningful than separate statements of the component legal entities
   >
   > They are *usually* necessary when one of the group owns (directly or indirectly) *over 50%* of the outstanding voting stock
   >
   > The information is presented as if it were *a single enterprise.*

7. The Equity Basis
   > For unconsolidated subsidiaries (where over 50% is owned) *and for investments in 50% or less* of the voting stock of companies in which the investor has significant influence over investees. 20% or more ownership presumes this influence, unless proved otherwise
   >
   > The investor's share of the net income reported by the investee is picked up and shown as income and an adjustment of the investment account—for all earnings subsequent to the acquisition. Dividends are treated as an adjustment of the investment account.

8. Translation of Foreign Branches
   > Translated into U.S. Dollars by conventional translation procedures involving foreign exchange rates.

9. Classification and Segregation:
   (Must separately disclose these important components)
   A. *Income Statement*—Sales (or other source of revenue); Cost of Sales; depreciation; Selling and Administration Expenses; Interest Expense; Income Taxes.
   B. *Balance Sheet*—Cash; Receivables; Inventories; Plant and Equipment; Payables; and Categories of Owners' Equity:
      > Par or stated amount of capital stock; Additional paid-in capital
      > Retained earnings: (affected by—
      >> Net income or loss
      >> Prior period adjustments
      >> Dividends
      >> Transfers to other categories of equity).
      >
      > Working Capital—current assets and current liabilities should be classified as such to be able to determine working capital—useful for enterprises in: manufacturing, trading, some service enterprises.
      >> Current assets—include cash and other assets that can reasonably be expected to be realized in cash in one year or a shorter business cycle.

Current liabilities—include those that are expected to be satisfied by the use of those assets shown as current; or the creation of other current liabilities; or expected to be satisfied in one year.

Assets and liabilities should *not* be offset against each other unless a *legal* right to do so exists, which is a rare exception.

Gains and loses—arise from other than products or services, may be combined and shown as one item. Examples: write-downs of inventories, receivables, capitalized research and development costs, *all sizable*. Also, gains and losses on: temporary investments, non-monetary transactions, currency devaluations are a few typical items.

Extraordinary items or gain or loss—should be shown separately under its own title, distinguished by unusual nature and infrequent occurrence—should be shown net of taxes.

Net Income—should be separately disclosed and clearly identified on the income statement.

10. Other disclosures: (Accounting policies and notes)
  A. Customary or routine disclosures:
    1. Measurement bases of important assets
    2. Restrictions on assets
    3. Restriction on owners' equity
    4. Contingent liabilities
    5. Contingent assets
    6. Important long-term commitments not in the body of the statements
    7. Information on terms of equity of owners
    8. Information on terms of long-term debt
    9. Other disclosures required by AICPA
  B. Disclosure of changes in accounting policies.
  C. Disclosure of important subsequent events—
       between balance sheet date and date of the opinion.
  D. Disclosure of accounting policies ("Summary of Significant . . . ").

11. Form of Financial Statement Presentation:
    No particular form is presumed better than all others for all purposes. Several are used.

12. Earnings Per Share:
    Must be disclosed on the *face of the Income Statement*. Should be disclosed for:
    A. Income before extraordinary items
    B. Net Income.
    Should consider:
    A. Changes in number of shares outstanding
    B. Contingent changes
    C. Possible dilution from potential conversion of:
           Convertible debentures
           Preferred stock
           Options
           Warrants.

END OF GAAP OUTLINE

3

Business Structures

[¶301] **BUSINESS STRUCTURE CONSIDERATIONS**

Any business enterprise is internally composed of two distinct human elements:

Employers—the owners of the business;

Employees—those employed by the owner.

(Sometimes, an owner is an employee of his own firm, but his classification as an owner is unaffected.)

The owner (employer) of a business may be the founder—the one who initially organized and funded the operation—or a successor to that original founder. The founder, in starting the business, has several, but limited, options as to the *type* of legal business-structure format to be used for the operation. (Also, the founder or his successor may choose to change the structure from one type to another at a subsequent date.)

The primary considerations are:

1. The extent of personal liability should the business fail;
2. The comparative tax advantages offered by different methods of organization.

And the available options are:

1. Sole proprietorship
2. Partnership—in combination with one or more other owners
3. Corporation—in combination with others for legal formation, but he might in fact be subsequently the sole owner
4. Sub-chapter S Corporation—with others, or alone
5. Professional Corporation or Association—with others, or alone.

25

(A Joint Venture is merely a stop-gap entity from which profits flow to one of the above types of entity.)

If the owner places a priority on *tax-savings,* any format would be chosen in preference to the corporation format, which historically has been taxed on both the *earnings* and the *distribution (dividends)* of those same earnings. The Sub-S corporation and the Professional corporation (if electing the Sub-S option) do eliminate the double-taxation feature (and also offer the advantage of full corporate deductions for executive salaries, if paid timely), but they also involve personal taxation on all the undistributed earnings, which pass through to the individuals (with certain exceptions) effectively as in a partnership.

If the owner places priority on the *limitation* of personal liability, he will choose the corporate form (possibly with the Sub-S option). But he cannot choose the Professional corporation to limit liability, since most states prohibit this limitation by law (as for doctors, accountants, etc.).

Once the legal format is set, the method of financial accounting and reporting for that particular type of business is applied.

Most accounting textbooks and guidelines seem to be directed toward the corporate method of accounting. The standards of maintaining records for most assets, liabilities and items of income and expense are generally applicable to any type of business structure. Whatever guidelines apply to the corporation also apply to most of the other forms of business entity, *except* in these areas:

1. The Capital or Equity section:
   A. Initial investment
   B. The sharing of profits/losses
2. Salaries/Drawings of owners
3. Income tax on the entity's profit
4. How to account for investments in subsidiaries or controlled nonsubsidiaries
5. Dissolution of the entity.

Here, in brief, are the major differences to recall or research for the various structures:

Clearly distinguish between *personal* expenditures and business expenditures. In proprietorships and partnerships, personal items are to be treated as drawings or withdrawals or as loans. In a corporation, treat as a loan or dividend.

In partnerships, the *partnership agreement* takes precedence and establishes all the rules, especially of distribution. The agreement should spell out: Capital contributions requirements and basis of assets or liabilities assumed, duties of the partners, time to be spent in the business, limitations on drawings, the ratio of sharing profits and losses, death provisions, insurance protection, loans and interest on loans. Salaries might, for example, be alloted to each working partner before the ratio-splitting of profits, but the salary plus the split-share of the remaining profit effectually go into that partner's capital account and are reduced by *actual drawings* (salary plus profit-withdrawal).

In *dissolution* of partnerships, liabilities to/from partners are paid before distribution, and *no* distribution is made in excess of each partner's just share needed for liquidation of liabilities.

Death usually dissolves a *partnership,* unless the agreement makes specific contingent provisions.

Financial statements for either a proprietorship or partnership should provide a "Statement of Capital Changes" (similar to a corporation's "Changes in Retained Earnings").

The valuation of assets (and/or liabilities) at original cost should be stated at fair value, in any structure. Goodwill is set up, if pertinent, and the Capital or Capital Stock section credited for the agreed ownership portion. (Law requires corporations sometimes to distinguish between "par value" and "excess of par.") "Negative goodwill" should be used to write down non-current (fixed) assets in an immediate proportion. Goodwill, if any, should be amortized for financial purposes over 40 years unless there is proof of a shorter benefit period. Goodwill is not deductible for tax purposes.

The *trade name,* if any, should be used on proprietorship or partnership statements, with disclosure of the type of business structure.

The "cash basis" of accounting is *not* a generally accepted accounting principle, and proper financial statements, when carrying an independent auditor's opinion, are either qualified ("subject to") or with a disclaimer, depending on the materiality of the difference had the accrual method been used.

Financial accounting for sole proprietorships and partnerships *should not* record accruals or deductions for the income tax which that owner or co-owner must pay on his respective share of the earnings. However, financial footnotes should make such a disclosure if the funds for such payment may deplete those belonging to the entity (as future "withdrawals").

The *equity method* of accounting for investments in subsidiaries or controlled non-subsidiaries is *not* permitted for sole proprietors, trusts or estates. Proprietors should carry investments *at cost.* Partnerships and joint-ventures should use cost adjusted for accumulated undistributed earnings.

Deferred taxes on undistributed earnings of subsidiaries or non-subsidiaries should *not* be set up for partnerships, because of the factor of "personal taxing" mentioned above.

Financial statements for sole proprietorships may show a "reasonable" salary allowance for the owner to arrive at a financial operating income. But the salary is still a withdrawal.

Consolidations are permitted a proprietorship (over 50% ownership):

1. If owning 100%, the investment is eliminated against equity;
2. If less than 100%, the minority interest is shown on the income statement before extraordinary items, and on the balance sheet between liabilities and net worth.

Other eliminations should be as in consolidations.

Joint ventures are usually not majority-controlled by any of the participants. Hence, consolidation is not in order. The equity method is used by partnerships or corporations that participate in a joint venture. Proprietors should use the cost method of investment. Sometimes, however, upon proper disclosure, ''proportionate'' consolidation is used. Here, a pro-rata share of assets, liabilities and income is consolidated.

4

Employee Benefits

INTRODUCTION

Over the years, the types of fringe benefits offered employees have evolved as methods of helping employees avoid or delay the impact of individual income taxes. At the same time, government has effectively paid about half of the costs, because for every corporate deductible expense-dollar, there is the corresponding maximum federal tax saving of 46%, plus state tax savings.

The competition to provide higher benefits represents an increasing awareness of the value of human resources (labor) and the costs of training and keeping good personnel. Both monetarily and psychologically, the employer tries to satisfy by providing favorable motivation for extended, continued employment.

The inducements are many: Modern equipment, comfortable working conditions, medical facilities, lounges and restaurants, employee discount stores, year-round temperature control, use of the telephone, and, more lately, staggered hours or optional choice of working time.

Among the dollar inducements are the following:

Annual (or short-term) benefits:

1. Bonuses—with timed-deferral of cash payment to be most beneficial to the employee (shifting income);
2. Transfers of property, rather than cash;
3. Wage continuation plans (sick pay);
4. Expense reimbursement or allowances;
5. Meals and lodging away from home;
6. Moving and relocation expenses, including guarantee of non-loss on home sale;
7. Courtesy discounts on products handled;
8. Hospitalization and health insurance;
9. Medical reimbursement plans;
10. Group life term-insurance coverage.

29

Long-term benefits:

    1. Deferred compensation arrangements;
        A.   Stock option compensatory plans
        B.   Pension and Profit-Sharing plans
        C.   Other deferred compensation contracts;
    2. Key-person (non-term) life insurance.

The discussion following centers on these long-term benefits.

[¶ 402]   DEFERRED COMPENSATION PLANS

STOCK OPTION PLANS

[¶ 402.1]   Non-Compensatory Plans

A plan is considered to be non-compensatory when it possesses all four of the following characteristics:

    1. Almost all full-time employees may participate;
    2. Stock is offered to employees equally based on a uniform percent of wages;
    3. The time for exercise is limited to a reasonable period;
    4. The discount from the market price of the stock is not greater than would be reasonable in an offer to stockholders or others.

An example of a non-compensatory plan is one that qualifies under Section 423 of the IRS Code. (See Section Two—Taxes.)

[¶ 402.2]   Compensatory Plans

Stock issued to an employee under any plan *except* a non-compensatory plan (above) is considered to be a compensatory plan and calls for the recognition of *compensation expense* by the employer.

The time of earliest measurement (issuance, date of grant) is the determining factor as to when to record the compensation. The fact that the employee may not be able to receive or sell the stock for some years does *not* affect the compensation.

At the time of issuance (the date of the agreement), if the facts of the option price and a market price are known, the difference between a *higher* market price and the option price (the price at which the employee may buy the stock from the company) is considered to be compensation—at that time, not later. However, if the granting of the options is predicated upon the rendering of *future services,* the compensation calculated may be deferred to the period of future benefit (to be derived from those services). The excess (or bargain) is the theoretical benefit availed to the employee for his services, past, present or future.

For example, assume the employee's services would extend over two years (current and next year), the entry would be:

Current Year

Employees Compensation (current expense)	50.	
Unearned Compensation (holdover)	50.	
Capital Surplus		100.

Market Price at issuance	$ 10.	
Option price	9.	
Excess per share	$ 1.	
100 shares @ $ 1.	$100.	

Next Year

Employees Compensation (expense)	50.	
Unearned Compensation		50.

Any "unearned compensation" should be shown as a separate reduction of stockholders' equity.

No compensation is recognized if the option price equals or exceeds the market price at option issuance date.

Note again that the *exercise* date is not pertinent—yet.

For *tax* purposes, the amount deductible by the corporation is not applicable or determinable until the time the employee must pick up ordinary income, a factor which varies according to the plan as specified under IRS regulations. Thus, both the period and amount of expensing will probably differ for tax purposes, thus creating timing differences. Also, the difference between the compensation originally recorded and the tax-deductible amount goes to Capital Surplus.

[¶ 402.3]   Earnings Per Share

All shares which could be issued under the arrangement are considered "as if" issued, and considered to be common stock equivalents and outstanding for earnings per share computations. If applicable, the treasury stock method is used to determine the incremental shares.

Compensatory stock options may thus affect *both* factors in the EPS formula: The numerator, for the compensation expense; and the denominator, by the addition of the equivalent shares.

Both primary and fully diluted computations are affected, if 3% or more.

[¶402.4] Tandem (Alternate) Stock, Elective Plans, Phantom Stock

Sometimes, stock plans for employees contain provisions for an election of alternative rights or options. These plans which combine rights are called "tandem stock" or "alternate stock" plans. If the election to acquire stock under either right decreases the other right, it is called a "phantom stock" plan.

[¶ 403] PENSION (AND PROFIT SHARING) PLANS*

This text *does not* concern itself with the accounting requirements for maintaining and reporting the position and activities of and within the fund itself.

This discussion deals with the *expense* portion which a company may or may not claim for financial accounting and reporting purposes—the accounting for the *cost* of the plans, which may or may not coincide with the allowable tax deduction permitted the corporation, or with the amount required for funding.

(Non-corporate entities, as well as self-employed individuals, should examine ERISA provisions—the Employees Retirement Income Security Act of 1974, P.L. 93-406, with updates—for a comprehensive detailing of the extended deferment privileges now available.)

Pension commitments made by employers to employees have become increasingly significant in business and industry starting about in the mid-1930's, or about 50 years ago. It is not uncommon for an individual's largest single asset to be the vested interest in a retirement plan.

In 1974, Congress passed the Employee Retirement Income Security Act (ERISA) which mandated many pension plan requirements for virtually every private retirement plan in the United States. The objective of ERISA is to protect workers' pension rights, specifically the rights associated with funding, participation, and vesting.

ERISA requirements affect employers' costs importantly. How?

1. Annual funding is no longer discretionary. A plan *must* be funded based upon an actuarial cost which over time will be sufficient to pay all future pension obligations.

2. Tax deductions for the employer will be disallowed, and fines imposed by the government, if plans are not funded in compliance with ERISA requirements.

---

*See FASB Statement No. 35. *Accounting and Reporting by Defined Benefit Pension Plans*, March, 1980. Also, APB Opinion No. 8. *Accounting for the Cost of Pension Plans*, November, 1966, as amended by FASB Statement No. 36. *Disclosure of Pension Information*, May, 1980.

3. Comprehensive terms of a pension plan and detailed annual reports and schedules must be published.

4. All reports, schedules, statements, and other required information are subject to audit by independent certified public accountants.

An important section of the Act created the Pension Benefit Guaranty Corporation (PBGC) which protects pension plan participants from the cost of plan benefits. The operation of the PBGC is, essentially, the power to impose a lien on the assets of an employer for unfunded pension liabilities, and for the excess of the present value of guaranteed vested benefits over the pension fund assets. Also, Congress gave this lien equal status with a tax lien, which takes priority over most other creditor claims.

PBGC has the legislative authority to force an involuntary termination of a plan if it appears there is a reasonable possibility for nonpayment of the pension obligations. Congress, with a view to forcing ERISA administrators to monitor plans rigorously, restricts liens to 30% of an employer's net worth.

[¶ 403.1] Defined Contribution, Defined Benefit Plans

Pension plans are broadly defined as Defined Contribution and Defined Benefit Plans.

Defined Contribution Plan:

• The employer contributes a percentage of its income or a percentage of employees' income to a pension fund.

• Contain provisions which require employers to determine exactly the amount that must be contributed to the plan each year.

• Once the "defined" contribution is made, the employer has no additional pension liabilities.

• The contribution is made to a third party trustee.

• Pension expense for the year is the amount of the contribution.

• A liability is accrued at statement date for any part of the contribution that has not been paid to the trustee. (The liability is classified as current because it must be paid promptly.)

• Because the contributions as they accumulate belong to the employees, the employees assume the risk of a poor investment performance, but also share in the gains from wise investment management through increased future pension benefits.

• The retirees' benefits are based upon 1) the level of the defined contributions, and 2) the earnings of the plan's investment portfolio.

Defined Benefit Plan:

• Specifies the benefits to be received by retirees.

• Benefits based upon employee's age, years of service, and income during employment.

• The annual pension cost is based upon a formula that consists of a percentage rate times the number of years service times the income at the year of retirement, or an average of several years' income.

• The expense of a plan for the employer is based on the estimates of the benefits to be paid.

• Employer and employee contributions to the plan and accumulated earnings from plan investments are estimated to pay the benefits as provided in the plan.

Employer assumes the investment risks associated with the plan. Different from the Defined Contribution Plan, the employees do not own the plan assets, rather the employees accept a contractual amount of pension upon retirement. If the investment performance is favorable, the employer may reduce the contribution; if the investment performance is unfavorable, the employer must make additional contributions to assure that estimated benefits are funded.

[¶ 403.2]   Other Types of Plans

Qualified Plan is one which meets the criteria set forth in the Tax Code and, therefore, give the employer certain tax benefits. Likewise, the benefit to the plan participant is a deferral of taxes on the benefits until they are received in retirement. (The employer's contribution to the plan can be deducted when made to the fund.) Earnings of the fund are not taxed until they are distributed to beneficiaries years into the future.

Funded Plan is one the assets of which have been transferred to a trustee. If the total amount recognized as an expense has been given to the trustee, the plan is *fully* funded; if only a part of the expense has been recognized, the plan is a *partially* funded plan.

Insured Plan transfers the risk of the future commitments to an insurance company. The employer funds the plan by purchasing an annuity contract from an insurance company, with the insurance company contracting to pay the defined benefits as they come due. The company agrees to contractual premium payments.

Unfunded Plan does not require the company to transfer funds to a third party trustee. Such plans can be thought of as pay-as-you-go plans. There is a significant accounting aspect to these plans, e.g., funding takes place when the benefit is paid to the retiree, so no pension expense is recognized during the years of the employee's employment.

[¶ 403.3]   Accounting Standards

FASB Statement of Financial Accounting Standards No. 35 "Accounting and Reporting by Defined Benefit Pension Plans" sets forth the standards for pension fund accounting. Before FASB No. 35 was promulgated, accounting and reporting for pension plans was inadequately developed. ERISA stimulated the need for professional guidance by requiring annual reporting and other requirements (as noted above).

The primary objective of FASB No. 35 is to provide all the information necessary to determine the soundness of the plan, which in turn means the resources necessary to meet the future obligations of the plan. A summary of the requirements follow:

• FASB No. 35 applies to all defined benefit plans, except terminated plans.

• GAAP applies meaning that accounting principles not included in the statement apply.

• Information about the assets available to pay benefits.

• Information about the participants accumulated benefits.

• Information about the plan's investment performance.

• Information about all other factors that may affect the plan's ability to pay accumulated benefits.

• Statement of net assets available for benefits.

• Information giving the present value of accumulated benefits.

• Information concerning significant changes in accumulated benefits.

• The accrual basis of accounting is required.

• Fund investments are disclosed at their current value.

• Operating assets, if any, are disclosed at their cost less accumulated depreciation.

• Changes in the current value of investments since the last reporting period.

• Investment income must be reported.

• Contributions from employers and employees must be disclosed.

• Benefits paid since the last statement date must be disclosed.

• Administrative expenses must be reported.

• Actuarial present value of accumulated plan benefits attributable to employee service prior to the benefit valuation date must be disclosed.

• The measurement rules for accumulated benefits and the basis for the calculations should be explained.

• Cost-of-living adjustments included in the plan should be disclosed.

35

• FASB No. 35 and FASB No. 36 "Disclosure of Pension Information" both contain a number of actuarial and present value computations related to various aspects of a plan, i.e., probability of payment, withdrawals, disability, rates of return, discounting future cash flow, vested benefits, nonvested benefits, current investment values, etc.

[¶ 403.4]   Timing of Payments into Funds

An important tax factor which must be considered by the employer and the statement-preparer is the timing of actual payments into the pension or profit sharing fund.

All claimed expenses must have been actually disbursed (not merely accrued) by the legally required tax-return filing date, *including* all permissible extensions. Thus, a late filing of an 1120, without extension, would bring about disallowance of the claimed expense contribution to a pension plan, if the payment had not actually been made by March 15 (calendar year taxpayer).

Preparers of financial statements should be aware of the possibility of a "subsequent event" disclosure, or a timing difference note-requirement for known late payments.

[¶ 403.5]   The Expensing Standards

In the absence of convincing evidence that the company will reduce or discontinue the benefits called for in a pension plan, the cost of the plan should be accounted for on the assumption that the company will continue to provide such benefits. This assumption implies a long-term undertaking, the cost of which should be recognized annually whether or not funded. Therefore, accounting for pension costs should not be discretionary.

The cost of *all* benefit payments made to the fund should be charged to income, none to retained earnings. The annual provision for pension cost should be based on an accounting method which uses:

1. *An acceptable actuarial cost method,* which is rational and systematic and consistently applied, resulting in reasonable measure of pension costs from year to year (assigning separate portions to past or prior service cost). These methods may be based on the accrued benefit cost method or several projected benefit cost methods.

   and

2. The actuarial cost determined above should fall *between* the following *minimum* and *maximum* computations:

MINIMUM

Should *not* be *less* than the total of:

A. Normal cost, and

B. Interest on unfunded prior service cost, and

C. A provision for vested benefits, but *only* if the actuarially computed value of the vested benefits *exceeds* the total of:

    1. The pension fund, and

    2. Balance sheet pension accruals (*less*)

    3. Balance sheet pension prepayments or deferrals
       But only if this excess is not at least 5% less than the same year's beginning excess.

This provision for vested benefits should be the *lesser* of:

    1. The amount, if any, by which 5% of the beginning excess is greater than the amount of the *reduction* in excess for the year, or

    2. The amount needed to aggregate:

        A) Normal cost, and

        B) Equivalent 40-year amortization (cost per year) of past service costs—unless fully amortized—*plus* consideration for amortizing applicable amendments thereto, and

        C) Interest equivalents based on what would have been earned had prior year provisions been funded.

MAXIMUM

Should *not* be *greater* than the *total* of:

A. Normal cost, and

B. 10% of past service costs until fully amortized, and 10% of applicable amendments, and

C. Interest equivalents on the difference between provisions and amounts funded.

The complicated formula presented above will not usually pertain to those professionally administered plans engaging the services of professional actuaries. For an independent auditor, confirmation by the actuary is usually enough to substantiate the required corporate contribution. The guidelines should be more carefully observed by those companies which self-administer their own plans.

The difference between the amount expensed and that actually paid into the fund should be shown on the balance sheet as accrued or prepaid pension costs.

If the company has a legal obligation in *excess* of the amounts paid or accrued, the excess should be shown as both a deferred charge and a liability.

Except to the extent above, unfunded *prior* service cost is *not* a liability for the balance sheet.

All employees who would reasonably be expected to receive benefits under a pension plan should be considered in the cost calculations, considering turnover also.

[¶ 404]   PROFIT SHARING PLANS

Contributions are based upon independent action taken by the corporate Board of Directors, tied to the profit of the year, under a profit sharing agreement approved by both management and employees. The authority for the contribution is reflected in the minutes of the corporation. The IRS also approves the plan.

The IRS imposes a combined maximum tax-deductible limit for companies having *both* plans.

[¶ 405]   ACTUARIAL GAINS AND LOSSES

Reported gains or losses within the plans should be considered, generally on the average method, and only to the extent that they might necessitate a change in the contribution requirement. These gains or losses are usually reflected in the computations made by the fund administrator in the determination of the amount needed to be contributed by the corporation to keep the plan properly funded, subject to the minimum and maximum considerations.

[¶ 406]   DEFINED CONTRIBUTION PLANS

These plans specify either:

1. Benefits will be based on defined *contributions,* or
2. Contributions will result in defined *benefits.*

In circumstance (1), the contribution is the pension cost for the year. Circumstance (2) requires the determination of pension cost in the same detailed manner described above.

[¶ 407]   INSURED PLANS

Usually the amount of net premium payment determined by the insurance company is the proper pension cost for the employer, provided dividends, termination costs and other factors are handled properly by the insurance company.

[¶ 408] COMPANIES WITH MORE THAN ONE PLAN

Actuarial methods may differ, but accounting for each plan should follow the stated standards.

[¶ 409]   **SOCIAL SECURITY BENEFITS**
              AND PENSION PLANS

Some pension plans provide for reduced benefits to the extent of Social Security benefits. In estimating future benefits for present value purposes under the plan, estimate must also be made for the Social Security benefits applicable.

[¶ 410]   **ERISA REQUIREMENTS**

No change in accounting standards is necessitated by the new participation, vesting or funding requirements of the 1974 Act, because the determination of proper cost still falls under the minimum-maximum rules. However, significant increases in the dollar amount of the pension cost contribution caused by the requirements should be disclosed when the plan first becomes subject to the Act.

[¶ 411]   **OTHER DEFERRED**
              COMPENSATION CONTRACTS

Other contracts should be accounted for individually on an accrual basis, with the estimated amounts to be ultimately paid systematically, and rationally allocated, over the period of active employment from the time the contract is effective until services are expected to end or the contract expire. However, deferring expenses is permissible to match future services.

For annuity or lump-sum type settlements in these plans, the annual accrual should still be accrued over the time of active employment. Thus, the total expenses booked to the end of employment should equal the estimated present value of the money to be paid the employee (or beneficiaries).

When payments extend beyond the period of active employment (such as annuity payments to a beneficiary), the present value of all said payments should be accrued and expensed.

[¶ 412]   **KEY-PERSON LIFE INSURANCE**

The acceptable method of accounting for premium costs incurred in buying key-person (non-term) life insurance is to first charge an asset account for the period's increase in the cash surrender value of the policy, and then expense the difference between that increase and the premium paid. The ratable charge method is not acceptable. This procedure applies only to those policies under

39

which the corporation is the ultimate beneficiary. But the procedure also applies to those policies which may be taken on "debtor-corporation" officers.

A loan on a life insurance policy of an officer can be shown in either of two ways:

1. As a current liability if the company intends to repay it within the current year; or

2. As a deduction from the amount shown as cash surrender value if the company does *not* intend to repay it within a year. If it runs to the death of the insured, it is deducted from the proceeds, if the corporation transmits them to the survivors.

Although the corporation is the beneficiary of these funds on a pay-out of the policy, the proceeds are usually used to pay benefits to the employee's family, to redeem stock, or for some other purpose beneficial to the employee.

[¶ 413]   MISCELLANEOUS CONSIDERATIONS

In a business combination, the rule for assigning an amount for the assumption of pension cost accruals should be the greater of:

1. The accrued pension cost computed in conformity with the accounting policies of the acquiring company, or
2. The excess, if any, of the actuarially computed value of the vested benefits over the amount of the fund.

In the disposal of a business segment, costs and expenses directly associated with the decision to dispose should include such items as:

1. Severance pay;
2. Additional pension costs;
3. Employee relocation expenses.

In pooling of interest, employee compensation and stock option plans, if reasonable, may carry over to the acquiring company without violating the precepts of pooling.

[¶ 414]   401 (k) PLANS

Definition: Section 401 (k) of the Internal Revenue Code authorizes an employee benefit plan, under which an employee can elect to defer current taxes on the portion of his taxable income contributed on his behalf by his employer.

The main features of 401 (k) plans follow:

• Current tax savings for employers and employees.

• Employees can accumulate a substantial retirement fund by putting a portion of their income into a tax-deductible plan.

• Suitable for companies with a high percentage of employees who are willing to save a portion of their pay. 70 percent of all employees, or 80 percent of eligible employees, must choose to participate in the plan.

• Companies contributing to a profit-sharing plan can also contribute to a 401 (k) plan, as the plan can be combined with an existing pension or profit-sharing plan.

• Employee's contribution can be a portion of pay, or in lieu of a pay increase.

• All funds placed in the plan are deductible by the employer. And the employee's contribution and subsequent earnings on the plan's investments are tax free to the employee until withdrawal.

• Lump-sum withdrawals qualify for 10-year averaging.

• Employer and employee's contributions can be as much as 15 percent of the employee's pay, up to an annual dollar limit on profit-sharing plans.

• Employer's costs associated with establishing and administering the plan are deductible as ordinary business expenses.

• 401 (k) plans must be part of a qualified profit-sharing or stock bonus plans. A qualified plan must meet the following requirements:

1. The plan must permit the employee to elect to have the employer's contribution made to an employee trust.

2. The plan must prohibit a distribution of trust benefits attributable to employer contributions made merely because of the completion of a stated period of participation, or the lapse of a fixed number of years.

3. The employee's right to the accrued benefit derived from employer contributions must be nonforfeitable.

4. The plan must meet nondiscrimination rules pertaining to employee coverage.

A plan meets the nondiscrimination rule if:

1. The plan prohibits contributions and benefits from discriminating in favor of employees who are officers, shareholders, or highly compensated employees.

2. The plan either covers a certain minimum percentage of employees, or does not discriminate in its coverage.

3. The plan must cover a certain minimum percentage of eligible employees.

4. The contributions made to the plan must satisfy one of two *actual deferral percentage* tests: 1) The test for eligible highly compensated employees

must not be more than the deferral percentage of all other eligible employees multiplied by 1.5; or 2) The excess of the actual deferral percentage for the highly compensated employees must not be more than the actual deferral percentage of all other eligible employees multiplied by 2.5.

[¶ 414.1]   Definitions

Highly Compensated Employee: An eligible employee who receives more compensation than two-thirds of all other eligible employees.

Eligible Employee: An employee who in any year is eligible for employer contributions under the plan for that year.

Actual Deferral Percentage: For the eligible highly compensated employee (top ⅓) and all other eligible employees (lower ⅔) for a plan year: the average of the ratio, calculated separately for each employee in such group, of the amount of employer contributions paid under the plan on behalf of each employee for such year to the employee's compensation for the same year.

Employee Compensation: An employee's compensation is the amount taken into account under the plan prior to calculating the contribution made on behalf of the employee under the deferral election.

Covered Employees: Those employees in any year whose accounts are credited with a contribution under the plan for that year.

• Employees *may* borrow from the plan, but under strict guidelines set forth in the Code and in IRS regulations.

• 401 (k) plan may impact other qualified plans. If an employee is a participant in a 401 (k) plan and elects to defer a portion of his pay into the plan, the reduction in his compensation for federal income tax purposes may affect his potential benefits under other plans in which he is a participant. For example, if the employee is in a profit-sharing plan under which employer contributions are geared to pay, a reduction in pay due to a 401 (k) contribution may reduce the employer's contribution to the profit-sharing plan. The same is true with defined benefit pension plans in which potential benefits are based upon current compensation, and which could be affected by deferrals into a 401 (k) plan.

• Participation in a 401 (k) plan does not affect an employee's right to set up an IRA.

• The plan cannot discriminate in favor of "key" or highest-paid officers, executives, the "highly compensated," or shareholders.

5

Information Systems

THE FLOW OF DOCUMENTS

Paper. The forest primeval—milled and pressed to industrial use.

Contracts, certificates, invoices, correspondence, memos, rules, ledgers, machine-tapes, flow charts, advertising catalogs, computer runs, time-cards, checks, statements, tags, cards, sheets, rolls—scratch paper—envelopes, boxes, cartons. Unused paper supplies; paper-in-process; paper filed. Microfilm. Tax returns. Tape and red tape.

An avalanche, if uncontrolled.

Logic, purpose and usefulness, when held in check. A systematized schematic designed to control the economic current which generates the power of the business entity. Periodically to be monitored and tested for resistance, weakness, stability and storage capacity.

The aim—the goal—is to focus all paper into a group picture—one still-life, the photo at a given moment in time—the year-end for the financial statements, as posed by the figures in the general ledger, adjusted and dressed for that split-second closing moment. The numerical characters in a tableau, arranged and described in narration in conformity with professional standards.

Throughout the year, the numerical characters which will ultimately be stilled for one moment—to be counted and accounted for—to be placed in proper perspective for that financial statement group photograph—these characters keep moving, refusing to stand still, adding, accumulating, building, sometimes detracting and withdrawing—darting in and out of the books of account.

A firm hand is needed to guide these figures, to direct their movements, to prevent the inanimate from taking on life of its own, stop the machine before it becomes the master.

The chart of the anatomical business blood-line, in terms of recorded circulation, must be clearly directed, delineated and controlled:

The veins: through which information flows to the heart—

43

The books of original entry:

1. General Journal
2. Cash Receipts Book
3. Cash Disbursements Book
4. Sales Book with its corollary Accounts Receivable sub-ledger
5. Purchases Book with its corollary Accounts Payable sub-ledger
6. Payroll Register and Summaries.

The heart: which stores and pumps out the information—
The general ledger (with its associated valves):

7. General Ledger and Subsidiaries:
   Inventory Control
   Fixed Assets Ledger
   Cost Sub-Ledger Control
   Schedules to supplement

The arteries: which take that flow for digestion to the body and members of the community—owners, bankers, creditors, government, the general public—*The financial statements:*

8. Balance Sheet
9. Income Statement
10. Statement of Changes in Financial Position
11. Statement of Changes in Retained Earnings (or Capital interests)
12. Financial notes.

The following pages outline an approach to the development of an information system, which is sufficiently broad in its components, so that the accountant can apply it as a starting point for a study. Following this general outline are the components of an accounting information system in detail.

[¶ 502]   AN ACCOUNTING INFORMATION SYSTEM OUTLINE

WHAT IS AN INFORMATION SYSTEM?

I. A network of *procedures* for processing raw data in such a way as to generate the information required for management use.

(A) Procedures—the logical steps for accomplishing a job.

(B) System—a network of related procedures, the sum of which result in the accomplishment of the objective.

OBJECTIVE OF AN INFORMATION SYSTEM

I. To reduce the range of uncertainty in the decision-making process.

THE NATURE OF INFORMATION

I. Understanding the nature of information.

   (A) What is information?

   1. Information includes *all* the data and intelligence—financial and nonfinancial—that management needs to plan, operate and control a particular enterprise.

   2. Information is not just the accounting system and the forms and reports it produces. An efficient information system must move beyond the limits of classical accounting reports, and conceive of information as it relates to two vital elements of the management process—planning and control.

      (a) Information about the future.

      (b) Data expressed in nonfinancial terms, e.g., share of market, performance of personnel, adequacy of customer service.

      (c) Information dealing with external conditions as they might bear on a particular company's operations.

   (B) Data is not information. Information *is* data presented in a useful form.

   1. A report is a device which communicates information, not data.

II. Information is quantitative (statistical) or qualitative (nonstatistical).

   (A) Quantitative information—concerns selected data; data selected with respect to the problem, the user, time, place and function.

   (B) Qualitative—concerns information that can be expressed in nonstatistical terms; i.e., adequacy of customer service, environmental conditions.

THE ECONOMICS OF INFORMATION

I. Think of information as a *resource* used in a way that improves the organization's other resources—its personnel and physical facilities. Proper information can help to achieve the goals of the organization in the most efficient manner.

II. Like any other resource, information is not a free commodity. Accordingly, the same criteria should be applied to the development of an information system as to the development of any other resource.

   (A) Will the additional benefits expected from an information system justify the additional costs of developing and implementing the system (marginal cost vs. marginal utility)?

III. In regard to paragraph II, information is available to the organization at some cost. Generally, the initial information is of great value. However, as more and more information is ''bought,'' it becomes increasingly difficult to make use of these incremental units. Therefore, the utility of additional information decreases as more and more information becomes available.

IV. As more information is searched for, the cost of each *additional* unit of information tends to increase.

V. *The Problem*: Determining the amount of information you need from an information system becomes a balancing act. The maximum amount of information that the system can provide isn't necessarily the best. The additional costs of *one* more unit of information should be *exactly* equal to the assigned monetary value of the last unit of information provided.

IMPACT OF THE INFORMATION SYSTEM
ON ORGANIZATIONAL STRUCTURE

I. The system must tie together information requirements of the organizational structure.

II. The information system will produce changes in personnel working environment.

III. Usually, there is a gap created by a changing organization structure and a static information system.

THREE ELEMENTS OF AN INFORMATION SYSTEM

I. Syntheses of three subsystems of an information system.

    (A) The computer

    (B) Data processing

    (C) The language

APPROACH

I. Cornerstone for developing a management information system is the determination of the organization's information needs.

    (A) Requires a clear understanding of each decision-maker's role in the organization. This includes responsibilities, authority, and relationships with other executives.

        1. This cannot be accomplished by the open approach of simply asking an executive what information he requires.

        2. Information systems analyst must help management determine its information needs.

        3. Must be related to the manager's planning and control functions.

II. Analyze and evaluate the system *currently* in use.

    (A) Procedures

    (B) Forms used

    (C) Costs

PLANNING INFORMATION

I. Planning means setting objectives, formulating strategies, and deciding among alternative courses of action.

    (A) The information required to do planning is of three basic types.

        1. *Environmental Information.* Describes the social, political, and economic aspects of the climate in which a business operates, or may operate in the future.

        2. *Competitive Information.* Explains the past performance, programs, and plans of competing companies.

        3. *Internal Information.* Indicates a company's own strengths and weaknesses.

II. Planning information.

    (A) The strategic (as opposed to operating) information about critical business problems.

    (B) Flows to the top executive level.

    (C) The information required for executive-level decisions, e.g., policies.

    (D) Policy maker will be faced with less uncertainty, in the sense that he is better informed about what is going on.

    (E) Organization discipline is tightened as operating methods and results come under instantaneous observation of top management.

III. Determine the decision-making levels in the organization. How many "tiers" are to be included in the information system?

IV. Is the current system adequate?

    (A) Twenty tests to determine if current system is adequate.

      1. Does the current system produce useful reports, or just listings of numbers?

      2. Do all individuals, or stations, who receive reports use them for decision-making purposes, or do they receive them because they are interesting, or because it is ego-filling to be on the distribution list?

      3. Does the same report go to different levels of decision makers? Does the information system take into account the different needs for information at the different organizational levels?

      4. If an organization has automated, is the data processing subsystem simply a bookkeeping tool of the conventional accounting system? Is the automatic data processing system being used for information purposes, or merely as computing hardware?

      5. Are the managing officers completely familiar with the current system? Are they devoting personal interest and talent to this area?

      6. Is the system viewed as a decision-making resource, or narrowly as only a means to reduce accounting costs?

      7. Is the fact realized that conventional accounting systems fail to provide *all* the information necessary for the decision-making process?

      8. When was the system last analyzed?

      9. Is the information system centralized or decentralized? If the latter, is there a duplication of information processing?

     10. Can stored information be retrieved efficiently by users?

     11. How good are the internal data for planning purposes?

     12. How do costs behave in response to volume changes?

     13. Are the factors that condition success in the organization explicitly stated and widely communicated among the management group?

     14. Has the organization's structure remained *unchanged* during the past 15 years?

     15. Does the organization regularly collect and analyze information about population, price level, labor, and other important trends affecting the general profitability of the organization?

     16. What analyses are currently reported to operating management? Are they reported in a manner that permits their utilization in the planning process?

     17. Is significant information about competitors regularly collected and analyzed?

     18. How is current information "factored into" the planning process?

     19. To what extent are decisions based upon fact vs. belief and opinion?

     20. How is current information communicated? In a formal or informal manner?

V. Analyze current system to discover weaknesses.

(A) Analyze the flow of information through the system.

(B) Analyze the operations (termed "events") performed by individuals (or stations) in the system.

(C) Combine (A) and (B) by locating the *origin* of documents, measuring the effort needed to produce them, data needed for correct preparation, number of individuals, or stations, in the system that need copies, and the events that cause documents to be prepared.

   1. Compare the output that results with the output desired.

   2. Consider modifications that can reduce input, or will result in more desirable output, or both.

(D) Study all the operations of the business in order to understand clearly the *processes* within the company.

USE OF LINEAR PROGRAMMING

I. Linear programming can be used to maximize resource allocation.

(A) Linear programming is a systematic way of finding the best course of action when many variables and many conditions must be taken into consideration.

(B) An approach to maximizing an objective (profits) which is subject to many restrictions—legal, safety, service, policy.

(C) Four advantages of using linear programming:

   1. Construction of the model will give management additional insight into its everyday operations.

   2. The model gives management a way of testing and quantifying the effects of policy decisions.

   3. Linear programming stimulates the setting of goals and criteria for evaluating performance.

   4. Linear programming is an effective technique for long-range planning in the face of uncertainty.

FEEDBACK CONTROL

I. Controls involve *techniques* such as financial controls, costs, and other types of controls.

II. Based on pertinent and timely information.

III. Information for Feedback Control. Three basic flows of information needed.

(A) Provides a constant check on day-to-day results to be compared with expected, or forecasted standards.

(B) Fulfills most of the decision-making information for middle and lower echelons of operating personnel.

(C) The information provided is usually historical in nature—deals with money, materials, people, performance.

(D) Introduces management by exception techniques.*

   1. Establishes criteria, standards, forecasted or expected performance.

---

*Incidentally, this technique is hardly new in concept. See Exodus XVIII, Jethro to Moses, " . . . every great matter they shall bring to you, but any small matter they shall decide themselves."

2. Directs management attention *only* to off-target performance. Keeps useless information from the top. Only relevant facts, as they arise, will reach management, enabling control of circumstances as they are developing.

3. Reduces volume of information needed, because on-target performance can proceed without further action.

(a) Relieved of unnecessary data-gathering and other unproductive routines, so manager is freed for other work—particularly where his human abilities are needed, such as working with and helping employees under him.

[¶ 503]   SUB-LEDGERS AND SCHEDULES

Some accounts in the general ledger are, by their very nature *summaries* of important supplemental data which, because of bulk alone, would, if not entered in summary form, make the physical ledger too huge to handle. Items such as individual accounts receivable and payable, inventory units, machinery and equipment—though each represents an individual asset or liability—are best displayed in one or more summary accounts, with full details being maintained in a separate book or ledger, individually tended, the total of which ties to the control account.

Some, like accounts receivable and accounts payable, are automatic products of the internal system. (The computer updates the accounts receivable file with sales and with payments received, with the monthly summaries of changes going to the general ledger control account.) Sometimes, a one-write system updates subsidiaries simultaneously. Others must be maintained manually, like the fixed asset ledger or the manual inventory control card-system. Others may be generated by outside sources, like payroll records and summaries. Others are as basic as a petty cash summary.

[¶504]   SYSTEMS—MANUAL, MECHANIZED OR COMPUTERIZED

The number of different methods used for keeping records is almost as varied as the personalities of the people designing, operating and maintaining the system. With the exception of those larger entities where work is so divided that each employee performs only one small function in a huge system overviewed by few, except top management and outside auditors—few businesses use a standard text-book approach.

Most private systems are the result of accumulations of changing bit-by-bit adaptions to the needs and demands of the business itself and outside influences (taxes, AICPA and SEC guides and requirements, state and federal laws, competitive practices, advanced technology, market conditions, good-bad sales/ profit results, etc.). Except where the availability of funds and skills is unlimited (practically nowhere), most systems in use today are evolvements and combinations of good old basic hand-written techniques, now partitioned into piecemeal refinements, combining mechanical, electronic and manual skills.

Complete automation of the *entire* accounting process is a rarity.

Ultimately, the nature of the system used depends upon one or more of these factors:

Time and expediency

Skill required

Cost

Facilities and space available

The degree of in-depth coverage *wanted* by owners/management.

Note the emphasis on the word "wanted." Many weaknesses need correction for better tax-review backup or for more efficient reporting, but management, in weighing the costs involved, wisely chooses not to refine. For example, if the *cost* of instituting a highly complex standard costing system outweighs the advantages to be gained from it, management may choose to retain its current, less complex, less specific costing system, which has understandable, but controllable tolerances of error.

[¶504.1]   The Evolutionary Process of the Machine

The evolutionary process of systematized accounting record maintenance might use the following piecemeal add-on progression:

[¶504.2]   All Manual System

1. The *"shoebox" system*. The owner transacts all business in cash— buying, selling, paying expenses—and tosses invoices, documents, receipts into a box.

2. The *check book*. The owner stops paying bills with cash, now pays by check. Still uses shoebox for receipts for sales. Notes deposits in checkbook.

3. *Cash disbursements book*. Has now hired someone to do his payroll tax reporting. Lists each check in a book, from which he can obtain a columnar breakout distribution of each type of expense.

4. *Payroll register*. Supplements the above by transferring the weekly payroll items to separate sheets for each employee where total earnings and deductions are accumulated as required for payroll tax reports.

5. *Cash receipts book.* Owner now lists each day's receipts separately and distributes to columns by type of sale or income.

6. *General ledger.* Owner sets up a ledger sheet for each column category in his disbursements and receipts book. "Posts" summary totals periodically.

7. *General ledger expanded.* The owner goes back to the old shoebox and digs out the cost information needed to set up the value of permanent items bought then (assets: equipment, fixtures, etc.). Sets up asset accounts, long-term liabilities and a balancing net worth account.

8. *Sales book/accounts receivable ledger.* To get more sales, owner finds he must start giving credit. He uses sequentially numbered invoices, lists charge sales daily in numerical order in Sales Book. Makes a separate page for each customer in an accounts receivable subsidiary ledger. For this, he uses a carbonized two-part preprinted statement, which he updates manually every day or so.

In the Cash Receipts Book, he adds a column for "received on account" from customers. Line-by-line, these credits are posted to the above subsidiary ledger-statement. Also, he includes a column for cash discounts and allowances taken by customers. At month-end, he mails original to customer and keeps the copy of the statement as his ledger sheet and starts a new sheet for the new month with the balance from the old sheet.

9. *Periodic financial statements.* Owner now wishes to see how he progresses. Finds he needs further information for an accurate statement. He must, in a side computation, compute or estimate:

Any unpaid bill to creditors

Inventory on hand

Taxes due to date on payrolls, etc.

Possible bad debts among his stated receivables

Depreciate his equipment.

At this point, he probably seeks outside assistance.

10. *Purchase book/accounts payable ledger.* As business expands, his debts accumulate, and he wants to know the exact status of when and to whom payments are due. He adds these books to the system. In the Cash Disbursements Book, he puts a column for payment on account to accounts payable and another for cash discounts taken.

11. *Perpetual inventory cards.* His on-hand stock of unsold items grows daily, and he can no longer trust his memory to recall the exact cost of items in stock, nor the quantities on hand. He sets up one card for each type of merchandise on hand, goes to the storage area, counts and lists everything, checks his purchase invoices and assigns a cost to each item. On the card, he provides all the details pertaining to that item, so that he knows what's on hand and what cost it represents. Periodically, he takes a physical count to verify the perpetual cards.

12. *General journal.* He rounds off the system by putting in here any entry which does not appropriately go in the other books of original entry. He posts from here and the other books directly to the General Ledger.

13. *Worksheet entries and worksheet trial balance.* As an adjunct to the preparation of the now monthly financial statements, accruals, recurrent adjustments and accrual reversals (when necessary) are made to the balances taken from the ledger—all on workpapers—to determine monthly position and progress.

14. *Imprest petty cash system.* Adds this to tighten up on loose expenditures.

15. *Fixed asset subsidiary ledger.* To better detail them for depreciation investment tax credit, gains or losses on dispositions, basis on trade-ins.

[¶ 504.3]   Mechanizing

16. *A one-write system for check disbursements.* Here, he combines the old check book and his Cash Disbursements Book into one writing process, instead of two. He also opens a separate bank account for the payroll and uses a one-write system for it also. At month-end, he summary posts to the General Ledger.

17. *A billing machine.* Rented or bought. Mechanizes his invoices, customer statements, sales book and subsidiary receivable ledger.

18. *Service bureau.* He assigns numbers to his general ledger accounts in an ascending series covering assets, liabilities, equity, income, costs and expenses in that order. He is assisted in setting up framework numbers for captioning and totaling functions so the computer-produced financial statement conforms with the special format he wants. Monthly, he sends to the service bureau:

> A copy of his one-write check listing, with account numbers assigned for the debiting (in lieu of the columnar distribution spread);
>
> Manual summary entries for each other book of original entry;
>
> Manual entries for accruals, adjustments, recurrent monthly entries, reversals of accruals.

All this is submitted in simple debit/credit style with account numbers indicated. He adds each page, gets totals for debits, credits and *account numbers,* gets an overall batch control total for each. The Service Bureau cross-checks the inputting to the batch totals, and posting to wrong accounts is virtually eliminated.

He receives from the Service Bureau a printed Cash Disbursements listing, a General Ledger with alpha description (brief, as inputted), and financial statements with detailed supporting schedules.

19. *Computer terminal.* A typewriter-like console, which is hooked via telephone lines into an outside-owned computer. He may put his sales and receiva-

bles on it, his check-processing and disbursements run, his purchase-vendor invoices and purchase book, his inventory, the payroll, or general ledger—practically anything desired, depending upon the programming availability and the costs. The techniques used are compatible with those learned in the use of the service bureau, with the addition of a few typewriter-input techniques.

20. *Video scope.* May supplement the above terminal, so he can call for almost instantaneous display of that off-premises storage in the central processor's electronic file. He may request a printout for later delivery.

21. *The in-house computer.* The final decision is made. He rents or buys a computer for total in-house use. The extent of options available is vast. Basically, the type of in-house computer obtained should depend upon the more important of the following features:

The output wanted.

The capacity of the central processing unit for permanent program storage.

The additional adjunct program storage possibilities.

The type of storage—cassette, disc, tape and on down to magnetic cards or punched-paper tape, with each having advantages in terms of cost or access.

The type of input—punched cards, direct input from console, intermediate from console-to-tape-to computer, etc.

The extent of printout capabilities and demands (speed, size of paper, etc.).

The adaptation of video screens at the console or remote locations—branches, warehouse.

The cost factor—initial investment, machine and programs, maintenance, personnel needed, space necessitated.

The extent of skill needed.

The imagination of the owner or management—willingness to learn, try, develop new methods, new talents.

[¶ 505] PAYROLLS AND PAYROLL TAXES

Legal requirements have made the maintenance of accurate earnings records a mandatory function of any financial accounting system. The preparation of payrolls is now, in many companies, a segregated division of duty. Regular periodic summary information from detailed payroll records is needed for entry into the general ledger.

Details of each payroll are usually summarized monthly in a general journal entry and posted to the general ledger with distribution of the debits going to various salary-expense areas (for the gross salary) and the credits going to various withholding accounts (sometimes netted against corresponding employer-expense accounts, such as unemployment insurance) and the cash account upon which the net payroll checks are drawn.

The employer later pays the amounts withheld (hopefully as due) to the various taxing or other authorities, including his employer's added share (expense) as determined in the preparation of the required form for filing.

To support the filings, each payroll item must be isolated and collated for *each* individual employee to accumulate that individual's record of earnings as required for these quarterly, semi-annual and annual reports to federal, state and city taxing arms. The Fair Labor Standards Act and state laws also set standards of minimum pay for work hours and overtime for some or all employees.

Many payrolls are now prepared by outside processors, such as banks and service bureaus. Controls should be as strong as possible to assure accurate, protected input and output. All voided checks, for example, should be surrendered to the employer and accounted for in bank reconciliations.

Individual personnel permanent files should be maintained and would probably include:

> Name and address. Social Security number, date of birth, date hired, occupation, work week, regular and overtime rates, basis of pay (day, week, month), authorized increases, vacation time, bonuses, injuries and compensation claims and settlements, pension and profit-sharing information (deductions, rights and vested interests), W-4 and other withholding authorizations, references and correspondence, educational transcripts, unemployment claims and reports, medical records, health claims, exense-account authorizations, separation information (date, circumstances, etc.) and other information.

Time cards are usually filed separately and tied to specific payrolls by reference identification.

Payroll tax reports usually required are:

Federal:

Card-form 501 for payroll tax deposits with local bank
Quarterly 941 for witholding and FICA

W-2's

W-3

Annual 940 (Federal Unemployment)

1099—information returns with summary 1096

State:

Withholding tax—interim and annual

Unemployment insurance—usually quarterly

Disability insurance—usually quarterly, sometimes combined with unemployment report

Annual reports covering individual earnings; possibly annual information returns also.

The entire process of payroll preparation is an area which is conducive to effective statistical sampling techniques. Management (as well as outside auditors) should periodically sample all phases of the payroll routine, from initial authorizations through to the canceled-check returns. The discovery of one flaw might prove significant.

[¶506] THE GENERAL LEDGER, CHART OF ACCOUNTS AND TRIAL BALANCE

In the world of mechanical figures, uniformity offers many advantages, especially the one of eliminating hard-knock costly errors experienced by forerunners in the field of experimentation. One such area of "uniformity" in standard usage, which is most beneficial, is the conventional layout of the general ledger.

As shown below, accounts in the general ledger are most useful if arranged and numbered in the order sequence indicated. Any firm which has gone to an outside computer service or installed its own in-house computer for the generation of machined financial statements will attest to the necessity for this format. The machines, unthinking as they are, can easily be programmed to add, subtract, combine, sub-total, total, balance and print these accounts according to numerically sequential instructions each step of the way down the line-by-line financial balance sheet and income statement. (Moreover, sub-ledgers can be added as needed.)

Assets:
  Current
  Non-current
  Other
Liabilities:
  Current
  Long-term
Equity:
  Capital stock
  Retained earnings
Income—revenue from operations
Cost of sales items
Expenses:
  Selling
  Administrative
Non-operating income and expense
Federal income tax
Extraordinary items:
  Less applicable income tax
  Net income.

Limitations and definitions of the entries into each account should be spelled out for anyone with responsibility for booking entries into the general ledger. Most large firms have drawn up internal "charts of accounts" which pin-

55

point exactly which accounts should be debited or credited and the sources from which the entry might come. At the least, someone should be charged with the responsibility of making the decision, and written authorizations (sometimes, voucher-type general journal entries) should be prepared and signed by that authority.

Many modern systems call for the manual booking of summaries of all the books of original entry, recurrent monthly journal entries, adjustments, accruals and reversals onto loose-leaf-type numbered journal sheets, batch-totaled, with a copy going to the computer department for processing to monthly hard-copy ledger cards. Sometimes, a yearly re-run is made showing all the action in each account for the entire year. A trial balance is usually a by-product of the computer-run general ledger.

Summary entries may be by-passed for cash disbursements, sales or purchases, if the input of this material is programmed for direct summation of monthly activity, being stored and posted to the general ledger when run with the other input from the summary general journal sheets.

Some systems in use today even by-pass the use of a general ledger, producing all the same pertinent information and references in comprehensive, detailed financial statements. Controls here should assure proper input, output and traceable audit trails.

[¶ 507] LONG-TERM CONSTRUCTION CONTRACTS

> Revenue is usually recognized at the time of exchanges in which cash is received or new claims arise against other entities. However, exceptions are made, for example . . . for long-term construction-type contracts.

There are two methods available to commercial organizations engaged wholly or partly in the contracting business for handling long-term construction contracts:

1. The completed-contract method; and

2. The percentage-of-completion method.

These contracts generally entail the construction of a specific project.

[¶ 508] THE COMPLETED-CONTRACT METHOD

The completed-contract method recognizes income only when the contract is completed or substantially completed. Costs of contracts in process and current billings are accumulated, but there are no charges or credits to income except for provisions for losses. If remaining costs are not significant in amount, a contract may be regarded as substantially completed.

General and administrative expenses are not charged off to periodic income but are allocated to the contract. This is especially important when no contracts are completed in a year in which there are general and administrative expenses. It is not as important when there are numerous contracts. However, there should be no excessive deferring of overhead costs which might occur if total overhead was assigned to few or small contracts in process.

Even though the completed-contract method does not permit recording any income before completion, provision should be made for expected losses. Any excess of accumulated costs over related billings should be shown in the balance sheet as a current asset. Excess of accumulated billings over related costs should be shown in most cases as a current liability. Where there are many contracts, and costs exceed billing on some and billings exceed costs on others, the contracts should be segregated so that the figures on the asset side include only those contracts in which costs exceed billings and on the liability side, only those in which billings exceed costs. The assets should be described as "costs of uncompleted contracts in excess of related billings" rather than as inventory or work in process. On the liability side, the item should be described as "billings and uncompleted contracts in excess of related costs." The standards state that the excess accumulated billings over related costs should be shown as a current liability *in most cases*. Noncurrent classification is discouraged, but would nevertheless be within GAAP.

The advantage of the completed-contract method is that since it is based on results as finally determined, it is generally more accurate than if it were based on estimates for unperformed work which could involve unforeseen costs or other possible losses. It is generally used for contracts lasting less than one year. But where accurate estimates of completion costs aren't available, it may be used for longer term contracts. The disadvantage of the completed-contract method is that in a period where no contract has been completed, current performance is not reflected. This results in showing high profits one year and little or no profits in other years.

[¶ 508.1]   Percentage-of-Completion Method

The percentage-of-completion method recognizes income as work on a contract goes along. Recognized income should be *that percentage of estimated total income* that either (a) incurred costs to date *bear to total costs* after giving effect to estimates of costs to complete based upon most recent information or (b) which may be indicated by such other measures of progress to completion as may be appropriate (see illustration). Under the percentage-of-completion method current assets may include costs and recognized income not yet billed for certain contracts, and liabilities (usually current liabilities) may include billings in excess of costs and recognized income with regard to other contracts.

The principal advantages of the percentage-of-completion method are (1) periodic recognition of income instead of the irregular recognition of income on completed contracts, and (2) the reflection of the status of the uncompleted contracts through the current estimates of costs to complete or of progress toward completion. In the *completed-contract method* there is no reflection of status of uncompleted contracts.

The chief disadvantage of the percentage-of-completion method is that it depends upon estimates of ultimate costs and, consequently, of currently accruing income which is subject to uncertainties inherent in long-term contracts.

ILLUSTRATION

Income reflected under percent-of-completion method:

	Accumulated Percent Completed (1)	Expenses allocable to contract (2)	Year's assigned portion of contract (1)	Net income to report
Year 1	30%	$ 305,000	$ 300,000	$ (5,000)
Year 2	75%	385,000	450,000	65,000
Year 3	100%	210,000	250,000	40,000
Totals		$ 900,000	$ 1,000,000	$ 100,000

Total contract price is $1,000,000.

(1) Percentage of completion is a certified percentage furnished by the architect. The percent increases each year until 100% is completed. The difference between one year and the next is that year's completed portion.

(2) Includes supplies used during year, with consideration given to opening and closing inventories. Expenses are those ascertainable as incurred to bring the contract to the stage of completion.

Note that *billings* are not shown because reportable income is *not* predicated on them, though in some cases billings may coincide with the percentage completed.

[¶ 508.2]   Income Under the "Completed Contract" Method

Using the same example above, the net income of $100,000 would be reported only in the final year (Year 3), together with details. No reflection of partial completion is shown on the income statement for the first and second year. (See Tax Section of this book also.)

[¶ 509]   INSTALLMENT, COST RECOVERY AND RETAIL METHODS

Recognizing revenue and expenses if proceeds are collectible over a long period without reasonable assurance of collection: The terms of an exchange transaction or other conditions related to receivable collectible over a long period may preclude a reasonable estimate of the collectibility of the receivables. Either an installment method or a cost recovery method of recognizing revenue may be used as long as collectibility is not reasonably assured.

[¶ 509.1]   Installment Method

If there is no basis for estimating the *degree* of collectibility because of a contract running over an extended period of time, the installment method or cost recovery method may be used (as opposed to recording the entire sales figure combined with a provision for bad debts).

However, at that time of sale, if collectibility is assured and there is no question of recovery, the installment method is unacceptable.

[¶ 509.2]   Cost Recovery Method

Under the same logic which permits the use of the installment method, the cost recovery method is also permitted. Here, equal amounts of revenue and expense are recognized as collections are made until all costs have been recovered, postponing recognition of all profit until all costs have been recovered.

(See Timing Difference and Appendix E.)

[¶ 509.3]   Retail Method

The terminology, "retail method," is properly used only in connection with the pricing of retail store inventories, not with the method of accounting practiced by retail stores, which is properly called "in the installment sales method," as described previously.

For more discussion of the "Retail Method" for inventory, see this text's chapter on Current Assets (Inventory).

[¶ 510]   THE NOT-FOR-PROFIT ORGANIZATION

(Fund Accounting)

Most not-for-profit organizations derive their funds from the public-at-large. Gifts, donations, bequests and endowments (in most cases tax deductible to the donor) are the main source of income for non-profit organizations, which are organized under special state and federal laws for the purpose of accomplishing a specific goal—education (colleges), research (foundations), hospitals and childcare.

Sometimes, government provides grants and aid for these institutions.

In general, the tax laws and other statutes endeavor to limit these institutions from encroaching on the profit-making activities which are characteristic of the business enterprise. Under current law, certain gains and profits on *unrelated-to-function* activities are now taxable to the not-for-profit organization (such as publishing revenue, security income—interest and capital gains).

The chief accounting characteristic which differentiates the non-profit organization from the profit organization is the strict distinction which must be made and accountability provided for each donation or grant received and disbursed.

There are two broad types of delineation:

1. *Unrestricted funds*—monies received with no restrictive use specified by the giver—to be used for the current continuing operation of the organization in fulfilling the general purpose for which it was organized; and

2. *Restricted funds*—monies received and spent for *specific* purposes with designated strings attached—such as government funds provided for student loans, or endowment portfolios where the principal is not to be touched, but the income thereof may be used for current or designated purposes.

    In addition, permanent property acquisitions are segregated into a "plant fund." Rules for capitalization and writeoff usually depend upon government's participation or non-participation in its funding.

Because of the public and governmental accountability required and the right-to-know how the donated funds are being used, it is imperative that *each fund* (each restrictive gift/grant and the non-restricted fund) be explained, both as to the status of assets, liabilities and fund balance, as well as detailing the income and expenses generated by or in that fund during the period. Moreover, an overall summary of changes in fund balance is also prepared.

The AICPA has guideline recommendations in industry audit guides for many of these institutions, such as: Colleges and Universities, Hospitals, State and Local Governmental Units, Voluntary Health and Welfare Organizations and Medicare Facilities. The trend in accounting standards for the not-for-profit organizations is toward the use of full accrual accounting.

[¶ 510.1]   Tips on Fund Accounting

Definition: A fund can be defined as a fiscal and accounting entity with a self-balancing set of accounts recording cash and other financial resources, together with all related liabilities and residual equities and balances, and changes therein, which are segregated for the purpose of carrying on specific activities, or attaining certain objectives, or attaining certain objectives in accordance with special regulations, restrictions, or limitations.

Governmental accounting has similarities and dissimilarities as compared to commercial accounting:

Similarities

- Uses the double-entry system
- Journals
- Ledgers

- Trial balances
- Financial statements
- Internal controls

Dissimilarities

- Revenues and expenses cannot always be matched
- There is no profit entry
- Restrictions on the raising and spending of revenues
- The emphasis is upon accountability of the public officials
- The recording of budgets in the accounting system for the governmental fund
- The application of modified accrual accounting rather than full accrual accounting

[¶ 510.2]   Eight Types Of Funds

1. The *General Fund* which accounts for all transactions not accounted for in any other fund.

2. *Special Revenue Fund* which accounts for revenues from specific sources or to finance specific projects.

3. *Debt Service Fund* which accounts for the payment of interest and principal on long-term debt.

4. *Capital Project Fund* which accounts for the receipt and disbursement of funds used for the acquisition of capital facilities.

5. *Enterprise Funds* which account for the financing of services to the public paid for by the users of the services.

6. *Trust and Agency Funds* which account for assets held by a governmental unit as trustee or agent for individuals, private organizations, or other governmental units.

7. *Intragovernmental Service Funds* which account for the financing of special projects and services performed by one governmental entity for an organization unit within the same governmental entity.

8. *Special Assessments Funds* which account for special assessments levied to finance public improvements or services which benefit the property against which the assessment has been made.

The accountant should:

- Maintain complete and adequate files for the initial documentation which established or restricted the fund, together with any special reporting requirements demanded.

• Keep separate detailed books of entry for each fund, separate bank account for that fund, separate identification of all property and securities.

• Under *no* circumstances should assets of separate funds be commingled. Transfers between funds should not be permitted without documentary authorization, and inter-fund receivables and payables should, in contra-effect, be equal and clearly identified, always maintaining the original integrity of each fund.

• Interest accruals, cooperative-share funding (example: government 80%—college 20% in Work Study Program), expense allowances or allocations—all should be made timely.

• Federal, state and local reporting requirements should be studied, met and reported as due to avoid stringent penalties, interest and possible loss of tax-exempt status. Options may exist regarding the handling of payroll and unemployment taxes; they should be studied and explored for money-saving possibilities.

• Independently audited annual financial statements by fund are usually required both by organizational charter and governmental departments (especially where grant-participation is involved). Publication of the availability of these statements is sometimes mandatory (foundations).

• One area of discussion and dispute is the ''compliance'' feature of audits involving certain governmental agency grants. Here, the independent auditor is called upon to measure the agency's compliance with certain non-accounting rules, such as eligibility of money-recipients, internal controls and other matters not ordinarily associated with a financial audit. The integrity of the auditor's financial opinion should never be compromised by peripheral compliance requirements. In most cases, he should qualify his opinion indicating the results and *extent of tests* made for compliance. The AICPA, to some extent, has spelled out guidelines for ''compliance'' opinions in Section 9641 of its ''Statements on Auditing Standards.''

• Municipal accounting techniques, procedures, format and demands are not discussed here. Their overall application involves the use of fund accounting. The main distinction is the entering of the budget—the anticipated revenues and the appropriations thereof—directly on and as part of the books of account. Progress reports then show how actual compares with anticipated. The estimates are then zeroed out at year-end. The meaning and use of ''encumbrances'' should also be understood. Reports for some local subdivisions, such as school-boards, usually involve a strict accounting of each receipt and disbursement, including the detailing of outstanding checks.

[¶ 510.3]   **Terminology**

Here is a listing of definitions applicable only to fund accounting:

Abatement. Cancellation of amounts levied or of charges made for services.

Accrued Assets. Assets arising from revenues earned but not yet due.

Accrued Expenses. Expenses resulting in liabilities which are either due or are not payable until some future time.

Accrued Revenues. Levies made or other revenue earned and not collected.

Allotment Ledger. A subsidiary ledger which contains an account for each allotment showing the amount allotted, expenditures, encumbrances, the net balance, and other related information.

Appropriation. An authorization granted by the legislative body to make expenditures and to incur obligations for specific purposes.

Appropriation Expenditure. An expenditure chargeable to an appropriation.

Appropriation Ledger. A subsidiary ledger containing an account with each appropriation.

Assessment. The process of making an official valuation of property for the purpose of taxation.

Authority Bonds. Bonds payable from the revenues of a specific public authority.

Betterment. An addition or change made in a fixed asset which prolongs its life or increases its efficiency.

Budget. A plan of financial operation embodying an estimate of proposed expenditures for a given period or purpose, and the proposed means of financing them.

Budgetary Accounts. The accounts necessary to reflect budget operations and condition, such as estimated revenues, appropriations, and encumbrances.

Capital Budget. An improvement program and the methods for the financing.

Clearing Account. An improvement program and the methods for the financing.

Clearing Account. An account used to accumulate total charges or credits for the purpose of distributing them among the accounts to which they are allocable, or for the purpose of transferring the net difference to the proper account.

Current Special Assessment. Assessments levied and due during the current fiscal period.

*Current Taxes.*Taxes levied and becoming due during the current fiscal period—from the time the amount of the tax levy is first established, to the date on which a penalty for nonpayment is attached.

Debt Limit. The maximum amount of gross or net debt legally permitted.

Debt Service Requirement. The amount of money necessary periodically to pay the interest on the outstanding debt and the principal of maturing bonded debt not payable from a sinking fund.

Deficit. The excess of the liabilities of a fund over its assets.

Delinquent Taxes. Taxes remaining unpaid on and after the date on which a penalty for nonpayment is attached.

Direct Debt. The debt which a governmental unit has incurred in its own name, or assumed through the annexation of territory.

Encumbrances. Obligations in the form of purchase orders, contracts, or salary commitments which are chargeable to an appropriation, and for which a part of the appropriation is reserved.

Endowment Fund. A fund whose prinicpal must be maintained inviolate, but whose income may be expended.

Expendable fund. A fund whose resources, including both principal and earnings, may be expended.

Expenditures. If the fund accounts are kept on the accrual basis, expenditures are the total charges incurred, whether paid or unpaid, including expenses, provision for retirement of debt not reported as a liability of the fund from which retired, and capital outlays.

Franchise. A special privilege granted by a government permitting the continuing use of public property.

Full Faith and Credit. A pledge of the general taxing body for the payment of obligations.

Fund Accounts. All accounts necessary to set forth the financial operations and financial condition of a fund.

Fund Group. A group of related funds.

Governmental Accounting. The preparation, reporting, and interpretation of accounts for governmental bodies.

Grant. A contribution by one governmental unit to another unit.

Gross Bonded Debt. The total amount of direct debt of a governmental unit, represented by outstanding bonds before deduction of sinking fund assets.

Indeterminate Appropriation. An appropriation which is not limited either to any definite period of time, or to any definite amount, or to both time and amount.

Inter-Fund Accounts. Accounts in which transactions between funds are reflected.

Inter-Fund Loans. Loans made by one fund to another fund.

Inter-Fund Transfers. Amounts transferred from one fund to another.

Judgment. An amount to be paid or collected by a governmental unit as the result of a court decision, including a condemnation award in payment for private property taken for public use.

Lapse. As applied to appropriations, this term denotes the automatic termination of an appropriation.

Levy. To impose taxes or special assessments.

Lump-Sum Appropriation. An appropriation made for a stated purpose, or for a named department, without specifying further the amounts that can be spent for specific activities or for particular expenditures.

Municipal. An adjective applying to any governmental unit below or subordinate to the state.

Municipal Corporation. A body or corporate politic established pursuant to state authorization, as evidenced by a charter.

Net Bonded Debt. Gross bonded debt less applicable cash or other assets.

Non-Expendable Fund. A fund the principal, and sometimes the earnings, of which may not be expended.

Non-Operating Income. Income of municipal utilities and other governmental enterprises of a business character, which is not derived from the operation of such enterprise.

Operating Expenses. As used in the accounts of municipal utilities and other governmental enterprises of a business character, the term means the costs necessary to the maintenance of the enterprise, or the rendering of services for which the enterprise is operated.

Operating Revenues. Revenues derived from the operation of municipal utilities or other governmental enterprises of a business character.

Operating Statement. A statement summarizing the financial operations of a municipality.

Ordinance. A bylaw of a municipality enacted by the governing body of the governmental entity.

Overlapping Debt. The proportionate share of the debts of local governmental units, located wholly or in part within the limits of the reporting government, which must be borne by property within such government.

Prepaid Taxes. The deposit of money with a governmental unit on condition that the amount deposited is to be applied against the tax liability of the taxpayer.

Proprietary Accounts. Accounts which show actual financial condition and operations such as actual assets, liabilities, reserves, surplus, revenues, and expenditures as distinguished from budgetary accounts.

Public Authority. A public agency created to perform a single function, which is financed from tolls or fees charged those using the facilities operated by the agency.

Public Trust Fund. A trust fund whose principal, earnings, or both, must be used for a public purpose.

Quasi-Municipal Corporation. An agency established by the state primarily for the purpose of helping the state to carry out its functions.

Refunding Bonds. Bonds issued to retire bonds already outstanding. The refunding bonds may be sold for cash and outstanding bonds redeemed in cash, or the refunding bonds may be exchanged with holders of outstanding bonds.

Related Funds. Funds of a similar character which are brought together for administrative and reporting purposes.

Reserve for Encumbrances. A reserve representing the segregation of surplus to provide for unliquidated encumbrances.

Revenue Bonds. Bonds the principal and interest on which are to be paid solely from earnings, usually the earnings of a municipally owned utility or other public service enterprise.

Revolving Fund. A fund provided to carry out a cycle of operations.

Special Assessment. A compulsory levy made by a local government against certain properties, to defray part or all of the cost of a specific improvement or service, which is presumed to be of general benefit to the public and of special benefit to the owners of such properties.

Special District Bonds. Bonds of a local taxing district, which has been organized for a special purpose—such as road, sewer, and other special districts—to render unique services to the public.

Suspense Account. An account which carries charges or credits temporarily pending the determination of the proper account or accounts to which they are to be posted.

Tax Anticipation Notes. Notes issued in anticipation of collection of taxes, usually retired only from tax collections as they come due.

Tax Levy. An ordinance or resolution by means of which taxes are levied.

Tax Liens. Claims which governmental units have upon properties until taxes levied against them have been paid.

Tax Rate. The amount of tax stated in terms of a unit of the tax base.

Trust Fund. A fund consisting of resources received and held by the governmental unit as trustee, to be expended or invested in accordance with the conditions of the trust.

Unencumbered Appropriation. An appropriation or allotment, or a part thereof, not yet expended or encumbered.

Utility Fund. A fund established to finance the construction, operation, and maintenance of municipally owned utilities.

Warrant. An order drawn by a legislative body, or an officer of a governmental unit, upon its treasurer, directing the treasurer to pay a specified amount to the person named, or to the bearer.

6

Internal Control

**INTERNAL ACCOUNTING AND
                ADMINISTRATIVE CONTROL**

Internal control, according to the Professional Auditing Standards, is subdivided as follows:

(a) Accounting control, which comprises the plan of organization and all methods and procedures that are concerned mainly with, and relate directly to, safeguarding assets and the reliability of the financial records.

(b) Administrative control, which comprises the plan of organization and all methods and procedures that are concerned mainly with operational efficiency and adherence to managerial policies, such as sales policies, employee training and production quality control. This is usually only indirectly related to the financial records.

Administrative control includes, but is not limited to, the plan of organization and the procedures and records that are concerned with the decision processes leading to management's authorization of transactions. Such authorization is a management function directly associated with the responsibility for achieving the objectives of the organization, and is the starting point for establishing account control of transactions.

Accounting control comprises the plan of organization and procedures and records that are concerned with safeguarding assets and the reliability of financial records, and consequently are designed to provide reasonable assurance that:

(a) Transactions are executed in accordance with management's general or specific authorization.

(b) Transactions are recorded as necessary (1) to permit preparation of financial statements in conformity with generally accepted accounting principles or any other criteria applicable to such statements, and (2) to maintain accountability for assets.

(c) Access to assets is permitted only in accordance with management's authorization.

(d) The recorded accountability for assets is compared with the existing assets at reasonable intervals and appropriate action taken with respect to any differences.

[¶601.1] Fundamentals of a System of Internal Accounting Control

(1) Responsibility: There should be a plan or an organizational chart which places the responsibility for specified functions on specific individuals in the organization.

The responsibility for establishing and maintaining a system of internal accounting control rests with management. The system should be continuously supervised, tested and modified as necessary to provide reasonable (but not absolute) assurance that objectives are being accomplished, all at costs not exceeding benefits.

(2) Division of Duties: The idea here is to remove the handling and recording of any one transaction from beginning to end from the control of any one employee. Further, making different employees responsible for different functions of a transaction actually serves as a cross-check which facilitates the detection of errors, accidental or deliberate.

(3) Use of Appropriate Forms and Documents: Efficient design of forms and documents aids in the administration of the internal control system. Mechanical or electronic equipment can also be used to expedite the process of checking. Both of these methods provide control over accounting data.

(4) Internal Auditors: Periodic review of all the above elements of the internal control system should be carried out by an internal audit staff. The function of this staff would be to periodically check the effectiveness of above items (1), (2), and (3).

There is a relationship between the size of an organization and the degree of development of its system of internal control. Complete separation of functions and internal auditing department may not exist in smaller companies. The objective in these smaller companies is to divide the duties in the way that creates the greatest amount of internal check.

[¶601.2] Elements of a Satisfactory System of Internal Accounting Control

The elements of a satisfactory system of internal control include:

(1) A plan of organization which provides appropriate segregation of functional responsibilities.

(2) A system of authorization and record procedures adequate to provide reasonable accounting control of assets, liabilities, revenues and expenses.

(3) Sound practices to follow in the performance of duties and functions of each of the organizational departments.

(4) Personnel of a quality commensurate with responsibilities.

One important element in the system of internal control is the independence of the operating, custodial, accounting and internal auditing functions. There should be a separation of duties in such a way that records exist outside each department to serve as controls over the activities within that department. Responsibilities for various functions and delegation of authority should be clearly defined and spelled out in organizational charts and manuals. Conflicting and dual responsibility is to be avoided. The function of initiation and authorization of an activity should be separate from the accounting for it. Custody of assets should be separated from the accounting for them.

[¶601.3] Relationship of Your Internal Control System to Your Outside Accountants

The efficiency of your internal control system becomes important to your outside, independent auditors. Before determining how much of an audit they should make, they must review the internal control system. An efficient system may do away with certain audit procedures which might otherwise be necessary. A poor internal control system may necessitate greater checking on the part of the auditor with a consequent additional cost for the audit.

[¶602] INTERNAL CONTROL FOR INVENTORIES

Some internal control procedures that can be used in conjunction with different types of inventories — finished goods, work in process, materials, goods for resale — are detailed in the paragraphs that follow.

[¶602.1] Inventories of Merchandise Purchased for Resale and Supplies

(1) The purchasing department approves the purchase orders for merchandise to be bought. In a small company, the owner or manager may be the one to approve these purchase orders. Purchase orders should be sequentially numbered and traced to final disposition.

(2) After okays from purchasing manager have been received, requests for price quotations are usually sent out. These requests should go to various companies, and the company quoting the lowest price will be the one from which the purchases are made, unless there are other overriding considerations.

(3) In the selling department, an updated individual quantity record for each type of unit is kept on perpetual inventory stock cards. It is usually the responsibility of inventory clerks to keep these cards up to date. These stock cards indicate the need for reorders and they should be checked against purchase requisition by the manager of the selling department or other person in control of the merchandise stock. In a business too small to have a separate selling department, the owner or manager is the one to perform these functions. The number of units of merchandise

ordered is then entered on the inventory stock cards by one clerk. The number actually received is entered from the receiving list by another clerk. The number sold or used is entered on the stock cards by still another clerk from sales lists or salesmen's orders. After giving effect to the number ordered, received and issued on the inventory stock records the balance represents the number of units actually on hand. A well-rounded perpetual card system usually includes detailed unit costs for ready computation under either LIFO, FIFO, or average methods.

(4) In the receiving department, the receiving clerk should not be allowed to see purchase order records or purchase requisitions. Receiving reports are checked against the perpetual inventory stock records and a notation is made on these stock record cards indicating the date, order number and quantity received. Even where a business is too small to have a perpetual inventory, a receiving report should be made, which should then be checked against the purchase orders and a notation as to the day and quantity received made on those purchase orders.

(5) In the accounts payable department, the receiving report is checked against the merchandise stock record, then sent to the accounts payable department where it is verified against the seller's invoice. The purchasing agent should have approved the price on the seller's invoice before that invoice was sent to the accounts payable department. A clerk in the accounts payable department should verify all extension totals on the invoice. If the vendor's invoice and receiving report are in agreement the invoice is then entered into a purchase journal or voucher register for future payment. Any discrepancy between quantity received and quantity on the seller's invoice will hold up payment until an adjustment is made by the seller.

The departments involved in internal control in merchandise and supplies inventories are purchasing, sales, receiving, accounts receivable and accounts payable.

[¶602.2]   Finished Goods Inventories

(1) Ascertain the quantity of units which have been completed from the production record and transferred to the shipping department or warehouse. The daily report of finished goods units transferred to the warehouse or shipping department indicates the number of finished units available to the sales department.

(2) Compute the unit cost of finished goods delivered to the sales department. This information is obtained from the unit cost sheet (for a process cost accounting system) or from the job-order cost card (in a job order cost accounting system).

(3) Set up finished goods inventory cards and for each item record the quantity received at the warehouse, the quantity shipped on orders and the balance remaining at specified unit costs. The number of finished goods units in the warehouse or stockroom should tie in with this finished goods inventory file.

(4) Periodically, physically count the finished goods inventory and see that it ties in with the finished goods inventory file.

The departments involved in internal control of finished goods inventories are manufacturing, cost accounting, accounts receivable and sales.

[¶602.3]　Raw Materials and Supplies Inventories

(1) In the stores department, the storekeeper must safeguard the raw materials and supplies inventories — both physically and by accounting control. No raw materials or supplies can leave without a stores requisition. Quantity control at minimum levels is also the responsibility of the storekeeper.

The storekeeper should keep a stores record for each item, listing the maximum and minimum quantities, quantity ordered and number, quantity received, quantity issued, and balance on hand. When stores cards show minimum quantities, a stores ledger clerk pulls those cards from the file to make sure that materials or supplies are ordered to cover the minimum needs. Quantities shown on the stores record should be verified by making an actual count of the stores items which are to be ordered; then a purchase requisition is filled out from the stores records. The quantity of each item ordered is approved by the storekeeper. He knows the average monthly consumption of each item. The ordering of special equipment by department heads also goes through the storeroom after having the necessary executive approval. The purchase requisition is then sent to the purchasing agent.

In the stores department, a receiving report is prepared in triplicate by the receiving clerk. One copy goes to the stores ledger clerk, another to the accounts payable department; the third is kept by the receiving clerk. The receiving clerk puts the stores items in proper places within the storeroom after preparing his receiving report. Sometimes, location numbers are used to facilitate ready accessing.

The stores ledger clerk gets a copy of the receiving report and makes a record of the quantity and the order number on the stores ledger card affected by the items received.

(2) In the purchasing department, the purchase agent places the order for the quantity needed on the quantity requisition. If he feels the quantity ordered is excessive, he may look into the storekeeper's purchase requisition. He then requests price quotations from various supply companies, placing his order with the lowest bidder. The purchase agent also verifies the prices on the seller's invoices by comparing them with the price quotations.

(3) In the accounts payable department, no bill should be approved for payment until materials ordered have actually been received, are in good condition, and the prices of the seller's invoice match his quotations.

(4) In the manufacturing department, different individuals have authority to sign stores requisitions to withdraw materials from the storeroom. Usually, a foreman prepares a stores requisition where raw materials or supplies are needed in any of the manufacturing departments. This requisition contains the account name and number, department name and number, job order number, quantity of material issued, the stores item name and classification symbol, the name of the person to

withdraw materials from the storeroom, the unit price of the item and the total cost of items withdrawn from the storeroom.

The departments involved in internal control for raw materials and supplies inventory are stores, purchasing, accounts payable and manufacturing.

[¶602.4]   Work-in-Process Inventory

(1) In the manufacturing department, stores requisitions are prepared by shop foremen for materials which are to be charged to the work-in-process inventory account. Quantities of materials are obtained from engineering or administrative departments. Specifications for raw materials are usually shown on a bill of materials (a list of different items required to complete an order). The stores requisition will specify the quantity, price, cost of each item of raw material requisitioned and the job order number.

Time tickets are prepared by the workmen and approved by a foreman in the department in which work is performed before it is charged to the work-in-process inventory account. Each labor operation may have a standard time to perform a certain operation which has been predetermined by the engineering department. There also may be a predetermined standard wage rate, determined by the head of the manufacturing department and known by the payroll department. The cost accounting department is responsible for the amount of manufacturing expense charged to the work-in-process inventory account.

(2) In the cost department, raw material cost is computed from sales requisitions, direct labor costs from time tickets, and manufacturing expense is estimated from prevailing overhead rates.

Internal control methods for the work-in-process inventory account depend on whether the firm has a process cost accounting or job-order cost accounting system.

The chief point of internal control for work-in-process inventories is computing costs. Product costs are analyzed by operations, departments and cost elements. This permits measurement of the cost of products at different stages of completion. The number of partly finished units when multiplied by a cost at a particular stage should come close to the value in the work-in-process inventory account.

The departments involved in internal control of work-in-process inventories are manufacturing and cost accounting.

[¶602.5]   Taking Count—The Physical Inventory

The two most significant factors of inventory control are:

1. Knowing what *should* be on hand, based on paper controls; and

2. Verifying *what actually is on hand;* by a physical count.

[¶602.6] The Perpetual System—Knowing What Should Be on Hand

In many firms, not enough effort and emphasis are put into the timely keeping of detailed perpetual inventory stock records, thus ignoring the most basic control available.

The nature and extent of the records to maintain vary from company to company. At the least, there should be a constant updated record of the *units* handled — a card or a loose-leaf sheet to which are posted the "ins" and "outs" always showing the new morning's balance on hand — or rather, the balance which *should* be on hand. If expanded to the fullest, the system would also include unit-costs of acquisitions (or, in manufacturing, detailed material, labor and overhead costs assigned), unit-sales deleted at cost (based on the company's "flow-of-cost" assumption of LIFO, FIFO or average costs) and balance on hand extended at cost. Also, the individual record would show back-order positions, write-downs, destructions, and, most importantly, locations in the storage area (by location number or description). It may show the total sales income for that particular unit, displaying unit gross profits. Retail stores using the gross profit method of valuing inventories usually maintain controls over entire departments, or sections of departments, rather than by individual units, and extended values are at retail, showing markups and markdowns, as well as bulk cost figures.

The general ledger summary inventory asset account should (where the system provides cost-flowing movement) always tie to the total of the subsidiary perpetual system (at least monthly). They should be matched as often as possible and all differences traced to eliminate any weaknesses in the system.

The point is — know what *should be on hand!*

[¶602.7] The Physical Count—Verifying What Is Actually on Hand

At least once a year, a physical count of the entire inventory should be taken, usually as of the balance sheet date. Management, not the auditor, is responsible for taking this physical inventory. The auditor is an *observer* of methods, count and valuation, but he may help establish the system of counting, the tags to use, the methods of assuring a full count, the cutoff procedures, the pricing, etc., so as to satisfy himself of the reasonability of the total value he can accept for his attestation.

The method of tagging, counting, weighing or measuring, locating, recounting — the assignment of personnel — all the procedures should be set in advance and followed (unless properly authorized changes develop).

The auditor should familiarize himself with the nature of the products handled, the terminology, the packaging, the principles of measurement. His "education" in the client's processes should not be obtained at the sacrifice of counting-time.

The auditor is concerned with the final evaluation of that *physical* inventory. The perpetual records, as such, and errors therein are not a necessary part of the audit process, though weaknesses should be commented upon in the management letter.

However, a history of *accurate* internal paper control of inventory can substantially reduce the extent of testing by the auditor. When it can be expected that variations from perpetual inventories will be small and within tolerable limits, the auditor may choose to use statistical random sampling in testing either an immediately prior physical count or in counting only those items *drawn by the auditor* (without advance notice) for random selection. If the sample then indicates a rate of error unacceptable to the auditor, he may request another (or full) physical count, or he may, with management's consent, adjust the overall value of the inventory to an amount indicated by the sample (see Journal Entries in Appendix A), with management promising to investigate the error in the ensuing fiscal year.

When an effective perpetual inventory control is in use, management usually ''cycle'' counts the inventory once, or several times over, during the year, testing bits and pieces throughout the year, covering it entirely at least once.

There are often *portions* of an inventory which may require more time and effort to physically count than the relative merit of those portions warrants. Such items may be *reasonably* estimated (with joint approval of management and auditor), based on such elements as: last year's value, movement during the year, space occupied, weight, or, considering sales and purchases, using an estimated gross profit method.

[¶602.8]   Summary Thoughts

The accuracy of a physical inventory even with the most sophisticated computerized system, may always be in doubt if there is *no* perpetual record for comparison. A perpetual inventory is meaningless unless tested periodically to a physical count. A history of accurate perpetual records can be justification for an auditor's using statistical sampling for year-end evaluation. Moreover, management itself can use statistical sampling techniques for cycle counting. Tie-in to the general ledger asset account should be made regularly by management. The financial statement value of the inventory must be at cost or market, whichever is lower. Standards are *not* acceptable, unless approximating cost.

[¶603]   INTERNAL CONTROL FOR EXPENSES

Each of the various types of expenses requires special internal control procedures. These procedures are covered in the following paragraphs.

[¶603.1]   Manufacturing Expenses

(1) In the manufacturing service and producing department, small tools which are not constantly being used should be kept in the toolroom. Each workman requiring such tools is given metal checks, each stamped with his number. The toolroom attendant will release a tool to a workman in exchange for a metal check bearing the workman's number. The check is kept in the toolroom until the tool is

returned, at which time the check is returned to the workman.

The department foreman has the responsibility for approving a requisition for a new tool when one wears out.

(2) Charges for freight and shipping on incoming supplies should be charged to the account to which the supplies are charged. Copies of the freight or shipping bills should be attached to supply invoices. Supplies inventory is, therefore, charged for these freight and shipping charges instead of an expense account.

(3) Numerous types of shop supplies, such as brooms, oil, waste, solder, wire, are part of the raw materials and supplies inventory. They should be kept in the storeroom and issued only by a stores requisition, signed by an authorized individual. The individual who indicates the need for such supplies (usually a foreman) should indicate the job order number or departmental expense account number to which the material is to be charged on the stores requisition.

(4) Workmen categorized as indirect laborers should have an identification number when they work in a specific department. A time clock card should be kept and verified by a foreman or timekeeper.

The departments involved in internal control of manufacturing expenses are factory production, factory service and accounts payable.

[¶603.2]   Selling Expenses

(1) Salesmen's salaries should be okayed by the sales department manager before a summary is sent to the payroll department. The basis for the summary is the salesmen's daily report. Commissions earned by salesmen are verified from duplicate sales invoices mailed to the customer. These are computed in the sales department and approved by the sales department manager.

(2) To prevent padding of travel expenses, many companies allow flat rates or maximum amounts for each day of the week. Unusual amounts should require an explanation from the salesman.

(3) The office manager retains control over outgoing mail and postage. A mail clerk usually affixes the postage. A point to keep in mind as a control of postage expenses is not to permit every office worker access to stamps or a postage meter.

(4) Telephone expenses can be controlled by having the switchboard operator record all outgoing calls by departments on a call report sheet. Long distance calls should be reported on a special form indicating the party making the call and where the call is going to. From the long distance call record, telephone expenses are distributed by departments.

(5) Subscriptions to publications and dues of various organizations and professional societies should be approved by the sales manager before a voucher is prepared for them.

(6) All bills approved by the sales manager are sent to the accounting department for payment.

The departments involved for internal control of selling expenses are sales and accounts payable.

[¶603.3]   Administrative Expenses

Internal control for administrative expenses is very similar to the material for the sales department. Bills for administrative expense items should be approved by an administrative department executive before they are sent to the accounts payable department for payment.

The departments involved in internal control of administrative expenses are administrative and accounts payable.

[¶603.4]   Financial and Other Expenses

In corporations which have special departments to control financial problems in the company, a treasury department or similar department will handle expenses in the nature of interest, discount and dividends and may even supervise handling of cash. The financial department may also have the responsibility for authorizing credit extended to customers.

(1) A credit manager in the financial department should have the responsibility for approving sales orders above a specific amount. The manager should be in constant touch with the accounts receivable department to determine whether or not a customer has been regular in his payments. The treasurer has the responsibility for authorizing bad debt writeoffs. The writeoff itself should be made by someone in the accounts receivable department on the authority of the financial department executive — not the sales manager.

(2) The financial department executive or office manager approves expenditures such as interest and bank discounts, office expenses and supplies. After approval of these items, invoices are sent to the accounts payable department.

The departments involved in internal control for factory payrolls are timekeeping, payroll, accounts payable and the particular manufacturing division.

[¶603.5]   Salaries and Wages

(1) In the timekeeping department each workman is given an identifying number which will serve to identify the department within which he works. A badge with this number indentifies him when his presence within the factory is checked each day.

(2) It is the duty of a time clerk to check the presence of each workman once or twice a day, every day. This is to eliminate the possibility of one man punching the time clock for another workman who is absent. Absences are noted in a time book. These are then checked against the employee's time ticket, time clock card or payroll sheet at the end of each specific pay period.

(3) Care should be taken to prevent one worker punching another worker's time clock card. The time clock card indicates the number of hours the workman is present each day in the plant. The time clock card can be used to verify the hours shown on daily time tickets. This may be done daily or weekly.

(4) In the manufacturing department, a time ticket which lists the workman's name, number of hours worked on different jobs and labor operations and total hours worked is prepared. It must be approved by the foreman of the department in which work is performed.

(5) In the payroll department, time tickets are verified against the time clock cards and the time keeper's time clock book. The time ticket is then given to a clerk who inserts the hourly or piece-work rate of each workman. Another clerk computes the earnings. The time tickets are then used for working up the payroll sheet. Then, the time tickets are sent to the cost accounting department to prepare a payroll distribution sheet. The payroll sheet becomes the record by which the workman is paid. After the payroll sheet has been completely okayed, it is sent to the accounts payable department for payment. Payment to each worker, either by check or cash, should be receipted.

In the accounts payable department the payroll sheet serves as the basis for payment.

The departments involved in internal control for factory payrolls are time-keeping, payroll, accounts payable and the particular manufacturing division.

[¶603.6] Office Payroll

(1) In the sales department, the sales manager approves the daily sales reports. From these reports, a record of the salesperson's days is prepared. The record is sent to the payroll department after approval by the sales manager. The manager in the sales department also approves the records of work performed by the sales office force before sending it to the payroll department.

(2) In the administrative department, the office manager approves time worked by the office force and then sends it to the payroll department. Salaries of top executives are often placed on a special payroll. Their salaries are usually known by the paymaster who prepares their checks and sends them directly to the executives' offices.

(3) The treasurer or financial department office manager similarly approves the work performed by the clerical personnel in his department.

(4) Upon receiving these authorized reports from the various departments, the paymaster sets them up on a payroll sheet and after computing the applicable salary for each office worker, takes all applicable deductions and indicates a net salary for each employee.

(5) In the accounts payable department, payment for these office workers' salaries is prepared from the payroll sheets.

[¶604] INTERNAL CONTROL FOR CASH

Where currency is available, internal control is needed the most. Incoming checks may be used in manipulating accounts receivable and must be controlled. Accounts receivable control becomes part of cash control, and vice versa. Cash disbursements and petty cash also need special internal controls. The details on internal control for these cash or cash-connected items follow.

[¶604.1] Cash receipts

(1) In the selling department, cash sales should be recorded in a register. A numbered sales slip should be made up for each sale. These slips should be used in numerical order.

(2) In the cashier's department, an employee should count the cash in each register at the end of the day. Except for a small amount left to make change, all cash should be removed. The total daily cash receipts should be recorded on slips and placed in the same pouch as the cash itself. The pouch should then be turned over to a clerk (a different employee from the one who counted the cash in the register) who will make out a bank deposit slip. Still another clerk in the cashier's department should read the cash register totals of the day or remove the cash sales slips. The cash removed from the register must agree with the tape and the total of cash slips which are numbered sequentially (all numbers must have been accounted for). The sales readings are then compared with the amount of cash removed from the registers by the cashier. Small discrepancies are charged to a cash, short or over account. Larger discrepancies call for an explanation.

(3) In the accounts receivable department, incoming mail should be opened by a bonded clerk. All checks, currency, money orders are listed by this clerk on a cash-received record. The cash-received record lists date of receipt, name of sender and amount. The record and totals are then sent to the accounts receivable department to be properly applied to the customers' accounts. The cash is sent to the cashier's office and subsequently given to the deposit clerk.

(4) In the accounts receivable department, the record of cash received is used to credit against customers' accounts. This record then goes to the general accounting department where it is compared with daily deposit slips of cash received from customers before it is entered on the books.

The departments involved in internal control of cash receipts are selling, treasury or cashier's and accounts receivable.

[¶604.2]   Cash Disbursements

In the accounts payable department, purchase of any item must have prior approval from the authorized person in charge of the department in which the expenditure originates before it comes to the accounts payable department. Where a voucher system is in operation, vouchers are prepared for each expenditure. Information on the voucher matches that shown on the seller's invoice. Vouchers are entered in the voucher register after having been approved by the head of the voucher department and then placed in a pending file for future payments.

The departments involved in the internal control of cash disbursements are accounts payable and voucher.

[¶604.3]   Petty Cash

In any department where it is necessary to have a petty cash fund, at least two individuals should have the responsibility for handling petty cash. One individual inspects and approves the item for payment. The other has charge of the petty cash fund and pays the vouchers as they are presented. Each petty cash voucher should list the date, amount paid and name of the account to be charged. A bill or other receipt, if there is one, should be attached to the voucher. The employee who controls the petty cash fund should compare the receipts attached to the petty cash vouchers with the vouchers.

When the petty cash fund needs reimbursement, the person who controls the fund totals those petty cash vouchers which have been paid out and presents them to the accounts payable department, which then arranges for the necessary reimbursement.

The departments involved in the internal control of petty cash are selling, administrative, or others in which there is a need for such petty cash funds, and accounts payable.

[¶604.4]   Accounts Receivable

Copies of sales slips from the sales department are used to charge customers' accounts. Copies of any credits due customers come from the sales department. These records are sent to the accounts receivable department, where, if possible, one clerk should have the responsibility for entering only debits to customers' accounts and another for posting credits for returned merchandise, receipt of a note, etc. Still a third employee should enter the credit in the customer's account for cash received.

Sending statements at the end of each month is a good way to check the accuracy of the customers' accounts.

The departments responsible for internal control of accounts receivable are the accounts receivable and sales.

[¶604.5]   Notes Receivable

In the treasury department, a record of notes held from customers is made. A record is then sent to the accounts receivable division where a clerk makes the proper credits. A copy is sent to the general accounting department to reflect the charge to the control account — notes receivable. The treasurer keeps the notes until maturity date or until discounted with the bank. A subsidiary note register should be kept if the company receives a large number of such notes.

The departments responsible for internal control of notes receivable are treasury and accounts receivable.

[¶604.6]   Cash and Bank Reconciliations

Cash is the lifeblood of the company. It is the center upon which the whole circle of business activity is pivoted. Here is the reservoir into which all flows — in and out.

It is surprising to find that tests of cash receipts and cash disbursements are usually limited by management (through intermediaries) to monthly bank reconciliations.

Nothing is more effective than unannounced, non-routine, spot-tests of the cash-handling procedures (for that matter, *any* business procedure) by the highest working or non-working authority within the company. Think of the impact made on an employee when he *knows* he may be facing an impromptu test of his work by the president of the company — at any time! Called in, for example, to explain the purpose of a canceled check he now holds; imagine the psychological impact if this is done periodically, but irregularly? A test of application of payments on account — receivables and payables — almost any awareness of constant high-level review has an alerting effect. Peak, honest, performance is encouraged.

Bank reconciliations by and of themselves can not stand alone as proof of cash authenticity. They prove only the activity *within* that one period and serve to lend to prior reconciliations substantiation of then-listed outstanding checks. The current reconciliation is technically unproved until the outstanding checks and uncredited deposits in transit appear.

Reconciliations should be tested by someone other than the original preparer.

Block-proofs of cash should also be used occasionally to test an entire year's transactions. Here, all deposits are matched to all receipts recorded (in total); and all recorded disbursements are matched to total bank charges for cleared checks and minor items, with consideration, of course, given to opening and closing transit items.

The theory behind the mechanics of the bank reconciliation is to *update* the *bank* figures (on a worksheet) to reflect all transit items which have not yet cleared the bank, as follows:

Bank shows a balance of	$ 10,500
Add deposits in transit	2,000
	12,500
Less checks outstanding (itemized)	600
Adjusted bank balance	$ 11,900
Balance per books shows	$ 11,909
Difference	$ 9 (more on books)

Having taken the preliminary steps of determining the deposits in transit (by checking the bank credits against recorded receipts) and the outstanding checks (by checking off all returned canceled checks against the listing of those issued or carried over), we note a remaining difference of $9.

In *order*, the following are the *most expedient* ways of finding this difference:

1. Look at the bank statement for any bank charge (D/M's or combination) — not yet recorded in the general ledger;
2. Look at the books for any $9 debit (or combination) on the books and not on the statement;
3. $9 may be indicative of a transposition. Match the bank's opening pickup balance to the closing one on the last statement;
   Match deposits to receipts recorded;
   Check general ledger footings and subtraction;
   Check summary postings into the general ledger from the original source;
   Check footings in the books of original entry (Receipts, Disbursements, General Journal);

4. Having exhausted the above possibilities and still not having found the difference, check the face amount of each check to the amount charged by the bank (each check is canceled with a clearance date).

5. Now match your own listing of the check to the actual check. (Steps 4 and 5 are interchangeable)

6. Not yet? Prove the bank's additions.

7. If still elusive, you've probably missed it above or made a transposition error in listing transit checks or deposits; or, it may be an error made last month which was missed.

[¶605]   FILE MAINTENANCE

One of the most important, yet least emphasized, facets of the business enterprise is the establishment and proper maintenance of an effective, accurate filing system. How costly is the time wasted in frustrating searches for misfiled data, when initial precautions and firm rules might have assured quick access to and retrieval of needed documents by competent, authorized personnel!

[¶605.1]   Suggestions

Establish firm rules for filing.

Provide adequate accessible filing space for current files.

Pinpoint responsibilities for filing and accessing files.

Follow legal requirements for record retention. Establish an annual policy of removing out-dated files.

Utilize flow charts when appropriate.

Have sufficient copies of documents such as purchase orders, sales shipping papers, and all papers ultimately tied to a sales or vendor's invoice, to allow for a complete numerical file of each document.

[¶605.2]   A List of File Categories

Sales invoices to customers — both alphabetic and numeric files;

Vendor invoices — alphabetic, sometimes with copy of paid voucher check or numbered voucher. Some firms keep invoices segregated in an "unpaid" file until paid;

Canceled checks — keep by month in reconciled batches. Do not intermingle different batches;

Correspondence files — for customers, vendors, others;

Permanent files — organizational information, legal documents, leases, minutes, deeds, etc. Usually in fireproof areas, accessibility limited.

Other:

Tax files
Payroll and personnel files
Backup for journal entries
Investment files — security transactions
Petty cash voucher files

Purchasing department files — suppliers, bids, etc. (costs)
Credit department files
Prior years' books of entry
Data from subsidiary companies owned
Advertising programs, literature, etc.

[¶605.3]   Computer Files—Considerations

1. Security protection — access, codes, permanent tapes/discs of programs, updated balance files for accounts receivables, payables, general ledger, payrolls. Keep enough of these changing files for re-runs or accumulation runs, as needed for emergencies.

2. Keep hard copy until sure replacement hard copy is accurate, or as necessary for continuous file.

3. Be prepared for manual emergency work, if computer goes down suddenly.

4. Pinpoint responsibility for keeping logs, storage, etc.

[¶606]   THE FOREIGN CORRUPT PRACTICES ACT OF 1977*

One of the most significant developments in public accounting in recent years is the provision in the Foreign Corrupt Practices Act of 1977 (FCPA) requiring publicly-held companies to develop and maintain a system of internal accounting controls sufficient to provide:

1. That transactions are executed in accordance with management's general or specific authorization.

2. That transactions are recorded as necessary to permit preparation of financial statements in conformity with generally accepted accounting principles, or any other criteria applicable to such statements.

3. That the system maintains accountability for assets.

4. That access to assets is permitted only in accordance with management's general or specific authorization.

5. That the recorded accountability for assets is compared with existing assets at reasonable intervals, with appropriate action taken with respect to any difference.

Auditor's Objective: The significance of the Act, insofar as auditors are concerned, is the explicit statutory recognition given to accounting controls. The auditor's objective is to plan the examination to search for errors or irregularities that would have a material effect on the financial statements, and to use skill and care in the examination of the client's internal control system. While the independent auditor is not part of a company's internal accounting control system, the

---

*Appendix I is a reprint of the Foreign Corrupt Practices Act of 1977.

auditor must evaluate the effectiveness and monitor compliance of internal accounting control systems.

The fact that the statutory requirement applies to publicly-held corporations has led, initially, to the misunderstanding that it is of no concern to public accountants who are not involved in auditing public corporations. But auditors must be mindful of the *Statement on Auditing Procedure No. 1,* which applies to the scope of the examination of *all* companies, whether public or private corporations, partnerships, or other forms of business organizations. This Statement specifically references creditors, for example, who are a primary user of financial statements and to whom an auditor has a potential liability for materially misleading financial statements accompanying applications for credit to financial institutions, regardless of honest error or fraudulent intent.

[¶606.1] Compliance Problems

What can an accountant do to ascertain compliance with the 1977 Act? Compliance can be demonstrated by an *intent* to comply, since neither the Act nor the professional literature specify criteria for evaluating a system's adequacy or materiality levels. This makes it difficult for management, directors, independent auditors, and legal counsel to be sure of compliance with the Act.

The following suggestions may be helpful both to the accountant and to management for establishing intent to comply.

There should be:

1. Records of memos and minutes of meetings held by management, the board of directors, and the audit committee (if any) concerning internal accounting control concepts. The discussions should include legal counsel, internal auditors, and independent auditors.

2. Statements for the record of intention to comply.

3. A record of all meetings within the company of the accounting personnel and internal audit staff to ensure that they understand the importance of compliance and are able to monitor compliance.

4. A written program for continuing review and evaluation of the accounting controls system.

5. Letters from the independent auditors stating that no material weaknesses in internal accounting controls were discovered during the audit, or that suggested needed improvements have in fact been made. If necessary, the independent auditors' comments should include other deficiencies, and management's written plans to correct them should be included.

6. A record of periodic review and approval of the evaluation of the system by senior management, the audit committee, and the board of directors.

7. Instructional manuals for the development of methods and techniques for describing, testing, and evaluating internal controls.

8. Training programs conducted for internal auditors and other company personnel responsible for internal controls.

9. Changes in internal controls to overcome identified deficiencies that are initiated and documented.

10. A formal written code of conduct appropriately communicated and monitored. (Note: The SEC regards a corporate written code of conduct as imperative.)

11. Documentation that compliance testing was done by direct *visual* observations during the period being audited.

7

Current Assets

[¶701] CLASSIFICATION OF CURRENT ASSETS

Classification of current assets is important since the more the current assets exceed the current liabilities, the higher becomes the working capital. There is considerable variation and inconsistency among companies in the way assets are classified in financial statements.

For accounting purposes, the term "current assets" is used to designate cash and other assets or resources which are reasonably expected to be realized in cash, sold or consumed during the normal operating cycle of the business.

Here are some examples:

(1) Cash available for current operations and items which are the equivalent of cash; (2) inventories of merchandise, raw materials, goods in process, finished goods, operating supplies, and ordinary maintenance materials and parts; (3) trade accounts, notes and acceptances receivable; (4) receivables from officers, employees, affiliates and others if they are collectible in the ordinary course of the business within one year; (5) installment or deferred accounts and notes receivable if they conform generally to normal trade practices and business terms; (6) marketable securities representing the investment of cash available for current operation; and (7) prepaid expenses, such as insurance, rent, taxes, unused royalties, current paid advertising services not yet received, and operating supplies.

Prepaid expenses are not current assets in that they will be converted into cash, but in the sense that, if not paid in advance, they would require the use of current assets otherwise available during the operating cycle.

The operating cycle is defined as the average time between the acquisition of materials or services until the time that cash is finally realized on sale of the materials or services. Where there are several operating cycles occurring within a year, a one-year time period is used as the criterion for a current asset. Where the operating cycle is more than 12 months (i.e., in the tobacco, distillery, and lumber businesses), a longer period is used. Where a business has no clearly defined operating cycle, a one-year period is used.

[¶701.1]   Assets Excluded From "Current Assets"

The following types of items are to be excluded from the current asset classification:

(1) Cash and claims for cash which are (a) restricted as to withdrawal or use for other than current operations, (b) earmarked for expenditure in the acquisition or construction of noncurrent assets, or (c) segregated for the liquidation of long-term debts. Even though funds may not actually be set aside in separate accounts, funds that are clearly to be used in the near future for the liquidation of long-term debt, sinking fund payments, or other similar purposes should be excluded from current assets, unless the maturing portion of debt is being shown as a current liability.

(2) Investments in securities (marketable or not), or advances which have been made for the purposes of control, affiliation, or other continuing business advantage.

(3) Receivables arising from unusual transactions (e.g., sale of capital assets, loans or advances to affiliate companies, officers or employees) not expected to be collected within a one-year period.

(4) Cash surrender value of life insurance policies.

(5) Land and other natural resources.

(6) Depreciable assets.

(7) Long-term prepayments which are chargeable to the operations of several years or deferred charges, such as bonus payments under a long-term lease and costs of rearranging a factory or removal to a new location.

Accounts and notes receivable due from officers, employees or affiliated companies should not be included under the general heading "Accounts Receivable." They should be shown separately. The basic reasoning behind this is that accounts receivable are classified as a current asset presuming they will be converted into cash within one year. Except in the case where goods have actually been sold to them on account, for collection according to the regular credit terms, amounts due from officers, directors and stockholders are not likely to be collected within one year. Therefore, they should be shown under a noncurrent caption.

The same is true of accounts receivable from affiliated companies. These amounts are not likely to be paid off currently and are usually of a more permanent nature. Showing them as current assets is misleading. Also, there is an overstatement of current assets and consequently of working capital.

[¶701.2]   Valuation of Current Assets

Sometimes current assets are carried at values which do not represent realizable values. For example, accounts receivable should be net of allowances for uncollectible accounts or net of earned discounts when discounts are expected to give an *estimated* receivable value.

Also, some current assets should now reflect *unrealized* gains or losses. (See both Marketable Securities and Foreign Currency Translations in this Accounting Section.)

Assets and liabilities in the balance sheet should not be offset unless a legal right of setoff exists.

Inventory is valued at cost unless its utility value has diminished to a lower market replacement cost. Standard costing is acceptable, if it reasonably approximates actual cost. The flow of inventory costs may be predicated upon FIFO, LIFO, or average assumptions.

[¶702]   INVENTORY

The term "inventory" is used to designate tangible personal property which is: (1) held for sale in the ordinary course of business, (2) in the process of being produced for later sale, or (3) currently consumed directly or indirectly in the production of goods or services to be available for sale.

Manufacturing firms have many types of inventory; for example, finished goods, work in process, raw materials and manufacturing supplies. Finished goods of a manufacturing company are comparable to the merchandise of a non-manufacturing company. Excluded from inventory are long-term assets subject to depreciation and depreciable fixed assets retired from regular use and held for sale. Raw materials which become part of a finished product become part of that inventory cost. Trade practices and materiality are usually the determining factors in either inventorying production supplies on hand or expensing them as part of product costs.

In accounting for inventories we try to match appropriate costs against revenues. This gives a proper determination of realized income. Another way of putting it is to say that by applying the best method of costing inventory, we are measuring out "cost of goods sold," by associating cause and effect.

Inclusion of goods in inventory should follow the legal rule of title.

Whatever the location of goods, if title is legally held by the company, the goods should be included in inventory. If title to the goods has passed to a customer, the goods should not be included in inventory.

[¶702.1]   Cost of Inventory

The primary basis of accounting for inventories is cost. This means the sum of the expenditures and charges, directly or indirectly, incurred in bringing the inventory to its existing condition and location.

As applied to inventories, cost means acquisition and production costs. However, there are many items which, although related to inventory, are not included in the cost of the inventory; for example, idle facility expense, excessive spoilage, double freight, rehandling costs. If these costs are abnormal, they should be treated as expenses of the current period rather than carried forward as part of the inventory cost. General and administrative expenses should be treated as expenses of the period. Likewise, selling expenses should not be included in inventory. The cost of inventory, however, should include an applicable portion of manufacturing overhead. The exclusion of *all* overhead from inventory cost is not an acceptable accounting procedure.

Cost, however, *must not* be used when the *market* value of inventory items is lower than the cost.

[¶702.2]   Flow of Cost Assumptions

Costs for inventory may be determined under any one of several assumptions as to the flow of costs; for example, FIFO, average, and LIFO. The method selected should be the one which most clearly reflects periodic income.

The "flow of costs" and "flow of goods" are usually not the same. But we use a "flow of cost"—such as FIFO, average, or LIFO—because to identify the cost of a specific item sold is often impossible, impractical, or even misleading. Where similar goods are purchased at different prices at different times, it would be difficult to identify specific goods sold except in a case of valuable jewelry, automobiles, pianos or other large items. Even perpetual inventory records would not make identification possible. Therefore, an assumption is made with respect to the flow of costs in order to provide a practical basis for measuring period income.

LIFO is considered an appropriate method for pricing inventory during extended inflationary periods, when costs continue accelerating. When the economy is deflationary or relatively stable, the FIFO or average methods are usually preferred by management. Practices of the other companies in the same industry should also be considered. Financial statements would be more useful if all companies within a given industry used uniform methods of inventory pricing.

The method used must be consistently applied and disclosed in financial statements. (See Disclosures and Restatements in this text)

[¶702.3]   First-In, First-Out (FIFO)

This is probably the most common method of valuing inventories. The latest costs are assigned to the goods on hand; thus, the earliest costs become the costs of the goods sold. The theory here is that goods are disposed of in the same order as acquired.

Here is a simple illustration of FIFO. Opening inventory and purchases during the year were as follows:

Opening inventory	1,000 units at $10, or	$10,000
First purchase	800 units at $11, or	8,800
Second purchase	500 units at $14, or	7,000
Third purchase	400 units at $12, or	4,800
Fourth purchase	300 units at $13, or	3,900
Totals	3,000	$34,500

The closing inventory consists of 1,100 units. Under the FIFO method of costing, the closing inventory is considered to be made up of:

300 units of the fourth purchase (at $13)	$ 3,900
400 units of the third purchase (at $12)	4,800
400 units of the second purchase (at $14)	5,600
Cost of 1,100 units in closing inventory	$14,300

[¶702.4] Last-In, First-Out (LIFO)

In recent years, LIFO has become a very popular method. In years of rising prices and high taxes, the LIFO method keeps profits (and taxes) down. It has the virtue of applying the current price structure to the cost of goods sold, thus matching the high price structure of the sales with the high price structure of costs.

The basic approach to LIFO costing is to assign the *earliest* costs to the *closing* inventory, as if the latest-acquired items were the first sold. For example, if we use the figures set forth above in the FIFO illustration, the costs of our closing inventory of 1,100 units under the LIFO costing approach would be:

1,000 units of the opening inventory (at $10)	$10,000
100 units of the first purchase (at $11)	1,100
Cost of 1,100 units in closing inventory	$11,100

Note that the 100-unit incremental increase over the inventory might, in the LIFO method, have been valued under *any* one of the following four options:

1. In the order of acquisition (as illustrated)
2. At the most recent purchase cost
3. At an average cost for the year
4. At the "dollar-value" method which converts the incremental increase by means of an index based on the LIFO base year prices.

[¶702.5] Average Costs

A weighted average is sometimes used to determine the cost of the closing inventory. This method is generally not approved for tax purposes. Under the weighted average method, you determine an average unit cost and then multiply that average unit cost by the number of units in the closing inventory. To get the weighted average, the number of units in each purchase is multiplied by the unit price for that purchase. And the total units purchased and the total of all purchase costs are added to the units and costs in the opening inventory. Then the total of all the costs is divided by the total of all the units. The resulting figure is the average cost per unit.

For example, in the FIFO illustration above, the total number of units involved in the opening inventory plus the four purchases was 3,000. The total cost of the 3,000 units was $34,500. Dividing $34,500 by 3,000, we come up with an average cost per unit of $11.50. Since our closing inventory consisted of 1,100 units, if we priced it at average cost (1,100 × $11.50), the cost of our closing inventory would be $12,650.

Thus, depending on the method of cost used, our closing inventory could have been $11,100, $12,650, or $14,300.

[¶702.6]   The Retail Inventory Method

This method of inventory pricing is sometimes most practical and appropriate. It is used principally by retail establishments. This inventory valuation has as its initial starting point the retail or selling price of the merchandise rather than the cost. It arrives finally at the cost valuation entirely on the basis of average relationships of retail and cost figures over the period involved.

When merchandise is purchased, the retail selling price is placed on the price tag attached. At inventory time, the inventory is taken at the selling price. The cost is then arrived at by multiplying the inventory by the cost complement percentage, which is the difference between the mark-up % and 100%. It is arrived at as follows:

	Cost	Retail	Mark-up	Mark-up %	Cost Complement %
Beginning inventory	$ 50,000	$ 75,000	$25,000	33⅓%	66⅔%
Purchases	72,000	120,000	48,000	40 %	60 %
Total to Date	122,000	195,000	73,000	37.4%	62.6%
Markdowns		3,000	3,000		
Total to Date	$122,000	$192,000	$70,000	36.5%	63.5%
Sale for period		95,000			
Ending inventory		$ 97,000			

At the end of the period the retail inventory of $97,000 will be reduced to cost by applying the cost complement percent of 63.5. Thus the inventory figure at cost is $61,595.

The gross margin tabulation follows:

Sales		$ 95,000
Opening inventory	$ 50,000	
Purchases	72,000	
	122,000	
Closing inventory	61,595	
Cost of sales		60,405
Gross margin		$ 34,595

[¶702.7]   Lower of Cost or Market

A departure from cost basis of pricing inventory is *required* when the disposal of the goods in the ordinary course of business will be at less than cost. This calls for valuing the inventory at the lower of cost or market.

As used in the phrase, "lower of cost or market," market means current replacement cost (by purchase or reproduction) with the exception that: (1) market is not to exceed the net realizable value which is the estimated selling price in the ordinary course of business less reasonably predictable costs of completion and disposal, and (2) market should not be less than net realizable value reduced by an allowance for a normal profit margin. Here, for example, are the prices to be used in carrying out the lower of cost or market concept (the price to be used in each case is the one in bold face):

	1	2	3	4	5
(a) Cost	**.82**	.95	.95	**.78**	.94
(b) Market—cost to replace at inventory date	.86	**.90**	.80	.75	.94
(c) Selling price less estimated cost to complete and sell .	.92	.92	.92	.92	**.92**
(d) Selling price less estimated cost to complete and sell and normal profit margin	.83	.83	.83	.83	.83

In applying the cost or market rule, no loss should be recognized unless the evidence indicates clearly that a loss has been sustained. Where evidence indicates that cost will be recovered with a normal profit margin upon the sale of merchandise, no loss should be recognized even though replacement cost is lower. It should also be remembered that pricing goods at the lower of cost or market is not to be followed literally in all cases. Rather, it is to be applied realistically with regard to the form, content, and composition of the inventory.

There are three ways of applying the lower-of-cost-or-market rule: The rule may be applied on (1) each item in the inventory, (2) the total cost of the major categories in the inventory, or (3) the cost of entire inventory.

Each of these methods would produce different results, and all of them are considered acceptable for financial statement purposes. The method used should be the one which most clearly reflects periodic income. For example, if there is only one product, rule (3) would seem to have the greatest significance. Where there is more than one major product, rule (2) would seem to be the most useful. Rule (1), application of the lower of cost or market to each item of inventory, is the most common in practice.

When substantial and unusual losses result under the cost or market rule, it is desirable to disclose them separately from normal cost of goods sold.

Any procedure adopted for the treatment of inventory items should be applied consistently and disclosed in the financial statement. Without such consistency there is no basis with which to compare the results of one year with another. Any change in the basis of stating inventories will probably have an important effect on the statements, and full disclosure of such a change should be made.

There are some instances when inventories are properly stated above cost. Exceptions are made in the case of precious metals (e.g., gold and silver), agricultural or mineral products or the packing industry.

Where a company has firm purchase commitments for goods in inventory, losses which are expected to arise from such uncancellable and unhedged commitments for future purchase of inventory should be reflected in the current period in the same way as losses on inventory.

[¶703]   MARKETABLE SECURITIES

The traditional precept of stating assets at historical costs has, in the area of marketable equity securities, been changed by the AICPA. Effective for statements ending on or after December 31, 1975, marketable securities are to be shown at the *lower* of historical cost or current market value (statement date), through the use of offsetting valuation allowance accounts (separated as to current and noncurrent).

There are several ramifications to be considered in accomplishing this periodic write-down (or possible write-up) to historical costs:

1. Management decides whether to classify securities as current or noncurrent assets, *generally* basing the classification upon its intent or non-intent of one-year disposition.

2. All current equity securities held are considered to be a single portfolio. All noncurrent equity securities are considered to be another single portfolio.

3. In unclassified balance sheets, securities are considered to be noncurrent.

4. Entire portfolios are considered to be *one unit* for the purpose of determining the overall lump-sum value to be shown. This entails an *item-by-item comparison* between *cost* and *market price* for each holding. When an *entire* portfolio's market value sinks *below* its cost (some holdings may be *over* cost), a valuation allowance account is *credited* for the difference (and serves as an offsetting asset account for net balance sheet display purposes)—with the *debit* for the unrealized loss going to:

   A. An *income* statement unrealized loss account for those securities in the *current* portfolio;

   B. An *equity section* unrealized loss account for those securities in the *noncurrent* portfolio. This account is a separate (debit) component of retained earnings and is shown in the Statement of Retained Earnings, or in the more expansive Statement of Stockholders' Equity.

5. At each subsequent year end, the new market values are compared again with cost, and the valuation allowance accounts for the entire portfolios are adjusted for:

   A. Further declines, or

   B. Increases up to, but not exceeding, cost.

6. When securities are sold, the difference between *cost* and *selling price* becomes an income statement *realized* gain or loss, the asset cost being deleted from the portfolio and the valuation allowance account at year end being subsequently adjusted to reflect the temporary decline in the market value of the remaining securities held.

7. Permanent declines should be reflected immediately upon discovery as an income statement realized loss and a reduction of the asset cost account. The newly reflected written-down cost-basis becomes the portfolio value, and it should not be changed for later recoveries in market value.

8. When reclassifying portfolios from one category to another (current to noncurrent or vice-versa), permanent entries should be made to reflect the change as of the date of reclassification.

9. Timing differences should be recognized unless there is reasonable doubt that unrealized losses will be offset by subsequent capital gains.

10. Disclosure is required.

11. *No* restatement of prior year is necessary.

12. *Not* mandatory for not-for-profit organizations, except investor-owned hospitals.

13. *Not* applicable to immaterial items.

14. Equity securities do not include bonds, treasury stock, or redeemable preferred stock.

15. Does *not* pertain to those holdings treated under the equity method.

16. See illustrative journal entries in Appendix A.

8

Non-Current Assets

**CLASSIFICATION OF
NON-CURRENT ASSETS**

Noncurrent assets are assets which have a useful life of more than one accounting period. Equipment, land and buildings are examples of this category.

[¶802] **EQUIPMENT AND PLANT—
ACQUISITIONS AND DISPOSITIONS**

[¶802.1] **Acquisitions**

Assets acquired in exchanges are measured at the exchange price, that is, acquisition cost. Money and money claims are measured at their face amount or sometimes at their discount amount.

In exchanges in which neither money nor promises to pay money are exchanged, the assets acquired are generally measured at the fair value of the assets given up. However, if the fair value of the assets received is more clearly evident, the assets acquired are measured at that amount.

Under the above standards, equipment and plant are therefore valued:

1. At cost, if purchased for cash or its equivalent, or

2. If an exchange of non-cash property is involved (wholly or partially), preferably at the fair value of the asset acquired, or, if that is not clearly evident, of the asset surrendered (an example of the latter would be the use of the market price of the company's own stock given in exchange for an asset whose fair value cannot reasonably be determined), or

3. If a group of assets is acquired in one exchange, the total price is allo-

cated to the individual assets based on their relative fair values. Excess paid over fair value is treated as goodwill. In the opposite case, any excess of fair value of the assets acquired over the exchange price is used to reduce the value of the non-current assets (except investment securities) proportionately.

[¶802.2] Dispositions

Decreases in assets are recorded when assets are disposed of in exchanges.

Decreases in assets are measured by the recorded amounts that relate to the assets. The amounts are usually the historical or acquisition costs of the assets (as adjusted for amortization and other charges).

The disposing of equipment and plant assets usually results in a gain or loss and is reported as such on the financial statements. In an exchange, for financial purposes, losses should be recognized, but gains should be used to adjust the basis of the new acquisition.

On straight dispositions, depreciation is usually calculated to the date of disposal (approximately) and both the accumulated depreciation and the asset account are then netted to the amount recovered to arrive at the gain or loss, which, for tax purposes may require special consideration, such as recapture of depreciation and investment tax credits.

[¶802.3] Other Considerations

Self-constructed assets should not be depreciated while under construction. The cost basis should be determined not only by the material and labor expended, but also by apportionment of overhead items, such as depreciation on any fixed assets used in that construction process (which application in turn reduces the depreciation expense for that particular fixed asset).

Detailed sub-ledgers or worksheets should be maintained for all fixed assets, showing date acquired, cost or basis, investment tax credit, estimated life, salvage value (if any), depreciation taken by year, accumulated depreciation and gains or losses on dispositions or trade-in information.

Appraisal write-ups are contrary to generally accepted accounting principles, but when circumstances necessitate write-ups, the offset goes to "appraisal surplus" and becomes part of the equity capital. Depreciation then must be based on the higher, appraisal values.

[¶803] ACCOUNTING TREATMENT OF INVESTMENT TAX CREDIT

Two methods of accounting for the investment tax credit are suggested for use:

1. *The deferred method*—in which the credit is reflected in income over the depreciable useful life of the acquisition. The deferred credit unused may be shown as either deferred income or as a reduction of the asset value.

2. *The flow-through method*—in which the credit is used entirely in the year of acquisition and is reflected as a reduction of the income tax expense (as on the tax return).

A carryback of unused investment tax credit may be set up as a refund claim receivable with the corresponding reduction of tax expense shown separately on the income statement (but *not* as an extraordinary item). Carryforwards ordinarily are not recognized until they become allowable and available per the tax rules.

The effect of investment tax credits must also be determined, if relevant, in computing and disclosing timing differences pertaining to deferred taxes.

[¶804]   **DEPRECIATION***

> If an asset provides benefit for several periods, its cost is allocated to the periods in a systematic and rational manner in the absence of a more direct basis for associating cause and effect. . . . This form of expense recognition always involves assumptions about the pattern of 'matching costs to benefits' because neither can be conclusively demonstrated.

Depreciation is the term applied to the allocation of a fixed asset's cost over its beneficial useful life. It is a method of accounting which aims to distribute the cost or other value of tangible or capital assets, less salvage (if any), over the estimated useful life of the asset (which may be a single asset or a group of assets in a single account) in a systematic and rational manner. It is a process of allocation, not of valuation, applied on a consistent basis.

Rather than increasing expenses immediately, depreciation might also *increase* other asset values temporarily, such as in the application of overhead depreciation to inventory or to self-constructed assets.

From a tax viewpoint, the deduction for depreciation (which requires no annual cash outlay) reduces the amount of tax we have to pay. This has the effect of increasing the accumulation of cash at our disposal—i.e., the "cash flow."

Before we can determine the amount of our depreciation deductions, we have to know the following three elements: (1) the method of depreciation that we will use, (2) the amount we can recover (depreciable basis), and (3) the period over which we can take deductions (useful life).

The depreciation is usually applicable only to property which approaches, by wear and tear, business ineffectiveness. "Depreciation" and "repairs and

---

*For property placed in service prior to 1981, the above provisions apply. See section Two (¶2106) for coverage of the Accelerated Cost Recovery provisions that apply to property placed in service after 1980.

maintenance'' are not the same. It is necessary to distinguish between repairs and maintenance costs to keep the asset in operation and repairs which are capital expenditures and increase the life of the asset. The former are expense deductions in the year incurred; the latter must be amortized over the life of the asset. What repairs increase the life of the asset and what repairs are necessary for its operation is often a matter of judgment. Examples of repairs which are classified as capital expenditures are the costs of remodeling or reconditioning a building.

The determination, or estimation of useful life, may be based on: (1) IRS guidelines, such as in Bulletin F or ADR rules, basically determined by estimated physical durability, longevity or unit-productive capability; (2) statutory law, as in the case of a patent; (3) contract, as in the case of some leases; (4) utility, as in the case of an airport built for military training during war.

Although write-up of fixed assets to reflect appraisal, market or current values is not in accordance with GAAP, where such appreciation has been recorded, depreciation should be based on the written up amounts for financial statement purposes.

[¶804.1] Methods of Depreciation

Following the passage of the Internal Revenue Act of 1954, which permitted the use of the declining-balance and similar accelerated methods of depreciation, the AICPA stated such methods met the requirement of being systematic and rational and could be used for general accounting purposes, with appropriate disclosure to be made of any change in method when depreciation is a significant factor in determining net income.

The declining-balance and the sum-of-the-year-digits methods of depreciation are appropriate and most used in those cases where the expected productivity or revenue-earning power of an asset is greater during earlier years of life or when maintenance charges tend to increase during later years.

Accounting methods of depreciating assets may differ from tax methods used. It is the practice of many firms to use straight-line depreciation for accounting purposes and an accelerated one for tax purposes. When this happens, disclosure should be made of the timing differences. (See Appendix F for illustration of Methods of Depreciation. Also, see Tax Section.)

[¶805]   BASIS

Normally, the basis for depreciation (i.e., the capital amount on which you figure your depreciation deductions) is what you paid for property. To the cost of the property itself is added the cost of transporting the property to your premises, the cost of installation, acquisition related costs.

For tax purposes, the basis for depreciation can be different from the basis used for financial reporting purposes. This difference often arises when there are trade-ins involved. According to GAAP, the entity paying any monetary consideration on a trade-in should recognize losses immediately, but, for gains, should adjust the basis of the acquisition to the extent of the gain. For tax purposes, neither gain nor loss is usually recognized, with neither serving to adjust the basis of the new acquisition. Hence, there may be a timing difference with respect to the different bases used for depreciation.

[¶805.1]   Allocation of Basis

When property is acquired, it is often necessary to allocate basis. Here are the instances when allocation is necessary:

(1) When improved real estate is purchased, there must be an allocation made as to land (nondepreciable, because land doesn't wear out) and buildings;

(2) When more than one asset is purchased for a lump sum;

(3) When a group of assets (or possibly a business) is purchased for a single sum involving depreciable and nondepreciable assets.

Improved Real Estate: Whenever you acquire a piece of improved real property, you have an immediate need for an allocation. Land is not depreciable; and in order to determine your basis for depreciating the building, you have to reduce your overall basis by an amount which represents a reasonable basis for the land. The usual method of making the allocation is in proportion to the respective fair market values.

If you have in fact paid proportionately more for the building for some special reason and can establish the fact, you can use the higher amount as your depreciation basis. The best way to secure such an advantage, however, is by specific allocation in the contract which spells it out in detail.

If any of the contents of the building are included in the purchase transaction, you need a further allocation between the structure and the contents. Then the amount allocated to the contents must be further broken down among the various items which are included in the sale.

This latter allocation may require all parties to consider the investment credit and depreciation recapture provisions of the tax law.

Acquisition of more than one asset: In the purchase of more than one asset (mixed assets) the same rules which have been discussed above apply. The cost of a group of assets which is stated as a single sum must be broken down and allocated among the separate items or groups. This permits the proper allocation of useful lives to different assets or groups, and separates depreciable from nondepreciable assets. Again, the possible effects of the investment credit and depreciation recapture provisions must be watched.

[¶805.2]   Acquisition of a Going Business

Generally, in the acquisition of the assets of another entity in a business combination, the fair market value at acquisition is used for the assets acquired. (See Business Combinations later in this text.)

[¶805.3.]   Allocation in the Purchase Agreement

An allocation made at the time of the agreement and reduced to writing will ordinarily be accepted for tax purposes where it was bargained for at arm's length and in good faith.

[¶805.4]   Goodwill

The cost of an intangible asset including goodwill acquired in a business combination may not be written off as a lump sum to capital surplus or to retained earnings nor be reduced to a nominal amount at or immediately after acquisition.

Goodwill, which may be either an amount specified in a contract or determined to be that portion of cost applicable to unidentifiable assets, should be amortized over a period of forty years or less. However, if a lesser period of benefit can be definitely evidenced, that shorter period may be used.

Amortization of goodwill recorded for accounting purposes creates a permanent difference, since it is generally not allowable as a tax deduction.

[¶806]   ACQUISITION-RELATED COSTS

Interest costs must be capitalized as part of the cost of acquisition of certain assets, i.e., assets that are constructed or produced for a company's own use, or assets that are intended for sale or lease. Both regulated and non-regulated enterprises must comply. Generally, interest costs must be capitalized for all assets that require a period of time to get the assets ready for their intended use; except interest costs should not be capitalized for inventories.

The following is a listing (though not necessarily all-inclusive) of acquisition-related expenditures which *should be capitalized,* according to the AICPA publication, *Accounting For Depreciable Assets* (Accounting Research Monograph #1), by Charles W. Lamden, CPA, Ph.D.; Dale L. Gerboth, CPA; and Thomas W. McRae, CPA, 1975, 189 pages: (page 54).

1. Buildings:
    a. Original contract price or cost of construction.
    b. Expenses incurred in remodeling, reconditioning, or altering a purchased building to make it available for the purpose for which it was acquired.

   c. Cost of excavation or grading or filling of land for the specific building.

   d. Expenses incurred for the preparation of plans, specifications, blueprints, and so on.

   e. Cost of building permits.

   f. Payment of noncurrent taxes accrued on the building, at date of purchase if payable by the purchaser.

   g. Architects' and engineers' fees for design and supervision.

   h. Other costs, such as temporary buildings used during the construction period.

2. Machinery, equipment, and furniture and fixtures:

   a. Original contract or invoice cost.

   b. Freight and drayage in, cartage, import duties, handling and storage costs.

   c. Specific in-transit insurance charges.

   d. Sales, use, and other taxes imposed on the purchase.

   e. Costs of preparation of foundations and other costs in connection with making a proper *situs* for the asset.

   f. Installation charges.

   g. Charges for testing and preparation for use.

   h. Costs for reconditioning used equipment when purchased.

And, from the same source above, the following is a list of acquisition-related expenditures which *should not* be capitalized:

1. Expenditures for facilities and the renovation of buildings required in connection with specific contracts, which would not have been incurred except for such contracts and which are therefore specifically included in contract costs.

2. Repair of existing equipment, including replacement of component parts, reconstruction, or alteration except as outlined above.

3. Expenditures incurred in demolishing or dismantling equipment, including those related to the replacement of units or systems and the removal of parts in connection with a rebuilding or replacement project.

4. Expenditures incurred in connection with the rearrangement, transfer or moving of equipment within a plant or from one location to another.

5. Special test equipment, fixtures, cutting tools, shaping tools, and boring tools having a comparatively short term of effective life.

6. Extraordinary costs incidental to the erection of a building, such as those due to strike, flood, fire, or other casualty (although unanticipated expenditures, such as rock blasting, piling, or relocation of the channel of an underground stream, *should* be capitalized).

7. Cost of abandoned construction.

8. Cost incurred for bonus payments to contractors, temporary construction because of shortages of material for permanent construction, and so on, for the purpose of hastening completion. Extra payments, such as premium time to take advantage of management operating decisions, should be expensed.

The guiding principle is that "all incidental payments necessary to put the asset in condition and location for use" should be capitalized.

LEASES

In November, 1976, the FASB issued Statement No. 13, *Accounting for Leases,* which supersedes all prior Opinions, Statements, and Interpretations. In addition, the FASB has issued a number of Technical Bulletins to provide *guidance* (Technical Bulletins are not GAAP) on specific questions regarding the application of No. 13.

[¶807.1] Terminology

The terms associated with lease accounting are specifically defined in Statement No. 13.

Bargain Purchase Option. A payment at the end of the lease term by the lessee to the lessor, usually significantly below the estimated fair market value, which gives the lessee title to the property.

Bargain Renewal Option. Lessee's option to renew the lease at a bargain rental.

Capital Lease. Lease that meets one or more of the following four criteria:

• Lease transfers ownership to lessee during the term of the lease.

• Lease contains a bargain purchase option.

• Lease term is 75%, or more, of the economic useful life of the property.

• Present value of minimum lease payments equals 90%, or more, of the fair market value of the leased property, less the lessor's investment tax credit.

Contingent Rental. Rentals which can change in the future because the rental agreement is based upon unknown future events, i.e., future profits, future interest rates, future changes in a given price index.

Direct Financing Lease. Transfers substantially all of the risks and benefits of ownership of the leased property to the lessee. The lease does not result in any profit or loss to the lessor if the lessor is a manufacturer or dealer.

Estimated Economic Life. The useful life of the property, regardless of the term of the lease.

Estimated Residual Value. Estimated fair value of the property at the end of the lease; cannot be more than the estimated value at the inception of the lease.

Executory Costs. Costs such as taxes, insurance, and maintenance paid in connection with the leased property.

Fair Market Value. The price for which the property could be sold in an arm's-length transaction between unrelated parties.

Fair Rental. The rental for similar property in a similar neighborhood and geographic area.

Guaranteed Residual Value. An amount guaranteed by the lessee to the lessor for the estimated residual value of the asset at the end of the lease term.

Inception of Lease. The date of the lease agreement signed by all parties to the transaction.

Interest Rate Implicit. The interest rate that applies when the discounted present value of the minimum lease payments plus the unguaranteed salvage value is equal to the fair market value of the property, less any investment tax credit retained by the lessor.

Initial Direct Cost. Costs directly associated with the completion of a leasing transaction, i.e., legal fees, commissions, employee salaries (if any), credit investigations.

Lease Term. The fixed, noncancelable term of the lease agreement.

Lessor's Implicit Interest Rate. The lessor's rate of return on the leased property.

Lessee's Incremental Borrowing Rate. The interest rate the lessee would have to pay to borrow, for the same length of time as the lease, the funds necessary to have purchased the property.

Leverage Lease. The term applies only to lessors, as the lessee accounts for leveraged leases in the same manner as for nonleveraged leases. Leveraged leases can be considered to be direct-financing leases, but with four additional criteria:

• Three parties must be involved—a lessor, a lessee, and a creditor.

• The creditor's financing must be nonrecourse as to the credit of the lessor.

• Lessor's investment in the lease must decline in the early years of the lease and rise during the later years before final liquidation.

• Lessor's investment tax credit must be deferred and allocated to income over the life of the lease.

Minimum Lease Payment. Payments to be made during the term of the lease and must include a guaranteed residual value by the lessee, payment penalty for failure to renew the lease, and a bargain purchase option payment by the lessee at the end of the lease.

Minimum Rental Payment. The minimum payments to be made by the lessee to the lessor under the lease agreement.

Noncancelable Lease. A lease that is cancelable only upon some remote contingency, with the agreement of the lessor, or if a new lease is negotiated with the lessor.

Operating Lease. All of the different types of leases that are not a capital lease.

Related Parties. One or more persons or business entity with significant influence over the operating and financial policies of another person, or entity.

Sales-Type Lease. A lease that results in a profit or loss for a manufacturer or dealer. The benefits and risks of ownership are transferred to the lessee, the minimum lease payments are reasonably expected to be collected, and there are no uncertainties with respect to costs to be incurred by the lessor under the terms of the lease.

Unguaranteed Residual Value. The fair value of the leased property at the end of the lease that is not guaranteed by the lessee or by a third party.

[¶807.2]   Accounting Procedures

The main problem in accounting for leases is to determine whether the benefits and risks incident to ownership have been transferred from the lessor to the lessee. If so, the lessor treats the transaction as a sale, and the lessee as a purchase. Statement No. 13 reads:

> A lease that transfers substantially all of the benefits and risks incident to the ownership of property should be accounted for as the acquisition of an asset and the incurrence of an obligation by the lessee.

The matter becomes a question of substance over form. Some leases are nothing more than the right by a lessee to use the property of another (the lessor) for a limited period of time. GAAP does not recognize the obligations under such contracts as assets and liabilities in the financial statements of lessors and lessees. Other leases are essentially an installment purchase. In these instances, the substance of the transaction rather than the legal form determines the accounting requirements. Assets and liabilities, for example, for such a transaction would be taken into the accounting records of lessors and lessees in the same manner as any legal sale/purchase. The lessor would record the sale as a receivable for the future rent payments; the lessee would record the purchase as an asset and the rental obligation as the assumption of a liability.

[¶807.3]   A Summary of the Significant Accounting Considerations

The Lessor	*The Lessee*
Must classify the lease according to the substance of the transaction.	Must classify the lease according to the substance of the transaction.
Leases classified as either operating leases or one of three types of capital leases, i.e., direct-financing; sale-type; leveraged leases.	Classify leases as either operating or capital leases. Operating leases require a recognition of rent expense only. Capital leases require 1) recognition of the asset; 2) recognition of the liability incurred; 3) amortization of depreciation expense; and 4) interest expense on the liability.

In addition to meeting one of the four classifications test, lessor must apply two additional tests for a capital lease: 1) Rent collection must be reasonably certain; 2) future costs must be reasonably predictable.

Capital lease must meet one of the four tests (see definition of a capital lease).

Recognize rental income on a straight-line basis; depreciate the asset subject to operating leases.

Recognize interest income only on direct-financing and leveraged leases. Both gross profit and interest income are recognized on sales-type leases.

Recognize rent expense on operating leases on a straight-line basis. Recognize depreciation or amortization expense, interest expense, and executory costs on capital leases over the life of the lease. The recognized liability is separated into current and noncurrent items in the balance sheet.

[¶807.4]   Rules for Restatement:

1. Include the effects of leases in existence during periods covered by the financial statements

2. Balance sheets and income statements for periods beginning *after* Dec. 31, 1976, financial summaries and other data should be restated to conform with the new standards

3. All prior periods presented for comparative purposes should be restated where practicable per the new standards

4. For the earliest period *restated* (not *presented*), the cumulative effect on the beginning retained earnings should be determined and shown in the determination of net income for that entire earliest period restated. Disclose the amount and explain, if applicable, why it was impractical to restate any prior periods presented.

[¶808]   INTANGIBLE ASSETS

Intangible assets are categorized into two classes:

1. Identifiable intangible assets—those having specific identity and usually a known limited life. The limitation may be a legal regulation, a contractual agreement or the nature of the intangible itself; for example, a patent, copyright, franchise, trademark and the like.

2. Unidentifiable intangible assets—those having no specific identity and an unknown life. Goodwill is the most notable example.

Identifiable intangible assets should be recorded at their cost. If the asset is acquired in a transaction other than a purchase for cash, it is to be valued at its fair value or the fair value of the consideration given, whichever is more definitely determinable. If several identifiable intangible assets are acquired as a group, a separate cost should be established for each intangible asset. The cost or assigned basis should be amortized by systematic charges to income over the expected period of economic benefit usually set by law or by contract. If it becomes apparent that the period of economic benefit will be shorter or longer than that originally used, there should be an appropriate decrease or increase in annual amortization charges.

The costs of *unidentifiable* intangible assets (such as goodwill) are normally amortized on a straight-line basis over a period not exceeding forty years. Arbitrary shorter periods are not to be used unless specific factors pinpoint a shorter life.

Unidentifiable intangible assets are usually measured as the excess paid over the identifiable assets.

The cost of an intangible asset, including goodwill acquired in a business combination, should not be written off to income in the period of acquisition nor charged as a lump sum to capital surplus or to retained earnings, nor be reduced to a nominal amount at or immediately after acquisition.

The question of whether other costs of internally developed identifiable intangible assets are to be capitalized or expensed is not delineated by the Standards Board. Questions have arisen regarding the capitalization of the cost of a large initial advertising campaign for a new product or capitalizing the cost of training new employees. The interpretation is that there is no encouragement to capitalize these costs under existing standards.

[¶809] ## RESEARCH AND DEVELOPMENT COSTS (AND PATENTS)

Under the latest standards of financial accounting and reporting for research and development costs adopted in October, 1974, and the subsequent extensions of that section to cover applicability to business combinations accounted for by the "purchase" method, and applicability to computer software, research and development costs are to be *charged as expenses when incurred.* (Note that this is diametrically opposed to the old system of deferral and amortization.) (Note also that in changing to the direct expense method, previously amortized "R & D" costs should be treated as prior period adjustments.)

Research is planned search or critical investigation aimed at discovery of new knowledge with the hope that such knowledge will be useful in developing a new product or service or a new process or technique or in bringing about a significant improvement to an existing product or process.

Development is the translation of research findings or other knowledge into a plan or design for a new product or process or for a significant improvement to an existing product or process whether intended for sale or use. It includes the conceptual formulation, design and testing of product alternatives, construction of prototypes, and operation of pilot plants. It does not include routine or periodic alterations to existing products, production lines, manufacturing processes, and other on-going operations even though those alterations may represent improvements; and it does not include market research or market testing activities.

Typical activities which would be included in research and development costs (excluding those done for others under contract) are:

Laboratory research aimed at finding new knowledge

Searching for applications of findings

Concepts-forming and design of new product or processes

Testing of above

Modifications of above

Design, construction and testing of prototypes

Design of new tools, dies, etc, for new technology

Pilot plant posts not useful for commercial production

Engineering activity to the point of manufacture

Certain activities, however, are *excluded* from the definition of research and development and are either expensed or amortized depending upon the apparent periods benefited:

1. Engineering costs during early commercial production.
2. Quality costs during commercial production.
3. Break-down trouble-shooting costs during production.
4. Routine efforts to improve the product.
5. Adapting to a customer's requirement, if ordinary.
6. Existing product change-costs for seasonal reasons.
7. Routine designing of tools and dies, etc.
8. Costs of start-up facilities other than pilot plant or those specifically designed only for research and development work.
9. Legal work involved in patent applications or litigation, and the sale or licensing of patents.

In the following list, the *italicized* portions represent those elements of research and development costs and expenditures which should be *capitalized* and not expensed immediately. The non-italicized items are those which should be expensed immediately:

1. MATERIALS, EQUIPMENT AND FACILITIES: *The costs of materials (whether from the enterprise's normal inventory or acquired specially for research and development activities) and equipment or facilities that are acquired or constructed for research and development activities and that have alternative future uses (in research and development projects or otherwise) shall be capitalized as tangible assets when acquired or constructed.* The cost of such materials consumed in research and development activities and the depreciation of such equipment or facilities used in

those activities are research and development costs. However, the costs of materials, equipment, or facilities that are acquired or constructed for a particular research and development project and that have no alternative future uses (in other research and development projects or otherwise) and therefore no separate economic values are research and development costs at the time the costs are incurred.

2. PERSONNEL: Salaries and wages and other related costs of personnel engaged in research and development activities shall be included in research and development costs.

3. TANGIBLES PURCHASED FROM OTHERS: *The costs of intangibles that are purchased from others for use in research and development activities and that have alternative future uses (in research and development projects or otherwise) shall be capitalized and amortized as intangible assets in accordance with Section 5141.* The amortization of those intangible assets used in research and development activities is a research and development cost. However, the costs of intangibles that are purchased from others for a particular research and development project and that have no alternative future uses (in other research and development projects or otherwise) and therefore no separate economic values are research and development costs at the time the costs are incurred.

4. CONTRACT SERVICES: The costs of services performed by others in connection with the research and development activities of an enterprise, including research and development conducted by others in behalf of the enterprise, shall be included in research and development costs.

5. INDIRECT COSTS: Research and development costs shall include a reasonable allocation of indirect costs. However, general and administrative costs that are not clearly related to research and development activities shall not be included as research and development costs.

Research and development costs should *not* be charged as part of factory overhead because this handling would result in partial deferral to closing inventory. The standard requires expensing as incurred.

[¶809.1]   Writing Off a Patent

A patent has a legal life of 17 years. However, most companies write off patents in much shorter periods since their useful lives are generally shorter than 17 years. Reasons for writing off patents in less than 17 years are as follows:

(1) The patent could have been purchased many years after issuance.

(2) The patent is for a current-fad-type item and sales can be expected to last for only a year or two.

(3) A newer patented item appears on the market which puts an end to the economic usefulness of the patent.

Some companies buy a patent just to protect an older patent they have from becoming outmoded. The cost of the new patent purchase should be written off over the remaining life of the old patent.

[¶809.2]   Copyrights

A copyright has a legal life of 50 years after author's death, with those prior to December 31, 1977, renewable for 47 years. However, here, as in the case of patents, copyright costs are usually written off in a much shorter period since the economic usefulness of a copyright usually is only a few years. Since the cost of obtaining a copyright usually is nominal (unlike a patent), the amount is usually not amortized but is written off immediately to income. Publisher-held copyrights last 75 years, unless reassigned to the author.

[¶809.3]   Franchises

Franchises are identifiable intangibles and, by contract, have a certain number of years to run. They should be written off over that contractual period. Sometimes, a franchise can be terminated by the will of the licensor. In such case, an immediate write-off may be justified.

[¶809.4]   Trademarks

A trademark is an identifiable intangible, usually with an indeterminable life and should, therefore, be written off over forty years unless a shorter life can be determined with reasonable certainty.

In the same category are trade names, brand names, secret formulae and processes, designs, and the right to use certain labels.

[¶810]   GOODWILL

In acquiring a business in an exchange or combination, each individual asset is measured at its fair value. The excess exchange price over those values assigned to individual assets is termed and recorded as 'goodwill.'

Goodwill is an unidentifiable intangible asset. It has no permanent existence (such as land). It has no definite, measurable life. It has neither limited nor unlimited usefulness. Thus, delaying write-off until a loss is certain may cause a dilemma, as would an early write-off. Therefore, the AICPA, in recognition of this problem, has, for conformity, suggested the arbitrary period of write-off at forty years, or less. In addition, the straight-line method of amortization should be used in expensing goodwill.

The amortization of goodwill is not deductible for tax purposes. Since the expensing of goodwill creates a lower net income for financial statement purposes than the taxable income for tax purposes, there arises a *permanent* difference as opposed to a timing difference.

[¶810.1]   Establishing the Goodwill Factor

Goodwill is generally based upon the assumption that earnings will continue, but not forever. The good name and reputation of the sellers will continue to influence the business for a while in the hands of the new owners. It is this lingering influence which is the nature of goodwill. It may be the result of any of, or a combination of, the following:

1. A prized location;
2. Exceptional operating efficiency;
3. Unusually satisfactory relations with customers or personnel;
4. Special expertise in business techniques;
5. An unusual product with customer acceptance.

In negotiation to buy or sell a business, one of the problems is always the setting of a mutually satisfactory price on the value of goodwill—over and above the net fair value of the identifiable assets (minus liabilities).

Here are six varied methods of computing goodwill:

Assumed facts for computing the goodwill value; net assets, $1,000,000; profits of last 5 years: $190,000, $195,000; $190,000, $215,000, $210,000; total $1,000,000; average, $200,000

(1) *Years' purchase of past annual profits*

Profits of second preceding year	$ 215,000
Profits of first preceding year	210,000
Total and price to be paid for goodwill	$ 425,000

(2) *Year's purchase of average past profits*

Average profits of last 5 years (as stated above)	$ 200,000
Multiply by number of years of purchase	2
Goodwill	$ 400,000

(3) *Years' purchase of excess profits*

Year Preceding Sale	Profits	12½% of Net Assets	Excess
Third	$190,000	$125,000	$ 65,000
Second	215,000	125,000	90,000
First	210,000	125,000	85,000
Total Payment for Goodwill			$ 240,000

(4) *Years' purchase of average excess profits*

Average profits of past 5 years	$ 200,000
Deduct 12½% of $1,000,000	125,000
Excess	75,000
Multiply by number of years of purchase	3
Goodwill	$ 225,000

109

(5) *Capitalized profits, minus net assets*
Capitalized value of average net profits, or total value of business:
$200,000 ÷ 12½% $1,600,000
Deduct agreed value of net assets other than goodwill 1,000,000

Goodwill .... $ 600,000

(6) *Excess profits capitalized*
Average profits of past 5 years .... $ 200,000
Deduct profits regarded as applicable to net assets
acquired—12½% of $1,000,000 125,000

Remaining profits, regarded as indicative of goodwill .... $ 75,000

Goodwill = $75,000 ÷ 25% .... $ 300,000

[¶811] ORGANIZATION EXPENSES

When a corporation is created, there are numerous expenses involved in its creation. Among these are legal fees, stock certificate costs, underwriters' fees, corporation fees, commissions, promotion expenses, etc.

Under Section 248 of the tax law, organization expenses are to be written off over a minimum five-year period. This is the factor which causes many corporations to write organization costs off over that period, though the standards permit immediate write-off.

[¶812] SECRET FORMULAS AND PROCESSES

A formula or process known only to a specific producer may be a valuable asset even though there is no patent involved. Such property usually has economic benefit which continues indefinitely instead of a limited period.

In those instances in which the life is indeterminate, the forty-year period should be used, amortizing on a straight-line basis, as long as benefit continues and cannot be reasonably pinpointed or rejected.

[¶813] RETAIL LAND SALES*

For periods ending on and after Dec. 31, 1972, new requirements for financial reporting of retail land sales were promulgated by the Committee on Land Development Companies of the AICPA. Under the guides (which apply to retail lot sales on a volume basis with down payments smaller than those involved in

---

*Reference for this topic: *Accounting for Retail Land Sales* (An AICPA Industry Accounting Guide), AICPA 1973, 41 pages.

casual sales), payments made on such sales are treated as deposits and not recognized as sales under either the accrual method or the installment method until they equal at least 10% of the contract price, the cancellation period has expired, and promised performance becomes predictable.

[¶813.1]   Accrual Method

The accrual method is required on a project-by-project basis if *all* the following conditions are met:

1. The properties clearly will be useful for residential or recreational purposes without legal restriction when the payment period is completed, and

2. The project's planned improvements must have progress beyond preliminary stages and there is evidence that the work will be completed according to plan, and

3. The receivable cannot be subordinated to new loans on the property, except for construction purposes and collection experience on such contracts is the same as on those not subordinated, and

4. Collection experience of the project indicates that collectibility of receivable balances is reasonably predictable and that 90% of the contracts in force six months after sales are recorded will be collected in full.

All other contracts must be accounted for by the installment method under which revenue is recognized as payments are received, and related selling costs may be deferred.

There are three principal aspects with respect to reporting land sales. They are: (1) timing of revenue, (2) deferral of revenue for future performance obligations, and (3) measurement of revenue. The earlier practice was to count as income the full contract price at the time the contract was executed, even though a buyer made only a small down payment and the completion of the contract was uncertain.

For example, a buyer entered a contract with a land development company for the purchase of a $20,000 homesite. He made a $500 down payment and promised to pay the balance before completion. Under prior rules, the land development company would have counted the entire $20,000 as income, even though a large percentage of such contracts might never have reached completion.

[¶813.2]   Timing of Revenue

Under the present rules, the development company doesn't count the $20,000 as income unless there is a reasonable probability of completion and it collects a down payment of at least 10%.

Each company looks to its own experience to provide a reasonable prediction of the percentage of all the contracts that will be completed. The past sales experience will indicate how much should be deducted from the overall gross sales figure and provided for in an allowance for contract cancellations. When a contract is canceled, the receivable from the contract is charged to the allowance account.

The rules also include criteria for determining when a contract cancellation has occurred. According to the guidelines, a contract is considered canceled if less than 25% of the contract price has been paid and the buyer is in default for 90 days or more. If more than 25% but less than 50% of the contract price has been paid, the default period is 120 days; more than 50%, the default period is 150 days.

Where a company's collection experience cannot provide a reasonable prediction of completions, the installment method must be used, not the accrual method. Where refund period policies exist, no portion of the deposit receipts should be reported until the refund period has passed.

[¶813.3] Deferral of Revenue for Future Performance Obligations

Where there are significant future-performance requirements, the earning process is incomplete. Therefore, the portion of the income representing reasonable compensation for the improvement effort and risk must be deferred until the work is performed. The amount deferred is in the ratio of revenue that the unexpended costs bear to the total costs expected to be incurred.

[¶813.4] Measurement of Revenue

Here, we deal with the specific value that should be ascribed to long-term receivables where the interest rate is less than the prevailing rate for an obligation with similar terms, security, and risk.

The credit ratings of retail land purchasers generally approximate those of users of retail consumer installment credit provided by commercial banks and established retail organizations. Accordingly, the effective annual yield on the net investment in land contract receivables should not be less than the minimum annual rate charged to installment borrowers by commercial banks and established retail organizations.

9

Liabilities And Long-Term Debt

[¶901]   **IDENTIFICATION OF
                  CURRENT LIABILITIES**

The category of current liabilities normally consists of obligations which must be paid within one year. Some other current liabilities are as follows:

(1) Obligations whose liquidation is reasonably expected to require the use of existing current assets or the creation of other current liabilities.

(2) Obligations for items such as payables incurred in the acquisition of material and supplies which are to be used in the production of goods, or in providing services which are offered for sale.

(3) Collections received in advance pertaining to the delivery of goods or the performance of services which will be liquidated in the ordinary course of business by delivery of such goods or services. But note that advances received which represent long-term deferments are not to be shown as current liabilities. An example of this would be a long-term warranty or the advance receipt by a lessor of rentals for the final period of a ten-year lease as a condition to the execution of the lease.

(4) Debts which arise from operations directly relating to the operating cycle. Examples are accruals for wages, salaries, commissions, rentals, royalties, and income and other taxes; short-term debts which are expected to be liquidated within a relatively short period of time, usually one year; short-term debt arising from acquisition of capital assets; the current portion of a serial note; amounts required to be expended within one year under a sinking fund; loans accompanied by a pledge of a life insurance policy which by its terms is to be repaid within one year. When the intent is to repay a loan on life insurance from the proceeds of the policy received upon maturity or cancellation, the obligation should not be included as a current liability.

(5) Amounts which are expected to be required to cover expenditures within the year for known obligations, the amount of which can only approximately be determined. An example is a provision for accruing bonus payments. When an amount is expected to be required to be paid to persons unknown (for example, in connection with a guarantee of products sold), a reasonable amount should be included as a current liability.

It does not include debts to be liquidated by funds accumulated in non-current assets, or long-term obligations incurred to provide working capital for long periods. A contractual obligation falling due within a one-year period which is expected to be refinanced on a long-term basis should also be excluded from current liabilities. Bonds maturing within a one-year period which are to be refinanced by the issuance of new bonds should not therefore be included as current liabilities. Doing so would give a wrong impression of the company's working capital. The bonds should remain among long-term liabilities, with a footnote indicating the maturity date and the contemplated refinancing.

(6) Accounts payable for goods purchased before the end of the accounting period and for which title has passed but which have not been received.

(7) Liabilities for services rendered to your company before the end of the period but not yet billed.

(8) Dividends which have been declared but have not yet been paid.

(9) Liabilities to be liquidated in merchandise arising from the issuance of due bills, merchandise coupon books, and gift certificates.

(10) A liability must be accrued for employees' rights to receive compensation for future absences under certain conditions:

    a. If the employees' right to compensation for future absences is related to services already rendered to the company.

    b. The obligation relates to accumulated or vested rights.

    c. Payment of the compensation is probable.

    d. The amount of the compensation can be reasonably estimated.

Vacations, illness, and holidays are examples of liabilities to be accrued, if compensation is expected to be paid.

This rule does not apply to such items as termination pay, deferred compensation, stock (or stock options) issued to employees, nor to such fringe benefits as group insurance or long-term disability pay.

[¶902]   **LONG-TERM DEBT**

[¶902.1]   **Bond Premium or Discount**

Liabilities are measured at amounts established in exchanges, usually the amounts to be paid, sometimes discounted. Conceptually, a liability is measured at the amount of cash to be paid discounted to the time the liability is incurred . . . Bonds and other long-term liabilities are in effect measured at the discounted amount of the future cash payments for interest and principal.

The difference between the face amount of the liability to be paid in the future and the actual net proceeds received in the present for incurring of this debt is amortized over the period to the maturity due-date. When this amount of periodic calculated interest is combined with the nominal face-amount of interest actually paid to debt-holders, the difference is amortized, giving a level, "effective" rate, and is called the "interest" method of amortization and is an acceptable method to be used.

Statement presentation: Unamortized discount or premium or debentures or other long-term debt should be shown on the balance sheet as a direct deduction or addition to the face value. It should *not* be shown as a deferred item. The amortized portion of either premium or discount should be shown as an interest item on the income statement. Issue costs should be treated as deferred charges.

[¶903] EARLY EXTINGUISHMENT OF DEBT

Bonds and other long-term obligations often contain provisions giving the bond issuer an option to retire the bonds before their maturity date. This option is often exercised in connection with the issuance of new bonds at favorable rates (a refunding).

Usually, the amount paid for early extinguishment will be different from the face amount due and also different from the "net carrying value" of the debt. The "net carrying value" is the sum due at maturity plus or minus the remaining unamortized premium or discount (and cost of issuance).

On January 1, 1973, standards were adopted for the treatment of this early extinguishment of debt:

1. The difference between the reacquisition price and the *net carrying amount* of the debt (face value plus/minus unamortized items) should be recognized currently *in income* as gain or loss and shown as a separate item, and, if material, shown as an *extraordinary item*, net of related income tax effect.

2. Disclosure of pertinent details should be made.

3. Gains or losses should not be amortized to future periods.

4. The extinguishment of *convertible* debt before maturity should be handled in the same manner.

5. The criteria of "unusual nature" and "infrequency of occurrence" do *not* apply here for the classification of the early extinguishment of debt as extraordinary. The determining factor for classification is *"materiality."*

These existing standards, in effect, prohibit the old practice of applying gains or losses on debt refunded to any new issues of similar obligations.

[¶904] TROUBLED DEBT RESTRUCTURINGS

A restructuring of debt constitutes a troubled debt restructuring if the creditor, for economic or legal reasons related to the debtor's financial difficulties, grants a concession to the debtor that it would not otherwise consider. That concession stems either from an agreement between the creditor and debtor, or is imposed by law or a court.

Debtors: A debtor that transfers its receivables from third parties, real estate, or other assets to a creditor to settle fully a payable, shall recognize a gain on restructuring of payables. The gain shall be measured by the excess of (1) carrying amount of payable settled (the face amount increased or decreased by the applicable accrued interest and applicable unamortized premium, discount finance charges or issue costs), over (2) the face value of the assets transferred to the creditor. This difference is a gain or loss on the transfer of assets. The debtor shall include that gain or loss in measuring net income for the period of transfer, reported as provided in APB #30 (section 2012) ''Reporting Results of Operations.''

A debtor that grants an equity interest to a creditor to settle fully a payable shall account for the equity interest at its fair value. The difference between fair value of the interest granted and the carrying amount of the payable is recognized as a gain on restructuring of payables. Gains on restructuring of payables shall be aggregated and, if material, shall be classified as an extraordinary item, net of related income tax effect.

Creditors: When a creditor receives from a debtor in full satisfaction of a receivable, either (1) receivables from third parties, real estate, or other assets, or (2) shares of stock, the creditor shall account for those assets at their fair value at the time of restructuring. The excess of the recorded investment in receivables satisfied, over the fair value of assets received, is a loss to be recognized and included in net income for the period of restructuring and reported according to APB #30 (section 2012).

A creditor shall disclose the following information pertaining to troubled debt restructurings:

1. For outstanding receivables whose terms have been modified, by major category:
   (a) the aggregate recorded investment,
   (b) the gross income that would have been recorded in the period then ended, if those receivables had been current in accordance with their original terms and had been outstanding throughout the period, or since origination, if held for part of the period, and
   (c) the amount of interest income on those receivables that was included in net income for the period.
2. The amount of commitments to lend additional funds to debtors using receivables whose terms have been modified in troubled debt restructurings.

116

Commitments that are associated with a supplier's financing arrangements which involve an unconditional purchase obligation must be disclosed. These obligations are terms "take-or-pay" contracts.

The following must be disclosed:

1. The nature of the obligation.

2. The amount of the fixed and determinable obligation, in the aggregate and for each of the next five years.

3. A description of the obligation that is variable, and the purchases in each year for which an income statement is presented.

Disclosure of future payments on long-term borrowings and redeemable stock must also be disclosed. The maturities, sinking fund requirements (if any), and redemption requirements for each of the next five years must be shown.

For additional situations and more detailed information, see FASB Statement No. 15, *Accounting by Debtors and Creditors for Troubled Debt Restructuring*, June, 1977.

10

Equity

STOCKHOLDERS' EQUITY

"Stockholders' equity" is the most commonly used term to describe the section of the balance sheet encompassing the corporation's capital and retained earnings. Other terms used are "net worth" or "capital and surplus."

Stockholders' equity consists of three broad source classifications:

1. Investments made by owners:
   Capital Stock (Common and/or Preferred)—at par value (legal value) or stated amount
   Additional Paid-In Capital—"In Excess of Par," "Capital Surplus," etc.

2. Income (loss) generated by operations:
   Retained Earnings—the accumulated undistributed annual profits (losses), after taxes and dividends

3. Appraisal Capital—resulting from the revaluation of assets over historical cost (*not* in conformity with GAAP)

Changes in shareholders' equity, primarily in retained earnings, are caused by:

1. Periodic net income (loss) after taxes
2. Dividends declared
3. Prior period adjustments of retained earnings
4. Contingency reserves (appropriations of retained earnings)
5. Recapitalizations:
   A. Stock dividends and split-ups
   B. Changing par or stated value
   C. Reducing capital
   D. Quasi-reorganizations
   E. Stock reclassifications
   F. Substituting debt for stock
6. Treasury stock dealings
7. Business combinations
8. Certain unrealized gains and losses
9. Donations

118

[¶1002] CAPITAL STOCK

Capital stock is the capital contributed by the stockholders to the corporation.

[¶1002.1] Common Stock

The common stockholders are the residual owners of the corporation; that is, they own whatever is left after all preceding claims are paid off. By definition, common stock is "a stock which is subordinate to all other stocks of the issuer."

When a corporation has a single class of stock, it is often called "capital stock" instead of "common stock." The three aspects of stock ownership are (1) dividends, (2) claims against assets on liquidation, and (3) shares in management. As to these aspects of ownership, common stockholders have the following rights: to dividends, common stockholders have no fixed rights but, on the other hand, are limited to no maximum payment; their claim against the assets of the corporation on liquidation is last in the order of priority, following all creditors and all other equity interests. The common stockholders, by statute, must have a voice in management. Their voice is often to the exclusion of all other equity interests, but they may also share their management rights with other classes of stock.

Common stock may be classified:

(1) Par and No-Par Stock: Par stock is stock with a stated, legal dollar value, whereas no-par stock lacks such a given value. The distinction today is largely an academic one. However, state laws regarding stock dividends and split-ups and the adjustments of par value may affect the accounting treatment of such dividends.

(2) Classes of Common Stock: Common stock may be divided into separate classes—e.g., class A, class B, etc. Usually, the class distinction deals with the right to vote for separate directors, or one class may have the right to vote and one class may not. Class stock is a typical technique used where a minority group wishes to maintain control.

[¶1002.2] Preferred Stock

The second major type of capital stock is preferred stock, stock which has some preference with regard to dividend payments or distribution of assets on liquidation. In the usual situation, preferred stock will have a preference on liquidation, to the extent of the par value of the stock. In addition, its right to dividends depends on the following classification:

(1) Participating and Nonparticipating Right: If the preferred has a right to a fixed dividend each year but has not the right to share in any additional divi-

119

dends over and above the stated amount, it is nonparticipating preferred. If it is entitled to a share of any dividends over and above those to which it has priority, it is called participating. For example, a preferred may have the right to a 5% annual dividend and then share equally with the common stock in dividends after a dividend (equal to the preferred per-share dividend) has been paid to the common stockholders.

(2) **Convertible Preferred Stock:** Convertible preferred is stock which may, at the holder's option, be exchanged for common. The terms of the exchange and the conversion period are set forth on the preferred certificate. Thus one share of $100 par preferred may be convertible beginning one year after issue into two shares of common. If the preferred stockholder converts, he will own two shares of common at a cost to him of $50 per share (this assumes he purchased the preferred at par). A company will issue a convertible security at a time when it needs funds but for one reason or another cannot or does not wish to issue common stock. For example, in a weak stock market, common may be poorly received while a convertible preferred can be privately placed with a large institutional investor. The conversion privilege, from the point of view of the purchaser, is a ''sweetener'' since it affords the opportunity to take a full equity position in the future if the company prospers. The issuer may be quite satisfied to give the conversion privilege because it means that (assuming earnings rise) the preferred stock, with a prior and fixed dividend claim, will gradually be eliminated in exchange for common shares.

Accounting for a convertible preferred issue follows the usual rules. That is, when the preferred is first issued, a separate capital account will be set up, to which will be credited the par value of the outstanding stock. When conversion takes place, an amount equal to the par of the converted stock is debited to the preferred account. The common stock account will be credited with an amount equal to the par or stated value of the shares issued in exchange for the preferred. Any excess will go to capital surplus.

Both participating (1) and convertible (2) preferred stocks above must be considered in the computation of earnings per share.

(3) **Cumulative and Noncumulative:** A corporation which lacks earnings or surplus cannot pay dividends on its preferred stock. In that case, the question arises whether the passed dividend must be paid in future years. If past dividends do accumulate and must be paid off, the stock is cumulative; otherwise, noncumulative.

The preferred may share voting rights equally with the common stock, it may lack voting rights under any circumstances, or it may have the right to vote only if one or more dividends are passed. In the latter case, the preferred may have the exclusive right to vote for a certain number of directors to be sure that its interests as a class are protected.

For cumulative stock, the dividends must be accrued each year (even if upaid), unless issued with an ''only as earned'' provision. The effect on earnings per share is the extent of the reduction of net income for this accrual.

[¶1002.3]   Par Value, Stated Capital, and Capital Stock Accounts

The money a corporation receives for its stock is in a unique category. It is variously referred to as "a cushion for creditors," "a trust fund," and similar expressions. The point is that in a corporation which gives its stockholders limited liability, the only funds to which the creditors of the corporation can look for repayment of their debts in the event the corporation suffers losses is the money received for stock, which constitutes the stated capital account. Consequently, most state corporation statutes require a number of steps to be taken before a corporation can reduce its stated capital. These steps include approval by the stockholders and the filing of a certificate with the proper state officer, so that creditors may be put on notice of the reduction in capital.

Stated capital is actually divided into separate accounts, each account for a particular class of stock. Thus, a corporation may have outstanding a class A common, a class B common, a first preferred, a second preferred, etc. Each class would have its own account, which would show the number of shares of the class authorized by the certificate of incorporation, the number actually issued and the consideration received by the corporation.

It is at this point that the distinction between par and no-par stock becomes important. Par stock is rarely sold for less than its par value, although it may be sold for more. In many states, it is illegal to sell stock at a discount from par, and even when not illegal, there may be a residual stockholder liability for that original discount to the creditors. In any case, an amount equal to the par value of the stock must be credited to its capital account, with any excess going into a surplus account.

In the case of no-par stock, the corporation, either through its board of directors or at a stockholders' meeting, assigns part of the consideration received as stated capital for the stock and treats the rest as a credit to a capital surplus account. Treating part of the consideration received as stated capital is the equivalent of giving the stock a par value.

[¶1002.4]   Capital Stock Issued for Property

Where capital stock is issued for the acquisition of property in a non-cash transfer, measurement of owners' investment is usually determined by using the fair market value of the assets (and/or the discounted present value of any liabilities transferred).

When the fair value of the assets transferred cannot be measured, the market value of the stock issued may be used instead for establishing the value of the property received.

When the acquisition is an entire business, the principle of "fair value" is extended to cover each and every asset acquired (other than goodwill). If the fair value of the *whole* business is considered to be *more* than the individual values, that excess is considered to be goodwill.

121

The difference between fair value put on the assets received and the *par value* (stated) of the stock issued goes to the Capital-in-Excess of Par Value account (or Additional Paid-in Capital, etc.) as either a positive or negative (discount) amount. Note that this does *not* pertain to any "negative" goodwill which might have been created; said negative goodwill, if any, should be used to reduce, immediately, the non-current assets (except investment securities), proportionately to zero, if necessary, with any remaining excess to be deferred and amortized as favorable goodwill is amortized.

[¶1002.5] Capital in Excess of Par or Stated Value (Capital Surplus)

The term "capital surplus" is still widely used, although the preferred terminology is "capital in excess of par" or "additional paid-in capital."

The capital in excess of par account is credited with capital received by the corporation which is not part of par value of stated capital. It is primarily the excess of consideration received over par value or the amount of consideration received for no-par stock which is not assigned as stated capital.

In addition, donations of capital to the corporation are credited to this account. If stated capital is ever reduced as permitted by law, the transfer is from the capital stock account to this capital surplus account.

This account is also credited for the excess of market value *over* par value for stock dividends (which are not split-ups) and for the granting of certain stock options and rights.

[¶1003] RETAINED EARNINGS

Accounting Terminology Bulletin No. 1 (August, 1953) recommended the following (terminology bulletins do not have authoritative status, but are issued as useful guides):

1. The abandonment of the term "surplus;"
2. The term "earned surplus" be replaced with such terms that indicated the source such as:
   Retained Earnings
   Retained Income
   Accumulated Earnings
   Earnings Retained for Use in the Business

Retained earnings are the accumulated undistributed past and current year's earnings, net of taxes and dividends paid and declared.

Portions of retained earnings may be set aside for certain contingencies, appropriated for such purposes as possible future inventory losses, sinking funds, etc.

A Statement of Changes in Retained Earnings is one of the basic financial statements *required* for fair presentation of results of operation and financial condition to conform with GAAP. It shows net income, dividends, prior period adjustments. A Statement of Other Changes in Owners' Equity shows additional investments by owners, retirements of owners' interests and similar events (if these are few and simple, they are put in the notes).

Regardless of how a company displays its undistributed earnings, or the disclosures thereof, for tax purposes, the actual earnings and profits which could have been or are still subject to distribution as "dividends" *under IRS regulations* may, under some circumstances, retain that characteristic for the purpose of ordinary income taxation to the ultimate recipient. (See Tax Section of this book.) The AICPA has no requirement for this disclosure other than normal requirement for the "periods presented," which would usually show the activity in retained earnings for only two years and not prior.

[¶1004] PRIOR PERIOD ADJUSTMENTS

Under FASB Statement #16 *Prior Period Adjustments,* issued June 1977, only the following rare types of items should be treated as prior period adjustments and *not* be included in the determination of current period net income:

1. Correction of an error (material) in prior financial statements; and
2. Realization of income tax pre-acquisition operating loss benefits of *purchased subsidiaries.*

Corrections of errors are *not* changes in accounting *estimates.* Error corrections are those resulting from:

1. Mathematical errors;
2. Erroneous application of accounting principles;
3. Misuse of, or oversight of, facts existing at a prior statement period.

(Changes in accounting *estimates* result from *new* information or developments, which sharpen and improve judgment.)

Litigation settlements and income tax adjustments *no longer* meet the definition of prior period adjustments. However, for *interim periods only* (of the current fiscal year), material items of this nature should be treated as prior interim adjustments to the identifiable period of related business activity.

Goodwill may not be written off as a prior period adjustment.

Retroactive adjustment should be made of all comparative periods presented, reflecting changes to particular items, net income and retained earnings balances. The tax effects should also be reflected and shown. Disclosure of the effects of the restatement should be made.

[¶1005] CONTINGENCY RESERVES

A "contingency" is defined as "an existing condition, situation, or set of circumstances involving uncertainty as to possible gain or loss to an enterprise that will ultimately be resolved when one or more events occur or fail to occur."
Loss contingencies fall in three categories:

1. Probable
2. Reasonably possible
3. Remote.

In deciding whether to accrue the estimated loss by charging income or setting aside an appropriation of retained earnings, or merely to make a disclosure of the contingency in the notes to the financial statement, the following standards have been set:

Accrue a charge to income if *both* of the following conditions are met at the date of the financial statements:

1. Information available *before* the issuance of the financial statements indicates that probably the asset will be impaired or a liability incurred; and
2. A *reasonable* estimate of the loss *can* be made.

(When a contingent loss is probable but the reasonable estimate of the loss can only be made in terms of a range, the amount shall be accrued for the loss. When some amount within the range appears at the time to be a better estimate than any other amount within the range, that amount shall be accrued. When no amount within the range is a better estimate than any other amount, the minimum amount in the range shall be accrued.)

If discovery of the above impairment occurs *after* the date of the statements, disclosure should be made and pro-forma supplementary financial data presented giving effect to the occurrence as of the balance sheet date.

When a contingent loss is only *reasonably possible* or the probable loss cannot be estimated, an estimate of the *range* of loss should be made or a narrative description given to indicate that *no* estimate was possible. Disclosure should be made; but no accrual.

When the contingency is *remote*, disclosure should be made when it is in the nature of a guarantee. Other remote contingencies are not required to be disclosed, but they may be, if desired, for more significant reporting.

General reserves for unspecified business risks are not to be accrued and no disclosure is required.

Appropriations for loss contingencies from retained earnings must be shown, within the stockholders' Equity section of the balance sheet and clearly identified as such.

Examples of loss contingencies are:

1. Collectibility of receivables.

2. Obligations related to product warranties and product defects.

3. Risk of loss or damage of enterprise property by fire, explosion, or other hazards.

4. Threat of expropriation of assets.

5. Pending or threatened litigation.

6. Actual or possible claims and assessments.

7. Risk of loss from catastrophes assumed by property and casualty insurance companies including reinsurance companies.

8. Guarantees of indebtedness of others.

9. Obligations of commercial banks under "standby letters of credit."

10. Agreements to repurchase receivables (or to repurchase the related property) that have been sold.

Handling of these loss contingencies depends upon the nature of the loss probability and the reasonableness of estimating the loss.

[¶1006] RECAPITALIZATIONS

Essentially, a recapitalization means changing the structure of the capital accounts. It can also mean a reshuffling between equity and debt. A recapitalization may be done voluntarily by the corporation; or it may be part of a reorganization proceeding in a court, pursuant to a bankruptcy or a reorganization petition filed by the corporation or its creditors.

In almost all cases of recapitalizations, stockholder approval is required at some point during the process. This is because a recapitalization may affect the amount of stated capital of the corporation or change the relationships between the stockholders and the corporation or between classes of stockholders. The different categories of recapitalizations are discussed in the following paragraphs.

STOCK SPLIT-UPS, STOCK DIVIDENDS AND SPLIT-UPS IN THE FORM OF STOCK DIVIDENDS

[¶1006.1] Split-Up

A split-up involves dividing the outstanding shares into a larger number; for example, two for one. In a two-for-one split, each stockholder receives a certificate for additional shares equal to the amount of shares he is presently holding. The split-up is reflected in the corporate books by reducing the par value or the stated value of the outstanding shares. Thus if shares with a par value of $10 are split two for one, the new par becomes $5. No entry is necessary, other than a memo entry. The stockholder adjusts his basis for the unit number of shares.

Reverse Split: The opposite of a split-up is a reverse split, which results in a lesser number of outstanding shares. Stockholders turn in their old certificates and receive a new certificate for one-half former holdings. The par value or stated value is adjusted to show the higher price per share. A reverse split is sometimes used in order to increase the price of the stock immediately on the open market.

[¶1006.2]   Stock Dividends

As far as the stockholder is concerned, a stock dividend is the same as the stock split; he receives additional shares, merely changing his unit-basis of holding. But the effect is quite different from the point of view of the corporation. A stock dividend requires a transfer from retained earnings of the *market value* of the shares. Capital stock is credited for the par value and capital in excess of par value is credited for the excess of market price over par. (When the shareholder has the option of receiving cash, he must report the dividend as ordinary income.)

Dividends are presumed to be distributions which do not affect the market price because they are *less* than 20% to 25% of the number of previously outstanding shares.

[¶1006.3]   Stock Split-up Effected in the Form of a Dividend

Usually, a stock distribution is either a dividend or a split-up. However, there is another type of distribution, which, because of certain state legal requirements pertaining to the minimum requirements for or the changing of par value, necessitates a different nomenclature.

In those instances where the stock dividend is so great as to materially reduce the market value, it is by nature and AICPA definition a ''split-up.'' However, because certain states require that retained earnings must be capitalized in order to maintain par value, the AICPA standards recommend that those types of transactions be described by the corporation as a ''split-up effected in the form of a dividend.'' The entry would then be a reduction of retained earnings and an increase in capital stock for the *par value* of the distribution. For income tax purposes, the corporation may be required to show this reduction of retained earnings as a Schedule M adjustment and may technically still have to consider it as available for ordinary-rate ultimate distribution.

[¶1007]   CHANGING PAR OR STATED VALUE OF STOCK

This type of recapitalization involves changing from par to no par or vice versa. This is usually done in conjunction with a reduction of stated capital. A corporation, for example, may decide to change its stock from par stock to no-par stock in order to take advantage of lower franchise fees and transfer taxes. Or no-par shares may be changed to shares having par value to solve legal problems existing under particular state statutes. A par value stock which is selling in the market at a price lower than its par must be changed if the corporation intends to issue new stock, because of some state laws which prohibit a corporation from selling its par value stock for less than par value. In such case, the corporation may reduce par value or may change the par to no par, thereby, the new stock can be given a stated value equivalent to the price it can bring in the open market.

[¶1008]   QUASI-REORGANIZATIONS

Current or future years' charges should not be made against capital surplus (as distinguished from "earned surplus") however created, instead of the income accounts.

An exception to this rule (called "readjustment") occurs when "a corporation elects to restate its assets, capital stock and surplus and thus avail itself of permission to relieve its future income account or earned surplus account of charges which would otherwise be made there against." In which event, the corporation "should make a clear report to its shareholders of the restatements proposed to be made; and obtain their formal consent. It should present a fair balance sheet as at the date of the readjustment, in which the readjustments of the carrying amounts are reasonably complete, in order that there may be no continuation of the circumstances which justify charges to capital surplus."

As an example of how this readjustment might occur, suppose that a company has a deficit in its retained earnings (earned surplus) of $100,000. By revaluing its assets upward, it is possible for this company to create a capital surplus account for the write-up to fair value, then write-off the deficit in retained earnings to that account. From then on, a new earned surplus account should be established and the fact be disclosed for ten years.

[¶1009]   STOCK RECLASSIFICATIONS

Another category of stock recapitalization involves reclassifying the existing stock. This means that outstanding stock of a particular class is exchanged for stock of another class. For example, several outstanding issues of preferred stock may be consolidated into a single issue. Or, common stock may be exchanged for preferred stock, or vice versa. The object in this type of reclassification is to simplify the capital structure, which in many cases is necessary in order to make a public offering or sometimes to eliminate dividend arrearages on preferred stock by offering a new issue of stock in exchange for canceling such arrearages.

[¶1010] SUBSTITUTING DEBT FOR STOCK

One form of recapitalization that has become popular in some areas involves substituting bonds for stock.

The advantage to the corporation is the substitution of tax-deductible interest on bonds for nondeductible dividends on preferred stock. Of course, where we are dealing with a closely-held corporation, substituting debt for stock in a manner to give the common stockholders a pro rata portion of the debt may be interpreted for tax purposes as "thin" capitalization, and the bonds may be treated as stock anyhow.

Also, to attract new money into the corporation, it is advantageous to consider the issuance of convertible debt securities—bonds to which are attached the rights (warrants) to buy common stock of the company at a specified price. The advantages of this type of security are:

1. An interest rate which is lower than the issuer could establish for nonconvertible debt;

2. An initial conversion price greater than the market value of the common stock;

3. A conversion price which does not decrease.

The portion of proceeds from these securities which can be applied to the warrants should be credited to paid-in capital (based on fair value of both securities) and discounts or premiums should be treated as they would be under conventional bond issuance.

[¶1011] TREASURY STOCK

Treasury stock is stock which has previously been issued by a corporation but is no longer outstanding. It has been reacquired by the corporation and, as its name implies, held in its treasury. Treasury stock is not canceled because cancellation reduces the authorized issue of corporation stock.

In some circumstances, it is permissible to show treasury stock as an asset if adequately disclosed. However, dividends on treasury stock should not be treated as income.

[¶1011.1] Treasury Stock Shown at Cost

When a corporation acquires its own stock to be held for future sale or possible use in connection with stock options, or with no plans or uncertainty as to future retirement of that stock, the cost of the acquired stock may be shown separately as a deduction from the total of capital stock, capital surplus and retained earnings. Gains on subsequent sales (over the acquired-cost price) should be credited to capital surplus and losses (to the extent of prior gains) should be charged to that same account, with excess losses going to retained earnings. State law should be followed if in contravention.

[¶1011.2]   Treasury Stock Shown at Par or Stated Value

When treasury stock is acquired for the purpose of *retirement* (or constructive retirement), the stock should be shown at par value or stated value as a reduction in the equity section and the excess of purchase cost over par (stated) value should be charged to capital surplus to the extent of prior gains booked for the same issue, together with pro-rata portions applicable to that stock arising from prior stock dividends, splits, etc. Any remaining excess may be either applied pro-rata to common stock or to retained earnings.

[¶1011.3]   Treasury Stock as an Asset

If adequately disclosed, it is permissible in some circumstances to show stock of a corporation held in its own treasury as an asset. (This rule was adopted in 1934 upon recommendation of the New York Stock Exchange.)

For example, pursuant to a corporation's bonus arrangement with certain employees, treasury stock may be used to pay the bonus, and, in accordance with the concept of a current asset satisfying a current liability, that applicable treasury stock might be shown as current asset. However, dividends on such stock should not be treated as income while the corporation holds the stock.

[¶1012]   THE GOING CONCERN CONCEPT

There is an underlying presumption in the standards set for financial accounting that a business, once started, will continue functioning and operating as a going concern. For example, the use of historical costs for building and property, which are currently more valuable, presupposes that the *use* of that property will generate more advantages than would present disposition. Deferrals to future periods through systematic allocations also indicate a presumption of longevity.

This presumption of continuance as a going concern is never stated by the independent auditor—never worded in his own opinion. On the *contrary*, it is when there appears to be danger of the firm's *not* being able to continue as a going concern that the auditor makes the assertion that "the statements have been prepared on the basis of a going concern," and that he is *unable* to express an opinion because of major uncertainties, which he describes. Therefore, the actual use of the terminology, "going concern," in the auditor's opinion indicates trouble.

Some factors which may be indicative of *possible* failure to continue as a going concern are:

Inability to satisfy obligations on due dates.

Inability to perform contractual obligations.

Inability to meet substantial loan covenants.

A substantial deficit.

A series of continued losses.

The presence of major contingencies which could lead to heavy losses.

Catastrophes which have rendered the business inoperable.

11

Revenue (Income) and Expenses

REVENUE (INCOME)

The principles upon which net income is determined derive from the pervasive measurement principles, such as realization, and the modifying conventions, such as conservatism.

The entire process of income determination ("matching") consists of identifying, measuring and relating revenue and expenses for an accounting period. Revenue is usually determined by applying the realization principle, with the changes in net asset value interrelated with the recognition of revenue.

Revenue arises from three general activities:

1. Selling products;
2. Rendering services or letting others use owned resources, resulting in interest, rent, etc;
3. Disposing of other resources (not products), such as equipment or investments.

Revenue does not include proceeds from stockholders, lenders, asset purchases or prior period adjustments.

Revenue, in the balance sheet sense, is a gross increase in assets or a gross decrease in liabilities recognized and measured in conformity with GAAP, which results from those profit-directed activities that can change owners' equity.

Revenue is considered *realized* when:

1. The earning process is complete or virtually complete, and
2. An exchange has taken place.

The objectives of accounting determination of income are not always the same as the objectives used for tax purposes.

[¶1101.2]   Methods of Determining Income

There are various acceptable ways of determining income, all of which are discussed in other parts of this book:
Revenue (see three general activities above):

1. Accrual method—this is financial accounting and GAAP.
2. Cash method—this is *not* considered financial accounting, and not GAAP, since one of the characteristics of GAAP is the *accrual* of appropriate items.
3. Installment sale method—generally for retail stores.
4. Completion of production method—used for precious metals.
5. For long-term construction contracts:
   A. Completed contract method.
   B. Percentage-of-completion method.
6. For leasing activities:
   A. The direct financing method.
   B. The operating method.
   C. The sales method.
7. The cost recovery method (used for installment sales).
8. Consolidation method—for majority-owned subsidiaries (over 50%).
9. Equity method—for non-consolidated subsidiaries and for controlled non-subsidiaries.

Other types of income requiring special determination:

1. Extraordinary items of income.
2. Unrealized income arising from:
   A. Foreign currency holdings or transactions.
   B. Ownership of marketable securities shown as current assets.

A *shareholder* in a corporation does *not* have income when that corporation earns income (except for a Sub-S corporation). The shareholder has, and reports for tax purposes, income only upon *distribution* of that income in the form of dividends. Generally, distributions of stock—stock dividends and stock splits—are *not* income to the shareholder, but merely an adjustment of the number of shares he holds (for the same original cost plus token costs, if any). However, there are some situations which call for the stockholder to report stock dividends as income. (See Tax Section.)

If a buyer has a right of return to the seller, revenue is recognized if *all* of the following criteria are met:

1. Buyer is obligated to pay (and not contingent upon resale of the product) or has paid the seller.
2. Buyer's obligation would not be changed by theft, damage, or destruction of the product.
3. Seller does not have any significant obligation to buyer related to resale of the product by the buyer.

132

4. Buyer's business must have economic substance separate from the seller's business.

If these criteria are met, sales revenue and cost of sales reported in the income statement are reduced to reflect estimated returns; expected losses are accrued.

[¶1102]   EXPENSES

Expenses are one of the six basic elements of financial accounting, along with assets, liabilities, owners' equity, revenue and net income.

> Expenses are determined by applying the expense recognition principles on the basis of relationships, between acquisition costs [the term "cost" is commonly used to refer to the amount at which assets are initially recorded, regardless of how determined], and either the independently determined revenue or accounting periods. Since the point in time at which revenue and expenses are recognized is also the time at which changes in amounts of net assets are recorded, income determination is interrelated with asset valuation.

All costs are not expenses. Some costs are related to later periods, will provide benefits for later periods, and are carried forward as assets on the balance sheet. Other costs are incurred and provide no future benefit, having expired in terms of usefulness or applicability—these expired costs are called "expenses." All expenses, therefore, are part of the broader term "cost." These expired costs are not assets and are shown as deductions from revenue to determine net income.

> Expenses are gross decreases in assets or gross increases in liabilities recognized and measured in conformity with GAAP that result from those types of profit-directed activities that can change an owner's equity.

[¶1102.1]   Recognizing Expenses

Three pervasive principles form the basis for recognizing expenses to be deducted from revenue to arrive at net income or loss:

1. Associating cause and effect ("matching"):

For example, manufacturing cost of goods sold is measured and matched to the *sale* of the product. Assumptions must be made as to how these costs attach to the product—whether on machine hours, space used, labor expended, etc. Assumptions must also be made as to how the costs flow out (LIFO, FIFO, average costs).

2. Systematic and rational allocation:

When there is no direct way to associate cause and effect and certain costs are known (or presumed) to have provided benefits during the accounting period, these costs are allocated to that period in a systematic and rational manner and to appear so to an unbiased observer. The methods of allocation should be consistent and systematic, though methods may vary for different types of costs. Examples are: Depreciation of fixed assets, amortization of intangibles, interperiod allocation of rent or interest. The allocation referred to here is not the allocation of expired manufacturing costs within the "cost" area to determine unit or job costs; it is rather the broader area of allocation to the manufacturing area from the unexpired asset account: Depreciation on factory building, rather than overhead-depreciation on Product A, B or C.

3. Immediate recognition (period expenses):

Those costs which are expensed during an accounting period because:

A. They cannot be associated on a cause-and-effect basis with revenue, yet no useful purpose would be achieved by delaying recognition to a future period, or

B. They provide no discernible future benefits, or

C. They were recorded as assets in a prior period and now no longer provide discernible future benefits.

Examples are: Officer salaries, most selling expenses, legal fees, most general and administrative expenses.

[¶1103]   OTHER EXPENSES (AND REVENUE)

Gains and losses: Expenses and revenue from *other* than sales of products, merchandise or services may be separated from (operating) revenue and disclosed net separately.

Unusual items: Unusual items of expense or income not meeting the criteria of "extraordinary" should be shown as a separate component of income from continuing operations.

Extraordinary items: Extraordinary items are discussed elsewhere in this book. They should be shown separately—net of applicable taxes—*after* net income from continuing operations. If there are any disposals of business segments, they should be shown immediately prior to extraordinary items—also with tax effect.

12

Cost Accounting

[¶1201] **HISTORICAL AND STANDARD COST SYSTEMS**

Cost accounting systems vary with the type of cost (present or future) used. When present costs are used, the cost system is called an *historical* or *actual cost* system. When future costs are used, the cost system is called a *standard cost* system. In practice, combinations of these costs are used even in actual or standard systems. Where there is an intentional use of both types of costs, we sometimes refer to the system as a *hybrid cost* system.

Actual Cost System: Since an actual cost system uses only those costs which have already been incurred, the system determines costs only after manufacturing operations have been performed. Under this system the product is charged with the actual cost of materials, the actual cost of labor, and an *estimated* portion of overhead (overhead costs represent the future cost element in an actual cost system).

Standard Cost System: A standard system is based upon estimated or predetermined costs. There is a distinction between estimated and standard costs, however. Both are "predetermined" costs, but estimated costs are based upon average past experience, and standard costs are based upon scientific facts that consider past experience and controlled experiments. Arriving at standard costs involves careful selection of material, an engineering study of equipment and manufacturing facilities, and time and motion studies.

In either system, adjustment must be made at the financial statement date to the *closing inventory* so that it is shown at actual cost or reasonably approximate actual cost, or at market if lower. Also, the inventory must bear its share of the burden of overhead. "The exclusion of all overheads from inventory costs does not constitute an accepted accounting procedure."

For interim statements, estimated gross profit rates may be used to determine cost of goods sold during the interim, but this fact must be disclosed.

It must be emphasized that whatever cost accounting method is chosen by a company, its purpose is primarily an internal management tool directed at controlling costs, setting production goals, measuring efficiencies and variances, providing incentives and establishing realistic relationships between unit costs, selling prices and gross margins. Regardless of costing methods used, generally accepted accounting standards must be followed for the preparation of the financial statements, wherein the valuation must be cost or market, whichever is lower.

Also, either the FIFO or LIFO methods (or the average method) may be used under any cost system. These methods pertain to the assumption of the *flow* of costs, not to the actual costs themselves. Note that *both* methods may be used within one inventory, as long as the method is applied to that portion of the inventory consistently from period to period. Disclosures should be made of any change in method.

[¶1201.1]   Integrating Cost System

It is not essential to integrate a cost system with the rest of the accounting system, but it is highly desirable. A cost system is really an extension of the regular system. With an integrated system, entries in the inventory account in the general ledger should represent the sums of figures taken from the cost accounting data. The general ledger inventory accounts (e.g., finished goods, work in process, and raw materials) are the control accounts and they should tie in with the amounts of physical inventories actually on hand. Discrepancies may result from errors, spoilage, or thievery.

Elements of Cost: Production costs consist of three elements: direct materials, direct labor, and manufacturing (overhead) expenses:

Direct Materials: Those materials which can be identified with specific units of the product.

Direct Labor: That labor which can be identified with specific units of the product.

Manufacturing Expenses (Overhead): Those costs (including indirect material or labor) which can not be identified with specific units of the product. These costs represent expenses for the factory and other facilities which permit the labor to be applied to the materials to manufacture a product.

Sometimes, overhead is further subdivided into:

Direct overhead — Those manufacturing costs other than material and direct labor which specifically apply to production and require no allocation from other expense areas;

Indirect overhead — Those expenses which have been allocated into the manufacturing expense area from other more general areas.

For financial statement purposes, overhead should not include selling expenses or general or administrative expenses.

[¶1201.2] Cost Terminology (for quick reference)

Here are some brief definitions of various types of costs:

(1) *Historical* — measured by actual cash payments or their equivalent at the time of outlay.

(2) *Future* — expected to be incurred at a later date.

(3) *Standard* — scientifically predetermined.

(4) *Estimated* — predetermined.

(5) *Product* — associated with units of output.

(6) *Period* — associated with the income of a time period.

(7) *Direct* — obviously tradeable to a unit of output or a segment of business operations.

(8) *Prime* — labor and material directly traceable to a unit of output.

(9) *Indirect* — not obviously traceable to a unit of output or to a segment of business operations.

(10) *Fixed* — do not change in the total as the rate of output varies.

(11) *Variable* — do change with changes in rate of output.

(12) *Opportunity* — measurable advantage foregone as a result of the rejection of alternative uses of resources whether of materials, labor, or facilities.

(13) *Imputed* — never involve cash outlays nor appear in financial records. Involve a foregoing on the part of the person whose costs are being calculated.

(14) *Controllable* — subject to direct control at some level of supervision.

(15) *Noncontrollable* — not subject to control at some level of supervision.

(16) *Joint* — exists when from any one unit source, material, or process come products which have different unit values.

(17) *Sunk* — historical and not recoverable in a given situation.

(18) *Discretionary* — avoidable and unessential to an objective.

(19) *Postponable* — may be shifted to future period without affecting efficiency.

(20) *Out of pocket* — necessitate cash expenditure.

(21) *Differential* — changes in cost that result from variation in operations.

(22) *Incremental* — those added or eliminated if segments were expanded or discontinued.

(23) *Alternative* — estimated for decision areas.

(24) *Replacement* — considered for depreciation significance.

(25) *Departmental* — production and service, for cost distributions.

[¶1202] JOB ORDER OR PROCESS COST SYSTEMS

There are distinctions between cost systems other than the use of present or future costs.

137

A *job order system* compiles costs for a specific quantity of a product as it moves through the production process. This means that material, labor, and overhead costs of a specific number or lot of the product (usually identifiable with a customer's order or a specific quantity being produced for stock) are recorded as the lot moves through the production cycle.

A *process system* compiles costs as they relate to specific processes or operations for a period of time. To find the unit cost, these figures are averaged for a specified period and spread over the number of units that go through each process. Process costing is used when large numbers of identical products are manufactured, usually in assembly-line fashion.

Keep in mind that actual or estimated costs can be used with either a job order or process cost system.

[¶1202.1]   Benefits and Drawbacks

Whether the job order or process system is used depends on the type of operation. The job order system is rarely used in mass production industries. It is invariably used when products are custom made. Process costing is used where production is in a continuous state of operation as for: Paper, baking, steel making, glass, rubber, sugar, chemicals, etc. Here are some of the relative merits and shortcomings of each method:

Advantages

Job Order	*Process*
(1) Appropriate for custom-made goods	(1) It is usually only necessary to calculate costs each month
(2) Appropriate for increasing finished goods inventory in desired quantities	(2) Minimum of clerical work required
(3) Adequate for inventory pricing	(3) If there is only one type of product cost computation is relatively simple
(4) Permits estimation of future costs	
(5) Satisfies "cost-plus" contract requisites	

Disadvantages

Job Order	*Process*
(1) Expensive to use — a good deal of clerical work required	(1) Use of average costs ignores any variance in product cost
(2) Difficult to make sure that all materials and labor are accurately charged to each specific job	(2) Involves calculation of stage of completion of goods in process and the use of equivalent units
(3) Difficult to determine cost of goods sold when partial shipments are made before completion	

[¶1203]   HOW TO USE STANDARD COSTS

Smith Company manufactures only one product, glubs — a household article made out of a certain type of plastic. Glubs are made from D raw material which goes through a single process. Glubs are turned out from D material in a fraction of a day. Smith Company has a process-type cost setup integrated with its other financial records. D material is charged to work in process through requisitions based upon actual cost. Direct labor is charged to work in process based upon payroll. Manufacturing expense is charged to work in process based upon the number of payroll hours. Each day a record of the number of glubs manufactured is kept. This is the responsibility of the production department.

Here's the way the Smith Company process cost system operates: Every month, total figures are worked up for raw material, payroll, factory expenses. Each of these figures is then divided by the total number of glubs produced for that month to arrive at a unit cost per glub. Here is what the unit cost accumulation for the four months shows (this example assumes no work-in-process inventory and no equivalent units):

Unit Cost per Glub Manufactured

	First Month	Second Month	Third Month	Fourth Month	Weighted Average
Material D	$ .94	$ .91	$ .97	$1.10	$ .95
Direct Labor	1.18	1.22	2.00	.70	1.29
Manufacturing Expenses	1.22	1.47	2.11	.82	1.42
	$3.34	$3.60	$5.08	$2.62	$3.66

Right now, glubs are being sold at $4.30, and the present profit appears sufficient. T.O. Smith, the president and major stockholder of the corporation, feels that if glubs were sold at $3.30 each, four times as many could be sold. He also reports that he has learned that Glubco, Inc., Smith's competitor, is going to market glubs for $3.60. Smith thinks that $3.30 is a good sales price since the cost records indicate that glubs were manufactured for as low as $2.62 in the fourth month. Smith Company's accountant says the president is incorrect. He points out that the average cost is somewhere in the area of $3.55 to $3.80 based upon the cost records for six months. Selling glubs for $3.30 would create losses. The factory foreman says that during the third and fourth months there was an error in calculating the number of glubs put into finished goods inventory. From the figures for the fourth month, it appears that the foreman is correct. The unit cost per glub is unusually low. Mr. Smith wants to know the lowest at which he can sell glubs and still make a reasonable profit. The accountant suggests setting up a cost system based upon standard costs. He outlines the following steps:

(1) Purchasing department records indicate that material D should cost no more than 15¢ per pound. (According to the chief engineer, it takes approximately two pounds of D to produce one glub.) The 15¢ figure takes future market conditions into account.

(2) A time study of half a dozen workers who produce glubs is made. The average time it takes each of these six men to produce one glub is one-third of an hour. The average hourly wage of these men is $3.00.

(3) Based upon reasonable level of production for the following year, a departmental manufacturing expense or overhead is estimated to be 100% of direct labor.

Based upon the above determinations, the standard cost per glub is $2.30. It is calculated as follows:

Raw Material D: two pounds at 15¢ per pound	$ .30
Direct Labor: ⅓ hour at $3.00 per hour	1.00
Manufacturing Expense: 100% of direct labor	1.00
Total	$2.30

In order to produce glubs at this cost, the following points are agreed upon:

(1) When more than 15¢ a pound is paid for raw material D, the excess is to be charged to a special variance account instead of the raw material account. These excesses are to be explained periodically by the purchasing department.

(2) Requisitions for raw material D are to be limited to two pounds of D for each glub to be manufactured. If more than two pounds per glub is issued to meet scheduled production, the excess over two pounds is to be charged to a separate variance account. The reason for any excess will also have to be explained.

(3) The daily number of direct labor hours spent making glubs is to be multiplied by three. This should equal the number of glubs produced that day. Any discrepancy here is probably due to inefficiency. The number of inefficient hours at the standard $3 rate times the 100% manufacturing expense rate is to be charged to a special variance account.

(4) Payroll over $3 an hour is to be charged to a variance account. Only $3 an hour is to be charged to the work-in-progress account. The factory foreman will have to explain hourly labor figures over $3 periodically.

(5) Departmental variations in the 100% of direct labor manufacturing expense burden are to be charged or credited to separate variance accounts. This is to be done each month.

Here's what happened each month after this system was instituted:

Variance Accounts	Fifth Month	Sixth Month	Seventh Month	Eighth Month	Ninth Month
(1) Material D Price	$ 2,100	$ 300	$ 750	$ 0	$ 0
(2) Material usage	19,500	13,000	5,000	500	400
(3) Labor efficiency ..	8,000	5,050	800	700	300
(4) Labor rate	400	150	(50)	400	100
(5) Mfg. Expense	0	5,000	1,000	300	(100)
	$ 30,000	$ 23,500	$ 7,500	$ 1,900	$ 700
Units Manufactured ...	48,000	48,000	48,000	48,000	48,000
Variance per Unit	.63	.49	.16	.04	.01
Standard Unit Cost	2.30	2.30	2.30	2.30	2.30
Actual Cost	$ 2.93	$ 2.79	$ 2.46	$ 2.34	$ 2.31

Here is what was elicited from discussion with the persons responsible for the different variance accounts:

(1) The purchase price for raw material D exceeded 15¢ per pound mainly because of the distance of Smith Company from where D is obtained in the south. The head of purchasing feels that D could be purchased for no more than 15¢ if he

could have a small office in the south with one assistant who would remain there. It was decided to go ahead and give him the office and the additional employee.

(2) The factory foreman, together with the chief engineer, has been going over the requisitions of raw material D. More D was needed because some of the glubs had air holes in them and weren't usable. It seems that the pressure used to extrude them wasn't sufficient. The chief engineer says that he can replace the present air die channels with larger ones so that these defects do not recur. The foreman knew that some glubs were scrapped in the past, but it wasn't until this switch to standard costs that he knew how much waste there really was.

(3) The foreman and the industrial engineer who performed the time and motion study discussed the labor efficiency loss. It was their opinion that there were more factory employees than needed to carry out various operations to convert D into finished glubs. It was also learned that some employees could use more training, while others were overskilled for their particular functions. Still others were not producing enough for some reason or other. Both men felt that a training program instructing employees in the efficient use of available tools would increase efficiency. Further time and motion studies on every phase of the production process were initiated.

(4) There was not much variance in labor rate, but it was hoped that the training program would release more technically skilled and higher paid employees for use in the more complicated production steps.

At the end of the seventh month, it was obvious that the steps taken were beginning to pay off. The additional costs incurred in carrying out these steps (for example, the additional employee in purchasing and the southern office) created a manufacturing overhead variance where none had existed before; but the success in other areas outweighed this.

At the end of the ninth month, everyone agreed that the switch to standard costs had exceeded expectations. The new lower production cost would help expand the market for glubs. Smith Company was also in a good competitive position compared with Blubco since it probably could now undersell it.

This illustration shows the advantages of standard costs:

(1) Control and reduction of costs;

(2) Promotion and measurement of efficiencies;

(3) Calculation and setting of selling prices;

(4) Evaluation of inventories;

(5) Simplification of cost procedures.

[¶1204]   **DIRECT COSTING**

Another type of cost accounting which is used for internal purposes but not for financial or tax reporting purposes is "direct costing." This is a method in which only those costs which are a consequence of production of the product are assigned to the product — direct material cost, direct labor cost, and only variable manufacturing overhead. All fixed manufacturing costs are treated as expenses of the period.

The methods of recording costs for direct material and direct labor are similar under direct costing and conventional costing. It is in the method of reflecting manufacturing overhead that the systems differ. In a direct costing system, overhead costs are classified as fixed or variable. In conventional costing, only one overhead control account is used. In direct costing, two control accounts are used — a direct overhead account and an indirect overhead account. The direct overhead account is for variable expenses — those that vary with the volume of production. The indirect overhead account is for fixed expenses — those that do not vary with production. These are charged as expenses of the period rather than as costs of the finished product. Research costs, some advertising costs, and costs incurred to keep manufacturing and nonmanufacturing facilities ready for use are considered expenses of the period. Under direct costing, direct labor, direct material, and overhead costs that vary with production find their way into the inventory. The other manufacturing overhead expenses are charged off currently against income. The important reason behind direct costing is not to value inventories, but to segregate expenses.

[¶1204.1] Effect of Direct Costing on Financial Statements

Direct costing, if used on the financial statements (for internal use), would produce the following results:

(1) Where the inventory of manufactured goods does not fluctuate from one accounting period to the next, there should be no difference between net income using direct costing or net income using conventional costing.

(2) Where the inventory does fluctuate and is increased, net income under direct costing will be lower. *Reason:* Fixed overhead costs under direct costing will have been charged to the current period instead of deferred by increasing the value of inventory. Under conventional costing, the value of the ending inventory will have been increased by these fixed overhead costs.

(3) Where inventory decreases, net income under direct costing will be higher than conventional costing. *Reason:* Fixed overhead costs included in the value of the inventory under conventional costing will now increase the cost of goods sold, thereby reducing income.

13

Extraordinary Items

[¶1301] IMPUTED INTEREST ON NOTES RECEIVABLE OR PAYABLE

[¶1301.1] Accounting Considerations

The AICPA sets forth the appropriate accounting when the face amount of certain receivables or payables ("notes") does not reasonably represent the present value of the consideration given or received in certain exchanges. The objective of these rules is to prevent the form of the transaction from prevailing over its economic substance.

(*Present value* is the sum of future payments, discounted to the present date at an appropriate rate of interest.)

The Opinion states that:

(1) When a note is received or issued solely for cash, the note is presumed to have a present value equal to the cash received. If it is issued for cash equal to its face amount, it is presumed to earn the stated rate of interest.

(2) When a note is received for cash and some other rights or privileges, the value of the rights or privileges should be given accounting recognition by establishing a note discount or premium account, with the offsetting amount treated as appropriate. An example is a five-year noninterest-bearing loan made to a supplier in partial consideration for a purchase of products at lower than prevailing market prices. Under such circumstances, the difference between the present value of the receivable and the cash lent to the supplier is regarded as (a) an additional cost of the purchased goods, and (b) interest income, amortized over the life of the note.

(3) When a note is exchanged for property, goods, or services and (a) interest is not stated, or (b) it is stated but is unreasonable, or (c) the stated face amount of the note is materially different from the current cash sale price of goods (or services), the note, the sales price, and the cost of the property (goods or services) should be recorded at their fair value, or at an amount that reasonably approximates the market value of the note, whichever is more clearly determinable.

Any resulting discount or premium should be regarded as interest expense or income and be amortized over the life of the note, in such a way as to result in a constant effective rate of interest when applied to the amount outstanding at the beginning of any given period.

The Opinion also provides some general guides for determining an "appropriate" interest rate and the manner of amortization for financial reporting purposes.

[¶1302]   CLASSIFYING AND REPORTING EXTRAORDINARY ITEMS

Income statement presentation requires that the results of *ordinary operations* be reported first, and applicable provision for income taxes provided for. In order, the following should then be shown:

1. Results of discontinued operations:

    A. Income or loss from the operations discontinued for the portion of the period until discontinuance—shown net of tax, with the tax shown parenthetically;

    B. Loss (or gain) on disposal of the business segments, including provision for phase-out operating losses—also shown net of tax parenthetically.

2. Extraordinary items.

    Should be segregated and shown as the last factor used in arriving at net income for the period. Here, the caption is shown net of applicable income taxes, which are shown parenthetically.

    Note that extraordinary items do *not* include disposal of business segments as such, because they are segregated and shown separately prior thereto (as above).

An example of the reporting of the above:

	1982	1981
Income from continuing operations before income taxes	$ xxx	$ xxx
Provision for income taxes	xx	xx
Income from continuing operations	$ xxx	xxx

Discontinued operations (Note):
Income from operations of discontinued
Division B (less applicable taxes of $xx) $xx

	1982	1981

Loss on disposal of Division B, including provision for phase-out operating losses of $xx (less applicable income taxes of $xx)

	xx	xx
Income before extraordinary items		xxx

Extraordinary items (less applicable income taxes of $ xx)
(Note)

	xx	
Net Income	$ xxx	$ xxx

Earnings per share:

Income from continuing operations	$ x.00	$ x.00
Discontinued operations	x.00	x.00
Extraordinary items	x.00	x.00
Net Income	$ x.00	$ x.00

Note that earnings per share should be broken out separately for the factors of discontinued operations and extraordinary items, as well as for income from (continuing) operations.

The criteria for classifying a transaction or event as an "extraordinary item" are as follows:

Extraordinary items are events and transactions that are distinguished by their unusual nature *and* by the infrequency of their occurrence. Thus, *both* of the following criteria should be met to classify an event or transaction as an extraordinary item:

1. *Unusual nature*—the underlying event or transaction should possess a high degree of abnormality and be of a type clearly unrelated to, or only incidentally related to, the ordinary and typical activities of the entity, taking into account the environment in which the entity operates.

2. *Infrequency of occurrence*—the underlying event or transaction should be of a type that would not reasonably be expected to recur in the foreseeable future, taking into account the environment in which the entity operates.

Items which are *not* to be reported as extraordinary, because they may recur or are not unusual, are:

1. Write-downs of receivables, inventories, intangibles, or leased equipment.
2. Effects of strikes.
3. Gains or losses on foreign currency translations.
4. Adjustment of accruals on long-term contracts.
5. Gains or losses on disposal of business segments.
6. Gains or losses from abandonment or sale of property, plant or equipment used in the business.

Note that some highly unusual occurrence might cause one of the above types of gains or losses and should be considered extraordinary, such as those resulting from: major casualties (earthquake), expropriations, and legal restrictions. Disposals of business segments, though not extraordinary in classification, should be shown separately on the income statement, just prior to extraordinary items, but after operations from continuing business.

Miscellaneous data pertaining to extraordinary items:

Bargain sales of stock to stockholders are *not* extraordinary items, but they should be shown separately.

A gain or a loss on sale of coin collections by a bank is *not* an extraordinary item.

14

Earnings Per Share

[¶1401]   REPORTING EARNINGS PER SHARE

It is mandatory that earnings per share (EPS) data be shown in conjunction with the presentation of financial statements, annual or interim, and that such data be shown on the face of the income statement. However, these requirements no longer apply to non-public enterprises. A non-public enterprise, as defined in FASB #21, is an enterprise other than one (a) whose debt or equity securities trade in a public market, on a foreign or domestic stock exchange, or in the over-the-counter market (including securities quoted only locally or regionally), or (b) that is required to file financial statements with the SEC.

When reporting for companies that are considered to be public enterprises, such amounts should be presented for:

1. Income before extraordinary items, and

2. Net income.

It is customary to show the earnings per share for the extraordinary items also.

There are basically two types of capital structure involved in the calculation of EPS:

1. A simple capital structure, or

2. A complex capital structure.

Corporations with complex capital structures should present two types of earnings per share data:

1. Primary earnings per share, based on outstanding common shares and those securities that are in substance equivalent to common shares; and

147

2. Fully diluted earnings per share which reflect the dilution of earnings per share that would have occurred if all contingent issuances of stock had taken place. (Reduction of less than 3% is not deemed sufficient to cause dilution.)

Earnings per share should be presented for all periods covered by the income statement. If a prior period has been restated, the earnings per share should also be restated for that period.

The underlying simple basic formula for calculating EPS is:

Net income (earnings) *divided by* number of shares outstanding (common only)

$$\frac{\text{Earnings (net income)}}{\text{Number of common shares outstanding}} = \text{EPS}$$

The *dollars* are always the numerator; the *number* of shares the denominator.

The complexity of determining either factor in the formula increases as the corporate's capital structure expands into more exotic types of equity security and potential types of equity security.

Refer now to the *Fact Sheet* presented next and to the illustrations which follow based on that fact sheet:

[¶1402] FACT SHEET FOR EARNINGS PER SHARE ILLUSTRATIONS

	(in thousands of dollars)		
INCOME STATEMENT	1984	1983	1982
Income before extraordinary item	$12,900	$ 9,150	$7,650
Extraordinary item—net of tax	900	900	—
Net Income	$13,800	$10,050	$7,650

SHARE INFORMATION			
Common stock outstanding:	(in thousands of shares)		
Beginning of year	3,300	3,000	3,000*
Issued during year	—	300(3)	—
Conversion of preferred stock (1)	500	—	—
Conversion of debentures (2)	200	—	—
End of year	4,000	3,300	3,000
Common stock reserved under employee stock options granted	7	7	—

Weighted average number of shares (see calculations):

       1982—3,000,000 shares weighted average
       1983—3,150,000 shares weighted average
       1984—4,183,333 shares weighted average

---

*issued at 1/1/82
(3) issued at 7/1/83

1. *Convertible preferred stock:* 600,000 shares issued at the beginning of the second quarter of 1983. Dividend rate is 20¢ per share. Market value was $53 at time of issue with a cash yield of 0.4% as opposed to bank prime rate of 18%. Warrants to buy 500,000 shares of common stock at $60 per share for a period of five years were, in addition, issued along with this convertible preferred. Each share of the convertible stock was convertible into one common share (exclusive of the warrants).

   During 1984, 500,000 shares of the preferred stock were converted because the common dividend exceeded the preferred. But, *no warrants were exercised during the year.*

2. *Convertible debentures:* 10% with a principal amount of $10,000,000 (due 1997) were sold at 100 in the last quarter of 1982. Each $100 debenture was convertible into *two* shares of common stock. The entire issue was converted at the beginning of the *third* quarter of 1984, when called by the company. (None were converted in 1982 or 1983.)

   The prime rate at issue in 1982 was 12%. The coupon face rate of the bonds was 10%. The bonds had a market value of $100 when issued.

Additional information:

Market price of the common stock: (average prices)

	1984	1983	1982
1st quarter	50	45	40
2nd quarter	60	52	41
3rd quarter	70	50	40
4th quarter	70	50	45
Dec 31 closing price	72	51	44

Cash dividends on common stock:

	1984	1983	1982
Declared and paid *each* quarter	$1.25	$ .25	$ .25

[¶1403]
ILLUSTRATIONS
(Based on the Fact Sheet)

1982—SIMPLE CAPITAL STRUCTURE

The simplest computation involves those companies with:

1. Only common stock issued, and
2. No change in outstanding number during the year, and
3. Net income arising without any extraordinary items.

For 1982, the first year of the company's operation on the fact sheet, the EPS would be:

$$\frac{\text{Income}}{\text{\# shares outstanding}} \text{ or } \frac{\$7,650,000}{3,000,000} \text{ or } \$2.55 \text{ per share.}$$

1983—EXPANDED SIMPLE CAPITAL STRUCTURE

The significant changes in 1983 affecting EPS:

1. The extraordinary item of income of $900M, requiring separate disclosure; and
2. The 300,000 shares issued during the year, requiring the computation of a weighted average.

Computing the weighted average—determine the number of shares outstanding at the end of each quarter and divide by four:

1st quarter	3,000,000
2nd quarter	3,000,000
3rd quarter	3,300,000
4th quarter	3,300,000

12,600,000 divided by 4, or 3,150,000 shares

The employee stock options are *under* 3% of the aggregate outstanding, so they are not considered dilutive and are ignored in the EPS calculation.

Proper *disclosure* for the 1983 EPS would be:

Earnings per common share:	1983	1982
Income before extraordinary items	$2.90(4)	$2.55
Extraordinary item	.29(5)	—
Net Income	$3.19	$2.55

(4) $9,150,000 divided by 3,150,000
(5)   900,000 divided by 3,150,000

(In the above example, the dilution factors used *below* are not applicable, appearing on the fact sheet merely for use in the complex structure example next.)

1984—COMPLEX CAPITAL STRUCTURE

The significant changes in 1984 affecting EPS:

1. The number of common shares (equivalents) represented by the warrants; and
2. The number of common share equivalents represented by the 600,000 shares of convertible preferred stock, issued in 1981; and
3. The additional EPS computation required for the full dilution assumption.

1. The number of common shares (equivalents) represented by the warrants:

$60 exercise price × 500,000 warrants or $30,000,000

$30,000,000 divided by $70 share market price   428,572 (shares)

500,000 shares minus 428,572   71,428 (shares)

Weighted average of the warrant shares: Not applicable for any quarter prior to the third quarter of 1982 because the market price did not exceed the exercise price:

First quarter 1984	—
Second quarter 1984	—
Third quarter 1984	71,428
Fourth quarter 1984	71,428

142,856 divided by 4
Warrant share equivalents—or 35,714 shares

2. The number of common share equivalents represented by the convertible preferred stock:

	1984	1983
Number of shares of preferred stock issued in 1978	600,000	450,000*
Less the number of shares of common stock issued on conversion in 1984 (500,000). But, these shares were issued at various times during the year. Based on even issuance, the weighted average is ½ or	(250,000)	—
The equivalent shares with potential issue factor	350,000	450,000

	1982	1981
The weighted average number of common shares and equivalents is therefore:		
Shares outstanding at beginning (incl. 7/1/83 issue)	3,300,000	3,150,000
Shares issued on conversion of preferred stock (as above)	250,000	—
Shares issued on conversion of the debentures—200,000 at 7/1/84 weighted average is 100,000	100,000	
Equivalents for the warrants (as prior)	35,714	
Equivalents for the convertible preferred stock above	350,000	450,000
Total weighted average (primary)	4,035,714	3,600,000

3. Additional share calculation to determine full dilution:

Remaining shares applicable to convertible debentures	100,000	200,000
Shares applicable to warrants	(35,714)	—
Shares applicable to warrants based on yearend price of $72 — $60 × 500,000 divided by $72, with result subtracted from 500,000	83,333	
Add primary weighted shares above	4,035,714	3,600,000
Shares for full-dilution EPS	4,183,333	3,800,000

Proper disclosure of EPS for 1984 would then be:

	1984	1983
Primary earnings per common share and common equivalent shares (Note _):		
Income before extraordinary item	$ 3.20(1)	$ 2.54(1A)
Extraordinary item	.22(2)	.25(2A)
Net Income	$ 3.42(3)	$ 2.79(3A)

---

*Based on weighted average from start of second quarter

Fully diluted earnings per common share (Note _)

Income before extraordinary item	$ 3.11(4)	$ 2.46(7)
Extraordinary item	.21(5)	.24(8)
Net Income	$ 3.32(6)	$ 2.70(9)

(1) $12,900,000 divided by 4,035,714 or $3.20
(2)   900,000 divided by 4,035,714 or   .22
(3)   13,800,000 divided by 4,035,714 or $ 3.42

(1A) 9,150,000 divided by 3,600,000 or $ 2.54
(2A)   900,000 divided by 3,600,000 or   .25
(3A) 10,050,000 divided by 3,600,000 or $ 2.79

(4)   13,004,000 divided by 4,183,333 or $ 3.11
      (above includes $104,000 addback for debenture
      interest)
(5)   900,000 divided by 4,183,333 or   .21
(6)   13,904,000 divided by 4,183,333 or $ 3.32
(7)   9,358,000 divided by 3,800,000 or $ 2.46
      (includes $208,000 for interest or debentures)
(8)   900,000 divided by 3,800,000 or   .24
(9) $10,258,000 divided by 3,800,000 or $ 2.70

The illustrations here do *not* cover the following topics:

1. Disclosure requirements for financial notes.
2. Handling of dividends paid or unpaid on convertible stocks.
3. Subsequent events which require supplemental calculations.
4. Anti-dilution.
5. The test for common stock equivalent status (including the treasury stock method).
6. Details of calculating dilution under the treasury stock method.
7. Effect of stock splits or stock dividends on number of shares.
8. EPS in business combinations.
9. Discussion of the "if converted" method of computation.
10. Discussion of the "cash-yield" test for the consideration of equivalents.
11. Effect of contingencies involved in share issuance.
12. Securities of subsidiaries.

Some of the above topics may be illustrated best in financial statements issued by prominent public corporations.

15

Statement of Changes in Financial Position (Funds Statement)

[¶1501] ELEMENTS INCLUDED IN THE STATEMENT

One of the *required* basic financial statements (along with the balance sheet, statement of income, statement of changes in retained earnings and related notes and disclosures) is the "Statement of Changes in Financial Position" (formerly called the "Funds Statement"). The requirement applies to all profit-oriented businesses, regardless of whether they use "current assets/current liabilities" classifications or not.

As with other statements, information should be presented for at least two comparative periods. For interim reports, however, this statement is not required.

The complete statement of changes in financial position of a period "should include and properly describe all-important aspects of the company's financing and investing activities." This concept extends the elements of inclusion beyond those merely encompassing the factors in "working capital."

Earlier concept: The concept of *funds* in funds statements (Statement of Source and Application of Funds) was varied somewhat in practice, with resulting variations in the nature of statements. For example, *funds* were sometimes interpreted to mean *cash* or its equivalent, and the resulting funds statement was a summary of cash provided and used. Another interpretation of *funds* was that of *working capital* (current assets less current liabilities), and the resulting funds statement was a summary of working capital provided and used. The funds statement, therefore, excluded certain financing and investing activities because they did not directly affect cash or working capital.

153

Present concept: The standards now provide for the inclusion of the following elements in the Statement of Changes in Financial Position:

1. Working capital (or cash provided from or used in operations for the period):

   A. If the format shows the *flow of cash,* other components of working capital (inventory, receivables, payables) are then directed to the sources and uses of *cash* and should be so disclosed in detail.

   B. If the format shows the *flow of working capital,* the components of net change in working capital for the current period (and the comparative period presented) should be analzyed and shown in detail.

2. All other sources and applications of funds which affect (net) working capital.

Funds statements are required for each year income statements are presented, though detail is required only for the current year.

[¶1501.1]   Working Capital

The *components* of ''working capital'' are current assets and current liabilities. The term working capital in the professional parlance indicates the *excess* of current assets over current liabilities, and the more appropriate description is ''net working capital.''

Current assets include cash and other assets that can be expected to be turned into cash or consumed during the normal operating cycle—usually one year.

Current liabilities are basically those which will probably be satisfied within the same cycle (one year).

The flow of working capital: (This is the factor ''Funds Provided by Operations'' in the SOURCES OF FUNDS below.)

Working capital provided from operations for period:

1. Income (loss) before extraordinary items.

2. Add (or deduct) expenses not requiring outlay of working capital in the current period (such as depreciation).

3. Caption the total of above as ''Working Capital provided from Operations exclusive of extraordinary items.''

4. Add (or deduct) working capital provided by extraordinary items.

5. Add (or deduct), adjusting income for extraordinary items included which did *not* affect working capital.

6. (Total) Funds Provided by Operations (Working Capital).

[¶1501.2]   Other Sources and Applications

After the above has been determined, the other factors in the display are then calculated and displayed (overall) as follows:

SOURCES OF FUNDS:

Funds provides by operations (as above)	xx	
Other sources of funds	xx	xx

APPLICATION OF FUNDS   (xx)

Increase (or decrease) in funds
(Net change in working capital)   xx

The remaining information comes from the required disclosure of the following additional elements needed to arrive at and explain the net increase or decrease in (net) working capital for the period. Each factor should be classified as a "source" or an "application" as appropriate:

1. Outlays for purchases of long-term assets, detailed as to class;
2. Proceeds from sale of long-term assets (detailed as to class);
3. Reduction of long-term debt or preferred stock by conversion to common stock;
4. Issuance, assumption, redemption or repayment of long-term debt;
5. Issuance, redemption or purchase of capital stock for cash or for assets other than cash;
6. Dividends (except stock dividends and split-ups).

Working capital is a significant factor from several points of view. To creditors and credit grantors, it is an indication of the debtor's ability to repay. Management, stockholders and creditors want to know how it changes from year to year. Therefore, it is important to classify current assets and current liabilities properly.

[¶1501.3]   Information from Statement

The Statement provides management and stockholders with the following type of information:

(1) Where the profits were applied.

(2) The reason that dividends were not larger, or why the company was able to distribute dividends in excess of current earnings, or where there was a net loss for the period.

(3) The reason for the decrease in net current assets, although the net income is up, or vice versa.

(4) The reason money may have to be borrowed to finance purchases of new plant and equipment when the required amount is exceeded by the "cash flow"; i.e., the sum of the net income and depreciation.

(5) How increases in plant and equipment were financed.

(6) Where the proceeds of the sale of plant and equipment resulting from a contraction of operations were applied.

(7) Where the proceeds for the retirement of debt came from.

(8) What was done with the proceeds derived from an increase in outstanding capital stock or from the bond issue.

Hilton Hotels Corporation
and Subsidiaries

*Consolidated Statement
of Changes in Financial Position*

	Year Ended December 31,	1975	1974
Source of Funds	Net income	$ 42,381,000	17,279,000
	Depreciation	19,166,000	22,104,000
	Gain on sales of properties and write-down of investments (net of tax provision of $12,174,000 and tax benefit of $359,000)	(22,239,000)	(206,000)
	Deferred income taxes	719,000	1,721,000
	Equity in earnings of 17% to 50% owned companies	(5,904,000)	(2,446,000)
	Working capital provided by operations, exclusive of sales of properties and write-down of investments	34,123,000	38,452,000
	Sales of properties and write-down of investments		
	Proceeds	84,981,000	6,332,000
	Long-term portion of debt transferred	(18,808,000)	—
	Tax provision and benefit	(12,174,000)	359,000
	Long-term debt financing	—	8,000,000
	New Yorker property mortgage debt	—	6,847,000
	Reduction of investments	7,086,000	2,868,000
	Other — net	2,054,000	1,631,000
		97,262,000	64,489,000
Use of Funds	Property and equipment additions	15,254,000	35,705,000
	Reacquisition of New Yorker property	—	7,766,000
	Reduction of long-term debt	24,075,000	20,291,000
	Payment of cash dividends	7,450,000	7,757,000
	Purchase of treasury stock	25,463,000	5,208,000
	Additional investments	3,339,000	4,784,000
	Deferred taxes on casino receivables	971,000	928,000
	Settlements of prior income taxes	1,486,000	1,483,000
	Other changes in deferred tax liabilities	—	2,098,000
		78,038,000	86,020,000
Net Increase (Decrease) in Working Capital		$ 19,224,000	(21,531,000)

*Summary of Changes in
Components of Working Capital*

		1975	1974
Increase (Decrease) in Current Assets	Cash and temporary investments	$ 22,013,000	(25,271,000)
	Accounts and notes receivable	104,000	7,704,000
	Inventories	1,657,000	1,039,000
	Prepaid expenses and other	71,000	532,000
		23,845,000	(15,996,000)
Increase (Decrease) in Current Liabilities	Accounts and notes payable	(7,002,000)	5,587,000
	Accrued expenses and other	(3,085,000)	2,413,000
	Current maturities of long-term debt	(6,904,000)	580,000
	Federal and state income taxes	21,612,000	(3,045,000)
		4,621,000	5,535,000
Net Increase (Decrease) in Working Capital		$ 19,224,000	(21,531,000)

16

Foreign Currency Translations

[¶1601]   FOREIGN CURRENCY TRANSLATIONS FOR FINANCIAL STATEMENTS

The principle of conservatism *generally* requires the use of historical cost, and increases or decreases in assets or liabilities brought about by market conditions are not recorded until actual transfer or exchange occurs.

However, there are two exceptions, now accepted as standard procedure, which require the consideration of the *market price,* matching it to historical cost, and recording the *unrealized* loss or gain for the period, to reflect the market price of the asset (or liability), generally at balance sheet date.

This chapter is concerned with one of those exceptions—*foreign currency translations.* It reviews FASB Statement No. 52, *Foreign Currency Translation,* issued in December, 1981, effective for fiscal years beginning after December 15, 1982. Statement No. 52 replaces FASB Statement No. 8, *Accounting for the Translation of Foreign Currency* And Foreign Currency Financial Statements, dated October 1975. The other exception is in the handling of marketable securities, covered separately in the "Current Assets" portion of this section on accounting.

Why is translation necessary? It is not arithmetically possible to combine, add, or subtract measurements expressed in different currencies. It is necessary, therefore, to translate assets, liabilities, revenues, expenses, gains, and losses that are measured or denominated in a foreign currency.

[¶1601.1]   Definitions

Exchange Rate: The *ratio* between a unit of one currency (A) and the amount of another currency (B) for which currency A can be exchanged at a particular time.

Foreign Currency Transactions: Transactions whose terms are denominated in a currency other than the entity's functional currency.

Foreign Currency Translation: Disclosing in the reporting currency of the enterprise the amounts that are denominated in a different currency.

Foreign Entity: An operation whose financial statements are prepared in a currency other than the reporting currency, and accounted for on the equity basis in the financial statements of the reporting enterprise.

Functional Currency: The currency of the primary environment in which the entity operates, which in turn is considered to be the environment in which the entity primarily generates and expends cash.

Reporting Enterprise: An entity or group whose financial statements reflect 1) the financial statements of one or more foreign operations; 2) foreign currency transactions; 3) both.

Transaction Gain or Loss: Gains or losses from a change in exchange rates between the functional currency and the currency in which a foreign transaction is denominated.

Translation Adjustments: The translation of financial statements from the entity's functional currency into the reporting currency. (See para. 13 of FASB No. 52.)

Reporting Currency: The currency in which the reporting enterprise prepares its financial statements.

The application of Statement No. 52 (the "Statement") is to the financial reports of most companies with foreign operations. The essential requirements of the Statements are:

1. Transaction adjustments arising from consolidating a foreign operation which do not affect cash flows are *not* included in net income. Adjustments should be disclosed separately and accumulated in a separate classification of the equity section of the balance sheet.

2. Exchange rate changes on a foreign operation which directly affect the parent's cash flows *must* be included in net income.

3. Hedges of foreign exchange risks are accounted for as hedges without regard to their form.

4. Transaction gains and losses result from exchange rate changes on transactions denominated in currencies other than the functional currency.

5. The balance sheet translation uses the exchange rate prevailing as of the date of the balance sheet.

6. The exchange rate used for revenues, expenses, gains and losses is the rate on the date those items are recognized.

7. Upon sale (or liquidation) of an investment in a foreign entity, the amount accumulated in the equity component is removed and reported as a gain (or loss) on the disposal of the entity.

8. Intercompany transactions of a long-term investment nature are not included in net income.

9. Financial statements for fiscal years before the effective date of this Statement may be restated. If restatements are provided, they must conform to the requirements of the Statement.

10. The financial statements of a foreign entity in a highly inflationary economy must be remeasured as if the functional currency were the reporting currency. A "highly inflationary economy" is defined in the Statement to be an economy that has had a cumulative inflation rate of 100%, or more, over a three-year period.

17

Business Combinations and Investments in Subsidiaries

[¶1701] **BUSINESS COMBINATIONS AND ACQUISITIONS**

This chapter deals with the *accounting* treatment of dealings involved with the following types of business combinations and acquisitions:

1. Those *combinations* occurring when a corporation and one or more *incorporated* or *unincorporated* businesses *are united into one* accounting entity, with that single entity then carrying on the activities of the prior separate entities. Two methods of accounting are applicable here:

        A. The Purchase Method, or
        B. The Pooling of Interests Method.

2. Those *stock acquisitions* (or stock investments) wherein one corporation *buys the voting common stock* of another corporation—sometimes acquiring voting control, sometimes not—with both entities continuing as separate, individual, distinct operating corporations. Three methods of accounting are applicable here:

        A. The Consolidation Method (or the alternate Combining Method),
        B. The Equity Method, or
        C. The Cost Method.

In each of these methods, the investment in the subsidiary's stock appears on the books of the owning company as an investment asset.

In order to clarify the distinctions involved—as a quick reference—these major points should be considered:

1. Consolidation, the Equity Method and the Cost Method all pertain to the acquisition of *voting stock* by the buying company.
Pooling and Purchase pertain to the acquisition of *assets* and usually liabilities (inventory, plant, equipment, etc.).

2. How to distinguish between pooling and purchase:

   A. With *pooling*, the *acquiring* company uses its *own capital stock* to exchange for the capital stock of the acquired company. For example, a stockholder of Company B (the *acquired* company) will, after pooling, hold stock in Company A, the acquiring company. Company B's stock will have been cancelled. Or, a third Company C might be formed with both A & B companies folding into Company C. Pooling is usually a tax-free combination, provided all requirements are met.

   B. With *purchase*, the acquiring company buys the assets (usually net of liabilities), and the acquired company (the one selling the assets) must usually account for gain or loss on the sale of the individual assets, involving the recapture provisions of the tax law.

   C. Pooling involves the exchange of stock.
   Purchase can involve either stock, cash or property.

   D. In *purchase*, the assets are valued at *fair value*, usually creating goodwill. In *pooling*, there is no change in asset value, since they are picked up at net *book* value.

   E. Under both pooling and purchase, the acquired company is subsequently liquidated.

   F. A combination of *both* methods is unacceptable.

3. With *stock acquisitions*, all companies continue separate operations even though under new ownership or managerial control. Accounting records are maintained for each distinct company, and each company prepares financial statements independent of the other company. However, public release of those statements is guided by the rules of consolidation or the equity method.

4. With stock acquisitions:

   A. Use the *cost method* when owning less than 20% of the stock *and* exercising *no* effective managerial control.

   B. Use the *equity method* when owning 20% or more (influence is presumed)—or when owning less than 20% *but with substantial managerial* influence. Also, use the equity method when owning *over 50%* and *not using the consolidation method.*

   C. Use the *consolidation method* when ownership is *over 50%* (majority interest), *unless* conditions exist (described later) which constitute exception to the rules of consolidation and permit the use of the equity method.

   D. An acquiring enterprise should account for contingencies that can be reasonably estimated and considered probable as an allocation to the purchase price of the acquired company.

Note that financial accounting (and the SEC) require consolidation for over 50% holdings, with exceptions noted, but the IRS requires a minimum 80% voting control for consolidated tax returns.

Consolidation must also be used for subsidiaries whose principal activity is leasing property or facilities to the parent or other affiliates.

When *not* using consolidation, and the holdings are over 50%, the equity method must be used for all unconsolidated subsidiaries (foreign as well as domestic).

When holdings are 50% or under, down to 20%, you must use the equity method, since significant managerial voice is presumed (unless you prove the contrary).

Further details of each of these methods are now presented.

(See Journal Entries in Appendix A.)

[¶1702]   THE COST METHOD—STOCK ACQUISITIONS

The cost method: An investor records an investment in the stock of an investee at cost, and recognizes as income dividends received that are distributed from net accumulated earnings of the investee, since the date of acquisition by the investor.

Dividends from the investee's earnings are entered as income;

Dividends in *excess* of investee's earnings after date of investment reduce the cost of the investment;

Losses of the investee (after acquisition) should be recognized under the "marketable security" standards.

For the investor, under the *cost method*, dividends only are to be picked up as income (with cash being debited).

[¶1703]   THE EQUITY METHOD—STOCK ACQUISITIONS

The equity method: An investor initially records an investment in the stock of an investee at cost and adjusts the carrying amount of the investment to recognize the investor's share of the earnings or losses of the investee after the date of the acquisition. The amount of the adjustment is included in the determination of net income by the investor, and such amount reflects adjustments similar to those made in preparing consolidated statements including adjustments to eliminate intercompany gains and losses, and to amortize, if appropriate, any difference between investor cost and underlying equity in net assets of the investee at the date of the investment.

Proportionate share of earnings, whether distributed or not, increases the carrying amount of the investment and is recorded as income;

Dividends reduce the carrying amount of the investment and are *not* recorded as income;

After investment, a series of losses by the investee may necessitate additional reduction in the carrying amount.

Under the equity method, the proportionate share of earnings (losses) of the investee (subsidiary) is picked up as income (loss), with the investment asset account being debited (or credited for a loss). Dividends, when received, are thus merely a conversion of part of that increased investment value to cash.

Both the investment and the share of earnings are recorded as single amounts. Market devaluation is *not* applicable.

[¶1703.1] The Equity Method Should Be Used (For Foreign or Domestic Subsidiaries):

1. When owning *20% or more* of the voting stock of the investee (significant control is presumed); or

2. When owning *less than 20%* and the investor can demonstrate the exercise of significant control; or

3. When not consolidating those investees in which more than 50% is owned; but the equity method should not be used if consolidation is justified; or

4. For participant's share of joint ventures.

The equity method *should not* be used:

1. When consolidation is proper for over 50% control; or

2. When ownership is below 20% and there is *no* demonstrable control (use the cost method); or

3. When the principal business activity of the subsidiary is leasing property or facilities to the parent or other affiliates (consolidate instead).

"Voting stock interest" is based on the *outstanding* shares without recognition of common stock equivalents.

[¶1703.2] Applying the Equity Method

1. Follow the rules of intercompany profit and loss eliminations as for consolidations;

2. At purchase of stock, adjust investment to reflect underlying equity and amortize goodwill, if any;

3. Show investment as a single amount, and show income as a single amount, except for (4) below:

4. Show share of extraordinary items separately, net of tax;

5. Any capital structure change of the investee should be accounted for as in consolidations;

6. When stock is sold, account for gain or loss based on the carrying amount then in the investment account;

7. Use the investee's latest financial statement;

8. Recognize non-temporary declines in the value of the investee's stock by adjusting the investment account;

9. Do not write investment account below zero; hold over any losses until future gains offset them;

10. Before picking up share of investee's income, deduct any cumulative preferred dividends (paid or unpaid) not already deducted by the investee;

11. If the level of ownership falls to the point which ordinarily calls for the cost method, stop accruing earnings undistributed, but apply dividends received to the investment account;

12. If changing from the cost method to the equity method for any one investment (because of change in ownership), make the necessary retroactive adjustments;

13. If goodwill is created in (12) above, it should be amortized.

[¶1703.3] Income Taxes

1. Set up a deferred tax based on the investor's proportion of the subsidiary's net income (after tax), based on the investor's rate of tax, *unless*:
   If it appears that the *undistributed earnings* of the investee meet the *indefinite reversal criteria* (see elsewhere in this text), do *not* accrue taxes, but make disclosure.

2. For dividends received, pull applicable tax out of deferred taxes and put in tax payable account;

3. Disclose applicable timing differences.

(See also Journal Entries in Appendix A, Timing Differences and Disclosures in this text.)

[¶1704] THE CONSOLIDATION METHOD— STOCK ACQUISITIONS

There is a presumption that consolidated statements are more meaningful than separate statements and that they are usually necessary for a fair presentation when one of the companies in the group directly or indirectly has a controlling financial interest in the other companies.

Assets, liabilities, revenues and expenses of the subsidiaries are combined with those of the parent company. Intercompany items are eliminated.

Earned surplus of a subsidiary company from *prior* to acquisition does *not* form part of the parent's consolidated earned surplus, and dividends therefrom do not constitute income.

The purpose of consolidated statements is to present the financial data as if it were one single unit.

[¶1704.1] Rule for Consolidation

The usual condition for a controlling financial interest is ownership of a majority voting interest, and, therefore, as a general rule ownership by one company, directly or indirectly, of over 50% of the outstanding voting shares of another company is a condition pointing toward consolidation.

Do *not* consolidate:

1. When control is likely to be temporary; or

2. Where control does *not* rest with the *majority* holder (example: subsidiary is in reorganization or bankruptcy); or

3. Usually, for foreign subsidiaries (See later in this chapter); or

4. Where subsidiary is in a dissimilar business (manufacturer vs. financing); or

5. When the equity method or the cost method is more appropriate for the four conditions named above.

Note that the equity method should *usually* be used for all majority-held subsidiaries which are not consolidated, unless the cost method is necessitated by lack of influential control.

Foreign subsidiaries come under special standards and cost (with proper disclosure) may sometimes be used. (See later in this chapter.)

[¶1704.2] Other Considerations

A difference in fiscal period is no excuse for *not* consolidating. When the difference is no more than 3 months, use the subsidiary's fiscal-period report. Where greater than 3 months, corresponding period statements should be prepared for the subsidiary.

Intercompany items should be eliminated. (See later in this chapter.) For partial years:

1. The year of acquisition: Consolidate for the year and, on income statement, deduct pre-acquisition earnings not applicable to the parent.

2. The year of disposition: do not consolidate income; show only equity of parent in the subsidiary's earnings prior to disposal as a separate line item.

Shares held by the parent should *not* be treated as outstanding stock in the consolidation.

When a subsidiary capitalizes retained earnings for stock dividends or split-ups effected as dividends, such transfer is not required for the consolidated balance sheet which reflects the accumulated earnings and capitalization of the group (not the subsidiary).

[¶1704.3] Combined Statements

This is the showing of the individual company statements *plus* the combined consolidation, which combination reflects all intercompany eliminations.

Examples of when to use combined statements:

1. Where one individual owns controlling interest in several related corporations; or

2. Where several companies are under common management; or

3. To present the information of a group of unconsolidated subsidiaries; or

4. When it is necessary to show the individual operations of parent as well as subsidiaries, as well as the consolidated results—for creditors usually. This type is also called a ''Parent-Company'' statement.

[¶1704.4] Limitations of Consolidated Statements

Along with their advantages, consolidated statements have certain limitations:

1. The separate financial position of each company is not disclosed.

2. The dividend policy of each company cannot be ascertained.

3. Any financial ratios derived from the consolidated statements are only averages and do not represent any particular company.

4. A consolidated income statement does not show which companies have been operating at a profit and which have been losing money.

5. Creditors who are concerned with the financial resources of individual companies would not get the information they desire.

6. Disclosing liens or other particulars of individual companies may require extensive footnotes.

(See Journal Entries, Appendix A, for example of Consolidating Entries.)

[¶1705]   **THE PURCHASE METHOD—
BUSINESS COMBINATIONS**

The Purchase Method accounts for a business combination as the acquisition of one company by another. The acquiring company records at its cost the acquired assets less liabilities assumed. A difference between the cost of an acquired company and the sum of the fair values of tangible and intangible assets less liabilities is recorded as goodwill. The reported income of an acquiring corporation includes the operations of the acquired company after acquisition, based on the cost to the acquiring corporation.

The financial statements should be supplemented after purchase with pro forma statements showing:

1. Results of operations for the current period as if the combination had occurred at the beginning of the period; and

2. Results for the immediately preceding period, presented as if they had combined.

The AICPA has listed some general guides for the assigning of values to certain individual items, as follows:

Receivables at present values of amounts to be received, less allowances for uncollectibles.

Marketable securities at net realizable values.

Inventories:

Finished goods at selling prices, less disposal costs and reasonable profit to the acquirer;

Work in process at selling price, less cost to complete, disposal cost and reasonable profit;

Raw materials at current replacement prices.

Plant and equipment at current replacement cost if to be used or, if to be disposed of, at net realizable value.

Intangibles (identifiable, excluding goodwill) at appraised values.

All other assets at appraised values (including land).

Accounts and notes payable, long-term debt and other claims payable at *present values,* using current rates.

Accruals at present values.

Other liabilities and commitments, at present values, determined by using appropriate current interest rates.

Goodwill should be amortized on a straight-line basis over a period not to exceed 40 years, and only to a shorter period if benefit can be pinpointed.

[¶1706] THE POOLING-OF-INTERESTS METHOD— BUSINESS COMBINATIONS

The pooling-of-interests method accounts for a business combination as the uniting of ownership interests of two or more companies by exchange of equity securities. No acquisition is recognized because the combination is accomplished without disbursing resources of the constituents. Ownership interests continue and the former bases of accounting are retained. The recorded assets and liabilities of the constituents are carried forward to the combined corporation at their recorded amounts. Income of the combined corporation includes income of the constituents for the entire fiscal period for which the combination occurs. The reported income of the constituents for prior periods is combined and restated as income of the combined corporation.

A pooling involves the combination of two or more stockholder interests which were previously *independent* of each other.

The AICPA has said that a business combination which meets *all* of the following 12 conditions should be accounted for as a pooling:

1. Attributes of the combining companies:

    A. Each is autonomous and not a subsidiary or division for the prior two years; and

    B. Each is independent of the other combining companies.

2. Manner of combining interests:

    A. Effected within one year in a single transaction per a specified plan; and

    B. The corporation issues only common stock identical with its majority outstanding voting stock in exchange for substantially all of the voting common stock of the acquired company at the date of consummation; and

    C. None of the combining companies changes the equity interest of the voting common stock in contemplation of the combination within two years *before* the plan or between the dates the combination is initiated and it is consummated; and

    D. No company re-acquires more than a normal number of shares and only for purposes other than for business combinations between the dates of initiation and consummation; and

   E. The ratio of interest remains the same for each common stockholder, with nothing denied or surrendered, with respect to his proportion before the combination; and

   F. Stockholder voting rights are not restricted nor deprived of by the resulting combination; and

   G. The plan is resolved at the planned date and no provisions remain pending or carried over after the combination.

3. There is the absence of the following planned transactions:

   A. The combined corporation does not intend to retire or re-acquire any of the common stock issued to effect the combination; and

   B. The combination does not enter any financial arrangements to benefit former stockholders (such as a guaranty of loans secured by stock issued in the combination); and

   C. There is no intent or plan to dispose of any of the assets of the combination within two years after the combination, other than those in the ordinary course of business or to eliminate duplicate facilities of excess capacity.

Financial statements of the current period, and of any prior period, should be presented as though the companies had been combined at the earliest dates presented and for the periods presented.

Disclosure should cover all the relevant details.

[¶1707]   FOREIGN SUBSIDIARIES

The following are the possible methods of providing information about foreign subsidiaries:

1. Exclude foreign subsidiaries from consolidation. Include a summary of their assets, liabilities, income and losses for the year and the parent's equity in such foreign subsidiary. The amount of investment in the foreign subsidiary and the basis by which it was arrived should be shown. If the foreign subsidiary is excluded from consolidation, it is not proper to include intercompany profits (losses) which would have been eliminated by consolidating.

2. Consolidate domestic and foreign subsidiaries furnishing information of the foreign subsidiaries' assets, liabilities, income and losses, as stated above.

3. Furnish complete consolidated statements:

   A. Including only domestic companies, *and*

   B. Including the foreign subsidiaries.

4. Consolidate domestic and foreign subsidiaries and furnish, in addition, parent company statements showing the investment in and income from foreign subsidiaries separately from those of domestic subsidiaries.

DISCS

A Domestic International Sales Corporation (DISC) is typically a 100%-owned domestic subsidiary corporation of a parent manufacturing or sales company, created especially for the purpose of benefiting from special tax provisions under IRS Code Section 991-997, and electing to be taxed thereunder.

The DISC income is derived predominantly (95% by tax law) from export sales and rentals. The primary accounting aspects are:

1) A DISC is a wholly owned *domestic* subsidiary and should be consolidated with the parent's financial statement (the IRS prohibits it for tax purposes).

2) Portions of the DISC's earnings are considered to be distributed by the IRS and taxable to the parent. Therefore, for accounting purposes, clear distinction should be made on the DISC's books setting up a "previously taxed dividend payable." The parent should set up a contra "previously taxed dividends receivable" until such time as the cash transfer is made.

3) For the remaining portion of the DISC's earnings, which are not deemed distributed but which will be picked up as part of the consolidated income, *no entry* should be made for the deferral of applicable income taxes, *unless* there is indication of impending distribution of those earnings. Since the main purpose of the DISC option is to *defer* taxability of those undistributed earnings, the presumption of non-distribution prevails, and the indefinite reversal criteria apply.

Changes in the Tax Law have replaced the DISC system with the Foreign Sales Corporation system (FSC) starting in 1985 (see Internal Revenue Code sections 921-927). For further information on FSC tax treatment, see pages 294 and 295.

[¶1709] ## INTERCOMPANY TRANSACTIONS

[¶1709.1] ### In Consolidations:

Since consolidated statements reflect the position and results of operations of what is considered a single economic entity, all intercompany balances and transactions must be eliminated. Some of these are obvious. Others are not.

Here are some of the items to be eliminated (done on worksheets which combine the company and its subsidiary figures):

1. The investment account in the subsidiary and its corresponding equity offset (capital stock and applicable retained earnings).

2. Intercompany open account balances, such as loans, receivables, payables arising from intercompany sales and purchases.

3. Intercompany security holdings, such as bonds, including related bond discount or premiums.

4. Intercompany profits where goods or services are exchanged for over cost, such as profits on transfers of inventory or fixed assets. Intercompany profits on fixed asset transfers might also involve adjustments to the accumulated depreciation account. Intercompany profits on inventory may affect both opening and closing inventories of raw materials, work in process and finished goods, as well as cost of sales.

5. Intercompany dividends.

6. Intercompany interest, rents and fees.

7. Intercompany bad debts.

The amount of intercompany profit or loss eliminated is not to be affected by the existence of minority interests. Such items must be eliminated. However, in eliminating them, they may be allocated proportionately between the majority and minority interests.

If "bottom-line" accumulated losses occur to the extent of wiping out the minority interest, any excess losses should then be reflected against the *majority* interest, rather than showing a negative minority interest. However, future earnings should then first be applied to that excessive loss and the positive remaining earnings apportioned between the majority and minority interests.

[¶1709.2]   In the Equity Method

Intercompany gains and losses should be eliminated in the same manner as if the subsidiary were consolidated. It is not necessary to eliminate intercompany gain on sales to such subsidiaries if the gain on the sales does *not* exceed the *unrecorded* equity in the *undistributed* earnings of the unconsolidated subsidiary. However, do *not* eliminate intercompany holdings or debt.

[¶1709.3]   In Combined Statements

Intercompany transactions and intercompany profits and losses should be eliminated following the same manner as for consolidated statements.

[¶1710]   THE INDEFINITE REVERSAL CRITERIA AND UNDISTRIBUTED EARNINGS OF SUBSIDIARIES

The importance of accruing or not accruing income taxes for undistributed earnings picked up in either consolidating or using the equity method should be checked.

Ordinarily, the parent company must accrue its own rate of tax expense on all income shown on the income statement, including that income required for pickup under consolidating or use of the equity method. Timing differences are thus created until actual distributions (dividends) are received.

However, the AICPA standards recognize certain circumstances under which it is permissible to *omit* this accrual of deferred taxes. The theory is that the timing difference will not be reversed in the immediate future. The concept is known as *"The Indefinite Reversal Criteria,"* and it is based upon the assumption that the subsidiary's earnings will *not* be distributed.

The following reasons are sufficient to justify *non-accrual* of taxes on reflected undistributed earnings of investees:

1. The subsidiary has invested, or will invest, the undistributed earnings indefinitely; or

2. The subsidiary will remit the earnings in a tax-free liquidation; or

3. It is apparent, based on a history of non-dividend payment, that no distribution will be made (as in a DISC company).

However, full disclosure should be made showing:

A. The intention of reinvesting the undistributed earnings, or indefinitely postponing dividend distribution, *and*

B. The amount of the cumulative undistributed earnings and the extent of the tax not yet recognized.

[¶1711] GOODWILL IN BUSINESS COMBINATIONS

Goodwill arises only from the purchase method; no goodwill is created in the "pooling-of-interests" method of combining businesses, since assets and liabilities are carried forward to the combined corporation at their recorded amounts.

With respect to the purchase method and stock acquisitions treated under either the consolidation method or the equity method, accounting for goodwill requires its amortization over a period not in excess of forty years.

Goodwill is the amount assigned to the excess paid over the fair value of the identifiable net assets acquired.

[¶1712] NEGATIVE GOODWILL

When the fair value of the net assets acquired *exceeds* the purchase price, "negative" goodwill arises. The standards then call for a reduction in the noncurrent assets (excluding investment securities) on a proportionate basis to absorb that excess *immediately*. If, in this absorption, the non-current assets are reduced to zero value and an excess still exists, that amount should then, and only then, be shown as a deferred credit, not a part of equity, and amortized to income over an estimated benefit period not to exceed forty years. No part of that excess should be added to equity at time of acquisition.

18

Financial Statements—
Special Requirements

DISCLOSURES

"Financial information that meets the qualitative objectives of financial accounting also meets the reporting standard of adequate disclosure. Adequate disclosure relates particularly to objectives of relevance, neutrality, completeness, and understandability. Information should be presented in a way that facilitates understanding and avoids erroneous implications. The headings, captions, and amounts must be supplemented by enough additional data so that their meaning is clear but not by so much information that important matters are buried in a mass of trivia."

THE REQUIRED PRESENTATION AND DISCLOSURES:

[¶1801.1] **Required Basic Financial Statements For Comparative Periods:**

Balance Sheet—assets, liabilities, classes of owners' equity, components of working capital disclosed by the format;

Statement of Income—all revenue and expenses of the period per GAAP, gains, and losses distinguished from revenue, extraordinary items net of tax, net income and EPS on face of income statement;

Statement of Retained Earnings;

Statement of Changes in Financial Position;

Changes in other categories of equity;

(Consolidation or equity method for subsidiaries and translation of foreign currencies as applicable).

172

[¶1801.2] Description of Accounting Policies in a "Summary of Significant Accounting Policies"

With respect to:

Those principles materially affecting determination of financial position, changes in financial position and results of operation; should include the judgments regarding:

A. Recognition of revenue

B. Allocation of asset costs to current and to future periods

C. Principles and methods involving:

    1) Selection from acceptable alternatives

    2) Those peculiar to that industry

    3) Unusual applications of GAAP.

Examples are disclosure of methods of:

A. Consolidation

B. Depreciation

C. Amortization of intangibles

D. Inventory pricing

E. Recognition of profit on long-term construction contracts

F. Recognition of revenue from franchising

G. Recognition of revenue from leasing operations

H. Policy regarding profit or loss on sale of receivables with recourse.

Should not duplicate dollar information shown in body of statements;
Should cross-reference to financial notes when applicable;
These disclosures also apply to unaudited statements. Policy disclosures may be omitted on "internal use" statements, incomplete reports, certain special reports, or those without financial presentation.

[¶1801.3] Related Notes to the Financial Statements:

A. Disclosure of non-arm's-length transactions;

B. Disclosure of non-monetary transactions;

C. Any additional information which might affect the conclusions formed by an informed reader.

    1) Customary or routine disclosures:

        Measurement basis of important assets

        Restrictions on assets

        Restrictions on owners' equity

        Contingent assets

        Important long-term commitments, not in the body of the statements

        Terms of owners' equity

Terms of long-term debt

Disclosures required by regulatory bodies having jurisdiction.

2) Changes in accounting principles such as:

Change in method of inventory pricing

Change in depreciation method

Change in accounting for long-term construction contracts

Change from recording costs as an expense to method of amortizing and deferring them

Changes in accounting estimates when affected by a change in accounting principle

Change in the reporting entity

Consistent switch to straight-line method from accelerated method at specific life-points is *not* a change.

3) Subsequent events.

[¶1801.4]   Earning Per Share on the Face of the Income Statement: (not Applicable to Non-Public Enterprises)

A. For income before extraordinary items (and/or before disposals of business segments).

B. For net income.

Disclosures should cover number of shares outstanding, contingent changes, and possible dilution from potential conversions of convertible debentures, preferred stock, options or warrants.

[¶1802]   DISCLOSURES ITEMIZED

Here is an alphabetic listing of items *requiring disclosure* with short comments thereon, if applicable.

Accelerated Depreciation Methods—when methods are adopted.

Accounting Policies—see prior "Summary of Significant Accounting Policies."

Allowances (depreciation, depletion, bad debts)—deduct from asset with disclosure.

Amortization of Intangibles—disclose method and period.

Amounts Available for Distributions—note the needs for any hold-back retention of earnings.

Arrangements with reorganized Debtor—disclose if a subsequent event.

Arrears on Cumulative Preferred Stock—the rights of senior securities must be disclosed on the face of balance sheet or in the notes.

Assets (interim changes in)—only significant changes required for interims.

Business Segments.

Cash-Basis Statements—fact must be disclosed in the opinion with delineation of what would have been had accrual basis been used, if significant variance.

Change in Stockholders' Equity Accounts—in a separate schedule. This is not the changes in retained earnings statement, which is one of the basic required statements.

Change to Declining Balance Method—disclose change in method and effect of it.

Changes, Accounting—see text.

Commitments, Long-Term—disclose unused letters of credit, assets pledged as security for loans, pension plans, plant expansion or acquisition; obligations to reduce debt, maintain working capital or restrict dividend.

Commitments to Complete Contracts—only extraordinary ones.

Consolidation Policy—method used.

Construction Type Contracts—method used.

Contingencies—disclose when reasonable possibility of a loss, the nature of, and estimated loss. Threats of expropriation, debtor bankruptcy if actual. Those contingencies which might result in gains, but not misleading as to realization. Disclosure of uninsured risks is advised, but not required. Gain contingencies should be disclosed, but not reflected in the accounts.

Contingencies in Business Combinations—disclose escrow items for contingencies in the notes.

Control of Board of Directors—disclose any stock options existing.

Corporate Officer Importance—disclose if a major sales or income factor to the company.

Current Liabilities—disclose why, if any, omitted (in notes).

Dating (Readjusted) Earned Surplus—no more than 10 years is the term now required.

Deferred Taxes—disclose and also see Timing Differences in this text.

Depreciation and Depreciable Assets—disclose the following:
Depreciation expense for the period
Balances of major classes of depreciable assets by nature or function
Accumulated depreciation by classes, or in total
A general description of the methods used in computing depreciation.

Development Stage Enterprises—are required to use the same basic financial statements as other enterprises, with certain additional disclosures required. Special type statements are not permissible.

Discontinued Operations—disclose separately below continuing-operating income, net of tax, but before extraordinary items. Show separate EPS.

Diversified Company's Foreign Operations.

Dividends per Share—desirable, but not required.

Earnings per share—see prior section for presentation, but the following is also required in addition to the data stated there (does not apply to non-public enterprises):

1. Restatement for a prior period adjustment
2. Dividend preference
3. Liquidation preference

4. Participation rights

5. Call prices and dates

6. Conversion rates and dates

7. Exercise prices and dates

8. Sinking fund requirements

9. Unusual voting rights

10. Bases upon which primary and fully diluted earnings per share were calculated

11. Issues which are common stock equivalents

12. Issues which are potentially dilutive securities

13. Assumptions and adjustments made for earnings per share data

14. Shares issued upon conversion, exercise, and conditions met for contingent issuances

15. Recapitalization occurring during the period or before the statements are issued

16. Stock dividends, stock splits or reverse splits occurring after the close of the period before the statements are issued

17. Claims of senior securities entering earnings per share computations

18. Dividends declared by the constituents in a pooling

19. Basis of presentation of dividends in a pooling on other than a historical basis

20. Per share and aggregate amount of cumulative preferred dividends in arrears.

Equity Method—as follows:

1. Financial statements of the investor should disclose in the notes, separate statements or schedules, or parenthetically;
   The name of each investee and % of ownership
   The accounting policies of the investor, disclosing if, and why, any over 20% holdings are not under the equity method
   Any difference between the carrying value and the underlying equity of the investment, and the accounting treatment thereof;

2. Disclose any investments which have quoted market prices (common stocks) showing same—do not write down

3. Present summary balance sheet and operating information when equity investments are material;

4. Same as above for any unconsolidated subsidiaries where ownership is majority;

5. Disclose material effects of contingent issuances.

Extinguishment (Early) of Debt—gains or losses should be described, telling source of funds for payoff, income tax effect, per share amount.

Extraordinary Items—describe on face of income statement (or in notes), show effect net of tax after income from continuing operations, also after business disposals if any, show EPS separately for extraordinary item. May aggregate immaterial items.

Fiscal Period Differences (in Consolidating)—disclose intervening material events.

Fiscal Year Change—disclose effect only.

Foreign Items—Assets, must disclose any significant ones included in U.S. statements; gains or losses shown in body of U.S. statement; disclose significant "subsequent event" rate changes; operations, adequate disclosure to be made of all pertinent dollar information, regardless of whether consolidating or not (for foreign subsidiaries).

Headings and Captions—may be necessary to explain.

Income Taxes (and Deferred Taxes)—(see Timing Differences in this text.)

Income Taxes of Sole Proprietor or Partnership—may be necessary to disclose personal taxes to be paid if the money will come from and put a drain on the firm's cash position.

Infrequent Events—show as separate component of income and disclose nature of them.

Interim Statements—(see separate chapter in this text.)

Inventories—disclose pricing policies and flow of cost assumption in "Summary of Significant Accounting Policies"; disclose changes in method and effect on income. Dollar effect based upon a change should be shown separately from ordinary cost of sales items.

Investment Tax Credits—disclose method used, with amounts if material. Also, disclose substantial carryback or carryforward credits.

Leases—See Non-current Assets in this text.

Legal Restrictions on Dividend Payments—put in notes.

Liability for Tax Penalties—if significant, disclose in notes. May have to take exception in opinion.

Market Value of Investments in Marketable Securities—should be written down to market value and up again, but not to exceed cost for *entire* portfolio per classification—

Non-Cumulative Preferred Stock—should disclose that no provision has been made *because* it is non-cumulative.

Obligations (Short-Term)—disclose in notes reason any short-term obligations *not* displayed as current liabilities.

Partnerships, Limited—disclose fact that it's a limited partnership.

Patent Income—disclose if income is ending.

Pension Plans—must disclose the following:

1. Describe and identify employee groups covered by plan
2. The accounting and funding policy
3. The provision for pension cost for the period
4. Excess, if any, of vested benefits over fund-total; any balance sheet deferrals, accruals, prepays
5. Any significant matters affecting comparability of periods presented.

Pension Reform Act of 1974—must disclose the effect of future compliance for vesting in the first year *prior* to the date the plan is affected by the law's provisions.

Political Contributions—must disclose if material or not deductible for taxes, or if they are beneficial to an officer.

Pooling of Interests.

Price-level Restatements.

Prior Period Adjustments—must disclose with tax effects. Must disclose in interim reports.

Purchase Commit Losses—should be separately disclosed in dollars in income statement.

Purchase Method. (See Business Combinations.)

Purchase Option Cancellation Costs—yes, disclose.

Real and Personal Property Taxes—disclose if using estimates, and if substantial. All adjustments for prior year estimates should be made through the current income statement.

Real Estate Appraisal Value—for Development Companies, footnote disclosure might be useful.

Receivables, Affiliated Companies, Officers and Employees—should be segregated and shown separately from trade receivables.

Redemption Call of Preferred Stock—disclose in the equity section.

Renegotiation Possibilities—use dollars if estimable or disclose inability to estimate.

Research and Development Costs—"disclosure shall be made in the financial statements of the total research and development costs charged to expenses in each period for which an income statement is presented." Government regulated enterprises should disclose the accounting policy for amortization and the totals expensed and deferred. But do not disclose the confidential details of specific projects, patents, new products, processes or company research philosophy. Applies the above provision for disclosure to business combinations.

Restricted Stock Issued to Employee—disclose circumstance and the restrictions.

Retained Earnings Transferred to Capital Stock—arises usually with "split-ups effected as dividends" and with stock dividends; must disclose and include schedule showing transfers from retained earnings to capital stock. Also, must disclose number of shares, etc., for EPS; must show subsequent event effects.

Sale and Leaseback

Seasonal Business (Interim Statements)—must disclose, and advisable to include 12-month period, present and past.

Stock Dividends, Split-ups, etc.—must disclose even if a subsequent event and use as if made for and during all periods presented.

Stock Options—disclose status—(See Equity chapter in this text.) Has effect on EPS.

Stockholders Buy/Sell Stock Agreements—disclose.

Subleases—(See Leases in Non-Current Assets chapter in this text.)

Termination Claims (War & Defense Contracts)—shown as current receivable, unless extended delay indicated; usually shown separately and disclosed if material, in income statement.

Treasury Stock—(See Equity chapter in this text.) Shown in body of balance sheet (equity section ordinarily); should, in notes, indicate any legal restrictions.

Unconsolidated Subsidiaries—if using cost method, should also give independent summary information about position and operations.

Undistributed Earnings of Subsidiaries—(See disclosures required when not accruing deferred taxes under Indefinite Reversal Criteria in this text.)

Unearned Compensation—(See Stock Options in this text.)

Unremitted Taxes—disclose only if going concern concept is no longer valid.

(See next section for those disclosures which require *Restatement*.)

(Also, see sections on *Timing Differences and Taxes*, and *Permanent Differences*.)

[¶1803] RESTATEMENTS

The following alphabetic listing indicates those areas which *require* a restatement (with disclosure) for all prior periods presented in the comparative financial statements:

Appropriations of Retained Earnings—any change made to conform with Section 4311 for the reporting of contingencies requires retroactive adjustment.

Changes in Accounting Principle Requiring Restatement

1. Change *from* LIFO to another method.
2. Change in long-term construction method.
3. Change to or from "full cost" method in the extractive industries.

Must show effect on both net income and EPS for all periods presented.

Change in Reporting Entity—must restate.

Contingencies—restate for the cumulative effect applying the rules for contingencies.

Earnings Per Share—the effect of all restatements must be shown on EPS, separating as to EPS from continuing operations, EPS from disposals, EPS from extraordinary items and EPS from net income.

Equity Method—restatement required when first applying the method, even though it was not required before.

Extraordinary Items—if a similar one in prior period was not classified as extraordinary, but is now, reclassify now for comparison.

Foreign Currency Translations—restate to conform with adoption of standards; if indeterminable, use the cumulative method. Disclose nature of restatement and effect (or cumulative effect) on income before extraordinary items, on net income, and on related per share amounts.

Income Taxes (Equity Method)—restate to comply.

Interim Financial Statements—restate for changes in accounting principle and for prior period adjustments. If it's a cumulative type change, the first interim period should show the entire effect; if in later period, full effect should be applied to the first period and restated for other periods.

Leases—see Non-Current Assets chapter in this text.

Oil and Gas Producing Companies—in conforming with standards, restatement is not required, but it is permissible.

Pooling of Interests—A change in accounting method for pooled unit should be applied retroactively.

In initial pooling, combine year to date, restate prior periods presented, show separate information for independent operations and positions. Purchase method shows pro forma combine.

Until pooling is consummated, include the proportion of earnings in ordinary financials; *but* also present statements (retroactively applied) as if pooling had occurred.

Prior Period Adjustments—must restate the details affected for all periods presented, disclose and adjust opening retained earnings. Must also do it for interim reports.

Refinancing Short-Term Obligations—restatement is permitted, but not required.

Research and Development Costs—In conforming with standards, apply retroactively as a prior period adjustment.

No retroactive recapitalization of costs is permissible. Applies to *purchase* combinations also. Basic rule; expense as incurred.

Statistical Summaries (5 years, 10 years, etc.)—Restate all prior years involved in prior period adjustments.

Stock Dividends and Splits—Must restate earnings per share figures and number of shares to give effect to stock dividends and splits *including* those occurring *after* close of period being reported on (for all periods presented).

Revision based on FASB Opinions—retroactive restatement is not required *unless* the new standard *specifically* states that it is required.

Note that restatements are *not* required for a change from FIFO to LIFO, nor for a change in the method of handling investment tax credits.

[¶1804]   # TIMING AND PERMANENT DIFFERENCES—INCOME TAXES*

The corporation tax return form #1120 includes Schedule M on the back page of the form which calls for an explanation, detailed item by item, of the reasons for the difference between the taxable income shown on the tax return and the net income shown in the filer's financial statement.

This same difference between financial income and taxable income, which

---

*These unrealized gains or losses will probably reverse to the extent of the actual at date of finalization of transactions. However, there will always be some portion which will never reverse exactly as recorded. This irreversible portion must then be (theoretically) offset in that period, creating a reverse permanent difference in *that* period.

has for many years been shown on the tax return, must now also be explained for *financial* statement purposes. These are the "differences" in the terminology "timing difference" and "permanent difference."

The distinction between "timing" and "permanent" goes one step further: "Timing" differences are those which will someday reverse. "Permanent" differences will never reverse.

A permanent difference, for example, would be an expense taken on the financial statement, which is *never* allowable on the tax return.

A timing difference would be one, for example, which involves an expense taken *now* on the financial statement, but next year or later on the tax return, such as an excess contribution deduction, limited to 10% on the tax return, with carryover permissible.

[¶1805] PERMANENT DIFFERENCES

Those which will not reverse or "turn around" in other periods:

1. Specific *revenues exempt* from taxability (examples):
   Dividend exclusions

   Interest on tax exempt securities

   Life insurance proceeds

   Negative goodwill amortization

   Unrealized gains on marketable securities*

   Unrealized gains on foreign currency translations*

   Tax benefits arising from stock-option compensatory plans (when booked as income)

2. *Expenses* which are *not* tax deductible:
   Depreciation taken on appraisal increases or donated property

   Goodwill amortization

   Premiums on officer life insurance

   Tax penalties and fines

   Unrealized losses on securities or currency translations*

3. Those expenses which are predicated upon different bases for financial and tax purposes:
   Depreciation on trade-ins

   Statutory depletion vs. cost depletion

   Business combinations which treat purchase as "pooling for tax return or pooling as purchase."

---

*See FASB Statement NJ 37 *Balance Sheet Classification of Deferred Income Taxes*, July, 1980.

TIMING DIFFERENCES

Those which *will* turn around or reverse in one or more subsequent periods. Four broad categories:

1. Income—for Accounting NOW—for Taxes LATER
2. Expenses—For Accounting NOW—for Taxes LATER
3. Income—for Accounting LATER—for Taxes NOW
4. Expenses—for Accounting LATER—for Taxes NOW

1. Items of *income* included for accounting financial statement purposes NOW—not taken on the tax return until a LATER time (examples):

Gross profit on installment method date of sale/when collected on tax return.

Percentage of completion method on books/completed contract method for tax return.

Leasing rentals on books under financing method/actual rent less depreciation for tax return.

Subsidiary earnings reported now/as received for tax return.

2. Items of *expense* taken on financial statements NOW, not taken on tax returns until LATER (examples):

Accelerated depreciation used for financials/not for tax return.

Contributions on financials over 5% limit/carried over for taxes.

Deferred compensation accruals/taken when paid on tax return.

Estimated costs of various kinds/taken when cost or loss becomes actual and known, such as: guarantees, product warranties, inventory losses, legal settlements, segment disposals, major repairs.

Depreciation based on shorter life for books than for tax return.

Organization costs taken now/amortized for tax return.

3. Items of *income* taken into financial books LATER, but reported as income NOW on tax returns:

Rents and royalties deferred until earned/reported when collected for tax return.

Deferred fees, dues, services contracts/reported when collected for tax returns.

Intercompany consolidation gains and losses/taxed now if filing separate return.

Leaseback gains amortized gains over lease-term/date of sale for tax return.

4. Items of *expense* taken into financial books LATER, but taken NOW on tax return:

Depreciation; shorter lives used for tax purposes accelerated rates on tax return/straight-line on books certain emergency facility amortization taken on tax returns/later on books.

Bond discount, premium costs taken on return/amortized on books.

Certain costs which are taken for tax purposes/but deferred for financial purposes, as;

Incidental costs of property acquisitions

Preoperating costs

Certain research and development costs (deferred for financial purposes only those approved exceptions to those which must be expensed).

[¶1806.1]   Other Considerations Regarding Income Taxes:

Interperiod tax allocation should be followed under the deferred method.

Timing differences may be considered individually or grouped by similarity.

Tax carryback losses (including investment tax credit carrybacks should be recognized in the loss period in which the carryback originated). Carryforwards should not be recognized until realized (then show as *extraordinary* item) unless there is no doubt of realization (then show as part of operating profit or loss).

[¶1806.2]   Balance Sheet Presentation of Income Taxes:

Tax accounts on the balance sheet should be separately classified so as to show:

1. Taxes estimated to be paid currently.
2. *Net* amount of current deferred charges and deferred credits related to timing differences.*
3. *Net* amount of noncurrent deferred taxes related to timing differences.**
4. Receivables for carryback losses.
5. Where realization is beyond doubt, show an asset for the benefit to be derived from a carryforward of losses.
6. Deferred investment credits, when this method is employed.

[¶1806.3]   Income Statement Presentation of Income Taxes

All taxes based on income, including foreign, federal, state and local should be reflected in income tax expense in the income statement.

The following components should be disclosed separately and put on the income statement before extraordinary items and prior period adjustments:

1. Taxes estimated to be payable.
2. Tax effects of timing differences.
3. Tax effects of investment credits (either method).
4. Tax effects of operating losses.

---

*These unrealized gains or losses will probably reverse to the extent of the actual at date of finalization of transactions. However, there will always be some portion which will never reverse exactly as recorded. This irreversible portion must then be (theoretically) offset in that later period, creating a reverse permanent difference in *that* period.

**Not permissible netting.

[¶1806.4]   General Disclosures

In addition, the following general disclosures are required:

1. Amounts of any operating loss carryforwards not recognized in the loss period, with expiration dates and effect on deferred tax accounts;
2. Significant amounts of any other unused tax deductions or credits, with expiration dates;
3. Any reasons for significant differences between taxable income and pretax accounting income.
4. Deferred income taxes related to an asset or liability are classified the same as the related asset or liability. A deferred tax charge or credit is related to an asset or liability if reduction of the asset or liability would cause the underlying timing difference to reverse. Deferred income taxes that are not related to an asset or liability are classified according to the expected reversal date of the timing difference.

[¶1807]   REPORTING FOR BUSINESS SEGMENTS

According to FASB #14, it became mandatory for certain companies to report the results of operations by business segments.

The disclosure requirements generally pertain to: 1) enterprise operations in different industries, 2) foreign operations and export sales, 3) major customers. These disclosures are required for all complete annual statements per GAAP, including comparative presentations. However, these requirements do not apply to non-public enterprises per FASB #21 and do not apply to interim statements per FASB #18.

The purpose of the disclosures is to assist statement users in appraising past and future performance of the enterprise.

An industry segment is a component of a business enterprise engaged in providing a product or service primarily to unaffiliated customers. In order to determine whether a segment should be separately reported, the individual products and services must be identified and grouped into segments. A firm's profit centers are the starting point for determining segments. They are the smallest units of activity for which revenue and expense data are accumulated. Once the grouping has been completed, segments which are significant to the enterprise must be determined. An industry is considered to be significant when one or more of the following is true for the latest period: a) Revenue is 10% or more of the combined revenue from both unaffiliated customers and intersegment sales, b) operating profit or loss is 10% or more of either 1) the combined profit of all segments with profit or 2) the combined loss of all segments with loss, c) indentifiable assets exceed 10% or more of the combined indentifiable assets of all segments.

184

Revenue, operating profit and identifiable assets of unsegmented foreign operations (due to impracticability) are included in combined figures for the above tests.

When a segment, not usually reported separately, has abnormally high operating profit or revenue in one period, it should be reported separately if management considers it useful. Otherwise, it can be reported as in the past, but in any event, it should at least be disclosed.

In an attempt to keep matters practical, the number of reportable segments probably should not exceed ten. Closely related segments can be combined to bring the figure down.

When all segments have been identified and segregated, management must verify that combined sales to non-affiliated customers are at least 75% of total sales to non-affiliated customers. If they aren't, additional segments must be identified as reportable segments.

No segment information need be disclosed if 90% of revenue, operating profit, and identifiable assets are in a single industry and no other segment meets any of the 10% tests.

The following shall be presented for each reportable segment and in aggregate for the remaining segments not reported separately; disclose the effect of any changes: 1) Sales to unaffiliated customers and intersegment sales separately for each income statement presented, 2) operating profit (loss) for each income statement presented, 3) carrying amount of identifiable assets. Also for each segment: a) aggregate depreciation, depletion and amortization, b) capital expenditures, c) equity in vertically integrated unconsolidated subsidiaries and equity method investees.

Segment information may be presented a) in the body of the statements, b) entirely in the notes, or c) in separate schedules to the statements.

[¶1807.1]   Foreign Operations and Export Sales

Foreign operations revenue, operating profit, and identifiable assets (as per segments) shall be disclosed if either a) foreign operations revenue to unaffiliated customers is 10% or more of consolidated revenue, or b) foreign operations identifiable assets are 10% or more of consolidated assets.

The foreign operations disclosures shall be further broken down by significant foreign geographic areas and in aggregate for insignificant areas.

Export sales should also be disclosed in aggregate and by geographic area if sales to unaffiliated customers are 10% or more of consolidated sales.

[¶1807.2]   Customer Disclosures

If 10% or more of the revenue of an enterprise is derived from sales to any single customer, that fact and the amount of revenue from each customer shall be disclosed. Disclose similarly if 10% or more of revenue is derived from sales to domestic government agencies or foreign governments. The identity of the industry segment making the sales shall be disclosed.

Segment data should be restated for comparative purposes when the statements as a whole have been retroactively restated and when a change has occurred in grouping segments or foreign operations.

19

Interim Statements
(Prepared by Management)

[¶1901] GUIDELINES FOR INTERIM REPORTING

Guidelines for interim reporting by publicly traded companies have been established by the AICPA (and the SEC).

For those private companies which do not bear the same responsibility for full and adequate disclosure to public shareholders, the guideline for public disclosure should be studied and followed, where feasible and relevant, for possible self-protection against insurgent parties, since adherence to standards would probably be more defensible than non-adherence.

The following standards for determining information and the guidelines indicated for minimum disclosure have prevailed since December 31, 1973.

1. Results should be based on the same principles and practices used for the latest annual statements (subject to the modifications below).

2. Revenue should be recognized as earned for the interim on the same basis as for the full year. Losses should be recognized as incurred or when becoming evident.

3. Costs may be classified as:

    A. Those associated with revenue (cost of goods sold);

    B. All other costs—expenses based on;

        1) Those actually incurred, or

        2) Those allocated, based on:

            a) Time expired, or

            b) Benefits received, or

            c) Other period activity.

4. Costs or losses (including extraordinary items) should not be deferred or apportioned unless they would at year end. Advertised costs may be apportioned in relation to sales for interims.

5. With respect to inventory and cost of sales:

    A. LIFO basis should not be liquidated if expected to be replaced later, but should be based on expected replacement factor;

    B. Do not defer inventory losses because of cost or market rule; and conversely, later periods should then reflect gains on market price recoveries;

    C. With standard costs, variances which are expected to be absorbed by year-end should be deferred for the interim, not expensed. Unplanned purchase price or volume variance, not expected to turn around, are to be absorbed during the period;

    D. The estimated gross profit method may be used, but must be disclosed.

6. The seasonal nature of activities should be disclosed, preferably including additional 12-month-to-date information with prior comparative figures.

7. Income taxes:

    A. Effective yearly tax rate (including year-end applicable tax-planned advantages) should be applied to interim taxable income;

    B. Extraordinary items applicable to the interim period should be shown separately net of applicable tax and the effect of the tax not applied to the tax on ordinary net income.

8. Extraordinary and unusual items including the effects of segment disposals should be disclosed separately, net of tax, for the interim period in which they occur, and they should not be apportioned over the year.

9. Contingencies should be disclosed the same as for the annual report.

10. Changes in accounting practices or principles from those followed in prior periods should be disclosed and, where possible, those changes should be made in the first period of the year.

11. Retroactive restatement and/or prior period adjustments are required under the same rules applying to annual statements.

12. The effect of a change in an accounting estimate, including a change in the estimated effective annual tax rate, should be accounted for in the period in which the change in estimate is made. No restatement of previously reported interim information should be made for changes in estimates, but the effect on earnings of a change in estimate made in a current interim period should be reported in the current and subsequent interim periods, if material in relation to any period presented, and should continue to be reported in interim financial information of the subsequent year, for as many periods as necessary to avoid misleading comparisons.

[¶1901.1] Minimum Data to be Reported on Interim Statements Is as Follows:

1. Sales or gross revenues, provisions for income taxes, extraordinary items (including related tax), cumulative effect of changes in accounting principles or practices, and net income;
2. Primary and fully diluted earnings per share data for each period presented;
3. Seasonal revenue, costs and expenses;
4. Disposal of business segments and extraordinary items, as well as unusual or infrequent items;
5. Contingencies;
6. Changes in estimates, changes in accounting principles or practices;
7. Significant changes in balance sheet items;
8. Significant changes in tax provisions;
9. Current year-to-date, or the last 12 months, with comparative data for prior periods;
10. In the absence of a separate fourth-quarter report, special fourth-quarter adjustments and extraordinary, infrequent or unusual items which occurred during that fourth quarter should be disclosed in a note to the annual financial statement;
11. Though not required, condensed balance sheet data and funds flow data are suggested to provide better understanding of the interim report.

Interim reports are usually prepared by management and issued with that clear stipulation.

Accounting firms which issue reports for interim periods are to be guided by auditing standards set for "Reports on a Limited Review of Interim Financial Information" in Section 722 of Statements on Auditing Standards, April, 1981.

[¶1902] PRICE-LEVEL FINANCIAL REPORTING

One of the most discussed accounting problems today is price-level accounting. Even though the purchasing power of the dollar has been drastically reduced, financial reports treat the dollar as inflexible, presenting historical earlier values.

Considering the consumer price index as indicative of the dollar's purchasing power and applying that index to the net income of a corporation over a long period of time, we would see startling results. We'd find, for example, that the trend of profits might be downward, instead of upward as indicated by historical dollars. We'd also find that the annual depreciation taken on such items as buildings would be wholly inadequate (on a comparative basis) to match the replacement cost today. Yet, to up the value of the property and to raise the

189

annual depreciation charges to conform with the realities is *not* in conformance with GAAP.

Efforts to correct possible misleading distortions about the actual levels of income of business enterprise resulting from high inflation rates have long been studied. The result is a method of reporting that will, presumably, eliminate mis-interpretations of the results of operations and balance sheet valuations. In September, 1979, the FASB issued Statement No. 33, *Financial Reporting and Changing Prices,* which requires large publicly held companies to supplement their conventional financial statements with information about the effects of changing prices. While historical cost remains the basis for the "primary" statements, Statement No. 33 specifies the disclosures that must be presented as *supplemental* in annual reports to shareholders.

Inasmuch as the FASB considers the approach set forth in the Statement to be experimental, their approach includes a continuing assessment process to provide a basis for decisions on whether the requirements should continue as constituted, or whether any changes should be made.

[¶1902.1]   The "Dual"Approach

When the FASB was unable to obtain a consensus among the many interested parties concerned (sectors of the economy, shall we say) on a method to report the effects of inflation on business enterprises, the Board decided that companies should provide information utilizing *two* different measurement approaches:

1. Historical cost/constant dollar accounting which measures changes in the purchasing power of the dollar.

2. Current cost accounting, which discloses the effect of price *changes* on the enterprise's resources. Current costs can be thought of as reproduction costs for assets owned and in use.

Although there is continuing disagreement concerning the adequacy of the information required, there is general agreement among accounting and financial authoritative bodies that the effects of inflation are significant and have not been adequately disclosed. During the two years since the issuance of the Statements, various studies and surveys have shown:

1. Income from continuing operations measured on an inflation-adjusted basis is significantly lower than reported in the "primary" financial statements.

2. Inflation-adjusted measures of net assets have been much higher.

3. Rates of return adjusted are much lower.

4. Effective tax rates were considerably higher than the nominal ones.

Who must report? Public companies that have either (one *or* the other) $1 billion of assets or $125 million of inventories and gross properties (before accumulated depreciation) at the beginning of the fiscal year. All publicly-held corporations are encouraged to report the effects of inflation on their business.

[¶1902.2]   Definitions

Constant dollar accounting: A method of reporting financial statement items in dollars having the same purchasing power.

Current cost accounting: A method of measuring assets and related expenses at their current cost on the balance sheet date.

Monetary assets: Money or a claim to receive a sum of money, the amount of which is fixed or determinable without reference to future prices of specific goods or services.

Monetary liability: An obligation to pay a sum of money, the amount of which is fixed or determinable without reference to future prices of specific goods and services. (See Appendix H)

Note

1. Monetary items should not be confused with current items. Inventory, for example, is not a monetary item.
2. See Appendix H for the classification of certain asset and liability items as monetary or non-monetary.

The principal disclosures required by the Statement can be illustrated:

	Constant Dollar	Current Cost
Income from continuing operations	✔	✔
Purchasing power gain or loss on monetary assets and liabilities	✔	✔
Increases/decreases in current costs of inventories and properties, net of inflation		✔
Five-year summary of selected data	✔	✔
Footnotes and narrative explanation	✔	✔

[¶1902.3]   Guidelines for Preparing General Price-Level Statements

Here are the guidelines for the preparation of supplementary information:

1. Follow the same accounting principles as for historical statements except for changes in purchasing power.

2. Use the Urban Consumer Price Index to compute information on a constant dollar basis.

3. Inventories, property, plant, and equipment are measured at current cost or lower recoverable amounts.

4. Information on income from continuing operations for the current fiscal year on a historical cost/constant dollar basis, and on a current cost basis.

5. The purchasing power gain or loss or net monetary items for the current fiscal year.

6. Increases or decreases for the current fiscal year in the current cost amounts of inventory and property, plant and equipment.

7. Monetary items are already stated in dollars of current general purchasing power, so should appear at the stated amount.

8. Income tax is stated at the historical statement figure.

9. General price-level gains or losses should be shown as separate items.

10. Foreign statements, branches, or subsidiaries should be converted first to U.S. dollars, then to general purchasing power.*

11. Notes should explain the basis of preparation of the information and what the information purports to show.

The following information must be provided for each of the five most recent fiscal years:

1. Net sales and other Operating Revenues.

2. Historical Cost/Constant Dollar Information:

    a) Income from continuing operations;

    b) Income per common share from continuing operations;

    c) Net assets at fiscal year-end.

3. Current cost information:

    a) Income from continuing operations;

    b) Income per common share from continuing operations;

    c) Net assets at fiscal year-end;

    d) Increases or decreases in the current cost amounts of inventory and property, plant, and equipment net of inflation.

4. Other information:

    a) Purchasing power gain or loss on net monetary items;

    b) Cash dividends declared per common share;

    c) Market price per common share at fiscal year-end.

Footnote and narrative explanations are required:

1. Explanations of the information disclosed and its significance to the company's operations.

---

*This requirement is based upon FASB No. 8, which has been recently superseded by FASB No. 52 (See Chapter 16). The Board will issue an amendment to bring the requirements of FASB 33 into consistency with the new requirements of FASB No. 52. Until the amendment is issued, the reporting entity can prepare the information based on the application of Statement No. 8 and on the provisions of existing Statement No. 33.

2. An explanation of the calculation for the current cost of inventory and cost of goods sold, and for property, plant, and equipment and depreciation, depletion, and amortization expense.

3. The exclusion from the supplementary information of any adjustments or allocations of income tax expense.

SECTION TWO

TAXES

20

Taxes—Methods and Changes

"The art of taxation consists in so plucking the goose as to obtain the largest
amount of feathers with the least amount of hissing."
—**Jean Baptiste Colbert** (1693-1783)

[¶2001]   THE TAX REFORM ACT OF 1984

On July 18, 1984, the President signed into law what is considered by many
to be the most extensive tax legislation in the history of the country. The new law
affects every individual, business, nonprofit organization, and every other sector
of the economy to a significant extent.

There will be references throughout this section to the Tax Reform Act of
1984. Our concern in this tax section is with the Act's changes which affect business entities. In addition, you will find a summary explanation of the key provisions of the new law that affect you personally in the areas of gifts, estates, personal income taxation and retirement plants. (See Appendix J)

[¶2002]   THE ACCOUNTANT'S PROBLEM

In a landmark case, the court ruled:

"The essence of any effective system of taxation is the production of revenue ascertainable and payable to the Government at regular intervals. Only a
system of ascertaining income and tax at regular intervals, i.e., years, could
produce a regular flow of income to the Treasury and permit the application
of methods of accounting, assessment and collection capable of practical application by both the government and the taxpayer."

The determination of the proper timing for reporting income and deductions for
tax purposes is considered to be the most important function of accounting. The

197

timing of income and deductions involves determining the proper year in which each item of income and each deductible item should be reported. In a Tax Court case, the court ruled:

> "The annual reporting period is a necessity in administering the tax law, and the cornerstone of our tax structure."

There is not complete conformity between tax accounting and financial accounting, primarily because many financial accounting decisions are based upon estimates and opinions, while tax accounting decisions are based upon completed transactions and clearly identifiable events. For example, it is proper financial accounting practice to establish a reserve for a contingent warranty expense, based upon a manufacturer's experience for the estimate of future warranty expense. This approach complies with the matching principle, i.e., the income from the sale of the product is matched with one of the expenses of making the sale—the expense of fulfilling the warranty obligation. However, no tax deduction is allowed for tax accounting purposes until the estimated expense is actually incurred under the terms of the warranty.

Therefore, the main problem in tax accounting is the allocation of income and expense deductions to the maximum benefit to the taxpayer.

[¶2003]   ACCOUNTANTS' RESPONSIBILITY

Most everyone knows *something* about taxes. However, no one knows *everything* about taxes. Nonetheless, accountants are *presumed* to know taxes. Generally speaking, they probably are familiar with most of the overall, basic, more prominent features of the tax law—those sections which have been thoroughly tested in the courts and resolved into the traditional body of the law.

However, because of the intricate provisions and the relief loopholes provided and adjudicated, because of the often ambiguous legal wording and the necessity for interpretive regulations and further testing in the Tax Court, because of the very nature of the taxpayer/IRS adversary relationship, accountants, as well as others, merely serve as perhaps better-informed, but still "opinion-only" experts. Formerly, it was only the taxpayer who had to bear the burden— and the cost–and the responsibility.

Now, the Tax Reform Act of 1976, and subsequent amendments, subject preparers of tax returns to incur penalties if they do not comply with new standards and procedures. Accountants, and others, who prepare tax returns or give tax advice, should be familiar with the preparer's liabilities for penalties. These penalties are incurred for the following simple omissions:

1. The failure to sign a tax return for which they were paid;
2. The failure to give a copy of the tax return to the taxpayer;
3. Failure to maintain a list of tax returns prepared.

A more serious problem has been created by subjecting a preparer to a penalty for other negligence or the willful understatement of income tax. This has been interpreted by some Districts of the Internal Revenue Service to mean the failure to follow all the rules and regulations of the Service. The highlights of tax methods, procedures and considerations presented in this section are timely reminders of certain features of the tax law to be considered when advising a client. In no way should they be considered all-inclusive or all-instructive.

Further research into the tax law, the regulations, the interpretations and the court decisions is advised. Extensive tax publication services are available, constantly updating the ever-changing features of Federal and State tax laws and regulations.

Tax *evasion* is illegal.

Tax *avoidance* is legal. It is statutory.

Tax avoidance is on the books, in the courts—for you to find.

Research all pertinent topics.

[¶2003.1] Tax Return Preparation

For many corporations, assembling and analyzing the information needed to prepare the corporate tax returns can be a considerable task. Most, if not all, of the company's accounts have to be analyzed; provision often must be made for various types of allocations for state tax purposes; in the case of a corporation the activities of many branches, subsidiaries, or affiliates have to be coordinated (and the accounting records may be dispersed over many locations). In addition, the accounting personnel responsible for keeping the corporate books are not likely to be tax men, and the tax department may have to review the accounts with an eye to the tax significance of the various transactions.

How the tax return information will be assembled will depend in large part on the organization of the company. In a small company with few employees, the "tax man" may also be the one in charge of the books and may do all the analysis himself by direct examination of the company's books and records. In larger companies, the task of gathering the tax information may be more or less systematized, depending on the size of the company; the number and geographic location of the divisions, subsidiaries, or affiliates; the location and responsibilities for the accounting record; and the existence of a separate tax department.

In any event, however, the information is put together whether by direct examination of the books and records by the tax man, direct interviews of various accounting personnel by the tax department representatives, use of questionnaires (completed by the accounting personnel or by the tax department personnel after discussion with accounting personnel) some system should be developed to make sure all the pertinent information is gathered and analyzed in some systematic and usable form.

The accountant's task in finding tax opportunities (or pitfalls) may be greatly simplified by the use of a tax-planning checklist which points out some of the planning possibilities. The items on the checklist should be set up in financial audit format and suggest the action to be taken which would bring the desired tax results.

New Law: Accountant performing preparer services must require a written statement from a client that the client has adequate records to support claimed travel and entertainment deductions.

A tax preparer who colludes with a client in a willful misstatement of the client's tax liability is liable to a $1,000 fine, and loss of the privilege to practice before the Internal Revenue Service. A taxpayer can be assessed a 5% penalty for poor record keeping of deductions.

While it may not be necessary to analyze in detail each account for routine items, it probably is necessary to have some formal procedure for analyzing all items that have special tax significance. The checklists enumerate many of the items you may want to check (if they apply) and the reasons for wanting a special analysis of each. With these as starting points, you may readily find other areas of special significance that could be added.

[¶2004]   ACCOUNTING FOR INCOME TAXES

The tax consequences of business transactions are usually determined by their legal status, the accounting treatment of such items, or both. It therefore becomes imperative to plan accounting and legal techniques based upon legal requirements and generally accepted accounting principles and practices *before* entering into any transactions.

Once the transaction has occurred and the book entry has been made, it is usually too late to worry about the tax consequences. Even minor issues should be worked out in advance using proper procedures. For example, careful wording of purchase orders will often insure proper description on invoices, so that portions of work done that are deductible as repairs are properly described and billed separately from work done on permanent installations and improvements, that are required to be capitalized.

In order to plan properly, you must know the accounting techniques available to you. Here are the choices:

(1) Taxable year.

(2) Cash, accrual, or an approved hybrid accounting method.

(3) Last-in-first-out (LIFO) or first-in-first-out (FIFO) inventory method.

(4) Cost, or lower-of-cost-or-market, as method of evaluation of inventory.

(5) Method of handling time sales.

(6) Method of handling long-term contracts.

What the Tax Law Requires

Definitions

Gross Income: All income from whatever source derived, unless excluded by law. Includes income realized in any form whether in money, property, or services.

Income Taxes: Taxes based on income determined under the provisions of the U.S. Internal Revenue Code.

Taxable Income: For business, gross income reduced by all allowable deductions.

Income Tax Expense: The amount of income taxes (whether or not currently payable or refundable) allocable to a period in the determination of net income.

The law specifies only that you compute taxable income in accordance with the method of accounting you regularly employ in keeping your books; however, such method must clearly reflect your income.

Each taxpayer is authorized to adopt such forms and systems of accounting as, in his judgment, are best suited to his purpose. No uniform method is prescribed for all taxpayers. Nevertheless, the Regulations (Reg. §1.446-1) do provide that:

(1) All items of gross income and deductions must be treated with reasonable consistency.

(2) In all cases in which the production, purchase, or sale of merchandise is an income-producing factor, the accrual method of accounting must be used. Inventories of merchandise on hand (including finished goods, work in process, raw materials and supplies) must be taken at the beginning and end of the accounting period and used in computing taxable income of the period;

(3) Expenditures made during the fiscal year should be properly classified as between capital and expense. Expenditures for items such as plant and equipment which have a useful life extending over a number of years must be charged to capital expenditures rather than to expense;

(4) Where capital costs are being recovered through deductions for wear and tear, depletion, or obsolescence, expenditures (other than ordinary repairs) made to restore the property or prolong its useful life should be added to the property account or charged against the appropriate reserve, not to current expense;

Those who neither produce nor sell goods and consequently have no inventories can use either of the two regular methods of accounting, the cash or accrual. This includes artists; authors; artisans, such as carpenters and masons who either use their customers' materials or buy materials for specific jobs only; professionals, such as accountants, architects, attorneys, dentists, physicians and engineers; and brokers and agents rendering services of various kinds;

(5) Special methods of accounting are also prescribed in the Code. Such methods include the crop method, the installment method and the long-term contract method. There are also special methods of accounting for particular items of income and expense;

(6) A combination of methods (hybrid system) of accounting may also be used in connection with a trade or business, if consistently used;

(7) The fact that books are kept in accordance with the requirements of a supervisory agency does not mean that income for tax purposes is computed in the same manner.

[¶2005]   CHOOSING A TAXABLE YEAR

Definition

Taxable Year: The taxpayer's annual accounting period (including a 52- or 53-week year) which is the basis for which the taxpayer regularly computes his income in keeping the books.

The initial choice of an accounting period is generally within the control of the taxpayer. However, many taxpayers forfeit this right by giving the matter haphazard, last-minute consideration. The result is that they adopt an annual accounting period ill-suited to their business needs.

[¶2005.1]   Four Possible Choices

There are four types of taxable years recognized by the Code. They are (Reg. §1.441-1):

(1) *Calendar Year:* A 12-month period ending on December 31;

(2) *Fiscal Year:* A 12-month period ending on the last day of any month of the year other than December.

(3) *52-53 Week Year:* This is a fiscal year, varying from 52 to 53 weeks in duration, which ends always on the same day of the week, which (a) occurs for the last time in a calendar month, or (b) falls nearest the end of the calendar month.

(4) *Short Period:* A period of less than 12 months (allowed only in certain special situations such as initial return, final return, change in accounting period, and termination of taxable year by reason of jeopardy assessment).

The conditions for each type of annual accounting period may be summarized as follows:

Taxable Year	*Conditions*
(1) Calendar year *must* be used by a tax-payer if he	(a) keeps no books. (b) has no annual accounting period, or (c) has an accounting period (other than a calendar year) which does not qualify as a fiscal year.
(2) Fiscal year *may* be used by a taxpayer if	(a) he keeps books. (b) he has definitely established such fiscal year as his accounting period, and (c) his books are kept in accordance with such fiscal year.
(3) 53–53 Week taxable year *may* be used by a taxpayer if	(a) he keep books. (b) he regularly computes his income on a 52–53 week basis, (c) his books are kept on such 52–53 week basis.

[¶2005.2] Shift of Tax Year With Permission

In his first return a new taxpayer can select any taxable year permitted by the code. However, a taxpayer whose taxable year is a calendar year cannot adopt a fiscal year without the prior approval of IRS.

If a taxpayer does receive permission to change his accounting period, a return should be made for the short period beginning on the day after the close of the old taxable year and ending at the end of the day before the day designated as the first day of the new taxable year (§443). Generally, if a return is made for a short period, it is necessary that the income for the period be annualized and then divided by the number of months in the short period. The tax is then computed on that amount.

Example: Assume a taxpayer is filing a return for a three-month period and his net income for that period (April 1 to June 30) is $90,000:

$$\$ \ 90,000 \times 12 = \$1,080,000$$
$1,080,000 ÷ 3 (months in short period)　　= $360,000
Tax on $360,000　　　　　　　　　　　　$145,850*
Tax for short period is ¼ or　　　　　　　$ 36,462.50

---

*Corporate Income Tax Rates: 1982 rates—16% on 1st $25,000; 19% on next $25,000; 30% on next $25,000; 40% on next $25,000; 46% on anything over $100,000. In 1983 the first two will be 15% and 18%, respectively. Present law provides graduated corporate rates on the first $100,000 of taxable income, with the rate providing a maximum tax reduction of $20,250 in tax below the tax which would be imposed if the tax rate on that income were 46 percent. The new law phases out the benefits of the graduated rates on corporations with taxable income in excess of $1 million. An additional 5 percent tax is imposed on taxable income over $1 million, until the full $20,250 of tax benefit from the graduated rates is recaptured. (The new law rule applies to taxable years beginning after December 31, 1984.)

To prevent inequities, §443 provides that on the taxpayer's establishing the amount of his taxable income for the 12-month period, computed as if the period were a taxable year, the tax for the short period shall be reduced to the greater of the following;

(1) An amount which bears the same ratio to the tax computed on the taxable income for the 12-month period, as the taxable income computed on the basis of the short period bears to the taxable income for the 12-month period; or

(2) The tax computed on the taxable income for the short period without placing the taxable income on an annual basis.

Let us assume further that the taxpayer's net income from July 1 to March 31 was only $180,000—that the nine months after the short period showed a decrease in net profit.

Here's how the inequity is eliminated—

Tax on $270,000 = $104,450

$$\text{(three-months)} \frac{\$\ 90,000}{\$270,000} \times \$104,450 = \$34,781.85$$

Tax on $90,000 = $22,250
Since $34,781.85 is greater than $22,250, it will be used as the tax for the short period.
The taxpayer would then apply for a refund of $1680.65 ($36,462.50 − $34,781.85)

How to get permission: Application for permission to change must be made on Form 1128 by the 15th day of the second month following the short period needed to effect the change. The motive for the change must be a business reason and not one of tax avoidance.

[¶2006]   CHANGE OF ACCOUNTING METHOD

What is a change in accounting method? A change in accounting method occurs when an accounting principle is used that is different from the principle used previously for reporting purposes. The term "accounting principle" includes not only accounting principles and practices, but also the methods of applying them. For example, a change in inventory valuation from LIFO to FIFO is a change in method.

It should be noted that the correction of an error in previously issued financial statements (computational errors, oversights, misapplication of an accounting principle) is not an accounting change or change in method.

Income for tax purposes must be computed under the same method of accounting regularly used by you in keeping your books. If you have not used a method regularly or if the method regularly used does not clearly reflect income, the Commissioner can compute your income under a method which he considers clearly reflects your income.

Except for some special situations, you may not change your method of accounting without the prior consent of the Commissioner. If you make a change in your accounting method without prior consent, you will be required to make adjustments for pre-1954 Code years as well as post-1954 Code years. Pre-1954 Code year adjustments are not required if the change was initiated by the Commissioner.

It becomes important, therefore, to know whether a change constitutes a change in accounting method or merely a correction of an error (not requiring consent).

Consent is *required* for the following changes:

(1) From the cash to the accrual basis;

(2) Method of valuing inventory;

(3) From/to completed contract method, from/to percentage-of-completion method, or a change from/to any other method to the contract method;

(4) Those involving special methods, such as the installment method or crop method;

(5) Those specifically enumerated in the Code.

Consent is *not* required for the following changes:

(1) Correction of mathematical, posting or timing errors;

(2) Correction of bad debt reserves;

(3) Changes in estimated useful lives of depreciable assets.

The 1984 tax bill clarifies the Code with respect to changes in an accounting method. In the past, some taxpayers contended that there is no requirement to obtain IRS's permission to change from an *improper* to a proper accounting method; that a failure of IRS to consent to a change in this circumstance is a defense against an IRS charge of negligence and penalty assessment.

Congress in the new law has specifically provided that when a taxpayer fails to file a request to change its accounting method, the absence of IRS consent cannot be a defense to any penalty assessed by the taxpayer's failure to request a consent to the change.

Normally, a corporation is likely to use the accrual method of accounting. But some service companies will use the cash method. And in special types of businesses, specialized methods may be desirable. Appendix D summarizes the workings of the various accounting methods available for tax purposes and the advantages and disadvantages of each.

Form 3115
(Rev. Sept. 1983)
Department of the Treasury
Internal Revenue Service

Application for Change in Accounting Method
(See instructions)
Note: If you are applying for a change in accounting period, use Form 1128.

OMB No. 1545-0152

Expires 9/30/86

Name of applicant (If joint return is filed, show names of you and your spouse)	Identifying number (See instructions)
Address (Number and street)	Applicant's area code and telephone number
City or town, State, and ZIP code	District Director's office having jurisdiction
Name of person to contact (Please type or print)	Telephone number of contact person

Check one: ☐ Individual ☐ Partnership; Number of partners _____ ☐ Corporation ☐ S Corporation; Number of shareholders _____ ☐ Cooperative (Sec. 1381(a)) ☐ Ins. Co. (Sec. 801) ☐ Ins. Co. (Sec. 821) ☐ Ins. Co. (Sec. 831) ☐ Exempt organization; Enter code section ▶ .... ☐ Other (Specify):

Section A. Applicable To All Filers

NOTE: Are you making an election under section 458 or 466? . . . . ☐ Yes ☐ No

If "Yes," see Specific Instructions for Section J (Do not fill in Section A).

1 (a) Tax year of change begins (mo., day, year) .... and ends (mo., day, year) ....

  (b) Enter the 180th day of your tax year ▶ .... If this date is **earlier** than the date you signed this Form 3115 on page 5, see General Instructions for "Late Applications" before proceeding any further.

2 Nature of business and principal source of income (including type of business designation on your latest income tax return)
  ▶ ....

3 The following change in accounting method is requested (check and complete appropriate spaces):

  (a) ☐ Overall method of accounting: from .... to ....
  (b) ☐ The accounting treatment of (identify item) ▶ ....
  from (present method) ▶ .... to (new method) ▶ ....
  Attach separate statement providing all relevant facts, including a detailed description of your present and proposed methods. See also item 14 of Section A on page 2 regarding the "legal basis" for the proposed change.

  (c) If a change is requested under 3(b) above, check the present **overall** method of accounting:
  ☐ Accrual ☐ Cash ☐ Hybrid (if a hybrid method is used, explain in detail in a separate statement the overall hybrid method).

	Yes	No
(d) Is your use of your present method specifically not permitted by the Internal Revenue Code, the Income Tax Regulations or by a decision of the U.S. Supreme Court? See sections 4 and 6 of Rev. Proc. 80–51		
(e) Were you contacted in any manner by a representative of the Internal Revenue Service for the purpose of scheduling an examination of your Federal tax return(s) prior to the filing of this application? See sections 4 and 6 of Rev. Proc. 80–51		
(f) Are you a manufacturer to whom Regulation section 1.471–11 applies?		

  If "Yes," AND you are proposing to change the value of your inventories with this request, complete Section E-2 on page 4.

4 In the last 10 years have you requested permission to change your accounting period, your overall method of accounting or the accounting treatment of any item?		
(a) If "Yes," was a ruling letter granting permission to make the change issued? (if "Yes," attach copy) (if "No," attach explanation)		
(b) Regardless of your response to 4, do you or an affiliated corporation have pending any accounting method, accounting period, ruling or technical advice requests in the National Office?		

  (c) If 4(b) is "Yes," indicate the type of request (method, period, etc.) and the specific issues involved in each request.
  ▶ ....

5 If engaged in business or profession: (a) Enter your taxable income or (loss)* from operations for tax purposes for the five (5) tax years preceding the year of change:

1st preceding year ended; enter: mo. ___ yr. ___	2nd preceding year ended; enter: mo. ___ yr. ___	3rd preceding year ended; enter: mo. ___ yr. ___	4th preceding year ended; enter: mo. ___ yr. ___	5th preceding year ended; enter mo. ___ yr. ___
$	$	$	$	$

  (b) Enter the amount of net operating loss to be carried over to the year of change, if any . . .
  (c) Amount of investment credit carryover to year of change, if any . . . .
  (d) Other credit carryover, if any. (Identify) ▶

*Individuals enter net profit or (loss) from business; partnerships enter ordinary income or (loss); members of an affiliated group filing consolidated returns, see item 7(a) on page 2.

For Paperwork Reduction Act Notice, see instructions.

Form 3115 (Rev. 9–83)   Page **2**

	Yes	No

6 Do you have more than one trade or business? . . . .

  (a) If "Yes," do you account for each trade or business separately? . . . .

  (b) If "Yes," see Specific Instructions for Section A.

7 Is applicant a member of an affiliated group filing a consolidated return for the tax year of change? . . . .

  (a) If "Yes," state parent corporation's name, identifying number, address, tax year, and Service Center where the consolidated return is filed ▶

  and provide the information requested in item 5 on page 1 on a consolidated basis (attach schedule).

  (b) If "Yes," do all other members of the affiliated group employ the method of accounting to which the change is requested?
    ☐ Yes ☐ No. If "No," explain ▶

  (c) If 7 is "Yes," are any of the items involved in the calculation of the net section 481(a) adjustment attributable to transactions between members of the affiliated group? ☐ Yes (attach explanation) ☐ No

  (d) If 7 is "Yes," provide the information requested in items 4(a), 4(b), and 4(c) for each member of the affiliated group. Also, see General Instructions for "Signature".

	Yes	No

8 Is applicant a member of an affiliated group **not** filing a consolidated return for the tax year of change? . . . .

If "Yes," are any of the items involved in the calculation of the net section 481(a) adjustment attributable to transactions between members of the affiliated group or other related parties? (If "Yes," attach explanation) . .

9 If change is granted, will this method be used for financial reporting purposes? . . . .

If "No," attach explanation. Such explanation should include a discussion of whether your new method of accounting conforms to generally accepted accounting principles and why it will clearly reflect income.

10 Enter the net section 481(a) adjustment for the year of change, and the net section 481(a) adjustment which would have been required if the requested change had been made for each tax year of the 3-year period preceding the year of change. (See Specific Instructions for Section A.)

At the beginning of the year of change ending; enter: mo. ___ yr. ___	At the beginning of the 1st preceding year ended; enter: mo. ___ yr. ___	At the beginning of the 2nd preceding year ended; enter: mo. ___ yr. ___	At the beginning of the 3rd preceding year ended; enter: mo. ___ yr. ___
$	$	$	$

11 Has the net adjustment under section 481(a) for the year of change been reduced in any way by a pre 1954 amount? . . . . ☐ Yes ☐ No

12 Number of tax years present method has been used for which the change is requested in items 3(a) or 3(b). (See Specific Instructions for Section A.) . . . . ▶

13 Has your present method been designated by Rev. Rul. or Rev. Proc. more than 2 years prior to the filing of this Form 3115 as a change in method of accounting with respect to which section 5.12 2 of Rev. Proc. 80–51 applies? . . . . ☐ Yes ☐ No

14 State the reason(s) including the legal basis (statutes, regulations, published rulings, etc.) you believe approval to make the requested change should be granted. See item 7 of Rev. Proc. 80–51 ▶

Section B. Change in Overall Method of Accounting

1 The following amounts should be stated as of the end of the tax year preceding the year of change. If none, state "None." (Although some of the items listed below may not have been required in the computation of your taxable income under your present method of accounting, it is necessary that they be entered here for this form to be complete. Show amounts attributable to long-term contracts on page 4, Section F.) **Provide on a schedule the breakdown of the individual items which make up the "Amount" for lines 1(a) through 1(h).**

	Amount	Show by (√) how treated on last year's return	
		Included in income or deducted as expense	Excluded from income or not deducted as expense
(a) Income accrued but not received. . . .	$		
(b) Income received in advance of date on which it was earned. State nature of income and if discount on installment loans, see Section C on page 3			
(c) Expenses accrued but not paid			
(d) Other (specify)			
(e) Prepaid expense previously deducted . .			
(f) Supplies on hand previously deducted . .			
(g) Inventory on hand . . . . $ ___ Inventory reported on return $ ___ Difference			
(h) Reserve for bad debts (see instructions) .			
Net adjustment (Combine lines 1(a) through 1(h))	$		

2 Nature of inventory ▶

Form 3115 (Rev. 9–83)   Page **3**

3 Method used to value inventory . . . . ☐ Cost ☐ Cost or market, whichever is lower ☐ Other (attach explanation

4 Method of identifying costs in inventory . . . . ☐ Specific identification ☐ FIFO ☐ LIFO.

	1st preceding year ended; enter: mo. ___ yr. ___	2nd preceding year ended; enter: mo. ___ yr. ___	3rd preceding year ended; enter: mo. ___ yr. ___
5 Have any receivables been sold in the past three years? . . . . . ☐ Yes ☐ No			
If "Yes," enter the amounts sold for each of the three years. . . . . $	$	$	

6 Attach copies of Profit And Loss Statement (Schedule F (Form 1040) in the case of farmers) and Balance Sheet, if applicable, as of the close of the tax year preceding the year of change. State accounting method used when preparing balance sheet. If books of account are not kept, attach copy of the business schedule provided with your Federal income tax return or return of income for that period. If amounts in 1 above do not agree with those shown on profit and loss statement and balance sheet, explain on separate page.

Section C. Change in Method of Reporting Interest (Discount) on Installment and Other Loans

1 Change with respect to interest on: ☐ Installment loans, ☐ Commercial loans, and ☐ Other loans (explain) ▶ ....

2 Amount of earned or realized interest that has not been reported on your return as of the end of the tax year preceding the year of change . . . . $........

3 Amount of unearned or unrealized interest that has been reported on your return as of the end of the tax year preceding the year of change . . . . $........

4 Method of rebating in event of prepayment of loans ▶

Section D. Change in Method of Reporting Bad Debts. (See Specific Instructions for Section D before completing item 2 below.)

1 If a change to the Reserve Method is requested and applicant has installment sales, are such sales reported on the installment method? ☐ Yes ☐ No

If "Yes," show whether change relates to: ☐ Installment sales, ☐ Sales other than installment sales, or ☐ Both.

2 If a change to the Reserve Method is requested, provide the following information for the five tax years preceding the year of change:

	1st preceding year	2nd preceding year	3rd preceding year	4th preceding year	5th preceding year
Total sales					
Deductions for specific bad debts charged off					
Recoveries of bad debts deducted in prior years					
Year-end balances:					
Trade accounts receivable . . .					
Trade notes receivable					
Installment accounts receivable .					
Other receivables (explain in detail)					

3 If a change to the method of deducting specific bad debt items is requested, enter the amount in reserve for bad debts at end of the year preceding the year of change . . . . $..........

If your return was examined, enter amount allowed as a result of the examination.
If loan company, enter only capital portion.
Applicable only to receivables attributable to sales reported on installment method. Enter only capital portion of such receivables.

Section E–1. Change in Method of Valuing Inventories. (See Specific Instructions for Section E–1.)

1 Nature of all inventories ▶

2 Method of identifying costs in inventory . . . . ☐ Specific identification ☐ FIFO ☐ LIFO.

If "LIFO," attach copy of Form 970 adopting that method and copies of any Forms 970 filed to extend the use of the method.

3 Method used to value inventory . . . . . . ☐ cost ☐ cost or market, whichever is lower ☐ retail cost ☐ retail lower cost or market: ☐ other (attach explanation)

4 Show method and value of all inventories at the end of the tax year preceding the tax year of change under:

(a) Present method ▶ .... $ ......

(b) New method ▶ .... $ ......

(c) If changing to cost method are you going to elect LIFO for identifying costs? . . . . ☐ Yes ☐ No

Form 3115 (Rev. 9-83)   Page **4**

Section E-2. Change in Method of Inventory Costing by Manufacturers and Processors.
(See Specific Instructions for Section E-2.)

Please check ( ) the appropriate boxes showing which costs are included in inventoriable costs, under both the present and proposed methods, of all costs listed in Regulation sections 1.471-11(b)(2), (c)(2)(i) and (c)(2)(ii) for Federal income tax purposes, and all costs listed in or subject to Regulation section 1.471-11(c)(2)(iii) for tax and financial statement reporting purposes. **If any boxes are not checked, it is assumed that these costs are excluded from inventoriable costs.**

	Federal income tax purposes	
	Present Method Included (√)	Proposed Method Included (√)
Part I Direct Production Costs (Regulation section 1.471-11(b)(2)).		
1 Material		
2 Labor		

Part II Indirect Production Costs:

	Present Method Included (√)	Proposed Method Included (√)
1 Category One Costs (Regulation section 1.471-11(c)(2)(i))		
(a) Repairs		
(b) Maintenance		
(c) Utilities		
(d) Rent		
(e) Indirect labor		
(f) Production supervisory wages		
(g) Indirect materials & supplies		
(h) Small tools & equipment		
(i) Quality control & inspection		
2 Category Two Costs (Regulation section 1.471-11(c)(2)(ii)) (See also Rev. Rul. 79-25.)		
(a) Marketing		
(b) Advertising		
(c) Selling		
(d) Other distribution expenses		
(e) Interest		
(f) Research & experimental		
(g) Section 165 losses		
(h) Percentage depletion in excess of cost depletion		
(i) Depreciation & amortization for Federal tax purposes in excess of financial report depreciation		
(j) Local & foreign income taxes		
(k) Past service costs of pensions		
(l) Administrative (general)		
(m) Officers' salaries (general)		

3 Category Three Costs (Regulation section 1.471-11(c)(2)(iii)) (See also Rev. Proc. 75-40 and attach the data required by either section 5.02 or 5.03 (whichever is appropriate) of Rev. Proc. 75-40.)	Federal Income Tax Purposes		Financial Statements	
	Present Method Included (√)	Proposed Method Included (√)	Present Method Included (√)	Proposed Method Included (√)
(a) Taxes under section 164 (other than local & foreign income taxes)				
(b) Financial statement depreciation and cost depletion				
(c) Employee benefits				
(d) Costs of strikes, rework labor, scrap & spoilage				
(e) Factory administrative expenses				
(f) Officers' salaries (manufacturing)				
(g) Insurance costs (manufacturing)				

Section F. Change in Method of Reporting Income from Contracts

1 Are your contracts long-term contracts as defined in Regulation section 1.451-3? . . . . ☐ Yes ☐ No

2 Method to be used for reporting long-term contracts of substantial duration ☐ Completed ☐ Percentage of completion ☐ Accrual ☐ Other (explain)

3 Method to be used for reporting long-term contracts of less than substantial duration . . . ☐ Accrual ☐ Other (explain)

4 Net adjustment required under section 481(a) . . . .

Section G. Change in Method of Treating Vacation Pay. (See Specific Instructions for Section G.)

1 Is the plan(s) fully-vested as of the end of the tax year preceding the year of the change? . . . . ☐ Yes ☐ No

2 If "Yes," enter the amount of accrued vacation pay as of the end of the tax year preceding the year of change $ ....

3 Number of tax years plan(s) has been vested . . . . ▶

Form 3115 (Rev. 9–83)   Page 5

Section H. Change in Overall Method of Reporting Income of Farmers to Cash Receipts and Disbursements Method

NOTE: Also complete Section B.

		Yes	No
1	Is the taxpayer a corporation?		
2	Is the taxpayer a partnership with a corporation as a partner?		
3	If either 1 or 2 above is "Yes," has the taxpayer had gross receipts of $1,000,000 or less in each of its tax years beginning after 1975?		
	If "No," attach schedule showing which years taxpayer's receipts were in excess of $1,000,000.		

4 Provide the following information for the five tax years preceding the year of change:

	1st preceding yr.	2nd preceding yr.	3rd preceding yr.	4th preceding yr.	5th preceding yr.
(a) Gross receipts from farming .					
(b) Inventory: Crops, etc. . .					
Livestock held for sale:					
Purchased					
Raised					
Livestock held for draft breeding, sport, or dairy purposes:					
Purchased					
Raised					
Total inventory . .					

5 Method used to value inventory (check appropriate block):

☐ Cost   ☐ Cost or market, whichever is lower   ☐ Farm price   ☐ Unit livestock price   ☐ Other (explain on separate page)

Section I. Change in Method of Accounting for Depreciation

Applicants desiring to change their method of accounting for depreciation must complete this section. This information must be supplied for each account for which a change is requested. Note: Certain changes in methods of accounting for depreciation may be filed with the Service Center where your return will be filed. See Rev. Proc. 74–11 for the methods covered.

1 Date of acquisition ▶ ....

		Yes	No
2	(a) Are you the original owner or the first user of the property?		
	(b) If residential property, did you live in the home prior to renting the property?		
3	Is depreciation claimed under Regulation section 1.167(a)–11 (CLADR)?		
	If "Yes," the only changes permitted are under Regulation section 1.167(a)–11(c)(1)(iii). Identify these changes on the tax return for the year of change.		
4	Is the property public utility property?		

5 Location of the property (city and State) ▶ ....

6 Type or character of the property ▶ ....

7 Cost or other basis of the property and adjustments thereto (exclude land) . . . . $.....................

8 Depreciation claimed in prior tax years (depreciation reserve) . . . . $.....................

9 Estimated salvage value . . . . $.....................

10 Estimated remaining useful life of the property ▶ ....

11 If the declining balance method is requested, show percentage of straight line rate ▶ ....

12 Other information, if any ▶ ....

Section J. Change in Method of Accounting Not Listed Above (See instructions)

Signature—All Filers (See instructions)

Under penalties of perjury, I declare that I have examined this application, including accompanying schedules and statements, and to the best of my knowledge and belief it is true, correct and complete. Declaration of preparer (other than applicant) is based on all information of which preparer has any knowledge.

Applicant's name	Signature and title	Date

Signing Official's name (Please print or type)	Signature and title of officer of the parent corporation, if applicable	Date

Signature of Individual or firm preparing the application		Date

Form **3115** (Rev. 9–83)

General Instructions

(Section references are to the Internal Revenue Code, unless otherwise noted.)

When filing Form 3115, taxpayers are reminded to determine if IRS has published a ruling or a procedure dealing with the specific type of change since September, 1983 (the current revision date of Form 3115).

You should normally receive an acknowledgement on your application within 30 days. If you do not hear from IRS within 30 days of submitting your completed Form 3115, you may inquire about the status of your application by writing to: Control Clerk, CC:C:C; Internal Revenue Service, Room 5040; 1111 Constitution Ave., NW, Washington, DC 20224.

Paperwork Reduction Act Notice

We ask for this information to carry out the Internal Revenue laws of the United States. We need it to ensure that taxpayers are complying with these laws and to allow us to figure and collect the right amount of tax. You are required to give us this information.

Purpose of Form

File this form to request a change in your accounting method, including the accounting treatment of any item.

Generally, applicants must complete Section A. In addition, complete the appropriate section (B through J) for which a change is desired.

You must give all relevant facts, including a detailed description of your present and proposed methods. You must also state the reason(s) you believe approval to make the requested change should be granted. Attach additional pages if more space is needed for explanations. Each page should show your name, address, and identifying number.

State whether you desire a conference in the National Office if the IRS proposes to disapprove your application.

Time and Place for Filing

Generally, applicants must file this form with the Commissioner of Internal Revenue; CC:C:C, Washington, DC 20224, within the first 180 days of the tax year in which it is desired to make the change.

Note: If this form is being filed in accordance with Rev. Proc. 74–11, see Section I below.

Late Applications

If your application is filed beyond the 180 day period, it is "Late." The application will be considered for processing only upon a showing of "good cause" and if it can be shown to the satisfaction of the Commissioner that granting you an extension will not jeopardize the Government's interests. For further information see Rev. Proc. 79–63.

Identifying Number

Individuals.—Individuals should enter their social security number in this block. If the application is made on behalf of a husband and wife who file their income tax return jointly, enter the social security numbers of both. However, if an individual is engaged in a trade or business, enter the employer identification number instead of the social security number.

Other.—Applicants other than an individual should enter their employer identification number in this block.

Signature

Individuals.—An individual desiring the change should sign the application. If the application pertains to a husband and wife, the names of both should appear in the heading and both should sign.

Partnerships.—The form should be signed with the partnership name followed by the signature of one of the partners and the words "Member of Partnership."

Corporations, Cooperatives, and Insurance Companies.—The form should show the name of the corporation, cooperative, or insurance company and the signature of the president, vice president, treasurer, assistant treasurer, or chief accounting officer (such as tax officer) authorized to sign, and their official title. Receivers, trustees, or assignees must sign any application they are required to file. For a subsidiary corporation filing a consolidated return with its parent, the form should be signed by an officer of the parent corporation.

Fiduciaries.—The form should show the name of the estate or trust and be signed by the fiduciary, executor, executrix, administrator, administratrix, etc. having legal authority to sign, and their title.

Preparer other than partner, officer, etc.—The signature of the individual or firm preparing the form should appear in the space provided on page 5.

If a person or firm is also authorized to represent the applicant before the IRS, receive a copy of the requested ruling, or perform any other act(s), the power of attorney must reflect such authorization(s).

Affiliated Groups

Taxpayers that are members of an affiliated group filing a consolidated return, that seek a change to the same accounting method for more than one member of the group, must file a separate Form 3115 for each such member.

Specific Instructions

Section A.—(Item 5(a), page 1)—"Taxable income or (loss) from operations" is to be entered before application of any net operating loss deduction in section 172(a).

(Item 6, page 2)—If item 6(a) is "Yes," indicate on a separate sheet the following for each separate trade or business: Nature of business (manufacturer, retailer, wholesaler, etc.), overall method of accounting, whether in the last 10 years that business has changed its accounting method or is also changing its accounting method as part of this request or as a separate request.

(Item 10, page 2)—If providing the requested information relating to the 3 preceding years causes you financial hardship or other serious inconvenience, you may sign a statement under penalty of perjury that:

(1) Provides your best estimate of the percent of the net section 481(a) adjustment that belongs to each of the 3 preceding years; and
(2) Explains in detail why you cannot provide the requested information.

If we later examine your return for the year of the change or for later years, we have the right to verify your statement at that time. See section 5.06.2 of Rev. Proc. 80–51.

(Item 12, Page 2)—Insert actual number of tax years. Use of the term "since inception" is not acceptable. However, "more than 10 years" is acceptable.

Section B.—(Item 1(b), page 2)—Include any amounts reported as income in a prior year although such income had not been accrued (earned) or received in the prior year; for example, discount on installment loans reported as income for the year in which the loans were made instead of for the year or years in which the income was received or earned.

(Item 1(h), page 2)—If your change in accrual method involves a change to the reserve method for bad debts, see Rev. Proc. 82–19 for the steps to take in computing the section 481(a) adjustment.

Section D.—(Item 2, page 3)—When the only change in your method of accounting is for bad debts, from the specific charge-off method to the reserve method, you must follow the provisions of Rev. Proc. 82–19. Generally, if you comply with Rev. Proc. 82–19, you may assume the change has been approved.

Rev. Proc. 82–19 does not apply to your trade receivables that include items of unrealized income for Federal income tax purposes.

Section E–1.—Applicants must give complete details about the old method of valuing inventory and the proposed method. State whether all or part of your inventory is involved in the change.

Inventories of retail merchants.—The retail method of pricing inventories does not contemplate valuation of goods at the retail selling price. The retail selling prices of goods on hand must be reduced to approximate cost or market, whichever is lower, by the adjustments required in Regulation section 1.471–8.

LIFO inventory changes.—Attach a schedule with all the required computations when changing the method of figuring LIFO inventories. If you are changing from the LIFO to a non-LIFO method, attach a schedule with the following additional information:

(1) The specific types and classes of goods in the LIFO inventories involved in the proposed change and the comparative values of such inventories as of the end of the tax year preceding the year of change determined by (a) the LIFO method and (b) the proposed method and basis (such as FIFO cost or lower of cost or market).
(2) State whether the proposed method and basis conforms to the inventory method currently used with respect to non-LIFO inventories, if any, or that such method is otherwise consistent with Regulation section 1.472–6.

Section E–2.—Inventories of manufacturers and processors.—Applicants requesting to change to the full absorption method of inventory costing OR requesting permission to change a method of inventory valuation within the full absorption method MUST complete Section E–2 showing the treatment, under both their present and proposed methods.

Section F.—Regulation section 1.451–3(b)(1)(i) provides that, except as provided in Regulation section 1.451–3(b)(1)(ii), the term "long-term contract" means a building, installation, construction, or manufacturing contract which is not completed within the tax year in which it is entered into.

Section G.—When the only change in your method of accounting is for vested vacation pay plans, from the cash method to the accrual method, you must comply with the provisions of Rev. Proc. 82–32. Generally, if you comply with Rev. Proc. 82–32, you may assume the change has been approved.

Section I.—Rev. Proc. 74–11 provides a procedure whereby applicants are considered to have obtained the consent of the Commissioner to change their method of accounting for depreciation. You must file Form 3115 with the Service Center where your return will be filed within the first 180 days of the tax year in which it is desired to make the change. Also attach a copy of the form to the income tax return for the tax year of the change.

Section J.—Generally, this section should be used for requesting changes in a method of accounting for which provision has not been made elsewhere on this form. Attach additional pages if more space is needed for a full explanation of the present method used and the proposed change requested.

If you are making an election under section 458 or 466, show the applicable information required under Regulation section 1.458–10, or temporary Regulation section 5.466–1.

[¶2006.1]   Adjustments Required When a Change In Accounting Methods Is Made

A change in accounting method may be made either by the Commissioner or the taxpayer. If involuntary, the adjustments are based strictly on the 1954 Code years. If initiated by the taxpayer, all adjustments are necessary for the pre-1954 Code years. But the Code prescribes reliefs for the extent of the tax attributable to the increased income reportable for the year of change.

Also, the effect of some changes are prorated over a 10-year period (from the changeover year), such as:

(1) A change from cash to accrual method;

(2) A change in depreciation method;

(3) A change to the reserve method for bad debts;

(4) Changes necessitated by the regulations.

[¶2006.2]   When Changes Are Considered To Be Initiated by Taxpayer

Although the Regs are explicit in the specific procedure for requesting a change of accounting method, you may inadvertently cause a change. For example, it has been held that just changing the method on your return, or changing at the *suggestion* of a revenue agent, adds up to a change of method initiated by you. This is to be distinguished from the case where the agent *instructs* you to change.

Under the present procedure (effective for applications mailed after December 17, 1970), application for permission to change an accounting method or practice is filed on Form 3115 within the first 180 days of the year to which the change is to apply.

Adjustments resulting from the change are taken ratably "over an appropriate period, prescribed by the Commissioner, generally ten years," beginning with the year of change. Applications generally receive favorable consideration if the taxpayer agrees to the ten-year spread or any other approach suggested by IRS.

21

Assets

[¶2101]   CASH

Where the corporation has accumulated large amounts of cash, the possibility of the imposition of the accumulated earnings penalty should be checked. The penalty may be avoided if this situation can be corrected in time.

The penalty is not imposed if the accumulation is reasonable for purposes of carrying out the financial needs of the business. Also, the penalty may be avoided by a timely distribution of dividends or by a timely Subchapter S election.

Note that the accumulation problem can not be avoided by the investment of excess cash in tax-exempt bonds. Although the tax-exempt interest is not subject to the penalty, its accumulation may cause the imposition of the penalty.

Where the corporation's cash position is meager, the company might consider the use of a sale-leaseback of its plant or other real estate. This may produce additional funds from two sources: (1) from the sale of proceeds, and (2) from the tax benefits that may be derived from rental payments. There would be a tax benefit to the extent that the rental payments exceed the depreciation that the company was taking on the fixed assets.

Note that for cash basis taxpayers, certain types of income are considered to be constructively received for tax purposes, such as; interest credited on bank accounts, and matured interest coupons.

[¶2102]   ACCUMULATED EARNINGS TAX

An accumulated earnings tax is imposed on corporations that are formed for the purpose of avoiding the income tax with respect to shareholders, by permitting earnings and profits of the corporation to accumulate instead of being distributed. Where applicable, the tax is 27½ percent of the first $100,000 of accumulated taxable income for the taxable year and a rate of 38½ percent on accumulated taxable income in excess of $100,000.

213

The term "accumulated taxable income" means taxable income, with certain adjustments, less the accumulated earnings credit, reduced by a deduction for dividends paid. The accumulated earnings credit allowed is the *greater* of: (1) Earnings and profits of the tax year retained for the reasonable needs of the business *minus* net capital gains (reduced by the tax on such gains); or (2) $250,000 ($150,000 for certain personal service corporations) *minus* (accumulated earnings and profits at the end of preceding tax year reduced by dividends paid during the first 2½ months of the tax year). In determining accumulated taxable income, a corporation is permitted a deduction for net capital losses during the year in question. A corporation is also permitted a deduction for net capital gains during the year determined without regard to capital loss carryover or carrybacks, less certain taxes.

Whether or not a widely held corporation is subject to the accumulated earnings tax has been an unresolved issue, because no individual or small group of individuals was considered by the courts to have effective control of a widely held company, in contrast to one controlled by a few shareholders.

Under the new law, the fact that a corporation is widely held will not exempt it from the accumulated earnings tax.

The Act changes the determination of accumulated taxable income. The deduction from accumulated taxable income for net capital gains, less certain taxes, remains the same. However, in determining net capital gains for this purpose, net capital losses for any taxable year are treated as short-term capital losses during the next taxable year. The deduction for net capital losses also generally remains, but the deduction is reduced by any deduction from adjusted taxable income for net capital gains, less certain taxes, for preceding years beginning after the date of enactment of the Act (July 18, 1984). No such net capital gains, less certain taxes, are to be used to reduce the deduction for net capital losses more than once. In the case of corporations other than mere holding or investment companies, net capital loss carryovers are to be used only once in determining accumulated taxable income.

[¶2103]   ACCOUNTS RECEIVABLE

Here tax savings may be realized by switching to a more advantageous method of reporting income. A change to the installment method of reporting sales may defer taxes for a company that sells its products on an installment basis. This option is available under either cash or accrual method.

An installment sale is defined by the regulations as a "disposition of property where at least one payment is to be received after the close of the year in which the disposition occurs." The installment method permits the taxpayer to spread the income over the time-period of the installment contract. The logic underlying the regulation is that a taxpayer should not be expected to remit tax payments before receiving payment for the income on which the tax liability is based.

The accounting procedure is not complicated. Each payment collected is assumed to consist of two parts: 1) Costs; 2) Gross profit. The regulation reads: ". . . a person who regularly sells or otherwise disposes of personal property on the installment plan may return as income therefrom in any taxable year that *proportion* (italics provided) of the installment payments actually received in that year which the gross profit, realized or to be realized when payment is completed, bears to the total contract price."

> **Example:** A television dealer sells a TV for $300. His costs are $180; gross profit is $120. The gross profit percentage is 40%. The dealer would recognize 60% of each installment payment as a recovery of costs and 40% as realized gross profit.

Another possible tax-saving switch is to change from the strict write-off method for bad debts to the reserve method. The direct write-off method recognizes the bad debt expense when an account has proved to be uncollectible. This is not the most desirable method because it involves the assumption that the accounts receivable item in the balance sheet has no potential uncollectibles—an unrealistic assumption that results in a continuous overstatement of receivables.

A second procedure is the allowance method, so termed because a percentage of each period's sales (or period ending gross receiveables) is estimated to be an uncollectible amount. This approach more precisely matches bad debt expense with the related sales for the period. The amount determined is charged to a bad debt expense account, with the offsetting credit to a valuation account usually titled Allowance for Doubtful Accounts.

There is also the election to switch from the long-term contract to the completed contract method of reporting income. The completed contract method recognizes income only when the contract is completed, or substantially completed. (A contract is considered to be substantially completed if the remaining costs associated with fully completing contract performance are insignificant in amount.) All income and related expenses are deferred until completion of the job.

The percentage-of-completion method recognizes income as work on the contract progresses from accounting period to accounting period. Income is reported in proportion to the percentage of the work that has been completed as of the end of the accounting period.

[¶2104]   INVENTORIES

In an inflationary economy, a company will want to consider changing the method of valuation of inventories from FIFO to LIFO. The change, however, would affect the company's earnings for financial purposes because, if the company chooses to use LIFO for tax purposes, it *must* use the same method for financial reporting.

In the past, businesses were reluctant to adopt LIFO because of the complicated nature of the tax regulations associated with this method. The new tax law simplifies the requirements.

Particularly troublesome to small business was the IRS requirement that wholesalers, retailers, jobbers and distributors keep separate LIFO inventory accounts (termed "pools") for each product. After December 31, 1981, qualifying "small businesses," (defined as those with average annual gross receipts for the next preceding three years of $2 million or less), can elect a single dollar-value LIFO pool. In addition, a small business can use governmental indexes (under regulations yet to be issued) in pricing its inventory. (Note: The Treasury will issue appropriate governmental indexes to be applied. Formerly, businesses had to construct their own indices.)

A taxpayer who uses inventories must use the accrual method of accounting.

Supplies are not, in themselves, inventoriable. They become so only when acquired for sale or to be physically a part of merchandise intended for sale.

If you use the lower of cost or market for valuing inventory, the tax rule is that each item must be taken into consideration separately—i.e., the cost and market of each item must be compared. The Treasury does not recognize the right to value aggregates of similar inventory items on a total cost or market, whichever is lower, basis.

Taxpayer can elect in the first return the method of valuing inventory which conforms to the best accounting practice in the trade or business and which clearly reflects taxable income. The usual methods are: (1) cost, and (2) cost or market, whichever is less.

Taxpayer can elect, in the first return, the method of measuring cost [by specific identification, first-in-first-out (FIFO), LIFO, etc.]. Elections can be changed only with Commissioner's permission.

The Treasury does *not* for manufacturers, allow the use of "Prime Costing" (no overhead in inventory) or "Direct Costing" (the inclusion of only variable overhead).

Retailers can elect to use the retail inventory method. Other options are available in certain specialized fields (farming, security dealers).

The last-in-first-out method (LIFO) can be elected by making application on Form 970, filed with the return for the first year the method is to be used.

[¶2104.1]   Change of Inventory Method

Except for LIFO, which the taxpayer adopts by election, change in inventory method for tax purposes is treated as a change of accounting method, and the Commissioner's consent must be obtained. Since tax saving is not sufficient to justify a change, state in your request the business objective you seek to accomplish.

Recomputation of the opening inventory according to your new method will ordinarily be required.

Businesses that use LIFO must value their inventory at cost:

1. Any reductions of inventories, for whatever reason, must be restored to original cost.

Form **970**	**Application to Use LIFO Inventory Method**	OMB No. 1545-0042
(Rev. November 1981) Department of the Treasury Internal Revenue Service	▶ Attach to your tax return. ▶ For Paperwork Reduction Act Notice, see instructions on back.	Expires 11-30-84

Name	Identifying number (See instructions)

Address (Number, street, city, State and ZIP code)	CHECK ONE: ☐ Initial Election ☐ Subsequent Election

Statement of Election and Other Information:

A. I apply to adopt and use the LIFO inventory method provided by section 472. I will use this method for the first time (or modify this method) as of (date tax year ends) ...., for the following goods (give details as explained in instructions; use more sheets if necessary):

B. I agree to make any adjustments that the District Director of Internal Revenue may require, on examination of my return, to reflect income clearly for the years involved in changing to or from the LIFO method or in using it.

1. Nature of business

2. (a) Inventory method used until now

   (b) Will inventory be taken at actual cost regardless of market value? If "No," attach explanation. . . . . ☐ Yes ☐ No

3. (a) Was the closing inventory of the specified goods valued at cost as of the end of the immediately preceding tax year, as required by section 472(d)? If "No," attach explanation . . . . ☐ Yes ☐ No

   (b) Did you file an amended return to include in the prior year's income any adjustments that resulted from changing to LIFO? . ☐ Yes ☐ No
      See Rev. Proc. 76-6, 1976-1, C.B. 545. If "No," attach explanation.

4. (a) List goods subject to inventory that are not to be inventoried under the LIFO method

   (b) Were the goods of the specified type included in opening inventory counted as acquired at the same time and at a unit cost equal to the actual cost of the total divided by the number of units on hand? If "No," attach explanation . . . . . ☐ Yes ☐ No

5. (a) Did you issue credit statements, or reports to shareholders, partners, other proprietors, or beneficiaries, covering the first tax year to which this application refers? . . . . ☐ Yes ☐ No

   (b) If "Yes," state to whom, and on what dates

   (c) Show the inventory method used in determining income, profit, or loss in those statements

6. Method used to determine the cost of the goods in the closing inventory over those in the opening inventory. (See Regulations section 1.472-2.)
   ☐ Most recent purchases   ☐ Earliest acquisitions during the year   ☐ Average cost of purchases during the year   ☐ Other—Attach explanation

7. Method used in valuing LIFO inventories
   ☐ Unit method   ☐ Dollar-value method

8. (a) If you use pools, list and describe contents of each pool

   (b) Describe briefly the cost system used

   (c) Method used in computing LIFO value of dollar-value pools
     ☐ Double extension method   ☐ Other method (If other, describe and justify—see instructions.)

9. Did you change your method of valuing inventories for this tax year with the Commissioner's permission? If "Yes," attach a copy of the National Office's "grant letter" to this Form 970 . . . . ☐ Yes ☐ No

10. Were you ever on LIFO before? If "Yes," attach a statement to list the tax years you used LIFO and to explain why you discontinued it . . . . ☐ Yes ☐ No

Under penalties of perjury, I declare that I have examined this application, including any accompanying schedules and statements, and to the best of my knowledge and belief it is true, correct, and complete.

Date	Signature of taxpayer	
Date	Signature of officer	Title

Form 970. Application to Use LIFO Inventory Method.

Instructions

(References are to the Internal Revenue Code.)

GENERAL INSTRUCTIONS

Paperwork Reduction Act Notice.—The Paperwork Reduction Act of 1980 says we must tell you why we are collecting this information, how we will use it, and whether you have to give it to us. We ask for the information to carry out the Internal Revenue laws of the United States. We need it to ensure that you are complying with these laws and to allow us to figure and collect the right amount of tax. You are required to give us this information.

Purpose.—Form 970 is an optional form that you can file with your income tax return to adopt or expand the LIFO inventory method described in section 472. If you prefer, you can file a statement that gives the information asked for on Form 970. (See Regulations section 1.472–3(a).) File the application with your return for the first tax year for which you intend to use or expand the LIFO method.

Change from LIFO method.—Once you adopt the LIFO method, it is irrevocable. You must use it in all later years unless the Commissioner allows you to change to another method.

Note: Effective for tax years beginning after December 31, 1981, the Economic Recovery Tax Act of 1981 (Act) added the following new tax law:

1. Section 472(d)—Three-year averaging permitted for increase in inventory value.

2. Section 474—Election by certain small businesses to use one inventory pool.

The Act also added section 472(f) that authorizes IRS to issue regulations permitting the simplification of LIFO by use of Government Indexes. The regulations will specify the effective date for using the indexes.

SPECIFIC INSTRUCTIONS

Identifying number.—An individual's identifying number is the social security number. For all others it is the employer identification number.

Initial Election or Subsequent Election.—If this is your first election to use the LIFO inventory method, check the box for Initial Election. If you are expanding a prior LIFO election, check the box for Subsequent Election.

Statement of Election and Other Information.—If this is an initial election, enter the tax year you will first use the LIFO method and specify the goods to which you will apply it. If this is a subsequent election, enter the tax year you will expand the LIFO method and specify the goods to which the LIFO method is being expanded.

Attach a detailed analysis of all your inventories as of the beginning and end of the tax year for which you will use the LIFO method (tax year for which the LIFO method is being expanded if this is a subsequent election) and as of the beginning of the preceding tax year. Also, include the ending inventory reported on your return for the preceding tax year. Regulations sections 1.472–2 and 1.472–3 give more information about preparing this analysis.

Item 8.—Dollar-value method.—You may use the "dollar-value" LIFO method to determine the cost of your LIFO inventories, as long as you use it consistently and it clearly reflects income. Regulations section 1.472–8 gives details about this method.

If you are a manufacturer or processor who establishes dollar-value LIFO pools, you may use natural business unit pools, multiple pools, or raw materials content pools. See Regulations section 1.472–8(b).

If you are a wholesaler, retailer, jobber, or distributor, see Regulations section 1.472–8(c) for guidelines on establishing dollar-value LIFO pools.

To figure the LIFO value of a dollar-value pool, use a method described in Regulations section 1.472–8(e). If you do not use the "double-extension" or "index" method, attach a detailed statement to explain the method you do use and how it is justified under Regulations section 1.472–8(e)(1). For example, if you use a "link-chain" method, your statement should explain why the nature of the pool makes the other two methods impractical or unsuitable.

Signature.—Form 970 must be signed. If you are filing for a corporation, the form must be signed by the president, vice president, treasurer, assistant treasurer, chief accounting officer, or other corporate officer (such as tax officer) authorized to sign.

2. Under the former rules, taxpayers had to report any adjustments as taxable income in the year prior to the election of LIFO. Under the Act, adjustments must be taken into income over a 3-year period beginning with the year LIFO is adopted.

3. The "financial conformity" rule was not repealed. This means the LIFO-FIFO earnings comparisons are prohibited.

Statements of an inventory valuation basis in the first return is a binding election, even if there is no difference at that time between this method and some other method you try to use later. If permission to change is granted, but you fail to make the change for the year approved, you must request permission again if you want to make the change in a later year. However, the Commissioner cannot take advantage of an oversight to force the use of an inconsistent method.

[¶2104.2]   LIFO

For tax purposes, when LIFO is used, only cost—not the lower of cost or market—may be used.

The following LIFO rules pertain to the tax-law requirements. Since LIFO may be used for tax purposes only if also used in financial reports, the tax rules for LIFO influence the use of LIFO for financial reporting purposes, too.

How goods on LIFO are to be valued: Goods comprising the beginning inventory of the first year on LIFO must be valued at average cost. The average cost of units in each inventory class is obtained by dividing the aggregate cost of this inventory class, computed according to the inventory method previously employed by the taxpayer, by the number of units on hand. In effect, each unit is considered to have been acquired at the same time.

Goods of a specified type on hand at the close of a taxable year are treated as being, first, those included in the opening inventory of the taxable year in the order of acquisition and, second, those acquired in the taxable year. The taxpayer is given permission to value any physical increment of goods of a specified type at costs determined in one of the following ways:

(a) By reference to the actual cost of the goods most recently purchased or produced;

(b) By reference to the actual cost of the goods purchased or produced during the taxable year in the order of acquisition;

(c) By application of an average unit cost equal to the aggregate cost of all of the goods purchased throughout the taxable year divided by the total number of units so purchased or produced, the goods reflected in such inventory increase being considered for the purposes of the LIFO rules as having all been acquired at the same time.

Instead of applying costs as above, the taxpayer may use the "dollar-value" method which is the computation and application of an index.

(Note: The Treasury will issue appropriate governmental indexes to be applied. Formerly, businesses had to construct their own indices.)

[¶2104.3]   Retail LIFO for Department Stores

The Regulations permit department stores to use LIFO in connection with the retail method of inventory, on the basis of the semiannual price indices prepared by the Department of Labor.

The retail method of inventory valuation is suitable for retail establishments and businesses where selling prices are very closely related to cost. It isn't suitable to a manufacturing concern. It has found favor because it is relatively easy to use in the control of merchandise inventories, especially those that involve numerous items. For example, an average-sized supermarket has over 14,000 items on the shelves.

Where records of cost and selling prices are kept, this method permits a sound valuation for inventories. Compared with other methods, it is simple and inexpensive. Valuation is made by converting the current indicated retail value of an inventory into its related costs. Advantages are: (1) inventory for statement purposes can be obtained without a physical count; (2) the cost of each item of purchase is avoided; (3) ratios for merchandise turnover are more dependable because more inventory figures are available for ascertainment of average inventory methods.

[¶2104.4]   LIFO for Subsidiary Using FIFO

IRS says that an affiliated group may use the FIFO method of valuing the inventory of one of its members in preparing *consolidated financial statements* for credit purposes and for the purpose of reporting to stockholders even though the member corporation uses the LIFO method for tax purposes. While §472(c) requires the sub to use the LIFO method *in its financial statements* used for purposes of credit or stockholders, it does not require that the *consolidated statements* of the affiliated group be restricted in this same manner. The requirements of the statute are satisfied as long as the subsidiary uses a consistent method for valuing its inventory.

[¶2104.5]   Changes in LIFO Reserves—The New Tax Law

A corporation's earnings and profits are to be increased by the amount of any increase in the corporation's LIFO reserve for a taxable year. In addition, earnings and profits are to be decreased by the amount of any decrease in the corporation's LIFO reserve for a taxable year. However, decreases in reserve amounts below the LIFO reserve as of the beginning of the taxable year, beginning after the date of enactment of the new law, will not—except as provided by regulations—reduce earnings and profits.

In general, earnings and profits are to be increased or decreased by the amount of any increase or decrease in the LIFO recapture amount. This provision is designed to eliminate the impact of LIFO on earnings and profits. Under the present law, if a corporation's LIFO reserve increases $10, taxable income and earnings and profits are lower than they would have been had LIFO not been used. Under the new rule, $10 must be added back to earnings and profits.

An exception is provided, under regulations, for decreases below the amount of the reserve as of the close of the taxable year of the taxpayer, preceding the first taxable year to which the provision applies. Since the cumulative effect of the LIFO reserve has been to keep earnings and profits lower than they otherwise would have been, it is contemplated that the regulations will provide that in the event of a reduction in the LIFO reserve below its level as of the close of such taxable year (the pre-enactment reserve), earnings and profits will be increased as under present law without any offsetting reduction under the new rules. However, because a reduction in the reserve below the pre-enactment results in an increase in taxable income and earnings and profits, any subsequent restoration of the reserve up to the level of the pre-enactment reserve should result in an adjustment under the new rules.

Example: Let's assume that a taxpayer on a calendar year has a LIFO reserve of $100 at the end of 1984. Assume also that the reserve decreases to $95 at the end of 1985, and then increases to $105 at the end of 1986. Finally, assume that the reserve decreases to $90 at the end of 1987. The change in the reserve for 1985 results in an increase in taxable income and earnings and profits under present law, with no offsetting adjustment under the new rules. Under present law, the increase in the reserve in 1986 would reduce taxable income and earnings and profits. This reduction is offset by a $10 adjustment to earnings and profits under the new rules.

The $15 reduction in the reserve for 1987 increases taxable income and related earnings and profits by $15. This increase is offset, in part, by a $10 reduction in earnings and profits under the new rules. The adjustment for 1987 is $10, not $15, because the provision does not require an adjustment to offset the inclusion in earnings and profits. By the end of 1986, $10 (not $15) of the $100 pre-enactment reserve had been taken into account in determining earnings and profits.

(The provision applies to taxable years beginning after September 30, 1984.)

[¶2105] SECURITIES AND OTHER INTANGIBLES

Account for all on hand at beginning of year. Analyze acquisitions and dispositions during the year for gain or loss, long-term or short-term (depending on holding period). Determine whether any securities were written off as worthless during the year.

Income from investments may be increased by switching from taxable bonds paying ordinary interest to tax-exempt bonds. Also, switching from interest-bearing securities to dividend-paying stocks may boost income because of the special 85% dividend-received deduction. When the switch produces a capital loss, the loss may be carried back for a quick carryback refund (not, however, to increase a net operating loss of a carryback year).

Owning less than 80% of another company may provide tax savings through dividend deductions. But owning at least 80% of a company provides the special privilege of filing consolidated returns. Affiliated corporations which do not file consolidated returns are allowed a 100% deduction for "qualifying" dividends (as defined in the regulations) received from affiliates.

[¶2106] PROPERTY, PLANT AND EQUIPMENT

[¶2106.1] Accelerated Cost Recovery System (ACRS)

Congress recognized, when passing the Tax Act of 1981, that the useful-life depreciation rules developed over the past 50 years had become obsolete and very complex in their application. They, therefore, replaced the old system with a new one called the "accelerated cost recovery system" (ACRS).

As a result, the cost of most depreciable property placed in service after 1980—"recovery property"—will be recovered, using accelerated methods of recovery, over much shorter periods of time than was formerly the case. Furthermore, under the ACRS system, the methods of cost recovery and the recovery periods are the same for both new and used property.

Property placed in service before 1981 and certain public utility property will still be depreciated using the old methods.

Under ACRS, all eligible tangible property (real and personal) is assigned to either a 3-year, 5-year, 10-year, 15-year, or 18-year class, depending on the type of property. The asset's estimated useful life is no longer relevant. The full cost of the property—without reduction for salvage value—is recovered over the appropriate period, unless the taxpayer elects to use a longer recovery period.

[¶2106.2] Optional Recovery Periods

In lieu of accelerated recovery, a taxpayer may elect to use straight-line recovery over any of the following recovery periods for one or more classes of recovery property:

Class	Straight-Line Recovery Periods Available
3-year property	3, 5 or 12 years
5-year property	5, 12 or 25 years
10-year property	10, 25 or 35 years
15-year property	15, 35 or 45 years
18-year property	18, 35 or 45 years

If an optional straight-line recovery period is elected, the taxpayer must also elect it for all property of that class placed in service for the year the election is made. For 18-year real property, the election is made property by property. The longer recovery periods may not be used with an accelerated rate. Once made, the straight-line election may be revoked only with the permission of the IRS.

Computing Earnings Under ACRS: If corporations were allowed to use deductions computed under ACRS in figuring earnings and profits, they would have a substantial tax-free cash flow that could be passed along to shareholders as tax-free dividends, without any immediate tax impact. To minimize these tax-free payouts, the law provides that in computing earnings and profits, companies must use the straight-line recovery method over recovery periods that are longer than the periods used to compute deductions under ACRS for tax purposes.

[¶2106.3]   Computing ACRS Writeoffs

The ACRS deduction is computed by multiplying the unadjusted basis of the property by a statutory percentage (reproduced in the tables below). The percentage to be applied depends on the property's class and the number of years since the property was placed in service by the taxpayer. No deduction is allowed in the year of an asset's disposition.

The unadjusted basis of a property is its basis for determining gain. The basis is reduced by the portion of rehabilitated low-income housing being amortized and the portion being treated as an expense under Section 179. Special rules for real property: If placed in service after 1980 and before March 16, 1984, real property is depreciable over a 15-year ACRS period. Property placed in service after March 15, 1984 has an 18-year ACRS period. And property placed in service after June 22, 1984 uses the half-year convention for the year of acquisition and disposition. The 18-year table below is for property placed in service after June 22, 1984. It assumes a full year of ownership.

Recovery Percentages for the Property Classes*
(1981–1984 and subsequent years)

If the Recovery year is:	3-year	5-year	10-year	18-year real property
1	25	15	8	9
2	38	22	14	9
3	37	21	12	8
4		21	10	7
5		21	10	7
6			10	6
7			9	5
8			9	5
9			9	5
10			9	5
11				5
12				5
13				4
14				4
15				4
16				4
17				4
18				4
Total				100

(Author's estimates. IRS will issue a regulation for the recovery percentages, which is expected by the end of 1984.)

Recapture of Depreciation: Under prior law, gain on the disposition of real estate was treated as ordinary income only to the extent that depreciation claimed exceeded the amount that would have been allowable had straight-line depreciation been used. The 1981 Act changed the recapture rules with respect to real property. If an accelerated method is used for the depreciation of nonresidential real estate, then the entire amount of depreciation taken must be recaptured as ordinary income when the property is sold or disposed of (Act §1250).

Disposition of Recovery Property: Under the Act, if a taxpayer disposes of or retires recovery property during a taxable year, then he or she may not claim *any* depreciation deductions for the property for that year (IRC §168(d)(2)). A special provision, however, exempts real property from this rule. Under §168(b)(2)(B), depreciation deductions may be claimed for the taxable year in which the disposition or retirement occurs to reflect the months during which the property was in service during that year.

[¶2106.4] Election to Expense Property

A taxpayer, other than a trust or estate, may elect, in lieu of capital cost recovery, to deduct the cost of qualifying property in the taxable year it is placed in service. Qualifying property must be acquired by purchase for use in a trade or business, and must otherwise be eligible for the investment tax credit. No investment credit is allowable for the portion of the cost of property expensed under this rule.

For taxable years beginning in 1983, the dollar limitation on the amount that can be expensed is $5,000 a year, and was scheduled to increase to $7,500 for taxable years beginning in 1984 and 1985, and to $10,000 for taxable years beginning after 1985. The Act postpones for four years the scheduled increases in the maximum amount of property that can be expensed, so the amount that can be expensed will remain at $5,000 for taxable years beginning before 1988, increase to $7,500 for taxable years beginning in 1988 or 1989, and increase to $10,000 for taxable years beginning after 1989.

[¶2106.5] Safe Harbor—1984 Act

ERTA established ''safe harbor'' leasing provisions which stipulated that a lease of qualified property placed in service after 1980 would be considered as a bona fide lease for Federal income tax purposes, even though the lease had no non-tax economic substance. The lessor was treated as the owner of the property and was entitled to the ACRS deduction and, if applicable, any investment tax credit associated with the property. The provision also gave owners of property who could not use the tax benefits to sell those benefits.

The provision permitting the sale of the tax benefits resulted in a loss of revenue to the Treasury, as well as considerable controversy. Accordingly, the 1982 ACT—TEFRA—generally repealed safe-harbor leasing. In its place, TEFRA substituted a liberalized form of pre-safe harbor leasing termed "finance leasing." The finance lease rules provide that certain parts of the pre-safe harbor rules are not taken into account in determining whether an agreement with respect to a limited class of property is a lease for tax purposes. The pre-safe harbor rules therefore apply when finance lease rules are unavailable.

Finance Lease Property Defined: New recovery property which qualifies for ITC can be defined as finance lease property. *New* property is defined as property for which a lease arrangement has been completed within three months after the property is first placed in service by either the lessor or the lessee. Also defined is a "qualified lessor"—a corporation other than a Sub S or a personal holding company; a partnership of corporations none of which is a Sub S corporation or a personal holding company; a grantor trust where the grantor and all the beneficiaries of the trust are corporations or partnerships of corporations.

For a transaction to be a lease under the new rules, the lessee generally cannot hold title to or have a significant interest in the property. However, the fact that the lessor has title does not guarantee that the lessor is the owner for Federal income tax purposes. Both the courts and the IRS look to additional criteria in determining whether a transaction is a lease, with the criteria focusing upon the substance of the transaction rather than its form. To be entitled to depreciation deductions as the owner of the property, the lessor has to show that the property is being used for a business or other income-producing purposes. To have a business purpose, the person claiming ownership—the lessor—has to have a reasonable expectation that he will derive a profit from the transaction independent of tax benefits. This requirement eliminated a lease transaction intended merely to reduce the user's cost by utilizing the lessor's tax base.

The finance lease rules generally apply to agreements entered into after December 31, 1983, but four restrictions apply in 1984 and 1985:

• No more than 40 percent of property placed in service by a lessee during any calendar year before 1986 may qualify for finance lease treatment.

• A lessor may not use finance lease rules to reduce its tax liability for any taxable year by more than 50 percent.

• The 50 percent lessor cap does not apply to property placed in service after September 30, 1985 (in taxable years beginning after that date).

• The investment tax credit subject to a finance lease on property placed in service on or before September 30, 1985, is allowable ratably over five years rather than entirely in the year the property is placed in service.

The new law modified the above as follows:

• The effective date of the finance lease rules is postponed for four years. The rules will apply only to agreements entered into after December 31, 1987, and the four restrictions noted above will apply in 1988 and 1989. This means that the 40 percent lessee cap is extended to cover property placed in service by a lessee during any calendar year beginning before 1990.

• The 50 percent lessor cap is extended through September 30, 1989.

• The 5-year spread of investment credit for property subject to a finance lease is extended to cover property placed in service on or before September 30, 1989.

[¶2107] INVESTMENT CREDIT (ITC)

The ACRS and ITC work together. Having made the changes it did in the depreciation rules by introducing the ACRS concept, Congress had to make certain conforming changes in the investment credit setup. Formerly, for example, the investment credit was based on an asset's actual useful life. Now, for eligible recovery property placed in service after 1980, the credit is based on the recovery period of the property used in determining the deduction for depreciation.

100% of the cost qualifies for the full 10% credit if the property has a recovery period of five years or more. Moreover, 100% of the cost will also qualify for the full ESOP and Energy Credits. In the case of 3-year property, only 60% of the cost of the property qualifies for the regular investment, which results in a 6% credit.

[¶2107.1] Recapture—Two Sets of Rules

Old Law

1. Full cost of property, seven years useful life, qualified for the 10% investment credit.
2. For property held at least seven years, the credit was forever.
3. For property not held for seven years, some and perhaps all of the property was recaptured.
4. If the property was disposed of:
   a) Within the sixth or seventh year, 1/3 of the credit was recaptured.
   b) Within the fourth or fifth year, 2/3 of the credit was recaptured.
   c) Within three years, all of the credit was recaptured.

These old rules will continue to apply to investment credit property placed in service *before* 1981.

New Law

For investment credit property placed in service *after* 1980 a 2% recapture rule applies:

1. A 6% investment credit for 3-year recovery property.
2. A 10% credit for 5-year recovery property.

3. Recapture is reduced by 2% for each *full* year the property is held before disposition. Example: If 3-year property is not disposed of until the second year of ownership, the recapture is 4%.
4. The following table illustrates the 2% recapture rule.

If Disposed Of   Recapture Percentage

	3-Year Property	5-Year Property
Within 1 year	6%	10%
After 1 year	4%	8%
After 2 years	2%	6%
After 3 years	-0-	4%
After 4 years	-0-	2%
After 5 years	-0-	-0-

Used Property Limitation

Old law: $100,000 for the investment credit in any taxable year.

New law: $125,000 for taxable years beginning in 1981.

$150,000 for taxable years beginning after 1987.

[¶2107.2]   Luxury Automobiles

The new tax law limits the ITC and ACRS recovery deductions for passenger automobiles used in business and placed in service after June 18, 1984. The investment credit is limited to $1,000, unless the taxpayer elects to use a reduced investment credit percentage. In such a case, the credit limitation is reduced to two-thirds of what it would have been otherwise. The recovery expense deduction is limited to $4,000 for the taxable year that the vehicle is placed in service, and $6,000 for succeeding taxable years. These dollar figures will be inflation-indexed, beginning in 1985.

[¶2107.3]   Business-Use Test

For listed property (e.g., cars, trucks, computers) to be considered predominantly used in a qualified business, its business-use percentage must exceed 50%. If the business-use percentage is 50%, or less, no investment credit is allowed and depreciation must be calculated under the straight-line method over a longer than usual recovery period.

For more information on the new rules for cars, see Appendix J.

[¶2108]   LEASEHOLD IMPROVEMENTS

The costs of leasehold improvements are capital expenditures which are not currently deductible. For tax purposes, they are depreciated over their recovery periods or amortized over the remaining period of the lease, whichever is shorter. In some cases, however, improvements made by a tenant may be deducted, if they are made in lieu of rent.

If you are a lessee with an option to renew, the question arises as to whether the renewal period should be included.

For tax purposes, to avoid controversies as to probability of renewal, specific rules have been set down. Renewal periods are to be taken into account in determining the period over which amortization is to take place if the initial term of the lease remaining upon the completion of the improvements is less than 60% of the recovery period of the improvements. Even if you do not meet the 60% rule, you can still amortize over the initial term if you can establish that, as of the taxable year of the improvements, it is more probable that the lease will not be renewed than that it will be renewed.

[¶2109]   THE COST OF ACQUIRING A LEASE

The cost of acquiring a lease is amortized over the life of the lease. If less than 75% of the cost is attributable to the remaining term of the lease, you must take into account the renewal period as well as the remaining initial period for the purposes of amortization.

22

Liabilities

[¶2201] **TYPES OF LIABILITIES**

Liabilities to Stockholders: Interest, rent and salary owed by an accrual basis corporation to related parties (stockholders) should be given special attention. The payment cannot be deducted until the year it is actually paid out.

Deferred Income: Where income is received in advance of a sale or services to be rendered, the special election to defer sales should be considered.

Notes and Bonds Payable: Tax incentives favoring debt over stock capitalization should be considered.

Accrued Liabilities: A company on the accrual basis should consider the advantages of accruing employee bonuses in the current year and paying them in the next year. But the bonus must be paid within 2½ months after the close of the year (otherwise, the corporation loses its current deduction).

[¶2201.1] Reserves for Estimated Costs and Expenses

The general rule is that an expense is deductible by a cash-basis taxpayer when he pays it, and by an accrual-basis taxpayer when his liability is fixed.

Where a taxpayer receives income for services he is to perform in the future, the question arises as to when he may deduct the expenses attributable to such income.

If a liability is certain and all events to fix the fact have occurred, it may be accrued. Where uncertainty, or contingency exists, no liability may be accrued until the debt is certain. When a liability is fixed, with the amount uncertain, reasonable estimates may be used and the difference to actual accounted for in the year of exact determination.

229

[¶2201.2]   Contested Liabilities

How should you treat an expense which you pay in full but continue to contest because you believe you have no obligation to make payment?

The Supreme Court in *Consolidated Edison,* 366 U.S. 380, held that a contested property tax was not deductible until the contest was finally terminated, despite the fact that payment of the tax was made in a prior year. The Court stated that the tax could not be accrued because the payment was in the nature of a "deposit."

The Revenue Act of 1964 revised this rule by *requiring* the taxpayer to deduct the contest liability in the year it is paid, even though the contest is resolved finally in a later year.

As an example of how this provision works, assume the following situation: An accrual-basis taxpayer has a $100 liability asserted against it. It pays the $100, but later contests the liability in a court action. The court action is settled for $80. The law requires the taxpayer to deduct $100 initially, then pick up $20 in income in the later year of court decision.

When law doesn't apply: Where payment is not made until after the contest is settled, an accrual-basis taxpayer may accrue the deduction in the year in which the contest is settled, although the actual payment is made in a later year.

Example: An accrual-basis corporation has a $100 liability asserted against it. The corporation contests it. The contest is settled for $80. In the succeeding year it pays the $80. The company has to accrue the $80 in the year of settlement and deduct it then. If any portion of the contested amount is refunded, such refund must be included in income unless it comes within the "tax benefit" rule (§111). Under the tax benefit rule, to the extent a prior deduction did not result in a tax benefit, the recovery of that deduction item is not taxable.

Liabilities are included: Generally, the rule applies to contested local or state taxes. But it is equally applicable to any other contested liability.

Transfer of Funds Requirement: One of the requirements necessary for the deduction is that taxpayer transfer money or "other property" to satisfy the liability. When money is transferred to a bona fide escrow agent, you can usually take the deduction as long as the funds are no longer within your control.

Contingent Items: Reserves for contingent expenses, though used for financial reporting, are not usually deductible for tax purposes (except for bad debt reserve additions). Some may be deductible if the liability is fixed. An analysis must therefore be made concerning such items. Estimates of *amounts* may be used and deducted, so long as the fact of liability is fixed.

230

23

Equity

[¶2301]   **CAPITAL**

Dividend payments should be timed to suit the *stockholders'* tax situation whenever possible. Tax savings may be realized by having the corporation defer payment or split payment over two or more years.

Using appreciated property for dividends should be considered. A corporation realizes a taxable gain when it distributes appreciated property to redeem its stock. But this is not true when it distributes certain appreciated property used in the company's business as a dividend [See Sec.311(d)(2)].

[¶2302]   TAX BENEFITS IN CAPITALIZATION

In financing business operations we have these broad objectives, each of which has tax prospects, as follows:

(1) *Minimize the Risk*: This means cushioning against loss by getting the maximum charge-off against fully taxable income.

(2) *Maximize the Gain*: This means setting the stage for the best possible conversion of income into capital gain and for getting as much of the money back tax free as possible by way of a recovery of the investment.

(3) *Minimize the Cost of Capital*: This means making the carrying charges tax deductible: fully deductible interest or rent rather than nondeductible dividends.

[¶2302.1]   Tax Guidelines in Capitalization

Tax factors have vastly increased the costs and the risks of financing. In shaping the form and the capital structure of a business, we must consider:

231

(1) Dividends are paid out of after-tax earnings.

(2) Interest paid on debt is tax deductible.

(3) From the investor's viewpoint (and this becomes important in close corporations), losses on stock are subject to capital loss restrictions and can be used to offset ordinary income to only a limited extent. However, there is a special exception for small business stock (§ 1244) which allows ordinary losses on the worthlessness of the stock (see discussion below).

(4) Individual losses on debt are usually subject to the same restriction. Bad debts from nonbusiness operations will be short-term losses and thus will first offset short-term gains. (And losses on advances to a closely held business generally are treated as nonbusiness bad debts.)

(5) Worthless securities (stock, bonds, debentures, or notes with coupons or in registered form) owned by a domestic corporation in an affiliated corporation may be fully deductible as ordinary losses [§ 165(g)(3)].

(6) When a corporation starts to earn income, an investor will have to pay tax on the return he receives on his investment in stock. Even if part of the stock is redeemed, he is likely to be charged with having received a taxable dividend to the extent of the corporation's accumulated earnings.

On the other hand, corporate funds may be used to repay debt without tax to the investor. Thus an investor stands to recover the money he advances for bonds or notes without having taxes eat into his capital.

(7) A corporation can borrow money at a much lower net cost than it can take money for stock. The cost of servicing debt is tax deductible, while the cost of servicing equity money must come out of net after-tax money.

[¶2302.2]   Special Treatment for Small Business Stock ("1244 stock")

One problem with stock is that, should there be a decline in value and the investors realize a loss, normally the loss will be a capital loss. This form of loss, of course, has a limited tax value. However, it is possible to issue stock (within certain limits) so that it qualifies under § 1244 of the Internal Revenue Code. When this is done, losses realized may be deducted by the investor as ordinary losses.

The ordinary-loss rule of § 1244 applies whether the loss was incurred on sale of the stock or on its becoming worthless. It can be used only by the original purchaser of the stock. In order to qualify for this special treatment, the following requisites have to be met:

(1) Such stock cannot be issued in a total amount of more than $1,000,000. The one million dollar limit is determined by the total of the amount of money and the value of other property to be received by the corporation for stock, as a contribution to capital, and as paid in surplus at the time the stock is issued. For

this purpose, the value of the property is the corporation's adjusted basis for determining gain, less any liabilities assumed or taken subject to.

(2) The stock must be issued for money or property and not for stock or securities.

(3) The corporation issuing the stock must be an operating company.

(4) If § 1244 stock was issued for property in a tax-free exchange and the basis for the property was higher than its fair market value, the deductible loss on the § 1244 stock is limited to that fair market value.

(5) Ordinary losses on small business stock are limited to the basis originally acquired on its issuance. Such losses cannot be increased by increasing basis as a result of subsequent capital contributions. Any such increase must be applied to other stock.

The loss that an investor can take in any one year under § 1244 is limited to $50,000. (Where a joint return is filed, the maximum is $100,000.)

[¶2303]   SUBCHAPTER S CORPORATIONS

There have been several modifications of Sections 1361–1379 of the Internal Revenue Code over the years, culminating in the *Subchapter S Revision Act of 1982*, which essentially is an entire set of new rules and requirements effective for taxable years beginning after 1982.

[¶2304]   SUBCHAPTER S
TAX REVISION ACT OF 1982

[¶2304.1]   Background

The Subchapter S (Sub S) election was first legislated in 1958. The intent of Congress was to allow small corporations to have the advantage of the avoidance of double taxation, by structuring the tax status of Sub S corporations in a manner similar to partnerships.

Subsequent developments demonstrated that Sub S not only failed to achieve its original purpose, but also created tax "traps" which were not intended by the Congress. The three main traps were:

1. Unintentional violations of the eligibility rules resulting in retroactive termination of the Sub S election.

2. Declaring taxable distributions which were thought to be tax-free distributions of previously taxed income.

3. Shareholders having an insufficient basis to absorb their share of the corporation's losses resulting in the *permanent* disallowance of that loss.

SUBCHAPTER S CORPORATIONS—New Law vs. Old Law

	Old Law Sec. 1371-1379	New Law Sec. 1361-1379
1. New distinctions		S Corporation—a corporation which has elected to be taxed under Sec. 1362(a) (the new Subchapter S designation). C Corporation—a corporation which is not an S corporation.
2. Qualified shareholders a) Number	a) 25 The increase conforms with allowable partners in the private placement exemption under Federal securities law.	a) 35
b) Husband and wife	a) Treated as a single shareholder.	a) No change.
c) Other qualified shareholders	a) Estates. b) Voting trusts. c) Grantor trusts. d) Qualified Subchapter S trusts. (1371(e)). e) —	a) No change. e) Estate of a bankrupt individual now qualifies.
3. Nonqualified shareholders	a) Nonresident aliens. b) Foreign trusts. c) Corporation.	a) No change. b) No change. c) No change.
4. Multi-tier organizations disqualified to elect	a) Member of an affiliated group as defined in Sec. 1504—80% rule in effect b) Holding a subsidiary other than a DISC.	a) No change. b) Cannot elect if it owns a DISC. If DISC was in effect as of June 23, 1982, election will remain in effect until terminated or one-half of stock transferred.
5. Outstanding stock of corporation	a) One class of stock.	a) More than one class of common stock allowed if the only difference is in voting rights. (Sec. 1361(c)(4)).

234

#	Item	Old Law	New Law
6.	Income disqualification	a) Not more than 80% of gross receipts from sources outside U.S.	a) Repealed.
		b) Not more than 20% of its gross receipts from passive income.	b) Raised to 25%. If no prior accumulated earnings and profits, passive income may be taxed at corporate rate without terminating election. Passive income test modified to exclude interest in deferred payment sales of property to customers. (Sec. 1221(1)).
7.	Election period	a) Any time during preceding year.	a) Same.
		b) Any time during first 75 days of the taxable year.	b) On or before 15th day of third month of the taxable year.
8.	Electing shareholders	a) All shareholders must elect. Sec. 1372(a).	a) All shareholders must elect. Sec. 1362(a)(2).
9.	Election form	a) Form 2553.	a) No change.
		b) Need names, addresses and Social Security numbers of *all* shareholders, shares of stock owned and date acquired.	
		c) All shareholders must sign.	
		d) For a qualified Subchapter S trust, the single income beneficiary must sign rather than the trustee.	
		e) Where the owner of record is other than the beneficial owner, the beneficial owner is the proper person to sign. Rev. Rul. 70-615, 1970-2 CB 169; Rev. Rul. 75-261, 1975-2, CB 350.	
10.	Revocation period	a) First month of taxable year.	a) On or before 15th day of third month of the taxable year.
11.	Revocating shareholders.	a) All shareholders. Sec. 1372(e)(2).	a) Shareholders holding more than one-half of shares on day when revocation is made. Sec. 1362(d)(1)(B).

SUBCHAPTER S CORPORATIONS—New Law vs. Old Law (continued)

	Old Law Sec. 1371-1379	New Law Sec. 1361-1379
12. Effect of termination	b) New shareholder within 60 days. Sec. 1372(e)(1). c) Prohibited transactions. a) In effect for entire year.	c) Prohibited transactions. a) If made within 15th day of third month, for entire year. b) If made subsequent to revocation period, for next year. c) Revocation may elect a subsequent date when revocation is effective, creating a short S year and a short C year.
13. Termination where corporation ceases to be a "small business corporation." (Sec. 1361(b)).	a) Termination for entire year.	a) Creates a short year known as an S short year. Sec. 1362(e)(1)(A). and b) Creates a short year known as a C short year. Sec. 1362(e)(1)(B). c) Short years prorate items of income, loss, deductions and credits on a daily basis between S short year and C short year. Sec. 1362(e)(2). d) Shareholders (all) may elect to not use pro rata method and account for all items in time period in which they occurred. Sec. 1362(e)(3).
14. Inadvertent termination	a) Cannot re-elect Sub S status for 5 years.	a) If Service determines event was inadvertent and corporation timely corrects the event, and if the shareholders agree to be treated as though election remained in effect, the IRS is instructed to be reasonable in granting waivers. Sec. 1362(f).

15. Computation of corporations' taxable income

a) The taxable income of an electing small business corporation is computed in the same manner as it would be computed if no election had been made with exceptions for Sec. 172 net operating losses and special deductions related to dividends received, Sec. 241 to 247. Reg. 1.1373-1(c).

a) The taxable income of an S corporation shall be computed in the same manner as in the case of an *individual* except that all items will be distributed on a pro rata basis (Sec. 1366), and items not deductible in computing partnership income will also not be deductible (Sec. 703(a)(2):

   Personal exemptions, deduction for foreign taxes, charitable contributions, NOL's, additional itemized deductions, deduction for depletion on oil and gas wells under Sec. 611. Sec. 1363(b).

16. Pass through of income to shareholders

a) Sec. 1373.

b) The undistributed taxable income is included in the gross income of the shareholders. Undistributed taxable income (UTI) is basically the net taxable income of the corporation, less any dividends paid and less any taxes on capital gains.

a) Sec. 1366.

b) The shareholder will realize his pro rata share of "nonseparately computed income or loss" and receive items of income (including tax exempt income), loss, deduction, or credit, the separate treatment of which could affect the liability for tax of any shareholder. In other words, the conduit approach for income as used in partnership reporting, as in Sec. 702(a).

c) The UTI is distributed according to shareholdings as of the last day of the corporate taxable year.

c) The items of income, deductions, credits are divided on a daily basis to shareholders (similar to old rules of dividing losses). (Sec. 1377(a)(1) new).

17. Distribution by an electing corporation

a) UTI—a tax free distribution of undistributed taxable income if made within 2-½ months after the end of the corporate year.

a) Post 1982 earnings of an S corporation are not considered earnings and profits.

   Income is categorized as "accumulated adjustments account" and adjusts basis. Sec. 1368(e)(1).

SUBCHAPTER S CORPORATIONS—New Law vs. Old Law (continued)

Old Law Sec. 1371-1379	New Law Sec. 1361-1379
b) Dividend—distributions within the year to the extent of current year earnings and profits.	If there are no prior earnings and profits, distributions are made against basis (whenever made) to the extent of basis. Subsequent distributions are treated as proceeds from sale of stock.
c) PTI—previously taxed income left in the corporation. This must be distributed within the year and after the UTI and current year dividend out of current year earnings and profits.	
d) Dividend out of accumulated earnings and profits. E & P includes the E & P prior to electing Subchapter S status plus nontaxable income received by the corporation and certain adjustments.	d) If there are prior earnings and profits, the distribution is (1st) from the accumulated earnings account, (2nd) a dividend to the extent of earnings and profits, (3rd) proceeds from sale of stock.
e) Return of capital.	
18. Tax on capital gains	
a) Sec. 1378-	a) Sec. 1374-
b) If the net capital gain exceeds $25,000 and exceeds 50% of its taxable income for the year, and the taxable income of the corporation exceeds $25,000, there is a corporate tax on the gain in excess of $25,000.	b) No change in language.
19. Exceptions	
a) The tax is not imposed if the corporation had been a Subchapter S electing corporation for the current year and three preceding years under Sec. 1372(a).	a) The tax is not imposed if the corporation had been an S corporation for the current year and three preceding years under Sec. 1362(a).

	Old law	New law
20. Net operating losses	b) New corporations exempt if have been an electing corporation for all years.	b) New corporations exempt if have been an S corporation for all years under Sec. 1362(a).
	a) Sec. 1374.	a) Sec. 1366(d).
	b) Net operating losses are deductible by the shareholders.	b) Rules for losses and deductions: Losses and deductions are deductible by the shareholders.
	c) Allocation of loss is on a pro rata basis for stockholdings on a daily basis.	c) Same.
	d) Loss limited to shareholder's basis in stock and loans to corporation.	d) Same.
	e) NOL's in excess of basis and loans are lost. There is no carryover by corporation or shareholder.	e) Any loss or deduction which is disallowed because shareholder does not have sufficient basis or loans, shall be carried over to next succeeding year when the shareholder has sufficient basis. (Sec. 1366(d)(2)). The carryover term is indefinite, as long as the corporation is an S corporation.
21. Net operating losses deducted against shareholder	a) Basis in loan never reestablished. Gross income only increases basis in stock. (Sec. 1376(a)).	a) Gross income reported by a shareholder restores basis to loans prior to increasing basis in stock. (Sec. 1367(a)(2)(B)).
22. Tax year of corporation	a) Electing corporations continue the same tax year as a C corporation, either calendar or fiscal year.	a) Permitted year is a taxable year which (1) is a year ending December 31, (2) is any other accounting period for which the corporation establishes a business purpose to the satisfaction of the Secretary. b) Fiscal year: Corporations which are electing corporations for the year which included December 31, 1982 are not required to change until they have a change of stock ownership

239

SUBCHAPTER S CORPORATIONS—New Law vs. Old Law (*continued*)

Old Law Sec. 1371-1379	New Law Sec. 1361-1379
23. Coordination with partnership and individual rules a) None	of more than 50 percent. (Sec. 1378). Stock ownership changed by reason of death is excluded. a) S corporations treated like partnership for purposes of certain provisions: 613(c)(13)—Depletion in the case of oil and gas wells. 4996(a)(1)(C)—Windfall profit tax. 48(c)—Used property for purposes of investment credit. 108(d)—Income from discharge of indebtedness. 179(d)—Election to expense certain depreciable assets. 194(b)(2)—Amortization of reforestation expenditures. 267(b)—Treatment of losses in the case of transactions between S corporations and certain related entities where the same persons own more than 50% of the stock or value of the corporation. 267(f)—S corporations are placed on a cash basis of accounting for transactions with shareholders owning 2 percent or more of the corporate stock. Therefore, items of interest and expenses to a related shareholder are only deductible on the same day as the shareholder recognizes the gross income.
24. Family corporations a) Not identified in law.	a) Sec. 1366(e).

240

b) Income (loss) distributed according to shareholdings.

b) If an individual who is a member of the family of one or more of the shareholders of an S corporation renders service to the corporation or furnishes capital to the corporation without receiving reasonable compensation, an adjustment will be made to give to individual income to reflect the value of compensation or capital. Rules coordinated with the family partnership rules under Sec. 704(e)(3).

241

Summary
Tax and Legal Differences
S Corporations, C Corporations, Partnerships

Points to Consider	S Corporations	C Corporations	Partnerships
Separate Entity or Aggregation	An entity apart from the shareholders.		Sometimes treated as separate entity; generally considered an aggregation of members among partners.
Period of Existence	Continues until dissolution; not affected by disaffiliation of shareholders, or sale of their shares, unless sale is to ineligible shareholder.	Same as S Corporation except period of existence not affected by share transfers.	Termination by agreement, or on partner's death, retirement or other disaffiliation.
Transfers of Interest	Readily and easily marketable by transfer of certificate of stock. Sale of shares to partnership, corporation, certain trusts, or nonresident alien terminates election.	Same as S Corporation with no restriction on eligibility to own shares.	Addition of new partner or transfer of partner's interest often requires consent of other partners.
Non-Loan Capital Sources	Sale of only one class of stock to no more than 35 eligible shareholders. Differences in voting rights permitted.	Sale of multiple classes of stock or other securities to unlimited number of individuals, corporations, or partnerships.	Contributions by general or limited partners with unlimited number of partners permitted.
Ownership Limitations	35 shareholder limit and qualification requirements to be shareholders.	No limit on number or class of shareholders.	No limit on number of partners.
Liability Exposure	Except in rare circumstances, shareholders are only liable for capital contributions.		General partners are personally, jointly and severally liable for partnership obligations. Limited partner liable for

Points to Consider	S Corporations	C Corporations	Partnerships
			capital contributions only.
Loan Collateralization	Shares may be used as loan collateral.		Partnership interests cannot serve as loan collateral.
Ownership/ Management Responsibility	No requirement for shareholder participation in management		All general partners participate in management and share joint responsibility. Limited partners do not participate in management.
Organizational Expenditures	Option to amortize over at least 60 months or capitalize.		
Tax Year	S Corporation must use a calendar year unless business purpose shown for fiscal year.	Calendar or fiscal year permitted. Tax year does not have to match shareholders' tax years.	Same restrictions as S Corporations.
Federal Tax Return	Form 1120-S Information return.	Form 1120, Corporate income tax return. May have to file estimated tax returns.	Form 1065, Information return.
Treatment of Income and Losses	Corporate income determined at entity level and passed through to each shareholder and taxed at individual rates. Some S Corporations pay capital gains tax and tax on "excess net passive income." Income loss items that affect a shareholder's tax liability are separately stated-e.g. charitable contributions, depletion.	All corporate income taxed at corporate level and again taxed at shareholder level when distributed as dividends. Some C corporations taxed as personal holding companies and can be taxed on excess accumulated income.	Same as S Corporation except no partnership capital gains tax nor tax on passive income.

243

Points to Consider	S Corporations	C Corporations	Partnerships
Net Operating Losses	Losses pass through to shareholders and are deductible to the extent of their stock and debt basis. Losses may be carried back or forward.	Deductible only by the corporation in a year which it has offsetting income. Losses may be carried back or forward.	Same passthrough rules as S Corporation.
Tax-Exempt Income	Tax-exempt income earned by the corporation retains its character when passed through to the shareholders. It increases shareholders' stock bases.	Tax-exempt income increase corporate earnings and profits and is not taxed at corporate level. If distributed to shareholders as dividends, it is subject to tax.	Same passthrough rule as S Corporation.
Foreign Income	No restrictions.	No restrictions.	No restrictions.
Capital Gains	Capital and Sec. 1231 gains pass through to shareholders and retain their character at shareholder level. 60% of long-term gains are excluded from gross income but are subject to the alternative minimum tax. *Some* S Corporations subject to tax on capital gains in excess of $25,000.	Capital and Sec. 1231 gains taxed at regular corporate rate or the alternative 28% rate.	Same rule as for S Corporation except no tax at partnership level on capital gains.
Capital Losses	Capital losses pass through to shareholders and retain their character at the shareholder level. Losses offset capital gains and then up to $3,000 of ordi-	Capital losses deducted at corporate level only to the extent of capital gains. Losses may be carried back three years or forward 15 years.	Same rule as S Corporations.

Points to Consider	S Corporations	C Corporations	Partnerships
	nary income. May be carried forward indefinitely.		
Accumulated Earnings	After 1982, all income is passed through and taxed at shareholder level. S Corporations with carryover C corporation earnings and profits are subject to 46% tax on excess passive income and distributions of accumulated earnings and profits taxed as dividend income.	C corporations may accumulate income for reasonable business needs. Up to $150,000 for personal service corporations and $250,000 for other C Corporations may be accumulated without question. Unreasonable accumulations subject to tax.	All income taxed to partners whether distributed or not.
Distributions and Income Allocations	Distributions are taxed to the extent they exceed a shareholder's basis in stock and debts. Corporation recognizes gain on distribution of appreciated property. Income may only be allocated in proportion to shareholdings.	Distributions taxed as ordinary income and allocated on basis of shareholders. C corporation does not recognize gain on distribution of appreciated property.	Distributions taxed to the extent they exceed partner's basis in stock and partnership debt. Distributive income shares may be allocated by agreement of the partners. Partnership does not recognize gain on distribution of appreciated property.
Fringe Benefits	Owner of 2% or more of S Corporation shares cannot receive tax-free most fringe benefits including, employer-provided health care, meals and lodging and life insurance.	Shareholder employees may receive tax qualified fringe benefits without restriction.	All partners not eligible for tax-free fringes.

245

Points to Consider	S Corporations	C Corporations	Partnerships
Retirement Plans	Through 1983, S Corporations can only contribute $15,000 a year to a shareholder-employee's retirement plan. After 1983, S Corporations, C corporations and partnerships are governed by the same retirement plan rules.	C corporations can provide a broad variety of defined benefit and defined-contribution plans. After 1983, all corporations and partnerships governed by the same rules.	Through 1983, partners' Keogh, plan contribution limits were less than limits for C Corp. employees. After 1983, partnerships and corporations governed by the same rules.
Investment Interest Deduction	Shareholder deducts his share of the S Corporation's investment interest as if the $10,000 plus net investment income limit applied at the corporate level.	No Limitation.	Partner may deduct his share of partnership's interest up to $10,000 plus his net investment income.
Dividends Received	Income passes through to shareholders and is subject to the $100 dividend exclusion. Corporation does not get exclusion for dividends it receives.	C Corporation can exclude 85% of dividends received from domestic corporations.	Same rule as S Corporations.
FICA Taxes	Tax payable by the corporation and the employees.		Self employment tax applies to salary and drawings.

246

On the other hand, there were tax avoidance opportunities for the sophisticated taxpayer which, likewise, were not intended by the Congress. Examples:

1. The deferral of income resulting from the selection of a taxable year for the corporation different from that of a majority of the shareholders.

2. The use of the retroactive termination provisions to prevent the passthrough of a substantial amount of income to the shareholders.

The main objective of the new law (to quote the committee Report) is "to simplify and modify the tax rules relating to eligibility for Subchapter S status and the operation of Subchapter S corporations. This is accomplished by removing eligibility restrictions that appear unnecessary, and by revising the rules relating to income, distributions, etc., that tend to create traps for the unwary."

[¶2304.2]   General Tax Rule

Like a partnership, an S corporation is an income reporting entity and is not subject to the corporate tax. An exception is a tax-avoidance scheme to organize an S corporation on a *temporary* basis to pass capital gains through to shareholders. Likewise, an S corporation cannot be used to avoid the corporate tax on passive income which exceeds 25% of the corporation's gross receipts. An S corporation also will be taxed on an early disposition of property for which an investment credit has been taken *prior to* Sub S election (but the election will not be treated as a disposition of the property).

Specifically, the primary intent of Congress in revising the law is to bring the Sub S rules into closer conformity with the tax laws as they apply to partnerships. Again, to quote the Committee Report:

"For example, the partnership provisions provide a complete passthrough of the tax characteristics of the items of income and deduction incurred by the partnership, while the Subchapter S provisions do not provide such a passthrough (except for capital gains). Under the partnership provisions, a distribution that does not exceed a partner's basis in his or her partnership interest generally is treated as a nontaxable return of capital. In many instances, a similar distribution to a Subchapter S shareholder is treated as a taxable distribution. Under the partnership provisions, a loss carryover is allowed to the extent that losses exceed a partner's basis in his or her partnership interest as of the close of the year; in the comparable Subchapter S situation, no loss carryover is available."

To meet the objectives as set forth in the committee hearings, the Congress legislated partnershiplike rules which pass items of income and loss through to the corporation's shareholders, with distributions being a return of the shareholder's investment, including previously taxed earnings. The result is a less-complicated set of rules than prior to the Act's revision. Accordingly, the 1982 revision incorporates the partnership approach which treats all items, such as depletion, foreign income, and fringe benefits much the same as under partnership provisions. Continued is the advantage of a small business corporation to elect a single-level shareholder tax on the corporation's earnings and, most significantly, eliminates the "traps" that inadvertently developed from prior legislation.

Since the choice to elect Sub S status can be made only by a "small business," it was necessary for Congress to define a small business enterprise:

1. The corporation does not have more than 35 shareholders.

2. The corporation must be a domestic corporation.

3. A shareholder can be an individual, estate, or trust (as defined in the Code). A husband and wife are considered to be one shareholder, including their estates, if any.

4. No shareholder can be a nonresident alien.

5. The corporation cannot have more than one class of stock (but differences in voting rights among shares of common stock aren't treated as different classes).

The following corporations are prohibited from electing Sub S status:

1. A corporation that is a member of an affiliated group.

2. A financial institution which is permitted by the Code to deduct bad debts, i.e., banks, savings and loan associations, mutual savings banks.

3. Insurance companies that are taxable under Subchapter L of the Code, except casualty companies under certain conditions even though subject to Subchapter L.

4. Corporations electing tax credits of U.S. possessions.

5. A DISC or *former* DISC.

[¶2304.3]   Key Advantages of a Sub S Election

• The major advantage is the elimination of the double-taxation penalty of C corporation stock ownership.

• Prior to 1982, S stockholders were subject to be taxed as high as 70% of their share of the corporation's earnings. Now, all personal income is taxed at the same rate with a top of 50%, regardless of the source of the income, be it salary, dividends, or other investment income of some sort.

• If the S corporation loses money, it becomes in effect a tax shelter as the shareholders can deduct the losses against their income from other sources, up to their equity and debt basis. Oddly, the new law permits losses to be deducted from the salary income of shareholders who may be employees, or officers of the corporation.

• Usually, a newly organized corporation loses money in the early years of its existence. It is allowable for an S corporation to be organized for new products, for research and development, for virtually any new operation that is not explicitly prohibited by the law.

- Capital losses of the S corporation can be used by the shareholders.
- An S corporation can now have tax-exempt income distributable to shareholders.
- Deductions for depreciation, depletion, and amortization are allowable.
- The investment credit is allowable.
- The minimum tax on preference items will be lower for an S corporation shareholder than for a C corporation stockholder. This is because of the double-taxation penalty of C corporations.
- An individual taxpayer's estimate can be lower if an S election is made.
- The primary advantage of an S corporation is the avoidance of corporate taxes, as the net income of the corporation is taxed to the shareholders, whether distributed to them or not. What can be most important for a shareholder is the tax rule which permits the corporation to pass through its *losses* to the taxpayer. A regular (C corporation) cannot pass operating or capital losses through to its shareholders, but must either use these losses or permanently lose them. The law permits an operating loss to be carried back three years, and then forward, if necessary, for 15 years. Or, if the corporation chooses, an operating loss can be carried forward 15 years with no carryback. This means that a C corporation *must* have been profitable within the past three years, or *must* become profitable in the future.

[¶2304.4]   Some Disadvantages

- The most significant disadvantage is the shareholders' liability for taxes on the full amount of the corporation's earnings, *whether or not distributed to the shareholders*. Accordingly, shareholders have to pay taxes on income they did not receive.
- Usually, loss carryforwards and carrybacks result in less tax savings for S corporation shareholders than for a C corporation.
- There are deductible items for C corporations that are not deductible by S corporation shareholders.
- Capital loss savings are less for a S shareholder than for C corporations.
- More immediate tax savings result if tax credits are taken by a C corporation than by the shareholders of an S corporation.
- An S corporation is more limited to fringe benefits for the more than 2% shareholders.
- It is possible for a C corporation's taxable income to be lower if it selects a fiscal year that is not allowable for an S corporation.
- There are eligibility limitations for S corporation shareholders.
- An S corporation cannot sell preferred stock (the one class of stock limitation).
- S corporations cannot have wholly owned subsidiaries.

[¶2304.5]   Loss Passthroughs

The new law continues the rules of the old law, which limit the deduction an S corporation shareholder can claim for losses passed through to the shareholder. The limit is the basis of the stock investment of the shareholder, plus any debt of the corporation owed to the shareholder. A significant change in the new law permits the shareholder to carry losses forward indefinitely, and allows a deduction in any future year(s) up to the stockholder's aggregate stock and debt basis. Under the old law, an excess loss was permanently lost, i.e., no carryforward allowed. (This is exactly the same rule as for partners, with partnership losses in excess of their partnership interest basis.)

Can a deduction be bought? Yes, it can. Assume a shareholder with a loss in excess of his basis. All the shareholder has to do is contribute to the corporation an amount in stock or debt, or both, equal to the loss, or any part of it. Further, the stockholder can borrow the money for this purpose. There is no limitation on the number of years the stockholder can take to buy an excess loss that is outstanding.

[¶2304.6]   Passive Investment Income

Definition: Passive income is defined to include gross receipts from royalties, rents, dividends, interest, annuities, and sales or exchanges of securities to the extent of the *gains* from the sale or exchanges of securities. Excluded from the passive income rule are interest on obligations acquired in the ordinary course of an S corporation's business; income from a lending or finance business; any amount received in the liquidation of a corporation in which the S corporation owned more than 50% of each class of the liquidated corporation's stock.

The Rule: Passive income cannot exceed 25% of gross receipts for three consecutive taxable years of S corporations with accumulated earnings and profits attributable to Sub C status. Under the Act, the election of an S corporation with accumulated earnings and profits from a Subchapter C year will be terminated if its passive investment income exceeds 25% of gross receipts for each of three consecutive taxable years in which it has such earnings and profits at the close of the taxable year. Also, to the extent the electing corporation has passive income in excess of 25%, the excess above 25% will be taxed at the maximum corporate rate, presently 46%. However, beginning in 1983, a *new* S corporation can have an unlimited amount of passive income without losing S status.

A significant modification was made by Congress in the treatment of capital gains from the disposition of capital assets. Gross receipts from the disposition can include only the capital gain net income realized on the disposition. The reason for this modification is to prevent the "churning" of assets by the S corporation.

250

Under the old Act, gross receipts included the *entire amount* of the proceeds from the disposition of capital assets other than stock or securities, but *no* part of those proceeds was passive income. While proceeds from the sale of capital assets still are not included in passive income, the amount of the gross receipts is limited to realized gain.

Under the old Act, an S corporation could increase its gross receipts (with little or no tax effect) by exchanging assets whose fair market value are about the same basis. Since the corporation's passive income would not be increased by the exchange, the corporation could use churning to increase its realized passive investment income up to the 25% gross receipts limit.

[¶2304.7]   Inadvertent Terminations

In view of Congress' intent to remove the traps which under the old Act caused inadvertent noncompliance with the requirements for Sub S continuance, the IRS is authorized by the new Act to waive the termination penalty under certain circumstances, which are:

• a violation of the passive income requirement, if the Commissioner determines the violation was inadvertent.

• whatever the inadvertent event might have been, if the corporation has taken steps to correct the event.

• the corporation's shareholders agree to make whatever corrections the Commissioner requires.

The Ways and Means Committee explained: "The committee intends that the Internal Revenue Service be reasonable in granting waivers, so that corporations whose Subchapter S eligibility requirements have been inadvertently violated do not suffer the tax consequences of a termination if no tax avoidance would result from the continued Subchapter S treatment. In granting the waivers, it is hoped that taxpayers and the government will work out agreements that protect the revenues without undue hardships to taxpayers. For example, if a corporation, in good faith, determined that it had no earnings and profits, but it is later determined on audit that its election terminated by reason of violating the passive income test because the corporation in fact did have accumulated earnings, if the shareholders were to agree to treat the earnings as distributed and include the dividends in income, it may be appropriate to waive the terminating events, so that the election is treated as never terminated. Likewise, it may be appropriate to waive the terminating event when the one class of stock requirement was inadvertently breached, but no tax avoidance had resulted. It is expected that the waiver may be made retroactive for all years, or retroactive for the period in which the corporation again became eligible for Subchapter S treatment, depending on the facts."

[¶2304.8]   Safe-Harbor Rule—A Trap Eliminated

Under the prior law, the Internal Revenue Service ruled that debt of an S corporation that resulted in an obviously thinly capitalized company (very highly leveraged) was a tax avoidance scheme, because interest on a heavy debt structure could add to the corporation's losses and deduction from the shareholders' other sources of income. This created the problem of tax avoidance *intent*, and whether or not tax avoidance was, in fact, present in a given situation. To correct the problem, in order to prevent the corporation's S status from being terminated because a debt instrument could be classified as a separate class of stock, the 1982 Act's revision includes a "safe harbor" for *straight debt* obligations.

What is straight debt?

• The debt is a written unconditional demand to pay a fixed amount on demand on a specified date.

• The interest rate and the interest payment dates are not contingent on profits, nor at the corporation's discretion. However, a rate tied to the prime rate is an exception, because the prime rate is an external factor outside of the corporation's discretion.

• The debt cannot be convertible into stock.

• The creditor must be an individual (including an estate or trust) who is an eligible person to own stock (but does not have to) in the corporation.

In clarifying the safe-harbor rule, the Ways and Committee said:

> "It is intended that these rules will treat the instrument in such a way as to prevent tax avoidance, on the one hand, and also to prevent unfair, harsh results to the taxpayer. It is anticipated that these safe-harbor instruments will be treated as debt under Subchapter S, so that no corporate income or loss will be allocated to the instruments. Payments on the instruments shall be includible in the income of the holder and deductible by the corporation (subject to the rules of the bill relating to the accrual of upaid amounts). Payments on these instruments may be examined to determine whether the payments represent interest or other income in any situation where the treatment as interest might give the taxpayer an unwarranted tax advantage, such as under the net interest exclusion.
>
> "In the case of a regular corporation (with a straight debt instrument outstanding, which is treated as stock under corporate tax law principles) that elects Subchapter S, it is intended that the election not be treated as an exchange of debt for stock, but a later redemption of the instrument may be treated as a dividend if the corporation had remaining accumulated earnings and profits. Prior to the issuance of final regulations, it is intended that these general principles will apply to straight debt instruments.
>
> "The classification of an instrument outside the safe-harbor rules as stock or debt will be made under the usual tax laws classification principals."

[¶2304.9]   A Trust as a Shareholder

A "qualified Subchapter S trust" can be a shareholder of an S corporation. *Definition*: A qualified Subchapter S trust is a trust which owns stock in one or more electing small business corporations; all of the income is distributed to *one* individual; the *one* individual must be a citizen or resident of the United States (cannot be a nonresident alien); the corpus of the trust is distributable only to the income beneficiary; the beneficiary's interest terminates upon death or the termination of the trust; if the corporation is terminated before the death of the beneficiary, all assets of the trust must be distributable to the beneficiary.

If a qualified trust fails to meet any of these requirements, it will lose its qualified status.

[¶2304.10]   Technical Corrections

The 1984 Act incorporated a number of technical corrections to the Subchapter S Revision Act of 1982.

• Gain is recognized to an S corporation that makes a distribution of appreciated property with respect to its stock, as if the S corporation had sold the property to the distributee at its fair market value. The new law makes this rule inapplicable to distributions in complete liquidation of S corporations and of stock by an S corporation in a reorganization, where the receipt of such stock is tax free to the shareholder.

• If a shareholder contributed a debt to an S corporation as a contribution to capital after December 31, 1980, corporate income will not result to the extent that the debt had previously been reduced by the passthrough of losses from the corporation.

• Under the prior law, an S corporation could not own a subsidiary other than an inactive subsidiary, which was defined as a corporation which had no *taxable* income. The new law substitutes a *gross* income test for the *taxable* income test. Now an S corporation's election will terminate on the first day during the corporation's taxable year that the subsidiary has gross income.

• Under the prior law, passed-through S corporation losses were taken into account before any deductions for worthless stock. The new law extends this rule to situations where the shareholder's debt in the corporation becomes worthless. This means that if a shareholder has no basis in his S corporation stock, but does have a basis in debt owed by the corporation and that debt becomes worthless, corporate losses for the year will be allowed to the shareholder to the extent of the shareholder's basis in the debt. This in turn will reduce the amount of the short-term capital loss for the worthless debt.

• Under the prior law, the recapture of investment tax credits claimed in pre-S years is to be made at the corporate level. No adjustments to E & P were allowed for any investment credit recapture. Now, an S corporation can reduce accumulated E & P by the investment credit recaptured.

• Certain trusts that distributed income currently can qualify as shareholders in S corporations. Under prior law, the election could be retroactive for up to 60 days. Under the new law, the election may be retroactive for up to 2 months and 15 days, which conforms to the time provided the corporation to make an S election. In addition, under the new law, the disqualification of a "qualified

Subchapter S trust'' because of the failure to meet the distribution requirements is effective on the first day of the first taxable year after the distribution requirements are not met.

• The current law amended the passive income rules to prevent the termination of an S corporation because of excess passive income. Now, an S corporation with excess passive income can elect to terminate rather than paying both a corporate and shareholder tax on that income. If the S corporation does elect to terminate, it cannot reelect S corporation status within 5 years without the consent of IRS.

• Cash distributions by an S corporation during the one-year post-termination transition period are tax free. The new Act permits an S corporation to elect to treat such distributions as dividends, provided all shareholders agree. This enables the corporation to avoid the accumulated earnings and personal holding company tax.

• The corporate preference rules generally have not applied to S corporations. Now the corporate preference rules apply to the first 3 taxable years after a C corporation elects S status. This prevents a C corporation from electing S status to avoid the preference rules.

• Under the new law, interest and expenses owed by an accrual basis S corporation to a cash-basis related taxpayer are allowable deductions to the corporation no earlier than the day such amounts are includible in the gross income of the payee.

• Present law imposes a tax on S corporations with passive income and C corporation's earnings and profits. Under the new law, IRS can waive this tax if the corporation has in good faith determined that it had no such E & P, and the earnings are distributed after discovery.

• Present law requires the basis of debt that is reduced by losses to be restored to subsequent income. The new law clarifies that this applies only to the extent the basis in the debt was reduced in taxable years beginning after 1982.

[¶2305]   PROFESSIONAL CORPORATIONS

Organizations of doctors, lawyers, accountants and other professionals duly organized under state laws as professional associations or corporations are now generally recognized by the IRS as corporate entities.

They now have the choice of being taxed as:

1. Corporations, or

2. Sub-Chapter S Corporations.

In the past, combinations of professional persons were considered to be partnerships for tax purposes with all income earned, whether distributed or not, flowing through to the individual returns. In addition, deferment of income for flowing through to the individual returns. In addition, deferment of income for retirement purposes and later taxation was extremely limited in comparison with what could be deferred for corporate officials.

If they exercise the *Sub-S option,* professional corporations will:

1. Eliminate the corporate form of double taxation (on dividends) by being taxed on all earnings, whether distributed or not, effectively (with exceptions) being taxed as if it were a partnership, yet having some of the corporation-type benefits;

2. *Not be able to obtain key corporate fringe benefits:* In general, the following fringe benefits are taxable to Sub S shareholder-employees who own more than 2% of the stock; employer-funded medical reinbursement plan; employer-paid accident, health, and group-term life insurance. On the plus side, in tax years beginning after 1984, deductible contributions to a S Corp. retirement plan are the same as for a C Corp. retirement plan.

In other-than-tax considerations, and excluding the factor of personal liability for professional malpractice, the corporate structure for the professional group offers the same advantages and disadvantages of a regular corporation.

[¶2306]   RECAPITALIZATIONS

A recapitalization may be tax free or taxable, depending on how it is accomplished. An exchange of stock for stock—i.e., common for common or preferred for preferred—is tax free regardless of whether or not a reorganization or recapitalization is involved (§1036). In other cases, to get freedom from taxes, you need to meet the reorganization rules.

[¶2306.1]   Tax-Free Recapitalizations

Tax-free recapitalization should have a proper plan of reorganization and a "good business purpose" (other than just for a tax-saving purpose). In determining whether an exchange is tax free, you'll have to rely on your interpretation of the law and regulations; there is no complete listing of exchanges that are tax free or not tax free. Here is a brief summary of the types of changes and their tax results.

Stock for Stock: The following exchanges have been held to be tax free:

(1) A surrender to the corporation for cancellation of a portion of its preferred stock in exchange for no-par value common stock.

(2) A surrender of common stock for preferred stock previously authorized, but unissued. However, see §306 stock.

(3) An exchange of outstanding preferred stock, having priorities as to the amount and time of payment of dividends and the distribution of the corporate assets upon liquidation, for a new issue of common stock having no such rights.

(4) An exchange of common for common or preferred for preferred could also qualify as a recapitalization with no gain or loss resulting.

(5) An exchange of outstanding preferred stock with dividend arrearages, for a similar amount of preferred stock plus an amount of stock (preferred or common) applicable to the amount of the arrearages. But this exchange cannot be made solely for the purpose of effecting the payment of dividends for current and immediately preceding taxable years on the preferred stock exchanged. If it is, an amount equal to the value of stock issued in lieu of such dividends can become taxable.

Bonds for Bonds: An exchange of bonds for bonds in equal principal amounts is tax free. However, the fair market value of the excess of principal amount of bonds received over those surrendered is taxable as "boot," and if the securities are capital assets to the holder, this excess is taxed as capital gain.

Bonds for Stock: A discharge of outstanding bonds for preferred stock instead of cash is tax free (The same result could probably be achieved with any type of security.) The entire exchange is tax free with no allocation as to the interest on the arrearages. Further, stock worth less than the principal amount of bonds surrendered may be distributed to creditors with no taxable result.

Stock for Bonds: A distribution of bonds or other securities in exchange for the surrender of stock is taxable. In addition, if the corporation has substantial earnings on hand, a distribution of bonds to the common stockholders (whether or not pro rata) is likely to be taxed as a dividend. But where the distribution of bonds is to preferred stockholders (rather than pro rata to common stockholders) on a non-pro rata basis, capital gain or loss may result.

[¶2306.2]   Recapitalization Exchanges Taxed as Dividends

There are four reasons why a recapitalization exchange may be taxed as a dividend. It is important to avoid having your exchange fall into any one of these danger zones. The four possibilities are:

(1) *Distribution of "boot" where there are corporate earnings available for distribution.* Distribution of "boot" automatically means a tax of some sort; and if the corporation has undistributed earnings, the Treasury will be tempted to charge that distribution of the "boot" was a distribution of earnings.

(2) *Redemption of stock treated as a dividend.* To avoid this, the redemption must be one of the following: (a) not essentially equivalent to a dividend; (b) substantially disproportionate; (c) a complete termination of stockholder's interest.

(3) *Failure to meet "net effect" test.* Regardless of technical compliance with the law, a recapitalization can be taxed if it fails to meet the "business purpose" test. The "net effect" test is a refinement of the "business purpose" test. It means that the recapitalization will be taxed if its net effect is to accomplish a distribution of earnings.

(4) *Preferred stock bailout.* A preferred stock dividend followed by sale or redemption of the preferred stock is taxable as a dividend to the extent the corporation had earnings and profits.

[¶2306.3]   Elimination of Arrearages in Dividends or Interest

A recapitalization is often used as a means of eliminating back dividends on a preferred stock or back interest on bonds. Generally, the investor will be given a new security to replace the defaulted one plus something to take the place of the arrearage. Only some exchanges for this purpose will be tax free.

Dividend or interest arrearages could be eliminated tax free only by replacing them with new stock. In the case of dividend arrearages on preferred stock, the arrearage might be eliminated by issuance of new preferred in exchange for the old preferred, the amount issued being sufficient to cover both the old preferred and the back dividends. In the case of bond interest, the back interest might be eliminated by issuance of new bonds in the same amount as the old bonds, plus preferred stock to cover the back interest. However, there are exceptions if the arrearage pertains to the current or preceding taxable years.

[¶2306.4]   When to Use a Taxable Recapitalization

In most discussions of the tax effects of recapitalizations, the stress is placed upon avoiding taxability. This doesn't always produce the best result. For example, in the usual bonds for preferred stock recapitalization, there is no spread between the basis of the old securities and the value of the new ones. In this case, since there is no gain, it makes no particular difference whether the recapitalization is taxed. And where basis exceeds value, it will be desirable to have the exchange taxed in order to realize a loss.

Even where there is a tax, it will be at the capital gain rate unless the corporation has earnings and the recapitalization is equivalent to the payment of a dividend. Depending upon the circumstances, it may be advantageous to effect a taxable recapitalization, rather than a nontaxable one.

[¶2307]   DIVIDENDS

Cash Dividends, Stock Dividends, Rights and Split-ups: In making distributions to shareholders, corporations should be aware of the possible tax effect to the distributee (shareholder).

Cash dividends are taxable at ordinary rates to the recipient in the year of receipt, if the distribution is out of current profits or accumulated retained earnings. Portions of the dividend may be capital gain distributions; portions may be non-taxable distributions. Distinctions must be indicated on the 1099-DIV sent to the recipient ($10 or more).

Stock dividends are ordinarily non-taxable to the recipient at the time of distribution, merely adjusting his basis by changing the number of shares owned at the same prior total cost. Stock rights usually increase the cost-basis and the number of shares. However, there are some circumstances under which stock dividends/rights *may* be taxable in the year of issue, such as distributions when the recipient has an alternative option of receiving cash or property from the corporation, or in disproportionate distributions, or distributions involving preferred or convertible stocks—these instances may involve a pickup of income at the *market price* at the time of distribution.

"Stock Split-ups" and "Stock Splits Effected in the Form of a Dividend" (to conform with State laws) change the holding basis of the stock to the recipient. The corporation may have to make Schedule M adjustments on its Form 1120, if the stock distribution entailed an adjustment of retained earnings, because such earnings, if not taxable upon distribution, may still be considered available for cash dividend distribution by the IRS and, therefore, at some future day, taxable at regular individual rates when and if distributed in cash [§ 312(d)].

[¶2308]   OTHER EQUITY CONSIDERATIONS

Net Operating Loss Carryover: Determine the availability of carryover losses from prior years for possible reduction of current year's taxes.

Retained Earnings: Federal and many state returns require an analysis of the retained-earnings account.

"Schedule M" Adjustments: Gather the data needed to prepare Schedule M—the schedule that reconciles the company's income per its books with the income according to the tax return. Items involved may include losses (e.g., net capital losses); items not allowed as tax deductions; income items picked up in prior years for book purposes but for the current year for tax purposes, or vice versa; or deductions picked up currently for tax purposes but not for book purposes, or vice versa.

Form **1120**

Department of the Treasury
Internal Revenue Service

U.S. Corporation Income Tax Return

For calendar year 1983 or other tax year beginning .... 1983, ending .... 19 ....

► For Paperwork Reduction Act Notice, **see page 1 of the instructions.**

OMB No 1545-0123

19**83**

SCHEDULE M-1.—Reconciliation of Income Per Books With Income Per Return

Do not complete this schedule if your total assets (line 14, column (D), above) are less than $25,000

1 Net income per books.

2 Federal income tax

3 Excess of capital losses over capital gains

4 Income subject to tax not recorded on books this year (itemize) ----------------------

5 Expenses recorded on books this year not deducted in this return (itemize)

   (a) Depreciation . . . $ ----------------

   (b) Contributions carryover $ ----------------

6   Total of lines 1 through 5

7 Income recorded on books this year not included in this return (itemize)

   (a) Tax-exempt interest $

8 Deductions in this tax return not charged against book income this year (itemize)

   (a) Depreciation . . . $ ----------------

   (b) Contributions carryover $ ----------------

9   Total of lines 7 and 8

10 Income (line 28, page 1)—line 6 less line 9

SCHEDULE M-2.—Analysis of Unappropriated Retained Earnings Per Books (line 24 above)

Do not complete this schedule if your total assets (line 14, column (D), above) are less than $25,000

1 Balance at beginning of year

2 Net income per books.

3 Other increases (itemize) -----

4   Total of lines 1, 2, and 3

5 Distributions: (a) Cash.

          (b) Stock

          (c) Property

6 Other decreases (itemize) -----

7   Total of lines 5 and 6

8 Balance at end of year (line 4 less line 7)

☆U.S. Government Printing Office 1983—380-100   23-0916790

24

Income

CONFLICTS BETWEEN TAX AND BUSINESS ACCOUNTING

The conflicts between tax accounting and generally accepted business accounting center around the questions: (1) *when* is it income? and (2) *when* is it deductible? To illustrate the differences that have existed in these two areas, we include the following list which was submitted by the American Institute of Certified Public Accountants to the House Committee on Ways and Means in connection with the Hearings on the 1954 Code. (See the *Expense Section* following for listing of "Divergences involving the time of allowance of deductions.")

Divergences Involving the Time of Recognition of Revenues

(A) Revenues, deferred for general accounting purposes until earned, but reportable for tax purposes when received:

(1) Revenues susceptible of proration on a fixed-time basis or on a service-rendered basis:

Rentals.
Commissions.
Revenues from maintenance and similar service contracts covering a specified period.
Warehousing and trucking fees.
Advertising revenues.
Advance royalties on patents or copyrights.
Transportation ticket and token sales.
Sales of coupon books entitling purchaser to services.
Theatre ticket sales.
Membership fees.
Tuition fees.
Laboratory fees.

(2) Revenues susceptible of proration over average duration of demand:

Life memberships.

Revenues from service contracts extending over life of article serviced or period of ownership by original owner.

(B) Revenues deferred for general accounting purposes until right to retain them is substantially assured, but reportable for tax purposes when received:
  (1) Receipts under claim of right.

(C) Revenues accrued for general accounting purposes, but not reportable for tax purposes until collected:
  (1) Dividends declared.
  (2) Increase in withdrawal value of savings and loan shares.

[¶2401.1]   Income Received in Advance

Frequently, a taxpayer receives payment for services he has not yet performed (e.g., club membership dues, magazine subscriptions). The question then is, in what year does the taxpayer have to report these payments as income?

Accounting Rule: The accountant says that you have no income until it is actually *earned*; that the mere receipt of cash or property does not result in a realization of income. The accountant treats the prepayment as a liability which obligates the recipient to perform services before he can be said to have *earned* the payment. (This problem applies to accrual-basis taxpayers; cash-basis taxpayers are considered to have *earned* a prepayment when it is received.)

Tax Rule: You have income when you have the *right to receive* it, even though it is not earned. Thus, cash payments received in advance, negotiable notes received as advance payments, and contract installments due and payable are taxable to the recipient as advance income, even though these payments are for services to be provided by the taxpayer in a subsequent tax year. Here is a composite tax picture.

Type of Income	Basis	Extent Taxable	Authority
Cash receipts	Cash or accrual	Full amount	*American Automobile Association,* 367 US 687; *Schlude,* 372 US 128.
Negotiable notes	Cash	Fair market value	*Pinellas Ice Co.,* 287 US 462; Reg. § 1.61—2(d)(4).
	Accrual	Face Value	*Schlude,* 372 US 128; *Schlude,* TC Memo 1963-307; *Spring City Foundry Co.,* 292 US 182.
Unpaid contractual payments due and payable under terms of the contract	Cash	None—no fair market value	Est. of *Ennis,* 23 TC 799; *nonacq.,* 1956-2 CB 10; *Ennis,* 17 TC 465.
	Accrual	Face Value	*Schlude,* 32 TC 1271.

Type of Income	Basis	Extent Taxable	Authority
Unpaid contractual installments not due under the contract nor evidenced by notes	Cash	None	*Schlude*, 372 US 128.
	Accrual	None	*Schlude*, 372 US 128.

The tendency of the courts seems to be to require reporting prepaid receipts, but Sections 455 and 456 of IRC were enacted to provide special relief.

(1) *Accrual-basis taxpayers* may defer prepaid income from service contracts or from the sale of goods.

(2) *Publishers* may elect to spread prepaid subscription income.

(3) *Membership organizations* organized without capital stock which do not distribute earnings to any members and do not report income by the cash receipts and disbursements method may spread their prepaid dues income ratably over the period (not to exceed 36 months) during which they are under a liability to render services.

[¶2401.2] Repayment of Income Received Under Claim of Right

Since the tax law requires the accrual-basis taxpayer to include payments received (although not yet earned) in taxable income when received, it obviously disagrees with good accounting practice on how to treat such payments if they must be repaid.

If you are required to repay money received under a claim of right, the tax law says you can deduct it in the year of repayment.

[¶2401.3] Premature Accruals—New Law

Under the accrual method of accounting, an expense is generally deductible in the taxable year in which all the events have occurred that determine the fact of the liability, and the amount of the liability can be determined with reasonable accuracy (the so-called "all events test"). Whether an expense involving a future obligation can satisfy the all-events test in a year significantly earlier than the year in which the taxpayer must fulfill the obligation, has been the subject of controversy under present law. In general, the new law provides that in determining whether an accrual method taxpayer has incurred an amount during the taxable year, all the events which establish the taxpayer's liability for such amount will not be deemed to have occurred any earlier than the time when economic performance occurs. If economic performance has occurred, the amount will be treated as incurred for purposes of the Code. Amounts incurred are deductible currently only if they are not properly chargeable to a capital account, and are not subject to any other provision of the Code that requires the deduction to be taken in a taxable year later than the year when economic performance occurs. Effective date: Accruals after July 18, 1984.

The new law provides criteria for determining when economic performance occurs in the case of two categories of liabilities: 1) liabilities arising from another person providing goods or services or the use of property to the taxpayer; 2) liabilities of the taxpayer to provide property or services. Economic performance occurs with respect to the first category as the property or services are provided to the taxpayer. Economic performance occurs with respect to the second category as the taxpayer provides the property or service.

In the case of interest, economic performance occurs with the passage of time; that is, it occurs as the borrower uses, and lender foregoes use of, the lender's money—rather than as payments are made. Interest incurred by accrual method taxpayers, with respect to debts incurred after June 8, 1984, will be deductible only on a constant interest basis.

[¶2402] INCOME TAXES—TIMING INCOME AND EXPENSES

Once a corporation is in the 46% rate bracket in earnings, it has nothing to gain taxwise in shifting income from one year to another in terms of rates. Current corporate tax rates are 15% up to $25,000; 18% on the next $25,000; 30% on the next $25,000; 40% on the next $25,000; and 46% on the balance over $100,000. For tax years beginning after 1983, there's an additional 5% tax (up to $20,250 maximum) on corporate taxable income over $1 million.

There can be many reasons for shifting income and expenses. One year may have so many deductions already that additional income can be picked up tax free. True, if the income were not picked up, the current year's loss could be carried back three years and forward 15 years. But, perhaps the prior years were also loss years and no immediate benefit can be realized from the current year's loss (or if refunds will be available, the years may be subject to tax audit). On the other hand, the current year's deductions may be "light" but the following years' deductions are expected to be "heavy." Shifting income forward can match up the deductions with the income.

Similar results can be achieved by shifting expenses from one year to another. In a year when additional income is desirable, the same effect may be achieved by shifting expenses out of that year.

Where we have installment sales—whether the company is an installment dealer or makes a so-called casual sale of substantial property calling for payment over a number of years—the total tax paid on the income realized from the sale may be the same whether we use installment sale or accrual accounting. We may prefer to use the installment method of reporting the sale for tax purposes so as to match the actual tax payments with the receipt of income.

HOW TO HANDLE SALES

Gross sales are a decisive factor in determining the income level for a given year. The method of selling and the timing of shipments can control the tax year. In a cash-basis business, it is relatively simple to control the time of payment. Income can be increased for the year by accelerating collections; it can be reduced by either allowing payments to take their normal course or by a delay in billing. For accrual-basis businesses, a sale is taken into income when completed, which is when title has passed. As a general rule, title passes when delivery has been made, usually determined by reference to the invoice or bill of lading. Thus, an accrual-basis taxpayer can accelerate income by speeding up deliveries. Similarly, income can be reduced by holding off deliveries in the closing weeks of the year.

Long-Term Contracts: Taxpayer has the option of reporting on the percentage-completion method or the completed-contract basis.

Both the percentage-of-completion and the completed-contract methods of accounting are permitted for income tax purposes as long as more than one year elapses from the date of execution to the date of completion and acceptance of the contract (Reg. § 1.451-3).

Use of either of these methods is optional; the taxpayer may use the cash or accrual method for other operations although using the percentage-of-completion or completed-contract method for long-term contracts. But once the method of accounting is originally adopted, a change requires IRS approval.

[¶2403.1] Completed Contract Method of Accounting

A corporation that accounts for income and expenses attributable to a long-term contract on the completed contract method of accounting generally recognizes income and expense in the year in which the contract is completed. Under the new law, a corporation that accounts for income and expense on this method is required to compute earnings and profits as if it were accounting for income and expense attributable to long-term contracts on a percentage of completion basis.

This provision is effective for contracts entered into after September 30, 1984, other than for binding contracts entered into on or prior to that date.

[¶2403.2] Construction Period Interest, Taxes, and Carrying Charges

For purposes of computing a corporation's earnings and profits, construction period interest, taxes, and carrying charges are required to be capitalized as a part of the asset to which they relate, and written off as is the asset itself. This rule applies to all corporations. Further, it applies with respect to both residential and nonresidential real property, and to personal property.

"Construction period interest and taxes" include: property taxes (real and personal); interest paid or accrued on debt incurred or continued, to acquire, construct, or carry property; and other carrying charges, but only to the extent such taxes, interest, and carrying charges are attributable to the construction period for such property.

This provision is applicable to the effect on earnings and profits of amounts paid or accrued in taxable years beginning after September 30, 1984.

[¶2404] INSTALLMENT SALES

A company may be making installment sales and not using the installment method of reporting the income. Under the accrual method, it is picking up the entire income in the year of sale. Tax rules permit installment reporting of income on either a cash or accrual basis, thus spreading the tax effect over the period payments are received.

In addition to installment dealers, who can elect to use the installment method for their installment sales, casual installment sales of more than $1,000 and installment sales of real estate can be reported under the installment method for tax purposes on a sale-by-sale basis if certain rules are met. Payments in the year of sale, including demand bonds or notes or readily tradeable paper, cannot exceed 30% of the selling price, if the property was disposed of *before* October 20, 1980. For dispositions *after* October 19, 1980, the 30% test does not apply. Also, the two-or-more-payments requirement does not apply, as the IRS now defines an installment sale to be "a disposition of real property or a disposition of personal property when at least one payment is to be received after the close of the taxable year in which the disposition occurs" (Sec. 453(b)(1).

[¶2404.1] Installment Sales by Dealers

"Installment dealer" isn't defined in the tax law; no minimum percentage of installment sales is prescribed. Nor is frequency the decisive factor. Regularly engaging in installment selling and receiving payment of fixed sums at stated intervals are the important considerations.

On the installment basis, the income arising from an installment sale of real or personal property is reportable for tax purposes *proportionately* when and as the income is actually collected. The theory of the installment method is that each dollar collected includes a *pro rata* recovery of cost (nontaxable) and a *pro rata* receipt of *profit* (which is taxable in the year collected).

For tax purposes, the books of account needn't be kept on the installment basis; they can be kept regularly on the cash or accrual basis. But adequate records must be kept to provide the necessary information for computing the profit portion of the different installments.

The installment method applies only to *gains* from the sale of property. If the installment sale resulted in a *loss,* the loss must be deducted in the year of sale.

Expenses: A *dealer* must deduct the expenses in the year when paid (on the cash basis) or when incurred (on the accrual basis). He cannot apportion or spread the expenses over the years when the income from the installment sale is reported as collected.

[¶2404.2]   Choice of Installment Method by a Dealer

What is meant by "installment method?" This method allows the taxpayer to report gains over the entire time period of the installment sales contract. This enables the taxpayer to avoid the burden of paying the tax before receiving the cash. The essential element of this method is for each dollar collected to be partly recovery of costs and partly taxable profit. (This method does not apply to losses; losses on an installment sale must be deducted in the taxable year of the sale.)

For tax purposes, a dealer can switch to installment reporting without prior approval. All he needs to do is reflect the proper figures, with appropriate supporting schedules, in his return. A dealer can use the installment method for reporting installment sales and the accrual method for reporting sales on open account.

Change of Method: Once the taxpayer begins installment reporting, he needs the Commissioner's approval to switch to accrual reporting. (If changed within the first three years, the taxpayer can revoke his election automatically by filing amended returns for those years.) A dealer switching from accrual to installment reporting must report, when collected, the unrealized profit on receivables outstanding at the time of the switch. The fact that the entire profit was accrued and reported in the period the receivable arose doesn't change this.

Code §453 largely eliminates the double tax that arises from reporting the same income twice. You take the gross profit in the current year attributable to collections of items accrued in a previous year and divide it by the total gross profits of the year of collection. You then apply that fraction to the year's tax to find what percentage of the current tax is attributable to that collection. Next, take that same gross profit attributable to the prior year's collection and divide it by the total gross profit of the year of accrual. This results in the percentage of the prior year's tax that was attributable to the amount accrued then but collected now. The lesser of the two figures is then applied to reduce the current year's tax. (See Appendix E for example of "Adjustments in tax on change to Installment Method")

[¶2404.3] Installment Sale Treatment for Revolving Credit Sales

Since revolving credit sales sometimes are paid in one payment by the customer, not all such sales are eligible for treatment as installment sales; special rules apply for the determination of apportioning and determining the extent of those sales which may be treated as installment sales [Reg. § 1453-2(d)(2)(i)].

[¶2404.4] Casual Installment Sale of Personalty

The occasional, or casual, sale of a piece of equipment or other personalty can be reported for tax purposes by the installment method. No "installments" are required. One payment will qualify the transaction as an installment sale if the single payment is made *after* the end of the year of sale.

Payments in the year of sale include all payments made by the buyer in the year the sale is closed, whether in cash or property. The buyer's note or other evidence of obligation to pay in a later year is merely a promise to pay, not a payment; consequently, it is not applicable until paid.

However, if installment obligations are discounted or otherwise disposed of during the year of sale, they have to be considered as payments in that year. A buyer's note that becomes due and paid during the year is property and must be included as must readily traded bonds or debentures of the purchaser or securities payable on demand.

[¶2404.5] Depreciation Recapture—New Law

Depreciation recapture income is to be fully recognized in the year of an installment sale of depreciable property, regardless whether payments are received in the year of sale. Under the old law, gain did not have to be recognized until principal payments were received, with the gain treated as ordinary income up to the amount of recapture income.

Effect: Any gain associated with an installment sale can be recapture income which must be reported in the year of sale, even though no payments were received. The new law therefore eliminates an important tax advantage of an installment sale.

[¶2404.6] Discounting Installment Receivables

There are two types of arrangements a dealer can make with banks or factors to obtain advances on his installment receivables. He can: (1) pledge them; that is, borrow against the receivables as collateral, or (2) discount them; that is, sell them at less than face value.

Under a pledge, the dealer receives a loan of perhaps as much as 85% of the balance due on the installment sales contracts and pays interest on the loan monthly. By discounting, he receives about 85% of the balance due, less a service charge; the remaining 15%, known as a holdback, is placed in a reserve account to secure the dealer's contingent liability as guarantor that the installment balances will be paid.

The installment method of reporting is available to the dealer only if he uses the *pledging* arrangement. If he discounts, he must report all of the income in the year of sale, even though the bank or factor has full recourse against him in the event the purchasers don't pay their installment liabilities.

New Law: Deferred principal payments on *corporate* installment sales will be treated as received in the tax year the sale occurs. This will prevent corporations from converting taxable dividends into a tax-deferred return of capital by borrowing on the installment contract and distributing the loan proceeds *before* the profit on the installment sale is recorded in E&P.

[¶2404.7] Installment Sale of Real Property

An installment sale of real property is generally subject to the same rules as a casual installment sale of personal property. Also keep in mind that while a mortgage on the property isn't payment even if assumed by the buyer, a mortgage which the buyer assumes or takes subject to is treated as payment received in the year of sale where such mortgage exceeds the seller's basis for the property sold (Reg.§1.453-4(c).

[¶2404.8] Installment Computation for Sale of Realty

Total profit is divided by contract price; the resulting percentage is the percent of each payment received that must be reported by the seller as income. Contract price is the entire amount the seller will receive (excluding payments on existing mortgages except to the extent they exceed the seller's basis).

Suppose we have a selling price of $25,000 and a cost basis of $15,000. The buyer assumes an existing $5,000 mortgage and gives his own mortgage for the balance due, payable over a 20-year period. Down payment is $5,000, and payments in the first year total $1,000, of which $600 represents interest. The sale qualifies for installment reporting.

Here is the computation for the first year.

Selling price	$25,000	
Cost basis	15,000	
Gain	$10,000	
Payments received		$6,000
Less interest (reported as ordinary income)		600
Principal amount received		$5,400

Selling price	$25,000
Less mortgage assumed	5,000
Contract price	$20,000
Profit percentage ($10,000÷$20,000)	50%
Reportable gain (50% × 5,400)	$2,700

On the accrual method, the reportable gain would be $10,000 instead of only $2,700.

[¶2404.9] Disposition of Installment Obligation

If an installment obligation is sold or otherwise disposed of, there is gain or loss in the amount of the difference between the basis of the obligation and the proceeds in the case of a sale, and the fair market value of the obligation in the case of any other disposition. For example, if unrecovered cost is $75, unrealized profit is $50, and the dealer sells for $100, he has a $25 gain. If he gives the obligation away and it is worth $90, he has a $15 gain. In either case, the gain is capital gain if the original transaction gave rise to capital gain and ordinary income if the orginal transaction gave rise to ordinary income.

[¶2405] CONSIGNMENT SALES

Selling on consignment will defer income until sale by the consignee. Thus, delivery to distributors on consignment postpones income. Instead of taking sales into account upon delivery, as where sales are made on open account, income on consignment sales is deferred while the goods are held on the distributor's floor.

Thus, a manufacturer can defer income by placing his sales on a consignment basis. And, conversely, he can accelerate income by shifting to an open-account basis. He might do this, for example, in order to use up an operating loss which is about to expire. Consigned goods (out) remain part of the manufacturer's inventory until sold.

Approval and Return Sales: Sales on approval aren't reflected in income until the buyer decides to take the goods. The parties agree the buyer is to take possession of the goods temporarily, with the understanding that if the goods aren't satisfactory, he owes nothing to the seller except their return. New and perishable products are frequently sold this way. Title does not pass until buyer approves.

Substantially the same business result, but different tax consequences can be achieved by a transaction known as "a sale or return." Seller and buyer agree that the goods will pass to the buyer on delivery but that he may return them if they prove unsatisfactory. The income must be taken up immediately, even though the buyer may subsequently return the goods. Here, title passes on delivery. The form of the contract determines whether the transaction is a sale on approval or a sale with return privileges.

Application: If you have been using a contract which provides for sale with the privilege of return, you can defer a large slice of income simply by changing the contract to one for sale on approval. Or, if you have been selling on approval, you can bring a lot of additional sales into a given year by changing your contract to one providing for sale on delivery with the privilege of return.

Consignment and Approval Sales Under the Uniform Commercial Code: Where the term *consignment sale* or its equivalent is used but nothing else is said, the UCC says the transaction is treated as a sale or return. Thus, if the parties want the income postponed until the buyer resells the goods, merely using the *consignment sale* designation is probably not enough; the contract should spell out the details of when the title is to pass. Whether this is desirable in view of other consequences under the UCC—e.g., rights in the goods of the buyer's creditors—is something to be decided by the parties.

[¶2406]   OTHER FACTORS AFFECTING SALES

Here are some other areas involving sales where timing techniques may be employed for tax purposes.

Conditional Sales: In a conditional sale, the seller delivers merchandise to a buyer who contracts to pay for it over a period of time. The seller stipulates that title is not to pass until the price has been fully paid.

The sale is not legally complete until final payment is made and title has passed to the buyer. Nevertheless, for tax purposes, the sale price must be taken into income when the property has been transferred to the buyer.

Sales of Specific Goods on Which Work Must Be Done: When a contract for the sale of specific goods calls for the seller to do something to the goods to put them into a deliverable state, the property does not pass to the purchaser until such things are done unless the parties agree otherwise. Thus, the accrual seller will realize no taxable income until he places the goods in a deliverable state or title passes to the buyer, and to this extent he can control his receipt of taxable income.

Sales on Open Account: Where such goods, in a deliverable state, are "unconditionally appropriated" (i.e., "identified to," under the UCC) to the contract by either the buyer or seller with the consent of the other, the title in the goods passes to the buyer. Delivery of the goods to a *carrier* for shipment to the purchaser, even if such shipment is made C.O.D., constitutes an "unconditional appropriation." If the seller wants a larger taxable income in a particular year, he can realize it by simply increasing the rate of shipments. If, on the other hand, he wants to postpone taxable income, he can slow up on the shipments or other acts of "unconditional appropriation."

Sales Returns and Allowances: Where credits or refunds are made for damaged or unsatisfactory merchandise, the deduction becomes available when the liability is admitted.

[¶2407]   OTHER ORDINARY INCOME

Dividend Income: Breakdown between foreign and domestic payors of dividends is necessary for federal tax purposes—e.g., domestic dividends are generally subject to an 85% dividend deduction; foreign dividends may be subject to credit for foreign taxes paid. Intercorporate dividends of affiliated corporations should be earmarked for elimination on consolidated returns. 100% deduction is now allowed for qualifying dividends received by affiliated corporations from other affiliates in the group, as long as consolidated returns are *not* filed.

No dividend deduction is ordinarily allowed for DISC dividends. (See later discussion of DISC Corporations.)

Royalty and License Income: Allocation between foreign and domestic royalty or license income may be required for federal tax purposes (including foreign tax credit). It is important to have details about possible withholding of tax at the source. State allocations may also depend on source of the income.

Rental Income: It is very important to keep location information of properties throwing off the rental income for state allocation purposes. In addition, rent paid by related taxpayers (e.g., subsidiaries) may be subject to reallocation by IRS on audit unless they have good substantiation for amounts paid.

Interest Income: Source of payments is necessary for possible exemption of some of the income from either or both federal and state taxes.

Foreign Income, Blocked: In regard to income received or accrued in foreign currency which is not convertible into United States currency, a taxpayer has the election of deferring reporting the income until the restrictions are lifted or including it in his present year's income.

[¶2408]   IMPUTED INTEREST

Seller-held financing is often a key ingredient in real estate deals. Taking back a note for part of the sales price helps the seller get top dollar for his property. From the buyer's viewpoint, seller financing is an attractive alternative to often hard-to-get bank financing.

Tax angle: The seller pays tax in the year of sale on the profit paid to him in the year of sale. Assuming there is no recapture of depreciation, the balance of his profit is taxed in later years when he receives payments on the note from the buyer. The interest payments the seller receives on the note are fully taxable ordinary income. Generally, the buyer's tax basis in the property—for all purposes, including depreciation—is his cost, including the seller-held mortgage. The interest he pays on the note is deductible and not included in basis.

The 1984 Tax Law may have absolutely no effect on a seller-held financing deal. On the other hand, if a transaction is affected by the New Law, a seller may be required to pay more tax dollars sooner.

Background: Before 1985, a seller must charge at least 9% interest on his note. If he doesn't, the transaction is refigured as if 10% interest had been charged. Result: A portion of the note principal is transformed into interest. For the seller, that results in a reduced sales price—and less low-taxed profit and more high-taxed ordinary income. For the buyer, it means a lower cost basis and bigger interest deductions.

> **NEW LAW CHANGE:** Beginning in 1985, there is a higher minimum interest rate. It's set at 110% of the rate paid on Treasury obligations with maturities similar to the seller-held note. If the seller charges a lower rate on his note, the transaction is refigured at a new, higher "imputed" interest rate—120% of the Treasury rate.

While these rates change every six months, the rate in effect when a transaction is closed governs the interest rate for the life of the note.

Still another change: In general, if the sales price exceeds $250,000 and the minimum rate isn't met, the transaction is covered by the complex original issue discount (OID) rules. And even if the stated note interest equals or exceeds the minimum rate, the OID rules apply if payment of part or all of the note interest payments is deferred. Here, the results are especially harsh: The seller is taxed on interest income each year even though he may not receive a penny in interest for years. The buyer, on the other hand, can take current deductions for interest he hasn't yet paid.

Late-breaking development: As we went to press, Congress passed a measure that modifies the imputed-interest rules described above. Here are the highlights of the new law: (1) For sales of real property and used personal property before July 1, 1985, involving seller financing of $2 million of principal or less, no interest will be imputed if the parties state at least 9% compound interest. If the parties fail to state an adequate interest, interest will be imputed at a 10% compound rate; (2) Transactions involving seller financing of more than $2 million will be subject to a blended interest rate, based on a weighted average between 9% and 10%, and 110% and 120% of the Treasury borrowing rate; (3) Assumptions of loans in connection with sales of principle residences, vacation homes, farms, ranches and small business property will be permanently exempt from '84 TRA provisions applying imputed interest rules to assumptions. And assumptions made before October 16, 1984 will be permanently exempt from new assumption rules, except for assumptions in connection with transactions involving a purchase price of $100 million or more; (4) For sales before July 1, 1985, of real property and used personal property used in the active business of farming or ranching, with seller financing of $2 million or less of principal, interest income and deductions will be accounted for by both the buyer and seller on the cash method; (5) Under the permanent rules of '84 TRA, sales of all principal residences, and farms or ranches costing $1 million or less, will be permanently exempt from original issue discount rules. The sale of a principal residence to the extent the cost is less than $250,000, and the sale of land in connection with the sale of a farm or ranch costing $1 million or less, will be permanently exempt from the requirement to state interest at 110% of the Treasury borrowing rate. These transactions will be subject to interest rates established by Regs, currently 9% and 10%.

25

Expenses and Costs of Sales

[¶2501] **CONFLICTS BETWEEN TAX AND BUSINESS ACCOUNTING FOR EXPENSES**

As there are conflicts in the timing of entering and recognizing income, as indicated in the prior chapter, so too are there divergencies in the recognition of deductions. The following list of expense-timing differences was also included in the submission by the AICPA to the House Committee on Ways and Means in connection with 1954 Code Hearings:

Divergencies Involving the Time of Allowance of Deductions:

(A) Costs and expenses, recognized for general accounting purposes, on basis of reasonable estimates, in period of related revenues; but not deductible for tax purposes until established with certainty by specific transactions:

    (1) Sales returns and allowances.
    (2) Freight allowances.
    (3) Quantity discounts.
    (4) Cash discounts allowable to customers.
    (5) Allowances for customers' advertising.
    (6) Provision for return of commissions resulting from cancellations of related contracts.
    (7) Costs of product guarantees.
    (8) Deferred management compensation and incentive bonuses.
    (9) Vacation pay.
    (10) Pending injury and damage claims.
    (11) Rentals on percentage lease with minimum.
    (12) Provisions for major repairs and maintenance regularly done at intervals of more than a year.
    (13) Professional services rendered but unbilled.
    (14) Social Security taxes on unpaid wages.
    (15) Retailers' occupation taxes on credit sales.
    (16) Costs of restoration of property by lessee at termination of lease.
    (17) Contractors' provisions for restoration of property damaged during construction.

(18) Costs of handling, packing, shipping, installing, etc., of merchandise already sold.

(19) Provisions for future costs to be incurred in collection of accounts receivable arising from installment sales, where profit is reported in the year of sale.

(20) Provisions for losses on foreign exchange.

(21) Allowances for perpetual care of cemetery (where not actually segregated from receipts).

(B) Expenses, deferred for general accounting purposes to period of related benefit, but deducted for tax purposes in year of payment or incurrence of liability:

(1) Advertising expenses from which benefit has not yet been obtained, including costs of preparation of catalogs not yet put into use.

(C) Property taxes recognized for general accounting purposes ratably over the year for which they are levied, but deductible in total tax purposes on a certain critical date.

The foregoing differences do not include conflicts which result from Congressional policy decisions. These include, on the *income side:* tax-exempt interest, tax-free exchanges, exemption of life insurance proceeds, capital gains, etc.; and, on the *deduction side*: percentage depletion, amortization of emergency facilities, loss carryovers and the disallowance of excess charitable contribution, losses on wash sales, losses on sales between certain relatives or related business interests, capital losses, etc.

The special treatment accorded these items originates from social, economic, and revenue considerations which, in the main, are unrelated to accounting principles.

[¶2502]   INCOME TAXES—ELECTIONS

The taxpayer has an accounting election for tax purposes as to a variety of things. Following are listed the more important elections:

[¶2503]   BAD DEBT METHODS

Accrual-basis taxpayer can elect either to deduct specific bad debt losses or make additions to reserve for bad debts. Election is made on the first return on which a bad debt is claimed; it's binding for subsequent years. To make a change from one bad debt method to the other, the taxpayer must obtain permission from the Commissioner. (Usually, the change is from charge-off to reserve to get the charge-off deductions *plus* the deduction for setting up the reserve). However, you can get "automatic consent" if you're willing to spread the benefits. To apply for the automatic switch from specific writeoff to the bad debt reserve method, you must file Form 3115 (Application for Change in Accounting

Method) within 180 days of the beginning of the tax year for which you want to change with the District Director. You should attach a copy of Form 3115 to your return for the taxable year of change.

Then, unless you receive a letter from the District Director denying you permission because your application on Form 3115 wasn't timely filed, you may assume that the change has been granted.

Initial Reserve Limitation: The amount of reserve that you set up initially at the end of the year of change is to be determined by dividing total net losses on bad debts for the five years before the change year by the sum of the amounts of outstanding trade receivables at the end of each of these five years, and then multiplying the amount of outstanding trade receivables at the end of the year of change by this percentage. Receivables sold or to be sold shortly after the end of the change year are not to be included in computations.

Maximum Tax Benefit: The addition to your reserve for bad debts can only be deducted ratably over a ten-year period. So, the maximum added yearly tax benefit you get is 10% of the addition to the bad debts reserve account. For the year of change, your bad debt deduction will consist of your specific writeoffs plus 10% of the addition of your initial addition to the reserve. In the next nine years, your deduction will consist of your addition to the reserve for that year plus 10% of the addition of the year of change. The amount of reserve for the year of change must be considered in determining subsequent additions.

Partial worthlessness can either be charged off as it occurs, or the deduction can be postponed until the year in which the debt becomes entirely worthless. A mere decline in market value isn't sufficient to warrant a charge-off.

Analysis of ratios of reserves to sales for current year and average of previous five years is needed to substantiate current deduction if there is an examination by IRS.

[¶2504]   DEPRECIATION METHODS*

Note: This section applies to depreciable assets acquired *before* January 1, 1981.

Depreciation methods permitted by the tax law include: (1) straight-line method (equal annual installments), (2) declining-balance method (up to double the straight-line rate), (3) sum-of-the-years-digits method (rate is a fraction, the numerator being the property's remaining useful life at the start of the tax year and the denominator being the sum of all the years' digits corresponding to the estimated useful life at acquisition), and (4) any other consistent method which during the first two-thirds of the property's useful life does not give greater depreciation than under the declining-balance method (§167(b)).

---

*See Appendix F for illustrations of the different depreciation methods.

Method number (4) embraces use of a sinking fund, writeoffs on the basis of periodic appraisal, unit of production, etc. However, most taxpayers who do not use the classic straight-line method employ instead one of the acceleration methods, either the 200%-declining-balance method of the sum-of-the-years-digits methods.

Another possibility that should be mentioned is a combination of the straight-line method and the 200%-declining-balance method. With this method, you use the 200%-declining-balance method, which gives you extra large deduction in the early years. At this point where this starts to peter out, you switch to straight-line which can be accomplished without consent of the Commissioner (Reg. §1.167(e)-1).

A good deal of what you do here will depend on prior years' actions. But you will want to analyze the existing situation to see if special, quick writeoffs are justified as to special assets; whether it's time to switch from double-declining-balance to straight-line on certain assets. Where new assets were acquired during the year, whether accelerated depreciation should be used as to them even though you use straight-line as to your other assets; whether you are using adequate salvage provisions; and whether you are taking advantage of the right to disregard salvage where permissible.

The 1969 Tax Reform Act restricted the use of accelerated depreciation for real property to 150% and also tightened the recapture rules. It also provided quicker writeoffs for certain types of properties and improvements. Low-income housing rehabilitation may be depreciated over a 60-month period. Pollution control facilities which are certified by governmental authorities may also be amortized over a 60-month period (§169) and so may railroad rolling stock, child-care facility and on-the-job training facility expenditures.

The applicable allowable depreciation (or amortization in lieu of depreciation) methods and rates may be summarized as follows:

Declining-balance method, 200% rate is allowed for new tangible personal property with a useful life of three years or more; all types of newly constructed real estate structures acquired before July 25, 1969; only on new residential rental property where 80% or more of gross rentals are from dwelling units.

Declining-balance method, 150% rate is allowed for used tangible personal property and for new real estate bought or constructed after July 24, 1969. No accelerated depreciation is allowed for used realty bought after that same date, unless it is used residential rental property (see next paragraph).

Declining-balance method, 125% rate is allowed only for used residential rental property acquired after July 24, 1969, and having a useful life of 20 years or more, or if the Commissioner permits it on application for other types.

Sum-of-the-years-digits method is allowed only for new tangible personal property and new residential rental property.

Straight-line (useful life) method is allowed for all depreciable property, new or used, personal or real.

Straight-line method (no salvage value), 60 months applies to low-income rental housing rehabilitation expenditures; certified pollution control facilities; certain railroad rolling stock.

Additional first-year 20% depreciation write-off is also permitted (regardless of which method above is used) to the maximum extent of $2,000 depreciation (the same maximum applies to an *entire* affiliated group).

The taxpayer has a further election:

For assets placed in service after 1970, depreciation rates used may be based on either:

1) Estimated Useful Life, generally based on guidelines in Rev. Proc. 62–21 or prior IRS Bulletin F; or

2) The Class Life Asset Depreciation Range System (ADR).

Regulations regarding the use of ADR are quite extensive and detailed. Taxpayers should study this election further. It offers many taxable advantages.

[¶2505]   OTHER ELECTIONS

Leasehold Amortization: Improvement costs on leaseholds are recovered by one of two methods. You will need information about cost of improvement, useful life, remaining term of the lease, renewal options available. For example, if remaining life of lease is less than 60% of useful life of improvement, amortization must be over remaining lease life *plus* renewal periods, but not longer than useful life of improvement. Or, if lessor is an affiliate, shortest available life over which amortization may be taken is useful life of improvement. Location of leased property is also useful information for state allocation purposes.

Under ACRS, leasehold costs are recovered in about the same way, except instead of comparing the remaining years of the lease to the useful life, the remaining lease term is compared to the recovery period. This results in improvement costs being recovered either by straight-line amortization, or through ACRS recovery, whichever is shorter.

Trademark and Trade Name Amortization: Examine costs of trademarks or trade names incurred during the year (including cost of acquisition other than purchase), protection, expansion, registration (federal, state, or foreign), or defense of trademark or trade name; cost can be written off over at least a 60-month period rather than capitalized.

Patent Amortization: Examine patent data to determine whether there is any basis to increase deduction—e.g., patent has become worthless.

Bond Premiums: The bondholder can elect to amortize bond premium on wholly taxable obligations to maturity or to the date on which the bond is first callable if the deduction is smaller. The bond premium, which is deductible, reduces the basis of the bond. Taxpayer makes the election by claiming the deduction in the first taxable year for which he wishes it to apply. It applies to all bonds and can be revoked only with Commissioner's permission.

Every taxpayer must amortize premium on wholly-tax-exempt bonds, even though no tax deduction results, thus reducing the basis annually.

Carrying Charges: There is an election to deduct or capitalize taxes, interest and other carrying charges in connection with the following kinds of property:

(1) Unimproved and unproductive real property. The election is to deduct or capitalize taxes, interest and other carrying charges.

(2) Real property being developed or improved. The election is to deduct or capitalize costs up to the time construction or development has been completed. For instance: Social Security taxes on own employees, sale or use taxes on materials used in development or improvement of property, and other necessary expenditures paid or incurred in connection with this work.

(3) Personal property. The election is to deduct or capitalize interest on loans to purchase the property or to pay for transporting or installing, sales and use taxes paid on the property, Social Security taxes on own employees used in transporting and installing the property, paid or incurred up to the date installed or first put into use, whichever date is later.

Election to capitalize any item is made by filing a statement with the return, stating the items being charged to capital (Reg. §1.266- 1(c)(3)). Commissioner's consent is not required.

Circulation Expenditures: Publisher can elect to capitalize rather than deduct expenditures made to establish or increase circulation. Year-to-year expenditures to maintain circulation cannot be capitalized but must be deducted currently.

The election, if made, must be applied to all expenditures to increase circulation in the present or later years, except where the Commissioner permits change on written application.

The election is made by a statement attached to the first tax return to which it is applicable.

Depletion: Bear in mind that a taxpayer has no election, in the true sense of that word, in selecting a depletion method. What actually happens is that he must make a computation for depletion based on both the cost and percentage methods and then select the method which results in the greatest deduction, regardless of whether it will be a disadvantage to the taxpayer (Code Sections 612 and 613). This computation is to be made each year.

Cost depletion formula:

$$\frac{\text{Original Cost} + \text{Development Expense}}{\text{Estimated Units of Recovery}} = \text{Unit Depletion}$$

Unit Depletion × Units Extracted and Sold = Cost Depletion Allowed

Percentage depletion is the lesser of the statutory percentage of gross income (varies from 22% on down, depending upon the statutory classification and definition under Sections 613 and 613A, with gas and oil also having additional limitations) from the property, or 50% of the net computed without the depletion deduction.

Foreign Taxes: With respect to income, war profits and excess profits taxes paid or accrued to a foreign country, a taxpayer has the option to take credit against income taxes or a reduction from gross income. (Code Sections 901-905).

Involuntary Conversion: Taxpayer can use recovery to either replace or restore property and avoid tax or pay the tax and step up the basis of newly acquired property.

To avoid the tax, the taxpayer must replace or restore the property within the time beginning with first date of known imminence of condemnation or the actual date of destruction and ending two years after the end of the first taxable year, or a later approved IRS date (three years for real property).

Mining—Development Expenses (Excluding oil or gas well): Taxpayer can either deduct these in the year they were incurred or capitalize them and deduct them ratably over units of ore as produced or minerals as benefited. These expenses do not include exploration expenses or expenditures for depreciable property (§616). For a mine in the development stage, the election applies only to the excess of expenditures over the net receipts from ores or minerals produced during the year. Election, if made, applies to all development expenditures. It is made by a written statement, filed with the Director of Internal Revenue with whom the return is filed, or by a rider attached to the return. A new election is made each year.

Mining—Exploration Expenses: All such expenditures paid or incurred after 1969 are deductible (§617). Such expenditures made for the discovery of a new mine are subject to recapture when the mine begins producing, with some exceptions as under Section 1245.

Research and Experimentation Incentives: Under the old law, research expenditures which resulted in an asset having a useful life extending beyond the current taxable year had to be capitalized and amortized. The 1981 Act allows a nonrefundable credit, in addition to other allowable deductions. The credit will equal 25% of the excess of the qualified research expenses for the taxable year over the average of these same expenses of the previous three years (termed the "base period" research expenses). The credit applies to qualifying amounts paid or incurred after June 30, 1981 and before January 1, 1986. Special rules for the base period apply to the first two years of the credit. The computation for the amount of the credit must take into account that base period research expenses cannot be less than 50% of the expenses for the current year.

An individual can apply the credit only against his tax related to his business which conducted research and experimentation activities. The purpose of this restriction is to prevent the credit being used to shelter an individual taxpayer's other income.

Unused credits can be carried back three years (which means that the credit is assumed to have been in effect in an earlier year), and forward 15 years.

Rent Expenses: Examine rent agreements in first year of agreement to see if there are any purchase options that might warrant IRS treating the rental as a purchase. In this connection, compare the rent called for where there is an option with what the rent would have been without an option. Rents paid may also be needed for state allocation formulas.

[¶2506]   EMPLOYEE BENEFITS

[¶2506.1]   "Reasonable" Compensation

All payments to compensate an employee for services which are ordinary and necessary to the operation of the business are deductible *provided* they are "reasonable."

What Is Reasonable? Determining reasonable compensation is not an easy task. The courts themselves have a hard time determining what is reasonable under certain facts. Nevertheless, here is a list of the several factors usually considered by the courts in dealing with this problem: (1) The employee's special qualifications; (2) the nature, extent and scope of work; (3) the size and complexities of the business; (4) the prevailing general economic conditions; (5) comparison of salaries to dividends; (6) rates of compensation for comparable positions in comparable concerns; (7) the "arm's length" element in the compensation deal; (8) consideration for past services and compensation in prior years; (9) comparison of salaries paid with employee's stock ownership.

As a rule of thumb, you can say that reasonable compensation is the amount that would ordinarily be paid for like services by like enterprises under like circumstances.

[¶2506.2]   Cash and Stock Bonuses

The cash bonus is used to assure the employee of an immediate share of the company's profits over and above his regular compensation. In a noncontractual plan, the amount of the bonus, who is to get it, and, in what proportions, are usually determined on a year-by-year basis—depending on the amount of profits.

Under a formal contractual basis, the employee knows before-hand exactly what to expect. If a certain profit is reached, he gets a definite amount as his share.

The stock bonus plan is exactly like the cash bonus except, of course, that the payment is made in company stock. The big advantage of paying employee's bonuses in stock rather than cash is that the company can retain the cash to be used in the business. Furthermore, the corporation gets a compensation deduction for the market value of the stock.

[¶2506.3]   Stock Options

Qualified stock options are back, under a new name—"incentive stock options." Five years after abolishing the qualified stock option, Congress restored this executive tax break and made it better than ever. What's more, §251 of the Economic Recovery Act of 1981 (IRC §422A) makes it possible for nonqualified options granted on or after January 1, 1976, and exercised on or after January 1, 1981, to qualify retroactively as incentive stock options.

Incentive Stock Options: Prior to the 1981 Act, the taxation of stock options (other than qualified options) granted by an employer to an employee as compensation was governed by §83. If a nonqualified option itself had a readily ascertainable fair market value when granted, the value of the option was taxable to the employee as ordinary income at that time. If the option did not have a readily ascertainable value when granted, the employee reported as ordinary income the difference between the option price and the value of the stock when the option was exercised (or, if the stock was restricted, on the date the restrictions were removed).

An employee does not recognize any income upon the granting or exercise of an incentive stock option provided that the option is exercised no later than three months after termination of employment and the employee does not dispose of the acquired shares within two years after the date of grant and one year after the date of exercise.* Any gain realized upon disposition thereafter is treated as long-term capital gain. (A similar provision that applied to qualified stock options required a holding period of three years after the date of exercise.)

These are the requirements for an incentive stock option.

(1) The option must be granted in connection with employment and pursuant to a plan that includes (a) the aggregate number of shares that may be issued under the options and (b) the employees or class of employees eligible to receive options. The play must be approved by the stockholders of the granting corporation within 12 months before or after the plan is adopted. (An identical requirement applied to qualified stock options.)

---

*The 1982 Act makes the bargain element of the option a tax preference item for calculating the minimum tax.

(2) The option must be granted within 10 years after the plan is adopted or approved by the stockholders, whichever is earlier. (The same provision applied to qualified options.)

(3) The option cannot be exercisable more than 10 years after the date of grant. See, however, Special Rule (5) on the following page. (Qualified options had a 5-year limit.)

(4) The option price cannot be less than the fair market value of the stock at the time of grant* (The same provision applied to qualified options.) However, see Special Rule (1) on the following page.

(5) The option is nontransferable except by will or the laws of descent and distribution, and is exercisable only by the employee during his lifetime. (Same as qualified option.) Under the 1984 Tax Act, a change in the terms of an option to make it nontransferable (and thereby qualify as an ISO), will be treated as a new option. As a result, the option must be adjusted to meet ISO requirements.

(6) The employee does not own more than 10% of the voting stock of the employer corporation or of its parent or subsidiary. See, however, Special Rule (5). (For a qualified option, ownership could not exceed 5% of the voting stock if the corporation's equity capital was $2 million or more.)

(7) An option may not be exercisable while an incentive stock option that was granted earlier remains outstanding. (A similar restriction applied to qualified options.)

(8) No more than $100,000 worth of stock can be optioned to an individual in any one year. However, if less than $100,000 is granted in any year, one-half of the ungranted amount may be carried over to three succeeding years. (Qualified options had no such limitations.)

Special Rules

(1) There is *no penalty* if the option price is less than the fair market value of the stock on the date of grant, as long as there was an attempt, "made in good faith," to meet the requirement that the price be no less than the market value. (Qualified stock options had a similar "good faith" provision, but required the lucky optionee to include in income either 1½ times the difference between the option price and the value at the time of grant or the difference between the option price and the value at the time of exercise, whichever was less.)

(2) If an employee sells acquired stock within two years after the option is granted, the employee's gain will be included in his gross income and deductible by the corporation as compensation.

(3) A transfer by an insolvent individual to a trustee, receiver, or other fi-

---

*The 1984 Tax Act makes the determination of a stock's fair market value for both income and minimum tax purposes without regard to any restriction other than one which, by its terms, won't lapse.

duciary in a bankruptcy proceeding or other similar proceeding for the benefit of creditors will not be subject to the two-year or one-year holding period.

(4) An option may be treated as an incentive stock option if:

a) the employee may pay for the stock with stock of the corporation granting the option;

b) The employee has a right to receive property when the option is exercised, provided that IRC §83 applies to the property;

c) The option is subject to any condition that is not inconsistent with the requirements for an incentive stock option.

(5) An incentive stock option may be granted to an individual who owns more than 10% of the voting stock of the corporation or its parent or subsidiary if the option price is at least 110% of the fair market value of the stock at the time of grant and the option is not exercisable after five years.

(6) If an individual who received an incentive stock option is disabled, the option may be exercised as late as one year after employment is terminated because of disability.

[¶2506.4]   Deferred Compensation Arrangements

With the fantastic growth of business over the years, the arrival of high corporate and individual tax rates, and the increased public interest in retirement planning, there has been evolved a mass of intricate and involved deferred compensation plans to attract new employees or retain old employees.

Under a deferred compensation plan, payment of compensation presently earned is postponed to a future period. If the plan qualifies as an exempt trust under §401 IRC, the employer gets an immediate deduction for a contribution—even though the employee does not receive the sum until a later time. However, under a non-qualified deferred compensation contract, the employer gets a deduction only when he actually pays the deferred compensation to the employee (who is taxed at that time).

Under a nonqualified plan, the employer can pick and choose who will benefit; he is not committed to a class of employees or any other rigid requirement as provided for qualified deferred compensation plans. Generally, this arrangement is less ambitious than qualified plans and therefore more attractive to smaller organizations.

Most often, the nonqualified deferred compensation plan is used for a key executive. The ordinary plan is to have the company accumulate funds for the benefit of the executive and then pay them out when the executive reaches postretirement years and is in a lower tax bracket.

[¶2506.5]   Insurance Plans

Insurance is a significant vehicle for funding or providing employee benefits. Here are some of the most popular plans.

Key-Person Insurance: This is insurance on a key-person's life. It is deductible only if the *employer* is not directly or indirectly the beneficiary, and if the premiums are in the nature of compensation and are not unreasonable.

Split-Dollar Insurance: The employee pays a portion of the premium to the employer under this plan (life insurance), and that portion reduces the amount included in income (the includable amount would be, in effect, the employer's share of the premium). Any policy dividends received by the employee are also included in his income.

Group Term Life Insurance: This arrangement offers an employee an opportunity to acquire low-cost life insurance because it's purchased for a "group." Under a "group term" plan the employee can get up to $50,000 of insurance protection tax free; that is, all premiums paid on over that amount of insurance must be included in income. But the plan has to be a group *term* plan. Permanent insurance (whole life policies) does not qualify under this provision.

Group Health: This plan provides for the reimbursement of medical and hospitalization expenses incurred by an employee. Premiums are tax deductible by the employer and not taxable to the employee—even though the plan provides for the protection of the employee's family. This plan is widely used by many employers to provide their employees with at least the basic health and accident protection. Of course, individual health plans for particular employees are also used.

[¶2506.6] Qualified Pension and Profit-Sharing Plans

TAX ADVANTAGES OF QUALIFIED PLANS

(1) *Employer*: The employer gets a current deduction for amounts contributed to the plan, within specified limits, although no benefits may have been actually distributed to the participating employees that year. This permits an employer to accumulate a trust fund for his employees with 100-cent, before-tax dollars which, in effect, represent 54-cent after-tax dollars to the employer in the 46% tax surtax bracket. The employer expense for the contribution to a qualified plan may be accrued at year-end, but it must be paid no later than the legal time of filing the return (including extensions).

(2) *Employees*: The tax to the employee is deferred until the benefits under the plan are actually distributed or made available to him. If the employee receives a lump-sum distribution, a portion of it may be capital gains (based on years of participation prior to 1974) and the remaining taxable portion is subject to ordinary income rates, but there is a special 10-year averaging option available.

(3) *Trust Fund*: The income and gains on the sale of trust property of the trust fund are exempt from tax, in effect, being postponed until distribution. Funds, which are compounded tax free under a qualified plan, increase at a much

greater rate than if such funds were currently distributed to employees and personally invested by them. In the latter case, the amount received by the employees is subject to two tax bites—when he receives the benefits and again on the investment income earned on what is left.

CHOOSING BETWEEN PENSION AND PROFIT SHARING

Profit Sharing	*Pension*
(1) Generally favors younger employees.	(1) Generally favors older employees.
(2) Need not provide retirement benefits.	(2) Must provide retirement benefits.
(3) Contribution can be made only if profits exist.	(3) Contributions must be made for profitable as well as for loss years.
(4) Even in profitable years the amount of contributions, if any, can be left to discretion of management.	(4) Amount of contribution is not discretionary; it must be actuarially justifiable and tied to definitely determinable benefits.
(5) Contributed amounts generally cannot exceet 15% of year's payroll for participants.	(5) No maximum limit on contributions as long as they are actuarially justifiable and total compensation is within IRS 162 limitations.
(6) Forfeitures may be allocated in favor of remaining participants.	(6) Forfeitures must be used to decrease future cost to employer.
(7) No more than 50% of participant's account may be invested in life insurance.	(7) May be completely funded by investment in life insurance.
(8) Broad fringe benefits can be included (incidental accident and health insurance).	(8) Limited fringe benefits can be included (disability pension).
(9) Employer may never recover any part of contribution or income therefrom.	(9) Employer on termination of plan may recover excess funds which arose as a result of actuarial error.

ERISA

The Employee Retirement Income Security Act of 1974, commonly called ERISA, substantially changed the rules and set new minimum standards for employees' trusts, most notably in the following areas:

1) Participation rules.

2) Vesting rights.

3) Funding requirements.

In addition, the tax and information forms which are required to be filed with the IRS (and in some cases with the Department of Labor) were changed and are constantly being revamped.

Arguments both for and against the new law are being debated, and much confusion still surrounds its administration, regulation, interpretation and effect. Professional advice should be sought for updating old plans and for instituting new plans, as well as for assuring conformance with the required new regulations and reporting.

Non-corporate entities and individuals should also pursue the tax deferral opportunities now expanded for them under the new law.

[¶2507] HOW TO SHIFT BUSINESS EXPENSES

Here is how to shift expenses, depending on whether you want to boost the current year's or the following year's deductions:

(1) *A cash-basis taxpayer can pay all bills by December 31.* If it wants to defer expenses, it will hold off payment until January. You can't get a deduction for certain prepayments—even if you are on the cash basis (e.g., insurance premiums, rents)—especially if they cover more than one year's period.

(2) *Rush through repairs,* buy office supplies, pay research and experimental costs if you want the deduction this year. Hold off if you want it next year.

(3) *Accrual-basis taxpayers can pick up sales returns and allowances* by December 31, to get a deduction this year—after December 31, for a deduction next year.

(4) *Have your lawyer and accountant bill you* before year-end if you want to accrue or pay the bill for the taxable year.

(5) *Junk or abandon equipment, etc.,* before the year's end for deduction this year—next year for a deduction next year.

(6) *Switching from bad debt writeoffs to reserve* method brings more deduction into this year. Theoretically, this switch can double up your bad debt deduction. But, as a practical matter, since you need IRS' permission to switch, IRS will make you spread the additional deduction over a ten-year period. So you can only increase your deduction by 10% this year.

(7) *Corporate contribution deductions can be accrued* this year if paid within 2½ months after the end of the tax year. So, where the corporation is short of cash now but wants the deduction this year, make sure you pass the appropriate corporate resolution making the contribution and calling for payment no later than 2½ months after the end of your tax year. (*Caution:* The new premature accrual rules may affect this strategy. See Sec. 461.)

(8) *Items in dispute—contested taxes or other liabilities—*must be deducted when they are paid, even though a contest which finally determines the liability is resolved in a later year. This applies to accrual as well as cash-basis taxpayers. So, if you are anxious to get the deduction this year, pay the liability by year-end.

(9) *Losses on worthless assets* have to be shown by an identifiable event in the year the loss is taken. Where worthlessness may be difficult to prove, dispose of the asset in the year you want the loss.

Here are some other considerations that you should have at the end of the year.

[¶2507.1] Business Gifts at Year-End

Since year-end is often the season of making business gifts, it's important to check your lists carefully to be aware whether or not you are making total gifts to one person or more than $25—the deductible ceiling on a business gift. In addition, you ought to be aware of the definition of business gifts and where you can avoid falling within the definitions.

Maybe Your "Gift" Can Qualify as Entertainment: There's no ceiling on entertainment costs; but you have to have full substantiation.

Generally, says IRS, where an item might be either entertainment, on the one hand, or a gift or travel cost, on the other, it will be considered entertainment. But packaged food and beverages given to a customer, for example, for use at some other time are gifts.

As for theatre and similar tickets of admission, if you go along, it's entertainment, even if you give the tickets to your guest. If you don't go along, you can treat the expense either as entertainment or a business gift.

[¶2507.2] Audit Your Pay Setup at Year-End

Wages and salaries are by far the most compelling income and expense factor in many a business. The final months of the year provide the last opportunity to arrange compensation policies for minimum tax cost—both for employer and for employees.

Here are some important points you will want to watch:

Are Office-Stockholders Getting the Best "Tax" Salary? That's the amount at which any increase will cost the employee-stockholder more in taxes than the corporation will save by the increase and at which any decrease would cost the corporation more than the employee saves.

Bonus Declarations: Year-end bonus declarations and payments boost this year's compensation deductions. But you always have to be concerned with the problem of reasonableness. Suppose part of the compensation is disallowed as being unreasonable. The corporation loses the deduction and the employee still has income for what he received—so we have a double tax. If the corporation can use more deductions now but doesn't have the cash, it can accrue them (assuming, of course, the corporation uses the accrual method of accounting). It gets the deduction now, and the employee has income when he receives it.

But keep in mind the special rules; if the employee is a more-than-50%

stockholder, the corporation has to pay the accrued salaries or bonuses within 2½ months after the end of the year. Otherwise, it loses its deduction altogether.

Unusual Transactions: Check all transactions during the year of an unusual nature—outside the scope of what the corporation normally does—to determine whether any special tax problems exist as to any of these transactions.

Compensation: Details of officers' compensation are required for tax returns—name, Social Security number, address, title, time devoted to business, percentage of stock owned (common and preferred), amount of compensation and expense account allowances. As to other compensation, it's a good idea to reconcile the total compensation claimed on the tax return with the amounts shown on the payroll tax reports. Note that the compensation shown on the payroll tax reports is on a cash basis, so a reconciliation to the amounts of compensation claimed as deductions on the tax return which is on the accrual basis is necessary. This reconciliation will help justify your deduction if your tax return is audited.

Information on interest, rents and other payments to officers and stockholders may also be required for state tax returns.

Note the statutory definition of what must be included as "expense account allowance."

[¶2508] OTHER TAX-EXPENSE CONSIDERATIONS

Charitable Contributions: Examine charitable contributions in the form of donations of the company's own product. Deduction is based on market value plus ½ of appreciated value (not to exceed twice basis), since it is considered ordinary income property. Where deduction is based on accrual to be paid within two and a half months after close of taxable year, make sure the proper corporate resolution was passed before year end. The annual limit on a company's charitable contributions is 10% of taxable income.

Payroll Taxes: As in the case of compensation, the payroll taxes paid by the employer and deductible as expenses should be reconciled with the payroll taxes shown on the payroll tax returns, since the taxes on the payroll returns were computed on a cash basis and your deduction for income tax purposes may be deducted on the accrual basis.

Interest Expense: Examine basis for write-downs and keep sufficient backup information to support the write-down (or merchandise destruction), in the event of an examination.

Inventory Write-Downs: Examine basis for write-downs and keep sufficient backup information to support the write-down (or merchandise destruction), in the event of an examination.

Repairs: An analysis of the amounts expensed as repairs during the year should be made to see if all pass as repairs and are not likely to be held to be improvements. Where the items are very numerous, it is likely that a revenue agent will test the account. An analysis of the larger items—e.g., those costing $1,000 or more—made in advance, with sufficient data to back up the deduction of each of these items as a repair, may be very helpful if the return is audited.

Reimbursed Travel and Entertainment expenses: Make sure there is adequate substantiation by the employees who are reimbursed and that the accounting system used has sufficient internal control. The employee may also have to substantiate his deductions on his own tax return. The absence of proper backup in the form of vouchers, invoices, mileage reports, etc. on the corporation's part can jeopardize its deductions, since a prerequisite is adequate substantiation. Many companies use credit cards specifically to pinpoint these expenses by employees.

State Income and Franchise Taxes: These should be accrued on the federal tax return for the current year although not yet paid. Also check to see whether taxes that have been prepaid, and therefore deferred on the books, are nevertheless deductible for federal income taxes (as is allowed in many situations—e.g., property taxes may be deducted in the year they accrue even if the period of the tax extends beyond the taxable year). However, a few state franchise taxes specifically pertain to ensuing years and are not deductible until then (California).

Sales and Use Taxes: Where a company has a number of locations, it may be advantageous to review the policies at each location and make sure that only those sales and use taxes to which a particular location is subject and being paid or allocated.

Also, be informed as to the possibility of being liable for the sales tax in situations where "location" may not be a factor, such as direct mail sales or shipments.

[¶2509] INFORMATION FOR STATE ALLOCATIONS

Types of Locations: Determine whether the sales in any particular state are subject to any tax at all by the state. For example, where no offices are maintained within the state and orders are subject to acceptance outside the state and goods are shipped from outside the state, it may be that no franchise/income tax is due on sales made in that state. If you are subject to tax, however, consider the following data for the purpose of allocation under each state's own allocation formula:

Sales Data: For each state, you will want to know how much sales were billed to customers within that state, totals of sales reflected by shipments to all customers (wherever located) from points within the state, total sales reflected by shipments from within the state to customers within the state, total sales credited to a sales office within that state (a salesman who lives within the state and works out of his home, there being no "formal" office within the state, does not usually count as a sales office within the state).

Average Fixed Assets: For each physical location of the company, determine the balances at the beginning and end of the year (and the average by adding and dividing by two) of the net book values of the fixed assets—e.g., land, buildings, furniture and fixtures, equipment. Some states require the use of cost (California).

Inventories: For each physical location get the values of all inventories at beginning and end of year and average.

Payroll: For each state, determine the total payroll actually paid out during the year to employees in that state.

Officer/Stockholders: Determine if information is needed for separate disclosure of sums paid or accrued to officer/stockholders—salaries, rent interest— and the extent of loans to or from officers.

Taxes: Some states require separate itemization of all taxes by type paid everywhere and specifically within the state.

(See also State Tax Chapter which follows.)

26

Special Areas

[¶2601] TAXATION OF FOREIGN OPERATIONS

The availability of foreign tax shelters has been under heavy congressional attack in recent years. Building up corporate profits from foreign operations in a holding company in a country which does not subject such companies to any severe tax has been hard hit by provisions which tax "unrepatriated" foreign profits to the American investors.

The following paragraphs are a brief review of the tax rules applying to the various ways in which foreign operations may be conducted.

[¶2602] FOREIGN BRANCHES

For U.S. tax purposes, the branch operation represents only one part of a single entity and its results emerge in a single income tax return. Profits made from foreign sources are taxable immediately whether they are retained in the foreign country or returned to the U.S. In combining the income from the foreign country and the U.S., losses sustained abroad can be used to reduce U.S. income taxes if domestic profits have been earned.

Although segregation of branch profits is not necessary for computation of U.S. income taxes, it is necessary for foreign tax credit computation purposes since the credit is limited by the percentage of income from foreign sources.

[¶2602.1] Domestic Corporations

Resident foreign operations conducted through a domestic subsidiary corporation are handled by the subsidiary just as the parent handles its branch operation. Current profits brought to the parent via the dividend route are eligible for the 85% (in some cases 100%) dividend-received deduction, and, on liquidation, profits can be brought to the parent tax free.

Possessions Corporations: Domestic corporations deriving a large portion of their income from sources within U.S. possessions may, under certain circumstances, avoid U.S. income taxes with respect to all income derived from sources without the U.S.: 80% of the corporation's gross income must have been derived from sources within U.S. possessions and 50% must have been derived from the active conduct of a trade or business within that possession.

[¶2602.2]   Foreign Corporations

Foreign corporations fall into one of two basic categories. They are either controlled foreign corporations, or they are not. If they are not controlled foreign corporations, they are eligible for the advantages which have long been associated with foreign business operations; i.e., no current U.S. tax on foreign-source income, no problem under U.S. tax law in accumulating earnings, freedom to transfer funds from one foreign operating form to others, and capital gain on liquidation. On the other hand, if they are controlled foreign corporations, they are still not subject to U.S. tax on current foreign source earnings; but all or part of their current earnings can be currently includable in the gross income of their parent company or stockholders.

Foreign corporations are themselves taxable only on U.S.-source income, even though the worldwide operations of the company are entirely managed in the U.S. Resident foreign corporations—those engaged in a trade or business within the U.S.—are taxed on their entire gross income from U.S. sources less allowable deductions and credits. Nonresident foreign corporations—those not engaged in business in the U.S.—are taxed at a fixed flat rate of 30% on fixed or determinable, annual or periodical gains, profits and income from U.S. sources, such as interest, dividends, rents, salaries, wages, royalties, etc.

[¶2602.3]   Controlled Foreign Corporations

A controlled foreign corporation is one in which, after giving effect to various attribution-of-stock-ownership rules, more than 50% of the voting stock is owned on any one day in the taxable year by U.S. citizens, residents, corporations, partnerships, trusts and estates. A "U.S. shareholder," by definition, would be any U.S. citizen resident, domestic partnership, corporation, estate or trust which owns 10% or more of the voting interest (as part of 50% controlling interest).

The "U.S. shareholder" must include in its (his) gross income his share of the statutory defined: (1) Subpart F income, (2) previously excluded Subpart F income withdrawn from less developed countries, and (3) increases in earnings invested in U.S. property by the controlled foreign corporation.

Foreign Assets and ACRS: Special rules are provided in the Act for the application of ACRS to real and personal property used outside of the United States.

For foreign depreciable personal property, the cost recovery period is the midpoint life of the ADR guideline period for the property as of January 1, 1981. The recovery tables to be provided by IRS will be based upon the 200% declining-balance method for the early years, with a switch to straight-line in later years. There is no salvage value limitation.

For foreign depreciable real property the recovery period is 35 years. The recovery percentages tables to be determined by IRS will be based upon the 150% declining-balance method for the early years, with a switch to straight-line in later years. Salvage value can be ignored.

[¶2603] FOREIGN SALES CORPORATIONS (FSC)

Foreign Sales Corporation Replaces DISC: Congress has replaced the Domestic International Sales Corporation (DISC) system of tax deferral for U.S. exporters with the new, less favorable Foreign Sales Corporations (FSC). The change was made to resolve the General Agreement on Tariffs and Trade dispute over whether DISCs were an illegal export subsidy.

Under the new law, part of an FSC's export income will be exempt from U.S. income tax, if the FSC meets foreign management and foreign economic process requirements. In general, management must take place outside the U.S., *and* the solicitation, negotiation, etc., of the underlying contract occurs outside the U.S., as well as 50% or more of the foreign direct costs. Smaller exporters can use two alternatives to the FSC to avoid the foreign presence and economic activities requirements: the interest charge DISC and the small FSC. Also, a U.S. corporation will be allowed a 100% dividends-received deduction for FSC dividends from earnings attributable to certain foreign trade income. The FSC's income must be determined according to specified transfer prices.

A bargain. The accumulated deferred income of existing DISCs—literally billions of dollars—will be considered previously taxed income and therefore exempt.

Qualification: An FSC must: (1) Be created or organized under the laws of a foreign country (that meets certain requirements concerning exchange of information) or a U.S. possession; (2) Have no more than 25 shareholders at any time during the tax year; (3) Have no preferred stock outstanding at any time during the tax year; (4) Maintain permanent books of account at a non-U.S. office and records that the corporation must keep under Sec. 6001 at a U.S. location throughout the tax year; (5) Have a board of directors that includes at least one non-U.S. resident; (6) Not be a member of a controlled corporate group of which a DISC is a member, at any time during the tax year; and (7) Have made a timely election to be treated as an FSC.

Small FSC: An FSC is a small FSC for a tax year, if it has made a timely election to be treated as a small FSC, and isn't a member of a controlled corporate group that includes a FSC (unless the other FSC has also made such an election).

Election: A corporation may elect to be treated as an FSC or a small FSC for a tax year during the 90-day period immediately preceding the beginning of the tax year. IRS may consent to the making of an election at other times. All shareholders on the first day of the first tax year for which the election is effective must consent in writing.

The election is revocable after the first taxable year.

Interest Charge DISC: A small exporter can avoid the foreign presence and economic activity requirements of the FSC by using an interest charge DISC.

The DISC can continue to defer income attributable to $10 million or less of qualified export receipts subject to an interest charge on the DISC shareholders. The charge will be based on the tax otherwise due if the deferred income were distributed. The interest rate will be the base period Treasury bill rate. DISC taxable income attributable to qualified export receipts that exceed $10 million will be deemed distributed.

[¶2604] BUSINESS ACQUISITIONS— SALES AND PURCHASES

TAX CONSIDERATIONS

Much of the planning of the purchase or sale of a business is influenced by the tax consequences. What follows is a summary of the major tax considerations and the alternatives available to bring about the desired results.

[¶2604.1] How to Maximize Tax Benefits

If business assets are sold as a unit for a lump-sum consideration, the sales proceeds must be allocated among the individual assets of the business, and the gain or loss computed accordingly. The owner is not permitted to treat the sale of his business as the sale of a single capital asset. Moreover, the burden of proving that any portion of the sale proceeds is attributable to the goodwill and other capital assets of the business is on the vendor. The problem may be eased by drafting the contract or bill of sale to provide for specific prices for each individual asset in the business. The buyer will want to allocate as much of the purchase price as possible to depreciable assets. He may prefer to rely on an appraisal if he can't get a favorable allocation agreed to in the contract.

No gain is recognized to the corporation if it sells its assets and liquidates under IRC §337 (except for §1245 and 1250 property).

The following chart illustrates the tax effects and the conflicting desires of buyer and seller involved in allocating the purchase price of the business:

Asset	Price Benefiting Buyer	Price Benefiting Seller
(1) *Capital* (Goodwill, trade name, convenant not to compete ancillary to sale of goodwill)	Low (not depreciable)	High (capital gain)

Asset	Price Benefiting Buyer	Price Benefiting Seller
(2) *Property used in the trade or business:*		
(a) Machinery, fixtures, etc.	Medium (recoup cost via depreciation)	Medium (ordinary loss under §1231)*
(b) Land	Low (not depreciable)	High (capital gain or ordinary loss under §1231)
(c) Copyrights (purchased for use in the business)	Medium (recoup cost via amortization)	High (capital gain or ordinary loss under §1231)
(d) Patents	Medium (recoup cost via amortization)	High (capital gain under §1235)
(3) *Noncapital:*		
(a) Inventory and stock in trade	High (recoup via cost of goods sold)	Low (ordinary income)
(b) Accounts receivable	High (recoverable as collected)	Low (ordinary income)
(c) Copyrights and intellectual property sold by the creator	Medium (recoup cost via amortization)	Low (ordinary income)
(d) Covenant not to compete	Medium (usually recoup cost via amortization)	Low (ordinary income)
(e) Interest on deferred payment of purchase price	Medium (deduct as ordinary business expense)	Low (ordinary income)

[¶2604.2] Sale of Stock vs. Sale of Assets

Here are the opposing considerations of the seller and buyer on the sale of a corporate business.

The seller wants to sell stock because:

(1) He has a *clean* deal, realizing capital gains (unless he has a collapsible corporation).

(2) There is no problem of depreciation recapture at ordinary income rates under §1245 and 1250.*

(3) There is no problem of recapture of any investment credit.**

(4) It is easier to set up an installment sale; if the corporation makes the sale of assets, it can't then distribute the installment obligations to the stockholders without tax consequences.

The buyer wants to buy assets, because:

(1) He need not worry about any *hidden* or contingent corporate liabilities.

---

*May realize income if depreciation recapture is involved (§1245).
**See warning on page 298.

(2) He gets a basis for the assets acquired equal to their market values—i.e., what he paid for them. If he acquires stock, the corporation's basis for the assets does not change even if the assets have appreciated considerably. A corporation can, however, within 75 days of purchasing at least 80% of the stock of the corporation, make an election under Section 338 to have the purchase price of the stock assigned to the assets. The seller in this case may be stuck with recapture of depreciation (income) under §1245 or 1250.

[¶2604.3] Goodwill vs. Covenant Not to Compete

The buyer writes off the noncompete agreement over the period of its restriction. He gets no tax writeoff for goodwill. The seller, on the other hand, gets capital gain on the sale of his goodwill, but ordinary income for the covenant. The agreement should be as explicit as possible regarding the intent of the parties respecting either or both goodwill and a covenant not to compete. Courts will not usually set aside executed agreements.

[¶2604.4] Bird's-Eye View of Tax Rules

The following table sets forth the various ways in which a corporate business can be sold and the tax consequences to the buyer and seller in each case.

Type of Transaction	Tax Consequence to Seller	Tax Consequence
Sale of assets by the corporation.	Corporation realizes gain or loss in same manner as proprietorship. If proceeds are then distributed to the stockholders in liquidation, a second tax (capital gain) is paid by them. *But the tax at the corporate level can be avoided by a statutory liquidation.*	Purchase price is allocated in same manner as in purchase of sole proprietorship.
Sale by corporation after adopting a liquidation resolution and distribution within 12 months (§337).	Corporation pays no tax on its gain—stockholders pay a tax on liquidation. (But corporation can have income if depreciation or investment credit recapture is involved.) This method is not available if corporation is collapsible.	Same as above.

Type of Transaction	Tax Consequence to Seller	Tax Consequence to Buyer
Liquidation under §336 and distribution of assets to stockholders and subsequent sale of the assets by them.	Stockholders pay a capital gains tax on liquidation (unless corporation is collapsible). Corporation has no taxable income on liquidation unless there's depreciation or investment credit recapture. They get a stepped-up basis for assets received; so they have no gain or loss on the resale. But must make sure corporation didn't enter into sales negotiations before liquidations; otherwise the double tax will not be avoided.	Buyer's basis is what he pays for the assets—allocated in same manner as on purchase of sole proprietorship.
Liquidation by corporation within one month (§333).	No gain or loss recognized on liquidation, but corporation can have income if depreciation or investment credit recapture is involved. Basis for assets received is basis for stock. Gain is then recognized on subsequent resale—with nature of the gain on each item depending on the nature of the asset in the hands of the selling stockholder. *Warning*: If corporation has earnings and profits, there is a dividend on liquidation. Cash and securities distributed are immediately taxable, too.	Same as above.
Sale of stock in the corporation.	Seller generally gets capital gain—unless the corporation is collapsible. *Warning*: Depreciation and ITC recapture can result if a corporate buyer makes an election under Code Section 338.	Buyer has a basis for his stock equal to what he paid for it; the corporation retains the same basis for its assets as before the sale. But if the assets have appreciated in value and 80% or more of the stock was purchased by a corporation within a 12-month period, the

Type of Transaction	Tax Consequence to Seller	Tax Consequence to Buyer
		buyer can elect to have the basis stepped up to the purchase price of the stock, if such election is made within 75 days (Section 338).
Tax-free acquisitions via one of several types of reorganizations.	Seller usually acquires stock in the buying corporation; there is no gain or loss on the transaction recognized for tax purposes. In some types of reorganization transactions, *boot* (cash or other property other than the permitted stock) is received. Then, to extent the boot does not exceed the gain, it is taxable (usually as capital gain; where shown to be such, it may be a dividend). Seller's basis for his new stock is same as his basis for his old, increased by any recognized gain and decreased by boot received.	The buyer's basis for the property acquired is generally the same as the basis of the property to the transferor prior to the transfer. But if there was any recognized gain to the transferor on the exchange, then the buyer's basis is increased by that gain (§362(b)).

[¶2605] ACQUIRING COMPANIES WITH TAX LOSSES

At one time there was a considerable traffic in loss companies—a profitable operation would acquire a loss company in order to use the acquired company's carryover loss to offset its own income. A number of restrictions in the Code, plus IRS's strict interpretations in its regulations, make the acquisition of loss companies today very difficult.

[¶2605.1] Available Routes for Acquiring Loss Companies

Here is a rundown of the various routes that may be used, what you have to do, and the pitfalls you have to overcome:

(1) Acquisition of Stock of a Loss Company: Here, the general idea is to acquire control of the loss company, put profitable operations into it, and have the loss carryovers available to offset the profits of the new profitable operations. Two obstacles must be overcome—IRC §382(a), and 269. Assuming the acquition of the stock creates at least a 60-percentage-point change of ownership of the stock, the loss carryover is disallowed unless the company continues to carry on a trade or business substantially as it did before the 60-percentage-point change. The requirement for carrying on the same business applies for the two-year period beginning in the year of the change of ownership. The obvious strategy is to continue the old business for two years and add a new business at the same time.

(2) Acquiring a Loss Company via a Reorganization or Liquidation: Under §381(a), where a loss company is acquired in a reorganization (other than stock-for-stock—i.e., a so-called "B" reorganization), the loss becomes available to the acquiring company. Here, too, however, there are a number of limitations.

In the first place, the stockholders of the loss company must end up with at least 40% of the value of the stock in the acquiring corporation. For each percent less than 40% with which they end up, a percentage of the loss carryover is disallowed *(IRC §382(b))*. Here, too, we have to consider §269.

Another limitation involves acquisitions of companies via liquidation. A tax-free liquidation of a subsidiary under §332 qualifies.

[¶2605.2] How §269 Affects Loss Company Acquisitions

Even if you get over the hurdles of §382, you may be stopped by §269. This section disallows the carryover loss if the principal purpose of acquiring the loss corporation is the avoidance or evasion of tax. And §269 applies even though the acquired corporation (the one that had the loss) is the one that wants to use the carryover where there was no good business purpose in the acquisition.

[¶2606] OTHER CARRYOVER ITEMS FOR TAX PURPOSES

Although the net operating loss carryover is the most important one, it isn't the only one allowed. Twenty other permitted carryovers are listed in §381 (where there is a reorganization or tax-free liquidation) as follows:

(1) Predecessor's earnings and profits carried over to successor; deficit carried over to extent of successor's earnings accumulated after the transfer, earnings for year of transfer to be prorated for this purpose.

(2) Capital loss carryover, prorated similar to operating loss proration.

(3) Accounting method of distributor or transferor to be used by successor.

(4) Same with inventory method if inventories are taken over, unless several predecessors or predecessor and successor used different methods.

(5) If declining-balance, sum-of-the-digits, or similar method of depreciation other than straight-line was used by the transferor or distributor, the successor will be treated as the transferor or distributor for purposes of the depreciation

deduction on assets taken over, to the extent that the transferor's or distributor's basis is carried over.

(6) Gain from installment sales of the distributor or transferor must continue to be reported on the installment basis by the successor if the later receives installment obligations on the transfer.

(7) Amortization of bond discount or premium must continue to be reported or deducted where the transferor or distributor left off in the bonds are assumed by the successor.

(8) Deferred exploration and development expenditures of transferor or distributor must be deducted by the successor as if it were the transferor or distributor.

(9) Deductions for contributions to employees' trust or annuity plan and compensation under deferred payment plan continued by the successor as if it were the transferor or distributor.

(10) If the successor recovers bad debts, taxes, or delinquency amounts previously deducted by the transferor or distributor, it is taxable to the extent it would be taxable if it were the transferor or distributor.

(11) For the purpose of applying the nonrecognition rules in involuntary conversions, the acquiring corporation is to be treated as the distributor or transferor corporation after the date of the distribution or transfer.

(12) The dividend carryover allowed personal holding companies.

(13) Amounts used or set aside for pre-1934 indebtedness of personal holding companies deductible if paid or irrevocably set aside by the successor.

(14) If the amount of stock, securities, and property of the acquiring corporation was determined by including the assumed obligations of the transferor or distributor, subsequent payment of the obligation won't give rise to a deduction. Otherwise, the payment can be deducted if it would have been deductible by the distributor or transferor if paid or accrued by it and the assumption gives rise to a liability after the date of the distribution or transfer. This applies to amounts paid or accrued in taxable years beginning after December 31, 1953, even though the distribution or transfer occurred before the effective date of the 1954 Code provisions relative to liquidations or reorganizations.

(15) Deficiency dividend of a personal holding company allowable to the transferor or distributor if paid by the transferee.

(16) Percentage depletion on waste or residue of prior mining by the transferor or distributor allowed to the successor as if it were owner or operator of the mine.

(17) Charitable contributions paid by the transferor or distributor in the year ending on the date of the transfer and in the preceding year in excess of the amount deductible are allowable to the acquiring corporation in its first two taxable years which began after the date of transfer or distribution, subject to the 5% limitation and other limitations in §170(b)(2).

(18) Excess contributions which the wholly owned subsidiary had made to a qualified pension plan, in the same way as if the acquiring corporation were the subsidiary; this carryover privilege is limited (see §381(c)).

(19) Pre-1954 adjustments resulting from a change in method of accounting.

(20) Credit for investment in certain depreciable property.

[¶2607] CONSOLIDATED TAX RETURNS

Consolidated returns can be filed by affiliated groups of corporations. Basically, an affiliated group is one where there is a common parent and 80% control at each level of the chain of corporations. Thus, losses of one company can be set off against the income of another. In effect, all the corporations are being taxed as a single economic unit. Tax accounting with reference to *intercompany transactions* conforms closely to general consolidation accounting principles for financial statements.

Certain corporations are excluded from the affiliated group for this purpose and are thus ineligible to participate in the filing of a consolidated return. These corporations are: (1) corporations exempt under §501; (2) insurance companies; (3) foreign corporations; (4) possessions corporations; (5) China Trade Act corporations; (6) regulated investment companies and real estate investment trusts; (7) unincorporated businesses which have elected to be taxed as corporations under §1361; and (8) DISC or former DISC corporations.

One hundred-percent-owned Canadian or Mexican corporations can be treated as domestic corporations and thus be eligible to participate in the filing of a consolidated return, at the election of the domestic parent, if the corporations were organized and maintained solely for the purpose of complying with the laws of such country as to the title and operation of property.

Where consolidated returns are filed, the affiliated group is deemed by law to have consented to all the consolidated return regulations prescribed by the Internal Revenue Service. These regulations are extremely complex and in some cases, have been deemed a sufficient reason by affiliated groups for not filing consolidated returns.

Once consolidated returns are filed, they must be continued to be filed in succeeding years, unless IRS gives its permission to change. Note that some states (like New Jersey) do not permit the filing of consolidated returns for franchise/income taxes.

Includible corporations which are members of an affiliated group of corporations are generally entitled (or required) to file consolidated Federal income tax returns. The Code defines an ''includible corporation'' to mean any corporation. An affiliated group means one or more chains of includible corporations connected through stock ownership with a common parent for an affiliated group. There are two requirements: (1) At least 80% of all classes of voting stock, and at least 80% of each class of nonvoting stock of each includible corporation (except the common parent) must be owned directly by one or more of the other includible corporations; (2) The common parent must own at least 80 percent of the voting power of all classes of stock, and at least 80 percent of each class of the nonvoting stock of at least one of the other includible corporations.

For purposes of the definition, nonvoting stock which is limited and preferred as to dividends is disregarded, as is certain stock held under employee stock ownership plans. Once the stock ownership requirements cease to be met with respect to any one corporation, it can no longer be included in the consolidated return of its former affiliated group.

The new law adds a significant requirement. In addition to the 80 percent of voting power rule, one corporation is not an affiliate of another corporation unless one owns stock having a value equal to at least 80 percent of the total fair market value of the stock (disregarding certain preferred stock) of the other.

The Act specifies the kind of stock that can be ignored in testing for affiliated group status:

• Stock which is not entitled to vote.

• Stock limited and preferred as to dividends.

• Stock with redemption and liquidation rights that do not exceed the stock's paid-in capital or par value.

• Stock that is not convertible into any other stock.

With respect to consolidation after deconsolidation, the law reads that if a corporation is included in a consolidated return filed by an affiliated group for a taxable year which includes any period after December 31, 1984, and such corporation ceases to be a member of such group for a taxable year beginning after December 31, 1984, then such corporation (and any successor) may not be included in any consolidated return filed by that group or any other group having the same common parent (or a successor) before the 61st month after the cessation.

[¶2608] **MULTIPLE CORPORATIONS/ CONTROLLED GROUPS**

For tax purposes, "controlled" groups are of two kinds:

(1) Parent-subsidiary type, or

(2) Brother-sister type.

Each type is defined in Code Section 1563. In the latter type, the rules of attribution pertain and should be thoroughly examined for pertinence and applicability.

All individual members of controlled groups are, for the purposes of certain statutory tax advantage provisions, considered to be one aggregate unit, entitled to only *one* benefit in the following areas:

(1) *Surtax Exemption*—for 1979 and later, a total of only $25,000 in each of the rate brackets, for the first $100,000, is permitted by the entire group. The exemption may be divided in any fashion by consent (attached to the returns).

(2) *20% Additional First-Year Depreciation*—is limited to one maximum for the entire affiliated group.

(3) *Accumlated Earnings Credit*—for 1982 and later, only one $250,000 accumulated earnings credit is permitted to a controlled group, with the single credit divided *equally* unless approval is obtained from the Commissioner for unequal allocation.

(4) *Investment Tax Credit*—the credit must be apportioned among all members of the group.

Each member of the controlled group is still allowed separate and individual 100%-dividends-received deductions for dividends from affiliates.

[¶2609]   GOLDEN PARACHUTE CONTRACTS

The present law allows a corporation a deduction for all the ordinary and necessary expenses paid or incurred during the taxable year in carrying on a trade or business. Reasonable allowances for salaries or other compensation for personal services qualify as ordinary and necessary trade or business expenses.

A golden parachute contract generally is any contract entered into by a corporation with an officer, shareholder, or highly compensated individual, including any independent contractor—providing at the time of execution for contingent payment of cash (or property) which is to be made in the event of a change (or threatened change) in ownership or control of the corporation (or of a significant portion of its assets).

No deduction is allowable for ''excess parachute payments'' paid or accrued. A nondeductible 20 percent excise tax is imposed on the recipient of any excess parachute payments, in addition to income taxes and FICA withholding.

An excess parachute payment is an amount equal to the excess of the parachute payment over the portion of the base amount allocable to the payment. ''Base amount'' is an individual's annualized income for a base period, which is the most recent five taxable years ending before the date on which the ownership or control of the corporation changed, or the portion of the five years that the person was an employee of the corporation. Excess payment is quantified to be the aggregate present value of the payments that equal or exceed three times the base amount.

Example: Assume that an individual's base amount is $100,000. Assume also that a payment totalling $400,000 is made on the date of a change in control, which is four times the base amount. The excess payment amount is $300,000. The provision, therefore, applies. Further, assume that the taxpayer establishes by clear and convincing evidence that reasonable compensation for services compensated for by the parachute payments totals $150,000. Excess parachute payments equal $250,000—$300,000 less ($150,000—$100,000).

If in the example parachute payments totalled $290,000, the provision would not apply because the payments would not equal or exceed three times the base amount.

27

State Taxes

[¶2701] VARIOUS FORMS OF STATE TAXATION

Virtually all states impose some form of franchise and/or income tax on corporations. The basis for either or both taxes varies from state to state, as does the definition of the terminology. For the corporation involved in interstate commerce, these state taxes can present some onerous burdens. You need detailed records in order to work out the various allocation or apportionment formulas called for by the states involved (so as to avoid imposing a tax on more than what is applicable to that state). Sometimes with proper planning, taking into account the needs of the business, it is possible to avoid altogether the taxes of some of the states with which your company has contact.

In addition to an income or franchise tax, some states impose a capital values tax, and a large number have a sales and use tax. This can become a burden when the states insist that you collect the use tax from customers to whom you sell in that state, even though you have no office or other permanent contact within that state. In the paragraphs that follow, we consider these taxes, when they apply, and what you can do about them in some situations.

[¶2702] CORPORATE INCOME TAXES

There are three basic types of state corporate income taxes:

(1) A state may impose a tax on all income arising out of, or derived from, property located within the state. Often these taxes will be imposed without regard to whether business is conducted within the geographical confines of the state. Where a company has a manufacturing plant or real property located in a state which imposes taxes upon income from property located within the geographical confines of the state, it will be subject to the tax on the income which can be traced to that property.

(2) Some states which impose a corporation income tax, base it on income from business conducted in the state. If the state basis was restricted to business conducted within the state, it might be that investment-type income derived from property in the state would not be reached. The applicability of a tax imposed upon income from a business conducted within a state to income from real estate or other tangible property located within the state would generally depend upon the use to which the property is put, the language of the particular statute, and its administration.

(3) Some states impose a tax upon income attributable to, or derived from, sources within the state. This probably affords the widest possible tax base for a state attempting to tax foreign corporations.

Some states do not permit the filing of consolidated returns.

[¶2702.1]   Apportionment of Tax

Normally the federal taxable income is a starting point for determining the state income tax. The federal income is usually then modified by eliminating the deduction for local and state franchise and income taxes. There are other adjustments according to the state laws that are made to the federal income before allocating a portion of that income to the state. The most commonly used apportionment formula (or a variant of such), is:

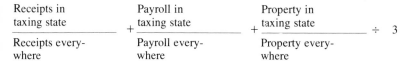

$$\frac{\text{Receipts in taxing state}}{\text{Receipts everywhere}} + \frac{\text{Payroll in taxing state}}{\text{Payroll everywhere}} + \frac{\text{Property in taxing state}}{\text{Property everywhere}} \div 3$$

Often the formula will provide for a separate allocation of items like capital gains income, rents, royalties, and dividends. Income of this type may be allocated to the situs of the property, the place of its use, the domicile of the owner, or the source of the income.

Unitary and Separate Businesses: Some states which impose an apportioned corporate income tax on foreign corporations apply the apportionment formulas only to unitary businesses. A unitary business is one which has basically one income-producing activity and its separate divisions are connected with, and directed toward, this activity. Thus, a company which both manufactured and sold its products, even though it operated through separate departments or divisions, would be a unitary business. Where two or more businesses of different types are conducted independently of each other, they are sometimes entitled to use their own separate accounting for purposes of apportioning income under state apportionment formulas.

[¶2702.2]   What Is a Sufficient "Nexus"?

A foreign corporation will have sufficient nexus or connection with the taxing state where it has assets or property within the borders of the taxing state. Similarly, where a foreign corporation qualifies to do business within a particular state by complying with the provisions of the state "qualification" statute, the corporation will be deemed to have established a domicile or residence within the state, giving that state a sufficient nexus for taxing that corporation.

Merely deriving income from within a state may be a sufficient nexus, unless:

(1) The corporation is engaged in truly minimal operations within the taxing state.

(2) The state's tax statute is not sufficiently broad to reach, in whole or in part, the particular type of activity which the foreign corporation is engaged in.

(3) The tax, although described as a corporate income tax, is not really a corporate income tax but essentially a privilege tax, so it may not be imposed upon a corporation which is engaged solely in interstate commerce as to the taxing state.

[¶2703]   HOW TO AVOID A STATE'S INCOME TAX

There are situations when a corporation can plan its operations so as to avoid all or part of the taxes imposed in one or more states from which it derives income.

[¶2703.1]   Planning Activities Within a State

Where a state taxes only companies doing business within the geographical confines of a state, the state's taxing authority may be avoided if you avoid activities which will bring your corporation within the definitions of the state tax law. Often this will mean that you cannot maintain an office in the state, maintain servicemen in the state, sell on consignment to in-state agents, and execute or perform contracts.

[¶2703.2]   Withdrawing from a State

Where your contacts with a state are reduced to the point that qualification is no longer required under the state's corporate statutes, you should consider withdrawing from the state. Most state corporate statutes have provisions whereby companies which have qualified under the laws of the state can subsequently withdraw.

[¶2703.3]   Taking Advantage of Apportionment Formulas

Often by carefully planning your activities and locating property, payroll, or other factors which enter into apportionment formulas in states which do not consider those factors in apportioning income, or minimize those factors in their allocation formulas, you can reduce the over-all tax bite.

[¶2704] **CAPITAL VALUES TAX**

Many states impose a tax upon the capital value of corporations. A capital values tax imposed on domestic corporations will generally tax the entire capital value of the corporation. However, apportionment is required when a capital values tax is imposed upon the property of a foreign corporation doing business in the state. The capital values taxes are generally based on the following factors: (a) actual value, (b) debt capital, and (c) capital stock.

Actual Value: A foreign corporation may be taxed on the entire property which it employs in a particular state. This would include physical property located in the state even though it is used primarily in interstate commerce. However, a state's authority to tax the intangible property of a foreign corporation is restricted. A state may tax the entire property—tangible and intangible—of a domestic corporation.

In some states credits are given in calculating the actual value on which the capital values tax is imposed for property which is reached by the state's property tax.

Debt Capital: In some states the amount of debt can be a factor in determining the basis for the capital values tax. Where a state seeks to use "debt capital" as a basis for a tax imposed upon foreign corporations, it must apportion the debt capital. A foreign corporation's tax liability will be limited to the proportion of the debt capital which may be apportioned to the state.

Capital Stock: A capital values tax can be based upon the capital stock of the corporation. Most states levy a tax of this form on domestic corporations (in the form of a franchise tax) and on foreign corporations which are qualified to do business within the state. Where a tax or fee based on the capital stock of the corporation is levied upon the capital stock of a foreign corporation, there is generally either a reasonable floor or minimum or provision whereby it is apportioned — i.e., a foreign corporation is required to pay the tax on only that portion of its authorized capital stock which would be apportioned to the activities or capital employed within the geographic confines of the state.

[¶2704.1] **Apportioning Intangible Property for Capital Values Tax**

Intangible property presents a special problem for a capital values tax. Where a capital values tax on foreign corporations must be apportioned, it is necessary to establish a situs of the intangible property owned by a foreign corporation. Several basic theories have arisen as to the situs of intangible property:

Domicile: The traditional theory is that corporate intangible property has a situs in the state where the corporation is incorporated. This is known as the domicile theory of situs. A few states have provided by statute that intangible property has a situs in the state where the principal office of the corporation is located, rather than the state of incorporation. Tangible property would have a situs where it is physically located.

Business Situs: In some states a doctrine of "business situs" for intangible property has developed. Under the business situs theory, intangible property may be taxed in the state where it has its situs or the intangible property came into existence. For example, an account receivable — a typical example of business intangible property — would have a situs in the state where the account arose. Other forms of business intangible property would have a situs where the business out of which they arose was conducted.

[¶2705]   SALES AND USE TAXES

Where a corporation makes sales to consumers within a state (i.e., not for resale) from goods located within the state, or it otherwise retains places of business within the state from which the sales are made, it is required to collect sales taxes in those states which impose this tax.

The big problem arises for companies engaged in interstate commerce which make interstate sales to customers in states imposing a sales tax. Usually, there is no basis for the state to impose a sales tax. But to "protect" the sales tax, the state imposes a "compensating use" tax. The tax is imposed on the buyer located in the state, on goods acquired from without the state and not subject to the sales tax, but which would have been subject to the sales tax had it been purchased within the state. Although the tax is imposed on the user within the state, the state in most cases would have difficulty enforcing the tax. The state attempts to find some basis for having the *seller* (who is located outside the state) collect the use tax from the buyer and remit it to the buyer's state.

It is very important that the corporation obtain and preserve the documentation where it is not required to collect sales tax. For example, if the buyer has an exemption certification because it resells the goods, the corporation should have a copy of the exemption certificate in its files.

SECTION THREE

MANAGEMENT

28

Capital Structure

[¶2801] MANAGEMENT'S RESPONSIBILITY

By capital structure, we mean the division of the corporation's capital between debt and equity and the various classes within those categories.

Essentially, the capital structure is a means of allocating risk of loss, participation in profits and financial control by management. The final decision on the capital structure is usually governed by the kind of money available (debt or equity money) and the terms on which it can be obtained. Nevertheless, in organizing a new corporation, or in raising additional financing for an existing company, management should make an effort to formulate the financial structure which will be most desirable for the business in the long run.

[¶2801.1] Basic Principles to Follow

It is easier to obtain money from both equity and debt sources if the financial plan reflects basic economic principles. Generally, bonds are issued when future earnings of a corporation promise to be large and reasonably certain; preferred stock is issued when earnings are irregular but show promise of exceeding preferred stock dividend requirements; common stock is issued when earnings are uncertain and unpredictable. These principles are not automatic. Tax considerations may alter them. Debt financing has tax advantages.

[¶2801.2] Highest Return on Capital

The highest potential return on equity capital investment and the largest potential for capital appreciation are produced by the combination of the smallest possible proportion of equity investment—common stock—and the highest proportion of fixed amount debt. This is called trading on the equity, also commonly termed "leverage." A business borrows money in the hope that the borrowed funds will produce more earnings than the interest rate paid for the money. The danger is that failure to earn a rate of return higher than the interest cost of the borrowed money will consume basic capital and possibly result in creditors taking the business assets.

313

As an illustration, a business with $100,000 in capital stock can make 10% on capital. If it borrows another $100,000 and keeps its 10% earnings rate on the capital it uses, common stockholders will get a 14% return after paying 6% on the borrowed money. If the earnings rate can be increased to 15%, common stockholders will get a 24% return. But if the earnings rate on the capital employed declines to 5%, common stockholders will receive only 4%. If the corporation earns only 2% on its $200,000, 6% will still be payable on the $100,000 of borrowed money and the common stockholders' capital will be dissipated by 2% a year.

Increased earning power, inflation, or any other factor which operates to increase the dollar value of assets benefits common stockholders exclusively — not the holders of fixed-value notes or bonds, or of preferred stock. So the owners of the business will profit to a greater degree from appreciation in value and sustain any loss at a faster rate when there is a low proportion of common stock and a high proportion of fixed value obligations.

[¶2801.3] Taking Minimum Risks

Maximum safety calls for all common stock and no fixed obligations to pay interest and redeem loans. But debt may be advantageous to raise capital and to maximize income and capital gain possibilities. So a business may have to make a judgment on how far it can go into debt. Caution and prudence of lenders may, to a considerable extent, determine this factor. In general, a lender will want the borrower to have as much money at risk as the lender has; so this may restrict borrowing to no more than equal to the amount of invested capital. Often the owners will want to advance money to their business on a temporary basis, and this could increase the proportion of debt to equity.

Wise limits on the proportion of capital to debt vary in each situation, depending on the earnings prospects, stability of the business, and the financial position and skill of its management. The presence of one or more of the following factors, where a loan is required, would suggest caution before lending funds:

(1) Instability of prices and volume.

(2) Abnormally high percentage of fixed cost.

(3) High rate of turnover.

(4) Low ratio of profits to sales.

For example, a retail store should borrow proportionately less than an apartment house venture or a printing plant with a large fixed investment in heavy machines.

When expansion seems necessary or advantageous, good financing requires a high ratio of stocks to debt to provide borrowing power for future needs. However, if the owners are sure of their future earnings prospects and earning power and feel that a relatively short operating period will prove their judgment, they may borrow as much capital as they need — or can get — and hold off issuing stock until they can get a higher price for it. Because the capital requirements of a successful business can be expected to increase sharply, it may be wise to hold back enough stock for future expansion needs without heavy dilution of the owner's interest and control.

[¶2801.4]   Maintaining Control of Company

A financing plan that will bring in enough outside funds and also maximize control is often accomplished by giving sole voting power to a small common stock issue. The danger always exists that the owners' control will be lost and their interest diluted if they do not foresee and prepare for the rising financial requirements that successful operation brings. When further capital is needed, the owners may have to release too large a portion of their stock holdings to keep full control.

A preferred stock issue is usually used to secure the investor's money when some of the investing group contribute intangibles such as services, special skills, patent rights, etc., and so are entitled to a share of the profits over and above the normal return for cash investment. Again the owner of the underlying equity must anticipate and make sure that the financial requirements of a successful business can be obtained without loss of his control and dilution of his interest. The use of preferred stock allows the owner to retain a larger proportion of the common. As the business grows, issuance of additional voting stock may reinforce the owner's control by making it more difficult for another to purchase a controlling stock interest.

29

Leases and Leasebacks

Leases today loom large in financing the acquisition of plant and equipment. The lease may be part of a sale-leaseback package or it may be the alternative to an outright purchase. A lease is preferred by some lessees because it does not usually require a large outlay of cash.

[¶2901]   **LEASE OR BUY?**

This is a decision that many taxpayers are often faced with. And it cannot necessarily be made on the basis of lowest net-after-tax cost alone — although, of course, the net-after-tax cost is a big consideration. Often the scales may be tipped in favor of rental, because (1) the burden of maintenance is usually on the lessor, and (2) it's easier to switch to a new machine. The latter option may be of great importance where the possibility of a newer machine may make the previous one obsolete.

But the cost is undoubtedly a big factor. And in arriving at the net-after-tax cost, we have to take into account the impact of the various tax factors on each type of acquisition.

Before making the comparison, however, let's get straight just what we are comparing. On the one hand, we have a rental of a machine we do not own. On the other hand, we acquire ownership. What's more, we can acquire ownership by financing our purchase—a very large initial cash outlay of company funds may not be necessary. Most acquisitions today are made via the financing route. So, in a sense, in comparing rentals with purchases, we are comparing two different costs of money—the interest factor that's built into the rental structure and the interest that is paid for the equipment loan. And the tax factors have a considerable effect on determining the net cost.

316

Making the Comparison: Insofar as the rent paid is concerned that's generally fully deductible for tax purposes. In addition, the lessor can pass through to the lessee the investment tax credit. Thus, the net cost is the gross rent less the tax benefit derived from both the deduction for rent and the investment credit.

On the purchase side, the buyer is paying both purchase price and interest. The interest is tax deductible. In addition, he gets an investment credit and depreciation deductions. Thus, his net cost is the total of purchase price and interest, reduced by the tax benefits derived from the investment credit, the interest deductions and the depreciation deductions.

[¶2901.1] How to Set Up the Figures to Make the Comparison

There are a variety of rental arrangements available, and there are numerous financing arrangements available, as well. Rather than attempt to deal with a specific illustration that may or may not apply to the type of equipment you are likely to rent or buy, we have set forth below two worksheets. One is for determining the first-year, after-tax cash cost of renting and the other for determining the first-year, after-tax cash cost of buying. Thus, you can insert your own figures on the worksheets and come up with a comparison that has meaning for you.

Worksheet for Determining First-Year, After-Tax Cost of Renting

1. Gross rent .... $ ____
2. Applicable tax rate .... ____
3. Tax saved via rent deduction (Line 1 × Line 2) .... $ ____
4. Net after-tax cost for first year (Line 1 minus Line 3) .... $ ____

Worksheet for Determining First-Year, After-Tax Cost of Buying

1. *Total cost of acquired assets¹* .... $____
2. Cash down payment in first year .... $ ____
3. Other first-year installments paid .... $ ____
4. Interest paid on unpaid balance .... $ ____
5. Total cash outlay in first year (total of Lines 2, 3, and 4) .... $ ____
6. Regular depreciation .... $ ____
7. Interest paid (same as Line 4) .... $ ____
8. Total deductible items (total of Lines 6 and 7) .... $ ____
9. Total tax saved by deductions (line 8 × tax rate) .... $ ____
10. Investment tax credit.. $ ____
11. Net after-tax, first-year cost (Line 5 minus Lines 9 and 10)................................... $ ____

¹Normally the total cost will be the contract price for the acquired assets. But if there is a trade-in, use adjusted basis — i.e., basis of the assets traded in plus balance paid or payable.

²If a trade-in is involved, substitute for the amount on Line 1 (for the purposes of this computation) the amount paid or payable for the equipment over and above the amount allowed by the seller for the trade-in.

[¶2902] PLANT FINANCING VIA LEASEBACKS

Here is a hypothetical example of a typical sale-leaseback deal. By working through it, we can see how the figures affect both buyer and seller.

A corporation uses a plant in its business which it has owned for 15 years. Original cost was $1,000,000, of which $700,000 was allocated to the building and $300,000 to the land. It has taken $440,000 of depreciation, so its basis for the whole property is now $560,000. In January 1984, it decides to sell the property to an investor corporation if it can get a 15-year leaseback. The sale price is $760,000, with a net rental under the lease equivalent to a 15-year amortization of the $760,000 at a 9% return — or a rental of $77,225. Assume that the investor corporation can allocate $500,000 of its purchase price to the building for depreciation purposes.

The Seller: The seller corporation has a $200,000 gain on the sale and pays a capital gains tax of $60,000. If it had borrowed $700,000 (the new amount it gets after the capital gains tax) at 9% interest payable over 15 years, on a constant payment basis, the yearly payment would have been $67,450. Over the 15-year period, the seller would have paid a total of some $1,012,000 instead of $1,158,000 (15 times $77,225) which it pays on the sale-leaseback. But in the case of the mortgage, the seller only gets a tax deduction for the $312,000 interest that it pays. This, together with the $260,000 depreciation that the seller had left on the property would have meant a total tax deduction of $572,000 or, at 46% corporate rates, a saving of $263,000. The mortgage would have cost the seller $749,000 ($1,012,000 minus the tax saving). But, under the leaseback, the seller gets a tax deduction for the entire rental paid, so it gets a saving of $533,000 (46% of the entire 15-year rental), which would mean a cost to the seller of the leaseback of $625,000 ($1,158,000 minus $533,000). The result is that the sale-leaseback costs the seller $124,000 less than what the mortgage would have cost.

The Buyer: The buyer, under the sale-leaseback, gets a deduction over the 15-year period of the lease of $500,000, the amount that it allocated to the building. This means that $500,000 of the rent income is protected from tax. The tax on the remainder is $302,000, so the net to the buyer on the sale-leaseback over the 15-year period is $856,000. If the buyer had taken a mortgage position in this particular property for $760,000 at 9% interest, it would have received $1,084,000 with $334,000 interest taxable to it (the remainder would have been mortgage amortization). This would have meant a total tax of $153,600 or a net after taxes to the buyer of $930,400. This is almost $74,400 more than the buyer's net in the case of the leaseback.

318

What the figures mean to both parties: Figures don't always tell the whole story. Here are some additional factors that can mean a great deal to one, or both, parties.

To the Seller: The seller pays $124,000 less (net after tax deduction) than it would in the case of a mortgage. But to get this, the seller has given up its ownership of the property at the end of the lease. At present, the land is valued at $260,000. So, it appears, the seller actually loses $136,000. But this is deceptive. The seller's building wears out at the end of the lease and, because of the favorable aspects of the deal to the buyer, the buyer would be able, at the time of the sale-leaseback, to give the seller an option to renew for, say, another 10 or 15 years at a very low rental. Any improvements constructed by the seller during the renewal term would be depreciated by the seller. Also, the sale-leaseback provides the seller with the maximum amount of financing, since with the property worth $760,000, it would be hard (due to legal limitations on the amount of the mortgage in relation to market value and to the desire by the mortgagees for protection), in most states, to get a mortgage for the full market value.

To the Buyer: In effect, the buyer has $74,400 of his investment left in the property at the end of the original lease term. The buyer has gotten out his 9% yield, plus the rest of his "principal" and will own the property worth at least $260,000, if land values don't change. The buyer can afford to give the seller a renewal lease at a rental of only $7,000 a year, and still get a 9% before-tax return on his $74,000. By this method, during the renewal lease term, the seller will have the land on a tax-deductible basis. And if the renewal lease is set up properly, any improvements will not be income to the buyer. At the end of the renewal term, or the original lease if the seller does not renew, the buyer still owns the land.

[¶2902.1]   Special Forms of Sale-Leasebacks

Besides the conventional sale-leaseback between two unrelated parties, there are some specialized forms of setting up this type of a transaction.

New Construction: Here a builder may arrange the financing for a new plant he is constructing for a business corporation by getting that corporation to agree to lease the property, and by interesting an investor in the purchase of the property upon completion. In the meantime, the builder will obtain construction financing unless the investor is an insurance company or pension trust which can handle the financing from commencement of construction.

Exempt Organizations: Educational and charitable organizations and other tax exempts have been heavy buyers in these deals. They enjoy a favorable tax status and so can afford to offer the seller a good deal — the seller deducts the rent, but the charity is not ordinarily taxed on it as income unless it is unrelated to its exempt functions. Consequently, the charity will be able to charge less rent than an ordinary investor. Also a charity or educational institution is exempt from local realty taxes, usually.

When you sell to a tax-exempt organization, it will pay you to hold on to the furniture and equipment and any other depreciable property which the buyer doesn't want. The buyer gets no benefit from the depreciation deduction since he pays no tax. You might as well keep these deductions for yourself.

30

Business Acquisitions

The accounting and financial officers of the company will be involved in any arrangements to buy a business or sell the existing business. Questions of value, technique (purchase or sale of assets or stock), accounting treatment (will the acquisition qualify as a "pooling of interest"?), tax consequences, desirability of the acquisition or sale all may be within the province of the chief financial officer and his staff.

[¶3001] **FORCES BEHIND BUSINESS SALES AND ACQUISITIONS**

Many businesses diversify and build up sales volume by acquiring other businesses. Capital values can be built by acquiring additional product lines, moving into new territory, etc. Financial statements may be improved. Taxes may be saved by acquiring companies with operating loss carry-forwards. This is done through tax-free exchanges.

We see an increasing use of a combination of methods that include leases, mortgage financing, and percentage and deferred purchase arrangements. They give a maximum retention of capital for regular business operations.

[¶3001.1] **Benefits of Merging**

Here's a list which will orient your own thinking and help you in any trade or negotiations with other firms:

(1) *Many young companies just don't have the cash* to realize their potential. This is particularly true in areas which require nationwide merchandising, heavy development work, and expensive productive equipment.

(2) *Diversification* is a major reason for acquisitions. The reasons for seeking diversification are numerous. For example, a company may be seeking to get into

321

the so-called areas of today; e.g., electronics, chemicals, atomic energy. By picking up a company already in one of these fields, it may get into the desired area much more economically than otherwise. Diversification may also be sought where a company needs funds to expand into a new field. By first diversifying, it hopes to broaden its profit base and increase its growth, with the new funds generated by growth used to get into the areas the company originally sought to enter. Diversification may also be sought by companies in cyclical business by acquiring companies not subject to severe ups and downs. In this way, the acquiring company hopes to make its financial problems less burdensome in the periods when it needs substantial financing and to overcome periods of low revenue when business is contracted.

(3) *Some firms merge with others to get into a new line because investors do not value the industry or its earnings very highly.* Unless such companies can substantially convert into another industry, they cannot realize a large mark-up in capital values.

(4) *Many companies realize that they must have more volume to carry the research and overhead staff necessary to stay competitive today.* The volume required to carry necessary research will vary industry by industry. For example, one company doing about $12 million a year acquired enough additional lines of business to bring its volume up to $20 million. Anything less would have made the firm hard-pressed to carry on the research and staff services needed to compete with others in its industry.

(5) *Plants become idle* as a result of a company's product lines becoming obsolete, or volume drops off for some other reason. The company finds itself with excess plant capacity. Where this plant capacity — e.g., machinery, equipment, etc.— is in good shape, and is not itself obsolete, acquiring a new business may be the best way of making use of this excess plant capacity. This may be a far better solution than a gradual shutdown and a contraction of the existing business.

(6) *Companies are sometimes acquired to get their special attributes.* For example, it may be desirable to get the key personnel of a particular company, and the only way is to get the company as well. In other cases, an acquired company may have special machinery already available which might cost a considerable amount in dollars and time to reproduce. Sometimes the acquired company may have a sales organization which would be just what the acquiring company needs. It may be more economical to acquire the company than to try to build up a similar sales organization.

(7) *Some new, successful companies are taxed so high that there's very little left for investors and expansion.* These make ideal buys for other firms with loss carryovers, which might be used to protect subsequent profits earned by the combined operation.

(8) *Some companies have found that it doesn't pay to continue a product line which doesn't yield a specified volume.* One company decided to dispose of all subsidiaries and divisions which did less than $10 million a year. Many companies are trying to earn the premium which investors pay for stability of earnings. They

seek diversification which will allow one line to hold up and balance off other lines which run through recessions.

(9) *Many companies go on the block because their owners are faced by a personal estate tax squeeze* and aren't able to get money out of a profitable business to make their personal portfolio liquid. The only solution is to sell part or all the business at capital gains rates or merge with a publicly traded company.

(10) *Many businesses don't want to distribute dividends* but would prefer to use accumulated earnings to acquire other products and expand into new territory or product lines.

(11) *Closely-held companies, or companies with cash and mortgagable assets locked up in the corporation, offer a good buying opportunity* — (a) to companies with fairly marketable stock, which can acquire the locked-up assets by an exchange of stock, or (b) to companies with a cash surplus which permits them to buy stock or assets at a discount (likely because the original owner has to pay a heavy tax rate if he taps the assets by taking a dividend distribution).

(12) *Some companies with strong earnings position can reap big advantages by picking up a smaller company.* Suppose the market values a firm 15 times earnings. If the firm can then pick up a smaller company for 5 or 6 times earnings (frequently possible), it will realize an automatic profit for its stockholders and still be able to plow some earnings into building up the new acquisition.

(13) *When two companies in the same business merge, they can often bring about a number of operating economies.* Bulk purchasing for both companies may cut the unit cost of purchases. In some cases, duplicating facilities may be eliminated — e.g., one warehouse may serve the purposes of both businesses and one warehouse may therefore be eliminated.

31

Financing—Short-Term

[¶3101] SOURCES OF SHORT-TERM FUNDS

Banks, finance companies and factors are the usual sources of short-term funds, although some finance company loans and bank term loans may run for a fairly long term or provide for a continuing line of credit.

Short-term credit may be available on the strength of the overall financial soundness of the borrower or for specific collateral — often, accounts receivable.

[¶3102] ARRANGING FOR CREDIT LINES WITH BANKS

The most readily available and frequently used source of money for a business is a bank loan. For most businesses, banks are only a source of temporary short-term money. To qualify for an unsecured bank loan, a company has to be substantially established and adequately supplied with equity money. The exceptions are cases in which the bank is lending on the strength of the personal credit of the proprietor, or principal stockholder, or somebody else who underwrites the loan for the borrowing business.

In dealing with banks, it is important to understand the nature of a commercial banking operation. The money it lends is that placed with it by depositors plus its own capital. A portion of the deposited money is set aside in reserves, another portion is held to meet the depositors' regular demands for cash, and the remainder is available for loans. Neither banking laws nor banking practice permit investment in a business or making capital loans in lieu of equity capital.

[¶3102.1] Selecting a Bank

The choice of a bank is important in the development of proper credit facilities, and a good banking connection once made is a valuable asset. As a general rule, it is not necessary to shop around for a banking connection — a local bank can usually meet the company's banking needs in a satisfactory manner. Some companies deliberately patronize more than one bank with the idea that if one bank turns down a request for a loan, the other will grant the loan. But this may backfire. One bank may want quick repayment for fear that the other will get repayment first. Where the local bank has restrictions which make it unable to meet the company's requirements, it is wise to go to another bank. But ordinarily it pays to give one bank all your business, in the expectation that the bank will take care of a good customer in time of financial stress. Banks prefer the exclusive arrangement. In times of financial need the bank whose officials have a good working knowledge of a company's operations and financial background can take care of its credit needs more quickly and effectively.

[¶3102.2] How the Banker Judges a Borrower

The banker will study the financial statements of the borrower, using many of the ratios described in this book.

In addition, he will want further information which he will get partially from discussion with the prospective borrower, partially from checking his credit files, and partially from checking with other creditors. The customer's or prospect's credit file, which contains the accumulated information about a particular business and its owner, is of tremendous importance in every loan decision. It is a marked trail which leads the experienced lending officer back through the history of the organization and its officers and enables him to uncover and evaluate information that might not otherwise be made available to him.

The banker will want to know these things about the prospective borrower:

(1) Its character, ability, and capacity.

(2) What kind of capital resources does it have?

(3) What kind of business organization is it? How good are its executives? What has been its sales trend?

(4) Will the loan be a sound one? Are any of the following conditions present to an extent which would throw doubt on the financial soundness of the business:
(a) Heavy inventories in relation to sales.
(b) Excessive dividends and salary withdrawals.
(c) Heavy loans to officers of subsidiary organizations.
(d) Large past-due receivables.
(e) Top-heavy debt.
(f) Too much invested in fixed assets.
(g) An overextended position — i.e., scrambling to apply income and funds to pay the most insistent creditors.

[¶3102.3] Types of Bank Accommodations

A company should familiarize itself with the various kinds of loan accommodations a bank is willing to extend, the interest rates, terms, and security requirements of each.

A Line of Credit: A line of credit is merely a declaration by a bank that, until further notice, it is prepared to lend up to a stated maximum amount on certain terms and conditions to the prospective borrower. Since the line of credit is only a declaration of intent, it can be canceled at any time. The availability of a line of credit is very valuable because, instead of fixed credits which call for continuing interest, only amounts of money actually used, plus a small commitment fee on any portion of the original commitment not actually borrowed, are charged, which add up to inexpensive financing.

The application for a line of credit is not an application for a loan but simply an arrangement under which the bank agrees to make loans if funds are needed. But even so, a bank conducts an intensive investigation before granting the line of credit.

Term Loans: A business loan which runs for a term of more than one year with provisions for amortization or retirement over the life of the loan is a term loan. Such a loan, even if secured, will depend upon the bank's appraisal of the long-range prospects of the company, its earning power and the quality of its management. The term is usually a maximum of ten years.

Short-Term Loans: Short-term bank loans are obtained either by individual borrowing or by obtaining a *line of credit* against which advances may be obtained. Short-term borrowing is available to companies that have sufficient credit to minimize the bank's risk. The loan is granted on the basis of a study and analysis of the financial position of the company. The security for these loans is a series of promissory notes which evidence the cash advance. These notes have maturity dates calling for repayment within one year, at which time they are reviewed, repaid, reduced or extended. Short-term loans are particularly effective for seasonal financing and the financing of inventories, or to keep things running smoothly during spurts of seasonal activity. Before granting a short-term loan, the bank may require that between 10% and 20% of the loan actually made be kept on deposit (called a compensating balance), or that the loan be cleaned up at least once a year to prevent the use of bank credit as permanent funds.

Character Loans: These are short-term, unsecured loans, generally restricted to companies or individuals with excellent credit reputations.

Installment Loans: Large banks generally grant this type of loan. Installment loans are made for almost any productive purpose and may be granted for any period that the bank allows. Payments are usually made on a monthly basis; as the obligation is reduced, it often may be refinanced at more advantageous rates. The installment loan can be tailored to the seasonal requirements of the company.

Equipment Loans: An increasingly popular method of raising funds is to borrow money against machinery and equipment. There are two main ways of handling equipment loans. The first is to pledge equipment to which the company has an unencumbered title as security for the loan. The second method is via an installment financing plan.

Time Purchase Loans: Many special types of time purchase loans are available to finance both retailer and consumer purchase of automobiles, household equipment, boats, mobile homes, industrial and farm equipment, etc., and are made for varying periods of time, depending on the product. This category also includes accounts receivable financing, indirect collections and factoring.

Inventory Loans: These loans are available if the merchandise or inventory can qualify as collateral. The requirements are stiff and the loans are limited to certain classes of inventory.

Accounts Receivable Loans: Small banks are not usually equipped to offer this type of loan, and the majority of their business customers are too small to take advantage of it. Under this loan, the bank takes over the company's accounts and notes receivable as collateral for the loan.

Warehouse Receipt Loans: Under this plan, goods are stored in warehouses and the warehouse receipts are used as security for a loan to pay off the supplier. As fast as the company is able to sell the merchandise, it pays off the bank loan. This loan permits the company to get along without a large amount of working capital.

Collateral Loans: A company may be able to obtain bank loans on the basis of such collateral as chattel mortgages, stock and bonds, real estate mortgages, and life insurance (up to the cash surrender value of the policy). Even with collateral, the bank will still give great weight to the company's ability to repay. The bank may turn down the application for a loan, no matter how good the collateral, if there is not a clear showing of ability to repay.

[¶3103] SHORT-TERM BORROWING FROM COMMERCIAL FINANCE COMPANIES

A commercial finance company will frequently step in where a commercial bank will not. Commercial finance companies charge a higher rate and will sometimes take more risk and almost always take on more clerical work to protect their money. Because many companies in the commercial finance field are also engaged in factoring, there is a tendency to confuse the two. Factoring is the service rendered through the assumption of the credit risk on sales purchased from the factored company and the acceptance of the bookkeeping and collection responsibilities for the resulting receivables. In contrast to factoring, the commercial finance company does not guarantee against credit losses on sales to customers.

Finance companies do not ''lend'' money — they provide revolving working capital. Perhaps this is a subtle distinction, but if a company requires borrowed money it should, if qualified, resort to the many commercial banks throughout the country to satisfy that need. Banks and commercial finance companies are not in competition with one another. Finance companies are among the largest borrowers of money from commercial banks, and commercial banks very frequently refer their customers to finance companies when the capital position of the prospective borrower is insufficient for the bank to grant the credit lines needed.

Funds advanced by commercial finance companies are secured by collateral — mainly accounts receivable — and the finance company has recourse to the borrowing firm. The decision to advance the necessary funds is based, among other things, upon the character and ability of the company's management, its diversification and performance, the quality of the assets pledged, and the ability of the company to operate at a profit if the funds are made available to it.

Commercial financing of accounts receivable and other collateral provides a flexible borrowing arrangement whereby a borrower will receive the funds needed, in the amounts needed, and at the time needed. The accounts receivable outstanding are self-liquidating through their collection. To keep interest charges at a minimum, the financed company may borrow only the funds it needs as and when needed. This method can be contrasted with the fixed-dollar loan, which carries a constant interest cost that must be met.

[¶3103.1]   Accounts Receivable Financing

Accounts receivable are accepted by some banks and most commercial credit companies as collateral for a line of credit. Individual banking practices vary, however, and the borrower should become familiar with local banking requirements. The financing of accounts receivable involves the assignment by the borrower to the lender of the borrower's accounts receivable. These accounts receivable are security for advances which the lender makes to the borrower simultaneously with each assignment. As the proceeds of the assigned accounts are collected, they are turned over to the lender and applied to reduction of the indebtedness, the excess being returned by the lender to the borrower. The borrower remains responsible for the payment of the debt, even though the primary source of payment are the proceeds of the assigned accounts receivable. If the proceeds of the assigned accounts receivable are insufficient to repay the amount advanced, the borrower is liable for the deficiency. This is one important difference between accounts receivable financing and factoring. The factor purchases the accounts receivable from the borrower and assumes the risk of loss from any bad accounts.

Accounts receivable may be financed on a notification or a non-notification basis. Under a notification plan, the receivables are pledged and payment is made directly to the lender, but the borrower remains responsible for the payment. The lender notifies the borrower's customers that their accounts have been assigned and directs them to make payments directly to him. Under the more satisfactory and more commonly used non-notification plan, the borrower collects as agent for the lender. This method is preferable because the relationship between the borrower and his customers is not disturbed and the financing arrangement remains confidential.

[¶3103.2]   Functions of Accounts Receivable Financing

The primary function of accounts receivable financing is to release funds tied up in these accounts, thereby giving a company working capital. Financing of receivables may put a borrowing company in a stronger position for sales expansion and may improve its credit standing by providing funds to discount its own payables.

Accounts receivable financing should be employed in conjunction with a cash forecast and financial plan. The financing will be used according to the plan's estimate of how much cash will be required before the expended cash comes back from customers. Whenever there is a shortage of working capital but available accounts receivable that are not yet due, the borrower is in a position to raise cash to meet his current needs. Of course, this financing aid is not the final answer to the problem of inadequate working capital; but it is a means of temporary relief, especially in seasonal industries where receivables are concentrated in a short period of the year and unacceptable collateral for long-term financing.

[¶3103.3] Mechanics of Accounts Receivable Financing

Before accepting accounts receivable as collateral, the lending agency will evaluate the risks and investigate the facts involved. Through analysis and investigation of the borrower's financial history and related factors, the lending agency can decide if it wants to assume the risk and how the risk can be minimized. At the outset it should be emphasized that certain types of businesses do not lend themselves to receivable financing. Most service enterprises fall into this category. This is because a serviceman may damage the customers' goods and offset any receivable that may be due. The same risk appears in businesses that furnish special orders. And generally factors do not look with favor on unstable industries.

Other considerations involve the accounts themselves. The lender will look to see if the accounts are acceptable for financing. Usually any account that represents a bona fide obligation owed to the borrower from a creditworthy customer, without the probability of setoff or the like, is available for financing. Under certain conditions, partial billings against unfinished contracts may be financed. The lender will have to be assured that these invoices are payable on regular terms and won't be unduly delayed. Under most circumstances, long-term dating will not disqualify the receivables unless there is undue hazard in their collection.

After the lender has satisfactorily completed his investigation, a basic contract between the lender and the borrower will be executed defining the rights and obligations of the parties. The contract is generally needed because accounts receivable financing contemplates a series of transactions rather than a single isolated loan. Many lenders require yearly contracts. While the agreements vary with the situations, a typical agreement might provide that the borrower assign all accounts receivable, or a selected group of them, to the lender as security. In return the lender agrees to advance funds up to 80% of the face value of the accounts receivable pledged, usually specifying a dollar maximum which can be borrowed. Periodically, schedules of customers' invoices are submitted to the lender to replenish borrowing power. Under this type of arrangement, the borrower, when cash is needed, simply lists the invoices which he wants to finance on the lender's standardized form and the lender advances the cash upon presentation of the form. The borrower should avoid arrangements where it is necessary to get clearance on each individual invoice. Blanket deals are much easier to administer, since invoice schedules are simply submitted periodically on accounts that have blanket approval and the lender worries about individual account limits.

[¶3103.4]   Equity Adjustments

Upon the collection of the accounts, the financing company generally receives a larger amount than the percentage advanced. The excess, known as "equity," is credited to the client's accounts. (However, the full difference between the gross amount of the invoice and the percentage advanced is seldom realized upon payment because of returns, allowances and discounts.)

[¶3103.5]   Cost of Accounts Receivable Financing

There are various methods of computing charges on open accounts receivable. The most common are:

(1) Straight interest on the amount of funds advanced expressed either as a rate per annum, per month or per diem. The rate of interest is applied to the average daily balances;

(2) A commission on the accounts assigned plus, in some cases, interest on the funds advanced. The logic behind the commission is that regardless of the amount of funds advanced against the assigned accounts, a major expense is incurred in handling the bookkeeping involved. The commission more accurately reflects the cost of maintaining the account;

(3) Charges may be expressed as a percentage of the average balance of the collateral assigned;

(4) A minimum charge may be required as assurance that the financing company will meet its expense in initiating and servicing the account;

(5) Gradually decreasing rates may be applied in any of the above methods, reflecting the decreasing operating costs per dollar advanced as the account grows larger.

Rates on the accounts receivable loan vary widely. Commercial bank rates may range from prime to 2% over prime or higher per annum on the balance in the loan account. Some banks add a small service charge to cover the sizable amount of clerical work involved, such as one-half of one percent based on total receivables pledged or a flat amount for originally setting up the loan. As pointed out, banks do not often go into accounts receivable financing, so that the borrower will probably have to turn to a commercial finance company for the loan. The cost of financing accounts receivable through a finance company is high. This may cost the borrower 2% to 4% over prime on a loan where the advance is 75% of the face value of the receivables. The rates may range from 4% to 8% over prime, or higher, depending on the overall interest cost of money.

[¶3103.6]   Split Loans

There may occasionally be a situation where a company's credit standing may no longer entitle it to unsecured borrowing, but its financial position may still be far better than that of the usual finance company client, and therefore the company may not be willing to pay the high finance company charge. In this case the finance company may be able to work a *split loan* with a bank at a reduced rate for the borrower. The finance company will approach the bank and do all the preliminary work of setting up the loan. The split loan is a three-way arrangement among the borrower, the finance company and the bank. Under this arrangement, the finance company advances half the needed funds and takes full charge of administering the accounts receivable, which are the security for the entire arrangement. The bank does no work except to lend the other half of the needed funds without guarantee by the finance company. The bank relies on the judgment of the finance company and is able to employ its funds at a good rate with no more expense than any unsecured loan would entail and with greater safety because both lenders are protected by the lien on the accounts receivable. The benefit to the borrower can be seen from the following figures:

Assume the finance company rate is 20%, the prime bank interest rate is 16% and the rate for a split loan is 18%. If the borrower had used the finance company exclusively, he would have paid 20%. Here, he pays 20% on half the loan and 16% on the other half, or a net rate of 18%.

[¶3104]   FINANCING THROUGH A FACTOR

Factoring is primarily a credit business in which the factor checks credits and makes collections for his client. He also purchases his client's accounts receivable without recourse, thereby guaranteeing the client against credit losses. This is the basic service of a factor for which the factor receives a fee. Normally the account debtor is notified that the account was purchased by the factor and that payment thereon is to be made directly to the factor.

In this operation the factor checks the credits, makes the collections and assumes the loss in the event the accounts are not paid. Up to this point, however, the factor has passed no funds to his client. He has purchased the accounts and has agreed to pay for them on their net due dates.

Under the standard factoring contract, the factor buys the client's receivables outright, without recourse, as soon as the client creates them by shipping merchandise to customers whose credit the factor has investigated and approved. Cash is made available to the client immediately on shipment; thus, in effect, he sells for cash and can turn his receivables into cash as fast as he creates them. The arrangement is flexible, however, to the extent that the client may withdraw the full proceeds of the sale or leave the proceeds with the factor until their due date. He is charged interest only for money withdrawn prior to the due date. Thus he has a 100% demand privilege on the funds available to him but pays interest only on funds actually used.

However, the factor will make cash advances to the client on the receivables prior to their maturity. For example, suppose that the factor purchases accounts receivable amounting to $40,000 from his client, without recourse, due in 60 days. In this case, the factor owes the client $40,000 which must be paid in 60 days. The factor, however, will advance, say, $35,000 to the client immediately, to make operating cash available. The other $5,000 will be paid when due. The factor will charge interest on the funds advanced to the client, and at current rates. If these advances are not enough to meet the needs of the client — and this occurs frequently in seasonal business — the factor will also make short-term, supplementary loans secured by inventory, fixed assets or other acceptable collateral.

[¶3104.1]   Non-Notification Factoring

Non-notification factoring is now available to clients in many fields who sell directly to customers in the retail trade. In this type of factoring, the factor purchases the receivables outright without recourse but does not assume the collection function without specific request. The client makes collections himself, and the customer is not notified of the factoring arrangements. The fee for non-notification factoring may be less than that charged for notification factoring.

[¶3104.2]   Bank and Factor in Combination

Frequently, a commercial bank can not provide all the loan funds a growing company needs. Its balance sheet is not liquid enough or it can't clear off the bank debt every six or twelve months. A factor can provide funds to clear off bank loans periodically or make additional bank credit possible by guaranteeing accounts or replacing accounts receivable with cash.

[¶3104.3]   When Should You Factor?

First, can you factor? Yes if:

(1) You sell on normal credit terms;

(2) 80 to 90% of your customers are rated;

(3) Your annual volume is sufficiently large for profitable factoring.

What will factoring do for you? It converts your sales into cash sales. It can give you additional working funds to expand, modernize or whatever will improve your business.

Now, what will it cost you? You pay a service charge and interest. Interest will be 22% or 24% or more per annum on money actually used on a daily basis. The service charge, depending on the risk in your accounts and the amount of handling required, will be from three-quarters of one percent to one and one-half percent of the receivables purchased. But against this, you can credit savings:

(1) On the salaries of credit and collection people;

(2) On the elimination of bad debt writeoff;

(3) On the interest on money borrowed to carry sales and accounts receivable.

[¶3104.4] What the Factor Wants to Know

The first points a factor considers are the type of sales and the selling terms of the borrower. The sales should be on open account, so as to create accounts receivable that can be sold. The terms of the sale determine the value of the account to the factor. The shorter the terms of payment, the faster the factor can expect to turn over his investment and the lower his rates. If payment terms are extended, the factor will have a long wait to realize his investment and will charge a higher rate, one that might be prohibitive.

Credit information on the accounts should be available. The credit rating determines the risk assumed by the factor when he purchases the accounts without recourse. The factor will expect some credit losses and will include a loss reserve in his charges. A factor will not enter into a factoring agreement unless almost all of the borrower's regular customers seem to be good credit risks.

The arrangement should continue over an extended period of time — something more than a few months. Factors do not like to get involved in short-term deals.

The volume of accounts is important. Just as in any business the larger the earnings propsect, the more attractive the deal is. It does not pay a factor to handle a small volume. The size of the individual accounts control the factor's costs. The greater the balance of the accounts, the smaller the percentage of fixed cost in its collection.

The factor will examine the records to determine if there is an abnormal percentage of returns and complaints. If the percentage of returns as compared with sales is too high, the factor may take this as a warning signal and back out of the transaction.

[¶3104.5] Provisions of Factoring Contract

The business of the present-day factor is to purchase accounts receivable upon much the same basis that tangible assets are bought and sold. The typical contract first provides that the client agrees to sell to the factor as absolute owner, and the factor agrees to purchase from the client without recourse to the client (with certain exceptions), all accounts receivables created by the client in the ordinary course of his business. The factor usually has recourse to the borrower for returns or allowance for bad debts or errors in pricing.

[¶3105] INVENTORY LOANS

Inventories are not as liquid as accounts receivable, and a bank or finance company will generally want to secure its advances by accounts receivable and go to inventories only after the business has exhausted its ability to borrow on receivables. Receivables convert into cash automatically, they present fewer legal

333

problems, they don't go out of style or become technologically obsolete or suffer drastic price declines. But inventory financing is important, particularly to businesses that must build up a stock to meet a seasonal demand.

Inventory is acceptable as collateral usually if the following conditions are met:

(1) The inventory is readily salable — that is, no great sales effort would be required to turn it into cash to satisfy the loan if that should become necessary;

(2) The inventory consists of basic commodities that will not deteriorate or become obsolete within the period of the loan;

(3) The necessary legal technicalities to protect the lender's position in the event of bankruptcy are available.

You will be able to borrow, if at all, only on your stock of raw materials or finished merchandise. Work in process has little value for borrowing purposes. No lender wants the responsibility for finishing up and selling work in process.

Here's what a lender will want to know about your inventory before he decides whether and how much he can lend on it:

(1) Is the price fairly stable or does it fluctuate sharply?

(2) How broad a market is there for the commodity?

(3) Are there any governmental restrictions on its sale?

(4) Under what conditions may the commodity be stored and for how long?

(5) Is the item closely graded by the trade?

(6) How does the condition of the commodity affect its value?

(7) Is the commodity usually sold in certain standard sizes, and does the commodity under consideration comply with those standards?

(8) Is there any danger of obsolescence in the near future due to technological changes?

(9) What should the costs of liquidation be, such as sales commissions, parking and transportation charges?

(10) Can the commodity be hedged by the purchase of futures?

[¶3105.1]   The Problem of Protecting the Lender

The Uniform Commercial Code, already adopted in most jurisdictions and all the leading commercial and industrial states, has eliminated a lot of legal problems that formerly existed in connection with inventory financing.

The Code rules relating to after-acquired property, future advances, dominion and control of the collateral by the debtor, commingling of goods, and transferring the lien on the collateral to the proceeds make possible so-called "floating liens." The concept of a floating lien is that of a lien on a shifting stock of goods or inventory; that is, a lien on collateral in more or less constant flux and undergoing quantitative and qualitative changes. It is a concept that responds to a long-felt need of businessmen for an effective device giving a lender a security interest on goods and materials which the debtor is permitted to retain, process, manufacture or otherwise change and sell, and also covering the proceeds of the sale and the new goods and materials bought by the debtor with the proceeds in a continuing cycle of business activity. The chattel mortgage has been unable to satisfy this need because of problems in connection with description of the property covered, after-acquired property, and the power of the debtor to sell the collateral and to use the proceeds.

The fact that the Code makes legally possible a floating lien does not mean that the secured creditor's interest in collateral covered by the lien will necessarily be entitled to priority over all liens subsequently attaching or perfected in the same collateral. It may be subordinate to subsequent purchase money interests, and there will be problems of priority as against federal tax liens.

Also, a purchaser from the debtor in the ordinary course of business will get good title. However, the lender's lien may attach to the proceeds of the sale or the resulting account receivable.

In jurisdictions that have not adopted the Code, the lender will be looking to protect his lien under a Factors' Lien Act or the Uniform Trust Receipt Act or by taking actual or constructive possession of the inventory. The lender's actual possession of the goods is rarely feasible, and it will not be often that he can be given constructive possession by having the goods placed in a regular public warehouse and having him hold warehouse receipts. This can be cumbersome and expensive because it necessitates transferring the goods to and from the borrower's premises, plus storage charges. Field warehousing may be a more feasible alternative. Both these continue to be used in Code jurisdictions, although the underlying legal requirements may vary somewhat from pre-Code law.

[¶3105.2] Field Warehouse Financing

A field warehouse is created by a warehouse company leasing, at a nominal rent, a portion of the buyer's premises where the pledged inventory is to be stored. This space is segregated from the rest of the buyer's premises by a partition, wire fence or other appropriate means. Separate locks are installed to prevent any person from entering the storage space without the consent of the warehouse company. Signs can be posted all about the leased premises indicating that the space is under the control of the warehouse company and not the borrower. The purpose of this is to assure that the borrower's creditors will not be misled into thinking that they can lay claim to this inventory, or that they are secured by the fact that this inventory is on the borrower's premises.

The warehouse company hires a custodian, usually putting on its payroll a stockman who has been looking after the inventory for the borrower. Warehouse receipts are issued to the lender.

Commercial finance companies have developed a method of handling the whole chain of transactions from the acquisition of raw material to finished inventory for accounts receivable. Withdrawals from the warehouse are replaced by a steady stream of new raw materials and finished goods going into the warehouse. The sales invoice goes into the hands of the commercial finance company to replace finished goods shipped out of the warehouse. The net effect is to add a substantial increment of working funds to the business. As the finance company furnishes funds to buy raw materials, it is repaid out of advances on the finished product and then gets repaid for these advances out of cash paid upon the collection of the accounts receivable created when the finished product is sold.

[¶3105.3]   The Factor's Lien

The use of a field or other warehouse is usually not practical where the borrower must retain possession of the inventory for further processing. Field warehousing is unnecessary in states where there are factor's lien laws, because the procedure where a factor's lien is available can be much less cumbersome and less expensive than field warehousing.

The lien agreement between the borrower and the lender must be placed on public record and usually provides that the borrower will report to the lender at frequent intervals the nature and value of the inventory in the hands of the borrower at that time. The borrower agrees that it will, upon a reduction in its inventory, make payments to the lender on its loans equal to or greater than the amount of the inventory reduction. The law usually requires that a notice, in a specified form, of the existence of the factor's lien be posted in a conspicuous place at the principal entrance to the place of business of the borrower. For obvious reasons, the lending agency usually requires a liberal margin of inventory values against its advances, inspects the inventories at frequent intervals and follows loans of this kind with exceptional care.

This procedure gives the lender a good lien on practically every piece of inventory located on the premises. A factor's lien is not operative against bona fide purchasers for value of the merchandise, who purchase it from the borrower in the ordinary course of business without actual notice of the lien. These purchasers get good title to the merchandise free and clear of the lien, but the lien of the lender attaches to the account receivable created by the sale. It is very important that the lender adhere strictly to the notice, posting, and filing requirements of the statute which makes the factor's lien available.

The usual transaction involving the financing of inventory on a factor's lien contemplates a combined inventory and accounts receivable financing operation. The lender expects the inventory advances to be repaid out of the proceeds of the accounts receivable created by the sale of the inventory after it has been processed. The borrower expects to finance part of his cost of production by receiving additional advances on accounts receivable as they are created and assigned to the lender.

[¶3105.4]   Trust Receipts

A trust receipt is a financing instrument in the form of an agreement between a bank (the lender), called the entruster, and a person, firm, or corporation (the borrower), called the trustee. It shows that certain goods or property, or evidence of title to these goods or property, having been acquired for financing purposes by the lender are released by it under specified conditions to the borrower.

While the goods are in the borrower's possession, the lender retains ownership until the goods or property, or the evidence of title to goods or property, are properly accounted for by the trustee to the entruster. This accounting is through payment or otherwise, as set out in the instrument.

The trust receipt is used for interim financing of staple commodities when it is necessary to release pledged goods from a warehouse in order to sell or process them. Another use is in financing, under a "floor-planning" arrangement.

Floor Planning: This term refers to the use of the trust receipt to finance the purchase by dealers or distributors of motor vehicles, household appliances and other products that may be readily identifiable as to specific units and that have other than a nominal unit value.

Under such a financing arrangement, the products are actually paid for by a bank or other lending agency, which obtains title through the payment of a draft with bill of lading attached, for the purchase price, or through a bill of sale or otherwise. In effect, the products are released by the lender to the borrower for inventory and sales purposes against the borrower's note and trust receipt. The trust receipt provides, in effect, that the borrower will hold the products in trust for the lender for the purpose of sale at not less than a specified minimum sale price per unit and will, pending sale, return the products to the lender upon demand. Or, upon sale, the borrower will keep the proceeds of sale segregated and deliver such proceeds to the lender immediately.

Floor Plan Terms: Frequently, the lender will advance for the original purchase no more than 90% or less of the invoice cost of the products to be financed. It will usually require the monthly curtailment of any advances outstanding at the end of three months, with complete liquidation required within six months after the date of purchase. Interest on daily loans outstanding is usually billed to the borrower at regular monthly intervals.

Floor Plan Procedures: During the period of outstanding advances, the lender will have a valid security interest (except against an innocent purchaser for value) in the products held by the borrower under trust receipt, provided they are clearly identifiable and the lender has observed all requirements of law surrounding trust receipt financing. These requirements may vary to some extent with the laws of each state but usually they include the necessity of placing on public record a "Statement of Trust Receipt Financing" which, in effect, is merely a notice that the borrower is engaged in trust receipt financing with a specified lender. At frequent but irregular intervals, the lender will make a detailed physical check of the products held by the borrower under trust receipt to establish their continued availability and to inspect their condition.

Observing Floor Plan Terms and Procedures: The business using this method of inventory financing must take exceptional care to see that, when floor-planned products are sold, the proceeds of sale are delivered promptly to the lender to apply on outstanding advances. As the name implies, a trust receipt arrangement requires the trust of the lender in the integrity of the borrower. The latter must avoid any appearance of irregularities that might lead to the destruction of the confidence.

32

Financing—Long-Term

[¶3201] DIFFERENCES BETWEEN LONG-TERM AND SHORT-TERM DEBT

The basic distinction within a corporation's capital structure is that between equity (common and preferred stocks) and long-term debt. Short-term debt, even though it is anticipated that it will be renewed, is normally considered a current liability.

Long-term debt is generally shown as a separate category of liabilities and is distinguished from a stock issue in the following ways: (1) the corporation makes an absolute promise to pay the full amount at maturity; (2) the corporation promises to pay a fixed interest at periodic intervals; (3) the debt is frequently, but not necessarily, secured by specific assets of the corporation or by its assets generally; (4) the debt is frequently, but not necessarily, issued under an indenture under which a trustee is appointed to act as the creditors' representative in dealing with the corporation. Long-term debt is ordinarily in the form of bonds, although there is today a greater use of notes.

[¶3202] LONG-TERM BONDS

Long-term bonds are normally issued either in registered or coupon form. A coupon bond contains a coupon for each interest payable date during the life of the bond. When the interest date is reached, the bondholder clips the coupon and sends it to the corporation and subsequently receives his interest payment. Coupon bonds are transferable merely by delivery (like cash) and, hence, create a problem of safekeeping for the bondholder. A registered bond is registered with the corporation, and interest payments will be made directly to the registered owner until such time as the corporation is notified of a transfer. Registered bonds can only be transferred by negotiation (i.e., endorsement by the present owner) and are therefore less risky to hold.

338

[¶3202.1] Principal, Interest, and Maturity of Long-Term Bonds

A bond issue will normally be made up of a large number of bonds identical in all respects (except sometimes as to maturity). The usual denomination (par value) for a bond is $1,000, although in some cases "baby bonds" of $100 denominations have been issued to appeal to the smaller investor. The bond's stated, or "nominal" interest rate is selected on the basis of two considerations: (1) the current scale of money rates; (2) the quality of the company issuing the bonds. If the interest rate is set too low, the bond issue will be salable only at a substantial discount from par or may not be salable at all. If the interest rate is too high, the corporation will be paying more than necessary for the money it obtains. Once the bonds have been issued, their price will fluctuate depending on changes in money rates and in the financial and operating condition of the company. It is unusual for a publicly traded bond to have the same market rate as the nominal rate—that is, it is unusual for the bond to be traded at exactly par value.

The current range of money rates plays a role in determining whether a long-term bond issue should be considered at all. Current interest rates are plotted on a graph according to the maturity of the various issues. This is called a "yield curve." An upsweeping yield curve means that the longer maturities yield the highest interest rates (the "normal" situation, since there must be some inducement for lenders to tie up their money for the longer periods). However, there are occasions when the yield curve will be downsweeping; i.e., interest rates for the shorter maturities will be higher than for the longer maturities. Obviously, the best time from the borrower's viewpoint for a long-term bond issue is when the yield curve is downsweeping, since long-term money is then cheaper than short-term money. On the other hand, if the yield curve is sharply upwards, short-term money may be so much cheaper that it would be wise to arrange the necessary financing through short-term loans (assuming they are available) with the intention of refinancing with long-term debt at some later date when the yield curve is more favorable.

The maturity of long-term debt may range anywhere from five years to 100 years. A bond issue may have a single maturity date for all the bonds or may be a serial issue, with a certain proportion of the bonds maturing at different dates. With a single maturity, the company must be prepared to pay off the entire issue at one time or refinance, called *refunding*. A serial issue spreads the corporation's obligation over a period of years and can be thought of as somewhat similar to a sinking fund.

[¶3202.2] Secured Bonds

For blue-chip corporations of the very highest quality, specific security for a bond issue is usually of little importance to the market because of the high credit standing of the company. But for other companies, the security underlying a bond may be an important factor in determining its marketability. Secured bonds can be divided into four classes:

339

(1) Real Property Mortgage Bonds: These are bonds secured by real estate owned by the corporation. The face amount of the bonds will normally not exceed two-thirds of the appraised value of the real estate in the case of first mortgage bonds. In addition, second or third mortgage bonds can be issued.

(2) Equipment Obligation Bonds: These are bonds secured by chattel mortgages on personal property owned by the corporation. A special form of such bond is the equipment-trust certificate under which title to the property remains with the lender who leases it to the corporation until such time as the debt is paid. Equipment-trust certificates are most often used in the railroad industry.

(3) Collateral Trust Bonds: These are bonds secured by investment securities in companies other than the borrower. The borrower is entitled to the interest or dividends from the securities, but they may be sold by the lender in case of the borrower's default.

(4) General or Blanket Mortgage Bonds: These are bonds secured by all of the corporation's assets. These bonds normally preclude any further issues of secured debt by the corporation unless they specifically provide that they may be subordinated to future bond issues secured by specified assets.

One major problem that frequently occurs in secured bonds is the inclusion of an after-acquired property clause. This clause provides that the mortgage securing the bond issue will automatically be expanded to include all property or specified property subsequently acquired by the corporation. Sometimes this is limited to new property which is acquired to replace property originally included under the mortgage, but on other occasions the clause covers all new property acquired by the corporation and thus increases the security of the bondholders. If a corporation has such a bond indenture in existence and wishes to avoid subjecting new property to the outstanding mortgage, it may be able to proceed in one of the following ways:

(1) Acquire the new property subject to a purchase money mortgage, which ordinarily has priority over the after-acquired property clause;

(2) Organize a subsidiary company to hold the new property;

(3) Lease instead of buy the new property;

(4) Acquire the new property in connection with a merger or consolidation, which frequently renders the after-acquired clause inoperative;

(5) As a last alternative, the outstanding bonds can be redeemed.

[¶3202.3]   Guaranteed Bonds

The guarantee is a less common form of creating security for a bond issue. A guarantee differs from a mortgage in that the creditor is entitled to look to another person rather than to specified property as additional protection for his loan. The three most common types of guarantee bonds are:

(1) Individual Guarantees: These are most often used in closed corporations where all or some of the stockholders may sign the bonds or notes individually. They assume personal liability in addition to the corporate liability.

(2) Guarantees by Corporate Parents: A corporation may decide to carry out some of its operations via subsidiary corporations. In that case, if the subsidiary sells a bond issue, the parent corporation by guaranteeing the bonds can sometimes make the bonds salable at a lower interest rate. Although corporations cannot, as a general rule, guarantee the obligations of others, most states make an exception for subsidiary corporations or for guarantees made within the scope of the corporation's business operations.

(3) Joint Guarantees: These are most common in the railroad industry where two or more railroad corporations may guarantee the bonds of a facility which is jointly used by them, such as a terminal building.

[¶3202.4]   Debenture Bonds

These are unsecured bonds backed only by the general credit of the corporation. In the case of small and many medium-sized companies, debenture bonds are considerably riskier than either secured or guaranteed bonds. There are two primary categories of debentures:

(1) Nonsubordinated Debentures: These, on their face, make no provision for subordination to any future bond issues. However, if the bond indenture says nothing further, these bonds will automatically be junior in lien to any future bond issues which are secured by specific corporate assets. To prevent this from happening, the lender may insist that the indenture contains a provision limiting the total amount of future debt which the corporation may issue or a provision that the debenture bonds will have an equal status with the claim of any future mortgage bonds or secured bonds issued by the corporation.

(2) Subordinated Debentures: Of all types of debt, these most resemble a stock issue. The subordination clause places the lender last among all the creditors of the company, past or future. The advantage to the corporation is that it preserves its future borrowing power, while at the same time creating deductible interest rather than nondeductible dividends. This type of bond issue will appeal to persons who are prepared to assume greater risk than the usual bondholder, but who also want a priority position as against the common stockholders. Debenture bonds are very similar, therefore, to preferred stock. In fact, the debentures will frequently carry a conversion privilege as a "sweetener," thus giving the bondholder the option to change his interest to stock in the event the company is successful.

[¶3202.5]   Discount Bonds

Sometimes bonds may be issued at a discount instead of calling for interest. For example, a bond with a face of $1,000 may be issued at $750. At maturity, the bond will be redeemed for $1,000.

This type of bond is not usually used except by closely-held companies. But tax problems may be created by a discount bond.

For bonds issued on or before July 18, 1984, to the extent there is an "original issue discount" and the bondholders realize this discount, either on redemption or through sale to other holders, the gain realized is treated as ordinary income. Gain not attributable to the original issue discount—i.e., gain that might arise from purchasing a bond as between bondholders, at a further discount— is treated as capital gain. Note: There's a major new law change for bonds issued after July 18, 1984 and purchased on resale at a discount. The gain is ordinary income to the extent of the accrued market discount.

From the corporation's point of view, discount should be amortized over the life of the bond, thereby increasing proportionately each year's interest expense. Where a premium is received, it too is amortized over the life of the bonds, thereby decreasing each year's interest expense.

[¶3202.6]   Special Features of Bond Issues

Any or all of the following special types of provision may be found in a bond issue:

(1) Sinking Funds: A sinking fund requires the corporation to set aside a certain amount of cash each year so that, at the maturity of the bond issue, there will be sufficient funds to pay off the bondholders. The annual contribution may be set up in one of several different ways. For example, an increasing amount may be required each year on the theory that the underlying asset becomes more productive. Or, higher amounts may be required in the earlier years because increasing maintenance charges are anticipated as the asset grows older. If the sinking fund reserve is retained by the corporation until the maturity of the bond issue, the corporation may invest the funds in some form of investment which is both safe and liquid, such as Treasury obligations. On the other hand, the indenture may provide that the sinking fund cash is to be used to purchase bonds on the open market or from individual bondholders drawn by lot. Whatever the specific use of the sinking fund, it acts to increase the security of the remaining bondholders.

(2) Restrictions on Cash Payments: A bond indenture frequently prohibits the corporation from paying out cash dividends or using cash to reduce working capital unless a minimum amount of surplus is retained. Stock dividends, however, are normally not prohibited since they do not involve the outflow of cash.

(3) Convertibility to Stock: This has already been mentioned in connection with debentures. In setting conversion terms (the price of conversion), the corporation determines whether or not it wishes to force conversion. If it is issuing the bonds only as a temporary measure, it will give relatively easy conversion terms so that the bondholders are encouraged to take stock as soon as possible. On the other hand, if the corporation prefers the bonds (for example, because the interest is deductible), it may set the conversion terms to be attractive only after a period of years.

(4) Call Feature: This is a provision frequently inserted in a bond indenture for the protection or benefit of the corporation issuing the bonds. It permits the corporation to redeem the entire bond issue by paying the call price, which usually is set somewhat above par. For example, if the bonds have a face value of $1,000, the corporation may be permitted to call (redeem) them at $1,050. The time at which the bonds may be called may begin either immediately or after a certain number of years. A callability provision has a disadvantage from the borrower's point of view since it puts a limit on the price potential of the bond. If interest rates decline, the bond price will rise as a consequence and, apart from the call price, may reach a level substantially above par. However, if the corporation has the call privilege, it will probably exercise it when bond prices begin to rise, because this means the corporation can refinance by issuing a new bond issue at lower interest rates.

[¶3203]   **TERM LOANS BY BANKS AND INSURANCE COMPANIES**

Term loans are a common way of providing intermediate financing, i.e., from one to five years and sometimes up to ten years. The parties frequently proceed on the assumption that a term loan will be renewed each time it becomes due, provided of course that the financial condition of the business warrants such renewals. While such debt may therefore remain on the company's books for very long periods of time, it is nevertheless classified as intermediate because the lender has the option at relatively frequent intervals to terminate the loan.

There are numerous purposes for intermediate borrowing. One of the most common is to provide adequate working capital. A company may be under-capitalized from the start, or it may find that in times of prosperity more capital than anticipated is tied up in inventory and accounts receivables. In such a case, a term loan can supplement the firm's own equity investment. Another common use of the term loan is to acquire equipment with relatively short lives. Depreciation of the equipment affords tax-free cash which is available to pay off the loans; when new equipment is again required, the loan can be renewed. Finally, a term loan is often used when the company is actually seeking long-term funds but decides that the time is not propitious for floating long-term debt or for a public issue of stock. Typically, companies are reluctant to issue long-term debt when interest rates are very high, or to issue common stock when the market is quite weak.

Interest rates on term loans will, as befits their intermediate status, fall somewhere between the extremes of the maturity yield curve. They will tend to rise during periods of business expansion as the commercial banks are called upon to increase their business loans, and conversely term loans will be in less demand during times of economic recession. Commonly, the interest is in the form of a discount, whereby the bank deducts annual interest at the inception of the loan. This will make the actual interest rate higher than the nominal (contract) rate.

As regards repayment of principal, a term loan may be a standing loan, a fully amortized loan or a partially amortized loan. In the last case, the loan is called a balloon loan since a portion of the principal will remain due at maturity despite regular payments of principal. Generally, unsecured term loans will require some amortization, particularly if they run for more than one year. On the other hand, if the loan is secured by stocks or bonds or by other assets of the borrower, no or very little amortization may be required even though the loan is for a longer term.

[¶3203.1] Restriction in Term Loan Agreements

A term lender will be particularly interested in the borrower's cash flow rather than net income after taxes. The reason is that over a relatively short period, a company may be fully capable of paying off a term loan out of its cash flow, even though it may go through a temporary period of declining or nonexistent earnings. Or under opposite circumstances, a company may anticipate a large net income but may have a very small cash flow due to the need to purchase new equipment, pay off other loans, etc. Important provisions in the term loan agreement which act to restrict the borrower include the following:

Additional Debt: The lender may impose restrictions on the borrower's right to incur additional debt. This is more likely where the term debt is unsecured and new debt, by virtue of security provisions, may place the term loan in a subordinated position.

Restriction on Dividends: A common provision is one forbidding dividends unless net profits and/or cash flow and/or working capital reach designated amounts.

Restrictions of Cash Payments: In addition to limiting dividend payments, the loan agreement may limit other cash payments. For example, surplus may not be used to retire existing stock or for investment in foreign subsidiaries.

Restrictions on Salaries: In the case of smaller companies, a lender may insist that salaries, bonuses and other compensation be restricted to stated amounts.

Minimum Working Capital: The effect of the preceding restrictions is to insure that the company has sufficient working capital for its needs. In addition, the loan agreement may specifically provide for a minimum working capital position.

Barring Merger or Consolidation: Finally, the lender may insist that no merger or consolidation take place while the term loan is outstanding. The reason is that such a combination may deprive the borrower of necessary cash or may place the term loan in a very subordinated position.

33

Investing Working Capital
for Short-Term Periods

[¶3301] **CONSERVING CASH**

The amount of current assets which must be maintained by the business to sustain its working capital needs will vary, depending on such matters as the rapidity of inventory turnover, the length of the collection period, and the extent to which current assets are reduced by capital replacement, dividends and similar needs of the business.

Regardless of the absolute amounts needed by a particular business, it is a general principle of business finance that cash should be conserved whenever possible. In other words, the amount of inventory should be no higher than needed to sustain the normal sales volume of the business and every effort should be made to collect receivables as soon as possible.

Until quite recently, this principle of conserving cash led most financial officers to favor large cash balances in corporate checking accounts, since this represented 100% liquidity. The view was taken that any type of investment represented an unnecessary business risk. But this is now regarded as too conservative and, since it denies the business any return on its cash, too costly a practice to follow.

[¶3301.1]   The Minimum Need for Cash

There are at least five reasons why a minimum cash balance must be maintained:

(1) Immediate Liabilities: The company must have cash for its payroll and for other liabilities, such as tax payments or trade accounts which must be paid in the next few weeks.

(2) Emergencies: It is possible that the business will need a sum of cash for some emergency purpose, or perhaps even to make a highly advantageous purchase which must be consummated at once.

(3) Purchase Discount: Companies like to have sufficient cash on hand to take advantage of all purchase discounts. While, today, many companies look upon the cost of merchandise or other items purchased as the net cost after discount, nevertheless, failure to pay a bill within a discount period can be quite expensive. For example, merchandise purchased on a 2%/ten; net/30-basis will, in effect, pay 2% interest for the use of the money for 20 days if the bill is not paid within the 10-day period. This is the equivalent of a 36% annual interest rate. Hence it becomes important to pay all bills within the discount period, so it is important to have sufficient cash on hand to take advantage of the discounts.

(4) Compensating Bank Balances: Most commercial banks require that borrowers maintain a compensating deposit with them. For example, a company borrowing $100,000 may be required to maintain a continuing deposit of $20,000. This increases the actual interest cost because the borrower has the use of $80,000 instead of $100,000.

(5) "Window-Dressing": This is a purely psychological factor but one which should not be overlooked. Even though a company has excellent reasons for maintaining an extremely low cash balance, such a figure on its balance sheet may prove disconcerting to stockholders and creditors, who may feel that the business is short of working capital, one of the most common reasons for business failure.

[¶3301.2]   Nature of Risks in Investing Cash

In theory, conversion of cash into any other form of investment creates three possible kinds of risks: credit, money, and liquidity.

(1) Credit Risk: This is the risk that the organization which issues the investment obligation will fail or will otherwise be unable to honor its obligation. Where the organization is the U.S. Government, this risk is almost nonexistent. The risk is small also for all practical purposes when the organization is a state, municipality or private organization which is insured by an agency of the government. Investors now, however, are more cautious of municipal obligations, after the experience of New York City. On the other hand, investing in common stock of a small enterprise obviously involves a high degree of risk.

(2) Money Risk: This refers to the risk of loss due to changes in interest rates. For example, the price of a U.S. Government bond may fall (even though no credit risk is involved) because interest rates rise, which in turn reflects changes in the supply and demand for money. The existence of money risk precludes any investment of cash in long-term obligations. However, there are forms of short-term investments (Government bills and certificates and time deposits, called "near-money") which involve such a minimum degree of money risk that it can be ignored.

(3) Liquidity Risk: This refers to the absence of a market for the investment. For example, a real estate mortgage may suffer no decline in price due to money risk or credit risk, but nevertheless may have no market at the time the holder wishes to sell it. To insure liquidity, corporate cash should be invested in obligations having an extremely active market, the most typical of which are U.S. Government securities.

[¶3301.3]   Types of Investments for Corporate Cash

Having defined the basic type of risk, we may briefly indicate the types of investments which may be appropriate for the investment of corporate cash balances:

(1) **Ninety-Day Treasury Bills:** Treasury bills are the shortest term obligation issued by the Federal Government and represent an obligation almost equal to actual cash in terms of the various risks outlined above. Treasury bills are issued for 91 or 182 days (there is normally a new issue every week), and their interest rate will vary depending on the degree of monetary ease which prevails. They are completely liquid, are sold by the government on a discount basis rather than on the basis of a face value plus accrued interest, and can be purchased only in minimum amounts.

(2) **Other Federal Obligations:** There are three other classes of Federal obligations: Treasury certificates (maturity of 6 to 12 months), Treasury notes (maturity of 1 to 5 years), and Treasury bonds (maturity of over 5 years). While these involve little credit risk or liquidity risk, they do involve a money risk as their prices will fluctuate in relation to the movement of interest rates.

(3) **Certificates of Deposit:** The institutions which were hurt most by the transfer of corporate funds from demand deposits to income-bearing investments have been the commercial banks. In an attempt to win back some of the lost funds, commercial banks now offer certificates of deposit. These are issued to a corporation on deposit of a minimum amount of funds (e.g., $15,000-$100,000) for a minimum period of time (e.g., six months) and carry an interest rate which substantially exceeds the current rate on savings accounts. Although the money deposited must remain for the minimum period in order to earn interest, the certificates themselves are negotiable in the money market so that from the point of view of the corporation, there is no problem as to liquidity. Because of the short-term nature of the deposit, there is similarly less risk of loss from changes in interest rates.

(4) **Savings and Loan Association Deposits:** Until commercial banks began issuing certificates of deposits, much of the corporate funds which were not invested in securities were placed in savings and loan associations. Here, they could earn high interest and normally could be withdrawn upon 30-day's notice. While such deposits normally create little money risks or credit risks (since deposits are insured by an agency of the Federal Government), there is some possibility of nonliquidity in the event of a severe economic downturn which could result in a high foreclosure rate, which in turn might mean that some savings and loan associations (which invest primarily in mortgages) might not be in a position to pay their depositors upon demand.

(5) Short-Term Commercial Notes: Finance companies and other monied corporations whose main assets are cash are constantly offering short-term notes to investors for the purpose of raising working capital. These notes, with maturities of from 90 days upwards, are suitable for many corporations since they provide a return slightly higher than that on Treasury obligations and, in the case of the largest finance companies, there is little risk.

(6) Short-Term Corporate Bonds: One type of investment that is used by corporate treasurers is corporate bonds which have only a short time until maturity. In the case of our largest and strongest corporations, their bonds involve small risk. If their bonds are bought at a discount a short time prior to maturity, this also reduces the money risk since even if money rates rise (causing a decline in bond prices generally), the investor knows he must receive at least par at the maturity of the bonds.

(7) Municipal Bonds: This type of investment may yield slightly less than some others, but income is exempt from tax at the corporate level. Such income cannot be distributed as a tax-free dividend.

(8) Commercial Paper: This is a short-term investment that usually pays interest at a rate higher than government obligations. The larger corporations borrow short-term funds in this manner with a 30-day maturity. If they are bought with discretion, the risk factor is moderate.

(9) Repurchase Agreements: Many financial institutions now offer to sell investors a package of government securities at a discount, with an agreement to repurchase the package at some later date, 30 days to 89 days, at a specified price. The risk factor is small if purchased from solid institutions.

(10) Money Market Funds: Money-market funds are simply portfolios of money-market instruments put together by a manager and made available to investors. Such funds are highly liquid and can be bought and sold daily. In some cases the funds are set up so that you may withdraw funds by merely writing a check. Risk can be minimized by buying funds which hold only government securities.

34

Financially Troubled Businesses

[¶3401]   **HANDLING A COMPANY
IN FINANCIAL DIFFICULTY**

The corporate accountant's need for handling a company in financial difficulty can arise when his own company is in trouble, or when a debtor of his company is the one that has the financial problems. In either case, he might, for example, be concerned with preparing or evaluating a statement of affairs. And he might be concerned with the rules of bankruptcy when his company or the debtor might be thrown into, or voluntarily go into, bankruptcy. More often, rather than outright bankruptcy, he might be involved in working out an arrangement for rehabilitating or reorganizing the company either as debtor or creditor.

[¶3401.1]   **Statement of Affairs**

The purpose of the statement of affairs is to determine how much the unsecured creditors can hope to get from the business if it is liquidated. The statement may be prepared by a trustee in bankruptcy to determine whether the business would be better off being dissolved or continued. It may also be prepared anywhere along the line where a business is in trouble (perhaps in trying to work something out with creditors) to determine the status of the unsecured creditors. (Note that we are referring here to an accounting statement of affairs as distinguished from a statement of affairs prescribed under the Bankruptcy Act, which is a comprehensive debtor's questionnaire.)

Included here is an illustration of a statement of affairs with a statement of the estimated deficiency to unsecured creditors.

X CORPORATION
Statement of Affairs
.............., 19....

Book Value	Assets	Appraised Value	Available to Unsecured Creditors	Estimated Shrinkage
$250,000	Fully Pledged Assets: Land & Building	$180,000		$70,000
	Less: Mortgage Payable (deducted contra)	150,000	$30,000	
	Partly Pledged Assets:			
30,000	Bonds of Y, Inc.	$32,000		
	(deducted contra)			
	Unpledged Assets:			
5,000	Cash	$5,000	5,000	
100,000	Accounts Receivable (less bad debts)	80,000	80,000	20,000
200,000	Inventories	120,000	120,000	80,000
1,000	Goodwill			1,000
$586,000	TOTALS		$235,000	$171,000
	Preferred Creditors (see contra)		55,000	
	Balance Available to Unsecured Creditors		$180,000	

Book Value	Liabilities and Stockholders' Equity	Unsecured Claims
	Preferred Creditors:	
$10,000	Wages Payable	$10,000
40,000	Taxes Payable	40,000
5,000	Estimated Administration Costs	5,000
	Deducted contra	55,000
	Fully Secured Creditors:	
150,000	First Mortgage Bonds and Accrued Interest (deducted contra)	
	Partially Secured Creditors:	
40,000	Notes Payable and Accrued Interest	
	Less: Appraised value of Y, Inc., Bonds	40,000
		32,000
		$8,000
	Unsecured Creditors:	
300,000	Accounts Payable	300,000
	Stockholders' Equity:	
200,000	Capital Stock	
(159,000)	Deficit	
$586,000	TOTALS	$308,000
	Available to Unsecured Creditors Contra	180,000
	Estimated Deficiency to Unsecured Creditors	$128,000
		$308,000

350

[¶3402] BANKRUPTCY

You may have contact with the Bankruptcy Reform Act of 1978 when:

1. You want to obtain for your company the status of a secured creditor in anticipation of the possible bankruptcy of the debtor.
2. You want to protect your company as creditor by putting the debtor in bankruptcy.
3. You want to press a claim against or recover an asset from a bankrupt estate.
4. Your company is the harassed debtor seeking to be discharged of its debt.
5. You want the protection of the court and an appointed trustee to rehabilitate your financially embarrassed business.

Chapter 11 of the Bankruptcy Code replaces Chapters X, XI, and XII of the Bankruptcy Act that applied to cases filed before October, 1, 1979.* Chapter 11 can be used as the means of working out an arrangement with creditors, with the debtor continuing or for a complete reorganization with the debtor or a trustee in charge of the business.

[¶3402.1] Avoidance of Preferences

The trustee or debtor in possession can avoid transfers that are considered preferences including the recovery of payments so considered. The elements of a preference are:

1. A transfer of the debtor's property,
2. To or for the benefit of a creditor,
3. For or on account of an antecedent debt,
4. While the debtor is insolvent,
5. Within 90 days before the petition (one year for insiders),
6. The creditor receiving the transfer receives more than he would have in a liquidation case without the transfer.

[¶3402.2] Making Claims Against a Bankrupt

A creditor establishes a claim in bankruptcy by filing what is known as a "proof of claim." You can go into almost any legal stationery store and buy appropriate forms. A creditor is not required to file a proof of claim if it agrees with the debt listed in the schedule submitted by the debtor to the court. However, creditors, who for any reason, disagree with the amount admitted on the debtor's schedules, or creditors desiring to give a power of attorney should prepare and file a complete proof of claim.

[¶3402.3] Putting a Debtor in Involuntary Bankruptcy

Three or more creditors (if there are 11 or fewer creditors, only one creditor is necessary) with unsecured claims of at least $5,000 can file to force a debtor into

---

*Prior law (Bankruptcy Act) used roman numerals for chapter identification while the new law (Bankruptcy Code) uses arabic numbers. There are eight chapters in the new law (all odd numbers) contained in Title 11 U.S. Code.

involuntary bankruptcy. Under prior law, before proceedings could commence, it was necessary for the debtor to have committed one of the acts of bankruptcy. The new law eliminates the acts of bankruptcy and permits the court to allow a case to proceed only (1) if the debtor generally fails to pay its debts as they become due, or (2) within 120 days prior to the petition a custodian was appointed or took possession (such as often happens with an assignment for the benefit of creditors). The latter excludes the taking of possession of less than substantially all property to enforce a lien.

Governmental units, estates, trusts, farmers and non-profit corporations cannot have an involuntary petition filed against them.

The petition can be filed under Chapter 7 (Liquidation) or under Chapter 11 (Reorganization).

There are several reasons why a creditor might want to force a debtor into bankruptcy:

1. There is a segregation of assets immediately without the risk of having the bankrupt dissipate or conceal the property available to pay his debts.

2. There is an orderly administration of the bankrupt's estate as well as a procedure under which claims against it can be expeditiously established.

3. If the bankrupt has made any substantial preferences—that is to say, if it has favored certain creditors—they can be required to return property to the estate for ratable distribution among all claims.

4. There is a provision for the examination of the bankrupt and witnesses to determine the nature of the acts, conduct and property of the bankrupt whose estate is in the process of administration.

[¶3402.4]   Procedure Steps in Bankruptcy Proceedings

The steps in a bankruptcy proceeding are these:

1. Filing of petition—a voluntary petition constitutes an adjudication; an involuntary petition may be contested. An answer to an involuntary petition would deny the allegations contained in the petition, generally the allegation that debts are not being paid when due.

2. The court will issue an order for relief which creates an automatic stay of the actions of creditors. As a result of the stay, no party, with minor exceptions, having a security or adverse interest in the debtor's property can take any action that will interfere with the debtor or his property until the stay is modified or removed.

3. A committee of creditors will be appointed as soon as practicable by the court in Chapter 11 proceedings. In Chapter 7 proceedings a trustee will be appointed by the court who may then appoint a committee of creditors. A meeting of the creditors committee can require the bankrupt to submit to a broad examination covering every phase of his operations.

4. The debtor must file an inventory of all his property and a list of all his creditors, secured and unsecured, showing the amount owed each. He must also file a "statement of affairs" giving information as to his financial history, the volume of business, his income and other pertinent information. The schedule must claim any exemptions the debtor believes he's entitled to, otherwise the exemption may be lost.

5. A trustee in bankruptcy may be elected at the first meeting of creditors by 20% of the unsecured creditors, both as to number and amount of claims, in a Chapter 7 proceeding. In a Chapter 11 proceeding, the appointment of a trustee is made only by petition to the court.

6. The trustee, if any, has a key role in bankruptcy proceedings. He must take over and gather together all the bankrupt's assets. To this end, he has the job of uncovering fraud and concealment and recovering preferences and fraudulent transfers. In Chapter 11 cases where the debtor is left in control of the business, the court may appoint an examiner to investigate if there has been fraud or concealment.

[¶3402.5] How the Assets of the Bankrupt Are Distributed

The Bankruptcy Code of 1978 modifies to a limited extent the order of payment of the expenses of administration and other unsecured claims. The Code provides the following priorities:

1. Administrative expenses.

2. Unsecured claims in an involuntary case arising after commencement of the proceedings but before an order of relief is granted.

3. Wages earned within ninety days prior to filing the petition (or the cessation of the business) to the extent of $2,000 per individual.

4. Unsecured claims to employees' benefit plans arising within 180 days prior to filing petition limited to $2,000 times the number of employees less the amount paid in (3) above.

5. Unsecured claims of individuals to the extent of $900 from deposits of money to purchase, lease, or rental of property or purchase of services not delivered or provided.

6. Unsecured tax claims of governmental units:

   a) Income or gross receipts tax provided tax return due (including extension) within three years prior to filing petition.

   b) Property tax last payable without penalty within one year prior to filing petition.

   c) Withholding taxes.

   d) Employment tax on wages, etc., due within three years prior to the filing of the petition.

   e) Excise tax due within three years prior to filing of the petition.

   f) Customs duty on merchandise imported within one year prior to the filing of the petition.

   g) Penalties related to a type of claim above in compensation for actual pecuniary loss.

[¶3402.6] Getting Debts Discharged

From the bankrupt's viewpoint, the discharge of his debts is the most important feature of the entire proceedings. He's entitled to a discharge as a matter of right unless proper objections are made and sustained. For everyone but a corporation, adjudication operates as an automatic application for discharge. A corporation may not obtain a discharge under Chapter 7 of the Code. This prevents the previous practice of maintaining the shell of a bankrupt corporation for latter use.

[¶3402.7] Grounds for Objecting to or Denying Discharge

There are ten statutory conditions that will deny the debtor a discharge:

1. Is not an individual.
2. Within one year prior to the filing of the petition, or after filing, transferred, destroyed, or concealed, or permitted to be transferred, destroyed, or concealed, any of his property with the intent to hinder, delay, or defraud his creditors.
3. Failed to keep or preserve adequate books or accounts or financial records.
4. Knowingly and fraudulently made a false oath or claim, offered or received a bribe, or withheld information in connection with the case.
5. Failed to explain satisfactorily any losses of assets or deficiency of assets to meet his liabilities.
6. Refused to obey any lawful order or to answer any material questions in the course of the proceedings after being granted immunity from self incrimination.
7. Within one year prior to the filing of the petition, committed any of the above acts in connection with another case concerning an insider.
8. Within the past six years received a discharge in bankruptcy under Chapters 7 or 11 of the Code or under the Bankruptcy Act.
9. Within the past six years received a discharge under Chapter 13 of the Code or Chapter XIII of prior law unless payments under the plan totaled 100 percent of the allowed unsecured claims or at least 70 percent of such claims under a plan proposed in good faith and determined to have been performed according to the debtor's best effort.
10. In addition, the discharge will be denied if, after the order for relief, the debtor submits a written waiver of discharge and the court approves.

It is interesting to note that the issuance of false financial statements to obtain credit, which was grounds for denial of discharge under the old law, will only prevent discharge for that particular debt rather than bar a discharge from all debts.

We can sum up these ten grounds by saying that a discharge in bankruptcy is available only to an honest debtor who has kept adequate records, cooperated in the bankruptcy proceedings, and hasn't been through bankruptcy proceedings for more than six years.

[¶3403] REHABILITATION

The financially embarrassed business can get relief under the Bankruptcy Code or by voluntary agreement with creditors.

[¶3403.1] Voluntary Agreements

We talk here about composition and extensions outside bankruptcy. In this connection, an arrangement under which the debtor is to pay a percentage of his debts is called a "composition." The main idea of an "extension" is that it gives the debtor more time to pay.

Either a composition or an extension involves two agreements: (1) one among two or more creditors and the debtor, and (2) one among the creditors themselves.

Why should the creditors want to approach the matter as a group rather than deal with the debtor on an individual basis? There may be a number of reasons, but certainly one of the more important is that, if a single creditor undertakes to collect the full amount owing him, he may precipitate bankruptcy proceedings either by the debtor or the other creditors. In those proceedings, he may have to return to the bankrupt's trustee any payment made by the debtor as an unlawful preference. And if no payment had been made but he had started legal proceedings which gave him sort of a lien, he would find that his lien was of no value to him, having been dissolved by the bankruptcy proceedings. Hence, a creditor might conclude that it would be better for him to try to work out some arrangement with the debtor and the other creditors rather than to engage in a race to collect his individual debt, especially since he could "win" the race in the first instance only to find himself disqualified in the end.

You can't have an effective composition or extension outside bankruptcy proceedings, however, unless all the creditors (or the great majority of creditors) are willing to go along with it and to overlook favored treatment to one or more creditors who won't go along. This is because the dissenting creditors won't be bound by the agreement and can proceed to the recovery of the amount due them by legal process. If you want a composition or extension that will bind the dissenters, the only way to get it is through bankruptcy proceedings or special local proceedings.

Effect of Agreement: A voluntary agreement will generally operate to discharge the debtor only when its terms have been carried out. Thus, a failure to pay notes given under the agreement may operate to revive the original debt even though the agreement doesn't expressly provide for its revival.

Care must be exercised to avoid discharging parties secondarily liable with the debtor. An extension of time of payment may, for example, discharge a surety unless he's agreed in advance to permit the extension.

Preferring Creditors: In a composition there's nothing wrong in "preferring" some types of creditors, where the preference has some rational or legal basis — e.g., the creditors "preferred" hold security or are entitled to some type of priority. Also, all the creditors who are parties to the composition should be told about the preference. A secret promise of a preference or other advantage made to one or more creditors will render the agreement fraudulent and void or voidable.

State Insolvency Laws: Before resorting to a composition outside bankruptcy, be sure to check the insolvency laws of your own state. They may operate as a limiting factor in the use of these agreements.

[¶3403.2]   Assignment for the Benefit of Creditors

The distinction between compositions and assignments for the benefit of creditors is not always clear. One distinction has been said to be that a composition requires the consent of the creditors while an assignment does not.[1] However, as a practical matter you can't have an effective assignment for the benefit of creditors unless the creditors at least passively acquiesce. If the creditors don't go along with the idea, they may be able to treat the assignment as an act of bankruptcy and throw the debtor into bankruptcy proceedings.

There's another big difference between a composition and an assignment. In a composition, the debtor holds on to his business and works out a readjustment of his debts with his creditors. In an assignment, he turns over his business and all his property to an assignee or trustee to be distributed in payment of his debts. Also, a composition contemplates release of the debtor from further liability; not so in the ordinary assignment, although the creditors can, of course, consent to a release or discharge.

In an assignment, the debtor has what is called "a resulting trust in any assets." This may remain after the creditors have been paid. But the debtor has no equity of redemption; that is, he can't come in at any stage after he's made the assignment and get his property back by paying off his creditors, unless, of course, all of them consent.

Local Variations in Law: Local variations in the law governing assignments must be checked out. Here are the main areas to be watched:

(1) Assignment of part of property. (In some states, a partial assignment is void; in others, it is valid if the part not assigned is open to the remedies of all of the creditors.)

(2) What property passes under a general assignment. [Generally, all property, real or personal, tangible or intangible, including goodwill, trademarks (not personal), patents, interest in insurance policies or assignor's life, and rights under trust; but property held in trust and property fraudulently obtained will not pass.]

(3) Necessity of acknowledging, filing or recording assignment. (Many states have provisions.)

(4) Inventory of property assigned and schedule of creditors who are to participate. (These will usually be included in assignment as a matter of course, but state law requirements should be checked for formal requirements.)

(5) Notice to creditors. (Statutes may prescribe time and form.)

(6) Reservation of control by debtor. (Assignment will be invalid if there is

---

[1] In Massachusetts consent of the creditors is required.

reservation of any degree of control. Debtor cannot reserve right to revoke or declare future uses or trusts to which assignment is to be subject.)

(7) Reservation of possession. (Some authorities hold that debtor's reservation of possession will invalidate an assignment.

(8) Intent to hinder or delay creditors. (Assignment made with a view to debtor's own advantage and to hinder and delay creditors in the just enforcement of their claims is vulnerable to attack as fraudulent.)

(9) Preferential treatment of creditors. (While there is nothing wrong with favoring creditors having recognized priorities, do not include a provision that those creditors will be first paid who will accept their pro rata share on condition that receipt constitutes a full release).

[¶3404] CORPORATE REORGANIZATION

Under the Bankruptcy Reform Act, Chapter 11 is designed to replace Chapters VIII, X, XI, and XII of prior law. Agreements under this Chapter can affect unsecured creditors, secured creditors, and stockholders. It is designed to provide the debtor with court protection while a plan is developed to rehabilitate the business and to minimize the substantial economic losses associated with liquidation (Chapter 7).

The new act favors the debtor in possession and will only appoint a trustee if requested by the party in interest and for cause. The term "cause" includes fraud, dishonesty or incompetence, or gross mis-management of affairs.

[¶3404.1] Who Can Start Reorganization Proceedings?

Reorganization proceedings can be instituted by the corporation (voluntary), or against it (involuntary) (1) by three or more creditors whose claims total $5,000 or more, are liquidated as to amount, and are not contingent as to liability, or (2) by an indenture trustee acting on behalf of the bondholders. If the corporation is to take the initiative, it can only do so with proper corporate authorization — usually a resolution of the board of directors.

[¶3404.2] Reclamation Proceedings

Reclamation proceedings are a quick way for a third party to get hold of property which belongs to him which is in possession of the trustee. Of course, in many situations where it is clear that the third party is entitled to property in possession of the trustee, he's not going to have to start a reclamation proceeding to get it; but if there's any doubt about the matter, chances are he'll resort to reclamation proceedings. He will not have to if he's the absolute owner of the property, because he'll win out as against a purchaser from the trustee if it comes to that unless, of course, the property in question is an intangible and negotiable. If the claimant holds a security interest only, the trustee will not hand it over if the property is worth more than the claim it secures. In that case he'll ask the court either to permit the secured creditor to sell the property outside bankruptcy and pay over the excess or to permit sale by the trustee, free and clear, and give the creditor an interest in the proceeds. The first course is likely to be followed only where the property in question is at some distant point and can't be conveniently sold with the other assets.

[¶3404.3]   Allowance Of Claims

At the first meeting of creditors, a provisional allowance of claims will be made for voting purposes, but this is not an allowance for purposes of dividend participation. However, as a general rule, claims filed at or before the first meeting will be allowed at that time if no objection is raised. If an objection is raised by either the trustee or one or more creditors, the referee will fix a date to hear and determine the points raised. There's no time limit on filing objections, but the referee may in his discretion refuse to entertain objections filed too late. Secured and priority claims will be allowed only to the extent they're unsecured. If a creditor has received a transfer, lien or preference which is voidable, his claim will not be allowed until he surrenders it to the trustee.

35

Budgeting for Profit Planning

[¶3501]   **BUDGETARY CONTROL**

A budget in its simplest terms is an estimate of future events. This is not a purely random guess, but a forecast which is computed from historical data that has been verified and assumed with some degree of credibility. The volume of sales for the following year, for example, may be estimated by using data from past experience, present-day market conditions, buying power of the consumer and other related factors.

Merely preparing the annual budget, then leaving it unaltered for the remainder of the budget period, is not the purpose. Preparation is only the first step. The second step is for management to control the operations of the firm and to adhere to the budget. Budgetary control is the tool of management for carrying out and controlling business operations. It establishes predetermined objectives and provides bases for measuring performance against these objectives. If variations between performance and objective arise, management alters the situation by either correcting the weakness in performance or modifying the budget. Firms that adopt budgetary control have a better control of operations and are better able to modify them to meet expectations.

[¶3501.1]   Types of Budgets

There are two principal types of annual profit budgets: the operating or earnings budget, and the financial or cash budget. The earnings budget, as its name implies, is an attempt to forecast the earnings of a company for a future period. To make such forecast, other estimates have to be made. Consequently, we have sales budgets, production budgets (which include labor budgets, materials budgets, purchases budgets, capital expenditure budgets, manufacturing expense budgets), administrative expense budgets, distribution expense budgets and appropriation-type budgets (e.g., advertising, research). The accuracy of each of these budgets determines the accuracy of the earnings forecast.

The cash budget, on the other hand, tries to forecast the utilization of the company's cash resources. It estimates the company's anticipated cash expenditures and resources for a period of operation. Cash budget forecasts, like the earnings forecast, depend heavily on sales forecasts. The amount of sales determines the amount of cash the company has for purposes of its operation.

[¶3502]   THE SALES BUDGET

The foundation of the entire budget program is the sales budget. If anticipated sales of a particular product (or project) do not exceed the cost to produce and market it by an amount sufficient to reward the investors and to compensate for the risks involved, the product (project) should not be undertaken. Sales forecasting must be continuous. Conditions change rapidly; in order to direct one's efforts into the most profitable channels, there must be a continuous review and revision of the methods employed.

[¶3502.1]   Forecasting Sales

A sales forecast represents the revenue side of the earnings forecast. It is a prediction as to the sales quantity and sales revenue. Sales forecasts are made for both short and long periods.

Forecasting sales with any degree of accuracy is not an easy task. For example, a firm which estimates sales with the expectation that a patent which it holds will not become obsolete may be disappointed.

In general, the business forecaster has two situations: (1) those which he can to some extent control, and (2) those where conditions created by others can only be observed, recorded, interpreted and applied to his own situation. A firm that has a monopoly due to an important patent which it owns is an example of a company which controls the situation. Forecasts made by such a company may be very accurate. In most cases, however, a company has no such control. It must attempt to interpret general conditions, the situation in its own industry, and future sales of its particular company before making forecasts.

Making the forecast is the responsibility of the sales manager, who, with the help of the district managers and the individual salesmen, determines the primary sales objectives for the year. Corrections of the forecast are made by the heads of the firm so that sales estimates will better reflect expected economic conditions. Before an estimate of sales is made, you must be reasonably sure that it is attainable. It must be based on the best evidence available. As conditions change, the forecast is revised.

If a firm desires to sell more than in the past, an analysis of past sales performances must be supplemented by other analyses. Consideration must be given to general business conditions. The effects of political and economic changes throughout the world are quickly reflected on individual business communities. Some of these factors which affect sales are wars, government regulations, and technological developments. This information should be used in appraising the probable effect of these changes on the sales of the firm for the budget period.

Market Analysis: A sales manager needs to know if his firm is getting its full share of potential customer demand as indicated by a market analysis.

The questionnaire is a popular method of reaching consumers, retailers and jobbers. Data collected gives the firm valuable information, essential in arriving at a forecast of sales possibilities.

A market analysis at a given time gives a picture of the present and potential consumption of a product. This picture provides only half the significant information. The other half can be obtained by continuing the survey over a period of time to discover market trends.

Pricing Policy: The sales budget is not complete until the firm decides on a practical policy as to what price can be secured for its product(s). Generally, estimates should be made to conform with the market prices during the budget period.

The next step is to formulate the sales policies of the firm. These policies should be established relative to such considerations as territorial expansion and selection, customer selection, types and quality of products and service, prices, terms of sales and sales organization and responsibility.

Only after a firm has thoroughly analyzed past sales experience, general business conditions, market potentials, the product to be sold and prices and has formulated its sales policies is it ready to develop the sales program.

Measuring Individual Performance: As a basis for measuring individual performance, a rewarding-merit sales standard could be established. A sales standard is an opinion of the best qualified judgment of performance which may reasonably be achieved under ideal conditions. By comparing this standard with the budget estimate (the figure expected) under normal conditions, management has provided the most important tool of sales control.

> An example of how a comparison between the standard and budget estimate may serve as a basis for reward is the following: A salesman may be told to produce sales of $150,000 (standard), but the firm may expect him to produce sales of only $125,000 (budget estimate). The salesman does not have to be told what the firm's budget figures are. In his endeavor to reach $150,000, he is trying to better what he believes is the budget figure. Depending on how close he comes to the $150,000, the firm may devise a method of rewarding him. It should be kept in mind, however, that the standard should not be set too high, since it may have a reverse effect if the salesman feels it is unreachable.

[¶3503] THE PRODUCTION BUDGET

After the sales budget has been prepared, the next step is to prepare the production budget which specifies the quantity and timing of production requirements.

While the sales budget is prepared in anticipation of seasonal fluctuations, the production budget endeavors to smooth out the fluctuations and thus make most effective use of productive capacity. This is accomplished by manufacturing for stock over the slow periods and using the stock to cover sales during busy periods.

There are different problems for a firm that sells stock products and one that produces special-order goods. The objective for a stock-order-type firm is to coordinate sales and production to prevent excessive inventories, but at the same time to have enough stock to meet sales. A forecast of production in such a firm should enable the executive to arrange to lay out the factory so as to handle the anticipated volume most conveniently. Production in such a firm must be as evenly distributed as possible over the year. It is uneconomical to manufacture the whole period's requirements within a relatively short period at the beginning of the budget period. This involves unduly heavy capital costs of carrying the large inventory. Also, distributing the work over the entire period spreads the labor costs.

With special-order items, the production department has to be prepared at all times to manufacture the goods as soon as possible after receiving the order. Production in this case has to be arranged for the best possible utilization of equipment and labor, so that idle time is reduced to a minimum.

[¶3503.1]   Budgeting Production Costs

Production budgets should be rigid as long as conditions remain the same, but they should be capable of prompt adjustment when circumstances change. For example, if a company operates at 70% of capacity in a period and the budget was based on a production volume of 80%, the budget is of little use. The budget will have to be altered to show what production costs will be at the 70% level. It is prudent when planning production at a particular anticipated percentage level to indicate in the budget the estimates of possible production costs at different levels.

[¶3503.2]   Preparing the Production Budget

The production budget period may vary in length. However, it is common practice among large corporations to use what is known as a ''product year.'' As an example, the automobile industry will usually start with the introduction of new models. The budget year should include at least one complete cycle of operations so that money tied up in raw materials and work-in-process materials may undergo one complete liquidation. Another factor influencing the budget period is the stability of general business conditions. It is more difficult to budget operations during an unstable period, and it is advisable at these times to shorten the budget period.

The production budget should be expressed in terms of physical units. To compute the physical quantities is simple. For example, a simple computation to estimate production required is:

	Units
Estimated sales	250,000
Less opening inventory	150,000
Total requirements	100,000
Add: Closing inventory	100,000
Production required	200,000

Before computing the quantity to be produced, it is necessary to decide quantities to be in the inventory at the end of the period. This decision should be based on factors such as:

(a) Adequate inventory to meet sales demands

(b) Evenly distributed production to prevent shortage of material and labor

(c) Danger of obsolescence

(d) High costs of storing large inventories.

Available Facilities: The production program must conform with the plant facilities available and should determine the most economical use of these facilities. The capacity of the plant is measured in two ways: maximum plant capacity and normal plant capacity. All other measurements are in percentages of maximum or normal capacity. Maximum capacity, of course, can never actually be attained. There are many unavoidable interruptions, such as waiting for setup of machines; time to repair machines; lack of help, tools, materials; holidays; inefficiency; etc. However, these interruptions should be looked into to determine how they can be minimized.

Management should also consider whether additional equipment is needed just to meet temporary sales demands. Later, such equipment may be idle. The replacement of old machinery with new high-speed equipment should also be considered. A careful study should help determine which step would be more profitable in the long run.

Records for each product showing the manufacturing operations necessary and a record of each machine, showing the operations capable of being performed by the machine together with its capacity, should be kept. Estimates must be made of material to be used, number of labor hours and quantities of service (power) required for each product. These estimates are called "standards of production performance." The establishment of these standards is an engineering rather than an accounting task. In this respect, these standards are similar to those used in standard cost accounting.

Cost of Production: The following is an illustration of how cost of production is determined: Assume a concern has a normal capacity of 100 units of product. Current production budget calls for 80 units. Only one product is made; and its production requires two operations, A and B. The standard costs are: variable costs per unit of product, one unit of direct material, $2; operation A (direct labor and overhead), $3; operation B (direct labor and overhead), $5; total $10. Fixed production costs for the budget period are $500, or $5 per unit based on normal capacity. This production cost budget would then be expressed as follows:

Variable cost (80 units @ $10)	$ 800
Fixed costs (80 units @ $5)	400
Costs chargeable to production	1,200
Cost of idle capacity (500 less 400)	100
Total budgeted costs	$1,300

There is a tie-in here between estimated costs, standard costs, and production budgets.

[¶3503.3]   Materials Budget

The purpose of the materials budget is to be sure that there are sufficient materials to meet the requirements of the production budget. This budget deals with the materials for the purchase of raw materials and finished parts and controls the inventory. How to estimate the material required depends on the nature of the individual company. A company manufacturing standard articles can estimate fairly accurately the amount of raw materials and the purchases required for the production program. Even where the articles are not standard, there is usually a reliable relationship between the volume of business handled and the requirements for the principal raw materials.

Tie-In to Standard Costs: In the preparation of the material budget, there is a tie-in to standard costs. Here is an example of how purchase requirements are computed:

Quantity required for production	300,000 units
Desired inventory at end of budget period	75,000 units
Total requirements	375,000 units
Less: Inventory at beginning of period	80,000 units
Purchase requirements	295,000 units

The next step is to express material requirements in terms of prices. Some firms establish standard prices based on what are considered normal prices. Differences between standard and actual purchase prices are recorded as a price variance.

Factors Affecting Policy: These are

(1) The time it takes the material to be delivered after the purchase order is issued.

(2) The rate of consumption of material as indicated by the production budget.

(3) The amount of stock that should be on hand to cover possible delays in inventory of raw materials.

On the basis of these factors, the purchasing department working with the production department can establish figures of minimum stocks and order quantities of raw materials and parts for each product handled. Purchases in large quantities are advisable if price advantages can be obtained. Bulk purchases are advisable during periods of rising prices but not during periods of declining prices. The unavoidable time lag between order and delivery of the material is also a reason to buy in advance.

Buying in advance does not necessarily involve immediate delivery. The deliveries may be spread over the budget period in order to coordinate purchases with production and to control inventory. To control inventory, it is desirable to establish minimum and maximum quantities for each material to be carried. The lower limit is the smallest amount which can be carried without risk of production delays. If materials can be obtained quickly, the inventory can be held near the lower limit. The advantage of keeping inventory at this lower limit is that it minimizes the cost of storage and possible obsolescence. If materials cannot be obtained quickly, there is the possibility of a rise in prices, and so it is advisable to carry more than minimum inventory.

Goods in Process: The time it takes for material to enter the factory and emerge as a finished product is frequently much longer than necessary for efficient production. Comparisons with other companies may reveal that a firm allows its goods to remain in process much longer than other firms. Investigations should be made to determine the causes of such delays and formulate remedies. These investigations are usually made in connection with the production budget.

Finished Goods: The budget of finished goods inventory is based on the sales budget. For example, if 100 units of an item are expected to be sold during the budget period, the problem is to determine how much must be kept in stock to support such a sales program. Since it is difficult to determine the exact quantity customers will demand each day, the finished goods inventory must maintain a margin of safety so that satisfactory deliveries can be made. Once this margin is established, the production and purchasing programs can be developed to re-plenish the stock as needed.

[¶3504] THE LABOR BUDGET

The labor budget deals only with direct labor. Indirect labor is included in the manufacturing expense budget. (The manufacturing expense budget includes the group of expenses in addition to indirect labor, expenses such as indirect material, repairs and maintenance, depreciation and insurance.)

The purpose of the labor budget is to ascertain the number and kind of workers needed to execute the production program during the budget period. The labor budget should indicate the necessary man-hours and the cost of labor required for the manufacture of the products in the quantities shown by the production budget.

[¶3504.1] Preparation of the Labor Budget

The preparation of a labor budget begins with an estimate of the number of labor hours required for the anticipated quantity of products. Before this can be done, it is necessary to know the quantity of items that are going to be produced. This information comes from the production budget. If the products are uniform and standard labor time allowances have been established, it is just a matter of multiplying the production called for by the standards to determine the labor hours required. If the products are not uniform but there is uniformity of operations, it is first necessary to translate production into operation requirements. Operation standards then should be established in terms of man- or machine-hours. The quantity of labor required may then be ascertained.

The next step in preparing the labor budget is to estimate the cost of direct labor. These estimates are computed by multiplying the number of units to be produced by the labor costs per unit. The problem then is to predetermine the unit labor costs. Some of the methods of determining these costs are:

(1)   Day rate system

(2)   Piece rate system.

(3)   Bonus system.

In firms where standard labor costs have been established for the products manufactured, it is necessary only to multiply the units of the product called for in the production budget by the standard labor costs.

A detailed analysis should frequently be made of the differences between actual and estimated labor costs. These should be investigated to detemine whether they are justified. An investigation may reveal inefficient workers, wasted time, defective materials, idle time, poor working conditions, high-priced workers, etc. Responsibility must be definitely placed and immediate action taken to correct those factors which are capable of being controlled.

The budgets for direct labor and manufacturing expenses are not complete until schedules of the final estimates are prepared. The form will vary, depending on the needs of the firm. The following is an example of a schedule of estimated direct labor costs where estimates are shown for each department of the firm:

X CORPORATION

ESTIMATED DIRECT LABOR COSTS
FOR THE PERIOD 1/1/xx to 12/31/xx

Dept.	Quantity to Be Produced	Standard Labor Cost per Unit	Total Estimated Labor Cost
1	127,600	$ .90	$115,000
2	127,600	1.60	204,000
3	127,600	1.12	143,000
		$3.62	$462,000

[¶3505]   CAPITAL EXPENDITURES BUDGET

Since capital expenditures represent a large part of the total investment of a manufacturing concern, the capital expense budget is of great importance. Unwise capital expenditures can seldom be corrected without serious loss to stockholders. The purpose of the capital expenditures budget is to subject such expenditures to careful examination and so avoid mistakes that cannot easily be corrected.

A carefully prepared capital expenditures budget should point out the effect of such expenditures on the cash position of the company and on future earnings. For example, too large a portion of total assets invested in fixed plant and equipment sooner or later may result in an unhealthy financial condition because of the lack of necessary working capital.

[¶3505.1]   Preparation of Capital Expenditures Budget

In preparing the capital expenditures budget, the following information is recorded:

(1) The amount of machinery, equipment, etc., on hand at the beginning of the budget period;

(2) Additions planned for the period;

(3) Withdrawals expected for the period;

(4) The amount of machinery, equipment, etc., expected at the end of the budget period.

Consideration should be given to estimates of additions planned for the period. Additions will be justified if they increase the volume of production and earnings, will reduce unit costs, and the money needed can be spared. Consideration should also be given to the percentage investment for fixed assets as compared with net worth of the firm for a number of years. Various business authorities have realized that an active business enterprise with a tangible net worth between $50,000 and $250,000 should have as a maximum not more than two-thirds of its tangible net worth in fixed assets. Where the tangible net worth is in excess of $250,000, not more than 75% of the tangible net worth should be represented by fixed assets. When these percentages are greatly exceeded, annual depreciation charges tend to be too heavy, the net working capital too moderate, and liabilities expand too rapidly for the good health of the business, alternative leasing should be considered.

The capital expenditures budget should include estimates not only for the budget period, but long-range estimates covering a period of many years. The ideal situation is where machinery is purchased at a time when prices are low. A long-range capital expenditures budget will indicate what machinery will be of use in the future. Then, machinery may be acquired when prices are considered low. Inefficient or obsolete machines can sometimes be made into satisfactory units by rebuilding them. If it is estimated that gains derived from rebuilding machinery will exceed the costs, then provision should be made in the capital expenditures budget to incur these expenses. Such expenditures are frequently called betterments and prolong the useful life of the machines. The preparation of detailed and accurate records is an essential part of the capital expenditures budget. The following information should be included in such a record:

(1) Description of machines;

(2) Date of requisition;

(3) Cost for depreciation rate.

From the above information, it is a simple matter to complete the depreciation for the budget period.

As with other budgets, actual expenditures should be compared with the

367

estimates, and any variation should be analyzed. In addition, a statement should be prepared showing the extent to which actual results obtained from the use of certain capital expenditures are in line with expectations. This is particularly important where substantial investments are made in labor-saving equipment, new processes or new machines.

[¶3506]　　　　　　THE CASH BUDGET

The cash budget is a composite reflection of all the operating budgets in terms of cash receipts and disbursements. Its purpose is to determine the cash resources that will be available during the entire budget program so that the company will know in advance whether it can carry out its program without borrowing or obtaining new capital or whether it will need to obtain additional capital from these sources. Thus, the company can arrange in advance for any necessary borrowing, avoiding emergencies and, more importantly, a cash crisis caused by a shortage.

A knowledgeable financial man goes into the market to borrow money when he can get the cheapest rate. The cash budget will tell the manager when he will need to borrow so he can plan accordingly. In a like manner, he can foresee when he will have sufficient funds to repay loans.

A cash budget is very important to a firm which does installment selling. Installment selling ties up cash resources, and a careful analysis of estimated future collections is needed to forecast the cash position of the company.

Other purposes of the cash budget are: (1) to provide for seasonal fluctuations in business which make heavy demands on funds to carry large inventories and receivables; (2) to assist the financial executive in having funds available to meet maturing obligations; (3) to aid in securing credit from commercial banks; the bank is more likely to lend funds for a definite plan that has been prepared, indicating when and how the funds will be repaid; and (4) to indicate the amount of funds available for investments, when available and for what duration.

[¶3506.1]　　Preparation of the Cash Budget

The main difference between a cash budget and other budgets is that in the cash budget all estimates are based on the dates when it is expected cash will be received or paid. Other budgets are prepared on the basis of the accrual of the different items (for accrual-basis companies). Therefore, in the cash budget, the budget executive cannot base the estimate of cash receipts directly on the sales budget for the obvious reason that all the cash will not be received from such sales in the same month in which they are billed. This is not true in the case of a business on a strictly cash basis. Depreciation is another item handled differently in the cash budget. Depreciation is a cost of doing business, and increases expenses and reduces net income for financial reporting purposes. It is not, however, a cash item and is ignored in preparing the cash budget, but the amount paid for a new plant or equipment in a single year or budget period is included in full in the cash budget.

Cash receipts of a typical firm come from cash sales, collections on accounts and notes receivable, interest, dividends, rent, sale of capital assets and loans. The cash sale estimate is taken from the sales budget. The estimate of collections on accounts should be based on the sales budget and company experience in making collections. With concerns whose sales are made largely on account, the collection experience should be ascertained with considerable care. As an illustration, assume the March account sales have actually been collected as follows:

Month	%
March	6.4
April	80.1
May	8.5
June	3.6
Cash Discount Taken	1.1
Bad Debts Loss	.3
Total	100.00

If the same experience is recorded for each month of the year, it is possible to resolve the sales estimates into a collection budget. It is sometimes desirable to develop the experience separately for different classes of customers for different geographical areas. Once these figures are ascertained, they should be tested from time to time.

Cash disbursements in a typical firm are made for payroll, materials, operating expenses, taxes, interest, purchases of equipment, repayment of loans, payment of dividends, etc. With a complete operating budget on hand, there is little difficulty in estimating the amount of cash that will be required and when it will be required. Wages and salaries are usually paid in cash and on definite dates. For purchases of material (from the materials budget), the purchasing department can readily indicate the time allowed for payments. Operating expenses must be considered individually. Some items, such as insurance, are prepaid. Others, such as commissions, are accrued. So, cash payments may not coincide with charges on the operating budget.

[¶3507] MANUFACTURING EXPENSE BUDGET

In preparing the manufacturing expense budget, estimates and probable expenses should be prepared by persons responsible to authorize expenditures. The general responsibility for variable expenses lies with the production manager. But the immediate responsibility for many of these expenses lies with the foremen of the several departments. Generally, expenses are estimated by those who control them. Each person who prepares a portion of the manufacturing expense budget is furnished with data of prior periods and any plans for the budget period which may affect the amount of expenses. With these data we can decide:

(1) Which, if any, of present expenses can be eliminated.

(2) Probable effect of the sales and production forecasts on those expenses which must be incurred.

No plans for the elimination or reduction of variable expenses should be made unless it is certain that the plan can be enforced.

The responsibility for many fixed manufacturing expenses is with the general executives. Such fixed expenses include long-term leases, pension plans, patents, amortization, salaries of major production executives, etc.

In preparing the budget estimates of manufacturing expenses, a common practice is to use percentages. Each expense is taken as a percent of sales or production costs. For example, if a certain expense is estimated to be 5% of sales, this percentage is applied to the sales estimate to obtain the amount of this expense. The fallacy with this method is that all expenses do not vary proportionately with sales or production. A sounder method of estimating manufacturing expenses is to give individual expenses separate treatment. In estimating the indirect labor expense, it is important to first analyze the expense for the period preceding the budget period. The requirements for additional help, or the possibility of eliminating some of the help, should be considered along with plans for increasing or decreasing any rates of compensation. Detailed schedules should be prepared, showing the nature of each job and the amount to be paid. By summarizing these schedules, an aggregate estimate can be determined. Indirect materials expense should be estimated by first analyzing the amount consumed in prior periods. This, together with the production budget showing the proposed volume for the budget period, serves as a basis for estimating the quantities of the indirect material requirements. The probable cost of such requirements estimated by the purchasing department is the amount to be shown in the manufacturing expense budget. Repairs and maintenance estimates are based on past experience data, supplemented by a report on the condition of the present equipment. If any additional equipment is to be installed during the budget period, recognition must be given to the prospect of additional repairs and maintenance charges. Electric power expense is in direct proportion to the production volume. The charges for depreciation of equipment can be estimated with considerable accuracy. Insurance expense for the budget period is estimated on the basis of the insurance in force charged to production with adjustments made for contemplated changes in equipment, inventories, or coverage of hazard incident to manufacturing.

To budget manufacturing expenses effectively it is important to establish standard overhead rates.

At frequent intervals during the budget period, comparison should be made between the actual expenses in each department and the amount estimated to be spent for actual production during the period. Variations should be investigated and steps taken to correct weaknesses in the production program.

A distinction should be made between controllable and uncontrollable expenses so that the responsibility of individuals can be more closely determined. To facilitate the estimating of expenses, a further distinction is made between fixed and variable expenses. Fixed expenses are those which remain the same regardless of the variations in sales or production. Variable expenses are those which increase or decrease proportionally with changes in volume, sales or production. Maintenance is seldom treated in a separate budget. It is usually regarded as part of the manufacturing expense budget.

Here is an example of a Schedule of Estimated Manufacturing Expenses for each operation of a particular product:

Y CORPORATION
FOR THE YEAR ENDED 12/31/xx

	Total	Operation 1	Operation 2	Operation 3
Variable expenses:				
Indirect materials	$ 20,000	$ 5,000	$ 10,000	$ 5,000
Indirect labor	100,000	10,000	15,000	75,000
Light and power	30,000	5,000	13,000	12,000
Telephone	5,000	3,000	—0—	2,000

	Total	Operation 1	Operation 2	Operation 3
Fixed and semi-variable:				
Factory rent	50,000	14,000	18,000	18,000
Superintendence	100,000	30,000	35,000	35,000
Depreciation	100,000	20,000	60,000	20,000
General and administrative expense	50,000	12,000	17,000	21,000
Total	$455,000	$99,000	$168,000	$188,000

After estimates of materials, direct labor and manufacturing expenses have been prepared, a Schedule of Estimated Cost of Production may be prepared as follows:

Z CORPORATION
FOR THE YEAR ENDED 12/31/xx

	Total	Product A	Product B	Product C
Cost Element:				
Materials	$200,000	$ 80,000	$ 50,000	$ 70,000
Labor	340,000	100,000	80,000	160,000
Manufacturing expenses	70,000	30,000	30,000	10,000
Total	$610,000	$210,000	$160,000	$240,000

[¶3508]   BREAK-EVEN POINT ANALYSIS

One type of budget which provides useful supplementary statistics is the break-even analysis. Although a complete and adequate budget may be developed without using a break-even analysis, its use adds to the understanding of estimates.

The break-even point is that amount of sales necessary to yield neither income nor loss. If sales should be less than indicated by the break-even point, a loss would result.

Where the total cost of goods sold and other expenses is less than sales and if this total varied in direct proportion to sales, operations would always result in net income. For example, in a company in which the cost of goods sold and expenses amounts to $1.80 per unit sold and the sale price is $2, on the first unit there would be net income of 20¢. On a million items, the net income would amount to $200,000.

As a practical matter, the simple example cited above is not realistic. The reason is that although some expenses may vary with volume of sales (e.g., salesmen's commissions, traveling expenses, advertising, telephone, delivery costs, postage, supplies, etc.), there are many other types of expenses which are not affected by the variations in sales. These expenses are called "fixed" expenses. Examples are depreciation, rent, insurance, heat, etc.

If, going back to the above illustration, we assume that fixed costs and expenses amount to $40,000, we have at least $40,000 of costs and expenses before even one unit is sold. If we sell a million units, however, we have an income before deducting fixed expenses of $200,000. After fixed expenses, our net income is $160,000. So, our income picture goes from a loss of $40,000 (where no units are produced) to a profit of $160,000 (where one million units are produced). Somewhere between these, however, is a point represented by a certain number of units at which we will have neither income nor loss — the break-even point.

[¶3508.1]   How to Compute the Break-Even Point

Here is how we determine the break-even point. Let S equal the sales at the break-even point. Since sales at this point are equal to the total fixed costs and expenses ($40,000) plus variable costs and expenses ($1.80 per unit or 90% of sales),

$$S = \$\ 40,000 + .9S$$
$$S - .9S = \$\ 40,000$$
$$.1S = \$\ 40,000$$
$$S = \$400,000$$

Even the above illustration oversimplifies the problem. It makes the assumption that all costs and expenses can be classified as either *fixed* or *variable*. However, in actual operations, expenses classified as fixed expenses may become variable where sales increase beyond a certain point, and some variable expenses may not vary in direct proportion to the sales.

Rent expense, for example, may not always be a fixed expense. A substantial increase in sales may create a need for additional showroom or salesroom space or, perhaps, salesmen's offices, or salesmen's commissions may rise unexpectedly when they have gone above a certain quota.

Then, there are types of hybrid expenses which may be classified as *semifixed*. For example, executives' salaries, association dues, subscriptions to periodicals and many other expenses are not in proportion to sales. Another unreality in the above problem is that as sales increase, there is a likelihood that sale prices will decrease because of larger orders. Now let's take a look at another situation:

Net sales		$ 2,500,000
Costs and expenses:		
Fixed	$ 250,000	
Variable	1,500,000	1,750,000
Net income		$ 750,000

This company currently has under consideration an investment in a new plant which will cause an increase in its fixed expenses of $200,000.

The present break-even point is as follows:

$$S = \$\ 250,000 + .6S$$
$$S - .6S = \$\ 250,000$$
$$.4S = \$\ 250,000$$
$$S = \$\ 625,000$$

If the company builds the plant, the break-even calculation will be:

$$S = \$\ 450,000 + .6S$$
$$S - .6S = \$\ 450,000$$
$$.4S = \$\ 450,000$$
$$S = \$1,125,000$$

If the plant expansion is undertaken, then the sales must be increased by $500,000 for the company to maintain its net income of $750,000, as follows:

$$S = \$\ 450,000 + .6S + \$750,000$$
$$S - .6S = \$1,200,000$$
$$.4S = \$1,200,000$$
$$S = \$3,000,000$$
$$\text{Increase} = \$\ 500,000\ (\$3,000,000\ \text{less}\ \$2,500,000)$$

Now let's analyze the situation under two alternatives. The maximum production with the present plant is 1,500,000 units. At an average sale price of $2 per unit, sales would be $3,000,000. With the new plant, sales are estimated to hit $5,000,000 (2,500,000 units @ $2 per unit).

	Without New Plant	With New Plant
Net sales	$3,000,000	$5,000,000
Less: Fixed costs and expenses	250,000	450,000
	2,750,000	4,550,000
Less: Variable costs and expenses (60% of sales)	1,800,000	3,000,000
Net income	$ 950,000	$1,550,000

If sales do not increase, the increase in fixed costs and expenses of $200,000 would cut the net income to $550,000. The break-even point will have been boosted $500,000, and the sales will have to be increased by this amount to produce the current $750,000 of income. Alternatively, the net income can be increased by $600,000 if the sales figure is increased by $2,000,000. Although these figures are based on an assumption that all costs and expenses are fixed or variable, the break-even analysis focuses attention on the factors involved in costs and income and provides a basis for consideration of various problems.

36

Financial Statement Analysis

[¶3601]   THE PURPOSE OF FINANCIAL STATEMENTS

Analysis techniques applied to financial statements are of interest to the corporate financial officer in a number of instances. For one thing, his own company's financial statements will be subject to analysis by creditors, credit grantors, and investors. Furthermore, he will want to analyze his own company's statements for internal management use. Also, he may be called upon to analyze other companies' financial statements for credit purposes and perhaps for investment purposes (where an acquisition is being considered).

[¶3602]   BASIC ANALYSIS TECHNIQUES

Much of the analytical data obtained from the statements are expressed in terms of ratios and percentages. (Carrying calculations to one decimal place is sufficient for most analysis purposes.) The basic analysis technique is to use these ratios and percentages in either a *horizontal* or *vertical* analysis, or both.

Horizontal Analysis: Here, we compare similar figures from several years' financial statements. For example, we can run down two years' balance sheets and compare the current assets, plant assets, current liabilities, long-term liabilities, etc., on one balance sheet with the similar items on the other and note the amount and percentage increases or decreases for each item. Of course, the comparison can be for more than two years. A number of years may be used, each year being compared with the base year or the immediate preceding year.

Vertical Analysis: Here, we compare component parts to the totals in a single statement. For example, we can determine what percentage each item of expense on the income statement is of the total net sales. Or, we can determine what percentage of the total assets the current assets comprise.

Ratios: Customarily, the *numerator* of the equation is expressed first, then the denominator. For example, fixed assets to equity means fixed assets *divided by* equity. Also, whenever the numerator is the larger figure, there is a tendency to use the word "turnover" for the result.

As indicated above, these techniques are widely used, generally in the course of one analysis.

[¶3603] BALANCE SHEET ANALYSIS

The significance of the balance sheet is that it shows relationships between classes of assets and liabilities. From long experience, businessmen have learned that certain relationships indicate the company is in actual or potential trouble or is in good financial shape. For example, they may indicate that the business is short of working capital, is undercapitalized generally, or has a bad balance between short- and long-term debt.

It must be emphasized that there are no fixed rules concerning the relationships. There are wide variations between industries and even within a single industry. It is often more valuable to measure these relationships against the past history of the same company than to use them in comparison with other businesses. If sharp disparities do show, however, it is usually wise not to ignore them. Many of the so-called "excesses" that in the past have led to recessions often show up in the balance sheets of individual companies. The most important balance sheet ratios and their implications for the business are discussed below.

[¶3603.1] Ratio Of Current Assets to Current Liabilities

The *current ratio* is probably the most widely-used measure of liquidity, i.e., a company's ability to pay its bills. It measures the ability of the business to meet its current liabilities. The current ratio indicates the extent to which the current liabilities are covered. For example, if current assets total $400,000 and current liabilities are $100,000, the current ratio is 4 to 1.

Good current ratios will range from about 2 to almost 4 to 1. However, the ratio will vary widely in different industries. For example, companies which collect quickly on their accounts and do not have to carry very large inventories can usually operate with a smaller current ratio than those companies whose collections are slower and inventories larger.

If current liabilities are subtracted from current assets, the resulting figure is the *working capital* of the company — in other words, the amount of free capital which is immediately available for use in the business. One of the most significant reasons for the failure of small businesses is the lack of working capital, which makes it difficult or impossible for the business to cope with sudden changes in economic conditions.

The details of working capital flow are presented in the two-year comparative Statement of Changes in Financial Position which is now a mandatory part of the financial statements.

An important feature of the ratios to remember is:

When you *decrease* both factors by the *same* amount, you *increase* the ratio:

	OLD	CHANGE	NEW
Current Assets	$100,000	$(25,000)	$75,000
Current Liabilities	50,000	(25,000)	25,000
Working Capital	$ 50,000	—0—	$50,000
Ratio	2 to 1		3 to 1

By paying off $25,000 worth of liabilities (depleting Cash), you have increased the ratio to *3 to 1* from *2 to 1*. Note that the *dollar* amount of *working capital* remains the same $50,000.

Conversely, should you borrow $50,000 on short-terms (increasing Cash and Current Liabilities), you would *reduce* the ratio to *1½ to 1* ($150,000/100,000), again with the dollar amount of working capital remaining at $50,000.

A variation of the current ratio is the *acid test*. This is the ratio of *quick assets* (cash, marketable securities, and accounts receivable) to *current liabilities*. This ratio eliminates the inventory from the calculation, since inventory may not be readily convertible to cash.

[¶3603.2]   Ratio of Current Liabilities to Stockholders' Equity

This ratio measures the relationship between the short-term creditors of the business and the owners. Excessive short-term debt is frequently a danger sign, since it means that the short-term creditors are providing much or all of the company's working capital. If anything happens to concern the short-term creditors, they will demand immediate repayment and create the risk of insolvency. Short-term creditors are most often suppliers of the business, and the company's obligation to them is listed under accounts payable. However, short-term creditors may also include short-term lenders.

A general rule occasionally cited for this ratio is that for a business with a tangible capital and earnings (net worth) of less than $250,000, current liabilities should not exceed two-thirds of this tangible net worth. For companies having a tangible net worth over $250,000, current liabilities should not exceed three-fourths of tangible net worth.

Tangible net worth is used instead of total net worth because intangible assets (such as patents and copyrights) may have no actual market value if the company is forced to offer them in distress selling.

[¶3603.3]   Ratio of Total Liabilities to Stockholders' Equity

The ratio differs from the preceding one in that it includes only long-term liabilities. Since the long-term creditors of a company are normally not in a position to demand immediate payment, as are short-term creditors, this ratio may be moderately greater than the preceding one without creating any danger for the company. However, the ratio should never exceed 100%. If it did, this would mean that the company's creditors have a larger stake in the enterprise than the owners themselves. Under such circumstances, it is very likely that credit would not be renewed when the existing debts matured.

[¶3603.4] Ratio of Fixed Assets to Stockholders' Equity

The purpose of this ratio is to measure the relationship between fixed and current assets. The ratio is obtained by dividing the book value of the fixed assets by the tangible value of stockholders' equity. A rule sometimes used is that if tangible net worth is under $250,000, fixed assets should not exceed two-thirds of tangible net worth. If tangible net worth is over $250,000, fixed assets should not exceed three-fourths of tangible net worth.

[¶3603.5] Ratio of Fixed Assets to Long-Term Liabilities

Since long-term notes and bonds are often secured by mortgages on fixed assets, a comparison of the fixed assets with the long-term liabilities reveals what "coverage" the note or bondholders have — i.e., how much protection they have for their loans by way of security. Furthermore, where the fixed assets exceed the long-term liabilities by a substantial margin, there is room for borrowing additional long-term funds on the strength of the fixed asset position.

[¶3603.6] Ratio of Cost of Goods Sold to Inventory— Inventory Turnover

One of the most frequent causes of business failure is lack of inventory control. A firm that is optimistic about future business, may build up its inventory to greater than usual amounts. Then, if the expected business does not materialize, the company will be forced to stop further buying and may also have difficulty paying its creditors. In addition, if a company is not selling off its inventory regularly, that item, or part of it, is not really a *current* asset. Also, there may be a considerable amount of unsalable inventory included in the total. For all these reasons, a business is interested in knowing how often the inventory "turns over" during the year. In other words, how long will the current inventory be on the shelves, and how soon will it be turned into money?

To find out how often inventory turns over, we compare the average inventory to the cost of goods sold shown on the income statement. (Typically, average is computed by adding opening and closing inventories and dividing the total by two.) For example, if average inventory is $2,000,000 and cost of goods sold adds up to $6,000,000, we have in the course of the year paid for three times the average inventory. So we can say the inventory turned over three times, and at year-end we had about a four months' supply of inventory on hand.

Another way to measure the same results is by using the ratio of net sales to inventory. In this ratio, net sales is substituted for cost of goods sold. Since net sales will always be a larger figure (because it includes the business's profit margin), the resulting inventory turnover will be a higher figure.

[¶3603.7] Ratio of Inventory to Working Capital

This is another ratio to measure over- or under-inventory. Working capital is current assets minus current liabilities. If inventory is too high a proportion of working capital, the business is short on quick assets — cash and accounts receivable. A general rule for this ratio is that businesses of tangible net worth of less than $250,000 should not have an inventory which is more than three-fourths of net working capital. For a business with tangible net worth in excess of $250,000, inventory should not exceed net working capital. The larger-size business can tolerate a condition where there are no quick assets because its larger inventory can be borrowed against; in addition, it presumably has fixed assets which can be mortgaged if necessary.

[¶3603.8]   Average Collection Period

An important consideration for any business is the length of time it takes to collect its accounts receivable. The longer accounts receivable are outstanding, the greater the need for the business to raise working capital from other sources. In addition, a longer collection period increases the risk of bad debts. A general rule for measuring the collection period is that it should not be more than one-third greater than the net selling terms offered by the company. For example, if goods are sold on terms of 30 days net, the average collection period should be about 40 days, though this varies from industry to industry. Special rules apply in the case of installment selling.

Another way of measuring the collection rate of accounts receivable is to divide the net sales by the average accounts receivable. This gives us the accounts receivable turnover; i.e., how many times during the year the average accounts receivable were collected. A comparison with prior years reveals whether the company's collection experience is getting better or worse.

[¶3603.9]   Ratio of Net Sales to Stockholders' Equity

A company acquires assets in order to produce sales which yield a profit. If tangible assets yield too few sales, the company is suffering from underselling; i.e., the under-utilization of its assets. On the other hand, the company may suffer from overtrading; i.e., too many sales in proportion to its tangible net worth. In other words, there is too heavy a reliance on borrowed funds to generate sales.

Another way of measuring the effective utilization of assets is to determine the ratio of net sales to total assets (excluding long-term investments).

In either case, comparisons of these ratios with similar ratios of other companies in the same industry can indicate the relative efficiency in utilization of assets of the company being analyzed.

[¶3603.10]   Ratio of Net Sales to Working Capital

This is similar to the preceding ratio, since it measures the relationship between sales and assets. In this case, the ratio measures whether the company has sufficient net current assets to support the volume of its sales or, on the other hand, if the capital invested in working capital is working hard enough to produce sales.

[¶3603.11]   Book Value of the Securities

This figure represents the value of the outstanding securities according to the values shown on the company's books. This may have little relationship to market value—especially in the case of common stock. Nevertheless, book value is an important test of financial strength. It is computed by simply substracting all liabilities from total assets. The remaining sum represents the book value of the equity interest in the business. In computing this figure, it is a good idea to include only tangible assets — land, machinery, inventory, etc. A patent right or other tangible may be given a large dollar value on the balance sheet, but in the event of liquidation may not be salable at all. The theory underlying the measurement of book value is that it is a good measure of how much cash and credit the company may be able to raise if it comes upon bad times. Book value is usually expressed per share outstanding.

Book value is also an important measure for the bondholders of the company. For them, the value has the significance of telling them how many dollars per bond outstanding the company has in available assets. Since they have a call on the company's assets before either the preferred stockholders or the common stockholders, a substantial book value per bond in excess of the face amount of the bond offers relative assurance of the safety of the bond — assurance that funds will be available to pay off the bonds when they become due. To find the book value of the bonds, add together the total stockholders' equity and the amount of the bonds outstanding.

For example, stockholders' equity totals $5 million. Bonded indebtedness is $2 million. From this $7 million total we subtract $1 million of intangibles. That leaves $6 million. This represents a coverage of three times the total bond indebtedness, usually a fairly substantial coverage.

[¶3603.12] Ratio of Long-Term Debt to Equity

This ratio measures the leverage potential of the business; that is, the varying effects which changes in operating profits will have on net profits. The rule is that the higher the debt ratio, the greater will be the effect on the common stock of changes in earnings because of increased interest expenses.

Many security analysts feel that in an industrial company equity should equal at least half the total of all equity and debt outstanding. Railroads and utilities, however, are likely to have more debt (and preferred stock) than common stock because of the heavy investments in fixed assets, much of which is financed by the use of debt and preferred stock.

[¶3603.13] Earnings Per Share (EPS)

Probably, the most important ratio used today is the earnings per share (EPS) figure. It is a *mandatory* disclosure on all annual financial (income) statements (for public companies) and mandatory for all interim statements (though unaudited) for public companies. Moreover, the EPS must be broken out separately for extraordinary items. The standards of calculation are quite complex where preferred stock, options and convertibility are involved.

The Accounting Section of this book discusses the factors involved in the computation and disclosure of a complex stock structure.

Basically, the EPS is the net income divided by the number of outstanding shares (including equivalent shares which are treated on an ''as-if-issued'' basis).

Investor reaction to the EPS figure — how it compares with other companies, with its own prior history, with the other investment choices (bonds, commodities, bank accounts, treasury notes, etc.)—is considered to be one of the significant factors in setting the market price of the stock, second only to dividends actually paid.

[¶3603.14] Return on Equity

This ratio is another method of determining earning power. Here, the opening Equity (Capital Stock plus Retained Earnings, plus or minus any other equity-section items) is divided into the net income for the year to give the percentage earned on that year's investment.

[¶3603.15] Return to Investors

This is a relatively new ratio used mostly by financial publications, primarily for comparison of many companies in similar industries. The opening equity is divided into the sum of the dividends paid plus the market price appreciation of the period. In addition, the ratio is sometimes extended to cover five years, ten years or more.

[¶3604] INCOME STATEMENT ANALYSIS

Just as with the balance sheet, most of the figures obtained from the income statement acquire real meaning only by comparison with other figures — either with similar figures of previous years of the same company or with the corresponding figures of other companies in the same or similar business.

For example, we could compare each significant item of expense and cost with net sales and get a percentage of net sales (vertical analysis) which we could then compare with other companies. Percentages are more meaningful to compare than absolute dollar amounts since the volume of business done by other companies in the same industry may vary substantially from the volume of our company.

We could also compare each of the significant figures on the income statement with the same figures for prior years (horizontal analysis). Here, too, comparisons of percentages rather than absolute dollar amounts might be more meaningful if the volume of sales has varied substantially from year to year.

Other significant comparisons are covered in the following paragraphs.

[¶3604.1] Sales Growth

The raw element of profit growth is an increase in sales (or revenues when the company's business is services). While merely increasing sales is no guarantee that higher profits will follow, it is usually the first vital step, so in analyzing a company, check the sales figures for the past four or five years. If they have been rising and there is no reason to believe the company's markets are near the saturation point, it is reasonable to assume that the rise will continue.

When a company's sales have jumped by the acquisition of another firm, it is important to find out if the acquisition was accomplished by the issuance of additional common stock, by the assumption of additional debt, or for cash. If the company paid by common stock and if the acquired firm's earnings are the same on a per-share basis as those of the acquiring firm, the profit picture remains exactly as it was before. The additional sales growth is balanced by the *dilution of the equity* — that is, the larger number of shares now sharing in the earnings.

The situation is quite different if the purchase was for cash or in exchange of bonds or preferred stock. Here, no dilution of the common stock has occurred. The entire profits of the new firm (minus the interest which must be paid on the new debt or the interest formerly earned on the cash) benefit the existing shareholders.

In any event, acquisitions of new companies often require a period of consolidation and adjustment and frequently are followed by a decreased rate of sales growth.

Consideration should be given to the effect of inflation on sales. A situation can exist where the increase in sales may be caused by the increase in prices. The result may be that unit sales have dropped in relation to the previous year's, but the dollar sales have increased. Comparing unit sales may be a better method of ascertaining the sales increase under certain circumstances.

[¶3604.2]   Computing Operating Profit

A company's costs of operations fall into two groups: *cost of goods sold* and *cost of operations*. The first relates to all the costs of producing the goods or services matched to the revenues produced by those costs. The second includes all other costs not directly associated with the production costs, such as selling and administrative costs (usually called period expenses).

Subtracting both of these groups of costs from sales leaves *operating profit*. Various special costs and special forms of income are then added or subtracted from operating income to get *net income before taxes*. After deducting state and federal income taxes, the final figure (which is commonly used for computing the profit per share) is *net income*. When analyzing a company, however, you will often be most interested in the operating profit figure, since this reflects the real earning capacity of the company.

The best way to look at cost figures is as a percentage of sales. Thus, a company may spend 90 cents out of every dollar in operating costs. We say its cost percentage is 90% or, more commonly, its operating profit margin is 10%. Profit margins vary a great deal among industries, running anywhere from 1% to 20% of sales, so don't compare companies in different industries. The trend of the operating profit margin for a particular company, however, will give an excellent picture of how well management is able to control costs. If sales increases are obtained only by cutting prices, this will immediately show as a decrease in the margin of profit. In introducing a new product it is sometimes necessary to incur special costs to make initial market penetration, but this should be only temporary.

The most used, examined and discussed ratio within a company is the Gross Profit Ratio. More significance is probably attached to this ratio than to any other, because increases usually indicate improved performance (more sales, more efficient production) and decreases indicate weaknesses (poor selling effort, waste in production, weak inventory controls).

The terminology in the gross profit percentages is sometimes confusing and misinterpreted, especially when the word "markup" is used. As an example:

	$	%
Sales	$ 100	100%
Cost of Sales	80	80%
Gross Profit	$ 20	20%

In conventional usage, there is a 20% Gross Profit or Margin on the sale (20/100)

However, if we were to determine the *markup*, the Cost of Sales is the denominator and the Gross Profit is the numerator (20/80 equals a 25% markup)

Sometimes, we start with Gross Profit *percentage desired;* we want to gross 20%, so what should the selling price be? (The only known factor is Cost).

	%	Known	As calculated
Selling price	100%	?	$ 150
Cost	80%	$ 120	120
Gross Profit	20%	?	$ 30

Selling price is always 100%. If cost is $120 and is equal to 80% of the selling price (it must be 80% because we've set a gross of 20%), divided $120 *by* 80% to get the 100% selling price of $150.

[¶3605]   EVALUATION OF FINANCIAL RATIOS

While most ratios are valuable in measuring the financial excellence of a business, certain ratios will be emphasized for particular purposes. The more common purposes for which ratios are used are the following:

[¶3605.1]   Management Evaluation

Management's primary interest is efficient use of the company's assets. Management will be particularly interested in the turnover ratios, such as the inventory turnover and the relationship of working capital to total sales. To the extent that assets are not being used efficiently, the company is overinvesting and consequently is realizing a smaller return than possible on its equity. On the other hand, excessive turnover is dangerous because it puts the company in an extremely vulnerable position. Management will also be particularly interested in trend relationships shown in the income statement for the past few years. Excessive selling expenses may indicate that commissions or other payments are out of line with the market. Management will also make a comparison between the company and its competitors in all areas to indicate where improvement in operations should be expected.

[¶3605.2]   Short-Term Creditors

A lender from whom short-term loans are sought will be particularly interested in the current ratio, since this is a measure of the borrower's ability to meet current debt and his margin of working capital. Also important is the net-worth-to-debt ratio, which shows the relationship of the stockholders' investments to funds contributed by trade creditors and others. It shows ability to stand up under pressure of debt. The sales-to-receivables ratio (net annual sales divided by outstanding trade receivables) shows the relationship of sales volume to uncollected receivables and indicates the liquidity of the receivables on the balance sheet. Another important ratio to the short-term lender is cost of sales to inventory, which shows how many times the company turns over its inventory. Among other things, this shows whether inventories are fresh and salable and helps evaluate the liquidation value of such inventory.

[¶3605.3]   Long-Term Creditors

Since the long-term lender is looking some periods ahead, he wants to be convinced, above all, that the company's earnings will continue at least at the same level. In addition, he will study the various working capital ratios to determine if the company will have sufficient cash when needed to amortize the debt. The ratio of total liabilities to the stockholders' equity is important because the long-term lender wants to be sure that the shareholder has a sufficient stake in the business. One ratio which is used almost solely by the long-term lender is the number of times fixed charges are earned. Fixed charges represent the interest payments on the lender's debt as well as any debt which has priority over it. When total earnings of the company are divided by total fixed charges (including preferred stock dividends, if any), the resulting figure represents the number of times fixed charges are earned.

[¶3605.4]   Stockholders

While stockholders are interested in the excellence of the company as a whole, they will tend to think in terms of per-share figures. Of these, probably the most important is the dividend return, since this represents the actual income which the stockholder will receive. For many years now, there has been greater emphasis on growth companies and capital appreciation, and far less emphasis on dividends. Consequently, to a stockholder in a growth company, earnings per share is a far more important figure than dividends. Investors who seek ''bargain'' situations will be on the lookout for stocks which sell at a price equal to or lower than book value per share. In theory, the liquidating value of such a company is at least equal to the price paid for the stock. An even more restrictive test is a stock which is selling at a price equal to net working capital per share. In such a company, the liquid assets alone are equal to the market value of the shares.

[¶3606]   CASH FLOW

The term "cash flow" refers to a variety of concepts, but its most common meaning in financial literature is the same as "funds derived from operations." The *concept* of cash flow can be used effectively as one of the major factors in judging the ability to meet debt retirement requirements, to maintain regular dividends, to finance replacement and expansion costs, etc.

In no sense, however, can the amount of cash flow be considered to be a substitute for, or an improvement upon, the net income as an indiciation of the results of operations or the change in financial position.

[¶3606.1]   Importance of Cash Flow

The concept of cash flow has been originated by security analysts. It has been stated that in evaluating the investment value of a company, cash flow is frequently regarded as more meaningful than net income as a measure of a company's ability to finance expansion without undue borrowing or holding back payment of dividends.

In using cash flow as an analytic tool, care is required. For example, Corporation X has been capitalized with straight common stock. Corporation Y, the same size as Corporation X and comparable in other respects, has been capitalized 25% with common stock and 75% with debt. A cash flow equivalent to, say, 20% of each corporation's gross sales will seem to be four times as large in relation to Corporation Y's stock when compared with the common stock of Corporation X. Cash flow as a meaningful tool, therefore, will have more significance when related to industries and companies in which long-term debt is limited.

One valid point in using cash flow is to put the profit margin squeeze into proper perspective. One of the most rapidly increasing costs is the depreciation charged against newly acquired plants and equipment. The use of accelerated methods of depreciation has created huge depreciation deductions which reduce profits. At the same time, accelerated depreciation creates additional cash flow and encourages further spending for facilities. In the opinion of some financial authorities, a showing of relatively high cash flow per dollar of capitalization is some compensation for a poor showing of net income per dollar of capitalization.

High cash flow is also the reason that some companies with relatively poor earnings per share are able to continue paying cash dividends per share; sometimes in excess of earnings. In addition to profits, the extractive industries get cash flow through depletion allowances, drilling writeoffs and amortization of development costs and depreciation.

Cash flow also helps analysts judge whether debt commitments can be met without refinancing, whether the regular cash dividend can be maintained despite ailing earnings, whether the extractive industries (i.e., oils and mining) will be able to continue exploration without raising additional capital, or whether additional facilities can be acquired without increasing debt or present capital.

Relative cash flow is an important factor in deciding whether to buy or lease. But it's not necessarily true that owning property creates funds for use in expansion. The cash made available to a corporation through operations will be similar whether the business property is owned or leased. Owned property acquired by borrowed capital will require periodic payments on the debt which will have to be met before funds are available for expansion.

37

The Securities and Exchange Commission

[¶3701]   ORGANIZATION AND OPERATION

In today's world of regulated business, it is important for accountants to have a working knowledge of the rules and regulations influencing SEC accounting.

In the late 1920s there was widespread speculation in the stock market. When the market crashed in 1929, the public demanded protective action from their legislators. Congressional committees held hearings into all phases of the securities industry, investment banking, and commercial banking activities prior to the market crash. As a result of these hearings, eight Federal statutes were enacted between 1933 and 1940 (with a ninth in 1970), bringing the securities markets and the securities business under federal jurisdiction. These laws are referenced as the "truth in securities" statutes. They include the Securities Act of 1933, the Securities Exchange Act of 1934, the Public Utility Holding Company Act of 1935, the Maloney Amendment to the Securities Exchange Act of 1934, and the Federal Bankruptcy Code. Also included are the Trust Indenture Act of 1939, the Investment Company Act of 1940, the Investment Advisers Act of 1940, the Securities Investor Protection Act (SPIC) of 1970, and the Securities Act Amendments of 1975.

[¶3701.1]   Truth in Securities Laws

The objectives of the laws are twofold. First is the protection of investors and the public against fraudulent acts and practices in the purchase and sale of securities. The second objective is to regulate trading in the national securities markets. For example:

1. "To provide full and fair disclosure of the character of securities sold in interstate and foreign commerce and through the mails, and to prevent fraud in the sale thereof, and for other purposes." (Securities Act of 1933.)

2. "To provide for the regulation of securities exchanges and the over-the-counter markets operating in interstate and foreign commerce and through the mails, to prevent inequitable and unfair practices on such exchanges and markets, and for other purposes." (Securities Exchange Act of 1934.)

3. "To provide for the registration and regulation of investment companies and investment advisers, and for other purposes." (Investment Company Act of 1940 and the Investment Advisers Act of 1940.)

[¶3702] SEC REPORTING
THE INTEGRATED DISCLOSURE SYSTEM

Overview: In September, 1980, the SEC adopted rules implementing an Integrated Disclosure System (hereinafter "IDS"). SEC registrants must follow the new rules in their Form 10-K report, certain other SEC filings, and in their annual reports to shareholders (hereinafter "annual report").

The new rules are lengthy and involved an extensive revision of Regulation S-X and commonly used SEC formats. The result is symmetry and consistency of financial statements and other disclosures among many public reports and filings.

An Historical Note: For years, the SEC researched and studied ways by which a single comprehensive financial reporting system could be achieved, not only between the 1933 and 1934 Securities Act, but also between these Acts and the annual shareholder report. It is this effort which led to the IDS.

To understand why the need developed for an IDS, an understanding of SEC registration and reporting form genesis may be helpful. Many 1933 Act registration forms were spawned in response either to the nature of the offering (e.g., stock option plans on Form S-8), or by virtue of the status of the offeror (e.g., Form S-7). Financial statement periods and content varied considerably among the many filings (forms). These differences developed over a long period of time by an evolutionary process as different perceived needs arose, even though the 1933 Act relates simplistically to the same transaction—the public sale of securities. With the passage of time since the enactment of the 1933 Act, a proliferation of SEC regulations, rules, reports, registration statement forms, and amendments to the Act occurred.

In the first 30 years of the SEC's existence, annual reports were exclusively a product of management decision. Until the early 1970's, the shareholder report financial statements were governed by Generally Accepted Accounting Principles (GAAP).

In the 1970s, however, the SEC added significantly to the shareholder report content by requiring disclosures such as a five-year summary of earnings and Management's Discussion and Analysis. Financial statements were expanded to include additional information such as quarterly operating data. Notwithstanding, the annual report to shareholders and the Form 10-K were typified as much by differences as by similarities. Since the differences were expanding and increasingly confusing, as well as compliance becoming increasingly expensive, an evaluation by the SEC of over 40 years of diverse rulemaking became necessary. The new IDS attempts to minimize these differences by achieving an interrelation among public financial reports.

For the SEC to achieve its goal of symmetry, a central framework of disclosure was necessary. SEC developed this framework only after evaluation of all elements of mandatory reporting (e.g., Regulation S-X, periodic filings, and shareholder reports) together with disclosures required by GAAP. This framework had to be adequate not only for annual reports, but also to meet the diverse disclosure requirements of the SEC—whether for the public sale of securities (1933 Act requirements) or for the Form 10-K annual report (1934 Act requirements).

Briefly, the IDS is based upon a "Basic Information Package" consisting of:

- Audited financial statements.
- Management's Discussion and Analysis.
- Selected income and balance sheet data.

This *Package* is common to the annual report, Form 10-K, and most 1933 Act filings

[¶3702.1]   Changes Affecting Independent Auditors

The significant changes affecting the independent auditor concern the financial statements appearing in the annual report to shareholders. Formerly, the SEC had no authority over the annual report; the statements in the annual report, therefore, did not have to conform to Regulation S-X (but, of course, had to comply with GAAP). The new S-K requirements now govern the annual report. This was accomplished by the requirement that all financial statements presented in annual reports must conform to the S-X accounting and disclosure requirements.

For example, and among other major changes, a shareholder report:

- Must contain three-year comparative financial statements prepared in conformity with Regulation S-X.
- A majority of the Board of Directors must sign the Form 10-K.
- Management's Discussion and Analysis is expanded, materially.

There are two significant consequences resulting from the requirements of the IDS. *First,* the SEC financial statement disclosure requirements will in many instances add considerable volume and detail to the filings. *Second,* the prior distinction between GAAP and S-X compliance disclosures will be thoroughly submerged. Historically, GAAP has been conceptually oriented, and the SEC often applied GAAP concepts as a springboard to specific S-X disclosures by applying rigid materiality criteria (most of which have been retained). Formerly, any audited financial statement disclosures appearing only in an SEC filing presumptively was an S-X compliance disclosure and not a GAAP requirement. This distinction disappears. GAAP no longer will be pristinely visible.

[¶3702.2]   The S-X Revisions

In order to reach the objective of uniformity of financial statements content, the SEC significantly revised S-X to bring the S-X requirements into conformity and consistency with GAAP.

• Transferring some of the information formerly required in the financial reports into schedules, which are not included in the annual report (but are included in the 10-K).

• Rules that duplicated GAAP have been deleted from the SEC rules.

• Obsolete S-X rules have been deleted.

• New disclosure rules have been added because of their informational value to the investing public, irrespective of the fact they may exceed GAAP requirements.

• Existing rules have been clarified, modified, and condensed.

A significant revision of the rules relates to the standardization of the financial statements in the individual forms. Article 3 of S-X are the general instructions for financial statement presentation in all disclosure documents. These uniform instructions require:

• Audited balance sheets as of the end of each of the *two* most recent fiscal years.

• Audited statements of income and changes in financial position for each of the *three* most recent fiscal years preceding the date of the *most recent* audited balance sheet being filed.

(NOTE: These requirements do not apply to Form S-18 which has been developed for "small business" offerings.)

[¶3702.3]   Aging

The new aging requirements synchronize with the time frame for a 10-K filing (within 90 days after the end of the registrant's fiscal year). Continuous updating synchronizes with the quarterly report Form 10-Q, which must be filed with the SEC within 45 days after the end of each of the first three (but not the fourth) fiscal quarters.

Interim statement requirements closely follow 10-Q requirements.

For registration statements, the SEC adopted 135 days as the critical date for determining the aging of financial statements at the expected effective date of the registration statement, or proposed mailing date of a proxy statement, which includes financial statements. Registration statements which are filed and are to become effective 90 days after the end of the fiscal year, but *before* the 135th day, must include audited balance sheets for the last two fiscal years and the three-year income and changes in financial position statements. If the filing or expected effective date is 135 days *or more* after the end of the fiscal year, they must be updated with an unaudited interim balance sheet as of a date within 135 days of filing, and expected effective date and unaudited income and changes in financial condition statements for the interim period, and for the corresponding period of the preceding year must be included.

[¶3702.4]   The Basic Information Package (BIP)

The new financial disclosure rule is termed the Basic Information Package (hereinafter BIP). The requirements of the BIP are common to Forms S-1, S-2, S-3, 10-K, and to the annual report to shareholders. The few differences are in the presentation of the financial information on the registration forms, i.e.:

Form S-1. The Form requires complete disclosure to be set forth in the prospectus, and permits *no* incorporation by reference. Form S-1 is to be used by registrant in the Exchange Act reporting system for less than three years.

Form S-2. Information can either be presented in the prospectus or in the most recent annual report, with the annual report delivered with the prospectus to shareholders. In the latter option, information is incorporated by reference *from* the annual report *into* the prospectus.

Form S-3. Information can be incorporated by reference *from* the 10-K.

[¶3702.5]   What Does the BIP Include?

Broadly, the Package requires information that the SEC considers to be essential for user decision making. Specifically, the following items constitute the substance of the BIP:

• Five years of comparative financial information.

• Management's Discussion and Analysis (MD&A) of the company's financial condition and results of operations.

• Information explaining the circumstances associated with a change in the registrant's independent auditor during the prior two fiscal years, if the change resulted from a disagreement on accounting practices and disclosure matters, or auditing scope or procedures.

- A description of the registrant's business and specified segmental information.

- Market and dividend record.

- Any material information necessary for a prudent investor to make an investment decision. Particularly, emphasis must be placed upon adverse information. "The SEC, in accord with the congressional purposes, specifically requires *prominent* emphasis be given in filed registration statements and prospectuses to *material adverse* contingencies." (Italics provided).

[¶3702.6]   Projections and Forward-Looking Information

Historically, the SEC has been opposed to projections and forecasts by registrants in their filings and annual reports. Over the years, however, there has been an increasingly widespread use of projections, estimates, forecasts, and other forward-looking information by private securities research organizations, with the projections based upon information originated with management in the first place.

Starting in 1963 with a *Special Study* reported to Congress, there have been a number of studies of this issue by various committees. Finally, in 1978, the SEC decided that as a practical matter the Commission should approve forward looking information because such information had become widely used. Accordingly, Securities Act Release No. 5992 and Securities Exchange Act Release No. 15305, both dated November 7, 1978, reads:

> "In light of the significance attached to projection information and the prevalence of projections in the corporate and investment community, the Commission has determined to follow the recommendation of the Advisory Committee and wishes to encourage companies to disclose management projections both in their filings with the Commission and in general."

[¶3707.7]   The Safe Harbor Rule

Concurrently, with the adoption of the forward looking rule, the Commission adopted a "safe harbor" rule which protects the registrant and independent auditor from lawsuits for a subsequently proved inaccurate projection *if* the projection was made in a:

> "good faith assessment of a registrant's performance" and that management "must have a reasonable basis for such assessment."

What is the significance of the safe harbor rule? It means that the plaintiff must carry the burden of proof to establish that the forecasts and projections did *not* have a reasonable basis, or were *not* disclosed in good faith. Heretofore, for the most part, the burden of proof was upon the defendants (the registrant, accountants, attorneys, and other signatories) to prove that they had, in fact, a reasonable basis for the projections, and had disclosed them in good faith.

[¶3702.8] The Information Covered By The Financial Forecasts Safe Harbor Rule

- Projections of revenues.
- Projections of earnings (losses).
- Projections of capital expenditures.
- Projections of dividend payments.
- Projections of capital structure and other financial items.
- Statements of management's plans and objectives.
- Statements of future economic performance in the MD&A.
- Disclosed assumptions underlying or relating to any of the projected financial information.

> NOTE: It should be clear that the Commission "encourages" forward-looking information; it is not required in either an SEC filing nor in the registrant's annual report.
>
> Also, the independent auditor does not have to certify the forward-looking information as presented by the management. However, the auditor must be mindful that many of the projections will be based upon certified information in the statements. Therefore, the auditor should take care to review management's forward-looking statements for consistency with the financial information in the certified statements.

The pages of SEC Release No. 33-6383, the Integrated Disclosure System, as appears in the Federal Register follow. Only the rules relevant to the independent accountant's responsibilities are reprinted here. The balance of the Release concern attorneys and legal matters only.

The information should be rigorously reviewed by the accountant because the new rules determine the accountant's preparation and presentation of the registrant's financial data.

[¶3703]　　　　　　SEC FORMS

The forms specify the financial and other information to be included in a filing and how the forms are to be prepared. The most frequently used forms are:

1. Form 10-K, the annual report structured as follows:
   a) Part I—Business, properties, legal proceedings, security ownership of certain beneficial owners and management.
   b) Part II—Market for the registrant's common stock and related security holders matters; selected financial data; management's

discussion and analysis; financial statements and supplementary data.

c) Part III—Directors and executive officers of the company; management remuneration and transactions.

d) Part IV—Exhibits, financial statement schedules and reports on Form 8-K.

2. Forms S-1, S-2, S-3. Required for new securities issues.

3. Form S-8. For employee benefit plans.

4. Form S-15. For certain business combinations.

5. Form S-16. For certain primary and secondary offerings.

6. Form S-18. For certain smaller offerings.

7. Form 10. For registration of securities traded over the counter.

8. Form 8-K. A current report to be filed after the occurrence of events expected to affect the company's operating results.

9. Form 10-Q. Quarterly report to the SEC.

[¶3703.1] Forms S-1, S-2, S-3

A significant part of the Integrated Disclosure System and revision of the rules was the adoption by the Commission of three new registration forms. These new Forms S-1, S-2, S-3 replace forms S-1, S-7 and S-16. The differences in the new forms related primarily to the extent that required information is actually delivered to potential investors.

New Form S-3: An abbreviated form, relies on the "efficient market theory"—information about companies using this form is already known or is so readily available it need not be repeated in a prospectus. The criteria for its use are designed to be indicative of a company's following in the market. The form allows maximum use of incorporation by reference of 1934 Act reports (contains minimal prospectus disclosure requirements). The qualifications for use of Form S-3 are:

• A registrant must have $150 million in *voting* stock held by holders not affiliated with the company.

• Or, registrant's having $100 million in voting stock and an annual trading volume in the stock market of 3 million, or more, shares.

The aggregate market value of the registrant's outstanding voting stock is computed by use of the price at which the stock was last sold, or the average of the bid and asked prices of the stock, as of a date within 60 days prior to the date of filing. Annual trading volume is the volume of shares traded in any continuous twelve-month period ended within 60 days prior to the date of filing.

Form S-3 also may be used for certain primary offerings of investment grade nonconvertible debt securities, secondary offerings other than by the issuer, offerings for dividend and interest reinvestment plans, and for exercise of certain conversions and warrants.

New Form S-2: This form is available for the registration of securities to be offered to a "middle range" of public companies. The qualifications for the use of Form S-2 are:

• The registrant has filed reports with the Commission for at least 36 calendar months immediately preceding the filing of the registrations statement (yet whose securities are not actively followed in the market to meet the test of Form S-3).

• The registrant has filed in a timely manner all reports required to be filed during the 12 calendar months immediately preceding the filing of the registration statement.

• Neither the registrant nor any of its consolidated or unconsolidated subsidiaries have, since the end of their last fiscal year for which certified financial statements of the registrant and its consolidated subsidiaries were included in a report: a) failed to pay any dividend or sinking fund installment on preferred stock; b) defaulted on any rental installment or installments on indebtedness for borrowed money; c) defaulted on any rental on one or more long-term leases, which defaults in the aggregate are material to the financial position of the registrant and its consolidated and unconsolidated subsidiaries, taken as a whole.

Form S-2 combines incorporation by reference of 1934 Act reports and delivery of the annual report to shareholders with the prospectus.

New Form S-1: This form is used for registration of securities of all issuers "for which no other form is authorized or prescribed, except that the form is not used for securities of foreign governments or political subdivisions thereof."

New Form S-1 is very similar to old Form S-1. New Form S-1 must be used by registrants in the 1934 Act reporting system for less than three years, and also may be used by any registrants who choose to do so, or for whom no other form in the reporting system is available. This Form requires complete disclosure to be set forth in the Prospectus and permits *no incorporation by reference.*

New Form S-1 is governed entirely by Regulation S-K for its nonfinancial substantive disclosure provisions. The Prospectus must include information about the registrant as is required to be reported in an annual report on Form 10-K. This information includes:

• The basic information package.

• The full Regulation S-K descriptions of business, properties, and legal proceedings.

• S-K disclosures with respect to management and security holders.

• All other S-K items where appropriate.

Regulation S-X: This regulation covers the form and content of financial statements filed with the SEC. Regulation S-X also covers the qualifications of accountants who report on financial statements and schedules filed with SEC.

Financial Reporting Releases: FRR's are a part of Regulation S-X which are issued periodically by the SEC. These releases cover individual topics concerning accounting requirements and reporting practices. The releases also give guidelines and examples of situations involving the independence of accountants.

The SEC has also developed a new release: Accounting and Auditing Enforcement Releases (AAER's) which are related to Commission enforcement actions.

[¶3704]   **GOING PUBLIC**

"Going Public" is a significant step in the business life of any company. It is a step which should be taken only after a rigorous appraisal of the advantages, disadvantages, consequences, and other sources of financing. Going public is an expensive means of raising capital, so the benefits must more than outweigh the disadvantages.

When considering a public offering, planning should begin long in advance. Many of the decisions associated with a first stock offering require a long period of time to implement. A well-planned public offering, therefore, requires the preliminary studies and implementing procedures to begin sometimes years before the securities are offered to the investing public.

The listing that follows are some of the more common advantages and disadvantages of going public. Following the listing are brief generalizations of the requirements and procedures in a public offering of securities.

[¶3704.1]   **Advantages**

1. Funds are obtained from the offering. When the securities are sold by the company, the money can be used for working capital, research and development of new products, plant and equipment expansion, retiring existing indebtedness, and for diversifying the company's operations.

2. Through public ownership of its securities, the company may gain prestige, become better known, and improve the business's operating results.

3. A company's customers and suppliers may become shareholders resulting in increased sales of the company's products or services.

4. Companies often consider expansion by the acquisition of other businesses. A company with publicly-traded stock is in a position to finance acquisitions with its own securities, instead of investing cash.

5. The business may be better able to attract and retain key personnel if it can offer stock having a public market (or options to purchase such stock).

6. A public offering of equity securities will usually improve a company's net worth, enabling the company to borrow capital on more favorable terms.

7. Once a public market is created for a stock and its price performs favorably, additional equity capital can be raised from the public, as well as privately from institutional investors on favorable terms.

8. Private ownership by one or a few persons of a fractional or even all of a closely-held business is an asset with no ready market, usually no market at all. Once the company becomes publicly owned and the after-market becomes well developed, there will be a ready market for even a small number of the majority owners' shares.

[¶3704.2]　Disadvantages

1. Public offerings are expensive, as registration with the SEC requires the retention of various professionals, i.e., investment bankers (underwriters), attorneys, accountants, and perhaps engineers, actuarials, and other experts.

2. Because of their responsibility to the public, the owners of a business lose some flexibility in management. There are practical, if not legal, limitations on salaries, fringe benefits, relatives on the payroll, and on operating procedures and policies. The authority to make decisions quickly may be lost, as many policies require prior approval by a board of directors, and in some instances by a majority of the shareholders.

3. There are many additional expenses and administrative problems for a publicly-owned company. Routine legal and accounting fees can increase materially. Recurring additional expenses include the preparation and distribution of proxy material and annual reports to shareholders, the preparation and filing with the Securities and Exchange Commission of reports required by the Securities Exchange Act of 1934, and the expenditure of fees for a transfer agent, registrar, and usually a public relations consultant. Added to the out-of-pocket costs is the cost in terms of executive time allocated to shareholder relations and public disclosures.

4. The owners of a privately-held business are often in so high a tax bracket that they prefer their company to pay either small dividends, or no dividends at all. The underwriters of an issue will usually require otherwise in order to increase the marketability and distribution of the first-time issue.

5. Once a company is publicly owned, research has demonstrated that management, some to a greater some to a lesser extent, tends to consider the effect on the market price of its stock when considering major decisions that will affect the profits. While it is generally acknowledged that management's preoccupation with day-to-day stock price fluctuations should be avoided, there are undoubtedly situations where a conscientious concern about the shareholders' investment quite properly should limit the decision-making alternatives for the management of a publicly-held company.

6. The one or few owners of a business possibly could be faced with a loss of control of the company if a sufficiently large proportion of the shares are sold to the public. Also, once a company's stock becomes publicly held, dilution of the prior owners' equity interest by subsequent public offerings, secondary financing, and acquisitions must be anticipated.

[¶3704.3]　Evaluating a Company for Public Financing

In evaluating the advisability of going public, as well as pricing the company's stock, the underwriters will consider:

1. The amount and trend of sales and earnings.

2. Present and projected working capital and cash flow.

3. The experience, integrity and quality of the company's management.

4. The growth potential of the business.

5. The nature and number of the customers.

6. The company's suppliers.

7. The company's competitive position in the industry.

[¶3704.4] Selecting an Underwriter

Once the decision has been made to go public, one of the most important decisions to be made is the selection of an underwriter. Investment banking firms vary widely in prestige, financial strength, and ability to provide various services which the company needs. Some underwriters are not interested in first offerings; others specialize in that phase of the underwriting business. Some underwriters specialize in certain industries; the large investment banking firms will usually accept business in all of the major industries. The company's attorneys, auditors, and bankers can be helpful in selecting the underwriter.

[¶3704.5] The Underwriting Agreement

It is customary for the company going public to sign a "letter of intent" for the underwriter. If used, the letter outlines the details and proposed terms of the offering and the underwriter's compensation. It is explicitly written into the agreement that it is not binding upon either party, except there usually is a binding provision spelling out the payment of expenses if one party withdraws from the offering.

[¶3704.6] What Securities to Offer

Once a company has decided to go public, it must determine with the advice of the underwriter what class of securities to offer. Most first offerings are common stock issues. A first offering can consist of a package including other securities, such as debenture bonds which may or may not be convertible into common stock; warrants to purchase common stock can be "attached" to the new offering; preferred stock with a conversion privilege can be included in the package.

[¶3704.7] The Registration Statement*

The registration statement is the disclosure document filed with the SEC that must accompany a registered offering of securities for sale to the public. This "filing" consists of two parts: Part I of the registration statement is the

---

*The SEC has recently adopted new rules (effective April 15, 1982) which significantly reduces the time and expense for "small" and new business enterprises to raise capital. The new Rules 501-506 are incorporated into Regulation D. The important aspect of Regulation D concerns exemption from registration for small offerings and private placements.

The SEC points out in Release No. 33-6389: "Regulation D is the product of the Commission's evaluation of the impact of its rules and regulations on the ability of small businesses to raise capital. This study has revealed a particular concern that the registration requirements and the exemptiive scheme of the Securities Act impose disproportionate restraints on small issuers."

Regulation D is essentially all legal and the text is far too lengthy to review here. Legal services should be retained for Regulation D offerings by small and new businesses.

prospectus, which is the information that must be distributed to the offerees (the investors) of the securities. Part II contains supplemental information about the company of specific interest to the SEC, but which is available for public inspection at the office of the Commission.

[¶3704.8]   Liabilities

It should be emphasized that management is responsible to determine that the factual information in the registration statement is accurate and complete. Management cannot assume a passive interest by relying entirely upon the attorneys and accountants to determine the information to be furnished, verify the information, and prepare the registration statement properly. It is reasonable, however, for management to rely upon counsel, accountants, and other experts associated with the registration for accuracy and completeness of the material in the statement, *assuming* management has properly disclosed factual information to the experts.

Under the Securities Act of 1933 (the governing statute for new security issues) and related statutes and regulations, civil and criminal liability can arise:

1. From material misstatements or omissions in a registration statement, including the final prospectus.
2. From failure to comply with applicable registration requirements.
3. From failing to supply a prospectus in connection with specified activities.
4. From engaging in fraudulent transactions.

Under various provisions of the Securities Act, company officers, directors, underwriters, controlling persons and experts who sign the registration statement are jointly and severally liable, and their civil liability can extend to the full sales price of the security; a criminal offense (fraud) can result in imprisonment for the signatory.

[¶3705]   REGULATION D

[¶3705.1]   Small Business Can Now Go Public

One of the primary sources of financing for small business public securities offerings is venture capital organizations. New venture capital investments have increased significantly in recent years, and the reduction in the capital gains rate in the Economic Recovery Tax Act of 1981 to 20% maximum tax on capital gains encourages risk-taking by venture capital firms. Small business enterprises are a significant investment for venture capital risk-takers. Access to venture capital financing, as well as to the money markets generally through investment bankers, has been made easier for the small entrepreneur by the *Small Business Issuers' Simplification Act* passed by Congress in 1980. The objective of this legislation is to enable small business enterprises to raise funds in the public market, with reduced registration and reporting requirements of the SEC.

In response to the small business legislation, the SEC adopted new rules effective April 15, 1982, which significantly reduces the time and expense for small and new "start-up" enterprises to raise capital. Regulation D was promulgated by the SEC to simplify the procedures for small business enterprises to enter the capital markets.

The SEC points out in Release No. 33-6389:

> Regulation D is the product of the Commission's evaluation of the impact of its rules and regulations on the ability of small businesses to raise capital. This study has revealed a particular concern that the registration requirements and the exemptive scheme of the Securities Act impose disproportionate restraints on small issuers.

The important aspect of Regulation D concerns exemption from registration for small offerings and private placements. The Regulation is implemented by Rules 501-506.

Rule 501: Defines 8 terms used in Regulation D.

1. Accredited investor.
2. Affiliate.
3. Aggregate offering price.
4. Business combination.
5. Calculation of number of purchasers.
6. Executive officer.
7. Issuer.
8. Purchaser representative.

Rule 502: Sets forth the general conditions which apply to the three exemptions under Regulation D. The conditions relate to integration, information requirements, limitation on manner of offerings and limitations on resale.

Rule 503: A uniform notice of sales form, designated Form D, is provided for in this rule. It is available for all offerings exempted by Regulation D. (Form D is reproduced immediately following the reprint of Regulation D.)

Rule 504: Permits any issuer, other than an investment company or an Exchange Act reporting company, to offer and sell a maximum of $500,000 of its securities to an unlimited number of persons during a twelve-month period.

Rule 505: Provides a registration exemption for any noninvestment company issuer, *whether or not* a reporting company under the Exchange Act. An eligible issuer can offer and sell up to $7,500,000 during a twelve-month period without general advertising or general solicitation. An offering under this rule can be made to an unlimited number of accredited investors, and to a maximum of 35 nonaccredited investors.

Rule 506: The transactional exemption provided by this rule does not restrict the dollar amount of securities offered. It is available to any issuer, whether or not a reporting company. A Rule 506 offering can be made to an unlimited number of accredited investors and to a maximum of 35 nonaccredited investors, but where the offering is to nonaccredited investors, the issuer must *reasonably* believe, *prior* to the sale, that each nonaccredited investor, either alone or with a purchaser representative, understands the merits and risks of the offering.

[¶3705.2] Definition of Small Business

In Release 33-6380 (January 28, 1982), the SEC defined the term "small business" or "small organization" as:

> . . . an issuer whose total assets on the last day of its most recent fiscal year were $3,000,000 or less, and that is engaged or proposing to engage in small business financing. An issuer is considered to be engaged or proposing to engage in small business financing . . . if it is conducting or proposes to conduct an offering of securities which does not exceed the dollar limitation prescribed by Section 3(b) of the Securities Act.

[¶3705.3] Form S-18

The qualified start-up company can register on Form S-18 when the total offering is not more than $7,500,000. This form can also be used for the registration of securities of any person other than the issuer (secondary offerings), provided the total offering price of the securities does not exceed $1,500,000, and the total offering price of the securities together with the total offering price of any securities to be sold by the issuer does not exceed $7,500,000.

[¶3705.4] Accountants Form S-18 Responsibilities

Financial Statement Requirements:

• An audited balance sheet for one year. (S-1 requires two years.)

• An audited income statement for two years. (S-1 requires three years.)

• An audited changes in financial position statement for two years. (S-1 requires three years.)

• Financial statements must be as of 90 days of the filing date.

• If a "stub" period (since the end of the last fiscal year) must be used to bring the financial statements into conformity with the 90-day requirement, the stub period can be unaudited, *but* must be presented on a comparative basis with the *same* stub period for the prior year.

• A consolidated balance sheet must be filed as of a date within 90 days prior to the date of filing the registration statement. This balance sheet need not be audited if it is not as of the latest fiscal year. If the balance sheet is not audited, an audited balance sheet must be filed as of a date within one year, unless the fiscal year of the registrant has ended within 90 days prior to the date of the filing, in which case the audited balance sheet may be as of the end of the preceding fiscal year.

• A consolidated balance sheet must be filed as of a date within 90 days prior to the date of filing the registration statement. This balance sheet need not be audited if it is not as of the latest fiscal year. If the balance sheet is not audited, an audited balance sheet must be filed as of a date within one year, unless the fiscal year of the registrant has ended within 90 days prior to the date of the filing, in which case the audited balance sheet may be as of the end of the preceding fiscal year.

• Consolidated statements must be filed of income, statement of changes in financial condition, and statements of other stockholders' equity for each of the two fiscal years preceding the date of the most recent balance sheet being filed and for the interim period, if any, between the end of the most recent of such fiscal years and the date of the most recent balance sheet being filed. These statements shall be audited to the date of the most recent audited balance sheet being filed.

• Aging requirements. Same as those applicable to the financial statements in other registration statements.

Information not required:

• No financial schedules to the financial statements are required.

• Management's Discussion and Analysis is not required because start-up companies have little or no financial history.

• Separate statements of unconsolidated subsidiaries and investees can be omitted.

• An index of financial statements and schedules need not be furnished.

• In general, Form S-18 departs from Regulation S-K requirements by requiring somewhat less detailed disclosures than Form S-1 concerning description of business, properties, officers and directors, legal proceedings, and management remuneration.

The financial statements of a Form S-18 filing do not have to comply with Regulation S-X requirements. However, they *must* be prepared in accordance with generally accepted accounting principles and practices (GAAP).

[¶3706]   SHELF REGISTRATION

Historically, every new security issue by a corporation had to undergo the complete registration process, regardless of how short or long the intervening time period between issues, including new issues of the same security.

The registration and marketing of a new issue is expensive; for a large company the cost of a new issue runs into seven figures.

On March 3, 1982, the SEC issued ASR 306 announcing a temporary rule—Rule 415—which established a procedure permitting "delayed or continuous offerings." The procedure is termed "shelf registration." The essential element in the shelf-registration process gives public corporations permission to register a security whether or not the new issue is to be sold immediately. Subsequent issues of the *same* security can be sold without a new registration for each issue.

[¶3706.1]   The Requirements

• Shelf registrations are limited to primary distributions made at the current market price of the security. Secondary issues do not qualify for shelf registration.

• Forms S-1-2-3- and S-8 (for employee benefit plans) can be shelf-registered, except that primary distribution "at the market" can be made only by S-3 qualified corporations.

(Note: At-the-market is defined by the SEC: "An offering into an existing trading market other than at a fixed price or through the facilities of a national securities exchange or to a market-maker otherwise than on an exchange.")

• There must be a reasonable expectation of selling shelf-registered shares within a two-year period. (The shares do not have to ever be sold, however.)

• The number of shares self-registered cannot exceed 10% of the float (Outstanding Stock) in the class of securities being shelf-registered.

• An underwriter(s) must be involved: 1) to provide an orderly distribution of the issue; 2) to ensure the accuracy of the Prospectus; 3) to assure compliance with the Prospectus delivery requirements.

[¶3706.2]   Purpose

As noted, the registration process is expensive for the issuer. By permitting continuous registration, a corporation will incur the expense of only one registration for several new issues of the *same* class of security.

Formerly, corporations sold a new issue on the effective date of the registration, which involved an unknown price for the security until (literally) a few hours before the sale. With shelf registration the issuer can take advantage of favorable changes in the market price of the security, and withhold an issue if market conditions have turned unfavorable.

[¶3706.3]   Updating the Shelf Registration

When necessary, a shelf registration is updated either by a supplement or amendment to the original registration. A supplement is simply a sticker attached to the Prospectus; it contains information relevant to the issue considered sufficiently material in nature by the issuer to be communicated to the public. Supplemental information is not passed upon by the SEC, nor is a part of the registration statement.

A post-effective amendment usually involves a revision of the original Prospectus. It is reviewed by the SEC, becomes a part of the registration statement, and must be declared effective by the SEC.

Rule 512 (a) (2) of regulation S-K:

> ". . . each such post-effective amendment shall be deemed to be a new registration statement relating to the securities offered therein . . . "

Amendments are required:

• When anytime after nine months after the effective date of the registration statement the Prospectus contains information *more than* 16 months old.

• The Rule provides that anytime after nine months subsequent to the effective date of a registration statement, a Prospectus can no longer be used if any information in the Prospectus is over 16 months old. This requirement is usually triggered by the age of the certified financial statements. Assume year-end (any year) certified financial statements and assume a registration statement became effective on June 1. An updated Prospectus would have to be filed and become effective prior to April 30 of the following year.

• When any "facts or events arising after the effective date of the registration statement which, individually or in the aggregate, represent a fundamental change in the information set forth in the registration statement."

• When there is a material change in the original distribution plan of the issue.

• When there is a change in the managing underwriter.

• When false or misleading information is discovered after the effective date of the original registration statement.

The shelf-registration procedure is an experiment for which the SEC has set a time limit of two years ending December 31, 1983. The Commission will, during that time period, continuously appraise the results of the application of the shelf-registration approach before making a final determination with respect to its use.

The proponents of the Rule believe that it makes it easier for companies trying to deal with volatile markets to seize advantageous moments in the market to sell new security issues.

The opponents of the process believe the procedure can disrupt the stock market, alter underwriting techniques, and is contrary to the interests of the investing public.

SECTION FOUR

APPENDIXES

Appendix A

INDEX FOR JOURNAL ENTRIES

References Are To Journal Entry Numbers

SAMPLE JOURNAL ENTRIES

OPENING INVESTMENT — Sole Proprietorship:
[1]

Cash	5,000	
Building (fair value)	45,000	
A. Able, Net Worth		50,000

OPENING INVESTMENT — Partnership:
[2]

Cash	30,000	
Inventory	30,000	
B. Baker (50%), Capital		30,000
C. Charles (50%), Capital		30,000

PARTNERSHIP INVESTMENT — with Goodwill:
[3]

Building (fair value)	45,000	
Goodwill	15,000	
A. Able (50%), Capital		60,000
Able contributes building for		
½ share of partnership.		

PARTNERSHIP INVESTMENT — Skill, no funds:
[4]

A. Able, Capital	3,000	
B. Baker, Capital	3,000	
C. Charles, Capital	6,000	
D. Dog, Capital		12,000
Dog gets 10% of partnership		
for the skill he'll contribute.		
Ratios will now be:		

Able	(25% less 10%)	22.5%
Baker	(same)	22.5%
Charles	(50% less 10%)	45.0%
Dog	(as granted)	10.0%
		100.0%

PARTNERSHIP INCORPORATES:
[5]

Cash	30,000	
Inventory — Raw Material	30,000	
Building (fair value)	45,000	
Capital Stock (par $10; 10,000		
shares issued; 100,000 auth.)		100,000
Additional Paid-in Capital		5,000
Shares issued: A. 2250; B. 2250;		
C. 4500; D. 1,000. Note that		
partnership goodwill is not carried		
over to corporation.		

CORPORATE INVESTMENT — with Goodwill:
[6]

Machinery & Equipment (fair value)	9,000	
Goodwill	1,000	
Capital Stock (1,000 shares)		10,000
Issuing 1,000 shares to E. Easy		
@ $10 par for machinery contributed.		

CORPORATION MONTHLY ENTRIES — The corporation

records all entries into the general ledger *through* summary entries made in the general journal from the books and sources of original entry:

[7] *Summary of Purchase Journal,* where all vendor invoices are entered:

Purchases — Raw Material	10,000	
Shop Supplies	2,000	
Office Supplies	1,000	
Office Equipment	3,000	
Utilities	1,000	
Freight Out	2,000	
Advertising	1,000	
Accounts Payable		20,000

[8] *Summary of Cash Disbursement, Regular Cash A/C:*

Cash — Payroll A/C	13,000	
Petty Cash	200	
Accounts Payable	14,500	
Federal Tax Deposits Made	5,100	
Bank Charges	2	
Cash — Regular A/C		32,602
Cash Discounts Taken		200

[9] *Summary of Cash Disbursements, Payroll A/C:*

Direct Labor — Shop	12,500	
Indirect Labor — Shop	1,500	
Salaries — Sales Dept.	2,000	
Salaries — G & A	4,000	
Cash — Payroll A/C (net pay)		13,000
W/H Tax Pay — Federal		4,400
FICA Tax Withheld		1,200
SUI & Disability W/H		300
State Income Taxes W/H		60U
Savings Bonds W/H		500

[10] *Summary of Sales Book:*

Accounts Receivable	35,000	
Sales Returns & Allowances	500	
Sales — Product L		18,000
Sales — Product M		16,600
Sales Taxes Payable		900

[11] *Summary of Cash Receipts Book:*

Cash — Regular A/C	30,500	
Cash Discounts Allowed	500	
Accounts Receivable		30,000
Machinery and Equipment		1,000

[12] *Summary of Petty Cash Box:*

Postage	40	
Entertainment	60	
Travel Expense	30	
Misc. Expense	20	
Petty Cash		150

[13] *General Journal Entries during month:*

Depreciation — M & E	10	
Machinery and Equipment	400	
Gain on Sale of Machinery		410

To correct entry from cash receipts:

Basis	$ 600	
Deprec.	10 (1/60th)	
	590	
S.P.	1000	
Gain	$ 410	

[14]

Depr.— Bldg (1/40x45,000x1/12)	94	
Depr.— M&E (1/5 x 8,400x1/12)	140	
Depr.— OE (1/5 x 3,000x1/12)	50	
Amortization (1/40x1,000x1/12)	2	
Accum Depr.— Bldg		94
Accum Depr.— M&E		140
Accum Depr.— OE		50
Goodwill		2

[15]

Real Estate Taxes	300	
Accrued Taxes — RE		300
1/12th of estimated $3,600 for yr		

[16]

Direct Labor (3125)	2,500	
Indirect Labor (375)	300	
Salaries — Selling (500)	400	
Salaries — G & A (1000)	800	
Accrued Salaries (5000)		4,000
To accrue 4/5 of last payroll in month.		

[17]

W/H Tax Payable — Federal	3,300	
FICA Tax Withheld	900	
FICA Tax Expense — employer	900	
Federal Tax Deposits Made		5,100
FICA Tax Expense — employer	300	
SUI & DISAB Expense	600	
FUI Expense	100	
Accrued Taxes — Payroll		1,000

To zero deposit account against withholding accounts and to book employer FICA expense and estimated unemployment tax for month.

[18]

Overhead	6,106	
Depr.— Bldg (60% of 94)		56
Depr.— M&E (all)		140
Indirect Labor (all)		1,800
Payroll Tax Exp (70% of 1900)		1,330
Shop supplies (all considered used)		2,000

Utilities (60% of 1000)		600
Taxes — RE (60% of 300)		180

To allocate expenses to overhead.
Taxes based on payroll proportion.
Other allocations based on space occupied.

[19]

Inventory — Raw Materials	(15,000)	
Inventory — Work in Process	none	
Inventory — Finished Goods	15,369	
Cost of Production — Inventory Change		369

To increase or (decrease) inventory
accounts to reflect new month-end
inventory as follows:

Raw Material:

Opening Inventory	$ 30,000
Purchases	10,000
Less used in production	(25,000)
Closing inventory	15,000
To adjust opening	$ (15,000)

Finished Goods:

Materials used (above)	$ 25,000
Direct labor costs	15,000
Overhead costs	6,106
3 units produced	46,106
1 unit unsold (⅓)	$ 15,369

(none at hand at beginning)
No work in process this month.

(The entries through here are all related with respect to the dollars shown. From here on, they are independent with respect to each CAPITAL HEADING, but related within the headed area.)

CUSTOMER'S CHECK BOUNCES
[20]

Accounts Receivable (Mr. A.)	100	
Cash (Disbursements)		100

To record bank charge for
Mr. A's check return — insufficient
funds.

[21]

Cash (Receipts)	100	
Accounts Receivable (Mr. A.)		100

For re-deposit of above, per
customer's instructions.

NOTES RECEIVABLE DISCOUNTED

[22]

Cash	9,900
Interest Expense	250

Notes receivable Discounted	10,000	
Interest Income	150	

For proceeds from customer note discounted,
due 90 days @ 6%, discount rate 10%.

[23]

Notes Receivable Discounted	10,000	
Notes Receivable		10,000

To offset. Customer note paid,
per bank notice.

FIRST-YEAR DEPRECIATION

[24]

Depreciation Expense — M & E	2,000	
Accumulated Depr — M & E		2,000

For maximum first-year depreciation
taken on 6/30 purchase of extruder.
See next entry for regular deprec.

[25]

Depreciation — M & E	400	
Accumulated Depr — M & E		400

To take straight-line on above:

Cost	$	10,000
Less 1st yr. Depr		(2,000)
S/L basis		8,000
Over 10 yrs — per yr	$	800
Six months this yr (no salvage value).	$	400

TAX LOSS CARRYBACK

[26]

FIT Refund and Interest Receivable	106,000	
Income Tax (Current Yr. Income Statement)		100,000
Interest Income		6,000

To set up receivable for carryback tax
refund due, plus interest.

SUB-CHAPTER S EQUITY ENTRIES

End of Year 1:

[27]

Net income for Current Year	30,000	
Undistributed Earnings — Post-Election		30,000

To close year's net income into
new Sub-S undistributed earnings
Equity account.

[28]

Retained Earnings	55,000	
Retained Earnings — Pre-Election		55,000

To retitle opening retained earnings
account and keep it separate from
earnings after Sub-S election.

[29]

Post-Election Dividends	10,000	
Cash		10,000

For cash distributions made of current earnings. (NOTE: State law may require a *formal* declaration of a dividend for corporations. If this is true, and there is no such declaration, this must be treated as a *loan receivable* from stockholders.)

INSTALLMENT SALES METHOD

[30]

Accounts Receivable	1,000	
Cost of Installment Sale		700
Deferred Gross Profit on Installment Sales		300

For original sale. (GP% is 30%)

[31]

Cash	300	
Accounts Receivable		300

For payment on account.

[32]

Deferred Gross Profit on Installment Sales	90	
Realized Gross Profit		90

To amortize 30% of above collection to realized income.

VOIDING YOUR OWN CHECK (Issued in a prior period)

[33]

Cash (Ck # 1601)	1,500	
Rent Expense		1,500

To void check #1601 (last month). Check reported lost. Payment stopped. Replaced with this month's check #1752. (See CD book)

INVESTMENT TAX CREDIT — THE DEFERRAL METHOD

[34]

Taxes Payable	7,000	
Deferred Investment Tax Credits		7,000

To set up investment tax credit under the deferred method. *Note:* The tax expense for this year on the income statement does *not* reflect the use of this credit.

Year 2:

[35]

Deferred Investment Tax Credits	700	
Income Tax Expense		700

To amortize 1/10th, based on 10-year life of asset to which applicable.

ACCUMULATED PREFERRED STOCK DIVIDENDS
[36]

Dividends (Income Statement)	30,000	
Dividends Payable (Liability)		30,000

To accrue this year's commitment,
6% of $500,000. *Note:* There was
no "only as earned" provision attached
to this issue.

DIVIDEND DECLARATION — COMMON STOCK
[37]

Retained Earnings	100,000	
Common Stock Extra Dividend Declared — (show in Equity Section)		100,000

To segregate common stock extra dividend
from accumulated earnings (until paid),
10¢ per share, 1,000,000 shares.

PAYMENT OF ABOVE TWO DIVIDENDS
[38]

Dividends Payable	30,000	
Common Stock Extra Dividend Declared	100,000	
Cash		130,000

For payment of dividends.

APPROPRIATION OF RETAINED EARNINGS
[39]

Retained Earnings	50,000	
Reserve Appropriation for Inventory Declines (Equity Section)		50,000

To set aside retained earnings for possible
inventory losses — per Board resolution.

[40]

Retained Earnings — (1/1 opening)	150,000	
Accounts Payable (XYZ Co.)		150,000

To record prior year billing error made
by supplier, XYZ Co., on invoice #_____,
dated 12/10. Error not discovered by
XYZ until after closing of our books and
issuance of statements. Error is considered
material enough to treat as prior period
adjustment. Item was not in inventory
at 12/31.

STOCK DIVIDEND
Usually:
[41]

Retained Earnings (at market)	45,000	
Common Stock (par $10, 3,000 shares)		30,000
Additional Paid-in Capital		15,000

For 3% stock dividend distributed on
100,000 shares — 3,000 shares issued.
Market value $15 at dividend date.

Sometimes:

[42]

Additional Paid-in Capital	30,000	
Common Stock (par $10, 3,000 shares)		30,000
For non-taxable distribution out of		
Paid-in Capital.		

SPLIT-UP EFFECTED IN THE FORM OF A STOCK DIVIDEND

[43]

Retained Earnings (at par)	1,000,000	
Common Stock (par $10, 100,000 shs)		1,000,000
For split in the form of a stock dividend		
(to conform with state law). One share		
issued for each share outstanding.		
100,000 shares at par of $10.		

STOCK SPLIT-UP

[44]

Common Stock (100,000 shares @ $10.)	memo	
Common Stock (200,000 shares @ $5.)		memo
Memo entry only. To record stock split-up		
by showing change in par value and in		
number of shares outstanding. One share		
issued for each outstanding. Par changed		
from $10 to $5.		

STOCK OPTIONS FOR EMPLOYEES AS COMPENSATION

PARTNERSHIP WITHDRAWALS

[45]

S. Stone, Withdrawals	15,000	
T. Times, Withdrawals	5,000	
Cash		20,000
For cash withdrawals.		

PARTNERSHIP PROFIT ENTRY

[46]

Net Income — P & L a/c		100,000	
S. Stone, Capital (50%)			50,000
T. Times, Capital (50%)			50,000
To split profit as follows:			
Per P & L closing account	$ 80,000		
Add back above included			
in P & L account	20,000		
Profit to distribute	$100,000		

[47]

S. Stone, Capital	15,000	
T. Times, Capital	5,000	
S. Stone, Withdrawals		15,000
T. Times, Withdrawals		5,000
To close withdrawal accounts		
to capital accounts.		

IMPUTED INTEREST (ON NOTES RECEIVABLE)

[48]

Notes Receivable (Supplier A — 6 yrs)	1,000,000	
Cash		1,000,000

For loan made to supplier. Received
non-interest bearing note, due 6 yrs.

[49]

Cost of Merchandise (from supplier A)	370,000	
Unamortized Discount on Notes Receiv.		370,000

To charge imputed interest of 8% on
above note, due in 6 years, to cost
of merchandise bought from A.

Year 2:

[50]

Unamortized Discount on Notes Receiv.	50,000	
Interest Income		50,000

To amortize this year's applicable
imputed interest on note.

BOND DISCOUNT, PREMIUM AND ISSUE COSTS

[51]

Cash	2,025,000	
Unamortized Bond Issue Costs	15,000	
Bonds Payable (8%, 10 yrs)		2,000,000
Unamortized Premium on Bonds		40,000

To set up face value of bonds, issue
costs and net cash proceeds received.

Year 2:

[52]

Unamortized Premium on Bonds	4,000*	
Unamortized Bond Issue Cost		1,500*
Interest Expense (difference)		2,500

To set up approximate amortization.
(*Should actually be based on present
values.)

[53]

Interest Expense	160,000	
Cash		160,000

To record actual payment of bond
interest. 8% of $2,000,000.

FEDERAL INCOME TAX — INTERIMS — AND EXTRAORDINARY ITEM

[54]

Income Tax (on continuing operations)	350,000	
Extraordinary Loss (tax effect)		50,000
Taxes Payable		300,000

To set up FIT at end of First Quarter
based on full year's 50% rate and
to segregate tax applicable to
extraordinary item.

Statement should show:
Net from continuing operations $700,000
Less FIT   (350,000)
    350,000

Extraordinary loss
  (net of $50,000 tax effect)   50,000
Net Income $300,000

CAPITALIZING A LEASE (LESSEE)

At contracting:
[55]

Capitalized Leases	1,920,000	
Long-Term Lease Liability		3,600,000
Unamortized Discount on Lease		(1,680,000)

To capitalize lease of $25,000 per
month for 12 years @ 12% imputed
interest rate. Estimated life of asset
is 15 years. Present value used, since
fair value is higher at $2,000,000.

(Note: The two credit items shown are
netted and shown as *one net liability*
on the balance sheet. The liability
(at present value) should always equal
the asset value, also at present value.
Future lease payments are broken out,
effectively, into principal and interest.)

Month-end 1:
[56]

Long-Term Lease Liability	25,000	
Cash		25,000

First payment on lease.
[57]

Interest Expense	18,950	
Unamortized Discount on Lease		18,950

For one month's interest.
1% of $3,600,000 less $1,680,000,
less initial payment on signing of
contract of $25,000 *(entry not shown)* or
$1,895,000.

[58]

Depreciation Expense	10,667	
Accumulated Depr of Capitalized Lease		10,667

One month:
$1,920,000 x 1/5 x 1/12

CASH SURRENDER VALUE — OFFICER LIFE INSURANCE
[59]

Officer Life Insurance — expense	1,500	
Cash		1,500

For payment of premium. *Note:* Expense

is not deductible for tax purpose and
is a *permanent* difference.

[60]

| Cash Surrender Value-Officer Life Ins. | 1,045 | |
| Officer Life Ins. expense | | 1,045 |

To reflect increase in C.S.V. for year

[61]

| Cash | 5,000 | |
| Loans Against Officer Life Insurance | | 5,000 |

(Displayed against the asset "C.S.V.")
To record loan against life policy. No intent
to repay within the next year.

STANDARD COST VARIANCES

[62]

Purchases — Raw Mat (at stand)	200	
Accounts Payable — actual		188
Variance — material price		12

[63]

Direct Labor — at standard	50	
Variance — Direct Labor rate	10	
Payroll — actual direct labor		58
Variance — Labor Time		2

[64]

Overhead — at Standard	75	
Variance — overhead	15	
Overhead itemized actual accounts		90

Adjusting Inventories:

[65]

Inventory — Raw Materials at standard	100	
Finished Goods — at standard	75	
Cost of Production — at standard		175

To adjust inventory accounts to reflect
end-of-month on-hand figures at standards.

[66]

Variance — material price	xx	
Variance — labor time	xx	
Variance — direct labor rate		xx
Variance — overhead		xx
Contra Inventory Asset a/c (variances		
to offset standard and reflect cost)		xx

To pull out of variance accounts that
portion which is applicable to inventory,
in order to keep an isolated contra account,
which in offset to the "standard" asset
account, reflects approximate cost.
The portion is based on an overall ratio
of variances to production and inventory
figures (at standard). (If normal, apply
to cost of sales for interims.)

ADJUSTING INVENTORY FOR SAMPLING RESULTS

[67]

| Cost of Sales | 50,000 | |

Inventory		50,000

To reduce inventory by $50,000 based
on sampling results:

Inventory per computer run	$ 1,000,000
Estimated calculated	
inventory per sample	950,000
Reduction this year	$ 50,000

Year 2:

[68]

Inventory	10,000	
Cost of Sales		10,000

To adjust inventory to actual
based on actual physical count
of entire inventory. Last year-end
sample error proved to be 4%,
not 5%.

ADJUSTING CLOSING INVENTORY FROM CLIENT'S STANDARD COST TO
AUDITOR'S DETERMINED (AND CLIENT AGREED) ACTUAL COST, AND TO
REFLECT PHYSICAL INVENTORY VS. BOOK INVENTORY DIFFERENCES

[69]

Inventory — Finished Goods (Standard)	25,000	
Cost of Sales		25,000

To adjust general ledger inventory
(at standard) to actual physical
inventory count, priced out at
standard. Actual is $25,000 more.

[70]

Cost of Sales	80,000	
Inventory — Finished Goods		
(Asset Contra Cost account)		80,000

To set up a contra account reducing
asset account, which is at standard
costs, effectively to audited actual
cost or market, whichever lower.

Year 2: (End of Year)

[71]

Inventory — Finished Goods (Asset		
Contra Cost account)	50,000	
Cost of Sales		50,000

To reduce the contra account to
the new year-end difference between
the "standard" asset account and the
actual cost determined for this new
year-end inventory.

PARTNERSHIP DISSOLUTION:

Balance Sheet

Cash	$ 20,000
Assets other	35,000

Liabilities	(25,000)
A Capital (50%)	(20,000)
B Capital (30%)	(14,000)
C Capital (20%)	4,000
	-0-

[72]

| Cash | 15,000 | |
| Assets other | | 15,000 |

For sale of some assets at book value.

[73]

A Capital (⅝)	2,500	
B Capital (⅜)	1,500	
C Capital		4,000

C cannot put in his overdraw —
to apportion his deficit.

[74]

| Liabilities | 25,000 | |
| Cash | | 25,000 |

To pay liabilities

[75]

Cash	10,000	
Loss on Sale of Assets other	10,000	
Assets other		20,000
A Capital (⅝)	6,250	
B Capital (⅜)	3,750	
Loss on Sale of Assets other		10,000

Selling remaining assets and apportioning loss

[76]

A Capital (remaining balance)	11,250	
B Capital (remaining balance)	8,750	
Cash		20,000

To distribute remaining cash
and zero capital accounts.

NOTE THE SHARING OF C'S DEFICIT
AND OF THE LOSS ON ASSET SALE
BEFORE DISTRIBUTING REMAINING
CASH.

MARKETABLE SECURITIES

Shown as Current Assets:
[77]

| Unrealized Loss — to P & L | 1,500 | |
| Valuation Allowance — Current | | 1,500 |

To write down 100 U.S. Steel:

Cost 1/1	$10,000
Market 12/31	8,500
Unrealized Loss	$ 1,500

Year 2:
[78]

| Cash | 4,500 |
| Realized Loss — P & L | 500 |

	Marketable Securities — Current		5,000
Sold 50 @ 90	$ 4,500	
Cost 50 @ 90	5,000	
Realized Loss	$ 500	

[79]

Valuation Allowance — Current	1,250	
Valuation Adjustment — Current (P&L Gain)		1,250*

To adjust valuation allowance a/c
(current) for remaining securities
left in portfolio:

	50 US Steel — cost 100	$ 5,000
Market, this year end — 95	4,750
Bal. should be	250 Cr.
Balance in valuation a/c	1,500 Cr.
Debit valuation a/c	$ 1,250 Dr.

*Note: Unrealized *gains* are called
"valuation adjustments." Unrealized
losses are called "unrealized losses."

Shown as Noncurrent Asset:

[80]

Unrealized Noncurrent Loss (Equity section)	1,000	
Valuation Allowance — Noncurrent		1,000

To write down 100 shares GM
from cost of 60 to market
value at 12/31 of 50.

Year 2:

[81]

Cash	2,900	
Realized Loss — P & L	100	
Marketable Securities — Noncurrent		3,000

	Sold 50 GM @ 58	$ 2,900
Cost 50 GM @ 60	3,000
Realized loss	$ 100

[82]

Valuation Allowance — Noncurrent	1,000	
Unrealized Noncurrent Loss (Equity Section)		1,000

To adjust valuation allowance a/c
(Noncurrent) as follows:

	Cost 50 GM @ 60	$ 3,000
Market now @ 65	N/A
(Higher than cost)	
Valuation a/c should be	-0-
(Because market is higher	
than cost)	
Balance in valuation a/c	1,000 Cr.
Debit to correct	$ 1,000 Dr.

TREASURY STOCK

Purchase of:

[83]

Treasury Stock — at Cost	125,000	
Cash		125,000

Purchase of 1,000 shares @ 125
market. Par value $50.
No intent to cancel the stock.

Sale of:
[84]

Cash	140,000	
Treasury Stock — at Cost		125,000
Additional Paid — in Capital		15,000

For sale of treasury stock @ 140.

APPRAISAL WRITE-UPS
[85]

Building	350,000	
Appraisal Capital (Equity Section)		350,000

To raise building from cost of $400,000 to
appraised value of $750,000 per require-
ment of the lending institution.

Year 2:
[86]

Depreciation — Building	21,667	
Accumulated Depreciation — Building		21,667

To depreciate based on appraised value:
(400,000 for 40 years; 350,000 for 30 yrs)
Building was 10 years old at appraisal.

FOREIGN CURRENCY EXCHANGE
[87]

Unrealized Loss (balance sheet)	10,000	
Accts Payable — Foreign		10,000

To adjust liabilities payable in
Swiss Francs to US Dollars at 12/31:

Exchange rate at 12/31 .40	$40,000
Booked at (100,000 frs) .30	30,000
More dollars owed	$10,000

[88]

Deferred Taxes	5,000*	
Unrealized Loss		5,000*

To show deferred tax effect (50% rate
times $10,000 above)
*Less Foreign or Domestic Dividend
Credits, if Applicable

Year 2:
[89]

Accounts Payable — Foreign	20,000	
Cash		19,000
Realized gain (Books, not Tax)		1,000

For payment of 50,000 Swiss Francs at exchange rate of .38

[90]

Accounts Payable — Foreign	500	
Balance Sheet		500

To restate liability at year-end:

50,000 Frs @ .39	$ 19,500	
Booked to last yr.	20,000	
(Gain)	$ (500)	

[91]

Taxes Payable	2,000	
Income Tax Expense	500	
Deferred Taxes		2,500

To transfer to actual taxes payable (from
deferred) that portion applying to the payment of $19,000. Original debt in dollars
was $15,000. 50% tax rate on $4,000 or
$2,000, plus $500 — to offset 2,500
booked to last 12/31.

[92]

Income Tax Expenses	250	
Deferred Taxes		250

To adjust deferred taxes to equal ½ of
4,500 (19,500 liability now, less original
liability of 15,000) for $2,250 tax deferral.

THE EQUITY METHOD

[93]

Investment — Oleo Co.	275,000	
Cash		275,000

Purchase of 25% of Oleo's stock,
at cost (25,000 shares @ $11).

[94]

Investment — Oleo Co.	40,000	
Deferred Good Will in Oleo		40,000

To set up additional underlying equity in
Oleo Co. at date of acquisition — to
write-off over 40 years.

[95]

Cash	5,000	
Investment — Oleo Co.		5,000

For receipt of 20¢ per share cash dividend
from Oleo.

[96]

Investment — Oleo Co.	27,500	
Income from Equity Share of Undistributed Earnings of Oleo continuing operations		25,000
Income from Equity Share of Undistributed Extraordinary Item of Oleo		2,500

To pick up 25% of the following
reported Oleo annual figures:

Net income after taxes, but before Extraordinary item	$100,000	
Extraordinary Income (net)	10,000	
Total net income reported	$110,000	

[97]

Income Tax Expense — Regular	12,500*	
Income Tax Expense — Extra Item	1,250*	

Deferred Taxes		13,750*

To set up 50% of above income as accrued
taxes. Expectation is that Oleo will
continue paying dividends.

*Dividend Tax Credit, if any, should reduce
these Amounts

[98]

Deferred Taxes	2,500*	
Income Taxes Payable		2,500*

To set up actual liability for tax on cash
dividends received.

*Dividend Tax Credit, if any, should reduce
these Amounts

CONSOLIDATION

Trial Balances
Now-at
12/31-End of Year

	A Co.	B Co.	Fair Value Excess at Acquisition
Cash	10,000	6,000	
A/R	20,000	10,000	
Inventory	30,000	5,000	
Equip	50,000	30,000	5,000
Investment Cost	40,000		
Liabilities	(30,000)	(5,000)	(1,000)
Common Stock	(20,000)	(10,000)*	
Retained Earnings	(50,000)	(20,000)*	
Sales	(80,000)	(40,000)	
Costs of Sale	20,000	14,000	
Expenses	10,000	10,000	
	-0-	-0-	
	(Parent)	(Sub)	

*Unchanged from opening balances.

*At year-end there were $5,000 intercom-
pany receivables*/payables. The parent had
sold $5,000 worth of product to the sub-
sidiary. The inventory of the subsidiary was
$1,000 over the parent's cost.

Consolidating
Entries:

[99]

Excess Paid over Book Value	10,000	
Investment Cost		10,000

To reduce investment cost to that of the
subsidiary's equity at time of purchase (unchanged at 12/31).

[100]

Equipment	5,000	
Liabilities		1,000
Excess Paid over Book Value		4,000

To reflect fair value corrections at time of
consolidation for the combination of current year-end trial balances.

[101]

B Co. Equity	30,000	
Investment Cost		30,000
Sales	5,000	
Costs of Sale		5,000
Costs of Sale	1,000	
Inventory		1,000
Liabilities	5,000	
Accounts Receivable		5,000
Excess paid over book value (expense)	150	
Goodwill		150

To eliminate intercompany dealings, debt,
investment, and to amortize goodwill.

Consolidated figures will then be:

Cash	16,000	
A/R	25,000	
Inventories	34,000	
Equipment	85,000	
Investment cost	—	
Goodwill	5,850	
Liabilities	(31,000)	
Common Stock	(20,000)	(Opening)
Ret. Earnings	(50,000)	(Opening)
Sales	(115,000)	
Cost of sales	30,000	
Expenses	20,150	
	-0-	

The year's consolidated net income (before
provision for income taxes) is $64,850.

PURCHASE METHOD OF BUSINESS COMBINATION

[102]

Accounts Receivable (present value)	50,000	
Inventory (current cost or market, lowest)	40,000	
Building (fair value)	110,000	
Equipment (fair value)	30,000	
Investments, non-current securities-market	5,000	
Goodwill	16,200	
Accounts Payable — (present value)		25,000
Long-term Debt — (face value)		30,000
Unamortized discount on long-term debt		

(to reflect present value)		(3,800)
Common Stock (Par $10; 10,000 shares)		100,000
Additional Paid-in Capital		100,000

To reflect, by the purchase method, the
purchase of Diablo Company assets and
liabilities for 10,000 shares of common
stock; total purchase price of contract
$200,000 based on market price of stock at
date of consummation of $20 per share
(1/1).

[103]

Amortization of Goodwill (1/40)	405	
Goodwill		405
Unamortized discount on long-term debt	760	
Discount Income (approx 1/5th)		760*

To amortize pertinent Diablo items, first
yearend. Goodwill on straight-line basis —
40 years. *Should be calculated present
value computation.

POOLING METHOD OF BUSINESS COMBINATION
[104]

Inventory	43,000	
Cash	5,000	
Accounts Receivable	60,000	
Reserve for Doubtful Accounts		7,000
Building	75,000	
Accumulated Depreciation — Building		15,000
Equipment	100,000	
Accumulated Depreciation — Building		60,000
Investments — non-current securities	4,000	
Accounts Payable		25,500
Long-Term Debt		30,000
Common Stock (10,000 shs @ par $10)		100,000
Additional Paid-in Capital		49,500

To reflect the pooling of Diablo items, per
their book value on date of consummation.

FUND ACCOUNTING

Initial transactions:
[105]

Cash	100,000	
Dues Income		100,000

For initial membership dues received.
[106]

Building	50,000	
Mortgage Payable		40,000
Cash		10,000

Purchase of building for cash and mortgage.
[107]

Interest Expense	2,400	
Mortgage Payable	2,000	

Cash		4,400

For first payment on mortgage.

[108]

Net income (100,000 less 2,400)	97,600	
Current Fund Balance		97,600

To close year's income

[109]

Mortgage Payable	38,000	
Current Fund Balance	12,000	
Building		50,000

To transfer building and mortgage to plant fund.

Plant Fund Entry:

[110]

Building	50,000	
Mortgage Payable		38,000
Plant Fund Balance		12,000

To set up building in plant fund.

Note that interest expense is to be
borne by the current fund every year
as a current operating expense used
in the calculation of required dues
from members. Also, the principal
sum-payments against mortgage are
to come out of current fund assets,
with no interfund debt to be set up,
until such time as a special drive is
held for plant fund donations for improvements and expansion.

MUNICIPAL ACCOUNTING — CURRENT OPERATING FUND

To book the budget:

[111]

Estimated Revenues	600,000	
Appropriations		590,000
Fund Balance		10,000

Actual year's transactions:

[112]

Encumbrances	575,000	
Reserve for Encumbrances		575,000

To enter contracts and purchase orders issued.

[113]

Expenditures — itemized (not here)	515,000	
Vouchers Payable		515,000
Reserve for Encumbrances	503,000	
Encumbrances		503,000

To enter actual invoices for deliveries received and service contracts performed and
to reverse applicable encumbrances.

[114]

Taxes Receivable — Current	570,000	
Revenues		541,500
Estimated Current Uncollectible Taxes		28,500

To enter actual tax levy and to estimate uncollectibles at 5%.

[115]

Cash	55,000	
Revenues		55,000

For cash received from licenses, fees,
fines and other sources.

[116]

Cash	549,500	
Estimated Current Uncollectible Taxes	8,000	
Taxes Receivable		549,500
Revenues		8,000

For actual taxes collected for this year.

To close out budget accounts:

[117]

Revenues	604,500	
Appropriations	590,000	
Estimated Revenue		600,000
Expenditures		515,000
Encumbrances		72,000
Fund Balance		7,500

To zero budget accounts and adjust
fund balance.

DISCS — DEEMED DISTRIBUTIONS (Parent's Books)

1975 — under old law

[118]

DISC Dividends Receivable (previously taxed)	110,000	
Deemed Distribution from DISC (income)		110,000

To pick up ½ of DISC's net of $220,000.

1976 — under the new law.

[119]

DISC Dividends Receivable (previously taxed)	189,375	
Deemed Distribution from DISC (income)		189,375

As follows:

Facts:

Gross export receipts average for 1972-1975	$1,100,000
Gross export receipts - 1976	$1,300,000
Net DISC income - 1976 only	$ 250,000

Since the 1976 net income is over
$150,000, the graduated relief in the 1976
law does not apply, and the calculation is:

67% of 1,100,000 = 670,000

670,000 ÷ 1,300,000 = 51.5%

51.5% × 250,000 = $ 128,750

250,000 − 128,750 = 121,250

121,250 × 50% =   60,625

        Total Deemed Distribution $ 189,375

[120]

Capitalization of Interest Costs
Qualifying Asset   10,000
    Accrued Interest   10,000

[121]

Employee Compensation   50,000
    Accrued Vacation   50,000

Appendix B
Guide to Record Retention
Requirements

Federal Register Office

GUIDE TO RECORD RETENTION REQUIREMENTS

REVISION AS OF JANUARY 1, 1978

This is a Guide in digest form to the provisions of Federal laws and regulations relating to the keeping of records by the public. It tells the user (1) what records must be kept, (2) who must keep them, and (3) how long they must be kept.

The citation appearing at the end of each entry represents Title number of Code of Federal Regulations and section affected (example: 20 CFR 38.1 would refer to Section 38.1 of Title 20 of the Code of Federal Regulations).

The Guide is derived from the regulations published by the various agencies in the Code of Federal Regulations, as amended in the daily issues of the FEDERAL REGISTER through December 31, 1977. Authority for the regulations is derived from the laws published in the United States Code, as amended by laws enacted during 1977.

This Guide was prepared under the editorial direction of Robert E. Lewis assisted by Rose Steinman, with Roy Nanovic and Carol Blanchard as Chief Editors. INQUIRIES, telephone 202-523-5227. SUGGESTIONS concerning this publication may be sent to Fred J. Emery, Director, Office of the Federal Register, National Archives and Records Service, Washington, D.C. 20408.

Coverage

In preparing the Guide it was necessary to establish boundaries in order to keep it from going beyond its intended purpose.

The Guide adheres strictly to the retention of records. It does not cover such matters as the furnishing of reports to Government agencies, the filing of tax returns, or the submission of supporting evidence with applications or claims.

The Guide is limited to provisions which apply to a class. Requirements applying only to named individuals or bodies have been omitted.

The Guide is confined to requirem which have been expressly stated many laws and regulations there i implied responsibility to keep copie reports and other papers furnishe Federal agencies, and to keep rel working papers. Such implied requ ments have not been included in Guide.

The following types of requirem have also been excluded from the Gu

(1) Requirements as to the kee of papers furnished by the Governm such as passports, licenses, permits, unless they are closely related to o records which must be kept.

(2) Requirements as to the displa posters, notices, or other signs in pl of business.

(3) Requirements contained in i vidual Government contracts, unless contract provisions are incorporate the Code of Federal Regulations.

NOTICE

The Guide to Record Retention Requirements does not have the effect of law, regulation, or ruling. It is published as a guide to legal requirements that appear to be in effect as of January 1, 1978.

18

. Internal Revenue Service
[Revised]

: The following items refer to re-
ents issued under the Internal Reve-
·de of 1954 which were in effect as of
y 1, 1978. All regulations applicable
·ny provision of law in effect on August
4, the date of enactment of the 1954
·are applicable to the corresponding
·ons of the 1954 Code insofar as such
·ions are not inconsistent with the
·de, and such regulations remain ap-
·e to the 1954 Code until superseded
·ulations under such Code. The In-
Revenue Service points out that the
·on from this compilation of any record
·lation issued thereunder shall not be
·ied as authority to disregard any such
·ment. The Service also points out
·rsons subject to income tax are bound

by the retention requirement given in item
4.1 regardless of other requirements which.
for other purposes allow shorter retention
periods.

The record retention requirements of the
Internal Revenue Service are divided into
the following categories: Income, Estate and
Gift, Employment, and Excise Taxes.

INCOME TAX

4.1 Persons subject to income tax.

(a) *General.* Except as provided in
paragraph (b), any person subject to
tax, or any person required to file a return of information with respect to income shall keep such permanent books
of account or records, including inventories, as are sufficient to establish the
amount of gross income, deductions,
credits, or other matters required to be
shown by such person in any return of
such tax or information.

(b) *Farmers and wage-earners.* Individuals deriving gross income from
the business of farming, and individuals
whose gross income includes salaries,
wages, or similar compensation for personal services rendered, are required to
keep such records as will enable the district director to determine the correct
amount of income subject to the tax,
but it is not necessary that these individuals keep the books of account or
records required by paragraph (a).

(c) *Exempt organizations.* In addition to the books and records required
by paragraph (a) with respect to the tax
imposed on unrelated business income,
every organization exempt from tax
under section 501(a) of the Code shall
keep such permanent books of account or records, including inventories,
as are sufficient to show specifically the
items of gross income, receipts, and disbursements, and other required information.

Retention period: The period that records should be kept varies from a few
years to a length of time that may cover
more than one taxpayer's lifetime. The
general requirement as stated in 26 CFR
1.6001-1 is that records must be kept "so
long as the contents thereof may become
material in the administration of any
internal revenue law." Some books and
records of a business may be "material"
for tax purposes so long as the business
remains in existence, and there may be
reasons other than the Federal tax consequences to the individual taxpayer for
retaining certain records for an indefinite period. However, the general requirements can be more precisely stated
in terms of (1) records of property subject to gain or loss treatment, and (2)
records supporting items of income, deductions, and credits.

Records of property for which a basis
must be determined to compute gain or
loss upon disposition (and depreciation,
amortization, or depletion allowed or allowable) must be retained until a taxable disposition is made. Thus, if property is given a substitute basis, i.e., the
basis it had in the hands of the prior
owner adjusted as required by the Code
or regulations, all records pertaining to
that property must be retained. After
a taxable disposition, the record reten-

tion rules explained below will generally
apply.

*Records of income, deductions, and
credits* (including gains and losses) appearing on a return should be kept, at a
minimum, until the statute of limitations
for the return expires. 26 CFR 301.6501
(a)-1 provides the general rule that the
amount of any tax imposed by the Internal Revenue Code shall be assessed
within three years after the return was
filed; 26 CFR 301.6511(a)-1 requires that
a claim for refund or credit must be
filed within three years from the date
of filing the return or 2 years after payment, whichever is later. However, there
are many exceptions. For example, a 6
year period of limitation applies for assessment if there has been a substantial
omission of income (26 CFR 301.6501
(e)-1), and a 7 year period applies for
filing a claim for credit or refund relating to bad debts or losses on securities
(26 CFR 301.6511(d)-1). The period of
limitations may be extended by mutual
agreement for any length of time, and
no statutory period applies if fraud is
established or if no return was filed (26
CFR 301.6501(c)-1).

Failure to retain records for a sufficient length of time could result, for example, in the assessment of additional
tax because of disallowance of deductions or a downward adjustment of basis
used in determining gain or loss on the
disposition of property.

The following record requirements
have not been assigned a specific record
retention period and the general "materiality" rule applies:

**4.2 Section 38 property; computation
of investment credit and qualified
investment.**

(a) *Component members of a controlled group on a December 31 apportionment of $25,000 amount.* To keep
as a part of its records a copy of the
statement containing all the required
consents to the apportionment plan. 26
CFR 1.46-1

(b) *Persons computing qualified investment in certain depreciable property.*
Maintain sufficient records to determine
whether section 47 of the Internal
Revenue Code, relating to certain dispositions of section 38 property, applies
with respect to any asset. 26 CFR 1.46-3

(c) *Recomputation of credit and
qualified investment.* Maintain records
which will establish with respect to each
item of section 38 property, the following facts: (1) The date the property is
disposed of or otherwise ceases to be
section 38 property, (2) the estimated
useful life which was assigned to the
property for computing qualified investment, (3) the month and the taxable
year in which property was placed in
service, and (4) the basis (or cost),
actually or reasonably determined, of
the property.

Taxpayers who, for purposes of determining qualified investment, do not use
a mortality dispersion table with respect
to section 38 assets similar in kind but
who consistently assign to such assets
separate lives based on the estimated
range of years taken into consideration

In establishing the average useful life of such assets, must, in addition to the above records, maintain records which will establish to the satisfaction of the district director that such asset has not previously been considered as having been disposed of. 26 CFR 1.47-1

(d) *Disposition or cessation of section 38 property.* Any taxpayer who seeks to establish his interest in a trade or business, a former electing small business corporation, an estate or trust, or a partnership, shall maintain adequate records to demonstrate his indirect interest after any such transfer or transfers. 26 CFR 1.47-3, 1.47-4, 1.47-5, 1.47-6

(e) *Persons selecting used section 38 property, $50,000 cost limitation.* To maintain records which permit specific identification of any item of used section 38 property selected, which was placed in service by the person selecting the property. Each member, other than the filing member, of a controlled group shall retain as part of its records a copy of the apportionment statement which was attached to the filing member's return. 26 CFR 1.48-3

(f) *Election of lessor of new section 38 property to treat lessee as purchaser.* The lessor and the lessee shall keep as a part of their records the statements filed with the lessee, signed by the lessor and including the written consent of the lessee. 26 CFR 1.48-4

4.3 Apportionment of the first $25,000 of the work incentive program (WIN) credit among members of a controlled group of corporations.

Each component member of the group shall keep a copy of the statement containing all the required consents. 26 CFR 1.50A-1

4.4 Persons claiming that a recomputation of the work incentive program (WIN) credit is not required by the early termination of a participating employee.

To maintain sufficient records to support claim that a termination of employment falls within the exceptions specified in the section cited. 26 CFR 1.50A-4

4.5 Persons maintaining that the transfer of an interest in a former small business corporation, estate or trust, or partnership or an interest in another entity does not result in a diminution requiring a recapture of the work incentive program (WIN) credit.

To maintain adequate records to demonstrate their indirect interest after any such transfer or transfers. 26 CFR 1.50A-5, 1.50A-6, 1.50A-7

4.6 Persons participating in employer accident or health plans.

To maintain records as are necessary to substantiate amount treated as their investment in their annuity contract. 26 CFR 1.72-15

4.7 Persons not totally blind claiming the additional exemption for blindness.

To retain a copy of the certified opinion of the examining physician skilled in the

disease of the eye that there is no reasonable probability that his visual acuity will ever improve beyond the minimum standards described in section 1.151-1 (d)(3) of the regulations. 26 CFR 1.151-1(d)(4)

4.8 Persons paying travel or other business expenses incurred by an employee in connection with the performance of his services.

To maintain adequate and detailed records of ordinary and necessary travel, transportation, entertainment, and other similar business expenses, including identification of amount and nature of expenditures, and to keep supporting documents, especially in connection with large or exceptional expenditures. 26 CFR 1.162-17

4.9 Persons claiming allowance for depreciation of property used in trade or business or property held for the production of income.

To keep records and accounts with respect to basis of property, depreciation rates, reserves, salvage, retirements, adjustments, elections, property excluded from elections, cost of repair, maintenance or improvement of property, agreements with respect to estimated useful life, rates and salvage, and other factors. 26 CFR 1.167(a)-7, 1.167(a)-11, 1.167(a)-12, 1.167(d)-1

4.10 Persons changing method of depreciation of section 1245 or section 1250 property.

To maintain records which permit specific identification of section 1245 or section 1250 property in the account with respect to which the election is made, and any other property in such account. The records shall also show for all the property in the account the date of acquisition, cost or other basis, amounts recovered through depreciation and other allowances, the estimated salvage value, the character of the property, and the remaining useful life of the property. 26 CFR 1.167(e)-1, 1.167(j)-1

4.11 Persons claiming depreciation with respect to residential rental property.

To maintain a record of the gross rental income derived from a building, and the portion thereof which constitutes gross rental income from dwelling units, in addition to records required under section 1.167(a)-7(c) with respect to property in a depreciation account. 26 CFR 1.167(j)-3

4.12 Persons claiming depreciation of expenditures to rehabilitate low-income rental housing.

To maintain detailed records which permit specific identification of the rehabilitation expenditures that are permitted to be allocated to individual dwelling units under the allocation rules and income certifications that must be obtained from tenants who propose to live in rehabilitated dwelling units after the close of the certification year. 26 CFR 1.167(k)-2, 1.167(k)-3

4.13 Persons claiming a dedu amounts expended in **ing certain students as a** of household.

To keep adequate records of actually paid in maintaining a as a member of the household. tain items, such as food, a r amounts spent for all member household, with an equal portio allocated to each member, wit ceptable. 26 CFR 1.170-2, 1.170

4.14 Persons claiming a deduc charitable contribution to nonoperating foundation th utes an amount equal to all tions received. [Added]

Obtain adequate records or o ficient evidence from such fo showing that the information i required qualifying distributior the time prescribed. 26 CFR 1.1 (4)

4.15 Persons electing to treat t or trade name expenditur ferred expenses.

To make an accounting segreg his books and records of trader trade name expenditures, for w election has been made, sufficien mit an identification of the c and amount of each expenditure amortization period selected i expenditure. 26 CFR 1.177-1

4.16 Persons electing additio year depreciation allowance tion 179 property.

To maintain records which per cific identification of each piece tion 179 property" and reflect from whom such property was 26 CFR 1.179-1

4.16a Election to deduct exp for removing architectural portation barriers to the and elderly.

To retain records and docum including architectural plans a prints, contracts, and building of all facts necessary to deter amount of any deduction to w taxpayer is entitled by reason of tion, as well as any adjustment made for expenditures in exces amount deductible. 26 CFR 7.1

4.17 Persons electing to dedu bilitation expenditures with to certain railroad rollin

To maintain a separate sectio record, as specified in the secti for each unit for which rehabilit penditures are deducted, and t tain records for expenditures ded incidental repairs and maintena CFR 1.263(e)-1

Retention period: See Item 4.1

4.18 Persons receiving any clas empt income or holding pro engaging in activities the from which is exempt.

To keep records of expenses o allowable as deductions which rectly allocable to any class or c exempt income and amounts

ts of items allocated to each class
R 1.265-1

Taxpayer substantiation of ex-
enses for travel, entertainment, and
ifts related to active conduct of
rade or business.

xpayer must substantiate each ele-
of an expenditure by adequate rec-
r sufficient evidence corroborating
wn statements. 26 CFR 1.274-1,
5

Persons who file a waiver of attri-
ution agreement with respect to a
edemption of stock in termination
f their interest.

retain copies of income tax re-
and any other records indicating
the amount of tax which would
been payable had the redemption
treated as a distribution subject to
n 301. 26 CFR 1.302-4

Corporations using different meth-
ds of depreciation for taxable in-
ome and earnings and profit.

maintain records which show the
ciation taken each year and which
llow computation of the adjusted
of the property in each account
depreciation taken. 26 CFR
-15(d)

Corporations receiving distributions in complete liquidation of subsidiaries.

keep records showing information
respect to the plan of liquidation
ts adoption. 26 CFR 1.332-5

Qualified electing shareholders re-
eiving distributions in complete
iquidation of domestic corporations
ther than collapsible corporations.

keep records in substantial form
ng all facts pertinent to the recog-
and treatment of the gain realized
shares of stock owned at the time
adoption of the plan of liquidation.
R 1.333-6

Persons who participate in a transfer of property to a corporation con-
rolled by the transferor.

keep records in substantial form
ing information to facilitate the
mination of gain or loss from a sub-
nt disposition of stock or securities
ther property, if any, received in
xchange. 26 CFR 1.351-3

Participant in exchange involving
a foreign corporation.

retain a copy of the ruling letter
ned from the Commissioner as au-
ty for treating a foreign corpora-
as a corporation in determining the
t to which gain on exchange is rec-
sed. 26 CFR 7.367(a)-1

Exchanges involving a foreign corporation that began after December
31, 1977.

corporation whose earnings and
s are required to be adjusted under
67(b)-4 through 7.367(b)-12 must

keep records adequate to establish the
adjustment.

A U.S. person owning a foreign corporation's stock to which an amount is attributed under §§ 7.367(b)-4 through
7.367(b)-12 must keep records to establish the amount so attributed. 26 CFR
7.367(b)-1.

4.27 Persons who participate in a tax-
free exchange in connection with a
corporate reorganization.

To keep records in substantial form
showing the cost or other basis of the
transferred property and other property
or securities and other property or
money received (including any liabilities
assumed upon the exchange, or any liabilities to which any of the properties
received were subject), in order to facilitate the determination of gain or loss
from a subsequent disposition of such
stock or securities and other property
received from the exchange. 26 CFR
1.368-3

4.28 Corporations which are parties to
reorganizations in pursuance of court
orders in receivership, foreclosure, or
similar proceedings, or in proceedings under Chapter X of the Bankruptcy Act.

To keep records in substantial form
showing the cost or other basis of the
transferred property and the amount of
stock or securities and other property or
money received (including any liabilities
assumed upon the exchange), in order to
facilitate the determination of gain or
loss from a subsequent disposition of such
stock or securities and other property
received from the exchange. 26 CFR
1.371-2

4.29 Persons who exchange stock and securities in corporations in accordance with plans of reorganizations
approved by the courts in receivership, foreclosure, or similar proceedings, or in proceedings under Chapter X of the Bankruptcy Act.

To keep records in substantial form
showing the cost or other basis of the
transferred property and the amount of
stock or securities and other property
money received (including any liabilities assumed upon the exchange), in
order to facilitate the determination of
gain or loss from a subsequent disposition of such stock or securities and other
property received from the exchange. 26
CFR 1.371-2

4.30 Railroads participating in a tax-
free reorganization.

Records in substantial form must be
kept by every railroad corporation which
participates in a tax-free exchange in
connection with a reorganization under
section 374(a) of the Internal Revenue
Code, showing the cost or other
basis of the transferred property and
amount of stock or securities and other
property or money received, including
any liabilities assumed upon the exchange, in order to facilitate the determination of gain or loss from a subsequent disposition of such stock or

securities and other property received
from the exchange. 26 CFR 1.374-3

4.31 Records required in computing
depreciation allowance carryovers of
acquiring corporations in certain
corporate acquisitions.

Records shall be maintained in sufficient detail to identify any depreciable
property to which section 1.381(c)(6)-1
of the regulations applies and to establish the basis thereof. 26 CFR 1.381(c)
(6)-1

4.32 Corporations and shareholders for
whom elections are filed with respect
to the tax treatment of corporate reorganizations.

To keep permanent records of all relevant data in order to facilitate the determination of gain or loss from a
subsequent disposition of stock or securities or other property acquired in the
transaction in respect of which the election was filed. 26 CFR 1.393-3

4.33 Qualified pension or annuity plans
with provisions for certain medical
benefits.

To keep a separate account for recordkeeping purposes with respect to contributions received to fund medical benefits described in section 401(h) of the
Internal Revenue Code. 26 CFR 1.401-14
Retention period: See Item 4.1.

4.34 Nonbank trustees, pension and
profit-sharing trusts benefiting
owner-employees.

To maintain separate and distinct fiduciary records, permanent records of
all fiduciary assets deposited or withdrawn from vault, full information relative to each account, and an adequate
record of all pending litigation in connection with exercise of fiduciary powers.
26 CFR 11.401(d)(1)-1(f)

4.35 Employers maintaining a pension,
annuity, stock bonus, profit-sharing,
or other funded plan of deferred
compensation.

To keep records substantiating all data
and information required to be filed with
respect to each plan. 26 CFR 1.404(a)-2,
1.404(a)-2A

4.36 Persons required to seek the approval of the Commissioner in order
to change their annual accounting
period.

To keep adequate and accurate records
of their taxable income for the short
period involved in the change and for
the fiscal year proposed. 26 CFR 1.442-1

4.37 Persons selling by the installment
method.

(a) Installment method. In adopting
the installment method of accounting the
seller must maintain such records as are
necessary to clearly reflect income. A
dealer who desires to compute income by
the installment method shall maintain
accounting records in such a manner as
to enable an accurate computation to be
made by such method.

(b) Revolving credit plan. The percentage of charges under a revolving

credit plan which will be treated as sales on the installment plan shall be computed by making an actual segregation of charges in a probability sample of the revolving credit accounts in order to determine what percentage of charges in the sample is to be treated as sales on the installment plan. The taxpayer shall maintain records in sufficient detail to show the method of computing and applying the sample. 26 CFR 1.453–1, 1.453–2

4.38 Prepaid dues income.

A taxpayer who makes an election with respect to prepaid dues income shall maintain books and records in sufficient detail to enable the district director to determine upon audit that additional amounts were included in the taxpayer's gross income for any of the three taxable years preceding such first taxable year. 26 CFR 1.456–7

4.39 Persons engaged in the production, purchase, or sale of merchandise.

(a) *General.* To keep a record of inventory, properly computed and summerized, conforming to the best accounting practices in the trade or business which clearly reflects income, enables inventories to be verified, and is consistent from year to year.

(b) *Manufacturers—full absorption method.* To maintain records and working papers to support burden rate calculations; and to preserve at his principal place of business all records, data, and other evidence relating to the full absorption values of inventory resulting from an election to change to the full absorption method. 23 CFR 1.471–1, 1.471–2, 1.471–11

4.40 Persons permitted or required to use the LIFO method of inventory valuation.

(a) *General.* To maintain such supplemental and detailed inventory records as will enable the District Director to verify the inventory computations.

(b) *Dollar-value method.* To maintain adequate records to support the appropriateness, accuracy, and reliability of the index or link-chain method. 26 CFR 1.472–2, 1.472–8

4.41 Controlled entities arm's length charges.

To maintain adequate books and records to permit verification of costs or deductions when a factor in determining the arm's length charge for services rendered to other members of a controlled group. 26 CFR 1.482–2(b) (3)

4.42 Supplemental Unemployment Benefit Trusts.

To maintain records indicating the amount of separation benefits and sick and accident benefits which have been provided to each employee. If a plan is financed, in whole or in part, by employee contributions to the trust, the trust must maintain records indicating the amount of each employee's total contributions allocable to separation benefits. 26 CFR 1.501(c)(17)–2(j)

4.43 Farmer's cooperative marketing and purchasing associations.

To keep permanent records of the business done both with members and nonmembers, which show that the association was operating during the taxable year on a cooperative basis in the distribution of patronage dividends to all producers. While under the Code patronage dividends must be paid to all producers on the same basis, this requirement is complied with if an association, instead of paying patronage dividends to nonmember producers in cash, keeps permanent records from which the proportionate shares of the patronage dividends due to nonmember producers can be determined, and such shares are made applicable toward the purchase price of a share of stock or of a membership in the association. 26 CFR 1.521–1

4.44 Corporation claiming deduction for dividends paid.

To keep permanent records necessary (a) to establish that dividends with respect to which the deduction is claimed were actually paid during the taxable year, and (b) to supply the information required to be filed with the income tax return of the corporation. To also keep canceled dividend checks and receipts obtained from shareholders acknowledging payment. 26 CFR 1.561–2

4.45 Mutual savings banks, etc., maintaining reserves for bad debts.

To maintain as a permanent part of its regular books of account, an account for: (1) a reserve for losses on nonqualifying loans, (2) a reserve for losses on qualifying real property loans, and (3) if required, a supplemental reserve for losses on loans. A permanent subsidiary ledger containing an account for each of such reserves may be maintained. 26 CFR 1.593–7

4.46 Mutual savings banks, etc., making capital improvements on land acquired by foreclosure.

To maintain such records as are necessary to reflect clearly, with respect to each particular acquired property, the cost of each capital improvement and whether the taxpayer treated minor capital improvements with respect to such property in the same manner as the acquired property. 26 CFR 1.595–1

4.47 Persons claiming allowance for cost depletion of natural gas property without reference to discovery value or percentage depletion.

To keep accurate records of periodical pressure determinations where the annual production is not metered. 26 CFR 1.611–2

4.48 Persons claiming an allowance for depletion and depreciation of mineral property, oil and gas wells, and other natural deposits.

To keep a separate account in which shall be accurately recorded the cost or other basis of such property together with subsequent allowable capital additions to each account and all other re-

quired adjustments; and, to ass segregate, and have readily avail his principal place of business, supporting data which is used in ing certain summary statements r to be attached to returns and suc records as indicated in sections c CFR 1.611–2, 1.611–5, 1.613–6

4.49 Persons claiming an allowa depletion of timber property

To keep accurate ledger accou which shall be recorded the cost c basis of the property and land t with subsequent allowable capita tions in each account and all oth justments. In such accounts ther be set up separately the quantity ber, the quantity of land, and the tity of other resources, if any, proper part of the total cost o shall be allocated to each after provision for immature timber The timber accounts shall be c each year with the amount of the each of the charges to the depletion ac of the charges to the depletion ac shall be credited to depletion r accounts. 26 CFR 1.611–3

4.50 Mineral property, taxable computation, allocation of 1245 gain.

Taxpayer shall have available nent records of all the facts neces determine with reasonable accur portion of any gain recognized und tion 1245(a)(1) of the Code wh properly allocable to the mineral erty in respect of which the income is being computed. In th sence of such records, none of th recognized under section 1245 shall be allocable to such mineral erty. 26 CFR 1.613–5

4.51 Persons computing gross i from mining by use of represe market or field price.

To keep records as to the source pricing information and relevan porting data. 26 CFR 1.613–4(c)(5

4.52 Partnerships claiming an ance for depletion of oil an property.

Each partner to keep separate ords of his share of the adjusted in each oil and gas property of the nership. 26 U.S.C. 613A as amend Pub. L. 94–455

4.53 Transfer of interest in oil property.

To retain records that show the of the transfer of an interest in or gas property, any geological an physical data in the possession of transferee or other explanatory with respect to the property trans and any other information that upon the question of whether at th of the transfer the principal value property transferred had been de strated by prospecting, exploration discovery work.

To keep records of the secondar tertiary processes applied and o

t of production so resulting. 26
613A-6.

Persons electing to aggregate sepa-
te operating mineral interests.

maintain adequate records and
that shall contain a description
aggregation and the operating
l interests within the operating
hich are to be treated as separate
ties apart from the aggregation.
eral description, accompanied by
riately marked maps, which ac-
y circumscribes the scope of the
ation and identifies the properties
are to be treated separately will be
nt. There shall also be included a
tion of the operating unit in suf-
detail to show that the aggregated
ing mineral interests are properly
a single operating unit. 26 CFR
2

Persons with separate operating
ineral interests in the case of mines.

maintain adequate records and
and statements of election as in-
d in the section cited. 26 CFR
3

Persons aggregating operating
ineral interests in oil and gas wells
a single tract or parcel of land.

btain accurate and reliable infor-
, and keep records with respect
, establishing all facts necessary
king the computations prescribed
e fair market value method of
ning basis on the aggregation. 26
.614-6

Persons electing to treat separate
perating mineral interests in oil and
as wells in a single tract or parcel
f land as separate properties.

maintain and have available rec-
nd maps sufficient to clearly define
act or parcel and all of the taxpay-
perating mineral interests therein.
R 1.614-8

Trustee of trust claiming charita-
le remainder interest deduction, in-
ompetent grantor.

retain certificate of incompetency
opy of the judgment or decree and
nodification thereof. 26 CFR 1.642
(b) (3)

Pooled income fund investing or
einvesting any portion of its proper-
ies jointly with other properties.

maintain records which identify
ortion of the total fund which is
d by the pooled income fund and
ncome earned by, and attributable
ch portion. 26 CFR 1.642(c)-5

Trusts-accumulation distribution
allocated to preceding years.

all taxable years of a trust, the
ee must retain copies of the trust's
he tax return as well as information
ining to any adjustments in the tax
u as due on the return. Trustee shall
retain trust's records required by
on 6001 of the Internal Revenue
and the regulations thereunder for
taxable year for which the period of
ations on assessment of tax under

section 6501 of the Code has not expired.
26 CFR 1.666(d)-1A

**4.61 Life insurance companies issuing
contracts with reserves based on segregated asset accounts.**

To keep such permanent records and
other data relating to such contracts as
is necessary to enable the District Director to determine the correctness of
the application of the separate accounting rules and the accuracy of the computations. 26 CFR 1.801-8(c)

**4.62 Life insurance companies distrib-
uting dividends to policyholders.**

Every life insurance company claiming a deduction for dividends to policyholders shall keep such permanent records as are necessary to establish the
amount of dividends actually paid during
the taxable year. Such company shall
also keep a copy of the dividend resolution and any necessary supporting data
relating to the amounts of dividends
declared and to the amounts held or set
aside as reserves for dividends to policyholders during the taxable year. 26 CFR
1.811-2

**4.63 Domestic mutual life insurance
companies with contiguous country
branches which make an election
under sec. 819A.**

To establish and maintain a separate
account for the various items attributable
to contracts insuring residents of a country contiguous to the U.S. U.S.C. 819A
as amended by Pub. L. 94-455

**4.64 Life insurance companies with re-
spect to the optional treatment of
policies reinsured under modified
coinsurance contracts.**

The reinsured and reinsurer shall
maintain as part of their permanent
books of account any subsequent amendments to the original modified coinsurance contract between the reinsured
and reinsurer. 26 CFR 1.820-2

4.65 Regulated investment companies.

(a) To maintain records showing the
information relative to the actual owners
of its stock contained in the written
statements to be demanded from the
shareholders.

(b) To maintain records showing the
maximum number of its shares (including the number and face value of securities convertible into stock) to be considered as actually or constructively
owned by each of the actual owners of
its stock during the last half of its taxable year.

(c) To maintain a list of persons failing or refusing to comply in whole or in
part with its demand for statements respecting ownership of its shares.

(d) To keep a record of the proportion of each capital gain dividend which
is gain described in section 1201(d) (1)
or (2) of the Internal Revenue Code of
1954 for taxable years ending after 1969,
and beginning before 1975.

(e) To keep a record of the proportion of undistributed capital gains which
are gains described in section 1201(d)
(1) or (2) of the Code for taxable years

ending after 1969, and beginning before
1975. 26 CFR 1.852-4(c) (3), 1.852-6,
1.852-9 (a) (1) (iii) and (c) (3).

**4.66 Shareholders of regulated invest-
ment companies.**

To keep copy C of Form 2439 furnished
for the regulated investment company's
taxable years ending after 1969, and beginning before 1975, to show increases
in the shareholder's adjusted basis of
shares of such company. 26 CFR 1.852-9

4.67 Real estate investment trust.

(a) To keep a record of the proportion of each capital dividend which is
gain described in section 1201(d) (1) or
(2) of the Internal Revenue Code of
1954 for taxable years ending after 1969,
and beginning before 1975.

(b) To maintain records showing the
information relative to the actual owners
of its stock contained in the written
statements to be demanded from its
shareholders.

(c) To maintain records showing the
maximum number of its shares (including the number and face value of securities convertible into stock) to be considered as actually or constructively
owned by each of the actual owners of its
stock during the last half of its taxable
year.

(d) To maintain a list of persons failing or refusing to comply in whole or in
part with its demand for statements respecting ownership of its shares. 26 CFR
1.857-4(e) (2), 1.857-6

**4.68 Persons claiming credit for taxes
paid or accrued to foreign countries
and possessions of the United States.**

To keep readily available for comparison on request the original receipt for
each such tax payment, or the original
return on which each such accrued tax
was based, a duplicate original, or a duly
certified or authenticated copy, in case
only a sworn copy of a receipt or return
is submitted. 26 CFR 1.905-2

**4.69 Western Hemisphere trade corpo-
rations.**

To keep records substantiating income
tax statement showing that its entire
business is done within the Western
Hemisphere and if any purchases are
made outside the Western Hemisphere,
the amount of such purchases, the
amount of its gross receipts from all
sources, and any other pertinent information. 26 CFR 1.921-1

**4.70 Persons or corporations seeking
to come within the exception to the
limitation on reduction in income tax
liability incurred to the Virgin
Islands, under section 934 of the Internal Revenue Code of 1954.**

Must maintain such records and other
documents as are necessary to determine
the applicability of the exception. 26
CFR 1.934-1

**4.71 United States shareholders of
controlled foreign corporations.**

To provide permanent books of account
or records which are sufficient to verify

for the taxable year subpart F, export trade, and certain other classes of income; gross income excluded from base company income and the increase in earnings invested in United States property; also, if the Commissioner has issued a determination letter granting authority for excluding certain income from foreign base company income, a copy of the letter shall be retained. 26 CFR 1.954–1(b)(4)(v), 1.964–3, 1.964–4

4.72 Domestic international sales corporations (DISCs); foreign investment attributable to producer's loans.

To keep permanent books or records as are sufficient to establish the transactions, amounts, and computations described in the section cited. 26 CFR 1.995–5 (f) and (g)

4.73 Election to use the average basis method for certain regulated investment company stock.

To maintain records as are necessary to substantiate the average basis (or bases) used on an income tax return in reporting gain or loss from the sale or transfer of shares. 26 CFR 1.1012–1

4.74 Executors or other legal representatives of decedents, fiduciaries of trusts under wills, life tenants and other persons to whom a uniform basis with respect to property transmitted at death is applicable.

To make and maintain records showing in detail all deductions, distributions, or other items for which adjustment to basis is required to be made. 26 CFR 1.1014–4

4.75 Persons making or receiving gifts of property acquired by gift after December 31, 1920.

To preserve and keep accessible a record of the facts necessary to determine the cost of the property, its fair market value as of the date of the gift, the gift tax attributable to the gift, and, if pertinent, its fair market value as of March 1, 1913, to insure a fair and adequate determination of the proper basis. 26 CFR 1.1015–1

4.76 Persons participating in exchanges or distributions made in obedience to orders of the Securities and Exchange Commission.

To keep records in substantial form showing the cost or other basis of the property transferred and the amount of stock or securities and other property (including money) received. 26 CFR 1.1081–11

4.77 Stock or security holders records of distribution pursuant to the Bank Holding Company Act of 1956.

Each stock or security holder who receives stock or securities or other property upon a distribution made by a qualified bank holding corporation under section 1101 of the Internal Revenue Code shall maintain records of all facts pertinent to the nonrecognition of gain upon such distribution. 26 CFR 1.1101–4

4.78 Gain upon sale or exchange of obligations issued at an original issue discount after December 31, 1954.

Taxpayer shall keep a record of the issue price and issue date upon or with each such obligation (if known or reasonably ascertainable by him). If the obligation held is an obligation of the United States received from the United States in an exchange upon which gain or loss is not recognized because of section 1037(a) of the Code (or so much of section 1031 (b) or (c) as relates to section 1037(a)), the taxpayer shall keep sufficient records to determine the issue price of such obligations for purposes of applying section 1.1037–1 of the regulations upon the disposition or redemption of such obligations. 26 CFR 1.1232–3(f)

4.79 Persons engaged in arbitrage operations in stock and securities.

To keep records that will clearly show that a transaction has been timely and properly identified as an arbitrage operation. Such identification must ordinarily be entered in the taxpayer's records on the day of the transaction. 26 CFR 1.1233–1

4.80 Grantors of straddles.

In the case of a multiple option where the number of options to sell and the number of options to buy are not the same or if the terms of all the options are not identical, the grantor must indicate in his records the individual serial number of, or other characteristic symbol imprinted upon, each of the two individual options which comprise the straddle, or by adopting any other method of identification satisfactory to the Commissioner. Such identification must be made before the expiration of the fifteenth day after the day on which the multiple option is granted and is applicable to multiple options granted after January 24, 1972. 26 CFR 1.1234–2

4.81 Record retention requirements for corporations and shareholders with respect to the substantiation of ordinary loss deductions on small business corporation stock.

(a) *Corporations.* The plan to issue stock which qualifies under section 1244 of the Internal Revenue Code must appear upon the records of the corporation. In addition, in order to substantiate an ordinary loss deduction claimed by its shareholders, the corporation should maintain records as indicated in section cited.

(b) *Shareholders.* Any person who claims a deduction for an ordinary loss on stock under section 1244 of the Code shall file with his income tax return for the year in which a deduction for the loss is claimed a statement setting forth information indicated in section cited.

In addition, a person who owns "section 1244 stock" in a corporation shall maintain records sufficient to distinguish such stock from any other stock he may own in the corporation. 26 CFR 1.1244(e)–1

4.82 Recomputed basis of section property and additional depr adjustments to section 1250 p when such property is so changed, transferred, or invol converted.

To maintain permanent record include (1) the date and mar which the property was acquire the basis on the date the proper acquired and the manner in wh basis was determined, (3) the and date of all adjustments to ba (4) similar information with res other property having an adjuste reflecting depreciation or amort adjustments by the taxpayer, or other taxpayer on the same or property. 26 CFR 1.1245–2, 1.1250– Retention period: See Item 4.1.

4.83 Foreign investment compan

To maintain and preserve suc manent books of account, record other documents as are suffici establish what its taxable income be if it were a domestic corpc Generally, if the books and recoi maintained in the manner prescr regulations under section 30 of t vestment Company Act of 1940, requirements shall be considered sa 26 CFR 1.1247–5 Retention period: See Item 4.1.

4.84 Persons involved in the liqu and replacement of life inver

To keep detailed records such enable the Commissioner, in his nation of the taxpayer's return f year of replacement, readily to ver extent of the inventory decrease cl to be involuntary in character a facts upon which such claim is bas subsequent inventory increases ar creases, and all other facts mate the replacement adjustment auth 26 CFR 1.1321–1, 1.1321–2

4.85 Unincorporated business e to be taxed as a domestic corpor

To keep records, render state and make returns in the same m as a domestic corporation and ma such other records as indicated i sections cited. 26 CFR 1.1361–10, 1 14

4.86 Records by small business co tions of (1) distributions o viously taxed income and (2) t tributed taxable income.

A small business corporation keep records of (1) distributions net share of the previously taxe come of each shareholder and (2) person's share of undistributed ta income. In addition, each sharel of such corporation shall keep a i of his own net share of previously income and undistributed taxabl come and shall make such record able to the corporation for its info tion. 26 CFR 1.1375–4; 1.1375–6

Persons required to withhold tax
n nonresident aliens, foreign cor-
orations, and tax-free covenant
onds on payments of income made
n and after January 1, 1957.

keep copies of Forms 1042 and
26 CFR 1.1461–2

Affiliated group; (1) intercom-
any transactions, accounting for
eferred gain or loss, and (2) aloca-
on of Federal income tax liability.

Maintain permanent records (in-
g work papers) which will properly
the amount of deferred gain or
d enable the group to identify the
ter and source of the deferred gain
s to the selling member and apply
plicable restoration rules. (2) If
liated group elects to use the
d of allocating Federal income tax
ty provided in section 1.1502–33(d)
of the regulations, it must main-
pecific records to substantiate the
bility of each member on a sepa-
eturn basis for purposes of para-
s (a)(1) and (b)(1) of such sub-
n (i). In addition, allocations of
bility may be made in accordance
any other method approved by the
issioner, but a condition of such
val shall be that the group main-
pecific records to substantiate its
tations pursuant to such method.
FR 1.1502–13(c)(5), 1.1502–33,
2–1

Tax-exempt organizations.

General. To keep records and
of account pertaining to informa-
ncluded in the annual return, in-
g items of gross income, receipts,
rsements, and contributions and
received, and to keep other perti-
information which will enable the
ct director to inquire into the orga-
on's exempt status. An organiza-
laiming an exception from the fil-
f an information return must main-
adequate records to substantiate
claim. 26 CFR 1.6001–1, 1.6033–1.
3–2

Employees' trusts. To keep as a
of its records for taxable years be-
ng after December 31, 1969, and
g before December 31, 1971, written
cation, or a copy thereof, from an
yer to the trustee that the employer
r will timely file the information re-
d under section 404 of the Internal
nue Code. 26 CFR 1.6033–1

Banking institutions, trust companies, or brokerage firms, who elect
to file Form 1087, Nominee's Information Return, for each actual owner
for whom it acts as nominee.

st maintain such records as will
it a prompt substantiation of each
ents of dividends made to the actual
r. 26 CFR 1.6042–1

Persons engaged in construction of
aircraft for the Army and the Air
Force.

keep books, records, and original
nces of costs pertinent to the deter-
tion of the true profit, excess profit,
ency in profit, or net loss from the
rmance of a contract or subcon-

tract, 26 CFR 16.13 (see 26 CFR 1.1471–1)

**4.92 Persons engaged in construction of
naval vessels or aircraft for the Navy.**

To keep books, records, and original
evidences of costs pertinent to the determination of the true profit, excess profit,
deficiency in profit, or net loss from the
performance of a contract or subcon-
tract. 26 CFR 17.14 (see 26 CFR 1.1471–1)

**4.93 Persons making payments of esti-
mated tax installments in foreign
currency.**

Maintain a copy of the statement certified by the foundation, commission, or
other person having control of the payments to the taxpayer in nonconvertible
foreign currency which are expected to
be received during the taxable year for
the purpose of exhibiting it to the disbursing officer when making installment
deposits of foreign currency. 26 CFR
301.6316–6

**4.94 Domestic building and loan asso-
ciations.**

To maintain adequate records to
establish to the satisfaction of the district
director that various assets tests are met
for taxable years beginning after
October 16, 1962, and ending before
November 1, 1964. 26 CFR 301.7701–13

A specified record retention period has
been established for the following income
tax records:

**4.95 Withholding agents making pay-
ment to nonresident aliens, foreign
partnerships, or foreign corporations
after December 31, 1971, which are
subject to a reduced rate or an exemption from tax pursuant to a tax
treaty.**

To maintain Form 1001, Ownership,
Exemption, or Reduced Rate Certificate.
Retention period: *Coupon bond interest* at least 4 years after the close of the
calendar year in which the interest is
paid; *Income other than coupon bond
interest or dividends* at least 4 years after
the close of the calendar year in which
the interest is paid; *Noncoupon bond interest* at least 4 years after the interest
is paid. 26 CFR 1.1441–6, 1.1461–1

4.96 Tax-exempt organizations.

(c) *Group returns.* The central organization shall retain the certified
statements of those local organizations
authorizing their inclusion in a group
return. 26 CFR 1.6033–2
Retention period: For taxable years
after December 31, 1969, until the
expiration of 6 years after the last taxable year for which a group return includes the local organization.

**4.97 Any trustee, insurance company,
or other person, which is notified
under section 6047(b) of the Code
that contributions to a trust or under
a retirement plan have been made
on behalf of an owner-employee.**

Shall maintain a record of such notification.

Retention period: Until all funds of
the trust or under the plan on behalf of
the owner-employee have been distributed. 26 CFR 1.6047–1

4.98 Income tax return preparers.

To retain a completed copy of the return or claim for refund, or record, by
list, card file, or otherwise, of the name,
taxpayer identification number and taxable year of the taxpayer (or nontaxable
entity) for whom the refund or claim for
refund was prepared and the type of return or claim for refund prepared and
the name of the individual preparer required to sign the return or claim for
refund. 26 CFR 1.6107–1, 1.6695–2

To retain the copy of a return or claim
for refund manually signed by the preparer that is photocopied together with
a record of arithmetical errors corrected
after signature; the information submitted with respect to a computer-pre-
pared return together with a record of
arithmetical and clerical errors corrected; and a manually signed copy of
the letter submitted to the Internal Revenue Service with respect to facsimile
signatures on a return or claim for a
nonresident alien individual together
with a record of arithmetical errors corrected after the signature is affixed.

Retention period: 3 years after the due
date of such tax for the return period
during which the return or claim for refund was presented for signature to the
taxpayer or 3 years following a late period in which the return became due. 26
CFR 1.6107–7, 1.6695–2.

ESTATE, GIFT, AND GENERATION-SKIPPING
TRANSFER TAXES

4.99 Executors and donors of estates.

Executors of estates are required to
keep records that will enable the district
director to determine accurately the
amount of the estate tax liability, and
they must be available for inspection
whenever required (26 CFR 20.6001–1).
Similarly, the donor of a gift is required
to keep records necessary to prepare the
gift tax return, and they must be available for inspection whenever required
(26 CFR 25.6001–1). Thus, an executor
must keep detailed records of the affairs
of the estate as will enable the district
director to determine the amounts of the
estate and the generation-skipping
transfer tax liabilities, including copies
of documents relating to the estate or
the transfer, appraisal lists of items included in the gross estate or trust, copies
of balance sheets or other financial statements relating to value of stock, and any
other information necessary in determining the taxes. Persons making transfers of property by gift must maintain
books of account or records necessary to
establish the amount of the total gifts
and generation-skipping transfers together with the deductions allowable in
determining the amounts of the taxable
interests and other information required to be shown in the tax returns.

EMPLOYMENT TAX

Retention period. Regulations requiring the retention of employment tax records usually specify the number of years
that such records must be retained. For
some employment tax records, however,
no specific retention period can be established and the "materiality rule" dis-

cussed in section 4.1 under *Income Tax* must be applied. Under the materiality rule, those records must be retained so long as they may become material in the computation of any tax.

Specific record requirements have not been assigned to the following and the materiality rule applies:

4.100 Vow-of-poverty religious orders electing social security coverage for its members.

To maintain records of the details relating to the retirement of each of its members. 26 CFR 31.3121(r)-1

A specific record retention period has been established for the following employment tax records:

4.101 Employers required to deduct and withhold income tax on wages which include sick pay.

To keep records with respect to payments (sick pay) made directly to employees under a wage continuation plan, and other informaton specified in the sections cited.

Retention period: 4 years after the due date of such tax for the return period to which the records relate or the date such tax is paid, whichever is later. 26 CFR 31.3401(a)-1, 31.6001-5 (retention: 31.6001-1)

4.102 General record retention requirement for employment taxes.

(a) Persons required by regulations or instructions shall keep copies of any return, schedule, statement, or other document as part of their records.

(b) Any person who claims a refund, credit, or abatement shall keep records as indicated in the section cited.

(c) While not mandatory (except in the case of claims) it is advisable for each employee to keep permanent accurate records as indicated in the section cited.

Retention period: 4 years after the due date of such tax for the return period to which the records relate or the date such tax is paid, whichever is later. In the case of claimants, at least 4 years after the date the claim is filed. 26 CFR 31.6001-1

4.103 Employers liable for tax under the Federal Insurance Contribuitons Act.

To keep records of all remuneration, whether in cash or in a medium other than cash, paid to his employees after 1954 for services (other than agricultural labor which constitutes or is deemed to constitute employment, domestic service in a private home of the employer, or service not in the course of the employer's trade or business) performed for him after 1936; and records of all remuneration in the form of tips received by employees after 1965 and reported to him. Records shall include information specified in section cited.

Retention period: 4 years after the due date of such tax for the return period to which the records relate, or the date such tax is paid, whichever is the later. 26 CFR 31.6001-2 (retention: 31.6001-1)

4.104 Employers and employee representatives subject to the Railroad Retirement Tax Act.

To keep records of all remuneration (whether in money or in something which may be used in lieu of money) other than tips, paid to his employees after 1954 for services rendered to him (including "time lost") after 1954 and such other records as specified in section cited.

Retention period: 4 years after the due date of such tax for the return period to which the records relate, or the date such tax is paid, whichever is the later. 26 CFR 31.6001-3 (retention: 31.6001-1)

4.105 Employers and persons who are not employers for purposes of the Federal Unemployment Tax Act.

To maintain records as specified in the section cited to determine the correct liability or nonliability for the tax.

Retention period: 4 years after the due date of such tax for the return period to which the records relate or the date such tax is paid, whichever is later. 26 CFR 31.6001-4 (retention: 31.6001-1)

4.106 Employers required to deduct and withhold income tax on wages paid.

(a) To keep records of all renumeration paid to such employees and tips received by employees and reported to him. Such records shall show with respect to each employee the information specified in the section cited.

(b) To retain the Internal Revenue Service copy and the employee copy of all undeliverable annual withholding statements.

Retention period: 4 years after the due date of such tax for the return period to which the records and statements relate, or the date such tax is paid, whichever is later. 26 CFR 31.6001-5, 31.6051-1(f)(3) (retention: 31.6001-1)

4.107 Employers claiming a refund, credit, or abatement of tax under the Federal Insurance Contributions Act or Railroad Retirement Tax Act.

Every employer who has filed a claim for refund, credit, or abatement of employee tax under section 3101 or section 3201 of the Internal Revenue Code, or a corresponding provision of prior law, collected from an employee shall retain as part of his records the written receipt of the employee showing the date and amount of the repayment, or the written consent of the employee, whichever is used in support of the claim. Where employee tax was collected under section 3101 of the Code, or a corresponding provision of prior law, from an employee in a calendar year prior to the year in which the credit or refund is claimed, the employer shall also retain as part of his records a written statement from the employee (a) that the employee has not claimed refund or credit of the amount of the overcollection, or if so, such claim has been rejected and (b) that the employee will not claim refund or credit of such amount.

Retention period: 4 years after the date the claim is filed. 26 CFR

31.6402(a)-2, 31.6404(a)-1 (rete... 31.6001-1)

4.108 Repayment by employer ... erroneously collected from em... under the Federal Insurance tributions Act or the Railroad ... ment Tax Act and of incon... withheld from wages.

(a) *Before employer files retu...* obtain and keep as part of his r... the written receipt of the em... showing the date and amount c... repayment.

(b) *After employer files return.* amount of an overcollection is rep... an employee, the employer shall ... and keep as part of his records the... ten receipt of the employee, showi... date and amount of the repaymer... in any calendar year, an employ... pays or reimburses an employee ... amount of an overcollection of em... tax under section 3101 of the In... Revenue Code, or a correspo... provision of prior law, which wa... lected from the employee in a pric... endar year, the employer shall c... from the employee and keep as p... his records a written statement (a... the employee has not claimed refu... credit of the amount of the overc... tion, or if so, such claim has bee... jected, and (b) that the employe... not claim refund or credit of ... amount.

Retention period: 4 years after th... date of such tax for the return ... to which the records relate, or the... such tax is paid, whichever is the ... The records of claimants shall be r... tained for a period of at least 4 ... after the date the claim is filed ... CFR 31.6413(a)-1 (retention: 31.60...

Appendix C
Financial Planning Tables

The following tables, involving the effects of interest factors, are useful in various forms of future business planning.

SIMPLE INTEREST TABLE

SIMPLE INTEREST TABLE

Example of use of this table:
Find amount of $500 in 8 years at 6% simple interest.
From table at 8 yrs. and 6% for $1   1.48
Value in 8 yrs. for $500 (500 x 1.48) $740

Number of Years	Interest Rate							
	3%	4%	5%	6%	7%	8%	9%	10%
1	1.03	1.04	1.05	1.06	1.07	1.08	1.09	1.10
2	1.06	1.08	1.10	1.12	1.14	1.16	1.18	1.20
3	1.09	1.12	1.15	1.18	1.21	1.24	1.27	1.30
4	1.12	1.16	1.20	1.24	1.28	1.32	1.36	1.40
5	1.15	1.20	1.25	1.30	1.35	1.40	1.45	1.50
6	1.18	1.24	1.30	1.36	1.42	1.48	1.54	1.60
7	1.21	1.28	1.35	1.42	1.49	1.56	1.63	1.70
8	1.24	1.32	1.40	1.48	1.56	1.64	1.72	1.80
9	1.27	1.36	1.45	1.54	1.63	1.72	1.81	1.90
10	1.30	1.40	1.50	1.60	1.70	1.80	1.90	2.00
11	1.33	1.44	1.55	1.66	1.77	1.88	1.99	2.10
12	1.36	1.48	1.60	1.72	1.84	1.96	2.08	2.20
13	1.39	1.52	1.65	1.78	1.91	2.04	2.17	2.30
14	1.42	1.56	1.70	1.84	1.98	2.12	2.26	2.40
15	1.45	1.60	1.75	1.90	2.05	2.20	2.35	2.50
16	1.48	1.64	1.80	1.96	2.12	2.28	2.44	2.60
17	1.51	1.68	1.85	2.02	2.19	2.36	2.53	2.70
18	1.54	1.72	1.90	2.08	2.26	2.44	2.62	2.80
19	1.57	1.76	1.95	2.14	2.33	2.52	2.71	2.90
20	1.60	1.80	2.00	2.20	2.40	2.60	2.80	3.00
21	1.63	1.84	2.05	2.26	2.47	2.68	2.89	3.10
22	1.66	1.88	2.10	2.32	2.54	2.76	2.98	3.20
23	1.69	1.92	2.15	2.38	2.61	2.84	3.07	3.30
24	1.72	1.96	2.20	2.44	2.68	2.92	3.16	3.40
25	1.75	2.00	2.25	2.50	2.75	3.00	3.25	3.50
26	1.78	2.04	2.30	2.56	2.82	3.08	3.34	3.60
27	1.81	2.08	2.35	2.62	2.89	3.16	3.43	3.70
28	1.84	2.12	2.40	2.68	2.96	3.24	3.52	3.80
29	1.87	2.16	2.45	2.74	3.03	3.32	3.61	3.90
30	1.90	2.20	2.50	2.80	3.10	3.40	3.70	4.00
31	1.93	2.24	2.55	2.86	3.17	3.48	3.79	4.10
32	1.96	2.28	2.60	2.92	3.24	3.56	3.88	4.20
33	1.99	2.32	2.65	2.98	3.31	3.64	3.97	4.30
34	2.02	2.36	2.70	3.04	3.38	3.72	4.06	4.40
35	2.05	2.40	2.75	3.10	3.45	3.80	4.15	4.50
36	2.08	2.44	2.80	3.16	3.52	3.88	4.24	4.60
37	2.11	2.48	2.85	3.22	3.59	3.96	4.33	4.70
38	2.14	2.52	2.90	3.28	3.66	4.04	4.42	4.80
39	2.17	2.56	2.95	3.34	3.73	4.12	4.51	4.90
40	2.20	2.60	3.00	3.40	3.80	4.20	4.60	5.00

COMPOUND INTEREST TABLE

Example of use of this table:

Find how much $1,000 now in bank will grow to in 14 years at 6% interest.

From table 14 years at 6%   2.2609

Value in 14 years of $1,000 $2,260.9

Interest Rate

Number of Years	6%	6 1/2%	7%	7 1/2%	8%	8 1/2%	9%	9 1/2%
1	1.0600	1.0650	1.0700	1.0750	1.0800	1.0850	1.0900	1.0950
2	1.1236	1.1342	1.1449	1.1556	1.1664	1.1772	1.1881	1.1990
3	1.1910	1.2079	1.2250	1.2422	1.2597	1.2772	1.2950	1.3129
4	1.2624	1.2864	1.3107	1.3354	1.3604	1.3858	1.4115	1.4376
5	1.3332	1.3700	1.4025	1.4356	1.4693	1.5036	1.5386	1.5742
6	1.4135	1.4591	1.5007	1.5433	1.5868	1.6314	1.6771	1.7237
7	1.5030	1.5539	1.6057	1.6590	1.7138	1.7701	1.8230	1.8875
8	1.5938	1.6549	1.7181	1.7834	1.8509	1.9206	1.9925	2.0668
9	1.6894	1.7625	1.8384	1.9172	1.9990	2.0838	2.1718	2.2632
10	1.7908	1.8771	1.9671	2.0610	2.1589	2.2609	2.3673	2.4782
11	1.8982	1.9991	2.1048	2.2156	2.3316	2.4531	2.5804	2.7136
12	2.0121	2.1290	2.2521	2.3817	2.5181	2.6616	2.8126	2.9714
13	2.1329	2.2674	2.4098	2.5604	2.7196	2.8879	3.0658	3.2537
14	2.2609	2.4148	2.5785	2.7524	2.9371	3.1334	3.3417	3.5628
15	2.3965	2.5718	2.7590	2.9588	3.1721	3.3997	3.6424	3.9013
16	2.5403	2.7390	2.9521	3.1807	3.4259	3.6887	3.9703	4.2719
17	2.6927	2.9170	3.1588	3.4193	3.7000	4.0022	4.3276	4.6777
18	2.8543	3.1066	3.3799	3.6758	3.9960	4.3424	4.7171	5.1221
19	3.0255	3.3085	3.6165	3.9514	4.3157	4.7115	5.1416	5.6087
20	3.2075	3.5236	3.8696	4.2478	4.6609	5.1120	5.6044	6.1416
21	3.3995	3.7526	4.1405	4.5664	5.0338	5.5465	6.1088	6.7250
22	3.6035	3.9966	4.4304	4.9089	5.4365	6.0180	6.6586	7.3639
23	3.8197	4.2563	4.7405	5.2770	5.8714	6.5295	7.2578	8.0635
24	4.0489	4.5330	5.0723	5.6728	6.3411	7.0845	7.9110	8.8295
25	4.2918	4.8276	5.4274	6.0983	6.8484	7.6867	8.6230	9.6683
26	4.5493	5.1414	5.8073	6.5557	7.3963	8.3401	9.3991	10.5868
27	4.8223	5.4756	6.2138	7.0473	7.9880	9.0490	10.2450	11.5926
28	5.1116	5.8316	6.6488	7.5759	8.6271	9.8182	11.1671	12.6939
29	5.4183	6.2106	7.1142	8.1441	9.3172	10.6527	12.1721	13.8998
30	5.7434	6.6143	7.6122	8.7549	10.5582	11.5582	13.2676	15.2203
31	6.0881	7.0442	8.1451	9.4115	10.8676	12.5407	14.4617	16.6662
32	6.4533	7.5021	8.7152	10.1174	11.7370	13.6066	15.7633	18.2495
33	6.8408	7.9898	9.3253	10.8762	12.6760	14.7632	17.1820	19.9832
34	7.2510	8.5091	9.9781	11.6919	13.6901	16.0181	18.7284	21.8816
35	7.6860	9.0622	10.6765	12.5688	14.7853	17.3796	20.4139	23.9604
36	8.1479	9.6513	11.4239	13.5115	15.9681	18.8569	22.2512	26.2366
37	8.6360	10.2786	12.2236	14.5249	17.2456	20.4597	24.2538	28.7291
38	9.1542	10.9467	13.0792	15.6142	18.6252	22.1988	26.4366	31.4583
39	9.7035	11.6582	13.9948	16.7853	20.1152	24.0857	28.8159	34.4469
40	10.2857	12.4160	14.9744	18.0442	21.7245	26.1330	31.4094	37.7193

Compound Interest Table (Con't.)

Number of Years	10%	11%	12%	13%	14%	15%	16%	17%
1	1.1000	1.1100	1.1200	1.1300	1.1400	1.1500	1.1600	1.1700
2	1.2100	1.2321	1.2544	1.2769	1.2996	1.3225	1.3456	1.3689
3	1.3310	1.3576	1.4049	1.4428	1.4815	1.5208	1.5608	1.6016
4	1.4647	1.5180	1.5735	1.6304	1.6389	1.7490	1.8106	1.8738
5	1.6105	1.6350	1.7623	1.8424	1.9254	2.0113	2.1003	2.1924
6	1.7715	1.8704	1.9738	2.0819	2.1949	2.3130	2.4363	2.5651
7	1.9487	2.0761	2.2106	2.3526	2.5022	2.6600	2.8262	3.0012
8	2.1435	2.3045	2.4759	2.6584	2.8525	3.0590	3.2784	3.5114
9	2.3579	2.5580	2.7730	3.0040	3.2519	3.5178	3.8029	4.1084
10	2.5937	2.8394	3.1058	3.3945	3.7072	4.0455	4.4114	4.8068
11	2.8531	3.1517	3.4785	3.8358	4.2262	4.6523	5.1172	5.6239
12	3.1384	3.4984	3.8959	4.3345	4.8179	5.3502	5.9360	6.5800
13	3.4522	3.8832	4.3634	4.8980	5.4924	6.1527	6.8857	7.6986
14	3.7974	4.3104	4.8871	5.5347	6.2613	7.0757	7.9875	9.0074
15	4.1772	4.7845	5.4735	6.2542	7.1379	8.1370	9.2655	10.5387
16	4.5949	5.3108	6.1303	7.0673	8.1372	9.3576	10.7480	12.3303
17	5.0544	5.8950	6.8660	7.9860	9.2764	10.7612	12.4676	14.4264
18	5.5599	6.5435	7.6899	9.0242	10.5751	12.3754	14.4625	16.8789
19	6.1159	7.2633	8.6127	10.1974	12.0556	14.2317	16.7765	19.7483
20	6.7274	8.0623	9.6462	11.5230	13.7434	16.3665	19.4607	23.1055
21	7.4002	8.9491	10.8038	13.0210	15.6675	18.8215	22.5744	27.0335
22	8.1402	9.9335	12.1003	14.7138	17.8610	21.6447	26.1863	31.6292
23	8.9543	11.0262	13.5523	16.6266	20.3615	24.8914	30.3762	37.0062
24	9.8497	12.2391	15.1786	18.7880	23.2122	28.6251	35.2364	43.2972
25	10.8347	13.5854	17.0000	21.2305	26.4619	32.9189	40.8742	50.6578
26	11.9181	15.0793	19.0400	23.9905	30.1665	37.8567	47.4141	59.2696
27	13.1099	16.7386	21.3248	27.1092	34.3899	43.5353	55.0003	69.3454
28	14.4209	18.5799	23.8838	30.6334	39.2044	50.0656	63.8004	81.1342
29	15.8630	20.6236	26.7499	34.6158	44.6931	57.5754	74.0085	94.9270
30	17.4494	22.8922	29.9599	39.1158	50.9501	66.2117	85.8498	111.0646
31	19.1943	25.4104	33.5551	44.2009	58.0831	76.1435	99.5858	129.9456
32	21.1137	28.2055	37.5817	49.9470	66.2148	87.5650	115.5195	152.0363
33	23.2251	31.3082	42.0915	56.4402	75.4849	100.6998	134.0027	177.8825
34	25.5476	34.7521	47.1425	63.7774	86.0527	115.8048	155.4431	208.1226
35	28.1024	38.5748	52.7996	72.0685	98.1001	133.1755	180.3140	243.5034
36	30.9128	42.8180	59.1355	81.4374	111.8342	153.1518	209.1643	284.8990
37	34.0039	47.5280	66.2318	92.0242	127.4909	176.1246	242.6306	333.3319
38	37.4048	52.7561	74.1796	103.9874	145.3397	202.5433	281.4515	389.9983
39	41.1447	58.5593	83.0812	117.5057	165.6872	232.9248	326.4837	456.2980
40	45.2592	65.0008	93.0509	132.7815	188.8835	267.8635	378.7211	533.8687

Compound Interest Table (Con't.)

Number of Years	18%	19%	20%	21%	22%	23%	24%	25%
1	1.1800	1.1900	1.2000	1.2100	1.2200	1.2300	1.2400	1.2500
2	1.3924	1.4161	1.4400	1.4641	1.4884	1.5129	1.5376	1.5625
3	1.6430	1.6851	1.7280	1.7715	1.8158	1.8608	1.9066	1.9531
4	1.9387	2.0053	2.0736	2.1435	2.2153	2.2888	2.3642	2.4414
5	2.2877	2.3863	2.4883	2.5937	2.7027	2.8153	2.9316	3.0517
6	2.6995	2.8397	2.9859	3.1384	3.2973	3.4628	3.6352	3.8146
7	3.1854	3.3793	3.5831	3.7974	4.0227	4.2592	4.5076	4.7683
8	3.7588	4.0213	4.2998	4.5949	4.9077	5.2389	5.5895	5.9604
9	4.4354	4.7854	5.1597	5.5599	5.9874	6.4438	6.9309	7.4505
10	5.2338	5.6946	6.1917	6.7274	7.3046	7.9259	8.5944	9.3132
11	6.1759	6.7766	7.4300	8.1402	8.9116	9.7489	10.6570	11.6415
12	7.2875	8.0642	8.9161	9.8497	10.8722	11.9911	13.2147	14.5519
13	8.5993	9.5964	10.6993	11.9181	13.2641	14.7491	16.3863	18.1898
14	10.1472	11.4197	12.8391	14.4209	16.1822	18.1414	20.3190	22.7373
15	11.9737	13.5895	15.4070	17.4494	19.7422	22.3139	25.1956	28.4217
16	14.1290	16.1715	18.4884	21.1137	24.0855	27.4461	31.2425	35.5271
17	16.6722	19.2441	22.1861	25.5476	29.3844	33.7587	38.7408	44.4089
18	19.6732	22.9005	26.6233	30.9126	35.8489	41.5233	48.0385	55.5111
19	23.2144	27.2516	31.9479	37.4043	43.7357	51.0736	59.5678	69.3889
20	27.3930	32.4294	38.3375	45.2592	53.3576	62.8206	73.8641	86.7361
21	32.3237	38.5910	46.0051	54.7636	65.0963	77.2693	91.5915	108.4202
22	38.1420	45.9233	55.2061	66.2640	79.4175	95.0413	113.5735	135.5252
23	45.0076	54.6487	66.2473	80.1795	96.8893	116.9008	140.8311	169.4065
24	53.1090	65.0319	79.4968	97.0172	118.2050	143.7880	174.6306	211.7582
25	62.6686	77.3880	95.3962	117.3908	144.2101	176.8592	216.5419	264.6977
26	73.9488	92.0918	114.4754	142.0429	175.9363	217.5368	268.5120	330.8722
27	87.2597	109.5892	137.3705	171.8719	214.6423	267.5703	332.9549	413.5903
28	102.9665	130.4112	164.8446	207.9650	261.8636	329.1115	412.8641	516.9878
29	121.5005	155.1893	197.8135	251.6377	319.4736	404.8072	511.9515	646.2348
30	143.3708	184.6753	237.3763	304.4816	389.7578	497.9128	634.8199	807.7935
31	169.1773	219.7636	284.8515	368.4227	475.5046	612.4328	787.1767	1009.7419
32	199.6292	261.5187	341.8218	445.7915	580.1156	753.2923	976.0991	1262.1774
33	235.5625	311.2072	410.1862	539.4077	707.7410	926.5496	1210.3629	1577.7218
34	277.9638	370.3366	492.2235	652.6834	863.4441	1139.6560	1500.8500	1972.1522
35	327.9972	440.7006	590.6682	789.7469	1053.4018	1401.7769	1861.0540	2465.1903
36	387.0368	524.4337	708.8018	955.5938	1285.1502	1724.1855	2307.7069	3081.4879
37	456.7034	624.0761	850.5622	1156.2685	1567.8833	2120.7482	2861.5566	3851.8598
38	538.9100	742.6505	1020.6746	1399.0849	1912.8176	2608.5203	3548.3302	4814.8248
39	635.9138	883.7542	1224.8096	1692.8927	2333.6375	3208.4800	4399.9295	6018.5310
40	750.3783	1051.6675	1469.7715	2048.4002	2847.0377	3946.4304	5455.9126	7523.1638

PERIODIC DEPOSIT TABLE

Example of use of this table:
How much is $1,000 a year invested at 6% worth in 20 years?
At 6% for 20 years, the figure is   38.993
For $1,000 a year, the amount is $38,993

Interest Rate

Number of Years	6%	7%	8%	9%	10%	11%	12%	13%
1	1.060	1.070	1.080	1.090	1.100	1.110	1.120	1.130
2	2.183	2.215	2.246	2.278	2.310	2.342	2.374	2.407
3	3.375	3.440	3.506	3.573	3.641	3.710	3.779	3.850
4	4.637	4.751	4.867	4.985	5.105	5.228	5.353	5.480
5	5.975	6.153	6.336	6.523	6.716	6.913	7.115	7.323
6	7.394	7.654	7.923	8.200	8.487	8.783	9.089	9.405
7	8.897	9.260	9.637	10.028	10.436	10.859	11.300	11.757
8	10.491	10.978	11.488	12.021	12.579	13.164	13.776	14.416
9	12.181	12.816	13.487	14.193	14.937	15.722	16.549	17.420
10	13.972	14.784	15.645	16.560	17.531	18.561	19.655	20.814
11	15.870	16.888	17.977	19.141	20.384	21.713	23.133	24.650
12	17.882	19.141	20.495	21.953	23.523	25.212	27.029	28.985
13	20.015	21.550	23.215	25.019	26.975	29.095	31.393	33.883
14	22.276	24.129	26.152	28.361	30.772	33.405	36.280	39.417
15	24.673	26.888	29.324	32.003	34.950	38.190	41.753	45.672
16	27.213	29.840	32.750	35.974	39.545	43.501	47.884	52.739
17	29.906	32.999	36.450	40.301	44.599	49.396	54.750	60.725
18	32.760	36.379	40.446	45.018	50.159	55.939	62.440	69.749
19	35.786	39.995	44.762	50.160	56.275	63.203	71.052	79.947
20	38.993	43.865	49.423	55.765	63.002	71.265	80.699	91.470
21	42.392	48.006	54.457	61.873	70.403	80.214	91.503	104.491
22	45.996	52.436	59.893	68.532	78.543	90.148	103.603	119.205
23	49.816	57.177	65.765	75.790	87.497	101.174	117.155	135.831
24	53.865	62.249	72.106	83.701	97.347	113.413	132.334	154.620
25	58.156	67.676	78.954	92.324	108.182	126.999	149.334	175.850
26	62.706	73.484	86.351	101.723	120.100	142.079	168.374	199.841
27	67.528	79.698	94.339	111.968	133.210	158.817	189.699	226.950
28	72.640	86.347	102.966	123.135	147.631	177.397	213.583	257.583
29	78.058	93.461	112.283	135.308	163.494	198.021	240.333	292.199
30	83.802	101.073	122.346	148.575	180.943	220.913	270.293	331.315
31	89.890	109.218	133.214	163.037	200.138	246.324	303.848	375.516
32	96.343	117.933	144.951	178.800	221.252	274.529	341.429	425.463
33	103.184	127.259	157.627	195.982	244.477	305.837	383.521	481.903
34	110.435	137.237	171.317	214.711	270.024	340.590	430.663	545.681
35	118.121	147.913	186.102	235.125	298.127	379.164	483.463	617.749
36	126.268	159.337	202.070	257.376	329.039	421.982	542.599	699.187
37	134.904	171.561	219.316	281.630	363.043	469.511	608.831	791.211
38	144.058	184.640	237.941	308.066	400.448	522.267	683.010	895.198
39	153.762	198.635	258.057	336.882	441.593	580.826	766.091	1012.704
40	164.048	213.610	279.781	368.292	486.852	645.827	859.142	1145.486

COMPOUND DISCOUNT TABLE

This table shows the present or discounted value of $1 due at a given future time. For example, assume property which will revert to a lessor in 10 years will then be worth $1,000. The present value of this reversion, computed at an assumed rate of 4% on the investment, is found by finding the factor on the 10-year line in the 4% column. The factor .6756 is multiplied by 1000 to obtain the answer of $675.60.

Years	4%	4-1/2%	5%	5-1/2%	6%	6-1/2%	7%	7-1/2%	8%	9%	10%	11%
1	0.9615	0.9569	0.9524	0.9479	0.9434	0.9390	0.9346	0.9302	0.9259	0.9174	0.9091	0.9009
2	.9246	.9157	.9070	.8985	.8900	.8817	.8734	.8653	.8573	.8417	.8264	.8116
3	.8890	.8763	.8638	.8516	.8396	.8278	.8163	.8050	.7938	.7722	.7513	.7312
4	.8548	.8386	.8277	.8072	.7921	.7773	.7629	.7488	.7350	.7084	.6830	.6587
5	.8219	.8025	.7835	.7651	.7473	.7299	.7130	.6966	.6806	.6499	.6209	.5935
6	.7903	.7679	.7462	.7252	.7050	.6853	.6663	.6480	.6302	.5963	.5645	.5346
7	.7599	.7343	.7107	.6874	.6651	.6435	.6227	.6027	.5835	.5470	.5132	.4816
8	.7307	.7032	.6768	.6516	.6274	.6042	.5820	.5607	.5403	.5019	.4665	.4339
9	.7026	.6729	.6446	.6176	.5919	.5673	.5439	.5216	.5002	.4604	.4241	.3909
10	.6756	.6439	.6139	.5854	.5584	.5327	.5083	.4852	.4632	.4224	.3855	.3522
11	.6496	.6162	.5847	.5549	.5268	.5002	.4751	.4514	.4289	.3875	.3505	.3173
12	.6246	.5897	.5568	.5260	.4970	.4697	.4440	.4199	.3971	.3555	.3186	.2858
13	.6006	.5643	.5303	.4986	.4688	.4410	.4150	.3906	.3677	.3262	.2897	.2575
14	.5775	.5400	.5051	.4726	.4423	.4141	.3878	.3633	.3405	.2992	.2633	.2320
15	.5553	.5167	.4810	.4479	.4173	.3888	.3624	.3380	.3152	.2745	.2394	.2090
16	.5339	.4945	.4581	.4246	.3936	.3651	.3387	.3144	.2919	.2519	.2176	.1883
17	.5134	.4732	.4363	.4024	.3714	.3428	.3166	.2924	.2703	.2311	.1978	.1696
18	.4936	.4528	.4155	.3815	.3503	.3219	.2959	.2720	.2502	.2120	.1799	.1528
19	.4746	.4333	.3957	.3616	.3305	.3022	.2765	.2531	.2317	.1945	.1635	.1377
20	.4564	.4146	.3769	.3427	.3118	.2838	.2584	.2354	.2145	.1784	.1486	.1240
21	.4388	.3988	.3589	.3249	.2942	.2665	.2415	.2190	.1987	.1637	.1351	.1117
22	.4220	.3797	.3418	.3079	.2775	.2502	.2257	.2037	.1839	.1502	.1228	.1007
23	.4057	.3633	.3256	.2919	.2618	.2349	.2109	.1895	.1703	.1378	.1117	.0907
24	.3901	.3477	.3101	.2766	.2470	.2206	.1971	.1763	.1577	.1264	.1015	.0817
25	.3751	.3327	.2953	.2622	.2330	.2071	.1842	.1640	.1460	.1160	.0923	.0736
26	.3607	.3184	.2812	.2486	.2198	.1945	.1722	.1525	.1352	.1064	.0829	.0663
27	.3468	.3047	.2678	.2356	.2074	.1826	.1609	.1419	.1252	.0976	.0763	.0597
28	.3335	.2916	.2551	.2233	.1956	.1715	.1504	.1320	.1159	.0895	.0693	.0538

Compound Discount Table (Con't.)

Years	4%	4-1/2%	5%	5-1/2%	6%	6-1/2%	7%	7-1/2%	8%	9%	10%	11%
29	0.3207	0.2790	0.2429	0.2117	0.1846	0.1610	0.1406	0.1228	0.1073	0.0822	0.0630	0.0485
30	.3083	.2670	.2314	.2006	.1741	.1512	.1314	.1142	.0994	.0754	.0573	.0437
31	.2965	.2555	.2204	.1902	.1643	.1420	.1228	.1063	.0920	.0691	.0521	.0394
32	.2851	.2445	.2099	.1803	.1550	.1333	.1147	.0988	.0852	.0634	.0474	.0354
33	.2741	.2340	.1999	.1709	.1462	.1251	.1072	.0919	.0789	.0582	.0431	.0319
34	.2636	.2239	.1904	.1620	.1379	.1175	.1002	.0855	.0730	.0534	.0391	.0288
35	.2534	.2142	.1813	.1535	.1301	.1103	.0937	.0796	.0676	.0490	.0356	.0259
36	.2437	.2050	.1727	.1455	.1227	.1036	.0875	.0740	.0626	.0449	.0323	.0234
37	.2343	.1962	.1644	.1379	.1158	.0973	.0818	.0688	.0580	.0412	.0294	.0210
38	.2253	.1878	.1566	.1307	.1092	.0914	.0765	.0640	.0537	.0378	.0267	.0189
39	.2166	.1797	.1491	.1239	.1031	.0858	.0715	.0596	.0497	.0347	.0243	.0171
40	.2083	.1719	.1420	.1175	.0972	.0805	.0668	.0554	.0460	.0318	.0221	.0154
41	.2003	.1645	.1353	.1113	.0917	.0756	.0624	.0515	.0426	.0292	.0201	.0139
42	.1926	.1574	.1288	.1055	.0865	.0710	.0583	.0480	.0395	.0268	.0183	.0125
43	.1852	.1507	.1227	.1000	.0816	.0667	.0545	.0446	.0365	.0246	.0166	.0112
44	.1780	.1442	.1169	.0948	.0770	.0626	.0509	.0415	.0338	.0225	.0151	.0101
45	.1712	.1380	.1113	.0899	.0726	.0588	.0476	.0386	.0313	.0207	.0137	.0091
46	.1646	.1320	.1060	.0852	.0685	.0552	.0445	.0359	.0290	.0190	.0125	.0082
47	.1583	.1263	.1009	.0807	.0647	.0518	.0416	.0334	.0269	.0174	.0113	.0074
48	.1522	.1209	.0961	.0765	.0610	.0487	.0389	.0311	.0249	.0160	.0103	.0067
49	.1463	.1157	.0916	.0725	.0575	.0457	.0363	.0289	.0230	.0147	.0094	.0060
50	.1407	.1107	.0872	.0688	.0543	.0429	.0339	.0269	.0213	.0134	.0085	.0054
51	.1353	.1059	.0831	.0652	.0512	.0403	.0317	.0250	.0197	.0123	.0077	.00488
52	.1301	.1014	.0791	.0618	.0483	.0378	.0297	.0233	.0183	.0113	.0070	.00440
53	.1251	.0970	.0753	.0586	.0456	.0355	.0277	.0216	.0169	.0104	.0064	.00396
54	.1203	.0928	.0717	.0555	.0430	.0333	.0259	.0201	.0157	.0095	.0058	.00357
55	.1157	.0888	.0683	.0526	.0406	.0313	.0242	.0187	.0145	.0087	.0053	.00322
56	.1112	.0850	.0651	.0499	.0383	.0294	.0226	.0174	.0134	.0080	.0048	.00290
57	.1069	.0814	.0620	.0473	.0361	.0276	.0211	.0162	.0124	.0073	.0044	.00261
58	.1028	.0778	.0590	.0448	.0341	.0259	.0198	.0151	.0115	.0067	.0040	.00235
59	.0989	.0745	.0562	.0425	.0321	.0243	.0185	.0140	.0107	.0062	.0036	.00212
60	.0951	.0713	.0535	.0403	.0303	.0229	.0173	.0130	.0099	.0057	.0033	.00191

PRESENT WORTH TABLE — SINGLE FUTURE PAYMENT

Example of use of this table:
Find how much $10,000 payable in 12 years is worth now at an interest rate of 6%.
From table for 12 years 6%
Present value of $10,000 in 12 years (10,000 × .4970)

.4970
$4.970

Interest Rate

Number of Years	6%	7%	8%	9%	10%	11%	12%	13%
1	0.9434	0.9346	0.9259	0.9174	0.9091	0.9009	0.8929	0.8850
2	0.8900	0.8734	0.8573	0.8417	0.8264	0.8116	0.7972	0.7831
3	0.8396	0.8163	0.7938	0.7722	0.7513	0.7312	0.7118	0.6931
4	0.7921	0.7629	0.7350	0.7084	0.6830	0.6587	0.6355	0.6133
5	0.7473	0.7130	0.6806	0.6499	0.6209	0.5935	0.5674	0.5428
6	0.7050	0.6663	0.6302	0.5963	0.5645	0.5346	0.5066	0.4803
7	0.6651	0.6227	0.5835	0.5470	0.5132	0.4816	0.4523	0.4251
8	0.6274	0.5820	0.5403	0.5019	0.4665	0.4339	0.4039	0.3762
9	0.5919	0.5439	0.5002	0.4604	0.4241	0.3909	0.3606	0.3329
10	0.5584	0.5083	0.4632	0.4224	0.3855	0.3522	0.3220	0.2946
11	0.5268	0.4751	0.4289	0.3875	0.3505	0.3173	0.2875	0.2607
12	0.4970	0.4440	0.3971	0.3555	0.3186	0.2858	0.2567	0.2307
13	0.4688	0.4150	0.3677	0.3262	0.2897	0.2575	0.2292	0.2042
14	0.4423	0.3878	0.3405	0.2992	0.2633	0.2320	0.2046	0.1807
15	0.4173	0.3624	0.3152	0.2745	0.2394	0.2090	0.1827	0.1599
16	0.3936	0.3387	0.2919	0.2519	0.2176	0.1883	0.1631	0.1415
17	0.3714	0.3166	0.2703	0.2311	0.1978	0.1696	0.1456	0.1252
18	0.3503	0.2959	0.2502	0.2120	0.1799	0.1528	0.1300	0.1108
19	0.3305	0.2765	0.2317	0.1945	0.1635	0.1377	0.1161	0.0981
20	0.3118	0.2584	0.2145	0.1784	0.1486	0.1240	0.1037	0.0868
21	0.2942	0.2415	0.1987	0.1637	0.1351	0.1117	0.0926	0.0768
22	0.2775	0.2257	0.1839	0.1502	0.1228	0.1007	0.0826	0.0680
23	0.2618	0.2109	0.1703	0.1378	0.1117	0.0907	0.0738	0.0601
24	0.2470	0.1971	0.1577	0.1264	0.1015	0.0817	0.0660	0.0532
25	0.2330	0.1842	0.1460	0.1160	0.0923	0.0736	0.0588	0.0471
26	0.2198	0.1722	0.1352	0.1064	0.0829	0.0663	0.0525	0.0417
27	0.2074	0.1609	0.1252	0.0976	0.0763	0.0597	0.0470	0.0369
28	0.1956	0.1504	0.1159	0.0895	0.0693	0.0538	0.0420	0.0326
29	0.1846	0.1406	0.1073	0.0822	0.0630	0.0485	0.0374	0.0289
30	0.1741	0.1314	0.0994	0.0754	0.0573	0.0437	0.0334	0.0256
31	0.1643	0.1228	0.0920	0.0691	0.0521	0.0394	0.0298	0.0226
32	0.1550	0.1147	0.0852	0.0634	0.0474	0.0354	0.0266	0.0200
33	0.1462	0.1072	0.0789	0.0582	0.0431	0.0319	0.0238	0.0177
34	0.1379	0.1002	0.0730	0.0534	0.0391	0.0288	0.0212	0.0157
35	0.1301	0.0937	0.0676	0.0490	0.0356	0.0259	0.0189	0.0139
36	0.1227	0.0875	0.0626	0.0449	0.0323	0.0234	0.0169	0.0123
37	0.1158	0.0818	0.0580	0.0412	0.0294	0.0210	0.0151	0.0109
38	0.1092	0.0765	0.0536	0.0378	0.0267	0.0189	0.0135	0.0096
39	0.1031	0.0715	0.0497	0.0347	0.0243	0.0171	0.0120	0.0085
40	0.0972	0.0668	0.0460	0.0318	0.0221	0.0154	0.0107	0.0075

PRESENT WORTH TABLE — PERIODIC FUTURE PAYMENTS

Example of use of this table:
To find the cost now of $1,000 of income per year for 20 years at 7%.
From table for 20 years at 7%   10.5940
Cost of $1,000 per year ($1,000 × 10.5940)   **$10,594**

Interest Rate

Number of Years	6%	7%	8%	9%	10%	11%	12%	13%
1	0.9434	0.9346	0.9259	0.9174	0.9091	0.9009	0.8929	0.8850
2	1.8334	1.8080	1.7833	1.7591	1.7355	1.7125	1.6901	1.6681
3	2.6730	2.6243	2.5771	2.5313	2.4869	2.4437	2.4018	2.3612
4	3.4651	3.3872	3.3121	3.2397	3.1699	3.1024	3.0373	2.9745
5	4.2124	4.1002	3.9927	3.8897	3.7908	3.6959	3.6048	3.5172
6	4.9173	4.7665	4.6229	4.4859	4.3553	4.2305	4.1114	3.9975
7	5.5824	5.3893	5.2064	5.0330	4.8684	4.7122	4.5638	4.4226
8	6.2098	5.9713	5.7466	5.5348	5.3349	5.1461	4.9676	4.7988
9	6.8017	6.5152	6.2469	5.9952	5.7590	5.5370	5.3282	5.1317
10	7.3601	7.0236	6.7101	6.4177	6.1446	5.8892	5.6502	5.4262
11	7.8869	7.4987	7.1390	6.8052	6.4951	6.2065	5.9377	5.6869
12	8.3838	7.9427	7.5361	7.1607	6.8137	6.4924	6.1944	5.9176
13	8.8527	8.3577	7.9038	7.4869	7.1034	6.7499	6.4235	6.1218
14	9.2950	8.7455	8.2442	7.7862	7.3667	6.9819	6.6282	6.3025
15	9.7122	9.1079	8.5595	8.0607	7.6061	7.1909	6.8109	6.4624
16	10.1059	9.4466	8.8514	8.3126	7.8237	7.3792	6.9740	6.6039
17	10.4773	9.7632	9.1216	8.5436	8.0216	7.5488	7.1196	6.7291
18	10.8276	10.0591	9.3719	8.7556	8.2014	7.7016	7.2497	6.8399
19	11.1581	10.3356	9.6036	8.9501	8.3649	7.8393	7.3658	6.9380
20	11.4699	10.5940	9.8181	9.1285	8.5136	7.9633	7.4694	7.0248
21	11.7641	10.8355	10.0168	9.2922	8.6487	8.0751	7.5620	7.1016
22	12.0416	11.0612	10.2007	9.4424	8.7715	8.1757	7.6446	7.1695
23	12.3034	11.2722	10.3711	9.5802	8.8832	8.2664	7.7184	7.2297
24	12.5504	11.4693	10.5288	9.7066	8.9847	8.3481	7.7843	7.2829
25	12.7834	11.6536	10.6748	9.8226	9.0770	8.4217	7.8431	7.3299
26	13.0032	11.8258	10.8100	9.9290	9.1609	8.4881	7.8957	7.3717
27	13.2105	11.9867	10.9352	10.0266	9.2372	8.5478	7.9426	7.4086
28	13.4062	12.1371	11.0511	10.1161	9.3066	8.6016	7.9844	7.4412
29	13.5907	12.2777	11.1584	10.1983	9.3696	8.6501	8.0218	7.4701
30	13.7648	12.4090	11.2578	10.2737	9.4269	8.6938	8.0552	7.4957
31	13.9291	12.5318	11.3498	10.3428	9.4790	8.7331	8.0850	7.5183
32	14.0840	12.6466	11.4350	10.4062	9.5264	8.7686	8.1116	7.5383
33	14.2302	12.7538	11.5139	10.4644	9.5694	8.8005	8.1354	7.5560
34	14.3681	12.8540	11.5869	10.5178	9.6086	8.8293	8.1566	7.5717
35	14.4982	12.9477	11.6546	10.5668	9.6442	8.8552	8.1755	7.5856
36	14.6210	13.0352	11.7172	10.6118	9.6765	8.8786	8.1924	7.5979
37	14.7368	13.1170	11.7752	10.6530	9.7059	8.8996	8.2075	7.6087
38	14.8460	13.1935	11.8289	10.6908	9.7327	8.9186	8.2210	7.6183
39	14.9491	13.2649	11.8786	10.7255	9.7569	8.9357	8.2330	7.6268
40	15.0463	13.3317	11.9246	10.7574	9.7791	8.9511	8.2438	7.6344

SINKING FUND REQUIREMENTS TABLE

Example of use of this table:
To find the amount of money which must be deposited at the end of each year to grow to $10,000 in 19 years at 8%.
From table for 19 years at 8%   .02413
Amount of each deposit ($10,000 × .02413) $241.30

Interest Rate

Number of Years	6%	7%	8%	9%	10%	11%	12%	13%
1	1.00000	1.00000	1.00000	1.00000	1.00000	1.00000	1.00000	1.00000
2	.48544	.48309	.48077	.47847	.47619	.47393	.47169	.46948
3	.31411	.31105	.30803	.30505	.30211	.29921	.29635	.29352
4	.22859	.22523	.22192	.21867	.21547	.21233	.20923	.20619
5	.17740	.17389	.17046	.16709	.16379	.16057	.15741	.15431
6	.14336	.13979	.13632	.13292	.12961	.12638	.12323	.12015
7	.11913	.11555	.11207	.10869	.10541	.10222	.09912	.09611
8	.10104	.09747	.09401	.09067	.08744	.08432	.08130	.07839
9	.08702	.08349	.08008	.07679	.07364	.07060	.06768	.06487
10	.07587	.07238	.06903	.06582	.06275	.05980	.05698	.05429
11	.06679	.06336	.06008	.05695	.05396	.05112	.04846	.04584
12	.05928	.05590	.05269	.04965	.04676	.04403	.04144	.03899
13	.05296	.04965	.04652	.04357	.04078	.03815	.03568	.03335
14	.04758	.04434	.04129	.03843	.03575	.03323	.03087	.02867
15	.04296	.03979	.03683	.03406	.03147	.02907	.02682	.02474
16	.03895	.03586	.03298	.03030	.02782	.02552	.02339	.02143
17	.03544	.03243	.02963	.02705	.02466	.02247	.02046	.01861
18	.03236	.02941	.02670	.02421	.02193	.01984	.01794	.01620
19	.02962	.02675	.02413	.02173	.01955	.01756	.01576	.01413
20	.02718	.02439	.02185	.01955	.01746	.01558	.01388	.01235
21	.02500	.02229	.01983	.01762	.01562	.01384	.01224	.01081
22	.02305	.02041	.01803	.01590	.01401	.01231	.01081	.00948
23	.02128	.01871	.01642	.01438	.01257	.01097	.00956	.00832
24	.01968	.01719	.01498	.01302	.01129	.00979	.00846	.00731
25	.01823	.01581	.01368	.01181	.01017	.00874	.00749	.00643
26	.01690	.01456	.01251	.01072	.00916	.00781	.00665	.00565
27	.01570	.01343	.01145	.00973	.00826	.00699	.00590	.00498
28	.01459	.01239	.01049	.00885	.00745	.00626	.00524	.00439
29	.01358	.01145	.00962	.00806	.00673	.00561	.00466	.00387
30	.01265	.01059	.00883	.00734	.00608	.00502	.00414	.00341
31	.01179	.00979	.00811	.00669	.00549	.00451	.00369	.00301
32	.01100	.00907	.00745	.00609	.00497	.00404	.00328	.00266
33	.01027	.00841	.00685	.00556	.00449	.00363	.00292	.00234
34	.00960	.00779	.00630	.00508	.00407	.00326	.00260	.00207
35	.00897	.00723	.00580	.00464	.00369	.00293	.00232	.00183
36	.00839	.00676	.00534	.00424	.00334	.00263	.00206	.00162
37	.00786	.00624	.00492	.00387	.00303	.00236	.00184	.00143
38	.00736	.00579	.00454	.00354	.00275	.00213	.00164	.00126
39	.00689	.00539	.00419	.00324	.00249	.00191	.00146	.00112
40	.00646	.00501	.00386	.00296	.00226	.00172	.00130	.00099

Appendix D — Accounting Methods — Advantages and Disadvantages

Who May Use	When Income Is Taxed	When Expenses Are Deductible	Advantages	Disadvantages
Cash Method				
Any taxpayer — unless inventories necessary to reflect income.	In year cash or property is received. For property, use fair market value.	Year in which payment is made in cash or property. Giving note is not payment; payment can be made with borrowed funds.	You don't pay taxes until you get the income.	You don't always match related income and expenses in one year, thur creating distortions.
Must be used if no records or incomplete ones.	Taxed in year of *constructive receipt*— even if there's no actual receipt (i.e., year income was available to you although you didn't take it).	Certain prepaid expenses must be spread over periods to which they apply even though full amount has been paid: *e.g.*, insurance premiums, rent. But payment for supplies bought in advance is currently deductible.	You can control each year's receipts and payouts and even out income over the years.	You may not have full control over receipts and income may pile up in one year.
Can use in one business although other method is used in other business.			You can keep simple records.	Liquidation or sale of business may create income bunching — all accounts receivable may have to be picked up at one time.
Accrual Method				
Anyone except those with no — or incomplete — books or records.	In year income is earned — i.e., year in which right to income becomes fixed, regardless of year of receipt.	In the year all events have occurred which fix the fact and the amount of your liability, regardless of the year of payment. Effective after 7/18/84, no deduction until "Economic Performance" occurs. See Sec. 461.	It matches income and related expenses and tends to even out your income over the years.	Have less leeway than cash-basis taxpayer to defer or accelerate income or deductions.

453

Who May Use	When Income Is Taxed	When Expenses Are Deductible	Advantages	Disadvantages
You must use if inventories are necessary to reflect income clearly — unless you can use one of the methods discussed below.	You do not accrue contingent, contested, or uncollectable items. Prepaid amounts are income when received — even if not yet earned. However, some relief is available by a special election to defer the income (see Rev. Proc. 71-21).	You do not accrue contingent or contested of liabilities. But if you pay a liability and still contest it, you deduct it when you pay it. If you get a recovery later, it's income when recovered.		Can still accelerate deductions, however, by: advancing repairs and advertising expenditures within desired period, purchasing supplies, getting bills for professional services before year-end.

"Hybrid" Method (see Reg. §1.446-(c) (1) (iv))

Who May Use	When Income Is Taxed	When Expenses Are Deductible	Advantages	Disadvantages
Any taxpayer if method clearly reflects income and is consistently used.	Accrual method is used in respect of purchases and sales, while cash method is used for all other items of income and expense.		Method is simple; it's not necessary to accrue income items such as interest, dividends. And the bother of accruing small expenses is removed.	Method is not entirely accurate. Since it is a "hybrid" it does not reflect true income. However, if consistently used, it gives a fairly good idea of how business is doing.

Who May Use	When Income Is Taxed	When Expenses Are Deductible	Advantages	Disadvantages
Installment Method				
Installment dealers who elect this method. Generally, seller in casual sale of personal property or of real property.	Each year that collections are made, a proportionate amount of each collection (equal to percentage of gross profit on entire sale) is picked up as gross income in the year of collection.	Dealer deducts expenses when paid (cash basis) or incurred (accrual basis). On casual sales, expense of sale reduces sales price, thereby having effect of spreading deduction over period of reporting income.	Income is spread over period of collection—so you do not pay taxes on amounts not yet received. If tax rates decline in future, part of profits will bear a lower tax.	Dealers who switch from accrual to installment basis may have to pay a double tax on some receivables — unless they sell off all receivables before the switch. Tax rates may go up; all depreciation recapture income is taxed in year of sale.
Deferred Payment Sales Method				
Any cash-basis taxpayer on sale of personal property. Any cash or accrual taxpayer on sale of real estate.	At time of sale, seller picks up cash and *fair market value* of buyer's obligations. If total exceeds basis of sold property, difference is taxable. In later years, as obligations are collected, difference between amount received and value at which obligations were picked up originally is taxable at time of collection.	Used generally with casual sales.	Useful in somewhat speculative deals where value of buyer's obligations are contingent on future operations and have little or no ascertainable present value.	You may be in for a long and costly argument with IRS as to value of obligations. Even though original sale gave capital gain, gain on collection of the obligations in future years will be taxable as ordinary income.

Long-Term Contract Methods

Percentage of Completion Method

Who May Use	When Income Is Taxed	When Expenses Are Deductible	Advantages	Disadvantages
Taxpayers who have long-term contracts more than a year to complete — usually construction contracts. There are two long-term contract methods — (1) percentage of completion and (2) completed contract — and IRS permission is needed to switch to or from either.	A portion of the total contract price is taken into account each year according to the percentage of the contract completed that year. Architects' or engineers' certificates are required.	All expenses made during the year allocable to that contract are deducted — with adjustments made for inventories and supplies on hand at the beginning and end of the year.	Income from long-term contract is reflected as earned. Income bunching in one year is avoided.	Accurate estimates of completion are difficult to make in some cases. If expenses are irregular as compared with income, there may be distortion of income in the interim years — although the final total will work out accurately.

Completed Contract Method

	The entire contract price is picked up as income in the year the contract is completed and accepted.	Expenses allocable to specific contracts (that would exclude general administrative cost) are not deductible until year of completion — when income is picked up.	Income can be reflected more accurately — all the figures are in when the computation is made. Avoids estimates in interim years which may turn out to be wrong.	Bunching of income or losses in one year is possible if a number of profitable or unprofitable contracts are all finished in one year. A steady flow of completed contracts from year to year overcomes this problem. There may be some argument with IRS as to proper year of completion in some cases.

Appendix E — Installment Method Examples

(1) ADJUSTMENTS IN TAX ON CHANGE TO INSTALLMENT METHOD

	Taxable Years Prior to Change		Adjustment Years After Change	
	Year 1	Year 2	Year 3	Year 4
Gross profit from installment sales (receivable in periodic payments over 5 years)	$100,000	$ 50,000	$ 20,000 [1] 10,000 [5] 80,000 [6]	$ 12,000 [4] 8,000 [5] 40,000 [6] 90,000 [7]
Other income	80,000	200,000	90,000	90,000
Gross income	$180,000	$250,000	$200,000	$240,000
Deductions	60,000	50,000	50,000	60,000
Taxable income	120,000	200,000	150,000	180,000
Tax rate assumed	30%	50%	40%	40%
Tax would be	$ 36,000	$100,000	$ 60,000	$ 72,000

Computation of Adjustment in Year 3
Year 1 Items

		Lesser Tax Portion
In Year 3 Portion of tax	20,000/200,000 × 60,000 = $6,000	
In Year 1 Portion of tax	20,000/180,000 × 36,000 = 4,000	$4,000

Year 2 Items

In Year 3 Portion of tax	10,000/200,000 × 60,000 = 3,000	
In Year 2 Portion of tax	10,000/250,000 × 100,000 = 4,000	3,000
Adjustment to tax of Year 3		$7,000

Computation of Adjustment in Year 4
Year 1 Items

In Year 4 Portion of tax	12,000/240,000 × 72,000 = $3,600	
In Year 1 Portion of tax	12,000/180,000 × 36,000 = 2,400	$2,400

Year 2 Items

In Year 4 Portion of tax	8,000/240,000 × 72,000 = 2,400	
In Year 2 Portion of tax	8,000/250,000 × 100,000 = 3,200	2,400
Adjustment to tax of Year 4		$4,800

[1] and [4] from Year 1 Sales
[2] and [5] from Year 2 Sales
[3] and [6] from Year 3 Sales
[7] from Year 4 Sales

(2) COMPUTATION BY DEALER UNDER INSTALLMENT METHOD

		First Year		Second Year		Third Year	
		(a) Cash Sales	(b) Installment Sales	(a) Cash Sales	(b) Installment Sales	(a) Cash Sales	(b) Installment Sales
(1)	Unit sales	40	80	60	100	70	120
(2)	Gross sales	$16,000	$40,000	$24,000	$50,000	$28,000	$60,000
(3)	Cost of goods sold	12,000	24,000	18,900	31,500	20,300	34,800
(4)	Gross profit	$ 4,000	$16,000	$ 5,100	$18,500	$ 7,700	$25,200
(5)	Gross profit accrual basis		$20,000		$23,600		$32,900
(6)	Rate of gross profit		40%		37%		42%
(7)	Receipts from installment sales:						
	First year		$15,000		$24,000		$ 1,000
	Second year				15,000		27,500
	Third year						22,500
(8)	Gross profit from installment sales:						
	First year 40%		$ 6,000		$ 9,600		$ 400
	Second year 37%				5,550		10,175
	Third year 42%						9,450
	Total		$ 6,000		$15,150		$20,025
	Gross profit from cash and installment sales (4a) plus (9b)		$10,000		$20,250		$27,725

(3) UNCOLLECTED INSTALLMENTS AND UNREALIZED GROSS PROFITS

An example showing how the dealer computes his profit if he uses the installment method follows. Our dealer runs an appliance store and has been selling refrigerators on the installment plan. The price is $400 cash or $500 on an 18-month installment basis, $50 down and $25 a month thereafter. Average cost per unit sold is $300 for the first year, $315 for the second, and $290 for the third.

If an installment account becomes uncollectible, there is no deduction for uncollected gross profit; but the portion of the uncollected balance that represents unrecovered cost is a bad debt. To use an extreme case, suppose the entire $45,000 in the example below became uncollectible. There would be no deduction for the $18,525 of unrealized gross profit; however, the balance of $26,475 would be deductible as a bad debt. Repossessions would reduce the deduction by an amount equal to the fair market value of the repossessed items. If the value of the repossessions exceeds the basis for the installment obligation, the difference, in the case of a dealer, is ordinary income.

Here are the uncollected installments and unrealized gross profits at the end of the third year:

	Uncollected Installments	Rate	Unrealized Gross Profit
2nd year's sales	$ 7,500	37%	$ 2,775
3rd year's sales	37,500	42%	15,750
Total	$45,000		$18,525

Appendix F —
Illustrated Depreciation Methods

STRAIGHT-LINE METHOD

The depreciation expense is the same from period to period. The formula followed for this method is:

$$\text{Depreciation expense} = \frac{(\text{Cost - Salvage Value})}{\text{Estimated Life}}$$

For example, if the asset costs $10,000, has a salvage value of $100, and an estimated life of ten years, the depreciation expense for the year would be computed as follows:

$$\frac{(\$10,000 - \$100)}{10} = \$990.$$

The straight-line method depends upon the hypothesis that depreciation will be at a constant rate throughout the estimated life.

200%-DECLINING-BALANCE METHOD

Under this method (also called the double-declining-balance method), the amount of depreciation expense decreases from period to period. The largest depreciation deduction is taken in the first year. The amount then declines steeply over succeeding years until the final years of estimated useful life when the depreciation charge becomes relatively small. Code §167 restricts the taxpayer to a rate not in excess of twice the straight-line rate if the straight-line method had been employed.

While true declining-balance method requires the application of a complex formula, if you are going to use the maximum declining-balance depreciation — i.e., the 200% method — you need not go through these mathematical computations. Just do this: (1) determine the straight-line percentage rate; (2) double it; (3) apply it against your full basis (undiminished by salvage value) to get your first

460

year's deduction. In the second year, (1) reduce your basis by the previous year's depreciation deduction; (2) apply the same percentage rate to the new basis you arrived at in step (1). In the third year and later years, repeat the same process.

Example: You buy a truck for the business. It costs $5,500 and has a five-year useful life. We'll assume you bought it January 1, 1979. Since it has a five-year life, the percentage of depreciation by the straight-line method is 20%. Using 200%-declining-balance, you'll use a 40% rate. So, for 1979, you'd deduct $2,200 (40% of $5,500). For 1980, you reduced your $5,500 basis (original cost) by the $2,200 1979 depreciation deduction. That gives you a basis for 1980 of $3,300. For 1980, your depreciation deduction would be 40% of that $3,300, or $1,320. That cuts your basis for 1981 to $1,980 and your depreciation deduction for that year becomes $792 (40% of $1,980). This process continues on for the future years you continue to hold this truck.

SUM-OF-YEARS-DIGITS METHOD

Here, diminishing rates, expressed fractionally, are applied to the total depreciable value (cost — salvage).

Under sum-of-the-digits, the annual depreciation charge decreases rapidly; since maintenance charges, on the other hand, increase rapidly, the effect is to level off the annual costs of depreciation and maintenance.

To use sum-of-the-digits, you proceed as follows. Using, for purposes of illustration, a depreciation account of $5,500 with a 10-year life and ignoring salvage, add the numbers of the years: $10 + 9 + 8 + 7 + 6 + 5 + 4 + 3 + 2 + 1 = 55$. Depreciation the first year will be 10/55 of $5,500, or $1,000. For the remaining years, you can follow one of two practices. Either you continue to base depreciation on original cost, using 55 as the denominator of your fraction and the number of the year as the numerator — 9/55 of $5,500, 8/55 of $5,500, and so on, or you apply a fraction with a diminishing denominator to unrecovered cost — 9/45 of $4,500, 8/36 of $3,600, and so on.

Note that in the second method, the amount by which the denominator for a given year diminishes is always the amount of the numerator for the preceding year. Denominator 45 in the second year is denominator 55 for the first year, less numerator 10 for the first year; denominator 36 for year 3 is denominator 45 for year 2, less numerator 9 for year 2.

Regardless of which method is used, annual depreciation will be the same: 9/55 of $5,500 and 9/45 of $4,500 both give $900 of depreciation; 8/55 of $5,500 and 8/36 of $3,600 both give depreciation of $800.

SINKING-FUND METHOD

The sinking-fund method of computing depreciation has been generally preferred by independent businessmen. An imaginary sinking fund is established by a uniform end-of-year annual deposit throughout the useful life of the asset. The assets are assumed to draw interest at some stated rate, e.g., 6%, sufficient to balance the fund with the cost of the asset minus estimated salvage value. The amount charged to depreciation expense in any year consists of sinking fund plus the interest on the imaginary accumulated fund. The book value of the asset at any time is the initial cost of the asset minus the amount accumulated in the imaginary fund.

Assume that an asset cost $1,000 and has no salvage value but has an estimated life of 25 years. The interest rate is assumed to be 6%. By using conversion tables, the sinking fund deposit is $1,000 × .01823 or $18.23. In the second year, the depreciation charge will be $18.23 + ($18.23 × .06) = $19.32; in the third year, it will be $18.23 + ($18.23 + $19.32) × .06 = $20.48, and so forth. The $18.23 represents the sinking fund deposit and remains the same for the period of depreciation. In other words, under this method the businessman anticipates earnings and profits on his capital investment and thus increases his capital.

This method is permissible for Federal income tax purposes provided it does not exceed the rate as computed under the declining-balance method, during the first two-thirds of the asset life.

UNIT-OF-PRODUCTION METHOD

This method is used for the depreciation of assets used in production. Under this method, an estimate is made of the total number of units the machine may be expected to produce during its life. Cost less salvage value, if any, is then divided by the estimated total production to determine a depreciation charge for each unit of production. The depreciation for each year is obtained by multiplying the depreciation charge per unit by the number of units produced. Here's how it works on a $10,600 machine good for 300,000 units of output:

$$R = \frac{\text{Cost - Salvage Value}}{\text{Estimated Units}}$$

$$R = \frac{\$10,600 - \$600}{300,000}$$

$$R = \$.03\tfrac{1}{3}$$

Units produced for 1 year = 24,000
Depreciation = 24,000 × $.03⅓ = $800

A severe obstacle to the use of this method is the difficulty of ascertaining the total number of units which the asset will produce. The production method is most applicable to fixed assets like airplane engines, automobiles, and machinery where wear is such an important factor. It is useful for fixed assets that are likely to be exhausted prematurely by accelerated or abnormal use.

Appendix G
Table of Contents — The Current Text*

VOLUME I

Current Text, published by the Financial Accounting Standards Board.

VOLUME II

Section
Disclosure Flowcharts—General Standards

Description and Instructions

INDUSTRY STANDARDS

Key Cross-Reference Guides

Co4 —Contractor Accounting:
Construction-Type Contracts

Co5 —Contractor Accounting:
Governmental Contracts

De4 —Development Stage Enterprises

Ed8 —Educational Organizations:
Colleges and Universities

Em6 —Employee Benefit Funds: Employee
Health and Welfare Benefit Funds

Fi4 —Finance Companies

Fo6 —Forest Products Industry

Fr3 —Franchising:
Accounting by Franchisors

He4 —Health Care Industry: Hospitals

In6 —Insurance Industry

In8 —Investment Companies

Mi6 —Mining Industry

Mo4 —Mortgage Banking Activities

Mo6 —Motion Picture Industry

No5 —Nonbusiness Organizations

Oi5 —Oil and Gas Producing Activities

Pe5 —Pension Funds: Accounting and Reporting
by Defined Benefit Pension Plans

Re1 —Real Estate: Sales

Re2 —Real Estate: Accounting for Costs and Initial Rental Operations of
Real Estate Projects

Re3 —Real Estate: Other

Re4 —Record and Music Industry

Re6 —Regulated Operations

St4 —Stockbrokerage Industry

Ti7 —Title Plant

Disclosure Flowcharts—Industry Standards

Description and Instructions

Yellow —Disclosure Directory

Blue —Specialized Industry Disclosures

Appendixes

Topical Index

Appendix H

MONETARY AND NONMONETARY ITEMS

The purpose of this Appendix is to provide guidance for the classification of monetary or nonmonetary asset and liability items. It is not intended to be absolutely definitive and followed regardless of the circumstances of the problem. If there is a doubt with respect to special circumstances involving a classification, the doubt should be resolved by reference to the definition in FASB. No. 33. (AC 1041.1).

Assets

	Monetary	Nonmonetary
Cash on hand and demand bank deposits (U.S. dollars)	X	
Time deposits (U.S. dollars)	X	
Foreign currency on hand and claims to foreign currency	X	
Securities:		
Common stocks (not accounted for on the equity method)		X
Common stocks represent residual interests in the underlying net assets and earnings of the issuer.		
Preferred stock (convertible or participating)		
Circumstances may indicate that such stock is either monetary or nonmonetary. See convertible bonds.		
Preferred stock (nonconvertible, nonparticipating)		
Future cash receipts are likely to be substantially unaffected by changes in specific prices.	X	

	Monetary	Nonmonetary
Convertible bonds		
If the market values the security primarily as a bond, it is monetary; if it values the security primarily as a stock, it is nonmonetary.		
Bonds (other than convertibles)	X	
Accounts and notes receivable	X	
Allowance for doubtful accounts and notes receivable	X	
Accrued losses on firm purchase commitments	X	
In essence, these are accounts payable.		
Deferred revenue		
Nonmonetary if an obligation to furnish goods or services is involved. Certain "deferred income" items of savings and loan associations are monetary.		
Refundable deposits	X	
Bonds payable and other long-term debt	X	
Unamortized premium or discount and prepaid interest on bonds or notes payable	X	
Inseparable from the debt to which it relates—a monetary item.		
Convertible bonds payable	X	
Until converted these are obligations to pay sums of money.		
Accrued pension obligations		
Fixed amounts payable to a fund are monetary; all other amounts are nonmonetary.		
Obligations under warranties		X
These are nonmonetary because they oblige the enterprise to furnish goods or services or (sic) their future price.		
Deferred income tax credits	X	
Cash requirements will not vary materially due to changes in specific prices.		

	Monetary	Nonmonetary
Deferred investment tax credits		X
Not to be settled by payment of cash; associated with nonmonetary assets.		
Life insurance policy reserves	X	
Portions of policies face values that are now deemed liabilities		
Property and casualty insurance loss reserves	X	
Unearned property and casualty insurance premiums		X
These are nonmonetary because they are principally obligations to furnish insurance coverage. The dollar amount of payments to be made under that coverage might vary materially due to changes in specific prices.		
Deposit liabilities of financial institutions	X	
Advances to supplier—not on a fixed price contract	X	
A right to receive credit for a sum of money; not a claim to a specified quantity of goods or services.		
Deferred income tax charges	X	
Offsets to prospective monetary liabilities		
Patents, trademarks, licenses and formulas		X
Goodwill		X
Deferred life insurance policy acquisition costs	X	
The portion of future cash receipts for premiums that is recognized in the accounts. Alternatively, viewed as an offset to the policy reserve.		
Deferred property and casualty insurance policy acquisition costs		X
Related to unearned premiums.		
Other intangible assets and deferred charges		X

Liabilities

	Monetary	Nonmonetary
Accounts and notes payable	X	
Accrued expenses payable (wages, etc.)	X	
Accrued vacation pay		
Nonmonetary if it is paid at the wage		
rates as of the vacation dates and		
if those rates may vary.		
Cash dividends payable	X	
Obligations payable in foreign currency	X	
Sales commitments—portion collected on		
fixed price contracts		X
An advance received on a fixed price		
contract is the portion of the		
seller's obligation to deliver goods		
or services that is recognized in		
the accounts; it is not an obligation		
to pay money.		
Advance from customers—not on a fixed		
price contract	X	
Equivalent of a loan from the customer;		
not an obligation to furnish a spe-		
cified quantity of goods or services.		
Variable rate mortgage loans	X	
The terms of such loans do not link		
them directly to the rate of infla-		
tion. Also, there are practical		
reasons for classifying all loans as		
monetary.		
Inventories used on contracts		
They are, in substance, rights to		
receive sums of money if the future		
cash receipts on the contracts will		
not vary due to future changes in		
specific prices. (Goods used on con-		
tracts to be priced at market upon		
delivery are nonmonetary.)		
Inventories (other than inventories used		
on contracts)		X
Loans to employees	X	
Prepaid insurance, advertising, rent,		
and other prepayments		
Claims to future services are non-		
monetary. Prepayments that are		

	Monetary	**Nonmonetary**
deposits, advance payments or receivables are monetary because the prepayment does not obtain a given quantity of future services, but rather is a fixed money offset.		
Long-term receivables	X	
Refundable deposits	X	
Advances to unconsolidated subsidiaries	X	
Equity investment in unconsolidated subsidiaries or other investees		X
Pension, sinking and other funds under an enterprise's control		
The specific assets in the fund should be classified as monetary or nonmonetary. (See listings under securities above.)		
Property, plant, and equipment		X
Accumulated depreciation of property, plant, and equipment		X
Cash surrender value of life insurance	X	
Purchase commitments—portion paid on fixed price contracts		X
An advance on a fixed price contract is the portion of the purchaser's claim to nonmonetary goods or services that is recognized in the accounts; it is not a right to receive money.		

Appendix I

TEXT OF PUBLIC LAW 95-213—
"FOREIGN CORRUPT PRACTICES ACT OF 1977"—
TITLE I

Be it enacted by the Senate and House of Representatives of the United States of America in Congress assembled,

TITLE I--FOREIGN CORRUPT PRACTICES

Short Title

Sec. 101. This title may be cited as the "Foreign Corrupt Practices Act of 1977".

Accounting Standards

Sec. 102. Section 13(b) of the Securities Exchange Act of 1934 (15 U.S.C. 78q(b)) is amended by inserting "(1)" after "(b)" and by adding at the end thereof the following:

"(2) Every issuer which has a class of securities registered pursuant to section 12 of this title and every issuer which is required to file reports pursuant to section 15(d) of this title shall--

"(A) make and keep books, records, and accounts, which, in reasonable detail, accurately and fairly reflect the transactions and dispositions of the assets of the issuer; and

"(B) devise and maintain a system of internal accounting controls sufficient to provide reasonable assurances that--

"(i) transactions are executed in accordance with management's general or specific authorization;

"(ii) transactions are recorded as necessary (I) to permit preparation of financial statements in conformity with generally accepted accounting principles or any other criteria applicable to such statements, and (II) to maintain accountability for assets;

"(iii) access to assets is permitted only in accordance with management's general or specific authorization; and

"(iv) the recorded accountability for assets is compared with the existing assets at reasonable intervals and appropriate action is taken with respect to any differences.

"(3)(A) With respect to matters concerning the national security of the United States, no duty or liability under paragraph (2) of this subsection shall be imposed upon any person acting in cooperation with the head of any Federal department or agency responsible for such matters if such act in cooperation with such head of a department or agency was done upon the specific, written directive of the head of such department or agency pursuant to Presidential authority to issue such directives. Each directive issued under this paragraph shall set forth the specific facts and circumstances with respect to which the provisions of this paragraph are to be invoked. Each such directive shall, unless renewed in writing, expire one year after the date of issuance.

"(B) Each head of a Federal department or agency of the United States who issues a directive pursuant to this paragraph shall maintain a complete file of all such directives and shall, on October 1 of each year, transmit a summary of matters covered by such directives in force at any time during the previous year to the Permanent Select Committee on Intelligence of the House of Representatives and the Select Committee on Intelligence of the Senate."

Foreign Corrupt Practices By Issuers

Sec. 103. (a) The Securities Exchange Act of 1934 is amended by inserting after section 30 the following new section:

"Foreign Corrupt Practices By Issuers

"Sec. 30A. (a) It shall be unlawful for any issuer which has a class of securities registered pursuant to section 12 of this title or which is required to file reports under section 15(d) of this title, or for any officer, director, employee, or agent of such issuer or any stockholder thereof acting on behalf of such issuer, to make use of the mails or any means or instrumentality of interstate commerce corruptly in furtherance of an offer, payment, promise to pay, or authorization of the payment of any money, or offer, gift, promise to give, or authorization of the giving of anything of value to--

"(1) any foreign official for purposes of--

   "(A) influencing any act or decision of such foreign official in his official capacity, including a decision to fail to perform his official functions; or

   "(B) inducing such foreign official to use his influence with a foreign government or instrumentality thereof to affect or influence any act or decision of such government or instrumentality,

in order to assist such issuer in obtaining or retaining business for or with, or directing business to, any person;

"(2) any foreign political party or official thereof or any candidate for foreign political office for purposes of--

"(A) influencing any act or decision of such party, official, or candidate in its or his official capacity, including a decision to fail to perform its or his official functions; or

"(B) inducing such party, official, or candidate to use its or his influence with a foreign government or instrumentality thereof to affect or influence any act or decision of such government or instrumentality,

in order to assist such issuer in obtaining or retaining business for or with, or directing business to, any person; or

"(3) any person, while knowing or having reason to know that all or a portion of such money or thing of value will be offered, given, or promised, directly or indirectly, to any foreign official, to any foreign political party or official thereof, or to any candidate for foreign political office, for purposes of--

"(A) influencing any act or decision of such foreign official, political party, party official, or candidate in his or its official capacity, including a decision to fail to perform his or its official functions; or

"(B) inducing such foreign official, political party, party official, or candidate to use his or its influence with a foreign government or instrumentality thereof to affect or influence any act or decision of such government or instrumentality,

in order to assist such issuer in obtaining or retaining business for or with, or directing business to, any person.

"(b) As used in this section, the term 'foreign official' means any officer or employee of a foreign government or any department, agency, or instrumentality thereof, or any person acting in an official capacity for or on behalf of such government or department, agency, or instrumentality. Such term does not include any employee of a foreign government or any department, agency, or instrumentality thereof whose duties are essentially ministerial or clerical."

(b)(1) Section 32(a) of the Securities Exchange Act of 1934 (15 U.S.C. 78ff(a)) is amended by inserting "(other than section 30A)" immediately after "title" the first place it appears.

(2) Section 32 of the Securities Exchange Act of 1934 (15 U.S.C. 78ff) is amended by adding at the end thereof the following new subsection:

"(c)(1) Any issuer which violates section 30A(a) of this title shall, upon conviction, be fined not more than $1,000,000.

"(2) Any officer or director of an issuer, or any stockholder acting on behalf of such issuer, who willfully violates section 30A(a) of this title shall, upon conviction, be fined not more than $10,000, or imprisoned not more than five years, or both.

"(3) Whenever an issuer is found to have violated section 30A(a) of this title, any employee or agent of such issuer who is a United States citizen, national, or resident or is otherwise subject to the jurisdiction of the United States (other than an officer, director, or stockholder of such issuer), and who willfully carried out the act or practice constituting such violation shall, upon conviction, be fined not more than $10,000, or imprisoned not more than five years, or both.

"(4) Whenever a fine is imposed under paragraph (2) of (3) of this subsection upon any officer, director, stockholder, employee, or agent of an issuer, such fine shall not be paid, directly or indirectly, by such issuer."

Foreign Corrupt Practices By Domestic Concerns

Sec. 104. (a) It shall be unlawful for any domestic concern, other than an issuer which is subject to section 30A of the Securities Exchange Act of 1934, or any officer, director, employee, or agent of such domestic concern or any stockholder thereof acting on behalf of such domestic concern, to make use of the mails or any means or instrumentality of interstate commerce corruptly in furtherance of an offer, payment, promise to pay, or authorization of the payment of any money, or offer, gift, promise to give, or authorization of the giving of anything of value to--

(1) any foreign official for purposes of--

    (A) influencing any act or decision of such foreign official in his official capacity, including a decision to fail to perform his official functions; or

    (B) inducing such foreign official to use his influence with a foreign government or instrumentality thereof to affect or influence any act or decision of such government or instrumentality,

in order to assist such domestic concern in obtaining or retaining business for or with, or directing business to, any person;

(2) any foreign political party or official thereof or any candidate for foreign political office for purposes of--

(A) influencing any act or decision of such party, official, or candidate in its or his official capacity, including a decision to fail to perform its or his official functions; or

(B) inducing such party, official, or candidate to use its or his influence with a foreign government or instrumentality thereof to affect or influence any act or decision of such governemnt or instrumentality,

in order to assist such domestic concern in obtaining or retaining business for or with, or directing business to, any person; or

(3) any person, while knowing or having reason to know that all or a portion of such money or thing of value will be offered, given, or promised, directly or indirectly, to any foreign official, to any foreign political party or official thereof, or to any candidate for foreign political office, for purposes of--

(A) influencing any act or decision of such foreign official, political party, party official, or candidate in his or its official capacity, including a decision to fail to perform his or its official functions; or

(B) inducing such foreign official, political party, party official, or candidate to use his or its influence with a foreign government or instrumentality thereof to affect or influence any act or decision of such government or instrumentality,

in order to assist such domestic concern in obtaining or retaining business for or with, or directing business to, any person.

(b)(1)(A) Except as provided in subparagraph (B), any domestic concern which violates subsection (a) shall, upon conviction, be fined not more than $1,000,000.

(B) Any individual who is a domestic concern and who willfully violates subsection (a) shall, upon conviction, be fined not more than $10,000, or imprisoned not more than five years, or both.

(2) Any officer or director of a domestic concern, or stockholder acting on behalf of such domestic concern, who willfully violates subsection (a) shall, upon conviction, be fined not more than $10,000, or imprisoned not more than five years, or both.

(3) Whenever a domestic concern is found to have violated subsection (a) of this section, any employee or agent of such domestic concern who is a United States citizen, national, or resident or is otherwise subject to the jurisdiction of the United States (other than an officer, director, or stockholder acting on behalf of such domestic concern), and who willfully carried out the act or practice constituting such violation shall, upon conviction, be fined not more than $10,000, or imprisoned not more than five years, or both.

(4) Whenever a fine is imposed under paragraph (2) or (3) of this subsection upon any officer, director, stockholder, employee, or agent of
a domestic concern, such fine shall not be paid, directly or indirectly,
by such domestic concern.

(c) Whenever it appears to the Attorney General that any domestic concern, or officer, director, employee, agent, or stockholder thereof,
is engaged, or is about to engage, in any act or practice constituting
a violation of subsection (a) of this section, the Attorney General may,
in his discretion, bring a civil action in an appropriate district court
of the United States to enjoin such act or practice, and upon a proper
showing a permanent or temporary injunction or a temporary restraining
order shall be granted without bond.

(d) As used in this section:

(1) The term "domestic concern" means (A) any individual who is a citizen, national, or resident of the United States; or (B) any corporation,
partnership, association, joint-stock company, business trust, unincorporated organization, or sole proprietorship which has its principal
place of business in the United States, or which is organized under the
laws of a State of the United States or a territory, possession, or com-
monwealth of the United States.

(2) The term "foreign official" means any officer or employee of a foreign government or any department, agency, or instrumentality thereof,
or any person acting in an official capacity for or on behalf of any
such government or department, agency, or instrumentality. Such term
does not include any employee of a foreign government or any department,
agency, or instrumentality thereof whose duties are essentially ministerial or clerical.

(3) The term "interstate commerce" means trade, commerce, transportation,
or communication among the several States, or between any foreign country and any State or between any State and any place or ship outside
thereof. Such term includes the intrastate use of (A) a telephone or
other interstate means of communication, or (B) any other interstate
instrumentality.

Appendix J
Concise Guide to the
Tax Reform Act of 1984

Featuring Special Help For Cashing In
On Its 32 Key Tax Changes

The huge new Tax Reform Act of 1984 is hundreds of pages long and makes critical changes in hundreds of sections of the Internal Revenue Code. On the one hand, this new law *boosts taxes* by eliminating a host of long-favored tax breaks. On the other hand, there are *important exceptions* to the tough new rules, and scores of vital *new tax-saving* opportunities.

This Emergency Handbook is set up to help taxpayers avoid the numerous pitfalls and to highlight ways for you to take advantage of the most useful changes in this all-encompassing New Law.

HOW TO GET TOP DEDUCTIONS
UNDER TOUGH NEW T&E SETUP

The New Law makes some of the biggest changes in travel and entertainment deductions in 22 years. In fact, the New Law actually represents a—

⋙TRIPLE THREAT TO T&E DEDUCTIONS → (1) One change may limit tax benefits if a business car is used for personal travel. (2) Another change imposes a brand-new dollar cap on the annual writeoff for a business car, even if it is used 100% for business. And finally, (3) the New Law sets up new, much more stringent recordkeeping requirements for T&E deductions.

How to Minimize the New Law Crackdown
On Personal Use of Business Cars

For years, self-employeds, partners and owners of closely-held corporations have treated the company car as a valuable fringe benefit. Under the New Law, it may cause a big increase in taxes.

⋙NEW TEST → If the car isn't used more than

50% for business, the car owner gets no investment tax credit and no fast writeoff (including up-to-$5,000 expensing).

Example: Early in 1984, your company provides you with a car; you use it 40% for business. The company claims a 6% investment credit—a dollar-for-dollar reduction in its tax bill—the year the car is put into service. It writes off the car under the accelerated cost recovery system (ACRS), deducting 25% the first year, 38% the second year, and the remaining 37% the third year.

≫**NEW LAW RULE** → All this changes under the New Law where a car is placed in service after June 18, 1984. Your company cannot claim the investment credit or use the three-year writeoff setup. Reason: The car is used only 40% for business. Your company does not meet the New Law's 50% business use test.

Special rule for employee-owned cars: If you use your own car on company business, you must also meet the 50% test to claim fast depreciation and an investment credit on your tax return. Employees must also meet two other new requirements: (1) The business use of your car must be for the convenience of your employer. And (2) the car must be required for you to do your job properly. If both tests are not met, you automatically fail the 50% test.

Suppose you flunk the 50% test. Are you out of luck? No. In some areas—for example, the business entertainment deduction for country club dues—you get no deduction if you fall short of the 50% business use test. That's not the case here.

≫**NEW WRITEOFF SCHEDULE** → If your personal use equals or exceeds 50%, the writeoff must be over five years on a straight-line basis (actually, it's six years: 10% the first year, 20% the second through the fifth year and 10% the sixth year). However, you get no investment credit.

In addition, there are moves you can make that can help you minimize the business use problem—or even eliminate it entirely. For example, there is a way for a company to meet the 50% test even if employees use their car extensively for family travel. However, a company can't use this idea for employees who own 5% or more of the company.

≫**IDEA IN ACTION #1** → If the employer is not doing it now, it can treat personal use as taxable compensation. The company withholds income tax and reports the compensation on your W-2.

Result: There is a trade-off. While employees have more taxable compensation, your company is once again entitled to an investment credit and three-year writeoff. Reason: Under the New Law, an employee's personal use counts as business use if (1) it is treated as taxable compensation and (2) the employee owns less than a 5% share of the employer.

Executives and professionals obviously don't want to overlook a single business mile that can help them meet the 50% test. For example, taking a customer in your car to lunch or to your club may provide the crucial business miles you need to go over the 50% mark.

≫**IDEA IN ACTION #2** → Combine a vacation with a trip taken primarily for business. As long as you are going anyway for business, you decide to bring the family along. Your trip counts as business travel for purposes of the 50% test. The fact that your family came along shouldn't make any difference — your mileage would be the same without them.

Effective date: Generally, cars placed in service or leased after June 18, 1984. But the new rules do not apply to cars placed in service on or before December 31, 1984, if acquired pursuant to a binding contract in effect on June 18, 1984.

How to Get Top Tax Mileage Under the New Law Cap On Automobile Tax Breaks

The New Law puts dollar limits on the investment credit and annual depreciation deduction for cars—even if you use your car 100% for business.

≫**NEW DOLLAR CAP** → The investment credit on a business car cannot exceed $1,000, regardless of how much business use you have. That's true even if the car costs $16,000, $20,000 or $40,000. And your depreciation writeoff cannot exceed $4,000 the first year and $6,000 in each year after that—again, regardless of your use or cost.

What this means: Your investment credit cannot exceed the credit normally available on a car costing around $16,000. And your depreciation deductions over the standard three-year writeoff period cannot exceed $16,000 ($4,000 in the first year and $6,000 in the second and third years). Any remaining cost has to be written off in later years at a rate no greater than $6,000 a year.

For example, suppose you pay $24,000 for a new car and use it 100% for business.

⋙**BEFORE NEW LAW** → You claimed an investment credit equal to 6% of your cost: $1,440. That cut your tax bill by $1,440 in the year you placed the car in service.

In addition, you wrote off your full cost (less one-half of your investment credit) over three years. If you were in the 50% tax bracket each year, that saved you another $11,640 in taxes. Total savings over three years: $13,080.

⋙**NEW LAW** → Your investment credit is limited to $1,000 and your depreciation deductions over the first three years cannot exceed $16,000. Total three-year tax savings in the 50% tax bracket: $9,000.

Of course, under the New Law, you can write off another $6,000 in the fourth year and the remaining cost in the fifth. You get the full writeoff. You simply have to wait longer to get the tax savings. But the extra investment credit is lost forever. And keep in mind that these are maximum figures. The new rules do not automatically allow you to claim $6,000 deductions each year. If you use your car for personal as well as business reasons, your deductions may be a lot less. For example, if you use your car 60% for business, your investment credit cannot exceed $600.

New Law strategy: The New Law dollar limits apply only to cars placed in service after June 18, 1984. The New Law does not—repeat, does not—affect the car you are currently using if it was acquired before then. So from a short-term tax standpoint, you might be better off making do with your present car instead of selling it and buying a new one.

Example: Mr. Vance, a sales executive, bought a car in 1983 that he uses 100% for business. The car cost $30,000. Vance sells the car in July, 1984 and buys a new one costing $40,000.

Result: Vance gets no depreciation deduction on his old car for 1984 (depreciation isn't allowed in the year of sale). And his depreciation deduction on his new car is limited to $4,000 for 1984, the first year of ownership. That's a mere $4,000 writeoff on a $40,000 car.

⋙**ALTERNATIVE MOVE** → Vance sticks with his 1983 car.

New result: He continues to write off the full cost of his car over three years. This gives him a 1984 depreciation deduction of $11,058—more than twice what he would get with a new $40,000 car.

Effective date: Cars placed in service after June 18, 1984. The transition rule for the 50% business use requirement applies here too.

How to Cope With the New Reporting and Recordkeeping Rules

Good records have always been a key to nailing down top-dollar T&E deductions, but under the New Law they are absolutely vital. Failure to keep the necessary records can not only cost you valuable deductions, you could be hit with—

≫**TAX PENALTIES** → Under the New Law, if you claim deductions that you cannot back up with adequate proof, you can automatically be hit with a 5% penalty for negligence.

What's more, the New Law stiffens the proof requirements themselves. Taxpayers get no business deductions or investment tax credits for cars (or other property, like computers) and cannot deduct business travel (including meals and lodging), business entertainment or gifts, unless the deductions and credits are backed up by contemporaneous records.

The New Law imposes an extra requirement on those who have a tax return professional fill out their return. They must sign a statement saying that they have the proper records and give the statement to the return preparer.

≫**WHAT TO DO** → Keep a current, up-to-date diary of your business driving that spells out where you travelled, when, the business purpose of your trip and the amount of each expense (backed up by receipts for expenditures over $25).

≫**SILVER LINING** → The log you keep could be worth big tax dollars. Suppose, for example, you find, in November, that you have driven 12,000 personal miles and 11,000 business miles. You will want to make sure that you use the car the rest of the year for business. By getting over the 50% mark—and having the log to prove it—you nail down (or keep) your credit and fast depreciation.

Effective date: The new recordkeeping rules apply to tax years beginning in 1985.

TOUGH NEW RULES FOR HOME COMPUTERS ALLOW TAX BREAKS

The tough new 50% rule for cars also applies to personal computers (and other assets such as planes, boats and trucks).

≫**WHAT'S AT STAKE** → Key tax breaks are lost if you don't use the computer more than 50% for business. You cannot claim the investment tax credit, expense the cost of the computer (i.e., currently deduct up to $5,000), or use the fast five-year depreciation deductions that computers ordinarily get.

Under the new rule, if you use the computer for business 50% of the time or less, you recover the depreciable portion of its cost at a slower rate—over 12 years instead of five.

What is business use? The rules are tricky. If you are an employee and own your own computer, the time it is used at home for business counts toward the 50% test only if your employer specifically requires home use to perform your employment duties properly. Using the computer for personal investment purposes is not considered business use for meeting the 50% test. The personal home use of a company-owned computer does count—but only if the employer treats it as compensation and declares it on your W-2 Form.

Typical example: Mr. Green uses his new $4,000 computer 40% of the time for business and 35% for analyzing and keeping track of his investments. It's used for the household budget and his children's video games the rest of the time.

Under the New Law rules: Green gets no investment credit, fast depreciation or expensing deduction. Reason: His direct business use misses the 50% mark. The 40% of the computer's cost that's attributable to business use and the 35% attributable to investment use—$3,000 in all—can be written off on a straight-line basis over twelve years. Green's annual writeoff: $250. If he had used the computer entirely for business, he could claim an immediate $4,000 deduction or, in the alternative, a $570 deduction and a $400 investment credit.

⋙**DEDUCTION BOOSTER** → Although use of the computer for investment purposes does not count toward reaching the 50% business use test, it *can* increase your deductions if you meet the 50% test. In our example, if Green used his computer for business use 51% of the time, his 35% investment use would be added to the business use—allowing him to take an investment credit and fast writeoffs on 86% of the computer's cost.

Suppose instead of buying his own computer, Green's company buys the computer and lets Green use it at home. Green still uses the computer only 40% of the time for business. Green's company treats the value of the personal use of the computer as compensation, and includes it on Green's W-2 Form.

⋙**WINNING RESULT** → The company can get a full investment credit and fast depreciation writeoffs for the computer. Reason: Green's non-business use of the computer that was treated as compensation now is considered to be business use, and the other 40% is actual business use. But if Green owned 5% or more of the company, personal use treated as compensation can never count as business use.

Word of caution: The 50%-business-use test must be met every year you use the computer. The first year it isn't met, you flunk the test. And you get no fast deductions in any succeeding year even if you then use the computer 100% for business. Part or all the investment credit and the fast depreciation you took in earlier years must be taken into income.

Final requirement: You must keep a contemporaneous diary that shows you used the computer more than 50% of the time for business. It's the same recordkeeping needed to claim deductions for the car you use in business. Tax idea: Use your computer to keep track of your business use. That's a business use in and of itself.

As with cars, if you find that you're falling behind on business use as year-end approaches, don't permit the computer to be used for anything but business. There are big tax dollars at stake. That way you can be sure to meet the more-than-50% test.

⋙**BIG EXCEPTION** → None of these tough new rules apply to a computer owned by and kept at an employer's regular business establishment.

Effective date: Property placed in service after June 18, 1984. The new rules do not apply if there was a binding contract to purchase the equipment in effect before June 19, 1984.

NEW LAW BOOSTS AUDIT-PROOF TRAVEL DEDUCTION BY 33%

⋙**EXTRA TAX SAVINGS** → The New Law increases by a full one-third the so-called automatic mileage deduction for charitable travel.

When you use your car for charitable volunteer work, you can write off your actual out-of-pocket expenses or use the automatic mileage deduction. With the mileage deduction, you don't have to keep a detailed record of your expenses. You need only prove the time, place and charitable purpose of your travel and your deduction can't be challenged as to amount by the Government. For 1984, the mileage deduction is 9¢ a mile.

⋙**NEW LAW BREAK** → The New Law boosts the mileage deduction to 12¢ a mile, starting in 1985. So a family with, say, 5,000 miles a year of charitable travel will be entitled to an additional $150 deduction. Added break: The 12¢-a-mile figure is for operating expenses only; parking fees and tolls continue to be deductible separately.

Effective date: January 1, 1985.

The new, bigger deduction is part of a growing list of audit-proof automatic deductions that save taxpayers time and trouble. Here are others:

● If you use your car for local and out-of-town business trips (including business-connected travel for education purposes), you can write off 20½¢ a mile for the first 15,000 annual business miles and 11¢ a mile above 15,000.

● When you use your car for trips to the doctor or other medical-related travel, you can add 9¢ a mile to your other deductible medical expenses.

● If you are transferred or get a new job, you can deduct 9¢ a mile for using your car in connection with the move.

● While you are away from home overnight on business, you can write off $14 a day for meal expenses ($9 a day if the trip lasts 30 days or more).

NEW LAW OPENS UP NEW BREAKS FOR IRAs

The New Law makes the Individual Retirement Account (IRA) a more attractive tax shelter than ever.

● IRA rollover: Before the New Law you could not take a retirement plan distribution and roll it over tax-free into an IRA while you were still working.

⋙**NEW LAW BREAK** → The New Law allows you to roll over most or all of the funds in your retirement plan into an IRA *before* you retire.

Net effect: The New Law gives you more control over where your retirement plan money is invested. For example, if you're not satisfied with the investments in your profit-sharing plan, you may be able to pull out what's in your plan account, roll it over into an IRA within 60 days and invest it as you prefer.

There are special rules that come into play—and they can be tough.

1. You cannot roll over this kind of distribution into another plan or annuity.

2. The distribution must be at least half your account balance.

3. The distribution cannot be one of a series of periodic payments.

4. Most important, the amount left in your plan

account—the part you did not roll over—is not eligible for the special 10-year income averaging or capital gain treatment that lump-sum distributions generally receive. What's more, the present rule still applies to what is rolled over: no ten-year averaging or capital gain treatment when the rolled over amount is distributed by the IRA.

Effective date: Distributions made after July 18, 1984.

• Eligible contributions: The New Law makes it much easier for divorced individuals to count alimony payments as earned income for IRA purposes. How it works: A person receiving taxable alimony—but no earned income—can put $2,000 of it into an IRA and get a $2,000 deduction. Before the New Law, a divorced person receiving alimony could make a deductible contribution only under very limited circumstances.

Effective date: January 1, 1985.

• Contribution deadlines: The New Law also changes the rules on the timing of IRA contributions. Starting with the 1984 tax year, you will have to make your IRA contribution by the April 15 tax return due date to get a deduction for that year. You can no longer extend your contribution deadline by getting a filing extension for your tax return. So your 1984 contribution must be made by April 15, 1985—period. On the other hand, if you got an automatic extension for your *1983* return, you were allowed to make your contribution on on before August 15, 1984, and deduct it on your 1983 return.

Effective date: Contributions for the 1984 tax year.

COMPANY INTEREST-FREE LOANS GET OKAY UNDER NEW TAX LAW

For all intents and purposes, no-interest loans to employees are still valid in the wake of the New Law. Loans can be made by the corporation without the actual payment of interest by employees. In most cases, what the New Law does is simply transform the no-interest loan into a series of bookkeeping transactions.

⫸**NEW LAW RULES** → The company is treated as paying the employee added compensation equal to the interest that would be owed on the loan. That "payment" is deductible by the company and taxable to the employee. However, the employee generally owes no income tax since he is entitled to an offsetting interest deduction for the interest he "pays" on the loan. The company comes out even too; its deduction is offset by the interest "payment" it receives.

Example: Employee Smith borrows $50,000 from his company for a year on a demand loan and pays back the money at the end of the year. The going interest rate is 10%. Result: Smith avoids paying $5,000 in interest that a bank would charge. And he pays no more income tax than he would before the New Law change. Reason: Although he now has $5,000 of extra income, he is entitled to an offsetting interest deduction. The company "payment" to Smith is, however, subject to Social Security and unemployment taxes under the New Law.

Note: A demand loan is used here for simplicity. But the same rules apply to loans for a fixed term if the loan becomes immediately payable should the employee leave the company. The New Law rules for other types of no-interest term loans are quite complex and could result in an employee having taxable compensation *without* a fully offsetting deduction.

Suppose the company "payment" cannot be treated as compensation. Either the no-interest loan is made to a shareholder, or it is made to a shareholder-employee whose total compensation is considered unreasonable by the Government. Under the New Law, the loan then has a—

⫸**DIFFERENT TAX RESULT** → The company "payment" is now considered to be a dividend. Result: The company cannot deduct dividends, so it has phantom income on the loan (the borrower's "payment" of loan interest). The borrower, on the other hand, pays no income tax because he still is entitled to an interest deduction that offsets his taxable dividend income. So, in effect, he receives a tax-free dividend from his company.

A no-interest company loan, whether made to an employee or to a shareholder, may qualify for this—

⫸**NEW LAW EXCEPTION** → There are no tax consequences to a no-interest loan if (1) total loans between the company and the taxpayer are less than $10,000, and (2) tax avoidance is not a principal purpose of the loan.

Effective date: Term loans made after June 6, 1984, and amounts outstanding on demand loans after June 6 (but a demand loan is exempt from the New Law if it is repaid by September 17, 1984.

YOU CAN STILL CASH IN ON INTEREST-FREE FAMILY LOANS

There are new gift and income tax rules for no- or low-interest family loans. Their impact on your situation depends largely on how big your loans are and why you made them.

≫**NEW RULES** → A loan from a parent to a child is treated in the following manner: (1) It's assumed that the parent is charging the going interest rate on the loan. (2) The rules then say the parent gives the child money to pay the interest. And (3) the child is treated as paying the interest back to the parent. With these three points in mind, it is important to note that no money changes hands—except for the loan principal.

Result: The parent makes a taxable gift, but this may be sheltered from gift tax by the $10,000 annual exclusion a taxpayer gets for each recipient ($20,000 if the taxpayer's spouse joins in the gift). Since the child is considered to return this gift in the form of interest, the parent must pay an income tax on it. The child does not take the gift into income, but he picks up a deduction for interest.

≫**NEW LAW EXCEPTIONS** → There are two important exceptions to the New Law rules. (1) There are no tax consequences to a no-interest loan if all loans between parent and the child come to less than $10,000 and the child doesn't use the loan to buy an income-producing investment. (2) If the total loans don't exceed $100,000 and the no-interest loan is not motivated by tax avoidance, the income taxed to the parent is limited. It cannot exceed the child's net investment income, and if that is less than $1,000, no income is taxed to the parent.

Effective date: Generally, June 6, 1984. But demand loans (the typical family loan) are exempt if they are repaid by September 17, 1984.

Effective date: Tax years beginning after March 1, 1984.

Does all this mean the end of family income splitting? No. Far from it. There's a long list of family income-splitting favorites that are untouched by the New Law. Maybe the best example is the short-term trust.

How it works: The parent transfers income-producing property—stock, for example—to a trust set up for his child. The trust lasts ten years and a day. The trust income is distributed and taxed to the low-bracket child. When the trust expires, the stock is returned to the parent. In effect, you have split income with your child for a ten-year period.

REAL ESTATE STILL FOUR-WAY FORTUNE BUILDING TAX SHELTER

Year in and year out, real estate has been a top source of tax-sheltered profit. Good news: Despite some important New Law changes, real estate still emerges a—

⫸**FOUR-WAY TAX WINNER** → You can continue to take advantage of the four key real estate tax shelter breaks: leverage, depreciation, tax-free swaps, and tax-sheltered capital gains. However, they've taken on an entirely new look because of the New Law. Here are some of the key changes.

Depreciation: Before the New Law, you could depreciate real property placed in service after 1980 over a fast, audit-proof 15 years.

⫸**NEW LAW CHANGE** → The New Law provides for a depreciation period of 18 years for property placed in service after March 15, 1984.

Major exception: Low-income housing is not affected by the New Law; the writeoff period remains 15 years.

Let's put things in perspective. It wasn't long ago that depreciation was based on a property's actual, useful life—which ranged up to 40 years for new property. So even with a 18-year writeoff period, you can still write off property in less than half the time.

Effective date: Property placed in service after March 15, 1984.

Leverage: You are often able to buy income property with a low downpayment—and borrow the rest. However, your tax deductions, including depreciation, are figured on the full purchase price. Result: Leverage multiplies real estate's profit potential and its tax shelter potential. The New Law does not change the fundamental advantages you get with leverage.

Tax-free swaps: If you swap business or investment property for like-kind property of equal value, there is no current tax on the exchange. You pay the tax when you sell the new property. That basic tax-free swap technique is untouched by the New Law.

But the New Law does crack down on so-called deferred exchanges. Before, you could immediately transfer property to another party and specify that the other party find property suitable to you within a period of, say, five years. The deal was closed when the actual tax-free exchange was made.

⫸**NEW LAW CHANGE** → Effective for transfers after the New Law's enactment date, you get tax-free treatment only if (1) the property suitable to you is identified within 45 days after you relinquish your property; and (2) you take title to the property within 180 days after you relinquish your property, or by the due date of your tax return (including extensions), whichever is earlier.

⫸**WHAT TO DO** → When the contract is drawn, set a closing date far enough in advance so that the other party has sufficient time to locate property you want.

Effective date: Generally, transfers of property after July 18, 1984. Special grace period: Transfers on or before July 18, 1984, are tax-free if the exchange property is received before January 1, 1987. (2) Where exchange property has been identified in a binding written contract entered into before June 14, 1984, the exchange property must be received before January 1, 1989.

Capital gains: If you sell real estate at a profit and you've held it long enough, all of it is low-taxed capital gain if you used straight-line depreciation. If you used accelerated depreciation, however, some of your gain may be treated as fully taxed ordinary income. The balance of your profit is treated as low-taxed capital gain.

Change for installment sales: It's common for sellers to take back a first or second mortgage when selling a commercial or investment property. That's a technique that often helps get the building sold at the right price.

But under the New Law, if a substantial amount of the sales price would be ordinary income, that could turn into a disaster. You could be badly hurt with—

≫**PHANTOM INCOME** → Effective for installment sales after June 6, 1984, sale profit treated as ordinary income is taxed in full in the year of sale—whether or not you receive payments in that year. Before the New Law, the recapture portion of your profit was taxed as ordinary income ratably—as you received installment payments from your buyer.

≫**WHAT TO DO** → (1) Try to help your buyer get a commercial mortgage. You'll still have ordinary income tax to pay, but at least you'll have the cash to pay it with. (2) If you must take back a mortgage, try to get as large a downpayment as possible. What you don't want is a situation where you, in effect, are a lender on the building—and are forced to be a borrower to pay the tax.

You should also consider using straight line depreciation when you buy real estate. That way you have no ordinary income—and therefore no phantom income—when you sell the property.

Effective date: Installment sales after June 6, 1984.

Another capital gain strategy: An owner who converts property to condominiums can turn high-taxed ordinary income into low-taxed capital gain. He sells the property at fair market value to a family corporation where he and his spouse own less than 80% of the stock. The corporation converts the building to condominiums and sells off units. Result: Profit from the sale to the corporation is low-taxed capital gain. Only the corporation's additional profit on condo sales is ordinary income.

Rehab credit liberalized: Owners of commercial or industrial property are eligible for a tax credit based on the cost of rehabilitating their buildings. The credit—a dollar for dollar reduction in the owner's tax bill—cuts the cost of the rehabilitation.

As a general rule, you qualify for the credit if at least 75% of the building's external walls are retained as external walls.

Good news: The New Law makes the credit—

≫**EASIER TO GET** → There is an alternative test for the credit. You get the credit if: (1) at least 50% of external walls are retained as external walls; (2) at least 75% of external walls are retained as external or internal walls; and (3) at least 75% of the building's internal framework is retained.

The rule was tougher before the change. At least 75% of a building's external walls had to be retained as external walls. Otherwise, a zero credit. There was no alternative test.

Effective date: Expenses incurred after December 31, 1983, in tax years beginning after that date.

BIG NEW LAW IMPACT ON REAL ESTATE FINANCING TECHNIQUE

The New Law hits hard at a "best of both worlds" real estate technique that accelerates deductions for buyers and defers taxes for sellers. Fortunately, there are a number of exceptions.

Technique in a nutshell: Seller wants $1 million for his income property. Buyer will pay that price only if Seller agrees to take back an $800,000 mortgage. The interest will accrue unpaid for five years. Suppose there's a five-year mortgage. If both parties are on the accrual basis, Seller has annual interest income and Buyer has annual interest deductions. And this is true, even if no cash is paid for five years.

More interesting results come when only Buyer is on the accrual basis. He takes current deductions for interest he won't pay for five years. Since Seller is on the cash basis, he defers paying tax until he actually receives the interest income.

≫**NEW LAW RESULT** → In effect, both Buyer and Seller are placed on the accrual basis as far as the mortgage interest is concerned. Buyer is entitled to current interest deductions. But Seller is treated as receiving taxable interest income each year—even though he is on the cash basis and doesn't get cash for five years!

For Seller the result is phantom income. He will have to pay tax on interest he hasn't yet received.

The good news: Many commercial and investment transactions are exempt from this new provision. To begin with, a sale that involves a standard self-liquidating note or mortgage (one that has annual principal and interest payments) is exempt. Key condition: The interest rate must equal or exceed the minimum test rate set by the Government. Here's a list of other key exempt transactions:

(1) Home mortgages.

(2) Notes received in a sale or exchange where the total amount paid for the property does not exceed $250,000.

(3) Generally, notes received for a farm (but sales price must be less than $1 million).

(4) Land sales between family members if sales price does not exceed $500,000 and at least 7% interest is charged.

≫**WHAT TO DO**→ If you have lined up a deferred interest deal with an accrual basis buyer and a cash basis seller, you may want to close the deal in 1984. Then these new rules will not affect you.

For transactions after 1984—whether buyer or seller—you may want to structure things differently. It will call for a different bargaining approach from both parties to the transaction. However, the important element will be to structure the deal to your benefit, not the Government's.

Effective date: Generally, these new rules apply to sales or exchanges after December 31, 1984.

NEW LAW OKAYS NEW TAX-FREE EMPLOYEE FRINGE BENEFITS

The New Law helps clear up the longstanding confusion over the tax treatment of employee fringe benefits:

Why the confusion? The Internal Revenue Code specifically exempts some fringe benefits from tax. For example, up to $50,000 of group-term life insurance coverage, contributions to pension and profit-sharing plans, employer-paid child care assistance and medical expense reimbursement plans, just to name a few. But for fringe benefits that aren't singled out by the Code— for example, employee discounts on merchandise— there has been no clear cut tax treatment. Court decisions and Government rules were sometimes contradictory.

≫≫NEW LAW RULES→ The New Law sets up special groups of fringe benefits that are tax-free. If a fringe benefit doesn't fall into one of these groups—and isn't exempted by any other Code provision—it is taxable.

Here's a quick rundown of some of the fringe benefits that get a thumbs up under the New Law:

• Employee discounts of up to 20% on services provided customers;

• Employee discounts on merchandise, as long as they don't exceed the employer's profit margin;

• Free or low-cost parking given to employees at or near their job;

• Personal use of company property (e.g., copiers) as long as the personal use by all employees doesn't exceed 15% of the property's total use;

• Monthly public transit passes sold to employees at a discount of no more than $15;

• Occasional company cocktail parties or picnics for employees;

• Taxi fares or supper money given employees once in a while for overtime work;

• Inexpensive holiday gifts to employees;

• Personal use of a demonstrator car by an auto salesperson;

• Occasional typing of a personal letter by a company secretary; and

• Employer-owned athletic facilities provided employees.

≫≫KEY REQUIREMENT→ In the case of employee discounts, the benefits are tax-free only if they are available to rank-and-file employees. The discounts can't be limited to owners or highly-paid employees. The same rule applies to athletic facilities unless the employer is willing to give up its business deductions for the cost of the facilities.

Effective date: The new fringe benefit rules generally take effect on January 1, 1985.

RESTRICTED STOCK
GETS BIG RETROACTIVE TAX BREAK

The New Law has a key retroactive election for executives who have bought stock from their companies subject to restrictions, either by exercising an option or buying the stock directly. In effect, it allows some owner-employees to convert fully-taxed ordinary income into—

⇒LOW-TAXED CAPITAL GAIN→ Without the new election, the appreciation in value on the restricted stock would be taxed as ordinary income. With it, the owner-employee can elect to treat the appreciation as capital gain.

Typical situation: Three entrepreneurs start up XYZ Corp. As part of their employment arrangement with XYZ, they each receive options to buy a substantial number of shares in XYZ at their fair market value. They exercise the options and acquire stock that is subject to a restriction: The stock cannot be transferred for three years. And if one of the employee-shareholders leaves XYZ's employment during the three years, XYZ can repurchase the stock at the original purchase price. XYZ does extremely well, and three years later, when the restrictions lapse, a conglomerate buys the stock from the three employees.

⇒TAX SURPRISE→ A recent Tax Court decision held that the profit from the stock is treated as ordinary income (taxed up to 50%), not capital gain (taxed up to 20%).

Court decision: Even though the employees paid the full market value, special tax rules apply because the original purchase price of the stock was tied to employment. The appreciation in the stock's value is taxed as ordinary income when the restrictions lapse. So the XYZ employees would have had to pay tax at ordinary income rates even if they hadn't sold the stock. That's another example of phantom income.

But none of this had to happen. The same special rules also include a special election. An employee can elect to be taxed at ordinary income rates when he buys the restricted stock. Taxable income: the difference between the stock's fair market value and what he paid for it. The difference was zero for the XYZ employees, so they would owe no tax if they make the election. The rules also say there would be no tax when the restrictions lapse. *And when the stock is sold, all appreciation would be capital gain.* The election, however, must be made within 30 days after buying the stock.

Then why didn't XYZ's employees make the election and nail down the capital gain for future appreciation? Answer: They—and many tax experts—didn't think it was necessary. The feeling was that the election only applied when restricted stock was bought for less than full market value. The XYZ people bought their stock for full fair market value. They got no discount.

⇒NEW LAW BREAK→ The New Law gives a second chance to owner-employees who have already bought restricted stock for full market value, and didn't make the election. If the stock was acquired after June 30, 1976, and on or before November 18, 1982 (the date of the Tax Court decision), the owner employee can make the election any time on or before April 15, 1985. The New Law requires the company to consent to the retroactive election.

Giant tax-saving results: The owner-employees defer the tax from the time the restrictions lapse to the time the stock is sold. And they convert ordinary income into capital gain.

Warning: The tough ordinary-income rule continues to apply to all restricted stock acquired for full market value after November 18, 1982. You have until thirty days after the purchase to make the election. So play it safe; when you do pay full market value, by all means make the election. The same election is available for those who buy for *less* than full market value. However, if they do elect, they will have to pay tax on the difference between the purchase price and full market value.

Effective date: Owners of restricted stock acquired for full value on or before November 18, 1982 must make the election by April 15, 1985.

NEW LAW CLEARS WAY FOR UNIVERSAL LIFE INSURANCE

The hottest new life insurance product to come around in a long time—universal life—may become even more popular. Reason: The New Law specifically approves it.

Background: Life insurance is entitled to important tax advantages. There is no current tax owed on a policy's cash value buildup; dividends are tax-free up to the amount of premiums paid; death benefits generally are income tax-free to beneficiaries. But when interest rates started to climb in the late seventies, insurance companies came up with flexible premium policies with investment returns higher than traditional policies.

≫**UNIVERSAL LIFE** → This kind of policy turns the standard insurance policy into a tax-sheltered investment. The insurance company guarantees a minimum return on the investment component of the policy, but when interest rates are high, the investment return exceeds the minimum. The policy holder can increase his premium payments, within limits, when he chooses. These extra payments don't necessarily increase his insurance coverage; instead, they can go to increase the cash value of the policy.

Green light: As long as a universal life policy meets

the definition of life insurance in the New Law, it gets all the tax breaks of a traditional whole life insurance policy.

The new rules eliminate from the life insurance category those policies that require disproportionately large investments. Typical example: Endowment policies.

Effective date: The new rules generally apply to insurance contracts issued after December 31, 1984.

HOW TO AVOID BIG CRACKDOWN ON DISCOUNT BOND TAX BREAK

If you buy a bond for less than its par value, then the bond is said to be selling at a "market discount." Before the New Law, you could count on this—

≫BIG TAX BREAK→ When the bond is redeemed or sold at a profit, the entire difference between the price paid and the amount received is taxed as tax favored long-term capital gain. In other words, 60% of the appreciation in the price of the bond escapes tax.

New Law crackdown: In general, gain from the sale or redemption of a market discount bond is treated as fully taxable interest income to the extent it's attributable to accrued market discount. There are also new rules that may limit your interest deduction if you borrow to buy market discount bonds.

≫KEY EFFECTIVE DATE→ The New Law crackdown that makes market discount ordinary interest income rather than capital gain applies only to bonds issued after July 18, 1984.

Result: Bonds issued on or before July 18, 1984, are not affected by the tough new rule. So, for many years to come, you will still be able to buy discount bonds and realize low-taxed capital gain at sale or redemption.

Suppose you have to pay tax on ordinary income when you dispose of a market discount bond. How do you compute your market discount? It's simple if you hold the bond to maturity. Market discount is redemption price less cost. But if you dispose of the bond before redemption, it's a rather complicated formula. Your broker should be able to help you here.

Tax surprise: The New Law also may require you to pay tax when you make a gift of a newly issued bond that you bought at discount.

Example: Mr. Black pays $5,000 for an ABC bond due in 20 years with a face value of $10,000. He gives the bond to his son ten years later when the bond has a fair market value of $7,500. In the usual gift situation, Black would owe no income tax on the transfer. Under the New Law, if the bond was issued after July 18, 1984, Black owes tax—at high ordinary income rates—on $2,500 ($7,500 fair market value when the gift is made minus $5,000 original purchase price).

The New Law provides an election that allows you to take a portion of the market discount into income each year the bond is held. This special election can open this—

⋙**NEW LAW STRATEGY** → Parents purchase a market discount bond and immediately give the bond to their child. The child elects to take the market discount into income each year. Result: The first $1,000 of income each year is completely sheltered by the child's personal exemption.

Important: The election to take market discount into current income applies to any market discount bond acquired on or after the date the election is made. It applies to all future tax years, and cannot be revoked without the consent of the Government.

The market discount rules do not apply to obligations that mature in one year or less. U.S. Savings Bonds and municipal bonds are also exempt from the crackdown. In fact—

TAX-FREE MUNICIPAL BONDS NOW HAVE ADDED ATTRACTION

Municipal bonds are an investment favorite for many reasons. The most important reason, of course, is that their interest is exempt from Federal income tax. And, in general, their interest also escapes income taxes imposed by the state or locality that issues the bond. The New Law doesn't change these tax advantages. And as a matter of fact, despite the new market discount rule, the investor with a discount municipal bond can still benefit from—

⋙**LOW-TAXED CAPITAL GAIN** → The New Law change that cracks down on other market discount bonds, leaves municipals untouched. If you buy a municipal bond at a discount and either sell it at a profit or hold it until maturity, the profit is still taxed as capital gain.

HOW TO TELL WHICH DIVIDENDS ARE STILL TAX-FREE

One New Law change will have an impact on dividends paid by public utilities. Some of these dividends are tax-free to the shareholders. Reason: They are not paid out of current earnings and profits and are therefore considered to be a tax-free return of capital.

The New Law cuts back on the availability of tax-free dividends by changing the definition of earnings and profits.

⋙**BRIGHT SPOT** → Shareholders in public utilities with dividend reinvestment plans continue to qualify for a popular tax break. Shareholders who file jointly can exclude up to $1,500 a year in cash dividends reinvested in new stock ($750 on a single return). In addition, when the new stock is sold, the proceeds can be treated as tax-favored long-term capital gains.

Effective date: In general, the earnings and profits definition changes take effect after September 30, 1984. Bottom line: More cash dividends will be subject to income tax.

The reinvestment break is in effect until 1986. A proposal to end this tax break after 1984 was deleted from the New Law at the last minute.

It is important to keep in mind that another type of dividend continues to be—

⋙**TAX FREE** → Dividends payable only in stock are generally not taxable when received.

NAIL DOWN LONG-TERM CAPITAL GAIN IN HALF THE TIME

The new shorter holding period for long-term capital gain treatment is a big break for investors. The New Law cuts in half the holding period for capital gains and losses. Before the New Law, the holding period was one year and a day. Now tax-favored long-term capital gain treatment will be available for gains on property held for only six months and a day.

⋙**TAX CUT** → On long-term capital gain, only 40% of the gain is taxed. So for someone in the 50% tax bracket, the top tax is 20% of the entire gain.

At some point this year, you may well wind up with stock that you've owned for six months that qualifies for long-term capital gain and stock you acquired nine months before that's still short-term.

Another big break: While the holding period for capital losses is also cut, there are built-in breaks here: (1) You still can offset up to $3,000 a year against ordinary income. (2) Where you acquired an asset before June 23, 1984, you have a year to take down short-term losses (worth twice as much as long-term losses).

Effective date: The six month holding period applies to assets acquired after June 22, 1984, and before January 1, 1988.

HOW TAX ACTION NOW CAN SALVAGE TAX-SHELTERED GAIN

The New Law eliminates a classic tax-saver that allowed your business to convert ordinary income into tax-sheltered capital gain. That's the bad news. The good news is that there is—

≫STILL TIME TO ACT → Some taxpayers may still be able to lock in capital gains for 1984. Reason: The New Law provision applies only to gains in tax years beginning after 1984.

Background: Under Section 1231 of the tax code, a sale of business property gets the best of both worlds: If the total gains from property sales in any one year exceed the total losses from that year, the net gain is treated as tax-favored long-term capital gain. If it's the other way around—the losses exceed the gains—the net loss is a fully deductible ordinary loss.

Before the New Law. a taxpayer could turn Section 1231 to his advantage by selling gain properties in one year and loss properties in another. Result: All the gains were treated as long-term capital gain and all the losses were fully deductible against ordinary income.

≫NEW LAW CRACKDOWN → Starting in 1985, the treatment of a net gain in the current tax year depends on what happened in the five previous years. When you have a net gain, it is fully taxed ordinary income to the extent of net losses in the five previous years; any remaining gain is tax-sheltered long-term gain. The tax treatment for net losses remains the same.

Result: Business taxpayers will find it more difficult to maneuver their Section 1231 gains to their advantage. However, the New Law does leave some room to maneuver this year.

Example: XYZ Corp., a calendar-year corporation, had a net Sec. 1231 loss in 1983 but no Sec. 1231 gains or losses for 1984. XYZ is currently negotiating to sell an office building (a Sec. 1231 asset). The closing will take place at the end of 1984 or the beginning of 1985.

≫TAX ACTION → XYZ is better off selling the building before the end of 1984, rather than in 1985. Here's why: The gain from the sale is treated as tax-sheltered long-term capital gain if the building is sold in 1984. If the building is sold in 1985, the gain is fully taxed ordinary income to the extent of the loss in 1983.

Reason: The 1984 gain is not affected by the 1983 loss. The 1985 gain comes under the New Law and is ordinary income because of the 1983 loss.

Effective date: Gains in tax years beginning after 1984.

IMPORTANT TAX CHANGES
FOR CLOSELY-HELD CORPORATIONS

Maybe the biggest news for closely-held corporations is the tax increase that didn't hit them.

≫**CORPORATE HEAVYWEIGHTS** → Corporations with taxable incomes of more than $1 million pay an extra 5% tax on income in excess of $1 million. There is a $20,250 cap on the increase, however.

Net effect: There is no graduated income tax for large corporations. It's as if they paid a 46% flat tax on all their taxable income.

Effective date: Tax years starting after December 31, 1983.

Here's a quick rundown on key New Law changes that do affect small, closely-held corporations:

Related taxpayers: Before the New Law, accrual basis corporations could deduct salary, bonuses or interest owed to a related cash basis taxpayer at the close of the current tax year, only if the related party was paid within 2½ months after the close of the tax year. A shareholder and a corporation are related if the shareholder owns more than 50% of the corporation's stock. If the 2½ month rule was not met, the deduction was lost forever.

≫**NEW LAW CHANGE** → The New Law says accrual basis corporations get no deduction for expenses owed to related parties until the tax year the expense is actually paid. And payment can be made more than 2½ months after the close of the tax year.

Effective date: In general, tax years beginning after 1983.

Distributions of appreciated property: Before the New Law, a corporation was better off distributing appreciated property as a dividend rather than paying a cash dividend. Reason: The property cost the corporation less than its present worth, and the corporation owed no tax on the property's appreciation in value. The cash dividend, however, was paid in after-tax dollars.

Under the New Law, corporations generally owe tax on a distribution of appreciated property. The distribution is treated as if it were a sale of the property at fair market value.

Effective date: Distributions on or after June 14, 1984.

Section 1244 stock: Investors in newly issued common stock in small companies get a big tax break that's written right into Section 1244 of the tax code. If things don't pan out, the loss from the sale of the stock is a deductible ordinary loss, rather than a capital loss of limited tax value. Sec. 1244 has no effect on gain. If stock of the same corporation is sold at a profit, the gain is tax-sheltered capital gain.

⋙**NEW TAX BREAK** → The rule on ordinary losses for Sec. 1244 stock is extended to preferred stock.

Effective date: Stock issued after July 18, 1984.

Payroll tax requirements: A payroll tax deposit is considered to be timely made if it is mailed two days prior to its due date. The two-day rule has enabled some employers to mail deposits to a distant depositary and have use of the money beyond the due date. For example, if a California-based employer mails a check to a depositary in New York, it may be four or five days before the funds are actually deposited.

⋙**NEW RULE** → A payroll deposit of more than $20,000 from an employer required to make deposits more than once a month must be made by the due date, no matter how the deposit is delivered.

Effective date: Deposits required to be made after July 31, 1984.

NEW LAW CREATES KEY CHANGES ON YOUR FORM 1040

The New Law makes important changes in the tax return you file for 1984, 1985, and future years. Let's take a look.

New medical expense deduction for lodging away from home: The cost of away-from-home travel for medical care is deductible as a medical expense. So is the additional travel expense of a companion (assuming a doctor says the companion is medically necessary). However, out-of-town lodging expenses incurred while obtaining outpatient medical treatment have been non-deductible.

⋙**NEW DEDUCTION** → Starting in 1984, lodging expenses while receiving outpatient medical care are deductible. What's more, a companion's lodging expenses are also deductible.

The new lodging deduction is limited to $50 per day per person. Key conditions: The cost of food remains non-deductible. The lodging must not be lavish or extravagant.

Effective date: January 1, 1984.

New tough rules for income averaging: Starting in 1984, income averaging is available only to those taxpayers who have a bigger increase in income (or a drop in deductions). New rules: You can income-average only if your taxable income for the current year exceeds 140% of your average taxable income for the preceding three years by at least $3,000. Before 1984, you qualified if your current taxable income was $3,000 more than 120% of the average for the previous four years.

For example, under the new rules, a taxpayer with an average taxable income of $40,000 in preceding years can use averaging only if his current taxable income exceeds $59,000. Before 1984, he would qualify if his taxable income exceeded $51,000.

⫸**TAX-SAVING SUGGESTION →** You can get the same tax-saving effect of income averaging. by spreading taxable income over a number of years. Examples: post-59½ IRA payouts over a period of years, real estate sales on the installment basis, bonuses over several years.

Result: The spread-out income may be taxed in a lower overall tax bracket.

New estimated tax rules: There is a penalty for the underpayment of estimated taxes. As a general rule, however, you avoid the penalty if withheld tax for the year is at least 80% of actual tax liability. There are also four so-called escape hatches that allow you to avoid the penalty even if you pay less than 80%.

⫸**NEW LAW CHANGE →** Starting in 1985, there are only two escape hatches: (1) You can use the prior year's tax as your estimated tax for the current year. If you make timely estimated tax payments equal to that amount, you are not liable for the penalty. (2) You owe no penalty if you pay 80% of the tax due on your annualized income. Your annualized income is what you would get if your income up to the payment date was received at the same rate for the entire year.

Another change: Starting in 1984, the Government can waive the penalty in case of casualty, disaster or "other unusual circumstances." The penalty can also be waived if there is reasonable cause for the underpayment of estimated tax during the first two years after a taxpayer retires after reaching age 62 or becomes disabled at any age.

Effective date: The new escape hatch rules take effect in 1985. However, the Government waiver of penalty applies in 1984.

HOW KEY EMPLOYEES CAN SIDESTEP OVERLOOKED NEW CRACKDOWN

Some retirement plan members now have less flexibility in timing their withdrawals from their plans. At the same time, other members gained in flexibility.

Background: If a pension or profit-sharing plan provides more than 60% of its benefits to key employees (i.e., officers and large shareholders), it is "top-heavy." And special rules apply to top-heavy plans. For example, they must provide faster vesting schedules and minium benefits and contributions to the lower level employees. In addition, top-heavy plan payouts to key employees under age 59½ are hit with an extra 10% tax. And key employees must begin taking payouts by the end of the year they become age 70½, even if they keep on working.

⫸**BIG NEW LAW CHANGE** → Starting with plan years beginning in 1985, *all* plan members who are also 5% shareholders are subject to both the 10% tax for pre-59½ distributions and the age 70½ withdrawal requirement—regardless of whether or not their plans are top-heavy! On the other hand, these rules are repealed as to key employees who are not 5% owners, even if their plans are top-heavy.

Another change: An employee can begin taking payouts as late as April 1 of the year after he or she attains age 70½. Starting with plan years beginning in 1984, fewer plans will be top-heavy. Here's why: Before the New Law, *all* officers were key employees. The New Law, however, says only some officers are. And since the definition of top-heavy plans is linked to benefits paid to key employees, some plans are no longer top-heavy.

⫸**GOOD NEWS** → An officer who earns less than one and a half times the contribution cap on defined contribution plans is no longer a key employee. The cap is $30,000 in 1984-1987, so that means a salary of $45,000. Beginning in 1988, that limit can rise with inflation.

Another benefit: Officers who are no longer key employees may start taking pre-59½ payouts immediately in 1984 (1) free of the 10% penalty tax and (2) regardless of whether their plans are top-heavy. In contrast, higher paid corporate officers who are not 5% shareholders remain classified as key employees and must wait until 1985 to get this same favorable treatment.

》》》**WHAT TO DO** → Some pre-age 59½ employees can time their retirement plan distributions to avoid the 10% penalty. Five per cent shareholders in non-top-heavy plans should accelerate payouts, taking them in 1984 rather than in 1985. On the other hand, employees who are not 5% shareholders, but who will retain their key employee status under the New Law, should hold off on taking distributions until 1985.

Effective dates: The rules for distributions to 5% shareholders apply to plan years beginning after December 31, 1984; the key employee definition change applies to plan years beginning after December 31, 1983.

TAX-DEFERRED ANNUITY STILL TOP TAX SHELTER

The New Law makes it tougher to take money out of a tax-deferred annuity before the annuity's starting date without paying a 5% penalty.

A deferred annuity operates like a long-term tax-sheltered savings account. The annuity owner pays a premium (or annual premiums) which accumulates tax-free earnings. No tax is owed until scheduled annuity payouts begin. But earnings withdrawn prior to the annuity starting date are subject to income tax. And before the New Law, a 5% penalty was also imposed if earnings were withdrawn by an owner under 59½ and if the earnings were attributable to an investment made within 10 years of the withdrawal.

Under the New Law, the 5% penalty is imposed on premature withdrawals, no matter how long ago the investment was made.

》》》**SPECIAL   BREAK** → The   new   tougher penalty provision applies only to annuity contracts issued after January 18, 1985. So if you buy an annuity on or before that date, you will be able to make penalty-free withdrawals ten years after the date of purchase.

Other exceptions: The New Law does not change existing exceptions to the 5% penalty. For example, no penalty is imposed on withdrawals made after age 59½. And no penalty is owed if the withdrawal is part of a distribution lasting at least five years.

Another annuity change: Before the New Law, if an

annuity owner died before the annuity starting date, no immediate income tax was owed by either the owner or the recipient of the annuity. The recipient was not subject to tax until payments were made to him.

≫**NEW LAW CHANGE** → If the annuity owner dies before the annuity starting date, the income in the contract is taxed as it is received, depending on who the beneficiary of the contract is.

The payout rules are similar to those for IRA's and qualified pension plans (see next article).

Effective date: Annuity contracts issued after January 18, 1985.

REVIEW FAMILY SECURITY PLAN TO SEIZE NEW OPPORTUNITIES

The New Law requires a fresh look at your estate plan. One New Law change gives you added flexibility in arranging your retirement plan payouts. Still another change freezes the top gift and estate tax rate.

Let's take a look at the key estate and gift tax changes in the New Law:

Retirement plan payouts: The New Law greatly liberalized a tough new rule that went into effect on January 1, 1984. For pension and profit-sharing plans, the rule basically said that you could not gear a plan payout to the life of a beneficiary who is not your spouse. In other words, a plan member generally could no longer use his retirement plan to provide a lifetime income for, say, his child. Under the tough rule, the child would have to be paid off within five years of the plan member's death. The same sort of rule also applies to payouts from Individual Retirement Accounts and Keoghs.

≫**NEW LAW CHANGE** → The New Law opens up a big exception in the five-year-rule for employees who die before payouts begin.

Starting in 1985, a plan of a deceased member can make payments over the life of any designated beneficiary, but only if payments begin within one year after the plan member's death. Exception: If the beneficiary is the plan member's spouse, payouts do not have to begin until the plan member would have been 70½ years old. The spouse can designate any individual to receive payments if he or she dies before the plan member would have reached 70½.

Effective date: The new one-year rule takes effect in 1985.

Estate tax exclusion: Before the New Law, there was a special $100,000 estate tax exclusion for lump-sum distributions from retirement plans where the employee died while still employed. The New Law does away with this special exclusion.

⋙**MINIMUM TAX COST** → (1) To get the $100,000 exclusion in the first place, a beneficiary had to agree to give up a big *income tax* break—the 10-year income averaging and capital gain treatment normally available on lump-sum payouts. (2) The elimination of the exclusion doesn't necessarily mean that the family will have to pay estate taxes on the plan payout. If the spouse is the plan beneficiary, the marital deduction will shelter the entire payout from estate tax. And if someone else is named as beneficiary, there is still the unified estate and gift tax credit to offset the tax that would be owed (see below).

Effective date: After December 31, 1984.

Estate and gift tax rates: The estate and gift tax rates are graduated, just like income tax rates. The top tax rate dropped from 60% in 1983 to 55% for the estates of decedents dying in 1984. The New Law fixes the top bracket at 55% through 1987; it will drop to 50% starting in 1988.

⋙**BIG BREAKS UNTOUCHED** → (1) You can still give and bequeath an unlimited amount of property to your spouse, free of estate and gift taxes (the marital deduction). (2) You can still make yearly lifetime gifts to anyone else of up to $10,000 ($20,000 if your spouse joins in) and pay no gift tax—it's completely excludable. (3) The unified estate and gift tax credit is currently enough to shelter $325,000 in 1984; the amount sheltered by the credit rises to $600,000 by 1987.

Estate tax result: In 1987 and years after, a decedent can leave $600,000 directly to his spouse and another $600,000 to his spouse in trust for his children and avoid estate tax on both his and his spouse's estates. That eventually provides $1.2 million to the children free of estate tax.

NEW LAW DRASTICALLY CHANGES RULES ON DIVORCE AND TAXES

The New Tax Law makes some big changes in the divorce taxation rules. Three key areas are affected: (1) property settlements, (2) alimony payments and (3) dependency exemptions.

Property settlements: The New Tax Law makes a 180-degree turn from the past in this area. Before the New Law, if, say, a husband transferred property to his wife as part of a divorce settlement, the husband could have been hit with an income tax. If the property had appreciated in value—its current value exceeded the husband's tax basis (usually cost)—he had to pay tax on the difference, just as if he sold the property to his wife. The big problem was he was paying tax on money he didn't receive—on phantom income.

The current value of the property became the wife's tax basis and she could sell the property tax-free immediately after the transfer.

Example: John Smith transfers $600,000-worth of his company's stock to his wife in a marital settlement. Result: If Smith's stock had cost him $100,000, he now has a long-term capital gain of $500,000—and receives no cash with which to pay the tax.

Mrs. Smith could turn around the next day, sell the stock for $600,000 and pay no tax because she shows no gain.

Under the New Law, property settlements are treated as gifts, not sales. Result: Property transfers made between spouses as part of a divorce are—

⋙**INCOME TAX-FREE** → The husband has no taxable gain or loss on the transfer. On the other hand, the wife carries over the husband's tax basis. So if she sells the property right away, she may now owe an income tax.

All things being equal, the transferring spouse will want to give low-basis property to his spouse and keep the high-basis property. Conversely, the spouse on the receiving end will want high-basis property to minimize her potential tax when the property is sold.

Effective date: The New Law generally applies to property transfers made after July 18, 1984. However, it will not apply to transfers after that date under prior settlements unless both parties agree.

⋙**IMPORTANT** → The parties can elect to have the New Law rules apply retroactively to transfers made between December 31, 1983, and July 18, 1984.

Alimony: Alimony payments continue to be deductible by the paying spouse and taxable to the receiving spouse. Say one spouse agrees to make payments to the other until either party dies or the receiving spouse remarries. This is deductible alimony to the paying spouse and taxable to the receiving spouse under both old and New Law.

But the New Law makes a change when the spouse makes payments of a fixed amount of money. Under the old law, payments of a fixed amount had to be "periodic" (made over a period in excess of ten years) in order to be treated as alimony for tax purposes. The New Law eliminates the "periodic" requirement. But annual alimony payments in excess of $10,000 must be made over at least six years. However, the divorce or separation instrument must state that there is no liability to make payments for any period after the death of the receiving spouse.

Another change: If alimony payments are scheduled to decrease when a child dies, marries or reaches majority, the paying spouse is penalized. The amount of each monthly payment equal to the scheduled decrease is treated as child support. It cannot be deducted by the paying spouse.

Effective date: The New Law's alimony provisions apply to agreements entered into after 1984. They also cover agreements entered into during or before 1984 if the agreements are modified after 1984 to provide that the New Law applies.

Dependency deduction: The old law had complicated rules to determine which divorced parent was entitled to a dependency deduction for the children. Sometimes the parent with custody of the children got the deduction and sometimes the noncustodial parent got it. The New Law simplifies things. The parent with a dependency deduction is now the—

➽**PARENT WITH CUSTODY** → The parent who has custody for the greater part of the year gets the deduction. Exception: The custodial parent can elect in writing to pass on the deduction to the non-custodial spouse.

Effective date: Tax years beginning after 1984.

HOW TO ESCAPE CRACKDOWN ON OIL AND OTHER TAX SHELTERS

A big source of oil and gas write-offs is the deduction for intangible drilling costs (IDCs). These are costs that go into the drilling of a well but have no salvage value after the well is completed. Typical intangible drilling costs: fuel, wages, hauling and supplies, construction of derricks, and other structures.

Up to now, a limited partnership could take a current deduction for these costs, as long as the drilling contract called for payments before the end of the year. The work didn't actually have to be performed until the next year. So an oil and gas partnership that paid for drilling on, say, December 20 could pass through a big first-year tax write-off to its limited partners.

➽**NEW LAW CRACKDOWN** → As a general

rule, effective after March 31, 1984, a tax shelter's prepaid expenses are deductible in the year the work is actually done—and not before.

Fortunately, the New Tax Law also includes a—

⫸GIANT ESCAPE HATCH → You can take a current deduction for prepaid expenses as long as: (1) the work is actually performed 90 days after the close of the current tax year; (2) the deduction for prepaid expenses does not exceed the taxpayer's cash investment (but cash investment does *not* include borrowings arranged by the tax shelter or its organizers or promoters); (3) the expense is a payment and not a deposit; (4) there is a business purpose for the prepayment; and (5) it does not result in a "material distortion of income."

Special bonus for oil and gas shelters: Although your drilling must *begin* in that 90-day period, the work need not be completed within 90 days for you to get a current deduction. Result: The door is still open to big first-year writeoffs in oil and gas.

Example: XYZ Limited Partnership is set up in December, 1984, to engage in oil and gas drilling. Bill Green buys a 10% limited partnership interest for $50,000. XYZ uses 85% of Green's cash (and the cash of the other limited partners) to pay for intangible drilling costs (the driller will pay for completion). The actual well drilling is begun before March 31, 1985 (90 days after the close of the 1984 tax year).

Result: Since the partnership has no income this year, Green winds up with a substantial tax loss of $42,500. If Green pays a 50% tax on his top dollars, that loss saves him $21,250 in tax dollars.

Next year—when the well is drilled and oil starts flowing—Green will start receiving income from the partnership. And a good chunk of that income will be—

⫸TAX-FREE → XYZ can offset part of the oil income with a depletion deduction for exhausting the oil reserves. Result: Tax-free cash for Green and the other limited partners.

Effective date: Prepayments made after March 15, 1984.

CHECKLIST OF OTHER VITAL NEW LAW CHANGES

● *Stiffer rules for deducting accrued expenses:* A taxpayer who uses the accrual method of accounting can deduct a business expense as soon as (1) the liability to pay it is fixed and (2) its amount can be estimated reasonably. The New Law adds another requirement starting after July 18, 1984: No deduction is allowed before "economic performance" has occurred. For example, if an accrual-basis taxpayer hires an outside firm to do research and experimental work, it can't deduct the payments until the work is actually performed—even if the liability and amount is determined beforehand. Exception: An accrued expense may be deductible in a tax year prior to economic performance if it is a recurring expense and economic performance occurs within 8½ months after the close of the year.

● *Tax credit for new product development:* The New Law did not extend this vital business credit. But there is still time to act. You can claim a 25% tax credit for qualified research and experimental costs paid or incurred before January 1, 1986.

● *New lease on life for mortgage subsidy bonds:* Under the New Law, a state or local government can continue to issue tax-free bonds to finance home mortgages. Effective date: Bonds issued after December 31, 1983 and before January 1, 1988. The authority to issue mortgage subsidy bonds had expired on December 31, 1983.

● *New limits for industrial development bonds:* An industrial development bond (IDB) yields tax-free interest if the proceeds are used to finance specific projects, such as low-income residential housing, sports facilities and airports. Under the New Law, IDBs issued by a state in any one year after December 31, 1983 cannot exceed the greater of (1) $150 per state resident or (2) $200 million. Under prior law, there were no dollar caps on IDBs.

● *Short-term CDs still offer tax-deferred income:* The New Law generally requires a taxpayer to report interest income as it is earned or accrued, whether or not the taxpayer is on the cash basis. Bank certificates of deposit with a maturity of one year or less escape this New Law crackdown. Interest on a short-term CD does not become taxable until you can withdraw it without incurring a penalty. For example, if you buy a CD in 1984 that matures a few months later in 1985 and no interest is credited to your account before the maturity date, tax is deferred until you file your 1985 tax return.

● *Charitable deduction crackdown:* The New Law contains tough new rules on charitable deductions for donations of property. These rules apply to (1) any single item valued over $5,000 and (2) similar items of property donations totalling more than $5,000 made in any year to one or more charities. The donor must obtain an independent written appraisal stating the property's fair market value on the date of contribution, the specific basis for valuation, a description of the property, and the qualifications of the appraiser. A summary of the appraisal, signed by the appraiser, must be attached to the donor's tax return. Charitable deductions will be cut back for those who do not comply with the new rules. Effective date: Charitable contributions made after December 31, 1984.

● *Finance leasing rules postponed:* The safe harbor rules for equipment leasing enacted in 1981 allowed unprofitable businesses to sell investment credits and super-fast depreciation writeoffs. Another tax law reduced tax benefits of the safe harbor rules in 1982. They were completely eliminated starting in 1984 and replaced by a somewhat similar substitute, finance leases. The New Law postpones the effective date of these finance leases to January 1, 1988.

● *Property contributed to partnership:* Under current rules, partners have an opportunity to shift tax burdens and benefits when they contribute to a partnership property with paper gains or losses. No tax is recognized on the transfer, and depreciation deductions and gain or loss on subsequent sale by the partnership can be spread among the partners. Under the New Law, the partnership must allocate depreciation deductions and gain or loss on a sale so that the contributing partner receives the tax benefits and burdens from gain or loss that occurred before the contribution to the partnership. Effective date: Property contributed after March 31, 1984.

● *Targeted jobs credit extended:* This allows an employer to get tax credits for part of the salary paid to new employees who are members of specific economically disadvantaged groups. Maximum credit: $3,000 in the first year of employment and $1,500 in the second year. The credit was due to expire at the end of 1984, but the New Law extends it for one year. It is now available for wages paid to members of targeted groups who begin employment on or before December 31, 1985.

● *Telephone excise tax extended:* The 3% excise tax currently imposed on telephone service was scheduled to expire at the end of 1985. The New Law extends this tax until December 31, 1987.

● *Brand-new tax break for homebuyers:* In lieu of issuing tax-free mortgage subsidy bonds, states can issue Mortgage Credit Certificates to qualifying homebuyers. These certificates, available beginning in 1985, entitle the homebuyer to a—

⫸**NEW TAX CREDIT** → The homebuyer can take a federal income tax credit equal to the greater of (1) 20% of interest paid or (2) $2,000. However, the credit can never exceed 50% of interest paid. The homebuyer can take an interest deduction only for the balance of his home mortgage interest. The brand-new Mortgage Credit Certificates are available to purchasers of principal residences where purchase price does not exceed 110% of the area's average purchase price. Homebuyers who obtain mortgage money raised through the sales of mortgage subsidy bonds are ineligible for the new Certificates.

Index